"Composed in the style of the great medieval *catenae*, this new anthology of patristic commentary on Holy Scripture, conveniently arranged by chapter and verse, will be a valuable resource for prayer, study and proclamation. By calling attention to the rich Christian heritage preceding the separations between East and West and between Protestant and Catholic, this series will perform a major service to the cause of ecumenism."

AVERY CARDINAL DULLES, S.J.
Laurence J. McGinley Professor of Religion and Society
Fordham University

"The initial cry of the Reformation was *ad fontes*—back to the sources! The Ancient Christian Commentary on Scripture is a marvelous tool for the recovery of biblical wisdom in today's church. Not just another scholarly project, the ACCS is a major resource for the renewal of preaching, theology and Christian devotion."

TIMOTHY GEORGE
Dean, Beeson Divinity School, Samford University

"Modern church members often do not realize that they are participants in the vast company of the communion of saints that reaches far back into the past and that will continue into the future, until the kingdom comes. This Commentary should help them begin to see themselves as participants in that redeemed community."

ELIZABETH ACHTEMEIER
Union Professor Emerita of Bible and Homiletics
Union Theological Seminary in Virginia

"Contemporary pastors do not stand alone. We are not the first generation of preachers to wrestle with the challenges of communicating the gospel. The Ancient Christian Commentary on Scripture puts us in conversation with our colleagues from the past, that great cloud of witnesses who preceded us in this vocation. This Commentary enables us to receive their deep spiritual insights, their encouragement and guidance for present-day interpretation and preaching of the Word. What a wonderful addition to any pastor's library!"

WILLIAM H. WILLIMON
Dean of the Chapel and Professor of Christian Ministry
Duke University

"Here is a nonpareil series which reclaims the Bible as the book of the church by making accessible to earnest readers of the twenty-first century the classrooms of Clement of Alexandria and Didymus the Blind, the study and lecture hall of Origen, the cathedrae of Chrysostom and Augustine, the scriptorium of Jerome in his Bethlehem monastery."

GEORGE LAWLESS
Augustinian Patristic Institute and Gregorian University, Rome

"We are pleased to witness publication of the
Ancient Christian Commentary on Scripture. It is most beneficial for us to learn
how the ancient Christians, especially the saints of the church
who proved through their lives their devotion to God and his Word, interpreted
Scripture. Let us heed the witness of those who have gone before us in the faith."

METROPOLITAN THEODOSIUS
Primate, Orthodox Church in America

"Across Christendom there has emerged a widespread interest
in early Christianity, both at the popular and scholarly level. . . .
Christians of all traditions stand to benefit from this project, especially clergy
and those who study the Bible. Moreover, it will allow us to see how our traditions are
both rooted in the scriptural interpretations of the church fathers while at
the same time seeing how we have developed new perspectives."

ALBERTO FERREIRO
Professor of History, Seattle Pacific University

"The Ancient Christian Commentary on Scripture fills a long overdue need for scholars and
students of the church fathers. . . . Such information will be of immeasurable
worth to those of us who have felt inundated by contemporary interpreters and novel theories
of the biblical text. We welcome some 'new' insight from the
ancient authors in the early centuries of the church."

H. WAYNE HOUSE
Professor of Theology and Law
Trinity University School of Law

"Chronological snobbery—the assumption that our ancestors working without benefit of
computers have nothing to teach us—is exposed as nonsense by this magnificent
new series. Surfeited with knowledge but starved of wisdom, many of us are
more than ready to sit at table with our ancestors and listen to their holy
conversations on Scripture. I know I am."

EUGENE H. PETERSON
Professor Emeritus of Spiritual Theology
Regent College

"Few publishing projects have encouraged me as much as the recently announced Ancient Christian Commentary on Scripture with Dr. Thomas Oden serving as general editor. . . . How is it that so many of us who are dedicated to serve the Lord received seminary educations which omitted familiarity with such incredible students of the Scriptures as St. John Chrysostom, St. Athanasius the Great and St. John of Damascus? I am greatly anticipating the publication of this Commentary."

FR. PETER E. GILLQUIST
Director, Department of Missions and Evangelism
Antiochian Orthodox Christian Archdiocese of North America

"The Scriptures have been read with love and attention for nearly two thousand years, and listening to the voice of believers from previous centuries opens us to unexpected insight and deepened faith. Those who studied Scripture in the centuries closest to its writing, the centuries during and following persecution and martyrdom, speak with particular authority. The Ancient Christian Commentary on Scripture will bring to life the truth that we are invisibly surrounded by a 'great cloud of witnesses.'"

FREDERICA MATHEWES-GREEN
Commentator, National Public Radio

"For those who think that church history began around 1941 when their pastor was born, this Commentary will be a great surprise. Christians throughout the centuries have read the biblical text, nursed their spirits with it and then applied it to their lives. These commentaries reflect that the witness of the Holy Spirit was present in his church throughout the centuries. As a result, we can profit by allowing the ancient Christians to speak to us today."

HADDON ROBINSON
Harold John Ockenga Distinguished Professor of Preaching
Gordon-Conwell Theological Seminary

"All who are interested in the interpretation of the Bible will welcome the forthcoming multivolume series Ancient Christian Commentary on Scripture. Here the insights of scores of early church fathers will be assembled and made readily available for significant passages throughout the Bible and the Apocrypha. It is hard to think of a more worthy ecumenical project to be undertaken by the publisher."

BRUCE M. METZGER
Professor of New Testament, Emeritus
Princeton Theological Seminary

ANCIENT CHRISTIAN COMMENTARY ON SCRIPTURE

OLD TESTAMENT
XIII

EZEKIEL, DANIEL

EDITED BY

KENNETH STEVENSON
AND MICHAEL GLERUP

WITH INTRODUCTION TO DANIEL
BY C. THOMAS McCOLLOUGH

GENERAL EDITOR
THOMAS C. ODEN

InterVarsity Press
Downers Grove, Illinois

InterVarsity Press
P.O. Box 1400, Downers Grove, IL 60515-1426
World Wide Web: www.ivpress.com
E-mail: mail@ivpress.com

InterVarsity Press˚ is the book-publishing division of InterVarsity Christian Fellowship/USA˚, a student movement active on campus at hundreds of universities, colleges and schools of nursing in the United States of America, and a member movement of the International Fellowship of Evangelical Students. For information about local and regional activities, write Public Relations Dept., InterVarsity Christian Fellowship/USA, 6400 Schroeder Rd., P.O. Box 7895, Madison, WI 53707-7895, or visit the IVCF website at <www.intervarsity.org>.

Scripture quotations, unless otherwise noted, are from the Revised Standard Version of the Bible, copyright 1946, 1952, 1971 by the Division of Christian Education of the National Council of the Churches of Christ in the U.S.A., and are used by permission.

Selected excerpts from Augustine, The Literal Meaning of Genesis, translated and annotated by John Hammond Taylor, Ancient Christian Writers 42, ©1982; John Cassian, The Conferences, translated and annotated by Boniface Ramsey, Ancient Christian Writers 57, ©1997; John Cassian, Conferences, translated by Colm Luibheid, The Classics of Western Spirituality, ©1985; Cassiodorus, Explanation of the Psalms, translated by P. G. Walsh, Ancient Christian Writers 51, 52 and 53, ©1990, 1991; Gregory the Great, Pastoral Care, translated and annotated by Henry Davis, Ancient Christian Writers 11, ©1978; Irenaeus, Against the Heresies, translated and annotated by Dominic J. Unger and John J. Dillon, Ancient Christian Writers 55, ©1992; John Chrysostom, Baptismal Instructions, translated by Paul W. Harkins, Ancient Christian Writers 31, ©1963; The Sermons of St. Maximus of Turin, translated by Boniface Ramsey, Ancient Christian Writers 50, ©1989; Methodius, The Symposium: A Treatise on Chastity, translated by Herbert Musurillo, Ancient Christian Writers 27, ©1958; Origen: An Exhortation to Martyrdom, Prayer and Selected Writings, translated by Rowan A. Greer, The Classics of Western Spirituality, ©1979; The Poems of St. Paulinus of Nola, translated by P. G. Walsh, Ancient Christian Writers 40, ©1975; Pseudo-Dionysius: The Complete Works, translated by Colm Luibheid, The Classics of Western Spirituality, ©1987; Pseudo-Macarius: The Fifty Spiritual Homilies and the Great Letter, translated by George A. Maloney, The Classics of Western Spirituality, ©1992; Symeon the New Theologian: The Discourses, translated by C. J. deCatanzaro, The Classics of Western Spirituality, ©1980; Tertullian, Treatises on Penance: On Penitence and On Purity, translated and annotated by William P. Le Saint, Ancient Christian Writers 28, ©1959. Reprinted by permission of Paulist Press, Inc. <www.paulistpress.com>.

Selected excerpts from Fathers of the Church: A New Translation, ©1947-, used by permission of The Catholic University of America Press, Washington, D.C. Full bibliographic information on volumes of Fathers of the Church may be found in the Bibliography of Works in English Translation.

Selected excerpts from The Homilies of St. Gregory the Great on the Book of the Prophet Ezekiel, translated by Theodosia Gray, ©1990. Reprinted by permission of the Center for Traditionalist Orthodox Studies.

Selected excerpts from Origen, On First Principles, translated by G. W. Butterworth, ©1973. Reprinted by permission of Peter Smith Publisher.

Selected excerpts from Jerome, Commentary on Daniel, translated by Gleason L. Archer Jr., ©1958. Reprinted by permission of Baker Publishing Group.

Selected excerpts from Gregory the Great, Forty Gospel Homilies, translated by David Hurst, Cistercian Studies 123, ©1990; Pachomian Koinonia: The Lives, Rules, and Other Writings of Saint Pachomius, translated by Armand Veilleux, Cistercian Studies 45, 46 and 47, ©1980-1982; The Syriac Fathers on Prayer and the Spiritual Life, translated by Sebastian Brock, Cistercian Studies 101, ©1987; Symeon the New Theologian: The Practical and Theological Chapters and the Three Theological Discourses, translated by Paul McGuckin. Cistercian Studies 41, ©1982; The Lives of Simeon Stylites, translated by Robert Doran, Cistercian Studies 112, ©1992. Used by permission of Cistercian Publications, Kalamazoo, Michigan. All rights reserved.

Selected excerpts from Theodoret of Cyrus, Commentary on Daniel, translated by Robert C. Hill, Writings of the Greco-Roman World 7, ©2006. Reprinted by permission of E. J. Brill Publishers.

Selected excerpts from Augustine: Later Works, translated by John Burnaby, The Library of Christian Classics 8, ©1955; Christology of the Later Fathers, translated by Archibald Robertson and edited by Edward Rochie Hardy, The Library of Christian Classics 3, ©1954; Cyril of Jerusalem and Nemesius of Emesa, translated by William Telfer, The Library of Christian Classics 4, ©1955; Early Christian Fathers, translated by Cyril C. Richardson, The Library of Christian Classics 1, ©1953; Early Latin Theology, translated by S. L. Greenslade, The Library of Christian Classics 5, ©1956. Used by permission of SCM and Westminster John Knox Presses, London, England, and Louisville, Kentucky.

Selected excerpts from The Works of Saint Augustine: A Translation for the 21st Century, edited by John E. Rotelle, ©1990-. Used by permission of the Augustinian Heritage Institute.

Selected excerpts from The Message of the Fathers of the Church, edited by Thomas Halton, ©1983-. Used by permission of The Liturgical Press, Collegeville, Minnesota. Full bibliographic information on volumes of The Message of Fathers of the Church may be found in the Bibliography of Works in English Translation.

Every effort has been made to trace and contact copyright holders for additional materials quoted in this book. The authors will be pleased to rectify any omissions in future editions if notified by copyright holders.

Cover photograph: Scala/Art Resource, New York. View of the apse. S. Vitale, Ravenna, Italy.

Spine photograph: Byzantine Collection, Dumbarton Oaks, Washington D.C. Pendant cross (gold and enamel). Constantinople, late sixth century.

ISBN 978-0-8308-1483-1

Printed in the United States of America∞

Library of Congress Cataloging-in-Publication Data

Ezekiel and Daniel/edited by Kenneth Stevenson and Michael Glerup;
general editor, Thomas C. Oden.
  p. cm.—(Ancient Christian commentary on Scripture. Old
  Testament; 13)
  Includes bibliographical references and indexes.
  ISBN-13: 978-0-8308-1483-1 (cloth: alk. paper)
  1. Bible O.T. Ezekiel—Commentaries. 2. Bible. O.T.
Daniel—Commentaries. I. Stevenson, Kenneth (Kenneth W.) II. Glerup,
Michael. III. Oden, Thomas C.
BS1545.53.E94 2007
224'.40609—dc22

                          2007031474

P	27	26	25	24	23	22	21	20	19	18	17	16	15	14	13	12	11	10	9	8	7	6	5	4	3	2	1
Y	31	30	29	28	27	26	25	24	23	22	21	20	19	18	17	16	15	14	13	12	11	10	09	08	07		

Contents

General Introduction

The Ancient Christian Commentary on Scripture has as its goal the revitalization of Christian teaching based on classical Christian exegesis, the intensified study of Scripture by lay persons who wish to think with the early church about the canonical text, and the stimulation of Christian historical, biblical, theological and pastoral scholars toward further inquiry into scriptural interpretation by ancient Christian writers.

The time frame of these documents spans seven centuries of exegesis, from Clement of Rome to John of Damascus, from the end of the New Testament era to A.D. 750, including the Venerable Bede.

Lay readers are asking how they might study sacred texts under the instruction of the great minds of the ancient church. This commentary has been intentionally prepared for a general lay audience of nonprofessionals who study the Bible regularly and who earnestly wish to have classic Christian observation on the text readily available to them. The series is targeted to anyone who wants to reflect and meditate with the early church about the plain sense, theological wisdom and moral meaning of particular Scripture texts.

A commentary dedicated to allowing ancient Christian exegetes to speak for themselves will refrain from the temptation to fixate endlessly upon contemporary criticism. Rather, it will stand ready to provide textual resources from a distinguished history of exegesis that has remained massively inaccessible and shockingly disregarded during the last century. We seek to make available to our present-day audiences the multicultural, multilingual, transgenerational resources of the early ecumenical Christian tradition.

Preaching at the end of the first millennium focused primarily on the text of Scripture as understood by the earlier esteemed tradition of comment, largely converging on those writers that best reflected classic Christian consensual thinking. Preaching at the end of the second millennium has reversed that pattern. It has so forgotten most of these classic comments that they are vexing to find anywhere, and even when located they are often available only in archaic editions and inadequate translations. The preached word in our time has remained largely bereft of previously influential patristic inspiration. Recent scholarship has so focused attention upon post-Enlightenment historical and literary methods that it has left this longing largely unattended and unserviced.

This series provides the pastor, exegete, student and lay reader with convenient means to see what Athanasius or John Chrysostom or the desert fathers and mothers had to say about a particular text for preaching, for study and for meditation. There is an emerging awareness among Catholic, Protestant and Orthodox laity that vital biblical preaching and spiritual formation need deeper grounding beyond the scope of the historical-critical orientations that have governed biblical studies in our day.

Hence this work is directed toward a much broader audience than the highly technical and specialized scholarly field of patristic studies. The audience is not limited to the university scholar concentrating on the study of the history of the transmission of the text or to those with highly focused philological interests in textual morphology or historical-critical issues. Though these are crucial concerns for specialists, they are not the paramount interests of this series.

This work is a Christian Talmud. The Talmud is a Jewish collection of rabbinic arguments and comments on the Mishnah, which epitomized the laws of the Torah. The Talmud originated in approximately the same period that the patristic writers were commenting on texts of the Christian tradition. Christians from the late patristic age through the medieval period had documents analogous to the Jewish Talmud and Midrash (Jewish commentaries) available to them in the *glossa ordinaria* and catena traditions, two forms of compiling extracts of patristic exegesis. In Talmudic fashion the sacred text of Christian Scripture was thus clarified and interpreted by the classic commentators.

The Ancient Christian Commentary on Scripture has venerable antecedents in medieval exegesis of both eastern and western traditions, as well as in the Reformation tradition. It offers for the first time in this century the earliest Christian comments and reflections on the Old and New Testaments to a modern audience. Intrinsically an ecumenical project, this series is designed to serve Protestant, Catholic and Orthodox lay, pastoral and scholarly audiences.

In cases where Greek, Latin, Syriac and Coptic texts have remained untranslated into English, we provide new translations. Wherever current English translations are already well rendered, they will be utilized, but if necessary their language will be brought up to date. We seek to present fresh dynamic equivalency translations of long-neglected texts which historically have been regarded as authoritative models of biblical interpretation.

These foundational sources are finding their way into many public libraries and into the core book collections of many pastors and lay persons. It is our intent and the publisher's commitment to keep the whole series in print for many years to come.

Thomas C. Oden
General Editor

A Guide to Using This Commentary

Several features have been incorporated into the design of this commentary. The following comments are intended to assist readers in making full use of this volume.

Pericopes of Scripture

The scriptural text has been divided into pericopes, or passages, usually several verses in length. Each of these pericopes is given a heading, which appears at the beginning of the pericope. For example, the first pericope in the commentary on Ezekiel is "1:1-3 Introduction." This heading is followed by the Scripture passage quoted in the Revised Standard Version (RSV) across the full width of the page. The Scripture passage is provided for the convenience of readers, but it is also in keeping with medieval patristic commentaries, in which the citations of the Fathers were arranged around the text of Scripture.

Overviews

Following each pericope of text is an overview of the patristic comments on that pericope. The format of this overview varies within the volumes of this series, depending on the requirements of the specific book of Scripture. The function of the overview is to provide a brief summary of all the comments to follow. It tracks a reasonably cohesive thread of argument among patristic comments, even though they are derived from diverse sources and generations. Thus the summaries do not proceed chronologically or by verse sequence. Rather they seek to rehearse the overall course of the patristic comment on that pericope.

We do not assume that the commentators themselves anticipated or expressed a formally received cohesive argument but rather that the various arguments tend to flow in a plausible, recognizable pattern. Modern readers can thus glimpse aspects of continuity in the flow of diverse exegetical traditions representing various generations and geographical locations.

Topical Headings

An abundance of varied patristic comment is available for each pericope of these letters. For this reason we have broken the pericopes into two levels. First is the verse with its topical heading. The patristic comments are then focused on aspects of each verse, with topical headings summarizing the essence of the patristic comment by evoking a key phrase, metaphor or idea. This feature provides a bridge by which modern readers can enter into the heart of the patristic comment.

Identifying the Patristic Texts

Following the topical heading of each section of comment, the name of the patristic commentator is given. An English translation of the patristic comment is then provided. This is immediately followed by the title of the patristic work and the textual reference—either by book, section and subsection or by book-and-verse references.

The Footnotes

Readers who wish to pursue a deeper investigation of the patristic works cited in this commentary will find the footnotes especially valuable. A footnote number directs the reader to the notes at the bottom of the right-hand column, where in addition to other notations (clarifications or biblical cross references) one will find information on English translations (where available) and standard original-language editions of the work cited. An abbreviated citation (normally citing the book, volume and page number) of the work is provided. A key to the abbreviations is provided on page xv. Where there is any serious ambiguity or textual problem in the selection, we have tried to reflect the best available textual tradition.

Where original language texts have remained untranslated into English, we provide new translations. Wherever current English translations are already well rendered, they are utilized, but where necessary they are stylistically updated. A single asterisk (*) indicates that a previous English translation has been updated to modern English or amended for easier reading. The double asterisk (**) indicates either that a new translation has been provided or that some extant translation has been significantly amended. We have standardized spellings and made grammatical variables uniform so that our English references will not reflect the odd spelling variables of the older English translations. For ease of reading we have in some cases edited out superfluous conjunctions.

For the convenience of computer database users the digital database references are provided to either the Thesaurus Linguae Graecae (Greek texts) or to the Cetedoc (Latin texts) in the appendix found on pages 315-23 and in the bibliography found on pages 345-54.

Abbreviations

ACW	Ancient Christian Writers: The Works of the Fathers in Translation. Mahwah, N.J.: Paulist Press, 1946-.
AF[1]	*The Apostolic Fathers:* Translated by J. B. Lightfoot. Editd by J. R. Harmer. London: Macmillan & Co., 1891. Reprint, Grand Rapids, Mich.: Baker book House, 1983.
AHSIS	*The Ascetical Homilies of Saint Isaac the Syrian.* Boston, Mass.: Holy Transfiguration Monastery, 1984.
ANCL	The Ante-Nicene Christian Library: Translations of the Writings of the Fathers down to A.D. 325. Alexander Roberts and James Donaldson, eds. Edinburgh: T & T Clark, 1867-1897.
ANF	A. Roberts and J. Donaldson, eds. Ante-Nicene Fathers. 10 vols. Buffalo, N.Y.: Christian Literature, 1885-1896. Reprint, Grand Rapids, Mich.: Eerdmans, 1951-1956. Reprint, Peabody, Mass.: Hendrickson, 1994.
AOV	Ambrose. *On Virginity.* Translated by Daniel Callam, CSB. Toronto: Peregrina Publishing Co., 1996.
AS	The Augustinian Series. Villanova, Penn.: Augustinian Press, 1988-.
BFG	*Be Friends of God: Spiritual Reading from Gregory the Great.* Translated by John Leinenweber. Cambridge, Mass.: Cowley Publications, 1990.
CCL	Corpus Christianorum. Series Latina. Turnhout, Belgium: Brepols, 1953-.
CER	Origen. *Commentarii in Epistulam ad Romanos.* Edited by T. Heither. 5 vols. New York: Herder, 1990-1995.
Cetedoc	Centre de Traitement Electronique des Documents.
CGSL	Cyril of Alexandria. *Commentary on the Gospel of St. Luke.* Translated by R. Payne Smith. Long Island, N.Y.: Studion Publishers, Inc., 1983.
CS	Cistercian Studies. Kalamazoo, Mich.: Cistercian Publications, 1973-.
CSCO	Corpus Scriptorum Christianorum Orientalium. Louvain, Belgium, 1903-.
ECTD	C. McCarthy, trans. and ed. *Saint Ephrem's Commentary on Tatian's Diatessaron: An English Translation of Chester Beatty Syriac MS 709. Journal of Semitic Studies* Supplement 2. Oxford: Oxford University Press, 1993.
EFHL	*The Enchiridion on Faith, Hope, and Love.* Translated by J. F. Shaw. Edited by Henry Paolucci. Chicago: Henry Regnery Company, 1961.
EKOG	Eznik of Kolb. *On God.* Translated by Monica J. Blanchard and Robin Darling Young. Leuven: Peeters, 1998.
ESOO	J. A. Assemani, ed. *Sancti patris nostri Ephraem Syri Opera omnia.* Rome, 1737.
FC	Fathers of the Church: A New Translation. Washington, D.C.: Catholic University of America Press, 1947-.
GCS	Die griechischen christlichen Schriftsteller der ersten Jahrhunderte. Berlin: Akademie-Verlag, 1897-.
HGE	*The Homilies of St. Gregory the Great on the Book of the Prophet Ezekiel.* Translated by Theodosia Gray. Etna, Calif.: Center for Traditionalist Orthodox Studies, 1990.
HOP	Ephrem the Syrian. *Hymns on Paradise.* Translated by Sebastian Brock. Crestwood, N.Y.: St.

Vladimir's Seminary Press, 1990.

INAL   St. Isaac of Nineveh. *On Ascetical Life*. Translated by Mary Hansbury. Crestwood, N.Y.: St. Vladimir's Seminary Press, 1989.

JCC   John Cassian. *Conferences*. Translated by Colm Luibheid. The Classics of Western Spirituality. Mahwah, N.J.: Paulist, 1985.

JCD   *Jerome's Commentary on Daniel*. Translated by Gleason L. Archer Jr. Grand Rapids, Mich.: Baker Book House, 1958.

JDDI   St. John of Damascus. *On the Divine Images*. Translated by David Anderson. Crestwood, N.Y.: St. Vladimir's Seminary Press, 1980.

KRBM   Marjorie Carpenter, trans. and ed. *Kontakia of Romanos, Byzantine Melodist*. 2 vols. Columbia, Mo.: University of Missouri Press, 1970-1973.

LCC   J. Baillie et al., eds. The Library of Christian Classics. 26 vols. Philadelphia: Westminster, 1953-1966.

LCL   Loeb Classical Library. Cambridge, Mass.: Harvard University Press; London: Heinemann, 1912-.

MFC   Message of the Fathers of the Church. Edited by Thomas Halton. Collegeville, Minn.: The Liturgical Press, 1983-.

MTS   Franz Zaver Seppelt, Joseph Pascher and Klaus Mörsdorf, eds. Münchener Theologische Studien, Historische Abteilung. Munich: Karl Zink, 1950-.

NJBC   *The New Jerome Biblical Commentary*. Edited by Raymond E. Brown, Joseph A. Fitzmeyer and Roland E. Murphy. Englewood Cliffs, N.J.: Prentice-Hall, 1990.

NPNF   P. Schaff et al., eds. A Select Library of the Nicene and Post-Nicene Fathers of the Christian Church. 2 series (14 vols. each). Buffalo, N.Y.: Christian Literature, 1887-1894. Reprint, Grand Rapids, Mich.: Eerdmans, 1952-1956. Reprint, Peabody, Mass.: Hendrickson, 1994.

OFP   Origen. *On First Principles*. Translated by G. W. Butterworth. London: SPCK, 1936. Reprint, Gloucester, Mass.: Peter Smith, 1973.

OHS   Basil of Caesarea. *On the Holy Spirit*. Translated by David Anderson, Crestwood, N.Y.: St. Vladimir's Seminary Press, 1980.

OSW   *Origen: An Exhortation to Martyrdom, Prayer and Selected Works*. Translated by Rowan A. Greer with Preface by Hans Urs von Balthasar. The Classics of Western Spirituality. New York: Paulist Press, 1979.

PDCW   *Pseudo-Dionysius: The Complete Works*. Translated by Colm Luibheid. The Classics of Western Spirituality. Mahwah, N.J.: Paulist Press, 1987.

PG   J.-P. Migne, ed. Patrologiae cursus completus. Series Graeca. 166 vols. Paris: Migne, 1857-1886.

PHF 1, 2   A. Isho, comp., 7th century. *The Paradise, or Garden of the Holy Fathers, being histories of the anchorites, recluses, monks, coenobites and ascetic fathers of the deserts of Egypt between A.D. CCL and CCCC circiter*. 2 vols. London: Chatto & Windus, 1907.

PMFSH   *Pseudo-Macarius: The Fifty Spiritual Homilies and the Great Letter*. Translated and edited by George A. Maloney, S.J. The Classics of Western Spirituality. Mahwah, N.J.: Paulist Press, 1992.

PO   Patrologia Orientalis. Turnhout, Belgium: Brepols, 1903-.

POG   Eusebius. *The Proof of the Gospel*. 2 vols. Translated by W. J. Ferrar. London: SPCK, 1920. Reprint, Grand Rapids, Mich.: Baker, 1981.

RSB   *The Rule of St. Benedict*. Edited by Timothy Fry, O.S.B. Collegeville, Minn.: The Liturgical Press, 1981.

SC   H. de Lubac, J. Daniélou et al., eds. Sources Chrétiennes. Paris: Éditions du Cerf, 1941-.

SCHO   *Selections from the Commentaries and Homilies of Origen*. Translations of Christian Literature, Series 1, Greek Texts. Translated by R. B. Tollinton. New York: The MacMillan Co., 1929.

SNTD   *Symeon the New Theologian: The Discourses.* Translated by C. J. de Catanzaro. The Classics of Western Spirituality. New York: Paulist Press, 1980.

TLG   L. Berkowitz and K. Squiter, eds. *Thesaurus Linguae Graecae: Canon of Greek Authors and Works.* 2nd ed. Oxford: Oxford University Press, 1986.

TTH   G. Clark, M. Gibson and M. Whitby, eds. Translated Texts for Historians. Liverpool: Liverpool University Press, 1985-.

WGRW   *Writings From the Greco-Roman World.* Atlanta: Society of Biblical Literature, 2001-.

WSA   J. E. Rotelle, ed. *Works of St. Augustine: A Translation for the Twenty-First Century.* Hyde Park, N.Y.: New City Press, 1995.

INTRODUCTION TO EZEKIEL

The Message of Ezekiel

The book of the prophet Ezekiel—a name that means "God strengthens"—is an unusual as well as an engaging read. It has been handled with long tongs by Jewish and Christian traditions from the beginning. Ezekiel the son of Buzi (Ezek 1:3) was a temple priest who appears to have been deported from Jerusalem to Babylonia in about 597 B.C., together with King Jehoiachin and other leading citizens of the defeated Judah. He received a call to be a prophet by the river Chebar, southeast of Babylon, a call that took the form of an overwhelming vision of the glory of God on a chariot (Ezek 1:4-28).

The fact that the book ends with a vision of the new temple (Ezek 40-48) probably reflects Ezekiel's memory of the Jerusalem temple where he could no longer offer priestly worship. His message is one of judgment, responsibility and hope to the people of Israel. It is a hard message, for Ezekiel prophesies the destruction of the temple and the wholesale deportation of the Jews from Jerusalem, which is what Nebuchadnezzar carried out in 586 B.C. Ezekiel's teaching has a strongly personal style throughout, with the elders regularly coming to him for advice (e.g., Ezek 14:1; 20:1; 33:31). His visions are full of sharp detail, and the style of the language, not without its difficulties whatever the translation, gives the impression of a strong and forceful personality. Unlike the other prophets (e.g., Hosea) Ezekiel dates the time of his call with precision, and unlike them (e.g., Jeremiah) he gives no personal details about his life, with one exception—the death of his wife, whom God commands him not to mourn (Ezek 24:15-18). He was probably aware of the teaching of Isaiah and Jeremiah. Daniel, his supposed contemporary, had a piety already proverbial in his time; we know this from two passages that the Fathers loved to use in their calls for personal responsibility—the three righteous men, Noah, Daniel and Job, cannot help the people of Israel unless they repent (Ezek 14:4, 28:3).

Ezekiel was accepted into the canon of Hebrew Scriptures with difficulty, and it is easy to see why. The prophet dares to claim to have seen God (Ezek 1:28), though the Fathers take care to point out that he saw only God's image, not his essence; his teaching about judgment seems at times harsher than the message of Isaiah and Jeremiah (Ezek 16-18); and Ezekiel even suggests that the Jewish law needed emendation (Ezek 20:25), which John Cassian, for example, used in order to point to Christ superseding it. Some of the rabbis forbade young people to read Ezekiel, particularly the opening vision of the heavenly chariot (Ezek 1), one of them even suggesting that fire would devour a child studying it; and some forbade the reading of Ezekiel 1 and Ezekiel 16 in public, because it became a foundation text primarily for mystical prayer and speculation.

And yet alongside this caution there also existed considerable enthusiasm. The Wisdom of Jesus ben Sirach refers explicitly to Ezekiel's vision of God (Sir 49:8). The heavenly chariot became an important inspiration for the *merkabah* ("chariot") mysticism of later Jewish piety, in which the chariot began to figure as a symbol in the instructions given to the devout in order to achieve heavenly visions; this explains why the chariot appears in various apocalypses (Dan 7-8, the *Apocalypse of Abraham* and 1 Enoch).

Ezekiel also leaves its mark on the New Testament. The image of Jesus as the shepherd (Mt 18:12-14; Jn 10:11-18) finds its inspiration in the prophecy about the shepherds and the sheep (Ezek 34), to which Augustine devoted two meaty sermons. More specifically, Revelation bears several significant traces of the influence of Ezekiel: the vision of the chariot from heaven with the four living creatures (Ezek 1:5-10) becomes the heavenly throne room with the four creatures surrounding Christ (Rev 4:1-8); the prophet is bidden to eat the scroll (Ezek 2:8-9), as is the seer (Rev 5:1, 10); the whore is condemned (Ezek 16:23; cf. Rev 17:1-6, 15-18); and each book ends with a vision of the new temple (Ezek 40-48; Rev 21-22). And yet just as Jews were nervous about Ezekiel, so were early Christians about Revelation, which became more widely read in the Christian West than in the East, where it has always been regarded as somewhat suspect. However, the four living creatures, as we shall see, take on an important symbolic role and are applied by the Fathers to the four Gospels, as well as to other aspects of the life of faith, both cosmological and psychological.

But what of the actual content of Ezekiel? The book falls approximately into four sections: Ezekiel 1-11; Ezekiel 12-32; Ezekiel 33-39; Ezekiel 40-48. These correspond to the selection of material we have made for this volume. The first part, Ezekiel 1-11, consists of Ezekiel's call and the beginning of his ministry; the vision of the heavenly chariot, the call of the prophet to speak to the rebellious house of Israel, his being told to eat the scroll and being silenced, his call to be the watchman, together with the nonverbal prophecies of the brick and the iron plate (Ezek 1:1-4:3); the marking of the innocent, and the vision of the punishment of ungodly rulers, culminating in the departure of the glory of the Lord from Jerusalem (Ezek 9:1-4; 11). This section sets the tone of the whole book, and it attracts considerable attention from the Fathers. They focus especially on the complexity of the opening vision, down to the details of the wings of the four creatures (Pseudo-Dionysius), as well as the image of the watchman, which is applied to the bishop's office in the church (Caesarius of Arles). More fundamentally, the off-beat character of the book is established at the outset, with its powerful vision of God, the effect of that vision on the prophet and the need for Ezekiel straightaway to find other means than speech in order to communicate with the people.

The next two sections of the book, Ezekiel 12-32 and Ezekiel 33-39, are about Ezekiel's verbal proclamation to the people. There is a gradual softening of tone from severe harshness at the beginning to the promise of hope later on. Words and parables of doom are the best description of the former, whereas promises of restoration characterize the latter. The theme of judgment, which dominates the whole book, is concentrated in the second section (see Ezek 13:1-4:5; 16-18; 20; 28). There are virulent prophecies against false prophets and against the hypocrisy of the elders (Ezek 13:1-14:5). Ezekiel 16 opens by describing Israel as a foundling child who is rescued by God and goes on to portray her as still determined to play the harlot, then ends on a message of hope, harbinger of things to come later in the book; Ezekiel 17 contains the allegory of the two eagles and the cedar, which also ends on a message of hope; Ezekiel 18 categorizes different attitudes to sin, stressing personal responsibility, since it does not matter who one's parents are or whether we once were righteous, because it is what we are doing now that matters; Ezekiel 20 casts the prophet's mind back to Israel's past disobedience in Egypt, the wilderness and Canaan (all was not rosy then), with a promise to purge Israel now, though God is ready to be merciful to the obedient; and Ezekiel 28 turns, by contrast, to Tyre and Sidon, as foreign nations, again promising recovery to Israel. Hard as much of this section sounds, with an almost merciless confrontation of people's motives, ambitions and actions, it is nonetheless shot through with an underlying hope for the future, once the reality of past and present are recognized for what they are. It is on these chapters that Origen concentrates his homilies on Ezekiel.

The atmosphere, however, turns increasingly towards a new future in the third section, Ezekiel 33-39 (see Ezek 33-34; 36-37). Ezekiel is to be a watchman again (see Ezek 3:17), speaking as commanded and not holding back, and Jerusalem will fall. The shepherds of Israel are scolded for failing to live up to their calling, and the Lord will become the shepherd, judging between them and providing a messiah as a new shepherd. Israel's oppressors will be judged, enabling the people to return so that they can be gathered together in a new covenant, with the Spirit written on their hearts of flesh, not stone. And Ezekiel has his vision of the valley of the dry bones, perhaps inspired by a battlefield, but now a place of resurrection, a vision unique to the Old Testament, and a passage that came to be used frequently at Easter.

The fourth and final part of the book, Ezekiel 40-48, is as self-contained as the opening vision. This time it is the vision of the new temple (Ezek 40; 43-44; 47). In some respects, this is the most complex part of the entire book; Ezekiel goes into considerable detail about the design of the building, its layout and its liturgical equipment. The only two writers whose work on this section has come down to us, Jerome and Gregory the Great, reacted somewhat differently. Jerome in his commentary shrinks from tackling such an extraordinary topic, whereas Gregory launches into a rich allegorical treatment in his homilies. Ezekiel 40 describes the outer court, the chambers around the court, the gates, the inner court, the tables of sacrifice and the vestibule. Ezekiel 43 portrays the return of the Lord to the temple and the offering of sacrifice on the altar once more. Ezekiel 44 returns to the theme of judgment: the gate of the sanctuary must be kept shut, and the uncircumcised and the idolatrous Levites are not to be allowed in. And Ezekiel 47 has the vision of water flowing through the temple, a symbol of the ever-new and ever-cleansing power of God.

Main Patristic Interpreters of Ezekiel

The main interpreters among the Fathers are comparatively few and far between, but we have more than enough to go on. This may be due in part to the fact that Ezekiel was regarded as a difficult book. But the evidence that we possess, we must remember, is by no means all that could be available. Four authors recur throughout, and each is important in himself.

The first is Origen, whose full-scale commentary has been mostly lost but who preached a course of fourteen homilies during his lengthy stay in Caesarea, between 239 and 242.[1] At Caesarea, where preaching was not restricted to bishops as it was elsewhere, there was a sermon on the Old Testament reading in the morning. The version that we have is Jerome's Latin translation, which was probably made in Constantinople (379-381), when Jerome, under the influence of Gregory of Nazianzus, became more interested in the

---

[1]For background material on Origen's homilies, see SC 352:7-22, 445-83.

controversial, allegorizing Alexandrian than he was later in his life. Whether the homilies were delivered exactly as they appear in Jerome's version is not clear, but Origen preached them as the passages were read in liturgical services at the time. His selection of passages from Ezekiel is instructive, for nearly all come from the words and prophecies of doom, except that the first homily expounds part of the opening vision (Ezek 1:1-6; 2:1ff.), and the concluding homily deals with the gate of the sanctuary of the new temple being kept shut (Ezek 44:1-3). Origen, not surprisingly, engages the *theoria* reading of Scripture, which is rich in typology. Ezekiel is the type of Christ; the marking of the saved on the forehead (Ezek 9:4-6) prefigures baptism; the struggles with false prophets are the early church's struggles with heresy; and the corruption of Jerusalem is the sinful character of the church. Origen's style is not always clear, though it is thought that Jerome stuck closely to the original Greek version that he possessed at the time. These homilies are uneven in length, and it may well be that the passages on which Origen preached were specifically at the behest of the local bishops (see Homily 13.1, on Ezek 28:12-23). They were probably not intended as popular Sunday preachments but delivered as weekday sermons, to a more educated gathering.

Jerome's commentary, by contrast, is a different kind of work altogether. By its nature, it is not selective.[2] Well-established in Bethlehem, Jerome began the commentary in the last decade of his life. He had already produced his Latin version of the Bible (the Vulgate) and was now writing commentaries on the Old Testament prophets. Having completed Isaiah, he decided—significantly, against the order of these books in the Scriptures—to write on Ezekiel before he dealt with Jeremiah, a commentary he never completed. The commentary on Ezekiel is a lengthy tome, which Jerome began in 411 but did not complete until 414. The interruptions were caused by a combination of refugees from the West to the Holy Land following the sack of Rome by Alaric the Goth, as well as theological controversies into which Jerome allowed himself to be drawn. From the outset, Jerome set himself the task of writing a straight exegesis of Scripture, avoiding becoming embroiled in rebutting heresies. And that, largely, is how the commentary reads, with its careful treatment of the text, in which he notes differences between the Septuagint (which he criticizes from time to time) and his own Vulgate version, as well as others.[3] Tantalizingly, he never names the Greek and Latin sources that he uses in his exegesis, and he refers to Jewish writers also. He stuck to his initial resolve for most of Ezekiel, explaining the text and drawing from it lessons of a moral, spiritual or theological nature. But when he reaches the vision of the new temple, he takes on a new lease of life. For example, the gate that is shut (Ezek 44:2) is the Law and the Prophets, the true interpretation of which can only come through Christ. Moreover, Jerome, the sharp-tongued scourge of the hierarchy, used the idolatrous Levites (Ezek 44:9) as the basis for an attack on lordly bishops.

Shortly after Jerome comes the commentary by Theodoret of Cyr, which was probably written between 433 and 438 in Antioch and may have been based on homilies.[4] In style much simpler and far shorter than Jerome, Theodoret's commentary follows more strictly the exegetical tradition of Antioch, which was suspi-

---

[2]See J. N. D. Kelly, *Jerome: His Life, Writings and Controversies* (London: Duckworth, 1975), 304-8.

[3]For a brief discussion of the Greek, Latin and Hebrew texts of the Old Testament used by the Fathers, see Andrew Louth's introduction in ACCS 1:xl-xlvi; the same background applies for Ezekiel. The textual variants among the various versions are considerable, but they do not alter the substantial meaning of the text; the main lxx variants are noted with the rsv in the commentary.

[4]For background material on Theodoret, see G. W. Ashby, *Theodoret of Cyrrhus as Exegete of the Old Testament* (Grahamstown: Rhodes University Publications Department, 1972) 94-96, 131-33.

cious of the allegorizing tradition of Alexandria. In the opening vision, he holds back any attempt to equate the four creatures with the Gospels, in the way of Jerome and others—they are instead about God's control of the universe. Theodoret's typology is far gentler than that of Origen. Interestingly, he skates over the vision of the new temple in a matter of pages.

The fourth major source is the series of the twenty-two homilies preached by Gregory the Great at the end of 593, perhaps extending to the beginning of 594.[5] They were delivered as a counterblast to the Lombard king Agilulf's march on Rome, just three years after Gregory left the Abbey of Saint Andrew to become pope. Not written down until some years after they were preached, these homilies come in two books. The first twelve consist of an introductory homily on the ministry of prophecy, and this is followed by eleven on the opening vision and the call of Ezekiel (Ezek 1:1-4:3). The second set is made up of ten homilies, exclusively on Ezekiel 40, the vision of the new temple. The selection of material preached on is quite different from Origen's, but the kind of audience appears to have been the same; they are demanding sermons, for a congregation of weekday adherents, which perhaps included monks and other religious officials. Like Origen, Gregory goes through the passages verse by verse. Behind Gregory's firm and clear prose we can discern the learning of Jerome, with a strong dose of Origen's allegorizing. The major themes are the depth and character of evil, the reality of Christ the Savior, the vision of God, the nature of contemplation, the need for compunction and tears in the face of God's judgment, the practice of virtues, the work of the church in preaching the good news and the need to live a life of contemplation and action, which is a favorite line of Gregory's elsewhere. There are times when one can sense the devastation by the Lombards, for example, at the end, when the preacher finds himself unable to say any more, because the contrast between the new temple and the sinful world is too great for him to bear (Homilies 2.10.24).

The Four Living Creatures

We have already mentioned the four living creatures—the man, the lion, the ox and the eagle. Because of the complex schemes that were developed in the patristic period, a word of fuller explanation is needed.[6] Comparison has already been made between Ezekiel and Revelation. There are some differences, principally that Ezekiel's creatures surround a chariot carrying the divine presence with the sequence of man, lion, ox and eagle, whereas Revelation (drawing also on Isaiah's temple vision [Is 6:1-4] and Daniel's judgment seat [Dan 7:9-14]) takes the seer himself into heaven through an open door in order to behold a heavenly throne room where Christ is in the center, surrounded by the four creatures—the lion, the ox, the man and the eagle—singing the Sanctus (Rev 4:1-8). The order in which the creatures appear is this time different, removing the man from first place perhaps in order to emphasize the centrality of Christ. Patristic preaching and commentary drew on Ezekiel and Revelation and produced a number of schemes, starting with three for the Gospels and the Evangelists.

The first scheme identified the lion as John, the ox as Luke, the man as Matthew and the eagle as Mark.

[5]For background material on Gregory's homilies, see SC 327:7-31, SC 360:11-32; see also Stephan Ch. Kessler, *Gregor der Grosse als Exegete: Eine theologische Interpretation der Ezekielhomilien*, Innsbrucker Theologische Studier 43 (Innsbruck-Wien: Tyrolia-Verlag, 1995). Also see Angela Russell Christman, "The Spirit and the Wheels: Gregory the Great on Reading Scripture," in In *Dominico Eloquio*, ed. Paul M. Blowers et al. (Grand Rapids: Eerdmans, 2002), 395-407.
[6]See Kenneth Stevenson, "Animal Rites: The Four Living Creatures in Patristic Exegesis and Liturgy," *Studia Patristica* 34 (2001):469-92.

This is what we come across in Irenaeus (*Against Heresies* 3.11.8), and it is followed by Victorinus of Petovium in his commentary on Revelation; Juvencus, the Spanish presbyter-poet; and Chromatius of Aquileia, in his commentary on Matthew. They all give the same rationale: the lion is John, because his Gospel begins full of confidence; the ox is Luke, because his Gospel begins with priestly sacrifice; the man is Matthew, because his Gospel begins with the genealogy of Jesus; and the eagle is Mark, because his Gospel begins with the prophecy of Isaiah (Is 43).

The second scheme becomes the standard one: the lion is Mark, the ox is Luke, the man is Matthew, and the eagle is John. This arrangement first appears in Epiphanius's *On Weights and Measures*, and he is followed by Jerome, Apponius and Gregory the Great. They all give a similar rationale and again use the opening words of each Gospel to support them; Matthew is the man because he begins with a genealogy; Mark is the lion, roaring in the desert, like his prophetic opening; Luke is the ox, because he begins with temple sacrifice; and John is the eagle, flying heavenwards like the divine Word.

The third scheme we first come across in the fragments of Hippolytus on Ezekiel, and he is followed by Augustine (who enters some caution about these schemes, observing that they should all point ultimately to Christ alone), Ambrose and Primasius of Hadrumetum. The lion is Matthew, because Christ is descended from the tribe of Judah; the ox is Luke, because Christ is shown in his priestly glory; the man is Mark, because of the humanity of Christ shown in that Gospel; and the eagle is John, because the mystery of the Word ascends to heaven.

It is interesting to speculate on why these schemes were worked out in the first place. Irenaeus may well have been following a tradition going back to Papias, and since the canon of the New Testament was in process of formation, such a typology, whether from Ezekiel or Revelation or both, could give support to there being no fewer and no more than four Gospels. At any rate, the fact remains that the aforementioned writers, representing both mainstream and out-of-the-way profiles, developed this tradition of interpretation. The standard scheme of Epiphanius, Jerome and Gregory is what won, and it took on an iconographical as well as a liturgical life of its own. For example, the Book of Kells (c. 800) has no fewer than three full-page depictions of all four creatures. The scheme became important in baptismal catechesis in the West. The rite of "exposition of the Gospels" found in the Gelasian Sacramentary, a book of prayers for the Eucharist and baptism falsely attributed to Pope Gelasius I that probably reflects liturgical usage at Rome as early as the sixth century, may well point to a still earlier tradition. This rite has a strong visual impact on the way that it teaches those to be baptized about each Evangelist, starting with the corresponding animal symbol. It is found in other later liturgical books, probably because of its popularity in catechesis.

Meanwhile, in the East, where the book of Revelation was more suspect, other ways of interpreting the creatures emerged. There are the four elements, with the lion as fire, the ox as earth, the man as air and the eagle as water. This is what we find in Methodius of Olympus and Novatian. Macarius and Ammonas avoid the book of Revelation and stick to Ezekiel when they interpret the creatures. For Macarius, the eagle is the king of birds, the lion is the king of the wild beasts, the ox is the king of domestic animals, while man is the king of all creatures in general. He also makes them correspond to the four ruling factors in the soul: the eagle is the will, the lion is the conscience, the ox is intelligence, and the man is love. Ammonas takes another psychological approach: the lion is a cherub, the Spirit of God resting on the soul to enable it to praise God; the man is the desire to inquire; the ox is faithfulness in struggle; and the eagle is the desire to ascend to the heights.

The important truth to grasp about these interpretations is that they are first and foremost the activity of the religious imagination and in no way can one be considered in some manner correct. For example, Jerome and Gregory the Great opted for the same Evangelist scheme (Jerome's authority was bound to carry weight in the West, in the face of others), but they could also envisage other ways of interpretation, along the lines of the psychological approach of Macarius. Indeed, Jerome adapted Plato's tripartite view of the soul (the rational, the emotional and the appetitive), adding as the fourth what he called conscience.[7]

Contexts of Teaching, Worship and Doctrine

There are many other examples of the distinctive use of Ezekiel. A summary of the opening vision (Ezek 1:1-28; 3:12-15) forms one of the readings from the Old Testament in the old Syriac lectionary for Ascension Day, a festival of doctrinal significance pointing to the heavenly priesthood of Christ that we encounter at the time of Cyril of Jerusalem in the holy city itself. While the date of the composition of this lection scheme is uncertain, it is assumed to be early, and the material in this particular lection is appropriate for the occasion—the chariot calling the prophet and leaving him among the people, just as Christ ascended into heaven, telling the disciples to proclaim the Good News on earth. An altogether different tradition is the feast of the four living creatures on November 4 in the Coptic and Ethiopic churches. Impossible to date, the mediaeval Ethiopic Synaxarium (a cross between a biblical and liturgical commentary) gives a rationale for the occasion almost identical to what we saw in Macarius, each creature being the king of a particular group. What we have here is quite different from the Evangelist schemes. It is, rather, a festival of the new creation, with representative creatures worshiping before God—arguably more in the spirit of the Ezekiel vision than Evangelists, and certainly pointing to a quite separate development.

Then, at the time of Caesarius of Arles, the call to be a watchman (Ezek 3:17-21) was the Old Testament reading at the consecration of a bishop, which was a passage used in conjunction with John 21:15-19, in which the risen Christ commands Peter to feed his sheep. Caesarius, who as metropolitan of Arles from 503 to 542 had considerable influence in Gaul, not only preached on this text in connection with an episcopal consecration but returned frequently in other sermons to the watchman ready to convict the people of their sins as the responsibility of the bishop; in this he follows Ambrose and Augustine. On a different note, around 411, Augustine, in the thick of the Donatist controversy, preached two homilies on the shepherds and the sheep. He preached through Ezekiel 34 verse by verse, warning the Christian community about the need for right order and proper teaching.[8]

There is also baptismal catechesis. A series of homilies preached by Cyril of Jerusalem in the holy city (c. 350) have come down to us.[9] Of these eighteen, there are two that use central passages from Ezekiel. The second is about repentance and is based on Ezekiel 18:20-21 (a much-commented-on text) as a basis. The

---

[7]See Norman Kretzmann, Anthony Kenny and Jan Pinborg, eds., *The Cambridge History of Later Medieval Philosophy* (Cambridge: Cambridge University Press, 1982), 688-89, for a discussion of how subsequent writers were misled by Jerome on this point.

[8]On the dating and context of these sermons, see *WSA* 3 2:292-93 n. 1 and 323 n. 1.

[9]See Edward Yarnold, *Cyril of Jerusalem* (London and New York: Routledge, 2000).

final catechesis, on the closing words of the Apostles' Creed, concerns the hope of resurrection, and its text is Ezekiel 37:1-14, the vision of the valley of the dry bones. Both these texts point to Cyril's use of two significant aspects of Ezekiel's teaching, the need for repentance and the promise of new life, both of which are fundamental to the baptismal life. The valley of the dry bones, moreover, understandably attracted attention as an Easter reading, for we find it later in the Jerusalem Easter vigil among the Old Testament readings, from where it spread through the Byzantine and Orthodox world. It is also found at Rome in the Gelasian Sacramentary at the vigil immediately after a reading from Ezekiel 36, the cleansing of the people and the new heart. To have two lections in succession during that central, lengthy baptismal liturgy is another indication of the use of Ezekiel as an important source of reflection and teaching. The evidence for lection schemes is very sparse in the early centuries. The Hippolytus fragments, for example, suggest a tradition of midrashes on Scripture somewhat akin to synagogue practice. What we do have overall for Ezekiel indicates local sequences, worked out for specific purposes, perhaps for the preachers themselves, as we have seen with Origen and Gregory the Great. But as far as Sundays and festivals are concerned, a few specific passages were selected. By the time these schemes were being worked out in the fourth, fifth and sixth centuries, the Old Testament reading begins to slip out of use at the Eucharist, in the fifth century in Constantinople and in the sixth century at Rome, though it survives elsewhere, as at Milan. The Roman rite held an increasingly strong influence in the West, and the lection schemes dating from the eighth century onwards point to what could be an already well-established practice, doubtless built on earlier exegesis, of using key passages during the weekdays of Lent, the season traditionally connected with baptismal catechesis. These are Ezekiel 18:1-9 (responsibility), Ezekiel 18:20-28 (conversion), Ezekiel 34:11-16 (feeding the sheep) and Ezekiel 36:23-28 (pouring out the Spirit, the heart of flesh). This latter passage did not always additionally appear at the long Easter vigil service.[10]

Ezekiel, like other books of the Old Testament, was used to illustrate and explain the Christian life—in Ezekiel's case with perhaps a slightly stronger accent on some of its contradictions and paradoxes, such as the reality of Christ from heaven among us, the responsibility of the believer, God's judgment as well as his determination to forgive sins, the resurrection of the body, the vision of heaven itself on earth and the way these truths are imparted to us in a spiritual reading of the Gospels. For example, the temple door that is shut (Ezek 44:2) is applied by Cyril of Alexandria and John of Damascus to the virgin birth, which probably explains why this passage came to be read in Jerusalem and subsequently all over in the Byzantine and Orthodox rites at vespers on the festivals associated with the Virgin Mary, including her birth (September 8). That is a clear example of the relationship between exegesis and liturgy. It also demonstrates the use of specially selected verses from Ezekiel in the context of the christological controversies of the time, as the same exegesis is found, for example, in Rufinus's *Commentary on the Apostles' Creed*. There are many other instances of the use of Ezekiel among the Fathers in other contexts, whether in what at the time was the public medium of writing letters (Jerome), defending belief in the resurrection (Ambrose), interpreting the Psalms (Cassiodorus), spelling out the importance of free will (Tertullian), exhorting Christians to follow

---

[10]On the Easter vigil, see A. J. MacGregor, *The Lections and Collects of the Vigils of Easter and Pentecost*, Ushaw Library Publications 1 (Ushaw, U.K.: Ushaw College Library, 1999); on the use of Ezekiel in Lent in the Roman lectionaries, see Antoine Chavasse, *Les Lectionnaires Romains de la Messe au VIe et au VIIIe: Sources et Dérivés 1 and 2*, Spicilegii Friburgensis Subsidia 22 (Fribourg: Editions Universitaires, 1993).

Christ more faithfully (Pacian of Barcelona) or wrestling with the question of free will (Theodoret of Cyr and Augustine).

All in all, Ezekiel emerges from this valley of rich interpretation as a challenging book, lovingly and thoughtfully reflected on. It is the result of much discernment and creativity, all the more nuanced because Ezekiel was used much more sparingly than the other two major prophets. The basic truths of the Christian message nonetheless stand out with a fresh clarity, particularly when one considers the difficulties Ezekiel's message encountered among his own people, during his own time and subsequently. No wonder the Fathers could find in certain key passages the heart of the Christian gospel. One gains a strong sense of Scripture as a rich pool in which to bathe rather than a rigid conceptual framework from which to write off specific propositions that are in some way logically vindicated forever. Using and interpreting Ezekiel thus becomes an activity of the religious imagination, the work of the Holy Spirit in the praying life of the church.

Kenneth Stevenson
Bishopsgrove
Fareham
Hampshire, U.K.

EZEKIEL

1:1-3 INTRODUCTION

¹*In the thirtieth year, in the fourth month, on the fifth day of the month, as I was among the exiles by the river Chebar, the heavens were opened, and I saw visions of God. ²On the fifth day of the month (it was the fifth year of the exile of King Jehoiachin), ³the word of the LORD came to Ezekiel the priest, the son of Buzi, in the land of the Chaldeans by the river Chebar; and the hand of the LORD was upon him there.*

OVERVIEW: The opening vision is unique and central to Ezekiel and formative to his message. Visions from heaven are unique and mysterious (GREGORY OF NAZIANZUS), but the Holy Spirit is omnipresent (BASIL). For this vision, all the angels descended, making it necessary for all the heavens to be opened (ORIGEN). The heavens opened at Christ's baptism (JEROME). The heavens are opened through contemplation (THEODORET). Ezekiel was thirty when the heavens were opened, the same age as Christ at his baptism (GREGORY THE GREAT).

Ezekiel, on whom the Spirit descended for a time only, is a type of Christ (ORIGEN), on whom the Spirit descended permanently (JEROME). In order to make any special revelations to mortals, God leads them away from distractions, so that they can be attentive (CHRYSOSTOM). The vision Ezekiel is about to have prefigures the mysteries of the gospel (JEROME). The hand that was on Ezekiel is Christ himself (GREGORY THE GREAT).

1:1 By the River Chebar

THE NATURE OF TRUE INSPIRATION. GREGORY OF NAZIANZUS: What would you say of Isaiah or Ezekiel, who was an eyewitness of very great mysteries, and of the other prophets: for one of these saw the Lord of Sabaoth sitting on the throne of glory and encircled and praised by the six-winged seraphim, and was himself purged by the live coal and equipped for his prophetic office;[1] and the other describes the cherubic chariot of God, and the throne on them, and the firmament over it, and him that showed himself in the firmament, and voices and forces and deeds. And whether this was an appearance by day, only visible to saints, or an unerring vision of the night, or an impression on the mind holding converse with the future as if it were the present or some other ineffable form of prophecy, I cannot say; the God of the prophets knows, and they know who are thus inspired. ON THEOLOGY, THEOLOGICAL ORATION 2(28).19.[2]

THE SPIRIT'S OMNIPRESENCE. BASIL THE GREAT: We believe that the Spirit is present everywhere, while the rest of the bodiless powers

---

[1]Is 6:1-8. [2]LCC 3:149.

are circumscribed by place. On the Holy Spirit 23.54.[3]

Many Heavens Opened. Origen: It was not enough for one heaven to be opened; a greater number was opened, so that the angels descended not from one, but from all the heavens on those who were to be saved. Homilies on Ezekiel 1.7.[4]

Baptism of Christ Foretold. Jerome: Truly our Lord and Savior Jesus Christ is prefigured, who came to baptism at the age of thirty years, which in a man is the perfect age. Commentary on Ezekiel 1.1.1.[5]

Maturity of Thirty Years. Gregory the Great: The statement that he received the spirit of prophecy in the thirtieth year indicates to us a point for consideration, namely, that the speech of teaching does not agree with the exercise of reason, except in ripe age. Homilies on Ezekiel 1.2.3.[6]

The Faith of the Believer. Jerome: You must understand that the heavens were opened not by the firmament being divided but by the faith of the believer, for the one to whom these things are heavenly is the one to whom mysteries are disclosed. At the baptism of the Savior, when the Holy Spirit descended on him in the form of a dove, we read that "the heavens were opened."[7] Commentary on Ezekiel 1.1.1-2.[8]

Contemplation. Theodoret of Cyr: He said that the heavens were open, not in reality or in deed but through spiritual contemplation. Commentary on Ezekiel 1.1.[9]

1:2-3 The Hand of the Lord

Ezekiel a Type of Christ. Origen: If you want to understand that this word is said about the Savior, do not hold back. The allegory has its own meaning as well, in this way: the Word of God comes to us as he who was born of the virgin, that is, man; as the Word who lives always in the Father. Homilies on Ezekiel 1.10.[10]

The Spirit a Temporary Gift to Humans Except Through Christ. Jerome: The Holy Spirit descended on Christ and remained; he descends on people, assuredly, but does not remain. Furthermore, in the scroll of Ezekiel, who is properly a type of the Savior—no other prophet, I mean of the major prophets, is called, "Son of man"; the title is given strictly to Ezekiel. Homilies on Mark 75 (Mk 1:1-12).[11]

God Leads Us from Tumult. Chrysostom: Whenever God is going to reveal some sight beyond all expectation to his servants, he leads them out of the cities to a place free from tumult. Against the Anomoeans 3.25.[12]

Future Mysteries Revealed. Jerome: To both Daniel and Ezekiel who were in Babylon by the river, the sacraments of the future were unfolded, I mean in the purest of waters, so that the power of baptism could be shown. Commentary on Ezekiel 1.1.3.[13]

Christ Is the Hand of the Lord. Gregory the Great: The hand or arm of the Lord signifies the Son, for by him all things were made. Homilies on Ezekiel 1.2.7.[14]

The Hand Is Strength. Jerome: So that we can discern and understand the visions of God, it is necessary for us to have the hand and strength of God on us. Commentary on Ezekiel 1.1.3.[15]

---

[3]OHS 85. [4]SC 352:70. [5]CCL 75:5. [6]HGE 22. [7]Mt 3:16. [8]CCL 75:5-6. [9]PG 81:820. [10]SC 352:76. [11]FC 57:130*. [12]FC 72:106*. [13]CCL 75:6. [14]HGE 24. [15]CCL 75:7.

1:4-14 THE APPEARANCE OF THE FOUR CREATURES

⁴*As I looked, behold, a stormy wind came out of the north, and a great cloud, with brightness round about it, and fire flashing forth continually, and in the midst of the fire, as it were gleaming bronze. ⁵And from the midst of it came the likeness of four living creatures. And this was their appearance: they had the form of men, ⁶but each had four faces, and each of them had four wings. ⁷Their legs were straight, and the soles of their feet were like the sole of a calf's foot; and they sparkled like burnished bronze. ⁸Under their wings on their four sides they had human hands. And the four had their faces and their wings thus: ⁹their wings touched one another; they went every one straight forward, without turning as they went. ¹⁰As for the likeness of their faces, each had the face of a man in front;^a the four had the face of a lion on the right side, the four had the face of an ox on the left side, and the four had the face of an eagle at the back.^b ¹¹Such were their faces. And their wings were spread out above; each creature had two wings, each of which touched the wing of another, while two covered their bodies. ¹²And each went straight forward; wherever the spirit would go, they went, without turning as they went. ¹³In the midst of the living creatures there was something that looked like burning coals of fire, like torches moving to and fro among the living creatures; and the fire was bright, and out of the fire went forth lightning. ¹⁴And the living creatures darted to and fro, like a flash of lightning.*

a Cn: Heb lacks *in front*   b Cn: Heb lacks *at the back*   c Gk Old Latin: Heb *And the likeness of*

OVERVIEW: The wind of God purifies us from sin (ORIGEN), spreads virtues on the church (GREGORY THE GREAT) and gives the new dispensation; the gleaming bronze is God himself (JEROME), with Christ, standing between God and humanity (GREGORY THE GREAT).

The four creatures provide a rich quarry from which different interpretations are developed, but throughout they are a unique way of linking heaven and earth and of driving the prophet on in his message to the people of Israel. The cherubim are the knowledge of God (ORIGEN). This vision in all its wonder shows us how incomprehensible is the glory of God (CYRIL OF JERUSALEM). The four creatures are the Gospels or the Gospel writers, in different schemes (HIPPOLYTUS AND IRENAEUS; EPIPHANIUS, JEROME AND GREGORY THE GREAT; AUGUSTINE). They are different aspects of the mystery of Christ's life (BEDE, JEROME, GREGORY THE GREAT). They can be the life of the preacher, strong in dedication and balanced in way of life (GREGORY THE GREAT). They can be related to the human personality (AMBROSE, JEROME, THEODORET, PSEUDO-MACARIUS, AMMONAS).

The four creatures are creatures of heaven (JEROME, PSEUDO-DIONYSIUS), which can be likened to the life of the preacher (GREGORY THE GREAT), though not everything heavenly can be understood (THEODORET).

1:4 The Stormy Wind

THE WIND PURIFIES. ORIGEN: When you have been purified by the sweeping wind, to the extent that it has swept away every evil from you and everything of evil character in your soul, then you will begin to benefit from the great cloud that envelopes the sweeping wind. HOMILIES ON EZEKIEL 1.12.[1]

---

[1]SC 352:86.

THE WARM WIND POSSESSES THE FAITHFUL.
GREGORY THE GREAT: When, at the Lord's command, the cold wind recedes, the warm wind takes possession of the hearts of the faithful, he who blows through the garden of God, holy church, so that reports of virtues flow out like spices for many people to hear about. HOMILIES ON EZEKIEL 1.2.9.[2]

A NEW DISPENSATION. JEROME: So that the exiled people can be comforted and the purpose of God revealed, the prophet saw a very great vision. As far as its interpretation is concerned, all the synagogues of the Jews are silent beyond what a person can say. COMMENTARY ON EZEKIEL 1.1.4.[3]

FIRE ON EARTH. JEROME: The Savior said that he had come to send fire on earth, and he wanted it to burn in us and in all believers. COMMENTARY ON EZEKIEL 1.1.4.[4]

THE LIKENESS OF GOD. JEROME: In the middle of the fire or the torments of God is the likeness of amber, which is more precious than gold or silver, and after judgment and torments, which seem awkward and hard to those who suffer them, a flash of lightning more precious than amber appears, while all things are steered by the providence of God and what is considered punishment is in fact a medicine. COMMENTARY ON EZEKIEL 1.1.4.[5]

CHRIST HIMSELF. GREGORY THE GREAT: What is meant by the resemblance of amber but Christ Jesus, the mediator of God and humankind? HOMILIES ON EZEKIEL 1.2.14.[6]

1:5-10 *The Appearance of the Four Creatures*

KNOWLEDGE OF GOD. ORIGEN: The cherubim are interpreted as the fullness of knowledge. Whoever is full of skill becomes a cherub that God drives. HOMILIES ON EZEKIEL 1.15.[7]

IMPOSSIBLE TO COMPREHEND GOD'S NATURE. CYRIL OF JERUSALEM: After this description of the prophet, we still cannot comprehend as we read. But if we cannot comprehend the throne that he has described, how will we be able to comprehend him who sits on it, the invisible and ineffable God? It is impossible to examine closely the nature of God, but for his works, which we see, we can offer him praise and glory. CATECHETICAL LECTURES 9.3.[8]

THE FOUR CREATURES AS THE FOUR GOSPELS. IRENAEUS: The cherubim have four faces, and their faces are images of the activity of the Son of God. For the first living creature, it says, was like a lion, signifying his active and princely and royal character; the second was like an ox, showing his sacrificial and priestly order; the third had the face of a man, indicating very clearly his coming in human guise; and the fourth was like a flying eagle, making plain the giving of the Spirit who broods over the church. Now the Gospels, in which Christ is enthroned, are like these. John expounds his princely and mighty and glorious birth from the Father, saying, "In the beginning was the Word, and the Word was with God, and the Word was God," and "All things were made by him, and without him was nothing made."[9] Therefore this Gospel is deserving of all confidence, for such indeed is his person. That according to Luke has a priestly character, and it began with the priest Zechariah offering incense to God. For the fatted calf was already being prepared that was to be sacrificed for the finding of the younger son.[10] Matthew proclaims his human birth, saying, "The book of the generation of Jesus Christ, son of David, son of Abraham,"[11] and "The birth of Jesus Christ was in this manner."[12] This Gospel is manlike, and so through the whole Gospel Christ appears as a man of humble mind and gentle. But Mark takes his beginning

---

[2]HGE 25*. [3]CCL 75:7. [4]CCL 75:9. [5]CCL 75:9. [6]HGE 27*. [7]SC 352:92. [8]FC 61:186*. [9]Jn 1:1-3. [10]See Lk 1:8ff.; 15:23. [11]Mt 1:1. [12]Mt 1:18.

from the prophetic Spirit who comes on people from on high, saying, "The beginning of the gospel of Jesus Christ, as it is written in Isaiah the prophet,"[13] showing a winged image of the Gospel. Therefore he made his message concise and immediate, for such is the prophetic character. AGAINST HERESIES 3.11.8.[14]

THE FOUR CREATURES ANNOUNCE THE COMING OF CHRIST. EPIPHANIUS OF SALAMIS: Four living creatures with four forms stand announcing the coming of Christ: the form of the man for one of them, because Jesus Christ was born at Bethlehem, as the Evangelist Matthew tells us; the form of the lion for another, as Mark proclaims him as having come from the Jordan, like the royal lion, as it is written, "Behold, like a lion coming up from the jungle of the Jordan";[15] the form of the bull for another, because Luke proclaims—and not only him, but all the Evangelists also—that at the appointed time, until the ninth hour, he was sacrificed on the cross as the ox for the world; the form of the eagle for the last, because John proclaims the Word that has come down from heaven and became flesh and has gone to heaven like an eagle, for a complete resurrection, full of the divine nature. ON WEIGHTS AND MEASURES 1.8-10.[16]

THE FOUR CREATURES AS THE EVANGELISTS. JEROME: The four-faced creature that we met in the Apocalypse of John[17] and in the beginning of Ezekiel's prophecy that had the face of a man, the face of a calf, the face of a lion, the face of an eagle, has also special significance for the text we are considering.[18] In Matthew, this human being has the face of a man; in Luke, an ox; in John, an eagle; in Mark, the lion crying in the desert. HOMILY ON MARK 75 (MK 1:1-12).[19]

THE FOUR WINGED CREATURES REPRESENT THE FOUR EVANGELISTS. GREGORY THE GREAT: The preface of each Gospel avers that these four winged creatures denote the four holy Evangelists. Because he began from the generations of

humankind, Matthew is justly represented by a man; because of the crying in the wilderness, Mark is rightly indicated by a lion; because he started from a sacrifice, Luke is well described as an ox; and because he begins with the divinity of the Word, John is worthily signified by an eagle, he who says, "In the beginning was the Word, and the Word was with God, and the Word was God";[20] while he stretched towards the very substance of divinity, he fixed his eye on the sun as if in the fashion of an eagle. But because all the elect are members of our Savior, for our Savior is indeed the head of all the elect, in that his members are thereby depicted, there is no obstacle to even him being signified in all these. For the only-begotten Son of God truly became man; he deigned to die like an ox at sacrifice for our salvation; he, through the virtue of his fortitude, rose as a lion. Moreover, the lion is said to sleep with open eyes because, in the very death in which our Savior could sleep through his humanity, by remaining immortal in his divinity, he kept vigil. Furthermore, ascending to heaven after his resurrection, he was carried aloft to the heights like an eagle. He is therefore wholly the same within us at the same time, who became a man by being born, an ox in dying, a lion in rising again and an eagle in ascending to the heavens. HOMILIES ON EZEKIEL 1.4.1.[21]

THE FOUR ANIMALS PRAISE GOD. HIPPOLYTUS: This is also how Ezekiel depicts those animals that praise God. In the four figures of the four Evangelists he demonstrates the glory of the Father and draws attention to his workings, in whom all four points of the compass are fulfilled. "The one animal," he says, "had four figures"; because each figure is a Gospel, it appears in a fourfold fashion. The first figure, he says, which was like an ox, indicates the priestly glory of Jesus, which Luke depicts. The second, which was like a lion, indicates the leadership and regal

---

[13]Mk 1:1-2. [14]LCC 1:382-83*. [15]Jer 49:19. [16]CSCO 461:40-41. [17]Rev 4:6-8. [18]Mk 1:1-12. [19]FC 57:121. [20]Jn 1:1. [21]HGE 40-41.

nature of the lion "of the tribe of Judah"; this is what Matthew depicts. The third was like a human being and shows the Son's capacity for suffering and the lowly nature of humanity; this is what Mark shows. However, the fourth, the eagle, teaches the spiritual secret of his power and might who flies up to the Father's heaven; this is John's message. FRAGMENT 1.[22]

THE ANIMALS EMPHASIZE THE KINGLY CHARACTER OF CHRIST. AUGUSTINE: It appears to me that those who have taken the lion to point to Matthew, the man to Mark, the ox to Luke and the eagle to John have made a more reasonable application of the figures than those who have assigned the man to Matthew, the eagle to Mark and the lion to John. For in forming their particular idea of the matter, they have chosen to keep in view simply the beginnings of the book, and not the full design of the several Evangelists in its completeness, which was the matter that should, above all, have been thoroughly examined. For surely it is with much greater propriety that the Evangelist who has brought to our attention most particularly the kingly character of Christ should be taken as being represented by the lion.... That Luke is intended under the figure of the calf, in reference to the sacrifice made by the priest, has been doubted by neither of the two sets of interpreters.... In this way it further follows that Mark, who has set himself neither to give account of the royal lineage nor to expound anything distinctive of the priesthood ... appears to be indicated simply under the figure of the man among those four living creatures. HARMONY OF THE GOSPELS 1.6.9.[23]

THE UNITY OF THE FOUR GOSPELS. JEROME: The Gospels are joined to each other. They stick together, and they run hither and thither in different ways in the whole circle of their flight. And they do not have an end to their flight, nor do they ever rise above and fall down, but they always move to higher places. COMMENTARY ON EZEKIEL 1.1.8-9.[24]

THE FOUR CREATURES AND THE LIFE OF CHRIST. BEDE: In the figure of the four living creatures the two designated by the man and the calf display the tokens of his passion and death, but the two prefigured by the lion and the eagle reveal the signs of the victory in which he destroyed death. For the man represents the Lord as he was made mortal through the incarnation; the calf stands for him as he was offered for us on the altar of the cross; the lion portrays him when he bravely conquered death; the eagle when he ascended into heaven. ON THE TABERNACLE 1.4.[25]

THE FOUR LIVING CREATURES AND THE GOSPELS IN GENERAL. JEROME: The face means the beginning of the Gospels, from which the man and the lion, that is, the nativity of Christ and the voice of prophecy crying in the wilderness, are on the right-hand side; but the ox, that is, about the victims and the sacrifice of the Jews, is on the left, is abolished and is transformed into a spiritual priesthood ... just so that all things may hold fast to him and be thought of as in one body; and the eagle, which is over the nativity and is over the prophecy that is fulfilled in the coming of Christ and over the priesthood that it surpasses, and is beyond all these things, refers to the spiritual nativity, how the Father is the Son and the Son is the Father. COMMENTARY ON EZEKIEL 1.1.10.[26]

LIKE AN EVANGELIST, A PREACHER. GREGORY THE GREAT: The sole of the foot in the holy preachers is like that of a calf, namely, advancing in due season, brave and cloven, because each possesses reverence in maturity, fortitude in action and division on the hoof in discernment. HOMILIES ON EZEKIEL 1.3.4.[27]

OBSERVE THE SYMBOLS OF THE CREATURES' BODIES. PSEUDO-DIONYSIUS: The feet are nimble in movement and speed in that perpetual

---

[22]GCS 1.2:183. [23]NPNF 1 6:80-81*. [24]CCL 75:14-15. [25]TTH 18:14-15*. [26]CCL 75:15. [27]HGE 32.

journey to the divine things. Hence the Word of God has fashioned wings on the feet of intelligent beings, for wings signify their uplifting speed, the climb to heaven, the ever-upward journey whose constantly upward thrust rises above all earthly longing. The lightness of wings symbolizes the freedom from all worldly attraction, their pure and untrammeled rising toward the heights. The bare feet and body signify detachment, freedom, independence, the fact of being untarnished by anything external, the greatest possible conformity to the divine simplicity. Celestial Hierarchy 15.3.[28]

An Active and Contemplative Life. Gregory the Great: There are two lives of holy preachers, the active, of course, and the contemplative, but the active precedes the contemplative in time, since contemplation ensues from a good work. For the contemplative confers greater merit than the active because the latter strives in the practice of instant labor, while the former tastes future rest with secret savor. Homilies on Ezekiel 1.3.9.[29]

The Position of the Creatures in Relation to the Life of Christ. Gregory the Great: Why are the four said to have a man and a lion on the right side and an ox on the left? Nor is it without wondrous reason that those two are said to be on the right and that one on the left. And, again, we must ask why the eagle is said to be not on the right or the left but above these four. Thus we present two questions that we must answer with the Lord's revelation. Indeed, a man and a lion are said to be on the right and an ox on the left. So, we have joys on the right and sorrows on the left. Hence we describe as our left that which we consider to be adverse. And, as we said before, the incarnation is represented by the man, the passion by the ox and truly the resurrection of our Creator by the lion. For all the elect were gladdened by the incarnation of the only-begotten Son, through whom we are saved; truly the holy apostles, the first of the elect, were sad-

dened by his death and rejoiced anew at his resurrection. Because, therefore, his nativity and his resurrection offer joy to his disciples, who were saddened by his passion, the man and the lion are described as being on the right and truly the ox on the left. For, indeed, these same holy Evangelists rejoiced in his humanity and were encouraged by his resurrection, they who had been saddened by his passion. Therefore, the man and the lion are on the right because the incarnation of our Savior gave them life, the resurrection established them. But the ox is to the left, because his death laid them low for a moment in faithlessness. But the place of the eagle is rightly defined not beside but above them, since, whether because it denotes his ascension or because it declares the Word of the Father to be with the Father, in the virtue of contemplation he surpasses the Evangelists; for, although speaking with them about Christ's divinity, he contemplates this more subtly than all of them. But if, when the eagle is joined with the other three, they are said to be four living creatures, is it any wonder that he is described as above these, because having seen the Word in the beginning, John even transcended himself? Homilies on Ezekiel 1.4.3.[30]

The Four Creatures as Four Affections. Ambrose: Now, in every sort of person, the astute Greeks have said, are to be found *logisticon, thymeticon, epithymeticon, dioraticon*; in Latin these are prudence, fortitude, temperance and justice. Prudence concerns the human reason. Fortitude bestows a certain power of fierce strength and contempt for death. Temperance, when it contemplates the heavenly mysteries and is retrained by consecrated chastity, cares nothing for bodily pleasures. And justice, from a certain high position of revelation, sees and searches out anything produced for others rather than itself; justice does not examine its own conveniences as much as what benefits society. It is appropriate that the

---

[28]PDCW 186. [29]HGE 34. [30]HGE 41-42*.

soul that has acted with justice is symbolized by an eagle. It should fly away from earthly things and be totally intent on the divine mystery of the sublime resurrection. It struggles for and attains glory insofar as it is impartial. On Virginity 18.115.[31]

The Four Creatures in Creation and Human Personality. Pseudo-Macarius:

The four animals that bore the chariot were a type of the leading characteristics of the soul. For as the eagle rules over all the other birds and the lion is king of the wild beasts and the bull over the tamed animals and humanity rules over all creatures, so the soul has certain dominant powers that are superior to others. I am speaking of the faculties of the will: conscience, the mind and the power of loving. For it is through such that the chariot of the soul is directed, and it is in these that God resides. In some other fashion also such a symbolism can be applied to the heavenly church of the saints. In this text of Ezekiel's vision it is said that the animals were exceedingly tall, full of eyes. It was impossible for anyone to comprehend the number of eyes or grasp their height since the knowledge of such was not given. And in a similar manner the stars in the sky are given for people to gaze on and be filled with awe, but to know their number is given to no one. So in regard to the saints in the heavenly church it is permitted to all who only enter into it and enjoy it as they strive to live in it. But to know and comprehend the number of the saints is given only to God. Fifty Spiritual Homilies 1.3.[32]

The Four Creatures in Human Personality. Ammonas: After I wrote the letter, I remembered what is written in Ezekiel, which he showed as an example of perfection. He saw an animal above the river Chebar that had four faces and four feet and four wings. The face of the cherub is when the Spirit of God rests in the soul and ensures that it gives praise with a pleasant and beautiful voice. When he wants to rise and

enquire of a person, he takes on himself the face of the man. But what is the ox? That is surely when the faithful soul is involved in struggle; the Spirit assists in the form of an ox, which is a strong animal, able to confound Satan. And what of the eagle? The eagle flies to the heights, higher than all the birds that fly. When the soul ascends to the heights, the Spirit comes and acts in the form of an eagle, so that it can remain on high and be near to God. Letter 13.8.[33]

The Eagle Represents the Human Conscience. Jerome: Most people interpret the man, the lion and the ox as the rational, emotional and appetitive parts of the soul. . . . And they come with a fourth part that is above and beyond these three and that the Greeks call συνείδησιν: that spark of conscience that was not even extinguished in the breast of Cain after he was turned out of paradise and by which we discern that we sin, when we are overcome by pleasures or frenzy and meanwhile are misled by an imitation of reason. They reckon that this is strictly speaking, the eagle, which is not mixed up with the other three but corrects them when they go wrong. Commentary on Ezekiel 1.1.6-8.[34]

Kingship, Priesthood and Prophecy. Theodoret of Cyr: The lion represents kingship (for it is the royal animal); the ox priesthood, for an ox was offered for the chief of the priests; prophecy is shown through the eagle, for it is the creature that flies high and has very sharp sight. The prophecy is of this kind: it contemplates the heights and looks very far into the future. It therefore teaches through what has been spoken, that the whole of human nature, together with its own leaders, has been subjected to the ruler and maker of all things, and he has instructed the human race in so many gifts. Commentary on Ezekiel 1.1.[35]

---

[31]AOV 50-51*. [32]PMFSH 38. [33]PO 10.6:612-13. [34]CCL 75:11-12. [35]PG 81:825.

1:11 *Their Wings*

MOVEMENT AND GOOD INTENTIONS. GREGORY THE GREAT: It must be remembered that every good deed that is done by good intention is always lifted up to the heavens. But one who seeks earthly glory by his good works dips his wings and faces downwards. HOMILIES ON EZEKIEL 1.4.4.[36]

MOVEMENT AND PREACHING. JEROME: Two are stretched out and lift themselves up on high and signify heavenly preaching, in everything that pertains to the majesty of God. Two cover their bodies, for human knowledge is excluded, and perfect consideration is not offered. COMMENTARY ON EZEKIEL 1.1.11.[37]

THE WINGS AND CONTEMPLATION. THEODORET OF CYR: He shows by these things not that everything is to be understood by divine power but that some things are clear to them and others are unknown, and they do not go beyond the limit set down for them. They stretch out two wings in their exultation, for the gift of contemplation has been granted, and they cover their bodies with two wings, covering those things that are hidden in happy ignorance, and they do not struggle in order to observe things that it is not right for them to see. COMMENTARY ON EZEKIEL 1.1.[38]

1:12 *Moving Without Turning*

THEY MOVE FOLLOWING THE HOLY SPIRIT. JEROME: This shows the secret of each Testament, because, in those four animals, the law and the gospel hasten toward the future and never make any motion back. COMMENTARY ON EZEKIEL 1.1.12.[39]

SELF-KNOWLEDGE. GREGORY THE GREAT: We should carefully examine ourselves as we do others and place our very selves, so to speak, before our eyes, so that unceasingly imitating the winged creatures, we always walk before our face, lest we be ignorant of what we are doing. HOMILIES ON EZEKIEL 1.4.9.[40]

1:13 *The Burning Coals*

FIRE AND THE DEITY. PSEUDO-DIONYSIUS: In general, whether reference is to high or low within the hierarchy, the Word of God always honors the representation of fire. And indeed it seems to me that this imagery of fire best expresses the way in which the intelligent beings of heaven are like the Deity. CELESTIAL HIERARCHY 15.2.[41]

PREACHING IS LIKE HANDLING THE BURNING COALS. GREGORY THE GREAT: Those who run to and fro in preaching, through love of the Lord, are the burning fire of his wheels, since they run through several places from desire of him, from whom they themselves burn and kindle others. HOMILIES ON EZEKIEL 1.5.10.[42]

1:14 *Darting To and Fro*

THE GOSPELS MOVE TOGETHER. JEROME: Whatever creature we will have looked at makes the knowledge of God shine forth, while the Creator recognizes it from his creatures. And from the midst of the animals splendor and fire and light go forth. For if the Gospels are at variance in themselves, you will find in the midst of their writings and worthy narratives the mysteries of the Holy Spirit. COMMENTARY ON EZEKIEL 1.1.13-14.[43]

A MIXTURE OF ACTIVE AND CONTEMPLATIVE. GREGORY THE GREAT: The living creatures in the vision went and turned not when they went, and they ran and returned, because holy people do not run headlong from the active life that they embraced to perform acts of injustice, and fall back from the contemplative, which they cannot continually retain, to the active life. HOMILIES ON EZEKIEL 1.5.12.[44]

---

[36]HGE 42*. [37]CCL 75:16. [38]PG 81:825. [39]CCL 75:16-17. [40]HGE 45*. [41]PDCW 183. [42]HGE 50*. [43]CCL 75:19. [44]HGE 52.

1:15-21 THE WHEELS OF THE CHARIOT

[15]*Now as I looked at the living creatures, I saw a wheel upon the earth beside the living creatures, one for each of the four of them.* [16]*As for the appearance of the wheels and their construction: their appearance was like the gleaming of a chrysolite; and the four had the same likeness, their construction being as it were a wheel within a wheel.* [17]*When they went, they went in any of their four directions without turning as they went.* [18]*The four wheels had rims and they had spokes; and their rims were full of eyes round about.* [19]*And when the living creatures went, the wheels went beside them; and when the living creatures rose from the earth, the wheels rose.* [20]*Wherever the spirit would go, they went, and the wheels rose along with them; for the spirit of the living creatures was in the wheels.* [21]*When those went, these went; and when those stood, these stood; and when those rose from the earth, the wheels rose along with them; for the spirit of the living creatures was in the wheels.*

d Heb *of their faces*   e Heb *on their four sides*   f Cn: Heb uncertain

OVERVIEW: The Fathers interpreted the wheels in different ways, mainly in reference to the Scriptures in themselves (BASIL, JEROME, THEODORET) or in the work of preaching (GREGORY THE GREAT). Others see the wheels cosmologically (ORIGEN, NOVATIAN, PSEUDO-DIONYSIUS) or psychologically (AMBROSE).

1:15 The Wheels

THE WHEELS SIGNIFY TIME. NOVATIAN: The wheels that lie beneath it signify the various periods of time in which all the component members of the world are constantly being whirled forward. Furthermore, feet have been given to these members that they may not always stand still but move on. All their limbs are studded with eyes because the works of God are to be contemplated with ever careful observation. And within their very bosom is a fire of glowing coals, to signify that this world is hastening to the fiery day of judgment or that all the works of God are fiery and not obscure. ON THE TRINITY 8.8-9.[1]

A ROUNDED LIFE. AMBROSE: I now understand more plainly what I have read, that one wheel runs within another and is not impeded. For a life lived without any offense is a rounded life, whatever the sufferings in which it is lived, and even within such it runs like a wheel. The law runs within grace, and the keeping of the law lies within the course of God's mercy; the more it rolls, the more it gains approval. JACOB AND THE HAPPY LIFE 2.11.49.[2]

THUNDER AND THE WHEEL. BASIL THE GREAT: Whoever is stretching forward, like a wheel, touching the earth with a small part of itself, is really such as that wheel was, about which Ezekiel spoke. HOMILIES ON THE PSALMS 13.3 (Ps 28).[3]

MOVING AND BEING REDOLENT OF THE GOSPEL. GREGORY THE GREAT: Indeed of one kind is the small flower of the grape, because great is the virtue and belief of the preachers that inebriate the minds of hearers; another is the smell of the olive flower, because sweet is the work of pity, which revives and glows like olive oil; another is

---

[1]FC 67:40-41. [2]FC 65:178. [3]FC 46:201*.

the smell of the rose, because wondrous is its fragrance, which shines and is redolent with the blood of the martyrs; another is the smell of the lily, because its fleshly life is white with the incorruption of virginity; another is the smell of the violet, because great is the virtue of the humble who, preferring to occupy far-off places through humility, do not raise themselves from the earth to the heights and serve in their minds the purple of the heavenly kingdom; another is the smell of spikenard when it is led to maturity, because the perfection of good works is prepared for the satisfaction of those who thirst for justice. HOMILIES ON EZEKIEL 1.6.4.[4]

PONDERING THE GOSPELS. JEROME: Everything that is earthly and heavenly and whatever falls under human understanding turns on its own wheels. . . . But if anyone considers the wheel and the movement of the Gospels—that is, of the four animals that breathe and live—and understands, [that person] will in a short space of time see that the world is completed by the teaching of the apostles. COMMENTARY ON EZEKIEL 1.1.15-18.[5]

MOVING STRAIGHT. PSEUDO-DIONYSIUS: As for the winged wheels, which go ahead with neither twist nor swerve, these have to do with the power to keep right on along the straight road, directly and without wandering off, and all this because the wheel of their intelligence is guided in a way that has nothing in it of this world. CELESTIAL HIERARCHY 15.9.[6]

1:16 Like a Wheel Within a Wheel

THE UNITY OF CREATION IN CHRIST. ORIGEN: If you consider the way in which the universe moves in different and contrary ways, whether you think it is in error or whether you think it is of a different nature from us, you see the meaning of "a wheel within a wheel." But as far as all that is concerned, the God of the whole universe directs everything and makes everything to move where he wills, in Christ Jesus, to whom be glory

and dominion for ever and ever. HOMILIES ON EZEKIEL 1.16.[7]

LAW AND GRACE. AMBROSE: The wheel within a wheel is life under the law, life under grace; inasmuch as Jews are within the church, the law is included in grace. For one is within the church who is a Jew secretly; and circumcision of the heart is a sacrament within the church. But that Jewish people are within the church of which it is written: "In Judah is God known";[8] therefore as wheel runs within wheel, in the same way the wings were still and the wings were flying. ON THE HOLY SPIRIT 3.21.162.[9]

THE WHEEL HAS FOUR FACES. GREGORY THE GREAT: The wheel has four faces because first it perceived the sins amid the peoples that must be restrained by the law, then it saw through the prophets, more subtly indeed through the gospel, and finally it observed through the apostles the things that must be stopped in the sins of people. HOMILIES ON EZEKIEL 1.6.12.[10]

1:17 Without Turning

THE TWO TESTAMENTS. JEROME: The two wheels are the New and the Old Testament; the Old moves within the New and the New within the Old. HOMILIES ON THE PSALMS 10 (Ps 76).[11]

THE NEW TESTAMENT INTERPRETS THE OLD. GREGORY THE GREAT: When our Savior came into the world, he made to be spiritually understood what he found to be carnally held. Thus wherever its letter is spiritually understood, all the carnal display in it comes to life. Truly the New Testament is also called the eternal Testament through the pages of the Old because the understanding of it is never changed. HOMILIES ON EZEKIEL 1.6.17.[12]

---

[4]HGE 55-56. [5]CCL 75:20*. [6]PDCW 190. [7]SC 352:96. [8]Ps 76:1 (75:1 LXX, Vulg.). [9]NPNF 2 10:157*. [10]HGE 59. [11]FC 48:75. [12]HGE 61*.

1:18 Full of Eyes

Wheels and the Teaching of the Gospel.
Jerome: Three things are equally indicated in the
animals and the wheels; when they stand, when
they walk and when they arise, what they do as
animals and wheels and what they do in common.
Commentary on Ezekiel 1.1.15-18[13]

Parts of the Human Body. Pseudo-Dionysius: I also think that each of the many parts of
the human body can provide us with images that
are quite appropriate to the powers of heaven.
One could say that the powers of sight suggest
their ability to gaze up directly toward the lights
of God and at the same time to receive softly,
clearly, without resistance but flexibly, purely and
openly the enlightenment coming from the Deity,
yet without emotion. Celestial Hierarchy
15.3.[14]

Watching and Ministry. Gregory the
Great: They who are superiors must be warned
to be earnestly on the watch, to have vigilant eyes
within and round about and to strive to become
living creatures of heaven. For the living creatures
of heaven are described as full of eyes round
about and within. Surely it is fitting that all who
are set above others should have eyes within and
round about, because they aim at pleasing the
judge within, and while giving outward examples
of living, they should detect what is to be corrected in others. Pastoral Care 3.4.[15]

1:19 Rising and Going with the Creatures

Acting Together. Jerome: When the animals stand, their wings are set down. For they are
not able to bear the voice of the Lord sounding in
the heavens, but they stand and marvel, and they
show by their silence the power of God, who sits
above the firmament. Commentary on Ezekiel
1.1.22-26.[16]

The Saints Carrying Lights. Gregory the

Great: Because the saints shrewdly examine
themselves as to the points on which they can be
judged by others, and strictly look at themselves
as they are often strictly scrutinized by others
and are not ignorant of the things that could lie
hidden, they carry the light on their backs. Homilies on Ezekiel 1.7.7.[17]

1:20 The Spirit in the Wheels

Propelled by God. Theodoret of Cyr: The
prophet also claims that the spirit of life was in
the wheels, its movement was spontaneous and of
its own free will. For the chariot was not placed
on some living creatures or on a yoke, but violent
clouds went before, and that mighty wind followed. The divine vehicle ran on its own accord
with the living creatures preceding it and the
wheels moving on their own. Commentary on
Ezekiel 1.1.[18]

The Spirit, the Scriptures and Virtues.
Gregory the Great: If the spirit of life touches
the soul of the reader to the observance of
patience, the wheels too immediately follow,
because he finds in holy Scriptures when Moses
and Aaron, although speaking rightly, suffered
persecution from the people, they ran to the tabernacle, yet they were still praying for the very
people from whom they fled. But their holy
minds endured the commotion of the haughty,
and they did not burst out against them in
hatred. True patience is that which loves whom
its bears. For to tolerate but to hate is not the virtue of mildness but is the veil of fury. Homilies
on Ezekiel 1.7.12.[19]

The Spirit and Prophecy. Gregory the
Great: If the spirit of life arouses the soul of the
reader to the study of prophecy, the wheels too
immediately follow, because he finds in holy
Scripture that Moses, at the Lord's command,

---

[13]CCL 75:21. [14]PDCW 185. [15]ACW 11:99 *. [16]CCL 75:23. [17]HGE
68. [18]PG 81:829. [19]HGE 71*.

rose against Pharaoh with so many words of bold prophecy. HOMILIES ON EZEKIEL 1.7.13.[20]

1:21 The Spirit in the Wheels

THE WAYS OF GOD ARE INCOMPREHENSIBLE.
JEROME: This is the whole vision: a spirit rising and a great cloud and four animals and four wheels following the animals and the spirit that is worthy to be above the firmament of God. COMMENTARY ON EZEKIEL 1.2.1.[21]

SPIRITUAL PROGRESS. GREGORY THE GREAT: There are those who advance as far as the point where they know to distribute well the earthly goods that they receive, to exert themselves in works of pity, to relieve the oppressed. These

manifestly go insofar as they strive for the benefit of their neighbor. Therefore the wheels progress with them because they arrange holy Scripture as the steps of their words on their journey. And there are others who in the faith that they have received are so strong to preserve it that they can resist all adversaries and are not only in no way drawn to the perversity of treachery but even rebuke those who speak perverse words and drag them to rectitude. When these stand the wheels too stand still, because the words of holy Scripture confirm their rectitude to them whenever they hear within themselves, "stand firm and hold to the traditions which you were taught by us."[22] HOMILIES ON EZEKIEL 1.7.15.[23]

---

[20]HGE 71*. [21]CCL 75:25. [22]2 Thess 2:15. [23]HGE 72*.

1:22-28 THE CREATURES, THE WHEELS AND THE VISION OF GOD

[22]*Over the heads of the living creatures there was the likeness of a firmament, shining like crystal, spread out above their heads.* [23]*And under the firmament their wings were stretched out straight, one toward another; and each creature had two wings covering its body.* [24]*And when they went, I heard the sound of their wings like the sound of many waters, like the thunder of the Almighty, a sound of tumult like the sound of a host; when they stood still, they let down their wings.* [25]*And there came a voice from above the firmament over their heads; when they stood still, they let down their wings.*

[26]*And above the firmament over their heads there was the likeness of a throne, in appearance like sapphire;[b] and seated above the likeness of a throne was a likeness as it were of a human form.* [27]*And upward from what had the appearance of his loins I saw as it were gleaming bronze, like the appearance of fire enclosed round about; and downward from what had the appearance of his loins I saw as it were the appearance of fire, and there was brightness round about him.[i]* [28]*Like the appearance of the bow that is in the cloud on the day of rain, so was the appearance of the brightness round about.*

Such was the appearance of the likeness of the glory of the Lord. And when I saw it, I fell upon my face, and I heard the voice of one speaking.

g Gk: Heb *awesome crystal* h Heb *lapis lazuli* i Or *it*

Overview: Ezekiel's vision moves from earth into heaven. The creatures take us there on a spiritual journey (Pseudo-Dionysius), as well as showing us the virtues of preaching (Gregory the Great). Christ, who is both God and man, is seen above the firmament (Jerome, Gregory the Great). Such a vision is beyond telling (Pachomius, Origen) and makes Ezekiel unique among the prophets (Jacob). Ezekiel saw only the likeness of the glory of God, not the real glory (Cyril of Jerusalem, Gregory the Great). God is not to be limited (Theodoret).

1:22 The Firmament

Christ Is There. Gregory the Great: It is possible, figuratively, to recognize in the name of the firmament our Savior himself, true God above all things, becoming perfect man among all things, in whom our nature is made strong with the Father. Homilies on Ezekiel 1.7.19.[1]

1:23 The Wings Stretched

Harmonious Life. Gregory the Great: Those virtues protect us in the face of almighty God that we bestow and join to our neighbors out of charity, and when we live in harmony with them we cover the sins we have committed. The two precepts of charity can thereby be understood by these two wings, namely, love of God and love of our neighbor. Homilies on Ezekiel 1.7.22.[2]

1:24 The Sound of the Wings

Understanding of God. Pseudo-Dionysius: Theology has transmitted to the people of earth those hymns sung by the first ranks of the angels whose gloriously transcendent enlighten-ment is by them made manifest. Some of these hymns, if one may use perceptible images, are like the "sound of many waters." Celestial Hierarchy 7.4.[3]

1:25 The Voice from the Firmament

Seeking the Voice. Gregory the Great: Transcending the soul, we seek the voice from the firmament when we examine what is the innumerable throng of holy angels in the sight of almighty God, what is their infinite joy at the jubilation of God, what joy without defect, what fervor of love not tormenting but delighting, how great is their desire for the vision of God with sufficiency and how great their sufficiency with desire. Homilies on Ezekiel 1.8.15.[4]

1:26 The Likeness of the Throne

Christ on the Throne. Gregory the Great: The firmament is beneath the throne, and the man is on the throne, because through assuming human nature he is born lower than the angels and is exalted above the angels. Homilies on Ezekiel 1.8.23.[5]

As Vision of God. Pachomius: When he came to the doorway of the church, he looked in and saw an apparition. Where his feet were, there appeared to him something like a sparkling sapphire, and he was unable to look at his face because of the great light that unceasingly flashed forth from him. Life of Pachomius (Bohairic) 184.[6]

1:27 Brightness

---

[1]HGE 74. [2]HGE 76*. [3]PDCW 165*. [4]HGE 84. [5]HGE 88*. [6]CS 45:219-20*.

ABOVE AND BELOW THE BRIGHTNESS. JEROME: In fact, even in Ezekiel, from what looked like from his waist upward God resembled amber, but from his waist downward he resembled fire. Whatever is above is gold, and whatever is below is ready for purgation in Gehenna. HOMILIES ON THE PSALMS 56 (Ps 146).[7]

CHRIST'S TWO NATURES. GREGORY THE GREAT: The brightness of gold is tempered there by the silver, and the appearance of silver is brightened by the splendor of the gold. In our Savior, then, the natures of divinity and humanity are united and joined. HOMILIES ON EZEKIEL 1.8.25.[8]

1:28 The Vision in Full

GOD'S GLORY INEFFABLE. ORIGEN: It is clear . . . that Ezekiel saw the cherubim and their course, and the firmament above them and the one seated on the throne. What could be more glorious and exalted than these things? COMMENTARY ON THE GOSPEL OF JOHN 6.23.[9]

NO OTHER PROPHET LIKE EZEKIEL. JACOB OF SARUG: The prophet wonderful-in-revelations told this account.

He who ate the scroll full of the symbols of creative power
Disgorged a *memra* at whose meaning intellects are dazzled.
He discoursed about the chariot and about its transformations
And about its forms and the faces that were joined in it.
About the faces and the wings and eloquent wheels
And the living spirit that was in the wheels being turned,
About the movement of service of the cherubs,
And about the high throne that is established on their backs,
And about the appearance of the image of the Son of God

Which was borne on the chariot with great awe;
And about the voice of that service that is the cherubs' own,
Which with great movement bless the most high in his place.
All these things from Ezekiel, the son of the exile,
Did the world learn about the chariot's awesome appearance.
For neither Moses nor David published this account
Nor any prophet told [of it] like Ezekiel. ON THE ESTABLISHMENT OF CREATION 1.4.[10]

ONLY THE LIKENESS OF GOD'S GLORY. CYRIL OF JERUSALEM: One might gather from a passage in Ezekiel that Ezekiel saw him, but what does Scripture actually say? He saw "the likeness of his glory"; not the Lord but only the likeness of his glory, not the glory as it really is. Yet, on beholding the likeness of his glory and not the glory itself, he fell to the earth in fear. But if the vision of the likeness of the glory inspired the prophets with fear and trembling, anyone attempting to look on God would surely lose his life. CATECHETICAL LECTURES 9.1.[11]

NOT THE GLORY ITSELF. GREGORY THE GREAT: He does not say, "the vision of the glory" but "the likeness of the glory," in order that it be truly shown that however great the will with which the human has strived, even though it prunes away the fantasies of bodily images from its meditation, yet still clad in mortal flesh it cannot avail to see the glory of God as it is. But whatever of that glory shines in the mind is the likeness and not the glory itself. There that preacher who was snatched to the third heaven said, "Now we see through a glass darkly."[12] HOMILIES ON EZEKIEL 1.8.30.[13]

---

[7]FC 48:407**. [8]HGE 89. [9]FC 80:174. [10]MFC 9:195. [11]FC 61:185*. [12]1 Cor 13:12. [13]HGE 92*.

BEYOND OUR COMPREHENSION. THEODORET OF CYR: When you have heard of various visions of God, do not think that the divine majesty has many forms. COMMENTARY ON EZEKIEL 1.1.[14]

THE DIVINE MAJESTY AND THE INCARNATION. THEODORET OF CYR: The godhead is empty of body and form; it is simple, and it has no part in composition and any form; nor can it be seen with eyes, nor can it be understood with the mind or limited within a boundary. He reveals visions just as it is necessary to make them appear. And in this place he shows these awesome things: he shows the favor that all people are to be granted, namely, of God and of our Savior in the dispensation of the flesh. Because of this, he says that human appearance is two natures: the one of amber, the other of fire, and the one carrying and the other being carried. In this way, the divine nature took on the human. COMMENTARY ON EZEKIEL 1.1.[15]

ONLY THE LIKENESS OF GOD'S GLORY. THEODORET OF CYR: He did not say this was the nature of the Lord or the glory of the Lord but that this was the likeness of the glory of the Lord. For as he willed, so he spoke, and creating the vision, he made me worthy of contemplating it. COMMENTARY ON EZEKIEL 1.2.[16]

---

[14]PG 81:833. [15]PG 81:833-36. [16]PG 81:836.

2:1-7 COMMISSION TO GO TO THE HOUSE OF ISRAEL

And he said to me, "Son of man, stand upon your feet, and I will speak with you." [2]And when he spoke to me, the Spirit entered into me and set me upon my feet; and I heard him speaking to me. [3]And he said to me, "Son of man, I send you to the people of Israel, to a nation[j] of rebels, who have rebelled against me; they and their fathers have transgressed against me to this very day. [4]The people also are impudent and stubborn: I send you to them; and you shall say to them, 'Thus says the Lord GOD.' [5]And whether they hear or refuse to hear (for they are a rebellious house) they will know that there has been a prophet among them. [6]And you, son of man, be not afraid of them, nor be afraid of their words, though briers and thorns are with you and you sit upon scorpions; be not afraid of their words, nor be dismayed at their looks, for they are a rebellious house. [7]And you shall speak my words to them, whether they hear or refuse to hear; for they are a rebellious house."

j Syr: Heb *nations*

OVERVIEW: Ezekiel falls on his face, a sign of his sinfulness (JEROME, GREGORY THE GREAT), and is commissioned to go to the rebellious people as a preacher, which is a heavy responsibility (GREGORY THE GREAT). But God gives the people a choice in the matter, and the scorpions among them are in their souls (CHRYSOSTOM). The preacher must live with the good and the bad (GREGORY THE GREAT), and not to be afraid (ORIGEN, SALVIAN).

2:1 Ezekiel Falls on His Face

BECAUSE OF SINFULNESS. JEROME: [Ezekiel] is not carried away by the greatness of the visions, but he falls on his own face through knowing the fragility of the human being. COMMENTARY ON EZEKIEL 1.2.1.[1]

HUMAN WEAKNESS SHOWN. GREGORY THE GREAT: What then would have become of this man if he had seen the Lord's glory as it is, who seeing the likeness of that glory but unable to bear it fell on his face? In this matter we must think with deep sorrow and ponder with tears to what wretchedness and weakness we have fallen who cannot bear that very good that we were created to behold. But here is something else for us to consider within ourselves from the prophet's act. For as soon as he saw the likeness of the glory of God, the prophet fell on his face. Since we cannot see this likeness through the spirit of prophecy, we must continually acknowledge it and punctiliously contemplate in holy Scripture, in divine counsels and in spiritual precepts. We, who when we perceive something of God, fall on our faces because we blush for the evil acts we remember committing. HOMILIES ON EZEKIEL 1.8.32.[2]

2:2 God's Purpose

ONLY THE SPIRIT CAN RAISE HIM. GREGORY THE GREAT: The divine voice commanded the prophet as he lay and bade him rise. But he could in no way have risen if the Spirit of the Almighty had not entered into him, because by the grace of almighty God we can indeed try to perform good works but cannot carry them through unless he who commands us helps us. HOMILIES ON EZEKIEL 1.9.2.[3]

2:3 Sent to a Nation of Rebels

A RESPONSIBILITY. GREGORY THE GREAT: The authority of preaching must not be offered to us who still lie in the confusion of infirmity. HOMILIES ON EZEKIEL 1.9.4.[4]

2:4 A Stubborn People

GOD IS GRACIOUS. JEROME: It is a mark of great mercy that God sends him to such as these and that he does not despair of their salvation; and it is a mark of the trust of the prophet that he does not fear to go to such as these also. COMMENTARY ON EZEKIEL 1.2.4.[5]

2:5 A Prophet Still Among Them

GOD CALLS HIS PEOPLE TO REPENTANCE. GREGORY THE GREAT: We see ruined cities, razed forts, ravaged fields, and nevertheless we still follow our ancestors in transgressions; we are not changed from this their pride that we saw. And they indeed at a time of pleasure. But we—which is more serious—sin at a time of being lashed. But almighty God, judging transgression, first snatched away our ancestors and then called them to judgment. He still awaits our penitence; he sustains us that we may return to him. HOMILIES ON EZEKIEL 1.9.9.[6]

GOD GIVES THE PEOPLE THE CHOICE. CHRYSOSTOM: He says "whether they hear or refuse," not out of ignorance but in case any of the obstinate should say that the prediction was what made them disobedient in the first place. He therefore expresses himself in terms of "whether they will" and "it may be." For though they had been obstinate towards his servants,[7] they ought to have shown reverence to the dignity of the Son. HOMILIES ON THE GOSPEL OF MATTHEW 68.1.[8]

---

[1]CCL 75:25. [2]HGE 93. [3]HGE 94. [4]HGE 95. [5]CCL 75:27. [6]HGE 97**. This is a reference to the Lombard invasions when these homilies were delivered (593). [7]Mt 21:35. [8]NPNF 1 10:415*.

2:6 Do Not Be Afraid

REVILINGS AGAINST THE PEOPLE. ORIGEN: Are there not revilings in Ezekiel directed against the people, when the Lord says, "you dwell among scorpions"? AGAINST CELSUS 2.76.[9]

SCORPIONS IN THE SOUL. CHRYSOSTOM: The soul that enjoys the watering that comes from the words of God produces in abundance, flourishes and teems with the fruit of the Spirit. But when a soul has become dry, is left uncared for and needs such watering, it becomes desert, its vines grow wild, it produces an abundance of thorns. And these thorns have the natural characteristics of sin. For where there are thorns, there will you find snakes, serpents, scorpions and every power of the devil. AGAINST THE ANOMOEANS 12.54.[10]

BEAR WITH THE BAD. GREGORY THE GREAT: There can be no bad without good, no good without bad in the church. My friends, before your time on earth is over, recall these examples. Strengthen yourselves to bear with the bad. If we are the offspring of God's chosen ones, we must live according to their example. The good have never refused to bear with the bad. FORTY GOSPEL HOMILIES 38.[11]

FEAR THEM NOT. SALVIAN THE PRESBYTER: Perhaps you fear the looks of your relatives sitting around and are afraid to offend them as they press and crowd around your beds. The Lord says through the prophet, "Be not afraid of them, be not dismayed at their looks, for they are a rebellious house." You must also be unafraid and constant; do not fear their faces or be broken by their display. FOUR BOOKS OF TIMOTHY TO THE CHURCH 3.19.[12]

THE HARDNESS OF THE UNBELIEVER. JEROME: Do not think yourselves to be deceived if you are sent to those who do not hear what you are saying. You must understand that I am preaching to you because they are of unsound mind and they gather together against you and they surround you, leaving no escape to you. For they do this because they are faithless and spurn the commands of God. COMMENTARY ON EZEKIEL 1.2.6.[13]

THE ATTITUDE OF THE ONE SENT. GREGORY THE GREAT: Humble authority must be in the superior and free humility in the inferior. HOMILIES ON EZEKIEL 1.9.12.[14]

2:7 Speak Whatever the Reaction

THE RESPONSIBILITY OF THE PREACHER. GREGORY THE GREAT: Every one who sins, what does he do but provoke the anger of his Creator against himself? We know that every time we sin in deed, in word, in thought, we make God angry with us. And yet he delays, he waits in mercy and first of all demands patience of himself, only then giving the word of exhortation to his preachers for us. Everyone who preaches rightly, if he is heard, appeases the anger of our Creator, who has been provoked by his sinful people. HOMILIES ON EZEKIEL 1.9.25.[15]

---

[9]ANCL 23:80. [10]FC 72:306. [11]BFG 116-17. [12]FC 3:352. [13]CCL 75:28. [14]HGE 98. [15]HGE 105*.

2:8–3:3 EZEKIEL COMMISSIONED
TO EAT THE SCROLL

[8]*"But you, son of man, hear what I say to you; be not rebellious like that rebellious house; open your mouth, and eat what I give you." [9]And when I looked, behold, a hand was stretched out to me, and lo, a written scroll was in it; [10]and he spread it before me; and it had writing on the front and on the back, and there were written on it words of lamentation and mourning and woe. [1]And he said to me, "Son of man, eat what is offered to you; eat this scroll, and go, speak to the house of Israel." [2]So I opened my mouth, and he gave me the scroll to eat. [3]And he said to me, "Son of man, eat this scroll that I give you and fill your stomach with it." Then I ate it; and it was in my mouth as sweet as honey.*

Overview: The prophet, who must not become like those to whom he is to preach (Jerome), has the scroll handed to him, which are the Scriptures. They are not always easy to understand; hence the importance of good preaching (Hippolytus, Gregory the Great). Although the Scriptures can be sweet to the taste, they become bitter when our understanding grows (Origen, Theodoret). The words of Scripture must be eaten before we can teach them (Jerome), for they are our real food, since they give us understanding (Gregory the Great), and like honey they teach us wisdom (Cassiodorus).

2:8 Do Not Be Rebellious

Do Not Imitate Them. Jerome: You must not imitate those whom you are sent to correct, in case the same sin should merit exactly the same punishment. Commentary on Ezekiel 1.2.8.[1]

2:9 The Hand with the Scroll

The Church Is Full of Sinners. Jerome: If God were to stand up as the avenger of sin, the church would lose many of its saints and certainly would be deprived of the apostle Paul. Letter 147.3.[2]

The Scroll Is Scripture. Hippolytus: The scroll symbolizes the prophets and the apostles. In it the Old Testament was written on the reverse and the New on the obverse. Moreover, the scroll symbolizes the secret, the spiritual teaching—and in such a dignified manner that it may be read on both sides. In reality it is of such a kind that there is a connection between reading the outside and understanding the inside. Fragment 3.[3]

The Book as Explained by the Preacher. Gregory the Great: As the order of preachers is signified by the prophet, so the pages of holy Scripture are meant by the book that he received. For the rolled book is the obscure speech of holy Scripture, which is enveloped in a profundity of sayings so that it is not easily penetrated by the understanding of all. But the book is spread out before the prophet because the obscurity of holy Scripture is opened for the preachers. Homilies on Ezekiel 1.9.29.[4]

2:10 Lamentation, Mourning and Woe

---

[1]CCL 75:29. [2]NPNF 2 6:291*. [3]GCS 1.2:184. [4]HGE 106*. This is probably also a reference to the reputation Ezekiel had for being hard to understand.

The Effect of the Message on the Prophet. Origen: I take it to be similar in the case of the book mentioned by Ezekiel, in which had been written lamentation, mourning and woe. The whole book contains the "woe" of those perishing, and the "mourning" of those being saved and the "lamentation" of those in between. John, too, who eats one roll on which there is writing on the back and the front,[5] considered the whole Scripture as one book, which is thought to be sweet at the start, when one chews it, but bitter in the perception of each of those who come to know it. Commentary on the Gospel of John 5.7.[6]

Do Not Be Downcast. Gregory the Great: Let not the multitude of our wounds reduce us to desperation, because the power of the healer is greater than the magnitude of our feebleness. Homilies on Ezekiel 1.9.35.[7]

3:1 Eat the Scroll

Ezekiel as Son of Man. Jerome: In the scroll of Ezekiel, who is truly a type of the Savior, no other prophet (I mean of major prophets) is called "Son of man." The title is given strictly to Ezekiel. In Ezekiel after almost every twenty or thirty verses it says regularly, "the word of the Lord came to the prophet Ezekiel." Someone may ask, "Why is that so frequently repeated in the prophecy?" Because the Holy Spirit descended on the prophet but again withdrew from him. Whenever it says "the word came," it indicates that the Holy Spirit departed from him and came back again to him. Homilies on Mark 75 (Mk 1:1-12).[8]

Scripture Is Our Real Food. Gregory the Great: In saying that without holy Scripture we shall be exhausted by hunger and thirst, he shows that its words are our food and drink. But it must be observed that they are sometimes food, sometimes drink. For in more obscure matters that cannot be comprehended unless they are explained, holy Scripture is our food, because whatever is expounded that it may be understood is as if chewed that it may be swallowed. But in plainer sayings it is drink. For we do not swallow drink by chewing. Therefore we drink plainer statutes because we attempt to understand them without exposition. Homilies on Ezekiel 1.10.3.[9]

We Have to Eat Before We Can Teach. Jerome: Unless we eat the open book first, we cannot teach the children of Israel. Commentary on Ezekiel 1.3.1.[10]

3:2 Ezekiel Receives the Scroll

The Will to Seek God. Jerome: With an open mouth the Lord has provided bread, so that the beginnings of his will may be in us and that we may reach the perfection of blessedness that comes from God. Commentary on Ezekiel 1.3.2-3.[11]

The Understanding Opened. Gregory the Great: Whenever almighty God offers his hand to the mouth of our hearts, he invariably opens our understanding and instills the food of holy Scripture into our senses. Homilies on Ezekiel 1.10.5.[12]

3:3 The Scroll Tastes Like Honey

The Digestion of Scripture. Jerome: The eating of the book is the initial reading and the simple narrative. But when we have done some hard meditating on it and when we have laid it in the treasure store of the memory, our belly is spiritually filled and our inward parts are satiated, so that like the apostle Paul[13] they are filled with compassion. Commentary on Ezekiel 1.3.3.[14]

---

[5]Rev 10:9. [6]FC 80:165. [7]HGE 109. [8]FC 57:130-31*. [9]HGE 110. [10]CCL 75:31. [11]CCL 75:31. [12]HGE 111**. [13]See Col 3:12. [14]CCL 75:32.

THE BELLY AS THE MIND. GREGORY THE GREAT: What are the bowels of the belly if not the interior of the mind, right intention, holy desire, a will humble before God and conscientious to its neighbor? HOMILIES ON EZEKIEL 1.10.6.[15]

HONEY AS WISDOM. CASSIODORUS: Honey can be understood as the explicit teaching of wisdom, whereas the comb can represent that known to be stored in the depth, as it were, of the cells. Undoubtedly both are found in the divine Scriptures. They added "to my mouth,"[16] for they were indeed proclaiming with their mouths the wisdom that they had swallowed with their throats. The prophet Ezekiel speaks in the same way of the Lord. EXPOSITIONS OF THE PSALMS 118.103.[17]

THE MESSAGE IS BETTER TO THE PROPHET'S TASTE. THEODORET OF CYR: Just as he contemplated that vision in spirit, so he now felt its taste in spirit. COMMENTARY ON EZEKIEL 1.3.[18]

---

[15]HGE 111*. [16]Ps 119:103 (118:103 LXX, Vulg.). [17]ACW 53:220-21*. [18]PG 81:844

3:4-11 COMMISSION TO SPEAK GOD'S MESSAGE TO THE HOUSE OF ISRAEL

[4]*And he said to me, "Son of man, go, get you to the house of Israel, and speak with my words to them. [5]For you are not sent to a people of foreign speech and a hard language, but to the house of Israel—[6]not to many peoples of foreign speech and a hard language, whose words you cannot understand. Surely, if I sent you to such, they would listen to you. [7]But the house of Israel will not listen to you; for they are not willing to listen to me; because all the house of Israel are of a hard forehead and of a stubborn heart. [8]Behold, I have made your face hard against their faces, and your forehead hard against their foreheads. [9]Like adamant harder than flint have I made your forehead; fear them not, nor be dismayed at their looks, for they are a rebellious house." [10]Moreover he said to me, "Son of man, all my words that I shall speak to you receive in your heart, and hear with your ears. [11]And go, get you to the exiles, to your people, and say to them, 'Thus says the Lord GOD'; whether they hear or refuse to hear."*

OVERVIEW: The prophet is sent to Gentiles and Israelites (GREGORY THE GREAT); clergy are prophets (AUGUSTINE), and they are to be ready to be firm in their preaching, regardless of the response they will get from the people (AUGUSTINE, JEROME), for exile is a place and state of confusion (GREGORY THE GREAT, CHRYSOSTOM). Hence there is the need to tell abroad what God instructs the prophet to preach (JEROME), though prophets are not the same as apostles (THEODORET).

3:4-5 Go to the House of Israel

GENTILES AND ISRAELITES INVOLVED. GREGORY THE GREAT: In the very beginning of this command, whereby the prophet is sent to preach, the calling of the Gentiles and the banishing of the people of Israel is clearly meant. HOMILIES ON EZEKIEL 1.10.15.[1]

CLERGY ARE PROPHETS. AUGUSTINE: What does that show, if not that God was speaking through the prophet? Now it is we clergy who were above all terrified by the prophet's words, that is, the leaders whom God appointed to speak to his people, and so we begin by seeing our own faces in those words. For as the reader intoned them we had a kind of mirror held up to us in which we could inspect ourselves, and inspect ourselves we did. Inspect yourselves, too, then. SERMON 17.2.[2]

PROPHETS AND APOSTLES DISTINGUISHED. THEODORET OF CYR: Here he clearly shows the distinction between apostolic and prophetic labors. Prophets have committed to them the responsibility of only one race, from which they were to have arisen and whose native language they knew. Apostles . . . have all the nations and peoples of the world entrusted to them, according to the command of the Lord.[3] COMMENTARY ON EZEKIEL 1.3.[4]

EASIER TO SPEAK TO OUR OWN PEOPLE. JEROME: Why should I speak of only one people? If I send you to different nations, my authority and power will still overcome every difficulty. COMMENTARY ON EZEKIEL 1.3.5-6.[5]

3:8 Faces to Be Hardened

RESIST SHAMELESSNESS. JEROME: From this we learn now and then that it is a mark of the grace of God to resist shamelessness. COMMENTARY ON EZEKIEL 1.3.8-10.[6]

HARDNESS NEEDS TO BE MET WITH HARD-NESS. JEROME: The Lord says to the prophets

that he has made their face a brazen city and a stone of adamant and an iron pillar,[7] so that they will not be afraid of the insults of the people but by their stern composure disarm the effrontery of those who sneer at them. A finely strung mind is more readily overcome by insult than by terror. LETTER 66.6.[8]

SHAME'S DIFFERENT RESULTS. GREGORY THE GREAT: Just as shame is laudable in a bad person, it is reprehensible in a good one. For a sinner to blush is a sign of wisdom, but for a good person to blush is a sign of foolishness. HOMILIES ON EZEKIEL 1.10.17.[9]

3:10-11 Speak to the Exiles

THE EXILE OF CONFUSION. GREGORY THE GREAT: When the prophet is sent to admonish the exiled people, this means not only the physical exile but also what has taken place in their mind. For they had come from Jerusalem to Babylon. And what is called Jerusalem, but the vision of peace, and what is Babylon but confusion? Whoever falls from right deeds to wicked actions comes, as it were, from Jerusalem to the city of Babylon, since he descends from a good endeavor to vice. For he has abandoned the summit of good contemplation and lives in the midst of the exile of confusion. HOMILIES ON EZEKIEL 1.10.21.[10]

WHAT GOD TELLS EZEKIEL HAS TO BE BROADCAST. JEROME: We must note that the teaching of God must first be fashioned in our heart and heard and understood carefully, and only then can it be laid before the people. COMMENTARY ON EZEKIEL 1.3.10.[11]

---

[1]HGE 115*. [2]WSA 3 1:367. [3]Mt 28:19. [4]PG 81:844. [5]CCL 75:33. [6]CCL 75:34. [7]Jer 1:18. [8]NPNF 2 6:136-37*. [9]HGE 116. [10]HGE 118*. [11]CCL 75:34.

3:12-15 COMMISSION TO VISIT BABYLON

[12]*Then the Spirit lifted me up, and as the glory of the* Lord *arose[k] from its place, I heard behind me the sound of a great earthquake;* [13]*it was the sound of the wings of the living creatures as they touched one another, and the sound of the wheels beside them, that sounded like a great earthquake.* [14]*The Spirit lifted me up and took me away, and I went in bitterness in the heat of my spirit, the hand of the* Lord *being strong upon me;* [15]*and I came to the exiles at Tel-abib, who dwelt by the river Chebar.[l] And I sat there overwhelmed among them seven days.*

k Cn: Heb *blessed be the glory of the* LORD   l Heb *Chebar, and to where they dwelt.* Another reading is *Chebar, and I sat where they sat*

OVERVIEW: The glory of God is reflected on in its own terms, as a journey to heaven (PSEUDO-DIONYSIUS) and as a reality that has the effect of making us aware of our need to repent (CHRYSOSTOM, JEROME, GREGORY THE GREAT). When the creatures shake their wings, that is seen as an indication of the two Testaments, as well as the virtues of the saints (GREGORY THE GREAT). Ezekiel goes forth, heavy in heart as a result of what he has been told but strengthened by this vision (JEROME, GREGORY THE GREAT).

3:12 The Sound of the Glory of God

THE TRINITY. JEROME: For the place of God is everywhere in which he finds hospitality, for surely the Son is the place of the Father as much as the Father is the place of the Son. COMMENTARY ON EZEKIEL 1.3.12.[1]

HEAVENLY GLORY. PSEUDO-DIONYSIUS: The first group of heavenly beings is particularly worthy of communing with God and of sharing in his work. They imitate, as far as possible, the beauty of God's condition and activity. Knowing many divine things in so superior a fashion they can have a proper share of the divine knowledge and understanding. Hence, theology has transmitted to the people of earth those hymns sung by the first ranks of the angels, whose gloriously transcendent enlightenment is thereby manifested.

Some of these hymns, if one may use perceptible images, are like the "sound of many waters,"[2] as they proclaim, "Blessed be the glory of the Lord from this place."[3] CELESTIAL HIERARCHY 7.4.[4]

THE DREAD OF HEAVEN. CHRYSOSTOM: Did you see how great is the holy dread in heaven and how great the arrogant presumption here below? The angels in heaven give him glory; these heretics on earth carry on meddlesome investigations. In heaven they honor and praise him; on earth we find curious busybodies. In heaven they veil their eyes; on earth the busybodies are obstinate and shamelessly try to hold their eyes fixed on his ineffable glory. Who would not groan, who would not weep for them because of this ultimate madness and folly of theirs? AGAINST THE ANOMOEANS 1.36.[5]

THE EFFECT OF THIS GLORY ON HUMAN BEINGS. GREGORY THE GREAT: The hearts of sinners were the place of the evil spirit, but when in their anger at themselves they return to life through penitence, they become the place of the glory of the Lord. For now they turn on themselves, now with tears of repentance they censure the evils that they have committed. Therefore the blessing of glory in praise of the Lord is heard where before resounded the injury of the Creator

---

[1]CCL 75:35. [2]Ezek 1:24. [3]Ezek 3:12 LXX. [4]PDCW 165*. [5]FC 72:66.

from love of this present age. And the hearts of sinners, which before had been an alien and sinful place, now become to the Lord his dwelling place. For those who are converted from their sins to the Lord not only bewail with tears the wicked deeds they have committed but also move on to the heights, through wondrous works, so that they become sacred creatures of almighty God. They are therefore able to fly to the heights on signs and virtues, so that they abandon the earth completely, and with the gifts that they have received, they reach for the heavens through sheer desire. Homilies on Ezekiel 1.10.29.[6]

3:13 The Sound of the Creatures and the Wheels

Shaken into Penitence. Jerome: It is better and truer to have understood the voice that one has heard than one that one has seen. Commentary on Ezekiel 1.3.13.[7]

They Beat Their Wings. Gregory the Great: Why is it that these winged creatures beat their wings in turn one to another? It is because all the saints by turns touch themselves with their virtues and rouse themselves to make progress through considering one another's virtue. For all things are not given to one person lest he fall through being puffed up with pride. But to this individual is given what is not given to you, and to you is given what is denied to that person, so that while that one considers the good that you have and he has not, he sets you before himself in his thoughts; and again, whereas you see that that one has what you have not, you set yourself behind him in your thoughts, and what is written is come to pass: "In humility count others better than yourselves."[8] Homilies on Ezekiel 1.10.32.[9]

The Two Testaments. Gregory the Great: The noise of the wheels is the speech of the Testaments. Then the noise of the wheels is heard after the noise of the sacred creatures' wings

because, after the speech of the preachers has been received, when the virtues of the saints fly up to pursue higher things and encourage each other on to progress, the posture of holy church is raised up, and the pages of the sacred Testaments are read throughout the world. Homilies on Ezekiel 1.10.37.[10]

Movement in Our Hearts. Gregory the Great: There are two movements through which our hearts are moved. One movement is from fear, the other from charity; the one results from the lamentations of the penitent, the other from the fervor of those who love. Therefore the first movement happens after the word of preaching, when we bewail the sins that we have committed; after the noise of the wings and the wheels, there is the second movement, when with much weeping we seek the heavenly blessings of which we hear. Homilies on Ezekiel 1.10.39.[11]

3:14 Lifted Up and Taken Away

Heaviness of Heart Lifted. Jerome: For the hand of the Lord was on the prophet, strengthening him, so that he could take the name of a sentinel and teach what he taught. Commentary on Ezekiel 1.3.14-15.[12]

The Prophet Is Strengthened. Gregory the Great: It is sweet to be among human beings, except for one who has tasted none of the joys of heaven, because the less he understands the eternal, the more delightfully he rests amid the temporal. But if anyone has already tasted with the mouth of his heart that sweetness of heavenly rewards, those choirs of angels singing hymns, the incomprehensible vision of the holy Trinity, for him what he sees within becomes sweeter the more that all he sustains outside turns bitter. Homilies on Ezekiel 1.10.43.[13]

---

[6]HGE 121*. [7]CCL 75:36. [8]Phil 2:3. [9]HGE 122*. [10]HGE 124-25 *. [11]HGE 125**. [12]CCL 75:37. [13]HGE 127*.

3:15 *Silence for Seven Days*

THE REASON FOR THE SILENCE. GREGORY THE GREAT: Speech is freely accepted by the hearer that is offered by the preacher with compassion of spirit. Thus when iron is joined with iron, it is first dissolved so that afterwards it is in turn held by itself. But if it does not first soften, it will in no way be able to hold itself strongly. Thus the prophet first sat with the captive people and showed himself mourning in their midst, so that when by making this gracious gesture out of charity he showed himself to them as gentle, he immediately held them through the firmness of his speech. HOMILIES ON EZEKIEL 1.11.2.[14]

[14]HGE 129**.

3:16-21 THE MESSAGE OF THE WATCHMAN GIVEN

[16]*And at the end of seven days, the word of the LORD came to me:* [17]*"Son of man, I have made you a watchman for the house of Israel; whenever you hear a word from my mouth, you shall give them warning from me.* [18]*If I say to the wicked, 'You shall surely die,' and you give him no warning, nor speak to warn the wicked from his wicked way, in order to save his life, that wicked man shall die in his iniquity; but his blood I will require at your hand.* [19]*But if you warn the wicked, and he does not turn from his wickedness, or from his wicked way, he shall die in his iniquity; but you will have saved your life.* [20]*Again, if a righteous man turns from his righteousness and commits iniquity, and I lay a stumbling block before him, he shall die; because you have not warned him, he shall die for his sin, and his righteous deeds which he has done shall not be remembered; but his blood I will require at your hand."* [21]*Nevertheless if you warn the righteous man not to sin, and he does not sin, he shall surely live, because he took warning; and you will have saved your life."*

OVERVIEW: The task of the prophet is described in terms of the watchman, which is applied to the work of any leader (AMBROSE, HIPPOLYTUS, JUSTIN, BASIL) but specifically to the office of bishop (AUGUSTINE, CAESARIUS, MAXIMUS); indeed, the word *bishop* means watchman (CASSIODORUS). The watchman's perspective gives him height for the ministry of prophecy (THEODORET). This launches the prophet into his work of warning both the wicked and the righteous of their responsibility to repent, whatever the nature of their sin (PHILOXENUS, JEROME, CHRYSOSTOM, SALVIAN), a task that requires great care (LEO), as well as detachment and the ability to use the right words (GREGORY THE GREAT).

3:16 *The Word of the Lord Comes*

TIME HELPS THE PROPHET TO SPEAK. JEROME: He who was to be a sentinel and to tell the words of God to the people had to be quiet for some time, and to grieve at the things he saw and have nothing in his consciousness in respect of which he would be reproved in other things. COMMENTARY ON EZEKIEL 1.3.16-17.[1]

[1]CCL 75:37.

25

3:17 The Prophet a Watchman

THE WATCHMAN WARNS. JUSTIN MARTYR: We do our very best to warn them, as you do, not to be deluded, for we know full well that whoever can speak out the truth and fails to do so shall be condemned by God. DIALOGUE WITH TRYPHO 82.[2]

CALLED TO HELP THE PEOPLE REPENT. HIPPOLYTUS: "Son of man, I have appointed you as a watchman for the members of the house of Israel, so that you may hear from my mouth and warn them." That means, "Look, I have made you a warning and a caution, so that you may say what I command to the just and to sinners, that the just may grow in discretion and the sinners in penitence." FRAGMENT 8.[3]

A BISHOP SPEAKS HIS OPINION. AMBROSE: An emperor ought not to deny freedom of speech, and a bishop ought not to conceal his opinions. Nothing so much commends an emperor to the love of his people as the encouragement of liberty in those who are subject to him by the obligation of public service. Indeed, the love of liberty or of slavery is what distinguishes good emperors from bad, while in a bishop there is nothing so perilous before God or so disgraceful before people as not to speak his thoughts freely. For it is written, "I spoke of your testimonies before kings and was not ashamed,"[4] and in another place, "Son of man, if I have made you a watchman for the house of Israel, to the intent (it says) that if a righteous person turns from his righteousness and commits iniquity because you have not given him warning (that is, not told him what to guard against), his righteousness shall not be remembered, and I will require his blood at your hand. Nevertheless, if you warn the righteous person not to sin and he does not, then the righteous shall surely live because you have warned him, and you shall deliver your soul." LETTER 40.2.[5]

THE HEIGHTS OF A WATCHTOWER. THEO-DORET OF CYR: "You must be," he says, "like a watchman, who is placed on top of some hill, with orders to announce for himself beforehand any invasions by barbarians. And you must be set up as if on a watchtower, on the highest point of prophecy, and what you foresee, you must tell out to the people." COMMENTARY ON EZEKIEL 1.3.[6]

THE BISHOP AAS A WATCHMAN. CAESARIUS OF ARLES: If we carefully heed the lessons that are read at the consecration of bishops, we have a means of rousing ourselves to the greatest compunction. What Gospel text is it, except the one I mentioned a little while ago? "Peter, Peter, tend my sheep," and again, "feed my sheep."[7] Did Christ say, cultivate the vineyards by your presence, arrange the country estates yourself, exercise the cultivation of land? He did not say this, but "feed my sheep." Now what kind of a prophetic text is read at the consecration of a bishop? It is this: "I have made you a watchman for the house of Israel." It did not say a steward of vineyards or country estates or the manager of fields; doubtless it is a watchman of souls. SERMONS 1.11.[8]

IT IS BETTER TO REBUKE THAN REMAIN SILENT. MAXIMUS OF TURIN: Sometimes when we preach, our sermons seem rather harsh to many, and what we speak about as a rule is taken by some as if it were produced from a hard attitude. For they say, "how severely and bitterly the bishop has preached!" not knowing that for bishops speaking is more a matter of obligation than of desire. Speaking, I say, is more a matter of obligation— not because the desire to preach the truth is lacking but because the silence that comes from not speaking is driven away by the punishment of the law. . . . This, then, is the preacher's situation—that he should not be

---

[2]FC 6:279. [3]GCS 1.2:185. [4]Ps 119:46 (118:46 LXX, Vulg.). [5]LCC 5:229-30. [6]PG 81:848. [7]Jn 21:17. The readings at episcopal consecrations at Arles in Caesarius's time clearly included Ezekiel 3:17 and John 21:17. [8]FC 31:11*.

silent with respect to the sins of another if he wishes to avoid sinning himself, and that he should correct his brother by reproving him so that he may not destroy what is priestly in himself. . . . Consequently it is better to correct the sinner by rebuking him than to accept the sinner's misdeed by keeping quiet. This is the position in which we have been placed: if we told sinners that their crimes were not their own, the guilt of their crimes would also implicate us. For this is in fact what the Lord says through the prophet: "And you, son of man, I have given you as a watchman to the house of Israel, and you shall hear the word from my mouth. When I say to the sinner, 'You shall die the death, and you do not speak so that the impious may beware of his way, the wicked himself shall die in his own wickedness, but I will require his blood from your hand,'" and so forth. Clearly these words are plain and obvious. They soil the watchmen with criminal blood when he keeps silence, and they are not satisfied that the evildoers' own evil doing condemns him unless they also incriminate the one who was unwilling to rebuke the evil in question. So, then, how great the iniquity of the sinner is! The sinner sins, and the bishop is convicted; he kills himself by his own sins, and his blood is required from the hand of the bishop. . . . What is a watchman? A watchman is one who, while standing (as it were) on a lofty pinnacle, looks out on the people around him so that no enemy falls unexpectedly on them but so that, as he keeps careful watch, the populace live in harmony and peace. SERMON 92.1-2.[9]

I HAVE MADE YOU A WATCHMAN. CASSIODORUS: The office of bishop is the highest order in the church. *Episcopos* means overseer, because with the help of divine grace he guards the Lord's flock from his high seat like a most careful shepherd. As the prophet Ezekiel says, "I have made you a watchman over the house of Israel." EXPOSITIONS OF THE PSALMS 108.8.[10]

THE WATCHMAN'S LIFE. GREGORY THE GREAT: The life of a watchman must always be high and circumspect. Let it be high lest he succumb to love of earthly things, and circumspect lest he be struck by the missiles of a hidden life from every side. HOMILIES ON EZEKIEL 1.11.7.[11]

THE WATCHMAN MUST BE CAREFUL. LEO THE GREAT: Just as the well-being of the churches causes us gratification, so we are deeply saddened whenever we learn of any liberties taken with, or acts committed against, canon law and ecclesiastical discipline. We cannot excuse ourselves to him who wished us to be on the watch if we do not repress such practices with the vigilance we should. We cannot excuse ourselves if we permit the unsullied body of the church (which we are bound to keep clean from all dirt) to be defiled by contact with those who pursue evil ends. For the very union of the members gets inharmonious elements in it through carelessness. LETTERS 4.[12]

SINNERS ARE EVERYONE. PHILOXENUS OF MABBUG: The words are addressed to the Jews, since it was to them that the prophet Ezekiel had been sent at that time; and today, too, after the coming of our Savior, the words apply to pagans and to Jews and to those who once believed but then denied their faith. The prophet's words are applicable to those who sin without perceiving their sin, since a sinner who has received baptism, even though he may be dead toward his soul, because he does not perceive his sin, yet he is alive to God because of the grace of baptism that he possesses. ON THE INDWELLING OF THE HOLY SPIRIT.[13]

3:18 The Wicked Must Be Warned

THOSE WHO LIVE PERSISTENTLY IN SIN. JEROME: A threat is not made against people but against sins, nor is it made against those who are

---

[9]ACW 50:213-14*. [10]ACW 53:105-6**. [11]HGE 131. [12]FC 34:23*. [13]CS 101:124.

converted from their imperfections but against those who remain in their sin. COMMENTARY ON EZEKIEL 1.3.18-19.[14]

THE WATCHMAN MUST SPEAK. GREGORY THE GREAT: We are constrained; we show ourselves to be defendants, we who are called priests, who above those sins that are our own also add the deaths of strangers, because we kill as many as we daily see go to their deaths, because of our silence and indifference. HOMILIES ON EZEKIEL 1.11.9.[15]

THE DANGER OF BISHOPS NOT SPEAKING OUT. AUGUSTINE: You have frequently heard in the holy Scriptures in what great danger bishops are placed, if they are unwilling to carry out what the apostle urges on them. . . . But when we reprove someone, if the person we reprove is bad, he fixes his attention on the one he is being reproved by and happily and more readily acknowledges what has to be put right in his reprover than in himself. And if he can find something true to say against the one who is reproving him, he is delighted. How much better to rejoice about his own healthy condition when he has been put right than about another person's illness when he is rebuked! SERMON 387.1.[16]

THE SUPERIOR MUST OFFER GUIDANCE. BASIL THE GREAT: It is of the greatest importance that the superior [in a religious community] be convinced that if he fails to offer his brother the proper guidance, he will draw on himself heavy and inescapable wrath, for his blood will be required at his hands. THE LONG RULES 29.[17]

PREACHING HARD THINGS. CAESARIUS OF ARLES: Whenever we preach something hard, we do not do so because we believe that you have done something of the sort, but we denounce things that you have not done, in order to be able to cure those matters in which you may have been overcome. It often happens that we fear to do great wrongs but more quickly fail to guard against slight ones. SERMONS 57.2.[18]

THE NEED TO REBUKE. CAESARIUS OF ARLES: It is necessary for us to rebuke, either in secret or in public, those who are careless. Now if the one whom we reprove is wicked, when we do so he will notice by whom he is rebuked, and he will more readily recognize what is being corrected in the one who is reproving him than in himself. SERMONS 145.1.[19]

3:19 By Warning the Wicked

THE PROPHET'S TASK ACCOMPLISHED. AUGUSTINE: If he does this, he goes out from there, not by physical withdrawal but defended by his behavior; he has done what he had to do, even if the other person did not heed the warning he should have heeded. SERMON 88.23.[20]

WARNING NECESSARY. CHRYSOSTOM: We learn from Ezekiel that, provided the guardian gives warning as to what it is necessary to avoid and it is necessary to choose, he delivers his own soul, even if no one pays any attention to him. HOMILIES ON THE GOSPEL OF JOHN 13.[21]

USING THE RIGHT WORDS. GREGORY THE GREAT: We must learn by experience how great must be the order and consideration of speech in the mouth of a shepherd. For a teacher must consider what he says, to whom he says it, when he says it, how he says it and how much he says. HOMILIES ON EZEKIEL 1.11.12.[22]

3:20 The Righteous Who Repent

ANYONE CAN SIN. SALVIAN THE PRESBYTER: Thus it happens that all things are changed, pass away and perish. No one considers anyone more

---

[14]CCL 75:38. [15]HGE 133**. The term "priests" at the time applied to bishops only. [16]WSA 3 10:397*. [17]FC 9:293. [18]FC 31:283. [19]FC 47:304*. [20]WSA 3 3:434. [21]FC 33:120*. [22]HGE 133-34.

base than himself or more lowly than God. If there is a time at which anyone can legally place God second to his blood and marriage relatives, there is no time in which God must lawfully be placed ahead of them. But if, because it is true, there is no time whatever in which he should not be given preference, there is no time when he can lawfully be placed second to them. Indeed, there is no time, not even at the point of death, because the prophet says that even the just person will perish on the day he errs. FOUR BOOKS OF TIMO-THY TO THE CHURCH 4.2.[23]

THE PREACHER MUST TRY TO SPEAK BEFORE-HAND. GREGORY THE GREAT: Because the

preacher was silent to the just person who fell into sin, he is held guilty of his blood. . . . But it may be asked whether the preaching should be given to the just person after he has fallen or before he falls. The preacher must watch lest he come into error and undoubtedly even before he falls. HOMILIES ON EZEKIEL 1.11.21.[24]

LOOKING OUT FOR THE RIGHTEOUS. JEROME: The one who does not hear perishes, but the other who hears and is converted to repentance saves his soul. COMMENTARY ON EZEKIEL 1.3.20-21.[25]

[23]FC 3:357. [24]HGE 137. [25]CCL 75:38.

3:22-27 COMMISSION TO CONFINEMENT

[22]And the hand of the LORD was there upon me; and he said to me, "Arise, go forth into the plain,[m] and there I will speak with you." [23]So I arose and went forth into the plain;[m] and lo, the glory of the LORD stood there, like the glory which I had seen by the river Chebar; and I fell on my face. [24]But the Spirit entered into me, and set me upon my feet; and he spoke with me and said to me, "Go, shut yourself within your house. [25]And you, O son of man, behold, cords will be placed upon you, and you shall be bound with them, so that you cannot go out among the people; [26]and I will make your tongue cleave to the roof of your mouth, so that you shall be dumb and unable to reprove them; for they are a rebellious house. [27]But when I speak with you, I will open your mouth, and you shall say to them, 'Thus says the Lord GOD'; he that will hear, let him hear; and he that will refuse to hear, let him refuse; for they are a rebellious house."

m Or valley

OVERVIEW: The prophet sees the glory once more, which gives him inner quiet (THEODORET), equips him for the difficult task ahead (JEROME) and makes him once more aware of his human frailty (GREGORY THE GREAT). The cords that will bind him are the Babylonians (HIPPOLYTUS), and these impose further disciplines on the work of

the preacher (GREGORY THE GREAT).

3:22 Go into the Plain

EZEKIEL, A SIGN FOR THE PEOPLE. HIPPOLY-TUS: "Go out into the plain, and you will be spoken to." This means that [Ezekiel] is made into a sign for them; or on this day he is ordered to go out into the plain, and he will be spoken to; and on the plain that face will be revealed to him that was shown to him at the river Chebar. FRAGMENT 9.[1]

CONFINEMENT WILL DEPRIVE HIM. JEROME: And notice this, that, standing himself in the middle of those who sat as captives, the prophet did not see the glory of God. COMMENTARY ON EZEKIEL 1.3.22.[2]

QUIET IS GRANTED TO THE PROPHET. THEODORET OF CYR: Quiet is afforded by contemplating divine things, when the mind is free from external cares, which makes it anticipate things, and it is distracted no more fully here or there, but it can take in divine things more exactly when it is turned in on itself. COMMENTARY ON EZEKIEL 2.3.[3]

3:23 Seeing the Glory

EZEKIEL WILL SURVIVE SEEING THE GLORY. JEROME: This is the meaning of the verse, "Because you have been strengthened by the sight of the majesty of the Lord, never fear anything and do not be frightened of anyone, and go back to your own house, whether it is for your bodily needs, as some people regard them, or as a sign of imminent danger." COMMENTARY ON EZEKIEL 1.3.23-24.[4]

THE PROPHET ONCE MORE FALLS ON HIS FACE. GREGORY THE GREAT: The glory of the Lord being manifest, the prophet falls on his face, because although a human being is raised up to understand the sublime, yet through contemplating the majesty of God he realizes the weakness of his own condition and (as it were) has no standing, he who sees himself as dust and ashes before the eyes of God. HOMILIES ON EZEKIEL 1.12.4.[5]

3:25 You Will Be Bound

THE BABYLONIANS ARE THE CHAINS. HIPPOLYTUS: "And look, they will bind you with chains and fetters." That is, the chains that will bind him, so that he might not go out and walk among them, are the Babylonians who encircle Jerusalem and its inhabitants and prevent them from going out and coming in. FRAGMENT 11.[6]

THE CORDS ARE THE HARDSHIPS TO FOLLOW. JEROME: So many are the struggles against God that they do not deserve to hear him rebuking them. From this it is clear that where there is a multitude of sinners, those who sin are unworthy, who are corrected by the Lord. COMMENTARY ON EZEKIEL 1.3.25-26.[7]

THE PREACHER'S DISCIPLINES. GREGORY THE GREAT: When each preacher is led back to the conscience of his house, bonds are put on him, and he is bound because the more he examines himself in thought, the more he realizes with what great infirmities of his mortality the soul of a righteous person is bound. HOMILIES ON EZEKIEL 1.12.13.[8]

3:26 You Will Be Silent

THE PREACHER'S SILENCE. GREGORY THE GREAT: This is what is meant: The word of preaching is taken away from you. As the people provoke me by their deeds, they are not worthy to have the encouragement of the truth. We cannot easily recognize whose vice causes the word to be withdrawn from the preacher. We know indeed that the shepherd's silence is sometimes harmful to him, but that it is always harmful to those subject to him. FORTY GOSPEL HOMILIES 19.[9]

3:27 When I Speak to You

PRIOR KNOWLEDGE HELPS EQUIP THE PROPHET. GREGORY THE GREAT: The prophet

---

[1]GCS 1.2:185. [2]CCL 75:40. [3]PG 81:852. [4]CCL 75:40. [5]HGE 142*. [6]GCS 1.2:186. [7]CCL 75:41. [8]HGE 146*. [9]CS 123:136*.

learns of the calamities beforehand so that he is prepared for all of them. For evils have less power over a mind when they do not come unexpected, and yet when calamities are known beforehand how great the virtue of obedience shown in him who both realizes that he is to suffer adversity and yet is not disobedient to the voice of God. HOMILIES ON EZEKIEL 1.12.15.[10]

[10]HGE 147*.

4:1-2 THE BRICK IS LAID

[1]*And you, O son of man, take a brick and lay it before you, and portray upon it a city, even Jerusalem;* [2]*and put siegeworks against it, and build a siege wall against it, and cast up a mound against it; set camps also against it, and plant battering rams against it round about.*

OVERVIEW: The prophet is unable to speak and communicates nonverbally to the people. The brick is Jerusalem (JEROME); the prophet is the preacher instructing the people (GREGORY THE GREAT).

JERUSALEM IS THE BRICK. JEROME: Jerusalem is to be represented on a brick, and the brick itself is to be placed before the prophet, so that when it looks like Jerusalem in the dust, it can portray the whole blockade against it. COMMENTARY ON EZEKIEL 1.4.1-2.[1]

THE PREACHER AND CORRECTION. GREGORY THE GREAT: There are some things that are to be reproved severely, so that when a fault is not recognized by the one committing it, he may appreciate its gravity by the verbal reproof, or when he glosses over to himself the evil he has done, he may have serious apprehension for himself owing to the asperity of the reproof given. It is, surely, the duty of the ruler to reveal the glory of our homeland in heaven by preaching, to show what great temptations of the ancient enemy are lurking in this life's journey and to correct with severe and zealous asperity those evils in his subjects that cannot be treated with forbearance, lest, being too little incensed against such faults, he himself be held guilty of all. PASTORAL CARE 2.10.[2]

THE INWARD SIEGE. GREGORY THE GREAT: When we know that one thing is accomplished according to history and we recognize that another lacks any reason according to history, we are to hold both in holy Scripture, since we are to believe that the siege of Jerusalem, which according to the meaning of the words happened later, is prefigured in the words and deeds of the prophet, and yet another siege, an inward one, is meant by it. HOMILIES ON EZEKIEL 1.12.21.[3]

THE PREACHER AND THE BRICK. GREGORY THE GREAT: Every teacher, when he accepts any earthly hearer of the teaching of the heavenly words, takes a brick. HOMILIES ON EZEKIEL 1.12.23.[4]

[1]CCL 75:42. [2]ACW 11:82-83. [3]HGE 150**. [4]HGE 151.

PREPARATION AGAINST TEMPTATION. GREGORY THE GREAT: A teacher ought to come to know which temptations beset the progressing soul in order that he may be able to prepare it to be on its guard against the traps of the evil spirit. HOMILIES ON EZEKIEL 1.12.25.[5]

[5]HGE 152*.

4:3 THE IRON PLATE

[3]*And take an iron plate, and place it as an iron wall between you and the city; and set your face toward it, and let it be in a state of siege, and press the siege against it. This is a sign for the house of Israel.*

OVERVIEW: The iron plate is the barrier between Israel and their God (JEROME), and the preacher's zeal must instruct the people about temptations (GREGORY THE GREAT).

THE ANGER OF GOD. JEROME: An iron plate, which is meant to be the image of the wall between the prophet and the city, represents the anger of God in all its fullness, which does not diminish as a result of any prayers, nor does it bend toward mercy in any way. COMMENTARY ON EZEKIEL 1.4.3.[1]

THE ZEAL OF THE PREACHER. GREGORY THE GREAT: Why is it that the prophet places this pan between himself and the city as a wall of iron? The meaning is that this strong zeal now at work in the mind of the teacher will be a witness on the day of the last judgment between him and the soul for which he is zealous against vices. Even if he who is taught is unwilling to hear, yet the teacher, by reason of the zeal that he exhibits, will not be answerable for the negligence of his hearers. HOMILIES ON EZEKIEL 1.12.30.[2]

THE TRAPS OF TEMPTATION. GREGORY THE GREAT: The teacher lays siege against the soul of the hearer when he proclaims that traps of temptations may be laid in everything that happens in this life, so that when the mind is everywhere fearful, everywhere circumspect, the more timidly it lives, the more vigilant it will be. HOMILIES ON EZEKIEL 1.12.32.[3]

THE SIEGE IN EACH SOUL. GREGORY THE GREAT: Just as the house of Israel physically underwent a siege, so each soul that now begins to serve almighty God perceives the traps the evil spirits are laying siege to it. HOMILIES ON EZEKIEL 1.12.33.[4]

[1]CCL 75:43. [2]HGE 154*. [3]HGE 155*. [4]HGE 155**.

4:4-6 THE PROPHET LIES ON HIS LEFT SIDE

[4]*Then lie upon your left side, and I will lay the punishment of the house of Israel upon you;[n] for the number of the days that you lie upon it, you shall bear their punishment.* [5]*For I assign to you a number of days, three hundred and ninety days, equal to the number of the years of their punishment; so long shall you bear the punishment of the house of Israel.* [6]*And when you have completed these, you shall lie down a second time, but on your right side, and bear the punishment of the house of Judah; forty days I assign you, a day for each year.*

n Cn: Heb *you shall lay . . . upon it*

OVERVIEW: Ezekiel's actions, strange as they may be, are intended by God to instruct the people (THEODORET).

THE PROPHET'S ACTIONS AND THEIR IMPACT. THEODORET OF CYR: Ezekiel was to lie down on his right side for 40 days and 150 on his left, to dig through a wall and flee, portraying in himself the captivity. Another time Ezekiel is to sharpen a sword to a point, shave his head with it and divide the hair four ways and assign a part here, a part there, without listing it all.[1] The ruler of the universe ordered each of these things to be done so that by the strangeness of this spectacle he might gather those who would not be persuaded by speech or give an ear to prophecy and so dispose them to hear the divine oracles. . . . So, just as the God of the universe providentially ordered each one of these things to be done for the good of those who live carelessly, so he arranged this extraordinary novelty to draw everyone by its strangeness to the spectacle and make his counsel persuasive to those who come. For the novelty of the spectacle is a reliable guarantee of the instruction it can give, and whoever comes to the spectacle leaves instructed in divine matters. LIVES OF SIMEON STYLITES 12.[2]

---

[1]Ezek 5:1-2. [2]CS 112:76**.

[4:7-8 EZEKIEL PROPHESIES TOWARD JERUSALEM]

[4:9-17 THE BREAD COOKED ON DUNG]

[5:1–7:27 ISRAEL'S PUNISHMENT FOR ABOMINATIONS]

[8:1-18 THE VISION OF ISRAEL'S FUTURE ABOMINATIONS]

9:1-4 THE MARKING OF THE INNOCENT

¹*Then he cried in my ears with a loud voice, saying, "Draw near, you executioners of the city, each with his destroying weapon in his hand." ²And lo, six men came from the direction of the upper gate, which faces north, every man with his weapon for slaughter in his hand, and with them was a man clothed in linen, with a writing case at his side. And they went in and stood beside the bronze altar.*

³*Now the glory of the God of Israel had gone up from the cherubim on which it rested to the threshold of the house; and he called to the man clothed in linen, who had the writing case at his side. ⁴And the LORD said to him, "Go through the city, through Jerusalem, and put a mark upon the foreheads of the men who sigh and groan over all the abominations that are committed in it."*

OVERVIEW: The man in linen is endowed with all manner of virtues (PSEUDO-DIONYSIUS). The mark on the foreheads of the innocent is a sign that saves them (ATHANASIUS), but it is an inward sign, on the heart, not just an outward sign on the forehead (AUGUSTINE). It is also a sign of repentance (CHRYSOSTOM) because of the saving power of the cross (CYPRIAN). The sign of the cross begins public prayer, as a way of recalling baptism (HORSIESI).

9:2 The Man Clothed in Linen

THE GARMENTS OF THE PRIESTHOOD AS VIRTUES. PSEUDO-DIONYSIUS: The priestly vestment signifies the capacity to guide people spiritually to the divine and mysterious sights and to consecrate one's whole life. And the cincture is an indication of the control exercised by these intelligent beings over their generative powers. They signify also their practice of gathering together, their unifying absorption, the harmo-

nious ease with which they tirelessly circle about their own identity. . . . The spears and the axes represent their discriminating skills amid the unlikeness of things, the sharp clarity and efficacy of their powers of discernment. CELESTIAL HIERARCHY 15.4-5.[1]

9:4 A Mark on the Foreheads of the Innocent

THE SIGN IS THERE TO BE SEEN. ATHANASIUS: Thus [the devil] suffers and is dishonored; and although he still ventures with shameless confidence to disguise himself, yet now, wretched spirit, he is detected rather by those who bear the sign on their foreheads; and he is even rejected by them, and is humbled and put to shame. For even if, now that he is a creeping serpent, he shall transform himself into an angel of light, yet his deception will not profit him; for we have been taught that "though an angel from heaven preach

---

[1]*PDCW* 186-87.

to us any other gospel than that we have received, he is anathema."[2] LETTER TO THE BISHOPS OF EGYPT 1.2.[3]

OUTWARD SIGN ON THE FOREHEAD. AUGUSTINE: But maybe that person wasn't yet a Christian. We at least, brothers and sisters, should listen; we to whom as believers the gospel is chanted, we by whom the one who said all this is worshiped, whose sign is worn by us on our foreheads and held in our hearts. It makes a great deal of difference, you see, where a person keeps the sign of Christ, whether on the forehead or both on the forehead and in the heart. You heard, when the holy prophet Ezekiel was speaking, how before God sent an exterminator of a wicked people, he first sent a marker and said to him, "Go and mark with a sign the foreheads of those who groan and grieve over the sins of my people, which are committed among them." Yet for all that they groan and grieve; and this is why they have been marked with a sign on the forehead— the forehead of the inner self, not the outer one. There is a forehead of the face, you see, and a forehead of the conscience. In fact, sometimes the inner forehead gets a knock, and the outer one blushes; it either blushes for shame or turns pale with fright. SERMON 107.7.[4]

THE CROSS A SIGN OF REPENTANCE. CHRYSOSTOM: I have heard many, after such experience, blame themselves and say, "What advantage is it that I have grieved? I have not recovered my money, and I have injured myself." But if you have grieved on account of sin, you have blotted it out and reaped the greatest pleasure. If you have grieved for your brothers who have fallen, you have both encouraged and comforted yourself and have also restored them; and even if you were not to profit them, you have an abundant recompense. And that you may learn that grieving for those who have fallen, though we should not at all benefit them, still brings us a large reward, hear what Ezekiel says, or rather, what God speaks through him. For when he had sent certain messengers to overturn the city and to consume all the dwellings with sword and fire, along with their inhabitants, God charges one of them, "Set a mark on the forehead of those that groan and are in anguish." And after charging the others and saying, "Begin from my holy ones," he goes on to add, "but do not touch whoever has the sign on him." HOMILIES CONCERNING THE STATUES 18.9.[5]

THE SAVING POWER OF THE CROSS. CYPRIAN: God says that only those can escape who have been reborn and signed with the sign of Christ; when sending his angels to lay waste the world and to destroy the human race he threatens more seriously than the last time.... This sign pertains to the passion and blood of Christ and that he is kept safe and unharmed whoever is found in this sign. To DEMETRIAN 22.[6]

PRAYERS BEGIN WITH THE SIGN OF THE CROSS. HORSIESI: At the beginning of our prayers let us sign ourselves with the seal of baptism. Let us make the sign of the cross on our foreheads, as on the day of our baptism, as it is written in Ezekiel. Let us not first lower our hand to our mouth or to our beard, but let us raise it to our forehead, sing in our heart, "We have signed ourselves with the seal." This is not like the seal of baptism, but the sign of the cross was traced on the forehead of each of us on the day of our baptism. REGULATIONS 7.[7]

---

[2]Gal 1:8. [3]NPNF 2 4:224*. [4]*WSA* 3 4:113. [5]NPNF 1 9:462**. [6]FC 36:187*. [7]CS 46:199*.

9:5-11 THE SLAUGHTER OF THE GUILTY

⁵And to the others he said in my hearing, "Pass through the city after him, and smite; your eye shall not spare, and you shall show no pity; ⁶slay old men outright, young men and maidens, little children and women, but touch no one upon whom is the mark. And begin at my sanctuary." So they began with the elders who were before the house. ⁷Then he said to them, "Defile the house, and fill the courts with the slain. Go forth." So they went forth, and smote in the city. ⁸And while they were smiting, and I was left alone, I fell upon my face, and cried, "Ah Lord GOD! wilt thou destroy all that remains of Israel in the outpouring of thy wrath upon Jerusalem?"

⁹Then he said to me, "The guilt of the house of Israel and Judah is exceedingly great; the land is full of blood, and the city full of injustice; for they say, 'The LORD has forsaken the land, and the LORD does not see.' ¹⁰As for me, my eye will not spare, nor will I have pity, but I will requite their deeds upon their heads."

¹¹And lo, the man clothed in linen, with the writing case at his side, brought back word, saying, "I have done as thou didst command me."

OVERVIEW: The guilty are to be slaughtered, and only those marked on the forehead will be saved (MAXIMUS) by the blood of the Lamb of God (BASIL). Even priests are among those to be killed, if they worship idols or can only think of their status (JEROME), for the inner self reveals the real character of a person (AUGUSTINE). Genuinely good people do not want others to be punished (CHRYSOSTOM), yet if they lack faith in the providence of God, they will receive no mercy whatever (JEROME).

9:5 Strike Them

PROTECTION ONLY FOR THOSE MARKED. MAXIMUS OF TURIN: In Ezekiel the prophet, when the angel who had been sent had slain everyone and the slaughter had begun at the holy places, only those whom he had signed with the letter tau—that is, with the mark of the cross— remained unharmed. SERMON 45.2.[1]

THE MARK OF THE LAMB OF GOD. BASIL THE GREAT: You have given a sign, the blood itself of a lamb without blemish, slain for the sin of the world. And Ezekiel says that a sign was given on the foreheads of the persons. HOMILIES ON THE PSALMS 20.3 (Ps 59).[2]

9:6 Slay the Priests

FALSE PRIESTS TO BE SLAIN. JEROME: This means priests who went to the temple and adored idols, or those who were called holy among the people because of their status as priests. It is time for judgment to begin on them from the house of God. COMMENTARY ON EZEKIEL 3.9.4-6.[3]

THE INNER SELF TELLS ALL. AUGUSTINE: So there is a forehead of the inner self. That is where those people were marked, to save them from being wiped out. Because even if they did not put right the sins that were committed among them, at least they were pained by them, and by their very pain they set themselves apart; while set apart for God, they were mixed together in the

---

¹ACW 50:250*. ²FC 46:338*. ³CCL 75:107.

eyes of people. They are marked with a sign in secret; they escape harm in public. The destroyer is sent next and is told, "Go, destroy, do not spare young, old, male, female; but do not go near those who have the sign on their foreheads." What a sure guarantee has been given you, my brothers and sisters, you among this people who are groaning and grieving over the wicked deeds committed in your midst and are not committing them! SERMON 107.7.[4]

9:8 Ezekiel Cried to the Lord

GOOD PEOPLE DO NOT WANT OTHERS TO BE PUNISHED. CHRYSOSTOM: You see, even if it is the wicked who perish, nevertheless the souls of good people are likely to show compassion when they see people being punished; and you will find each of the good people and the inspired writers making earnest supplication for them. HOMILIES ON GENESIS 25.12.[5]

THE PROPHETS GRIEVE FOR ALL. CHRYSOSTOM: It is, after all, the practice of the prophets and the just to grieve not only for themselves but for the rest of humanity. If you are inclined to

check that, you will find them all giving evidence of this compassion—for example, you can listen to Isaiah's words, "Don't put yourself out to comfort me for the destruction of the daughter of my people";[6] or Jeremiah, . . . "Who will pour water on my head and provide a fountain of tears for my eyes?"[7] or Ezekiel, "Alas, Lord, will you destroy what remains of Israel?" HOMILIES ON GENESIS 29.7.[8]

9:9 The People Are Guilty

LACK OF FAITH BRINGS DESTRUCTION. JEROME: The cause of so many crimes is this: The people thought that there was no such thing as providence on earth and that God did not look after mortal things at all. . . . They either thought that there was no providence, or if there had once been any, it had forsaken its own people. Therefore, not even the eye of the Lord will spare them, nor will he have mercy. COMMENTARY ON EZEKIEL 3.9.9-10.[9]

---

[4]*WSA* 3 4:113-14. [5]FC 82:133. [6]Is 22:4. [7]Jer 9:1 (8:23 LXX). [8]FC 82:203*. [9]CCL 75:110.

10:1-22 THE DEPARTURE OF THE LORD FROM THE SANCTUARY

Then I looked, and behold, on the firmament that was over the heads of the cherubim there appeared above them something like a sapphire, in form resembling a throne. [2]*And he said to the man clothed in linen, "Go in among the whirling wheels underneath the cherubim; fill your hands with burning coals from between the cherubim, and scatter them over the city."*

And he went in before my eyes. [3]*Now the cherubim were standing on the south side of the house, when the man went in; and a cloud filled the inner court.* [4]*And the glory of the LORD went up from the cherubim to the threshold of the house; and the house was filled with the cloud, and the court was full of the brightness of the glory of the LORD.* [5]*And the sound of the wings of the cherubim* was heard as far as the outer court, like the voice of God Almighty when he speaks.

⁶And when he commanded the man clothed in linen, "Take fire from between the whirling wheels, from between the cherubim," he went in and stood beside a wheel. ⁷And a cherub stretched forth his hand from between the cherubim to the fire that was between the cherubim, and took some of it, and put it into the hands of the man clothed in linen, who took it and went out. ⁸The cherubim appeared to have the form of a human hand under their wings.

⁹And I looked, and behold, there were four wheels beside the cherubim, one beside each cherub; and the appearance of the wheels was like sparkling chrysolite. ¹⁰And as for their appearance, the four had the same likeness, as if a wheel were within a wheel. ¹¹When they went, they went in any of their four directions^g without turning as they went, but in whatever direction the front wheel faced the others followed without turning as they went. ¹²And^h their rims, and their spokes,^i and the wheels were full of eyes round about—the wheels that the four of them had. ¹³As for the wheels, they were called in my hearing the whirling wheels. ¹⁴And every one had four faces: the first face was the face of the cherub, and the second face was the face of a man, and the third the face of a lion, and the fourth the face of an eagle.

¹⁵And the cherubim mounted up. These were the living creatures that I saw by the river Chebar. ¹⁶And when the cherubim went, the wheels went beside them; and when the cherubim lifted up their wings to mount up from the earth, the wheels did not turn from beside them. ¹⁷When they stood still, these stood still, and when they mounted up, these mounted up with them; for the spirit of the living creatures^j was in them.

¹⁸Then the glory of the LORD went forth from the threshold of the house, and stood over the cherubim. ¹⁹And the cherubim lifted up their wings and mounted up from the earth in my sight as they went forth, with the wheels beside them; and they stood at the door of the east gate of the house of the LORD; and the glory of the God of Israel was over them.

²⁰These were the living creatures that I saw underneath the God of Israel by the river Chebar; and I knew that they were cherubim. ²¹Each had four faces, and each four wings, and underneath their wings the semblance of human hands. ²²And as for the likeness of their faces, they were the very faces whose appearance I had seen by the river Chebar. They went every one straight forward.

g Heb on their four sides   h Gk: Heb And their whole body and   i Heb spokes and their wings   j Or of life

---

OVERVIEW: The glory of the Lord is portrayed in the clouds, in all its diversity and power (PSEUDO-DIONYSIUS), and the cherubim are the messengers of God (EZNIK, BEDE). The prophet, however, does not see the throne of God, only its likeness (ORIGEN, JEROME). The cherubim, whose movements are determined by God alone (PSEUDO-MACARIUS), are full of eyes because they have to see everything and make proper judgments ac-

cordingly (GREGORY THE GREAT). The departure of the glory of God from the temple leads to the foundation of the church (JEROME).

10:4 The Departure

THE GLORY OF GOD PORTRAYED IN THE CLOUDS. PSEUDO-DIONYSIUS: The Word of God represents the beings also as clouds. This is to show that the holy and intelligent beings are filled in a transcendent way with hidden light. Directly and without arrogance they have been first to receive this light, and as intermediaries, they have generously passed it on so far as possible to those next to them. They have a generative power, a life-giving power, a power to increase and completion, for they rain understanding down, and they summon the breast that receives them to give birth to a living tide. CELESTIAL HIERARCHY 15.6.[1]

CHERUBIM AS MESSENGERS OF GOD. EZNIK OF KOLB: To Ezekiel he made appear a driver in human form, flame-shaped and fire-tongued in a chariot composed of various forms. And he showed to him cherubim composed of various wild beasts, and a cherub's hand extended like a man's from the midst of the cherubim. ON GOD 118.[2]

ONLY THE LIKENESS. ORIGEN: The prophet did not see the throne but the likeness of the throne, just as he said earlier that he did not see the glory of the Lord but the likeness of the glory of the Lord.[3] EXCERPTS ON EZEKIEL 10.[4]

NOT THE REALITY. JEROME: Note, reader, how this higher vision both harmonizes and is at variance with what went before; if you compare each and take our suggestion, you understand divine mysteries and what I impressed on you previously, namely, how it is not truth that is meant on the firmament, on the throne and on the hand of the man, but only the likeness of the truth. COMMENTARY ON EZEKIEL 3.10.2-8.[5]

10:5 *The Sound of the Cherubim*

CHERUBIM AS ANGELIC POWER. BEDE: The prophet Ezekiel clearly declares that "cherubim" is the name of the angelic powers that he describes as having appeared to him with wings, according to the pattern in which they are ordered to be deployed here. ON THE TABERNACLE 1.5.25.18-21.[6]

10:12 *Full of Eyes*

BEING ON THE WATCH AND CAREFUL IN JUDGMENT. GREGORY THE GREAT: They who are superiors must be warned to be earnestly on the watch, to have vigilant eyes within and round about and to strive to become living creatures of heaven. For the living creatures of heaven are described as full of eyes round about and within. Surely it is fitting that all who are set above others should have eyes within and round about, inasmuch as they aim at pleasing the judge within, and while giving outwardly examples of living, they should detect what is to be corrected in others. Subjects are to be warned not to judge rashly the way of life of their superiors if, by chance, they observe anything reprehensible; otherwise, their just criticism of what is wrong may plunge them by pride into lower depths themselves. They must be warned that in observing faults in their superiors, they do not become too disrespectful to them. On the contrary, should the faults be of very serious nature, their private judgment should be such that constrained by the fear of God they still do not refuse to bear the yoke of reverence in subjection to them. PASTORAL CARE 3.4.[7]

10:18 *The Glory of the Lord*

THE FOUNDATION OF THE CHURCH. JEROME: I linger long in the land of the midday sun, for it was there and then that the spouse found her bridegroom at rest[8] and Joseph drank wine with his brothers once more.[9] I will return to Jerusalem and, passing through Tekoa the home of Amos,[10] I will look on the glistening cross of Mount Olive from which the Savior made his ascension to the Father.[11] Here year by year a red heifer was burned as an offering to the Lord, and its ashes were used to purify the children of

---

[1]*PDCW* 187-88. [2]*EKOG* 89*. [3]Ezek 1:28. [4]*PG* 13:801. [5]*CCL* 75:113. [6]*TTH* 18:17. [7]*ACW* 11:99. [8]Song 1:7. [9]Gen 43:16. [10]Amos 1:1. [11]Lk 24:50-51; Acts 1:9-12.

Israel.[12] Here also according to Ezekiel the cherubim after leaving the temple founded the church of the Lord. LETTER 108.12.[13]

10:21 *The Four Creatures*

MOVEMENT DETERMINED BY GOD ALONE.
PSEUDO-MACARIUS: Here God truly mounts and guides the soul. He always obtains the victory skillfully directing and leading with expertise the chariot of the soul to a heavenly mind forever.

God does not wage war against wickedness, but since he possesses all power and authority of himself, he brings about the victory by himself. Therefore the cherubim go not where they wish but where the rider in control directs them. Wherever God inclines them, there they go, and he supports them. FIFTY SPIRITUAL HOMILIES 1.9.[14]

---

[12]Num 19:1-10. [13]NPNF 2 6:200*. [14]PMFSH 42*.

11:1-21 UNGODLY RULERS OF THE NATION TO BE PUNISHED

[17]*Therefore say, "Thus says the Lord GOD: I will gather you from the peoples, and assemble you out of the countries where you have been scattered, and I will give you the land of Israel." [18]And when they come there, they will remove from it all its detestable things and all its abominations. [19]And I will give them one[n] heart, and put a new spirit within them; I will take the stony heart out of their flesh and give them a heart of flesh, [20]that they may walk in my statutes and keep my ordinances and obey them; and they shall be my people, and I will be their God. [21]But as for those[o] whose heart goes after their detestable things and their abominations, I will requite their deeds upon their own heads, says the Lord GOD."*

n Another reading is *a new*   o Cn: Heb *To the heart of their detestable things and their abominations their heart goes*

OVERVIEW: God will give his people a new spirit, a heart of flesh in their innermost being (JEROME), and any tendency to goodness on our part will be of his doing (THEODORET, CASSIAN). It will be a heart of true understanding, for a heart of stone obstructs the ways of God, and God's grace goes before us, in the way we use our free will, for the heart of flesh is not about carnal desire (AUGUSTINE). When we commit ourselves to God, he helps us on our way (ORIGEN), and the Spirit softens the hardness of our hearts (SAHDONA). The heart of flesh is su-

premely manifested in Christ (BARNABAS).

11:18-20 *A New Spirit*

THE NEW SPIRIT IN ISRAEL'S INNERMOST BEING. JEROME: I will gather you from the peoples, and I will return the land of Israel to you. When you have entered and taken away all the idols that caused offences to God, I will give you one heart, to fear and serve the Lord, so that you stop serving any kind of idols, even if they are different from the ones you had; and I will put a new spirit in your innermost being. COMMENTARY ON EZEKIEL 3.11.17-21.[1]

THE LORD'S DOING. JOHN CASSIAN: Quite obviously all this teaches us that the first good stirring of the will in us comes under the Lord's inspiration. He brings us along the road to salvation, either himself or by way of the exhortation of some person or through necessity. And our virtues are perfected also as a gift from him. Our task is, whether laxly or zealously, to play a role that corresponds to his grace, and our reward or our punishment will depend on whether we strove or neglected to be at one, attentive and obedient, with the kindly dispensation of his providence toward us. CONFERENCE 3.19.[2]

FREE WILL COOPERATES WITH THE GRACE OF GOD. JOHN CASSIAN: What does this all mean except that in each of these cases both the grace of God and our freedom of will are affirmed, since even by his own activity a person can occasionally be brought to a desire for virtue, but he always needs to be helped by the Lord. CONFERENCE 13.9.4.[3]

THE HEART OF FLESH IS MANIFEST IN CHRIST. EPISTLE OF BARNABAS: [God] says in another prophet, "I will take the stony heart out of their flesh and give them a heart of flesh" (that is, from those whom the spirit of the law foresaw) . . . because Christ himself was going to be manifested in the flesh and dwell among us. EPISTLE OF BARNABAS 6.14.[4]

A HEART OF TRUE UNDERSTANDING. AUGUSTINE: For by the heart of flesh and the fleshy tables is not meant a carnal understanding: but as flesh feels, whereas a stone cannot, the insensibility of stone signifies an unintelligent heart, and the sensibility of flesh signifies an intelligent heart. AGAINST FAUSTUS, A MANICHAEAN 15.4.[5]

A STONY HEART OBSTRUCTS GOD. AUGUSTINE: If God is not able to remove from the human heart even its obstinacy and hardness, he would not say, through the prophet, "I will take from them their heart of stone and will give them a heart of flesh." . . . Now can we possibly, without extreme absurdity, maintain that there previously existed in any person the good merit of a good will, to entitle him to the removal of his stony heart, when all the while this very heart of stone signifies nothing else than a will of the hardest kind and such as is absolutely inflexible against God? ON GRACE AND FREE WILL 29.[6]

GOD'S PREVENIENT GRACE WORKS WITHOUT FREE WILL. AUGUSTINE: Those and other divine testimonies, which it would take too long to enumerate, show that God by his grace takes away the stony heart from unbelievers and forestalls merit in people of good will in such a way that their will is prepared by prevenient grace, but not that grace is given through prevenient merit of the will. This is shown both by thanksgiving and by prayer: prayer for unbelievers; thanksgiving for believers. Prayer is to be made to him that he may do what we ask; thanksgiving is to be offered when he has done it. LETTER 217.[7]

NOT CARNAL IN DESIRE. AUGUSTINE: Flesh is not mentioned in this passage in order to signify carnal desire but rather in the way in which the prophet says that a heart of stone is taken away from the people and a heart of flesh is given them. ON GENESIS AGAINST THE MANICHAEANS 2.12.17.[8]

GRACE CAN BE POWERFUL. AUGUSTINE: This grace, which from divine generosity is bestowed secretly in human hearts, is rejected by no one, no matter how hard-hearted he may be. For it is given so that hardness of the heart may first be taken away. Therefore, when the Father is heard within and teaches, so that one may come to the Son, he takes away the heart of stone and bestows

---

[1]CCL 75:124. [2]JCC 97*. [3]ACW 57:475. [4]FC 1:200**. [5]NPNF 1 4:214. [6]NPNF 1 5:455. [7]FC 32:94*. [8]FC 84:113*.

a heart of flesh, as he promised by the word of the prophet. For it is thus that he makes them children of the promise and vessels of mercy that he has prepared for glory.[9] PREDESTINATION OF THE SAINTS 8.13.[10]

THE SPIRIT SOFTENS THE HARDNESS OF OUR HEARTS. SAHDONA: Truly great and mighty is the power of God's word. For the word of God has changed the "offspring of vipers"[11] into children of God. So let us constantly sow it within the hard soil of our heart,[12] waiting for [the word] to soften [our heart] so that the wheat ear of life may sprout up in it. For the word of God is at the same time the seed and the water; and even though we have a "heart like stone," it will be softened and split up by the water of the Spirit, so that it can bring forth holy fruit that is pleasing to God.

Therefore let no one neglect meditation on the divine words or the labor of reading the appointed measure. As our honored teacher said, from such meditation the soul acquires great benefit and finds salvation. BOOK OF PERFECTION 53-54.[13]

GOD REMOVES THE HEART OF STONE. ORIGEN: This might lead one to suppose that it was God who gave the power to walk in his commandments and to keep his judgments, if it was he who removed the stony heart, which hindered them from keeping the commandments, and who implanted in them the better and more sensitive one, which is here called a heart of flesh. ON FIRST PRINCIPLES 3.1.7.[14]

TO COMMIT OURSELVES TO GOD. ORIGEN: Now this is what is said by those who wish to prove by the authority of Scripture that nothing lies within our own power. We shall reply to them that these words must not be understood in that sense but as follows. It is as if an uneducated and uninstructed person becoming conscious of the disgrace of his condition, whether by being stirred at the exhortation of another or by a desire to rival those who are wise, should entrust himself to one by whom he is confident that he can be carefully trained and competently instructed. If then he, who had formerly hardened himself in ignorance, entrusts himself, as we have said, with full purpose of mind to a master and promises to obey him in everything, the master, on seeing clearly his purpose and determination, will on his part undertake to take away from him his lack of education and to implant in him education, not promising, however, to do this if the disciple withholds his assent and cooperation but only if he offers and pledges himself to entire obedience. ON FIRST PRINCIPLES 3.1.15.[15]

A DISPOSITION TO DO GOOD. THEODORET OF CYR: He calls it a new heart, as a force in the soul for honorable things. When they are disposed to contrary things, they refer to a change toward better things as a new spirit. Just as he spoke of another heart and did not mean a change in nature, but a disposition towards better things, so this is shared through a new spirit. COMMENTARY ON EZEKIEL 3.11.[16]

---

[9]Rom 9:23. [10]FC 86:234. [11]Mt 3:7. [12]Mt 13:5. [13]CS 101:224*. [14]OFP 167*. [15]OFP 187. [16]PG 81:901

11:22-25 THE GLORY OF THE LORD DEPARTS FROM THE EAST OF JERUSALEM

²²Then the cherubim lifted up their wings, with the wheels beside them; and the glory of the God of Israel was over them. ²³And the glory of the LORD went up from the midst of the city, and stood upon the mountain which is on the east side of the city. ²⁴And the Spirit lifted me up and brought me in the vision by the Spirit of God into Chaldea, to the exiles. Then the vision that I had seen went up from me. ²⁵And I told the exiles all the things that the LORD had showed me.

OVERVIEW: The cherubim lifted up their wings as a sign of the worship offered by all peoples (EUSEBIUS), for the Mount of Olives is the place where Christ ascended into heaven, a place of glory that is marked with the sign of the cross. The people are to be restored to their land in order to be God's people (JEROME).

11:22 The Cherubim Lifted Their Wings

AS THE WORSHIP OF ALL PEOPLES TODAY. EUSEBIUS OF CAESAREA: It is possible for us to see this literally fulfilled in another way even today, since believers in Christ all congregate from all parts of the world, not as of old time because of the glory of Jerusalem or that they may worship in the ancient temple at Jerusalem; but they rest there that they may learn both about the city being taken and devastated as the prophets foretold and that they may worship at the Mount of Olives opposite to the city, whither the glory of the Lord migrated when it left the former city. PROOF OF THE GOSPEL 6.18.[1]

THE MOUNTAIN OF THE ASCENSION OF CHRIST. JEROME: There is no doubt that the mount is the Mount of Olives, from which the Savior ascended to the Father, and the glory of the Lord, which had departed from the city of Jerusalem, stood on the Mount of Olives as a sign of resurrection and light. COMMENTARY ON EZEKIEL 3.11.22-23.[2]

THE SIGN OF THE CROSS. JEROME: It is wonderful that down to the present day the glory of the Lord, which had deserted the temple, stands on the Mount of Olives. Moving in the sign of a cross, it gazes at what was once the Jewish temple, destroyed in dust and ashes. COMMENTARY ON EZEKIEL 3.11.22-23.[3]

11:25 The Prophet Tells All

WALKING IN THE WAYS OF GOD. JEROME: Everything took place so that the captives should receive consolation, because they had to return to the land of Israel, in order to walk in the precepts of the Lord, and for them to be people for him and he to be a God for them. COMMENTARY ON EZEKIEL 3.11.24-25.[4]

---

[1]POG 2:29. [2]CCL 75:125. [3]CCL 75:125. [4]CCL 75:126.

[12:1-16 BAGGAGE FOR EXILE]

[12:17-20 EATING AND DRINKING WITH FEAR]

[12:21-28 THE WORD OF THE LORD PERFORMED]

13:1-16 PROPHECY AGAINST THE FALSE PROPHETS

The word of the LORD came to me: [2]*"Son of man, prophesy against the prophets of Israel, prophesy*[w] *and say to those who prophesy out of their own minds: 'Hear the word of the LORD!'* [3]*Thus says the Lord GOD, Woe to the foolish prophets who follow their own spirit, and have seen nothing!* [4]*Your prophets have been like foxes among ruins, O Israel.* [5]*You have not gone up into the breaches, or built up a wall for the house of Israel, that it might stand in battle in the day of the LORD.* [6]*They have spoken falsehood and divined a lie; they say, 'Says the LORD,' when the LORD has not sent them, and yet they expect him to fulfil their word.* [7]*Have you not seen a delusive vision, and uttered a lying divination, whenever you have said, 'Says the LORD,' although I have not spoken?"*

[8]*Therefore thus says the Lord GOD: "Because you have uttered delusions and seen lies, therefore behold, I am against you, says the Lord GOD.* [9]*My hand will be against the prophets who see delusive visions and who give lying divinations; they shall not be in the council of my people, nor be enrolled in the register of the house of Israel, nor shall they enter the land of Israel; and you shall know that I am the Lord GOD.* [10]*Because, yea, because they have misled my people, saying, 'Peace,' when there is no peace; and because, when the people build a wall, these prophets daub it with whitewash;* [11]*say to those who daub it with whitewash that it shall fall! There will be a deluge of rain,*[x] *great hailstones will fall, and a stormy wind break out;* [12]*and when the wall falls, will it not be said to you, 'Where is the daubing with which you daubed it?'* [13]*Therefore thus says the Lord GOD: I will make a stormy wind break out in my wrath; and there shall be a deluge of rain in my anger, and great hailstones in wrath to destroy it.* [14]*And I will break down the wall that you have*

daubed with whitewash, and bring it down to the ground, so that its foundation will be laid bare; when it falls, you shall perish in the midst of it; and you shall know that I am the LORD. ¹⁵*Thus will I spend my wrath upon the wall, and upon those who have daubed it with whitewash; and I will say to you, The wall is no more, nor those who daubed it,* ¹⁶*the prophets of Israel who prophesied concerning Jerusalem and saw visions of peace for her, when there was no peace, says the Lord GOD."*

w Gk: Heb *who prophesy*   x Heb *rain and you*

OVERVIEW: The prophetic ministry is close to the work of the preacher, who knows Scripture as containing teaching about sin, which can accuse anyone (ORIGEN). True and false prophets are alive in the church, and we must not be a law unto ourselves, since good prophets are wise, false prophets are stupid (JEROME) and greedy (JOHN CASSIAN). Ignorance is deep in the false prophet's life (BASIL), for the preacher must have the courage to speak out against worldly ways (GREGORY THE GREAT), though people can learn from their own mistakes (CLEMENT OF ALEXANDRIA). Flee the false peace of sinners (AMBROSE) and the whitewashed wall of hypocrisy (AUGUSTINE).

13:1-2 Prophesy

SIN IS TAUGHT ABOUT IN SCRIPTURES. ORIGEN: There is no kind of sin about which Scripture is silent and about which it does not teach its readers. HOMILIES ON EZEKIEL 2.1.[1]

FALSE PROPHETS TEACH AND LIVE FALSELY. ORIGEN: False prophets are teachers of the church whose words or life do not properly accord with the doctrine that they preach. HOMILIES ON EZEKIEL 2.1.[2]

SCRIPTURE CAN ACCUSE EVERYONE. ORIGEN: If the Word of God accuses me, I will try to be converted. HOMILIES ON EZEKIEL 2.2.[3]

THE WORD MUST BE ABOUT TRUTH. ORIGEN: The word of the present can agree with those who teach in the church, as long as they do not teach other than what the truth demands. HOMILIES ON EZEKIEL 2.2.[4]

PREACHING MUST BE BASED ON UNDERSTANDING. ORIGEN: If anyone reading the gospel fits its proper sense to the gospel without understanding that the Lord speaks, he is a false prophet speaking according to his own heart in the gospel. HOMILIES ON EZEKIEL 2.2.[5]

CHRIST IS PRESENT IN MOSES AND THE PROPHETS. ORIGEN: If I find in Moses and the prophets the thought of Christ, I speak not according to my own heart but from the Holy Spirit. HOMILIES ON EZEKIEL 2.2.[6]

TRUE AND FALSE PROPHETS IN THE CHURCH TODAY. JEROME: Whatever was said at that time to the people of Israel now applies to the church. The holy prophets are apostles and apostolic people, but the lying and raging prophets are all heretics, whose leaders invent things from their own heart; the people are led astray by them and acquiesce in the falsehoods of others. COMMENTARY ON EZEKIEL 4.13.1-3.[7]

WE MUST NOT BE A LAW TO OURSELVES. JEROME: The Ishmaelites represent those who are a law unto themselves, who yield to their own capricious hearts and evil desires. Ezekiel expresses the same thought: "Son of man, proph-

---

[1]SC 352:100. [2]SC 352:100. [3]SC 352:102. [4]SC 352:102. [5]SC 352:104. [6]SC 352:104. [7]CCL 75:137.

esy against the prophets that prophesy their own thought and do whatever their spirit impels." We, however, must not follow our own inclinations and be labeled Ishmaelites, "obedient to themselves," but rather be called Ishmael, "obedient to God." HOMILIES ON THE PSALMS 15 (Ps 82).[8]

13:3 Woe to the Foolish Prophets

TRUE AND FALSE PROPHETS KNOWN. ORIGEN: In the same way that a saint prays with the Spirit and prays with understanding and sings with the spirit and sings with understanding, so the false prophet prophesies according to his own heart and follows not the Spirit of God but his own spirit. HOMILIES ON EZEKIEL 2.3.[9]

GOD'S PROPHETS ARE WISE. JEROME: Since the name of prophets, according to the pattern of the Scriptures, is used of good and bad alike, they differ from each other in that good prophets are said to be wise and evil prophets are said to be stupid and senseless. The one refers to the people of the church, whereas the other refers to all heretics who depart from the Spirit of God and follow their own spirit, because in no way do they prophesy from divine impulse but from their own hearts. COMMENTARY ON EZEKIEL 4.13.3.[10]

13:4 Prophets like Foxes

A WICKED ANIMAL. ORIGEN: The fox is an animal good for nothing, sly, wild, ferocious. HOMILIES ON EZEKIEL 2.4.[11]

FALSE PROPHETS TEACH FALSEHOOD. JEROME: They observe empty things and divine falsehood and say that they have been sent by God, although have not; and they persist in their errors, keen on establishing only what they are saying. They argue because everything they have preached is empty. COMMENTARY ON EZEKIEL 4.13.4-7.[12]

THE FALSE PROPHET DOES NOT KNOW WHAT HE OUGHT TO TEACH. BASIL THE GREAT: At another time, because of his deceit toward his brother, he makes himself like the villainous fox. Truly, there is in him excessive folly and a bestial lack of reason, because, made according to the image of the Creator, he neither perceives his own constitution from the beginning nor wishes to understand such great dispensations that were made for his sake, so that he could learn his own dignity from them; he does not realize that, throwing aside the image of the heavenly, he has taken up the image of the earthly. HOMILIES ON THE PSALMS 19.8 (Ps 48).[13]

13:5-6 False Prophecy Not Fulfilled

THEY NEVER SEE THE TRUTH. ORIGEN: All that they want is false, and they can never see the truth. Take an example. To read the Scripture and to hear something other than what is written is to have an untruthful picture of Scripture; but to hear Scripture and interpret it in accordance with the truth, that is to see the truth. HOMILIES ON EZEKIEL 2.5.[14]

THE PROPHETS MUST OPPOSE WORLDLY POWERS. GREGORY THE GREAT: He complains of them, saying, "You have not gone up to face the enemy, nor have you set up a wall for the house of Israel, to stand in battle in the day of the Lord." Now, to rise up against the enemy is to oppose worldly powers with candid speech in defense of the flock. To stand in battle in the day of the Lord is to resist from love of justice evil people who contend against us. For if a shepherd was afraid to say what is right, what else is that but to have turned his back by not speaking? But when one places himself in front of the flock to defend them, he obviously is opposing a wall for the house of Israel against the enemy. PASTORAL CARE 2.4.[15]

AN ESSENTIAL WORK OF THE PROPHET. GREGORY THE GREAT: To go up in opposition

---

[8]FC 48:112-13*. [9]SC 352:110. [10]CCL 75:137. [11]SC 352:112. [12]CCL 75:139. [13]FC 46:325*. [14]SC 352:116. [15]ACW 11:52.

means openly to rebuke any powers that behave wickedly; and we hold fast in battle for the house of Israel on the day of the Lord and build a wall of resistance if we defend innocent believers against the unrighteousness of the wicked with the power of righteousness. Since a hireling does not do these things, he flees when he sees a wolf coming. FORTY GOSPEL HOMILIES 15.[16]

PROPHECY AND DIVINE AUTHORITY. JEROME: Whom does he mean by all those who have come before me? Those who say, "Thus says the Lord!" But the Lord has not sent them; they who have come on their own authority and have not been sent are the thieves and robbers. HOMILY 87 (ON JOHN 1:1-14).[17]

13:7-8 Delusive Visions

PREACHERS NEED PRAYERS. ORIGEN: Pray for us that our words may not be false. HOMILIES ON EZEKIEL 2.5.[18]

THE PRESENCE OF THE LORD IN TRUE TEACHING. ORIGEN: This is what we are looking for, that the Lord will be present as a witness to my words, that he may himself confirm what is said by witness of his holy Scriptures. HOMILIES ON EZEKIEL 2.5.[19]

HERETICS TEACH EMPTY THINGS. JEROME: The ministry of prophets is about speaking against heretics whose task is empty, whose visions are false and who persist in establishing their own words, because the Lord comes against them, rising up and lifting his hand over them to shake them, and he does not ensure that they are to be spared. COMMENTARY ON EZEKIEL 4.13.8-9.[20]

13:9 The Lord Is Against False Prophets

PROPHETS CORRUPTED. JOHN CASSIAN: Since [Judah] was corrupted by the plague of avarice and was cast down from a heavenly enrollment to earthly things, it is appropriately said of him . . .

"They shall not be in the council of my people, nor enrolled in the book of the house of Israel, and they shall not enter into the land of Israel." CONFERENCE 17.25.19.[21]

13:10 The People Misled

PEACE AND LOVE. AMBROSE: There is a peace that does not have a stumbling block and a peace that does. The one that does not have a stumbling block is from love; the one which does, from pretense. So also the prophet says, "Peace, peace; and where is peace?" Let us therefore run away from the peace of sinners, for they conspire against the guiltless person, they come together to oppress him who is just, they destroy the widow or overcome her modesty.[22] THE PRAYER OF JOB AND DAVID 3.3.6.[23]

THE PEOPLE MUST SING OF GOD'S HONOR. AUGUSTINE: They who choose to declare their own honor have refused to dwell in [God's] house; and therefore they do not sing a new song with all the earth.[24] For they do not share it with the whole world; and hence they are not building in the house but have erected a whitened wall. How sternly does God threaten the whitened wall? . . . What is the whitened wall but hypocrisy, that is, pretense? Outside it is bright; inside it is dirt. EXPLANATIONS OF THE PSALMS 96.3.[25]

WHEN PEOPLE ARE IGNORANT. JEROME: How is the cause helped by the people who dance attendance on these people with itching ears who know neither how to hear nor how to speak? They confound old mire with new cement and, as Ezekiel says, daub a wall with untempered mortar; so that, when the truth comes in a shower, they are brought to nothing. LETTER 133.4.[26]

13:13 The Wrath of the Lord

---

[16]CS 123:108-9. [17]FC 57:216-17. [18]SC 352:118. [19]SC 352:118. [20]CCL 75:140. [21]ACW 57:610. [22]Wis 2:12. [23]FC 65:372-73. [24]See Ps 96:1 (95:1 LXX, Vulg.). [25]NPNF 1 8:471*. [26]NPNF 2 6:275*.

Recognizing the Folly of Disobedience.
Clement of Alexandria: The words that follow describe and condemn some sin that has been
committed. The judgment contained in these
words is just, for it is as if he were giving notice in
the words of the prophet that, if you had not
sinned, he would not have made these threats. . . .

The inspired Word exists because of both obedience and disobedience: that we may be saved by
obeying it and educated because we have dis-
obeyed. Christ the Educator 1.2.5.[27]

---

[27]FC 23:7.

13:17-23 PROPHECY AGAINST
FALSE PROPHETESSES

[17]*And you, son of man, set your face against the daughters of your people, who prophesy out of
their own minds; prophesy against them* [18]*and say, Thus says the Lord God: Woe to the women
who sew magic bands upon all wrists, and make veils for the heads of persons of every stature, in
the hunt for souls! Will you hunt down souls belonging to my people, and keep other souls alive for
your profit?* [19]*You have profaned me among my people for handfuls of barley and for pieces of bread,
putting to death persons who should not die and keeping alive persons who should not live, by your
lies to my people, who listen to lies.*

[20]*Wherefore thus says the Lord God: Behold, I am against your magic bands with which you
hunt the souls,*[y] *and I will tear them from your arms; and I will let the souls that you hunt go free*[z]
like birds. [21]*Your veils also I will tear off, and deliver my people out of your hand, and they shall be
no more in your hand as prey; and you shall know that I am the Lord.* [22]*Because you have disheartened the righteous falsely, although I have not disheartened him, and you have encouraged the
wicked, that he should not turn from his wicked way to save his life;* [23]*therefore you shall no more
see delusive visions nor practice divination; I will deliver my people out of your hand. Then you
will know that I am the Lord.*"

y Gk Syr: Heb *souls for birds*   z Cn: Heb *the souls*

Overview: The face of the prophet must be
properly directed, and his words must avoid su-
perficiality or distortion of the truth (Origen).
All comfortable talk is to be avoided (Jerome),
for forgiveness can be costly (Gregory the
Great). Prophets can easily devalue true teaching (Chrysostom). Christ, however, the true

prophet, is yet to come (Ambrose).

13:17 Set Your Face Against Them

The Face of the Soul Needs Direction.
Origen: This face, that is to say the ruling faculty in our soul, if it is not fixed toward what it

should understand in the manner that it sees, it announces to its hearers that what it looks at has not in fact been seen. Homilies on Ezekiel 3.1.[1]

Prophets Need Determination. Origen: It should have a face that wants to be fixed toward what it is striving to understand, and for this reason the order is always first given to those who want to prophecy to make their face firm. Homilies on Ezekiel 3.1.[2]

Prophets Do Not Always Say Welcome Things. Origen: Soft are the souls and intentions of those leaders who always compose resonant and harmonious words. Homilies on Ezekiel 3.3.[3]

13:18 Woe to Their Dress

Prophecy Is About Daily Living. Origen: The Word of God must proclaim what is for the salvation of the hearer, what exhorts him to continence, to the practice of sensible actions, to all the things to which the person who is assiduous in works and not pleasures must apply himself in order to be able to obtain what God has promised. Homilies on Ezekiel 3.3.[4]

False Words as Fancy Dress. Origen: When the work of the speaker is deployed in licentious talk, a veil is placed on the head of everyone regardless of age, not just the children and the young but also the elderly. Homilies on Ezekiel 3.3.[5]

False Teaching Distorts. Jerome: Woe to those heresies and teachings! They promise respite and deceive every age and gender, in order to capture the souls of unhappy people, and they defame me to my own people until I am believed to desire nothing but my own pleasure. Commentary on Ezekiel 4.3.17-23.[6]

A New Prophet to Come. Ambrose: The prophet was lamenting the wretched frailty of our condition, which has no rest in this life and loses everything by death's sudden onset. For the Holy Spirit revealed to him that man would not arise for so long a time, until he should come who would refuse to stitch the old to the new or join new material[7] to the old but would make all things new, even as he said, "Behold, I make all things new!"[8] The Prayer of Job and David 1.7.25.[9]

Prophecy Breaks Physical Comforts. Origen: Allow me, O Christ, to break all pillows made for the luxury of souls. Homilies on Ezekiel 3.4.[10]

Comforts Are to Be Resisted. Gregory the Great: To put cushions under every elbow is to cherish with smooth flattery souls that are falling away from rectitude and are reclining in the pleasures of this world. It is as if a person reclined with a cushion under the elbow or a pillow under his head, is not reproved severely when he sins but is treated with enervating favoritism, in order that he may recline at ease in his error, the while no asperity of reproof assails him. Pastoral Care 2.8.[11]

13:19 Corrupting the People

Prophets Devalue True Teaching. Chrysostom: There were probably in the time of our ancestors also some who . . . "did the works of the false prophets"; . . . a thing, by the way, done (I think) by some even today. When, for example, we say that he who calls his brother a fool will go into hell fire, others will say, what? Impossible, they say. And again, when we say that the "covetous person is an idolater," in this too again they make excuses and say the expression is hyperbolical. And in this way they underrate and explain away all the commandments. Homilies on Ephesians 18.[12]

---

[1]SC 352:126. [2]SC 352:126. [3]SC 352:132. [4]SC 352:130. [5]SC 352:130. [6]CCL 75:147. [7]Mt 9:16. [8]Rev 21:5. [9]FC 65:345. [10]SC 352:136. [11]ACW 11:75-76*. [12]NPNF 1 13:132*. A reference to corporate penance, which involved excommunication for a time, under the direction of the bishop.

FORGIVENESS CAN BE COSTLY. GREGORY THE GREAT: Anyone who condemns a righteous person is putting to death one who is not dying; and one who tries to absolve a guilty person from his punishment is striving to bring back to life one who is not living. All cases must be carefully considered, and only then the power of binding and loosing used. The pastor must look at the sin and the repentance following after the sin, so that his sentence absolves those to whom almighty God grants the grace of sorrow. There is true absolution on the part of the one presiding only when it is in accord with the decision of the internal judge. FORTY GOSPEL HOMILIES 26.[13]

13:21 *Tearing Off Veils*

PLEASURE IS DANGEROUS. ORIGEN: We flee what is bitter, even though it is good for us, and we do not want to labor, because we are softened by pleasures, because we do not know that it is impossible to be a friend of pleasure and at the same time a friend of God. HOMILIES ON EZEKIEL 3.5.[14]

13:22 *The Wicked Have Been Encouraged*

AVOID EAR-TICKLING PREACHERS. ORIGEN: Let us pray that God will deliver us even from the hand of such leaders who, wherever they are, speak to please their hearers and cut and divide the church, because many are more fond of pleasures than they are of God. HOMILIES ON EZEKIEL 3.6.[15]

---

[13]CS 123:205*. [14]SC 352:136. [15]SC 352:138.

14:1-11 HYPOCRISY REBUKED AND REPENTANCE URGED

[1]*Then came certain of the elders of Israel to me, and sat before me.* [2]*And the word of the LORD came to me:* [3]*"Son of man, these men have taken their idols into their hearts, and set the stumbling block of their iniquity before their faces; should I let myself be inquired of at all by them?* [4]*Therefore speak to them, and say to them, Thus says the Lord GOD: Any man of the house of Israel who takes his idols into his heart and sets the stumbling block of his iniquity before his face, and yet comes to the prophet, I the LORD will answer him myself* [a] *because of the multitude of his idols,* [5]*that I may lay hold of the hearts of the house of Israel, who are all estranged from me through their idols.*

[6]*"Therefore say to the house of Israel, Thus says the Lord GOD: Repent and turn away from your idols; and turn away your faces from all your abominations.* [7]*For any one of the house of Israel, or of the strangers that sojourn in Israel, who separates himself from me, taking his idols into his heart and putting the stumbling block of his iniquity before his face, and yet comes to a prophet to inquire for himself of me, I the LORD will answer him myself;* [8]*and I will set my face against that man, I will make him a sign and a byword and cut him off from the midst of my peo-*

ple; and you shall know that I am the LORD. ⁹And if the prophet be deceived and speak a word, I, the LORD, have deceived that prophet, and I will stretch out my hand against him, and will destroy him from the midst of my people Israel. ¹⁰And they shall bear their punishment—the punishment of the prophet and the punishment of the inquirer shall be alike— ¹¹that the house of Israel may go no more astray from me, nor defile themselves any more with all their transgressions, but that they may be my people and I may be their God, says the Lord GOD."

a Cn Compare Tg: Heb uncertain

OVERVIEW: Hypocrisy is inflicted by ourselves alone, when we cannot tell the difference between the exterior and the interior person (ORIGEN); for hypocrisy is about impurity (JEROME). Therefore, we must be dissatisfied with ourselves, but not with God. God can deceive a prophet who is determined to teach what he wants, and he also allows some to go astray, because they can repent (AUGUSTINE). At root, however, these ills of the people are self-inflicted (JEROME), but God is still firm in his resolve to be their God (THEODORET).

14:3 On Hypocrisy

HYPOCRISY IS SELF-INFLICTED. ORIGEN: No one among us thinks that tortures are inflicted by anyone other than ourselves. HOMILIES ON EZEKIEL 3.7.[1]

INTERIOR AND EXTERIOR PERSON. ORIGEN: When the interior person perseveres according to the image of the Creator, then a person is born, and twice is the person made a person according to the exterior and the interior kind. HOMILIES ON EZEKIEL 3.8.[2]

HYPOCRISY IS IMPURITY. JEROME: This is the meaning: "Son of man, those people who sit before you have put impurities in their hearts, whether in their thoughts . . . or their idols—it is a scandal, and it means ruin and torment—and their iniquities are placed before their very faces." COMMENTARY ON EZEKIEL 4.14.1-11.[3]

14:6-10 Repentance Urged

WE MUST BE DISSATISFIED WITH OUR-SELVES. AUGUSTINE: Those dissatisfied with any facet of your creation are unsound in mind, as I was when many things that you made displeased me. Because my soul did not dare to be dissatisfied with my God, it would not identify as yours whatever dissatisfied it. In this way it had strayed into a belief in two substances, and it got no rest but recounted the opinions of others. Recoiling from that error, it had made for itself a god inhabiting the boundless area of all space, and it had considered that god to be you, and had "set it in its heart" and had become again the shrine of its idol, deserving of your loathing. But after you stroked my ignorant head and closed my eyes so that they should not see vanity, I retired from myself a little, and my madness was lulled to sleep. I awoke in you and saw you infinite in a different way, and that vision was not with the eyes of the flesh. CONFESSIONS 7.4.20.[4]

THE PROPHET WHO WAS DECEIVED BY GOD. AUGUSTINE: It is quite clear that God works in people's hearts to incline their wills to whatsoever way he wills: either to good in accordance with his mercy or to evil in accordance with their evil merits, and this, indeed, by his own judgments, sometimes manifest, sometimes hidden, but always just. You must keep this conviction firm and unshaken in your heart that in God there is no injustice. Accordingly, when you read the truth of the Scriptures and find that people are led astray by God or that their hearts are

[1]SC 352:140. [2]SC 352:144. [3]CCL 75:150. [4]MFC 17:29.

dulled and hardened by him, have no doubt that it was their previous evil merits that made them suffer their just penalties. ON GRACE AND FREE WILL 21.43.[5]

SO THAT THEY CAN REPENT. AUGUSTINE: You must believe that there were evil merits in that person whom God permits to go astray and to become hardened. But for the person on whom he has mercy, you must acknowledge with an unswerving faith that this is a case of the grace of God who is not rendering evil for evil but good for evil. ON GRACE AND FREE WILL 23.45.[6]

FALSE PROPHECY A SIN. AUGUSTINE: Which of the two, patience or power, do you find in the words of Scripture? Whichever you choose, even if you admit both, you must surely see that the false speech of this prophet is both sin and punishment for sin. Will you also say that the words, "I, the Lord, have deceived that prophet," should be interpreted as though God deserted him that he might be deceived in return for past misdeeds and thus err? Say what you will, he was punished for sin in such a way that he sinned prophesying something false. AGAINST JULIAN 5.3.13.[7]

14:11 The House of Israel Must Not Stray

SELF-INFLICTED EVILS. JEROME: Each one kindles the flames for himself and makes supplications, while he has no desire to correct his errors with penitence but remains in the areas that deserve to be burned in flames. COMMENTARY ON EZEKIEL 4.14.1-11.[8]

GOD'S DETERMINATION TO BE THEIR GOD. THEODORET OF CYR: I want to have them as my people and to be their God, attending to them with every care. COMMENTARY ON EZEKIEL 4.11.[9]

---

[5]FC 59:303*. [6]FC 59:307*. [7]FC 35:255. [8]CCL 75:152. [9]PG 81:924.

14:12-23 IF THERE WERE SOME RIGHTEOUS

[12]And the word of the LORD came to me: [13]"Son of man, when a land sins against me by acting faithlessly, and I stretch out my hand against it, and break its staff of bread and send famine upon it, and cut off from it man and beast, [14]even if these three men, Noah, Daniel, and Job, were in it, they would deliver but their own lives by their righteousness, says the Lord GOD. [15]If I cause wild beasts to pass through the land, and they ravage it, and it be made desolate, so that no man may pass through because of the beasts; [16]even if these three men were in it, as I live, says the Lord GOD, they would deliver neither sons nor daughters; they alone would be delivered, but the land would be desolate. [17]Or if I bring a sword upon that land, and say, Let a sword go through the land; and I cut off from it man and beast; [18]though these three men were in it, as I live, says the Lord GOD, they would deliver neither sons nor daughters, but they alone would be delivered. [19]Or if I send a pestilence into that land, and pour out my wrath upon it with blood, to cut off from it man and beast; [20]even if Noah, Daniel, and Job were in it, as I live, says the Lord GOD, they would

deliver neither son nor daughter; they would deliver but their own lives by their righteousness.

[21]*"For thus says the Lord GOD: How much more when I send upon Jerusalem my four sore acts of judgment, sword, famine, evil beasts, and pestilence, to cut off from it man and beast!* [22]*Yet, if there should be left in it any survivors to lead out sons and daughters, when they come forth to you, and you see their ways and their doings, you will be consoled for the evil that I have brought upon Jerusalem, for all that I have brought upon it.* [23]*They will console you, when you see their ways and their doings; and you shall know that I have not done without cause all that I have done in it, says the Lord GOD."*

OVERVIEW: There is no substitute for repentance, even in the face of the holiness of Noah, Daniel and Job (CLEMENT OF ROME, CYPRIAN, ORIGEN, JEROME, AUGUSTINE, CHRYSOSTOM). Repentance is like surgery, in that it inflicts pain and does us good (ORIGEN), and it is a prerequisite for turning to God (CHRYSOSTOM, SAYINGS). Righteous ancestors can do us no good (GREGORY OF NAZIANZUS, SALVIAN, JUSTIN), except as good examples (2 CLEMENT, BEDE, MARTIN), which means that we must pray for sinners (ORIGEN).

14:13 The Lord's Hand Stretched Out

IDOLATRY NOT PARDONED BY EVEN THE MOST RIGHTEOUS. CYPRIAN: It is not easy for God to pardon idolaters. . . . Ezekiel also denounces this wrath of God on those who sin against God. He says, "And the word of the Lord came to me saying, 'son of man, when a land shall sin against me so as to transgress grievously, I will stretch forth my hand on it, and I will break the staff of the bread thereof; and I will send famine on it and destroy man and beast out of it. And if these three men, Noah, Daniel and Job, shall be in it, they will not deliver sons or daughters; themselves alone shall be saved.'" EXHORTATION TO MARTYRDOM 5.4.[1]

THE PEOPLE AND THEIR LAND ALSO SINFUL. ORIGEN: Do you think it is true that the word applies not to the inhabitants of the earth but to the earth itself? HOMILIES ON EZEKIEL 4.1.[2]

THE CHURCH EXTENDS THROUGH ALL THE WORLD. ORIGEN: Thanks to the churches which reach to the limits of the world, the entire earth cries out with joy toward the God of Israel, and it is capable of good acts in its borders. HOMILIES ON EZEKIEL 4.1.[3]

THE EARTH CHASTISED. ORIGEN: Even though it is a punishment of the mother to be sent into exile, to be deprived of her children or at least to see her children bound for another province, in the same sort of way our mother the earth is chastised for her sins by God when people and beast are removed from her. HOMILIES ON EZEKIEL 4.3.[4]

SURGERY REQUIRES PAIN. ORIGEN: As the experts in medical art put it, in order to perform certain healings in the body, it is necessary to inflict not only a cut but also a burn. HOMILIES ON EZEKIEL 5.1.[5]

BAPTISM BY FIRE. ORIGEN: Those who are not healed by the baptism of the Holy Spirit, he baptizes with fire, because they are not able to be purified by the purification of the Holy Spirit. HOMILIES ON EZEKIEL 5.1.[6]

14:14 Noah, Daniel and Job Would Deliver Only Themselves

---

[1]FC 36:321-22**. [2]SC 352:156. [3]SC 352:164. [4]SC 352:168. [5]SC 352:192. [6]SC 352:192.

THE DESCENDANTS OF THE RIGHTEOUS CAN SIN. ORIGEN: Those who are of Abraham are not children of Abraham; although they are of his seed, they are not his children, because they are sinners. In the same way those whose actions resemble the wonder of Daniel are of Daniel, and those who imitate the patience of Job become Job. HOMILIES ON EZEKIEL 4.4.[7]

NOAH, DANIEL AND JOB CAN DO US NO GOOD NOW. JEROME: Noah was near to the world's flood, because the whole earth had polluted the ways of the Lord, but he was not able to spread it abroad; but his children, who happen to be of the same virtue and from the seed of the human race, he had protected. Daniel also calmed the captivity of the people of Israel without even crying. But Job, not because of his sins but because of his trial, freed neither house nor children. COMMENTARY ON EZEKIEL 4.14.12-23.[8]

WE HAVE TO TAKE RESPONSIBILITY FOR OUR OWN LIVES. CYPRIAN: Who was more righteous than Noah, who, when the earth was replete with sins, was alone found righteous on the earth? Who more glorious than Daniel? Who stronger in firmness of faith for enduring martyrdom, happier in God's favors, who when he fought so often conquered and when he conquered survived? Who was more diligent in good works than Job, stronger in temptations, more patient in suffering, more submissive in fear, more true in faith? And yet God said that, if they should ask, he would not grant. When the prophet Ezekiel interceded for the sins of the people, God said, "Whatever land shall sin against me, so as to transgress grievously, I will stretch forth my hand on it, and will break the staff of bread thereof, and will send famine upon it and will destroy people and beast out of it. And if these three men, Noah, Daniel and Job, shall be in it, they shall deliver neither sons nor daughters, but they only shall be delivered." Therefore, not all that is sought is in the prejudgment of the seeker but in the decision of the giver, and human opinion takes or assumes nothing to itself unless the divine pleasure also assents. THE LAPSED 19.[9]

THE CHARACTERISTICS OF NOAH, DANIEL AND JOB. DESERT FATHERS: The work of the monastic life is poverty and trouble and separation. . . . Noah must be taken as representing the personification of self-denial, and Job as representing labors and Daniel as representing separation; if a person possess these three rules of conduct the Lord dwells in him. SAYINGS OF THE DESERT FATHERS 193.[10]

DELIVERANCE FOR THEM. AUGUSTINE: Daniel is unique in being included among the three just men whom God says he will deliver, doubtless showing three special types of just people, when he says he will so deliver them as not to deliver their children with them, but they only shall be delivered: namely, Noah, Daniel and Job. LETTERS III.[11]

EXAMPLES OF RIGHTEOUSNESS FOR US. AUGUSTINE: Now I suppose it is not easy to find in God's Scripture so weighty a testimony of holiness given of any one as what is written of his three servants, Noah, Daniel and Job, whom the prophet Ezekiel describes as the only men able to be delivered from God's impending wrath. In these three men he no doubt prefigures three kinds of people to be delivered: in Noah, I suppose, are represented righteous leaders of nations, by reason of his government of the ark as a type of the church; in Daniel, people who are righteous in continence; in Job, those who are righteous in wedlock—to say nothing of any other view of the passage, which it is unnecessary now to consider. It is, at any rate, clear from this testimony of the prophet, and from other inspired statements, how eminent were these worthies in righteousness. ON THE MERITS AND FORGIVENESS OF SINS AND ON INFANT BAPTISM 2.12.10.[12]

---

[7]SC 352:172. [8]CCL 75:154. [9]FC 36:74. [10]PHF 2:196*. [11]FC 18:248*. [12]NPNF 1 5:49*.

THE EXAMPLES OF HOLY MEN CHALLENGE US. BEDE: Ezekiel the prophet mystically distinguishes them from one another when he foretells that there are only three men who will be delivered when the time of plagues comes, namely: Noah, Daniel and Job. For surely in Noah, who steered the ark over the waves, he shows those who are set over the church; in Daniel, who was zealous to live continently in the royal court, he shows the continent or virgins; in Job, who while married exhibited a wonderful example of patience to all, he shows the life of the virtuous married people. ON THE TABERNACLE 1.8.25.32.[13]

OUR REPENTANCE A PREREQUISITE. CHRYSOSTOM: No one may despair, though hitherto he may have been careless, of setting his hopes on nothing else, after God's mercy, but on his own virtue. For if these were no better for such a kindred, even though they were of the same house and lineage with Christ, until they gave proof of virtue, what favor can we possibly receive, when we plead with righteous kin and brethren, unless we are exceedingly dutiful and have lived in virtue? . . . But even if it is Ezekiel who does the pleading, he will be told, "though Noah comes, and Job and Daniel, they shall deliver neither sons nor daughters." . . . For it is true that the prayers of the saints have the greatest power, but only on condition of our repentance and amendment of life. HOMILIES ON THE GOSPEL OF MATTHEW 5.7.[14]

CHALLENGED BY HOLINESS. CHRYSOSTOM: Considering all these things, let us prepare for our departure from here. For even if the day of general consummation never comes to us, the end of each one is at the doors, whether they are old or young; and it is not possible for people, after they have gone from here, either to buy oil any more or to obtain pardon by prayers, though he who does the pleading be Abraham, or Noah, or Job or Daniel. While we have opportunity, let us store up for ourselves beforehand much confidence, let us gather oil in abundance, let us

remove all into heaven, that in the fitting time, and when we most need them, we may enjoy all; by the grace and love toward people. HOMILIES ON THE GOSPEL OF MATTHEW 20.6.[15]

HOLY DEEDS NECESSARY. PSEUDO-CLEMENT: Yes, if we do the will of Christ, we shall find rest, but if not, nothing will save us from eternal punishment, if we fail to heed his commands. Furthermore, the Scripture also says in Ezekiel, "Though Noah and Jacob and Daniel should rise, they shall not save their children in captivity." If even such upright men as these cannot save their children by their uprightness, what assurance have we that we shall enter God's kingdom if we fail to keep our baptism pure and undefiled? Or who will plead for us if we are not found to have holy and upright deeds? 2 CLEMENT 6.7-9.[16]

IF WE DO NOT REPENT. GREGORY OF NAZIANZUS: Who will cry aloud, spare your people, O Lord, and do not give your heritage to reproach, that the nations should rule over them: what Noah and Job and Daniel, who are reckoned together as men of prayer, will pray for us, that we may have a slight respite from warfare, and recover ourselves, and recognize one another for a while and no longer, instead of being a united Israel, be Judah and Israel, Rehoboam and Jeroboam, Jerusalem and Samaria, in turn delivered up because of our sins, and in turn lamented? IN DEFENSE OF HIS FLIGHT TO PONTUS, ORATION 2.89.[17]

SEPARATION FROM MATERIAL DISTRACTIONS. MARTIN OF BRAGA: Abbot Moses said, Separation from material things, that is, voluntary poverty, and endurance with patience and understanding are the possessions of a monk. . . . Noah is the personification of voluntary poverty, Job the personification of endurance with patience, Daniel the personification of under-

---

[13]TTH 18:34. [14]NPNF 1 10:34**. [15]NPNF 1 10:146*. [16]LCC 1:195*. [17]NPNF 2 7:222*.

standing. Accordingly, if the deeds of these three holy men are in any person, the Lord is with him, dwelling with him, receiving him and driving away from him every temptation and every tribulation that comes from the enemy. SAYINGS OF THE EGYPTIAN FATHERS 8.[18]

THE GOOD PERSON CANNOT SAVE THE WICKED. SALVIAN THE PRESBYTER: It is a crime, unbearably conceited and enormously wicked, that anyone should think himself so good that he supposes the wicked can be saved through him.

God, speaking of a certain land and a sinful people, said, "If these three men, Noah, Daniel and Job, shall be in it, they shall deliver neither sons or daughters; but they only shall be delivered." I think that nobody would be so presumptuous as to dare to compare himself with such men. Though a person tries to please God in this world, it is the greatest kind of unrighteousness to boast of his own righteousness. Hope is therefore removed in that false opinion by which we believe that a countless multitude of the damned can be saved by the intercession in this world of a few good people. THE GOVERNANCE OF GOD 3.11.[19]

14:20 Neither Son Nor Daughter

WE SHALL IMITATE THE VIRTUES OF FOREBEARS. CHRYSOSTOM: There will be no one then, the text is saying, able to rescue from there a victim of his own indifference, whether brother or father or mother. Why do I say brother or father or mother? Not even the just themselves, who have good grounds for confidence, will be of any assistance to us then if we have now been guilty of indifference.... See the magnitude of the threat and the kind of just people he brought forward as examples. These men, you see, at a critical time proved a source of salvation even to others: Noah saved his wife and sons when that terrible deluge overwhelmed the world; Job likewise proved a source of salvation even to others; and Daniel rescued many from death when that awful barbarian in his quest for things beyond

human nature wanted to do away with the Chaldeans, the magi and Gazarenes.... Rather, we should make this alone the object of attention: if we have virtuous forebears, to imitate their virtue; if the contrary is true and we come from disreputable forebears, not to think any handicap results from this but to fall to the labors virtue involves, no harm ensuing from this, to be sure. HOMILIES ON GENESIS 43.6-7.[20]

BEING DESCENDANTS IS NOT ENOUGH. JUSTIN MARTYR: You are sadly mistaken if you think that just because you are descendants of Abraham according to the flesh you will share in the legacy of benefits that God promised would be distributed by Christ. No one can in any way participate in any of these gifts, except those who have the same ardent faith as Abraham and who approve of all the mysteries.... As people who have cut your souls off from this hope, it is necessary that you know how to obtain pardon of your sins and a hope of sharing in the promised blessings. There is no other way than this, that you come to know our Christ, be baptized with the baptism that cleanses you of sin (as Isaiah testified) and thus live a life free of sin. DIALOGUE WITH TRYPHO 44.[21]

FAITHLESS SINNERS CANNOT RELY ON THEIR ANCESTORS. JUSTIN MARTYR: Those teachers deceive both themselves and you when they suppose that those who are descendants of Abraham according to the flesh will most surely share in the eternal kingdom, even though they are faithless sinners and disobedient to God, suppositions that the Scriptures show have no foundation in fact. DIALOGUE WITH TRYPHO 140.[22]

14:21 Acts of Judgment

PENANCE STILL NECESSARY. ORIGEN: All those who are sinners in the church, who have tasted

---

[18]FC 62:18-19. [19]FC 3:88*. [20]FC 82:438-39. [21]FC 6:214. [22]FC 6:363*.

the Word of God and have transgressed it, deserve prayers, but each one will be punished in accordance with his or her degree. HOMILIES ON EZEKIEL 5.4.[23]

RESPONSIBILITY IS UNAVOIDABLE. JEROME: As far as all these things are concerned, neither the teaching of spiritual parents nor political leaders were able to liberate us, unless the children approved and their imploring helped their own efforts; for justice for the just will be on him, and the iniquity and the sin of the sinner will linger on him. COMMENTARY ON EZEKIEL 4.14.12-23.[24]

---

[23]SC 352:200. A reference to public penance. [24]CCL 75:156.

[15:1-8 JERUSALEM A USELESS VINE]

16:1-14 THE FOUNDLING CHILD, ISRAEL

[1]*Again the word of the* LORD *came to me:* [2]*"Son of man, make known to Jerusalem her abominations,* [3]*and say, Thus says the Lord* GOD *to Jerusalem: Your origin and your birth are of the land of the Canaanites; your father was an Amorite, and your mother a Hittite.* [4]*And as for your birth, on the day you were born your navel string was not cut, nor were you washed with water to cleanse you, nor rubbed with salt, nor swathed with bands.* [5]*No eye pitied you, to do any of these things to you out of compassion for you; but you were cast out on the open field, for you were abhorred, on the day that you were born.*

[6]*"And when I passed by you, and saw you weltering in your blood, I said to you in your blood, 'Live,* [7]*and grow up*[b] *like a plant of the field.' And you grew up and became tall and arrived at full maidenhood;*[c] *your breasts were formed, and your hair had grown; yet you were naked and bare.*

[8]*"When I passed by you again and looked upon you, behold, you were at the age for love; and I spread my skirt over you, and covered your nakedness: yea, I plighted my troth to you and entered into a covenant with you, says the Lord* GOD, *and you became mine.* [9]*Then I bathed you with water and washed off your blood from you, and anointed you with oil.* [10]*I clothed you also with embroidered cloth and shod you with leather, I swathed you in fine linen and covered you with silk.* [11]*And I decked you with ornaments, and put bracelets on your arms, and a chain on your neck.* [12]*And I put a ring on your nose, and earrings in your ears, and a beautiful crown upon your head.* [13]*Thus you were decked with gold and silver; and your raiment was of fine linen, and silk, and embroidered cloth; you ate fine flour and honey and oil. You grew exceedingly beautiful, and came*

to regal estate. ¹⁴*And your renown went forth among the nations because of your beauty, for it was perfect through the splendor which I had bestowed upon you, says the Lord GOD."*

b Gk Syr: Heb *I made you a myriad*　　**c** Cn: Heb *ornament of ornaments*

OVERVIEW: The prophet speaks out with courage (ORIGEN), since punishment does good to the foundling child, Israel, to whom Christ offers freedom (CHRYSOSTOM). The spiritual rebirth of baptism represents cleansing; catechumens need to come to baptism and so experience the life of the Trinity. God's mercy will not pass us by (ORIGEN), but we need spiritual clothing (JEROME) as we move forward in spiritual growth (ORIGEN).

As we grow up, we become aware of the reality of temptation (ORIGEN) and consequently need to know the teaching that will help us to resist it (JEROME). God's mercy, however, knows no bounds (CHRYSOSTOM), for as the blood has been washed from us (ORIGEN), Christ was anointed with oil of a completely different kind that did not remove the pain that he suffered but still brought joy with it (JEROME). The paradox of God's love and our rejection of him is played out in the life of Christ (EPHREM). This challenges us to stand firm against temptation (JEROME), especially the temptation to pride (GREGORY THE GREAT), and to benefit from all kinds of spiritual clothing (THEODORET), including the ability to interpret the Scripture (ORIGEN) and to discern the life of the Trinity in us (JEROME).

16:2 Jerusalem's Abominations

THE COURAGE OF THE PROPHET. ORIGEN: Why is it that I admire Ezekiel? Because the order was given him to make known to Jerusalem its abominations, and he did not place before his eyes any danger that would result from his preaching, but in order to keep only the precepts of God, he spoke whatever he was told. Let us realize that there was a mystery, that there was the revelation of a mysterious kind on the subject of Jerusalem and all that is said against it. Nevertheless, he prophesied, and accused it of fornica-

tion. HOMILIES ON EZEKIEL 6.1.[1]

PUNISHMENT CAN BE GOOD. CHRYSOSTOM: What do you say, prophet? God punishes, and shall I grieve for those whom he is punishing? Certainly. For God, who punishes, wants us to grieve, since he does not want to punish us, and he grieves when carrying out punishment. Do not rejoice at this. One will say, "If they are justly punished, we ought not to grieve." What we ought to grieve for is this, that they were found worthy of punishment. When you see your son undergoing medical or surgical treatment, do you not grieve? You do not say to yourself, "What is this?" This cutting is for health, to speed his recovery; it is for his deliverance, this burning? But for all that, when you hear him crying out and unable to bear the pain, you grieve, and the hope of health being restored is not enough to carry off the shock to nature. HOMILIES ON THE ACTS OF THE APOSTLES 43.[2]

16:3 Born of the Canaanites

THE KNOWLEDGE OF GOD IN HIS CITY. ORIGEN: Which of the cities in the world were so elevated and so deep in knowledge as the city of God? HOMILIES ON EZEKIEL 6.3.[3]

MY RESPONSIBILITY. ORIGEN: If so many things are said in Jerusalem about which such great and wonderful things are written that have been promised to her, what future is there for unhappy me, if I sin? Who will I have for a father, who will I have for a mother? HOMILIES ON EZEKIEL 6.3.[4]

CHRIST COMES TO SET US FREE. CHRYSOSTOM: If we are on the alert, these evils that came

---

[1]SC 352:212-14. [2]NPNF 1 11:266*. [3]SC 352:216. [4]SC 352:218.

into life as a result of the sins of our forebears will in no way be able to harm us, because in fact they go no further than the level of terminology. It was the first formed human being who through the fall brought on the punishment of death and was responsible for spending his life in pain and distress, and it was he who was the cause of servitude. But Christ the Lord came and permitted all these evils to occur only at the level of terminology, provided we are of the right mind. You see, death is now not death but only carries the name of death—or, rather, even the very name has been abolished. HOMILIES ON GENESIS 29.23.[5]

16:4 *At Your Birth*

BAPTISM AS THE WASHING. ORIGEN: Not everyone is washed for salvation. We who have received the grace of baptism in the name of Christ are washed, but I do not know who is washed for salvation. HOMILIES ON EZEKIEL 6.5.[6]

CATECHUMENS ARE TO PREPARE FOR BAPTISM. ORIGEN: It is quite difficult that he who is washed should be washed in order to be saved. Listen, catechumens, listen, and from what is said, prepare yourselves, while you are catechumens, while you are not yet baptized, and come to the bath and be baptized for salvation. Do not be so baptized that you are washed but not for salvation. HOMILIES ON EZEKIEL 6.5.[7]

SALT HAS A SPIRITUAL QUALITY. ORIGEN: It is a great work to be rubbed with salt. If we are seasoned with salt, we are full of grace. HOMILIES ON EZEKIEL 6.6.[8]

THE NEWLY BAPTIZED IS DRIED. ORIGEN: The soul that is reborn is barely out of the bath before being enveloped with towels. HOMILIES ON EZEKIEL 6.6.[9]

THE WORK OF THE HOLY SPIRIT IN BAPTISM. ORIGEN: To take an example from human rela-

tionships, if the Holy Spirit gives, then I travel on to Jesus Christ and God the Father. HOMILIES ON EZEKIEL 6.6.[10]

WASHING FROM ALL KINDS OF DEFILEMENT. JEROME: That you were washed in water means washing not only from heretics but also from ecclesiastics who do not receive saving baptism with a full faith, about whom it is said that they will have received the water but not the Spirit. COMMENTARY ON EZEKIEL 4.16.4-5.[11]

16:6 *The Foundling Child Passed By*

WE ARE NOT FORSAKEN. ORIGEN: But see the mercy of God, see his extraordinary goodness. Even though Jerusalem was thrown into the open field, he does not look down on it as thrown out forever, he does not leave it in a state of perversion as entirely forgotten, as not in the end to lift up the fallen. You were thrown out, but I still return to you; my visit is not lacking after your ruin." HOMILIES ON EZEKIEL 6.7.[12]

SPIRITUAL CLOTHING NECESSARY. JEROME: When she is ready for marriage and her body is becoming beautiful, she did not have clothes to cover her, and she was not protected by the help of God. If people do not have clothing that Christ gives, they are naked; if people are not clothed inwardly with mercy, goodness, humility, chastity, gentleness and patience, they are cast on the earth, and their beauty is defiled in disorder and nudity. COMMENTARY ON EZEKIEL 4.16.6-7.[13]

16:8 *Passed By and Rescued*

AGE BRINGS AWARENESS OF TEMPTATION. ORIGEN: When we are of a greater age and can therefore sin, angels look for a chance to influence

---

[5]FC 82:214*. [6]SC 352:224. [7]SC 352:224-26. [8]SC 352:226. Salt was sometimes given to catechumens, following Mt 5:13. [9]SC 352:226. [10]SC 352:228. [11]CCL 75:164. [12]SC 352:232. [13]CCL 75:167.

us, and that is as true of the angels of God as it is of the angels of Satan. HOMILIES ON EZEKIEL 6.8.[14]

ALWAYS BE READY FOR MERCY. ORIGEN: Let us pray that the mercy of God will come on us and wash away the blood from our souls. HOMILIES ON EZEKIEL 6.9.[15]

AGE BRINGS THE NEED FOR PROTECTION. JEROME: As far as Jerusalem is concerned, let us compare it with our soul, which as long as it is in infancy is unable to sin; but when it comes to that age, many are the lovers of demons and heretics and perverse teachings, which desire to turn aside to it; they are driven away by the protection of the Lord, so that the soul receives not the attendance of the devil but the ministers of a savior. COMMENTARY ON EZEKIEL 4.16.8.[16]

GOD'S MERCY IS BOUNDLESS. CHRYSOSTOM: Do not infer from these things that it is about punishment only, but also about the boundless longsuffering of God. HOMILIES ON THE GOSPEL OF MATTHEW 43.5.[17]

16:9 Bathed with Water

CHRIST IS ANOINTED WITH ANOTHER KIND OF OIL. JEROME: Our Lord is anointed with another oil, which is not supposed to soften the grief caused by wounds but nonetheless brings with it joy. COMMENTARY ON EZEKIEL 4.16.8-9.[18]

THE LIFE OF CHRIST CONTRASTED WITH JERUSALEM. EPHREM THE SYRIAN: "Untie the donkey and bring it to me."[19]

He began with a manger and finished with a donkey, in Bethlehem with a manger, in Jerusalem with a donkey. This is like, "Rejoice, daughter of Zion, for behold, your king is coming to you, just and lowly and seated on a donkey."[20]

But the daughter of Zion saw him and was troubled. She looked at him and became sad. He the merciful One, and the Son of the merciful

One, had spread his benevolence over her like a father, but she conducted herself as perversely toward him as she had done toward the One who had sent him. Not being able to abuse the Father, she displayed her hatred against his Only Begotten. The daughter of Zion repaid him with evil for the immensity of his grace. The Father had washed her from her blood, but she defiled his Son with her spitting.[21]

The Father had clothed her with fine linen and purple, but she clothed him with garments of mockery.[22]

He had placed a crown of glory on her head, but she plaited a crown of thorns for him.[23]

He had nourished her with choicest food and honey, but she gave him gall.[24]

He had given her pure wine, but she offered him vinegar and soaked it with blood.[25]

The One who had introduced her into cities, she drove out into the desert. The One who had put shoes on her feet, she made hasten barefoot toward Golgotha.[26]

The One who had girded her loins with sapphire, she pierced in the side with a lance.[27]

When she had outraged the servants of God and killed the prophets, she was led into captivity to Babylon, and when the time of her punishment was completed, her return from captivity took place. COMMENTARY ON TATIAN'S DIATESSARON 18.1.[28]

STAND FIRM AGAINST TEMPTATION. JEROME: Our loins are girded with fine linen whenever the enticing incentives of lust have to be held back, and nothing of a heavy humor is left, and we are filled with the teaching of the apostle, when he says, "stand therefore, having girded your loins with truth."[29] COMMENTARY ON EZEKIEL 4.16.10.[30]

---

[14]SC 352:236. [15]SC 352:238. [16]CCL 75:168. [17]NPNF 1 10:276*. [18]CCL 75:170. [19]Mk 11:2; Mt 21:2. [20]Zech 9:9. [21]Mt 26:67. [22]Mt 27:28. [23]Mt 27:29. [24]Mt 27:34. [25]Jn 19:29. [26]Mt 27:33. [27]Jn 19:34. [28]ECTD 269. [29]Eph 6:14. [30]CCL 75:172.

16:11 Decked with Ornaments

WE CAN SERVE GOD WITH HIS GIFTS.
JEROME: When God has given us good works, he surrounds our hands with bracelets. COMMENTARY ON EZEKIEL 4.16.11.[31]

PETER'S DAY AN OCCASION FOR REJOICING.
JEROME: It is true that a festival such as the birthday of Peter should be seasoned with more gladness than usual; still our merriment must not forget the limit set by Scripture, and we must not stray too far from the boundary of our wrestling ground.[32] Your presents, indeed, remind me of the sacred volume, for in it Ezekiel decks Jerusalem with bracelets. LETTER 31.2.[33]

SPIRITUAL CLOTHING. THEODORET OF CYR: The priests are anointed with holy oil and are clothed with embroidered cloth and with silk. It means riches, which the people gained as a result of his providence, as much in spirit as in body. COMMENTARY ON EZEKIEL 5.16.[34]

16:12 The Crown upon Our Head

SPIRITUAL CROWNING. ORIGEN: Almighty God, grant to us to be worthy of the crown and glory on our head. HOMILIES ON EZEKIEL 6.10.[35]

THE CROWN OF LIFE. ORIGEN: We are not only anointed with this oil, but we also live. HOMILIES ON EZEKIEL 6.10.[36]

GOLD AND SILVER. JEROME: We have frequently said that gold relates to the mind and silver to eloquence. COMMENTARY ON EZEKIEL 4.16.13.[37]

THE SINGLE SWEETNESS OF THE TRINITY.
JEROME: After clothing, she shows what she has of food, so that Jerusalem may eat fine flour and honey and oil. This can be either individually or in a mixture of the three, which is a sweeter bread, the bread that comes down from heaven. The three names, as several think, indicate the mystery of the Trinity, not each within a separate substance but diversely, like fine flour and honey and oil, so that the single sweetness of the Father and the Son and the Holy Spirit can be made manifest. COMMENTARY ON EZEKIEL 4.16.13.[38]

16:14 Renowned Throughout the World

MADE PERFECT BY GOD ALONE. JEROME: In Ezekiel, God speaks to Jerusalem: "You were perfect through my beauty." And this is the meaning of the text: "You were not perfect through your own works or through your own knowledge and the boasting of your heart but through my beauty, which I had put on you freely through my mercy." AGAINST THE PELAGIANS 2.25.[39]

THE PREACHER MUST GUARD HIS OWN SOUL. GREGORY THE GREAT: Now, seeing that often when a sermon is delivered with due propriety and with a fruitful message, the mind of the speaker is exalted by joy all his own over his performance, he must take care to torment himself with painful misgivings: in restoring others to health by healing their wounds, he must not disregard his own health and develop tumors of pride. Let him not, while lifting up others, fall himself. In many instances the greatness of certain people's virtues has been an occasion of their perdition, in that they have felt inordinately secure in the assurance of their strength, and they died suddenly because of their negligence. For as virtue struggles against vice, the mind, as it were, exhilarated by this virtue, flatters itself; so that the soul of one actually engaged upon doing good casts aside all anxiety and circumspection and rests secure in its self-confidence. In this its state of inertia the cunning Seducer enumerates all that the person has done well and aggrandizes him with conceited thoughts about his preeminence over all others. . . .

---

[31]CCL 75:174. [32]This letter is dated to June 29, celebrated as the birthday of Peter. [33]NPNF 2 6:45. [34]PG 81:936. [35]SC 352:242. [36]SC 352:242. [37]CCL 75:177. [38]CCL 75:178. [39]FC 53:338-39.

The mind is lifted up in the confidence of its beauty, when with blithe self-assurance it glories over its virtues. But through this same confidence it is led on to play the harlot: that is, when by its thoughts the mind robs and deceives itself, evil spirits seduce and corrupt it with numerous vices. PASTORAL CARE 4.[40]

[40]ACW 11:234-35*.

16:15-34 THE IDOLATRY OF THE RESCUED FOUNDLING

[15]*But you trusted in your beauty, and played the harlot because of your renown, and lavished your harlotries on any passer-by.* [16]*You took some of your garments, and made for yourself gaily decked shrines, and on them played the harlot; the like has never been, nor ever shall be.* [17]*You also took your fair jewels of my gold and of my silver, which I had given you, and made for yourself images of men, and with them played the harlot;* [18]*and you took your embroidered garments to cover them, and set my oil and my incense before them.* [19]*Also my bread which I gave you—I fed you with fine flour and oil and honey—you set before them for a pleasing odor, says the Lord* GOD.[d] [20]*And you took your sons and your daughters, whom you had borne to me, and these you sacrificed to them to be devoured. Were your harlotries so small a matter* [21]*that you slaughtered my children and delivered them up as an offering by fire to them?* [22]*And in all your abominations and your harlotries you did not remember the days of your youth, when you were naked and bare, weltering in your blood.*

[23]*And after all your wickedness (woe, woe to you! says the Lord* GOD), [24]*you built yourself a vaulted chamber, and made yourself a lofty place in every square;* [25]*at the head of every street you built your lofty place and prostituted your beauty, offering yourself to any passer-by, and multiplying your harlotry.* [26]*You also played the harlot with the Egyptians, your lustful neighbors, multiplying your harlotry, to provoke me to anger.* [27]*Behold, therefore, I stretched out my hand against you, and diminished your allotted portion, and delivered you to the greed of your enemies, the daughters of the Philistines, who were ashamed of your lewd behavior.* [28]*You played the harlot also with the Assyrians, because you were insatiable; yea, you played the harlot with them, and still you were not satisfied.* [29]*You multiplied your harlotry also with the trading land of Chaldea; and even with this you were not satisfied.*

[30]*How lovesick is your heart, says the Lord* GOD, *seeing you did all these things, the deeds of a brazen harlot;* [31]*building your vaulted chamber at the head of every street, and making your lofty place in every square. Yet you were not like a harlot, because you scorned hire.* [32]*Adulterous wife, who receives strangers instead of her husband!* [33]*Men give gifts to all harlots; but you gave your*

gifts to all your lovers, bribing them to come to you from every side for your harlotries. [34]*So you were different from other women in your harlotries; none solicited you to play the harlot: and you gave hire, while no hire was given to you; therefore you were different.*

d Syr: Heb *and it was, says the Lord* GOD

OVERVIEW: The foundling child grows up into greater acts of idolatry, in which the mishandling of Scripture by preacher and people is prominent (ORIGEN), in which spiritual lust is prevalent (AUGUSTINE), in which heresy is rife (JEROME), in which those determined to forsake God do so (CHRYSOSTOM), in which the meaning of Scripture is distorted (ATHANASIUS), in which God shows that he demands purity of life (PACHOMIUS), in which true faith is corrupted (PETER CHRYSOLOGUS) and in which heretics follow the corrupt example of the adulterous woman (PACIAN).

16:17 Jewelry Misused

WE MUST HANDLE SCRIPTURE PROPERLY.
ORIGEN: The golden and silver vase, the censers, the cups and the rest of that kind we have in the holy Scriptures. But when we turn the meaning of Scripture into another that is contrary to the truth, we kindle the divine words and turn the things of God into other images. HOMILIES ON EZEKIEL 7.2.[1]

16:18 Embroidered Garments Used to Conceal Our Faults

EVEN HERESY CAN BE CONVINCING. JEROME: We do this whenever we surround our first heresy with prudence . . . and all the virtues. COMMENTARY ON EZEKIEL 4.16.18.[2]

FALSE GARMENTS CAN COVER HERESIES.
ORIGEN: These various clothes and beautiful garments that God has bestowed on us, if we cut them up and rip them and surround them with false teaching to deceive human beings, there is no doubt that we are covering idols with different clothing. HOMILIES ON EZEKIEL 7.3.[3]

TEMPTATIONS OF THE PREACHER. ORIGEN: To me who preaches the gospel in the church, the devil always stretches out a noose, in order to confuse the whole church with my conduct. HOMILIES ON EZEKIEL 7.3.[4]

IMITATE CHRIST. ORIGEN: We do not imitate anyone, but if we want to imitate anyone, we should imitate Jesus Christ. HOMILIES ON EZEKIEL 7.3.[5]

PRAYER ACCEPTABLE TO GOD. ORIGEN: Incense and oil are the prayer that is offered to God with understanding and in which God delights. EXCERPTS ON EZEKIEL 16.18.[6]

HERESY CAN BE TAUGHT. ORIGEN: Whoever is born in the teaching of heretics and has taken these principles for his own faith is a child of Jerusalem the fornicator and sinner. HOMILIES ON EZEKIEL 7.5.[7]

16:20 Sons and Daughters Sacrificed

LUST IS SINFUL. AUGUSTINE: By the name of such adulterers we are to understand every kind of carnal and lustful concupiscence. Indeed, since the Scriptures so constantly give to idolatry the name of fornication, and since the apostle Paul calls avarice idolatry,[8] who can doubt that every evil concupiscence may be rightly called fornication? SERMON ON THE MOUNT 1.12.36.[9]

THE SOUL CAN BE CORRUPTED. AUGUSTINE: When the soul disregards the higher law by which it is governed and prostitutes itself as

---

[1]SC 352:252. [2]CCL 75:183. [3]SC 352:254. [4]SC 352:256. [5]SC 352:258. [6]PG 13:812. [7]SC 352:262. [8]Col 3:5; Eph 5:5. [9]FC 11:55*.

though for a price, then it corrupts itself. SERMON ON THE MOUNT 1.12.36.[10]

16:22 Youthful Days Not Remembered

THE FORTUNES OF JERUSALEM IN HERESY.
JEROME: If our Jerusalem were tripped up by the lies of heresy, she would take her own sons who were stronger in the faith and her own daughters who were not as strong in the faith—whether they were sons who knew certain mystical things, or whether the daughters accepted straight history—to be handed over to be devoured by demons, and when she had killed them, she believed that she had made them live and please images and be satisfied by their massacre. COMMENTARY ON EZEKIEL 5.16.19-22.[11]

16:23 Abominations Continued

CORRUPTION CONTINUED. ORIGEN: Their bodies are corrupted, and the soul is wounded. HOMILIES ON EZEKIEL 7.6.[12]

THE WILLFULNESS OF THOSE WHO FORSAKE GOD. CHRYSOSTOM: I do marvel. You behave in the same way to me, who have been hitherto unknown to you, when even to the Father, of whom you have so much experience, you have done the very same. You have forsaken him, you have run to the devils, drawing to yourselves wicked lovers. With this Ezekiel too was continually upbraiding them. HOMILIES ON THE GOSPEL OF MATTHEW 43.1.[13]

16:25 Abominations Lead to Multiplication of Sin

THE SIN OF HERESY. ORIGEN: Possessing these things, she is of great beauty, but she is corrupted by the divisions of heretics and foreign religious systems. HOMILIES ON EZEKIEL 7.7.[14]

THE HERETIC CAN USE SCRIPTURE. ATHANASIUS: What then has persuaded you to contradict

each other and to procure to yourselves so great a disgrace? You cannot give any good account of it; this supposition only remains, that all you do is but outward profession and pretense. . . . And you make nothing of accusing the Fathers, and you complain outright of the expressions as being unscriptural; and, as it is written, "opened your legs to every one that passed by;"[15] so as to change as often as they wish, in whose pay and keep you are. Yet, though a person uses terms not in Scripture, it makes no difference, so that his meaning is religious. But the heretic, though he uses scriptural terms, because he is equally dangerous and depraved, will be asked in the words of the Spirit, "Why do you preach my laws and take my covenant in your mouth?"[16] ON SYNODS 39.[17]

THE DEPTHS OF SELF-CORRUPTION. JEROME: She will sit by the waters of loneliness, her pitcher laid aside, and open her legs to every one who passes by and be polluted to the crown of her head. It would have been better for her to have submitted to the yoke of marriage, to have walked in level places, than to aspire to loftier heights and fall into the depths of hell. LETTER 22.6.[18]

JERUSALEM THE WHORE. JEROME: A noble alternative only to be embraced in preference to Satan! In the old days even Jerusalem went whoring and opened her legs to everyone that passed by. It was in Egypt that she was first deflowered and there that her teats were bruised. LETTER 79.10.[19]

CHRIST IS CONCEIVED OF A VIRGIN. JEROME: Our Zion, in which at times there are Philistines and Tyre and Ethiopia; that watchtower, that meretrix, that harlot, that Rahab, that Babylon, that one who, according to Ezekiel, has prostituted herself to everyone on the crossroads; that meretrix, if she wills it, suddenly becomes a vir-

---

[10]FC 11:55*. [11]CCL 75:186. [12]SC 352:264. [13]NPNF 1 10:273*. [14]SC 352:266. [15]LXX. [16]Ps 50:16 (49:16 LXX). [17]NPNF 2 4:471*. [18]NPNF 2 6:24**. [19]NPNF 2 6:168*.

gin. A virgin she becomes, conceives the Son of God and brings him forth. "From your fear, O Lord, we conceived and suffered the pangs of childbirth, bringing forth the spirit of your salvation on the earth."[20] Understand, therefore, that [Jerusalem], who was a prostitute, conceives of God and is in labor and brings forth the Savior. HOMILIES ON THE PSALMS 18 (Ps 86).[21]

16:26 You Play the Harlot with Your Neighbors

HANDED OVER TO ALIENS. ORIGEN: You see that she is handed over to the souls of strangers, she who is unworthy to practice the law and the words of God. HOMILIES ON EZEKIEL 7.8.[22]

GOD DEMANDS PURITY. PACHOMIUS: If we have promised God purity, may we never be found in fornication, of which there are several forms. It is said that they prostituted themselves in a number of ways. My brothers, may no one ever catch us in deeds of this kind. May no one ever find us fallen below every other person. INSTRUCTIONS 1.39.[23]

16:28 Insatiable Harlotry

GOD'S COVENANT INVOLVES RESPONSIBILITY. ORIGEN: When God makes covenants with us and we consent to them, we are blessed. But when we prostitute ourselves to the spirits of evil, then we turn the covenants of God into the land of Canaan, and we make a pact with her. HOMILIES ON EZEKIEL 7.9.[24]

16:30 Your Heart Is Lovesick

GOD'S TEACHING CHALLENGES. ORIGEN: As the law is not made for the just but for the lawless and those who are not subjected to God, so the teaching that warns us away from fornication does not become chaste but is for the lawless and the fornicators and the disobedient. HOMILIES ON EZEKIEL 7.10.[25]

SPIRITUAL FORNICATION A REALITY. ORIGEN: If you understand fornication of the flesh and the soul and the spirit, and if you see someone fornicating in them, you will also see Jerusalem fornicating herself three times. HOMILIES ON EZEKIEL 7.10.[26]

THE PREACHER MUST SPEAK PRUDENTLY. ORIGEN: There is no doubt that the word of the orator provokes the hero to worse things when a heretic builds up his hero in the perversions of heresy by what he says. HOMILIES ON EZEKIEL 8.1.[27]

WE CAN APPEAR RELIGIOUS. ORIGEN: Those who have not completely gone away from religion but are conquered by sin and who want their sin to be hidden behave exactly like a prostitute who has been insulted. HOMILIES ON EZEKIEL 8.1.[28]

16:31 A Harlot Who Scorns Hire

TO DESERT THE WORSHIP OF GOD CAN BE EASY. JEROME: We can compare this with every single Christian soul who deserts the worship of God, indulges in vices and luxury and follows secular life, lest it does anything fruitful, and goes so far as destroying the riches of religion and does not even accept the riches of the world. There is no difficulty in her debauchery, for she herself rushes to her lovers. COMMENTARY ON EZEKIEL 5.16.30-31.[29]

THE HOUSE OF GOD IN THE FAITHFUL. ORIGEN: Ecclesiastics who are leaders in the church build the house of God, the church, in their own way of life as well as those of their faithful, and their work is the building of God. HOMILIES ON EZEKIEL 8.2.[30]

THE TRUE FAITH CORRUPTED BY POOR PHILOSOPHY. PETER CHRYSOLOGUS: These Gentile

---

[20]See Is 26:18. [21]FC 48:144*. [22]SC 352:268. [23]CS 47:32. [24]SC 352:268. [25]SC 352:270. [26]SC 352:274. [27]SC 352:278. [28]SC 352:282. [29]CCL 75:193-94. [30]SC 352:284.

peoples through their desire of worldly eloquence, through the brothels of the schools, through senseless disputation at the meeting places of the philosophical sects, dissipated the property of God the Father. By their conjectures they exhausted everything there was in the line of speech, knowledge, reason and judgment. But, even after that, these poor wretches still suffered the greatest need and most intense hunger to know the truth. Philosophy enjoined the task of seeking God, but of that truth to be learned it gathered no fruit. SERMON 5.[31]

16:32 *The Adulterous Wife*

HERETICAL PEOPLE ARE ADULTEROUS. PACIAN OF BARCELONA: A heretical congregation is an adulterous woman; for the Catholic congregation from the very beginning never left the marriage couch and nuptial chamber of her spouse or ardently desired unsuitable and strange lovers. You have painted a banished form with new colors; you have withdrawn your marriage couch from a long-standing marriage; you have left the body of a mother, the wife of one husband, adorning yourselves with new techniques of pleasing, new allurements of seduction. LETTER 3.22.1.[32]

HAVING NO PRICE WHATEVER. JEROME: When all fornicating women are accustomed to receive pay from their lovers, Jerusalem does the opposite, so that she may give more than she receives and so that she may show the abundance of her price; she burdened them, in order that they might come to her in a roundabout way, in case there was anyone near her who was not tainted by disgrace. COMMENTARY ON EZEKIEL 5.16.32-34.[33]

16:33 *Even the Gifts Given to Harlots Misused*

THE SOUL NEEDS TRUE LOVE. ORIGEN: The husband of the soul is the word of God, a spouse truly loving, who has given her chastity, justice and all the other gifts. HOMILIES ON EZEKIEL 8.3.[34]

---

[31]FC 17:47*. [32]FC 99:64. [33]CCL 75:196. [34]SC 352:290.

16:35-43 THE PROMISED PUNISHMENT FOR HARLOTRY

[35]*"Wherefore, O harlot, hear the word of the LORD:* [36]*Thus says the Lord GOD, Because your shame was laid bare and your nakedness uncovered in your harlotries with your lovers, and because of all your idols, and because of the blood of your children that you gave to them,* [37]*therefore, behold, I will gather all your lovers, with whom you took pleasure, all those you loved and all those you loathed; I will gather them against you from every side, and will uncover your nakedness to them, that they may see all your nakedness.* [38]*And I will judge you as women who break wedlock and shed blood are judged, and bring upon you the blood of wrath and jealousy.* [39]*And I will give you into the hand of your lovers, and they shall throw down your vaulted cham-*

ber and break down your lofty places; they shall strip you of your clothes and take your fair jewels, and leave you naked and bare. ⁴⁰They shall bring up a host against you, and they shall stone you and cut you to pieces with their swords. ⁴¹And they shall burn your houses and execute judgments upon you in the sight of many women; I will make you stop playing the harlot, and you shall also give hire no more. ⁴²So will I satisfy my fury on you, and my jealousy shall depart from you; I will be calm, and will no more be angry. ⁴³Because you have not remembered the days of your youth, but have enraged me with all these things; therefore, behold, I will requite your deeds upon your head, says the Lord God.

"Have you not committed lewdness in addition to all your abominations?"

OVERVIEW: God's anger is not a mark of senseless rage but is rather a sign of his deep love for us (CASSIAN, JEROME), since we need to be corrected and punished (ORIGEN).

16:42 The Fury of God

GOD'S LOVE PREVAILS. JOHN CASSIAN: Like a very skillful physician who has tried every treatment and sees that no remedy is left that could have an effect on their illness, the Lord is (as it were) overcome by the magnitude of their wickedness. He is forced to give up that merciful chastisement of his, and so he denounces them and says, "I will no longer be angry with you, and my jealousy has departed from you." CONFERENCE 6.11.8.[1]

GOD'S ANGER IS THE RESULT OF HIS LOVE FOR US. JEROME: Mighty is the wrath of the Lord when he is not angry with us here, for, then, he reserves us like a calf for slaughter. In fact, he says to Jerusalem, "Many are your sins and many your iniquities, but I will not be vexed with you." In other words, when you were only an adulteress, I loved you with a jealous love; but when you had many lovers, I despised you, and I will not be vexed with you. In this same way, a man is jealous of his wife when he loves her; but if he is not jealous, he hates her and does not imitate the words of him who says, "I will punish their crime with a rod"[2] but, "I will not punish your daughters for their harlotry."[3] HOMILIES ON THE PSALMS 51 (Ps 140).[4]

SPIRITUAL SIGHT MORE IMPORTANT THAN PHYSICAL. JEROME: It is when God shows no anger to sinners that his anger is great. So in the case of Ezekiel he said to Jerusalem, "Now I shall not be angry with you, my jealousy has left you." . . . So that I may not go too far and overrun the length of a letter by piling up instances from the Old Testament, I shall tell you a brief story that happened in the days of my childhood. When the blessed Antony was summoned by Athanasius, bishop of Alexandria, to the city of Alexandria to confute heretics, and Didymus, a most learned and blessed man, had a meeting with him, they had a discussion about the holy Scriptures. Antony admired the other's brain and praised his mental sharpness. Then he asked, "I imagine that your blindness does not depress you?" Didymus in his shame said nothing. But when Antony asked a second and third time, he finally succeeded in eliciting from Didymus a simple expression of grief. Antony said to him, "I am surprised at a wise man grieving at the loss of what ants, flies and gnats have rather than rejoicing at having what only the saints and apostles have deserved to get." From this you can realize that it is much better to see with the spirit than with the flesh and to possess the eyes that the mote of sin cannot enter. LETTER 68.[5]

---

[1]ACW 57: 230*. [2]Ps 89:32 (88:33 LXX, Vulg.). [3]Hos 4:14. [4]FC 48:368-69*. [5]MFC 17:97*.

WE NEED TO BE CORRECTED. ORIGEN: If you do not recover your senses when you have been chastised, if you are not corrected when you have been reproved, if you despise when you are beaten, you must realize that if you go on continually sinning his jealousy will depart from you and that which is said to Jerusalem by the prophet Ezekiel will be said to you: "Therefore my jealousy will depart from you, and I will no longer be angry with you." Behold the mercy and piety of the good God.... This is terrible! This is the end when we are no longer reproached for sins, when we offend and are no longer corrected. For then, when we have exceeded the measure of sinning "the jealous God" turns his jealousy away from us, as he said above, or my jealousy will be removed from you, and I will no longer be angry over you. HOMILIES ON EXODUS 8.5.[6]

---

[6]FC 71:328*.

16:44-52 SIN WORSE THAN THAT OF SODOM AND SAMARIA

[44]*Behold, every one who uses proverbs will use this proverb about you, "Like mother, like daughter."* [45]*You are the daughter of your mother, who loathed her husband and her children; and you are the sister of your sisters, who loathed their husbands and their children. Your mother was a Hittite and your father an Amorite.* [46]*And your elder sister is Samaria, who lived with her daughters to the north of you; and your younger sister, who lived to the south of you, is Sodom with her daughters.* [47]*Yet you were not content to walk in their ways, or do according to their abominations; within a very little time you were more corrupt than they in all your ways.* [48]*As I live, says the Lord GOD, your sister Sodom and her daughters have not done as you and your daughters have done.* [49]*Behold, this was the guilt of your sister Sodom: she and her daughters had pride, surfeit of food, and prosperous ease, but did not aid the poor and needy.* [50]*They were haughty, and did abominable things before me; therefore I removed them, when I saw it.* [51]*Samaria has not committed half your sins; you have committed more abominations than they, and have made your sisters appear righteous by all the abominations which you have committed.* [52]*Bear your disgrace, you also, for you have made judgment favorable to your sisters; because of your sins in which you acted more abominably than they, they are more in the right than you. So be ashamed, you also, and bear your disgrace, for you have made your sisters appear righteous.*

OVERVIEW: The sins of the people are terrible, for sin is found most easily in the crowd (ORIGEN), and we bear the consequences (JEROME). Divisions of the kingdom of Israel are the divisions of the church, pride being the greatest of all sins (ORIGEN). God's gifts are nonetheless to be found in repentance (CHRYSOSTOM), which means that we must devote ourselves to what benefits the soul (ISAAC). Christ, however, is the source of our justification (ORIGEN); we must take our punishment (JEROME), realizing that repentance matches every kind of sin (AUGUSTINE).

16:45 *Mutual Hatred Between Nations*

SIN AND VIRTUE OPPOSED. ORIGEN: Where there are sins, where there are multitudes of people, there are schisms, there are heresies, there are dissensions. But where there is virtue, there is unity, union, from which the single heart and spirit of all believers were made. HOMILIES ON EZEKIEL 9.1.[1]

WHERE EVIL FLOURISHES. ORIGEN: To put it more clearly, the origin of all evils is the multitude, but the origin of good things is to retire from the crowd and to confine oneself to the solitary life. HOMILIES ON EZEKIEL 9.1.[2]

UNITY IN THE TRINITY. ORIGEN: As the Father and Son are one, so those who have one Spirit are brought together in unity. HOMILIES ON EZEKIEL 9.1.[3]

THE CONSEQUENCES OF SIN. JEROME: When they have completed their crimes, they are cut into parts, and being no longer together, they plunge into the great crowd of people who are not able to ascend the mountain with Jesus. COMMENTARY ON EZEKIEL 5.16.45-47.[4]

16:46 *Like Samaria and Sodom*

FOLLOW CHRIST INSTEAD. ORIGEN: Virtue makes me to have Christ as my brother, so that I may be both good and well-mannered. HOMILIES ON EZEKIEL 9.1.[5]

THE DIVISIONS OF THE CHURCH. ORIGEN: What are these two sisters of Jerusalem the sinner? Schism and division of the people created Samaria. HOMILIES ON EZEKIEL 9.1.[6]

HERESY IS THE RESULT OF DIVISION. ORIGEN: This is to despise Zion and to trust in the mountain of Samaria. For if we ecclesiastics sin, heretics are certainly not strangers to us in the perversion of their teaching. HOMILIES ON EZEKIEL 9.1.[7]

16:49 *The Guilt of Sodom*

MANY AND VARIED. ORIGEN: To know that sins are unequal you only have to look at the teaching of the Scriptures, which will leave you in no doubt. HOMILIES ON EZEKIEL 9.2.[8]

THE GREATEST SIN. ORIGEN: What then is the sin most great of all sins? It is the one for which the devil fell.... Pride is greater than all sins, and the principal sin of the devil.... Often the reason for pride is for him who disregards having an ecclesiastical dignity. HOMILIES ON EZEKIEL 9.2.[9]

THE GIFTS OF GOD. CHRYSOSTOM: Do not ask those things from God that you receive from the devil. For it is God's part to give a contrite and humbled heart, sober, self-possessed and awestruck, full of repentance and compunction. These are his gifts, since it is these things that we most need. HOMILIES ON THE GOSPEL OF MATTHEW 6.9.[10]

DEVOTED TO PROFITABLE THINGS. ISAAC OF NINEVEH: The soul that devotes itself to the recollection of profitable things finds rest in its freedom; its cares are small, and it repents of nothing. It takes forethought for virtue, it bridles the passions, it keeps guard on excellence, and thus it enjoys growth [that is unhindered], joy free of solicitude, a good life and a haven without peril. ASCETICAL HOMILIES 40.[11]

DIFFERENT FORMS OF PRIDE. ORIGEN: Often having a fullness and an abundance of bread is the cause of arrogance. But often the sin of pride also

---

[1]SC 352:296. [2]SC 352:296. [3]SC 352:296. [4]CCL 75:203. [5]SC 352:298. [6]SC 352:300. [7]SC 352:300. [8]SC 352:302. [9]SC 352:304. [10]NPNF 1 10:42**. [11]AHSIS 199*.

arises over spiritual gifts, and discernment is needed to distinguish the one from the other. HOMILIES ON EZEKIEL 9.5.[12]

16:51 Samaria Has Committed Fewer Sins

JUSTIFICATION THROUGH CHRIST. ORIGEN: My Lord Jesus Christ is justified according to the dispensation of the flesh that he purified for our salvation, by Abraham, by Isaac, by Jacob and by the rest of the prophets. HOMILIES ON EZEKIEL 9.3.[13]

CHRIST CHANGES EVERYTHING. ORIGEN: Before Christ it was not possible for the light of the righteous to shine. HOMILIES ON EZEKIEL 9.3.[14]

16:52 Bear Your Disgrace

EXILE WITH PAIN. ORIGEN: O you who are subject to pain, do not go into exile with mourning. HOMILIES ON EZEKIEL 10.1.[15]

EXILE FROM THE CHURCH HURTS. ORIGEN: It is an infamy to be separated from the people of God and from the church; it is a dishonor in the church to leave the bench of presbyters, to be expelled from the rank of the diaconate. HOMILIES ON EZEKIEL 10.1.[16]

WE MUST TAKE OUR PUNISHMENT. ORIGEN: If we justify providence, we cleanse our disgrace; but if we do not receive the judgments of God, we will multiply our disgrace. HOMILIES ON EZEKIEL 10.1.[17]

NEARNESS TO GOD. ORIGEN: The more we come very near to God the more we come near the beatitude; and when we have sinned, we shall be far from it and very near terrible and very great punishments. HOMILIES ON EZEKIEL 10.2.[18]

THE MERCY OF GOD. ORIGEN: The person who is "very small" deserves mercy more quickly. HOMILIES ON EZEKIEL 10.2.[19]

BEAR YOUR PUNISHMENT. JEROME: One carries his disgrace who is racked with a proper conscience and bears his torture with a proper will, lest he should have to bear eternal torments. COMMENTARY ON EZEKIEL 5.16.52.[20]

REPENTANCE RELATIVE TO THE SINS COMMITTED. AUGUSTINE: It is one thing to have an action set forth as praiseworthy in itself and another to have it extolled in comparison with something worse than itself. We rejoice in one way when a sick person is cured and in another when he improves a little. Even in the sacred Scriptures, Sodom is spoken of as justified in comparison with the crimes of the people of Israel. LYING 5.7.[21]

---

[12]SC 352:320. [13]SC 352:310. [14]SC 352:310. [15]SC 352:328. [16]SC 352:330. [17]SC 352:332. [18]SC 352:334. [19]SC 352:336. [20]CCL 75:207. [21]FC 16:62.

16:53-63 THE PROMISE OF RESTORATION

[53]I will restore their fortunes, both the fortunes of Sodom and her daughters, and the fortunes of Samaria and her daughters, and I will restore your own fortunes in the midst of them, [54]that you may bear your disgrace and be ashamed of all that you have done, becoming a consolation to them.

⁵⁵*As for your sisters, Sodom and her daughters shall return to their former estate, and Samaria and her daughters shall return to their former estate; and you and your daughters shall return to your former estate.* ⁵⁶*Was not your sister Sodom a byword in your mouth in the day of your pride,* ⁵⁷*before your wickedness was uncovered? Now you have become like her*ᵉ *an object of reproach for the daughters of Edom*ᶠ *and all her neighbors, and for the daughters of the Philistines, those round about who despise you.* ⁵⁸*You bear the penalty of your lewdness and your abominations, says the* LORD.

⁵⁹*Yea, thus says the Lord* GOD: *I will deal with you as you have done, who have despised the oath in breaking the covenant,* ⁶⁰*yet I will remember my covenant with you in the days of your youth, and I will establish with you an everlasting covenant.* ⁶¹*Then you will remember your ways, and be ashamed when I*ᵍ *take your sisters, both your elder and your younger, and give them to you as daughters, but not on account of the covenant with you.* ⁶²*I will establish my covenant with you, and you shall know that I am the* LORD, ⁶³*that you may remember and be confounded, and never open your mouth again because of your shame, when I forgive you all that you have done, says the Lord* GOD.

e Cn: Heb uncertain f Another reading is *Aram* g Syr: Heb *you*

OVERVIEW: Restoration is promised, since God cannot be angry forever (ORIGEN). However, punishment is a way of dealing with all kinds and degrees of sin (JEROME), which is God's way of chastising us in order to redeem us (APHRAHAT).

16:53 Restoration of Fortunes

GOD AND ANGER ARE SEPARATE. ORIGEN: Anger is something other than God himself, so that it is never part of him, nor does he share in it in any way. HOMILIES ON EZEKIEL 10.2.[1]

16:54 Punishment Can Be Deserved

SINS COMMENSURATE WITH SINNER. JEROME: To whom is there any doubt that among three types of sinners, certainly wicked people, the Gentile, the heretic, the ecclesiastic, the one who deserves considerable punishment is the one who is of greater rank? COMMENTARY ON EZEKIEL 5.16.53-54.[2]

GOD ALONE IS JUST. ORIGEN: It is plain that the just and good God of the law and the gospels is one and the same and that he does good with justice and punishes in kindness, since neither goodness without justice nor justice without goodness can describe the dignity of the divine nature. ON FIRST PRINCIPLES 2.5.3.[3]

GOD CHASTISES IN ORDER TO REDEEM. APHRAHAT: Consider and observe, my hearer, that if God had given a hope to Sodom and to its fellows, he would not have overthrown them with fire and brimstone, the sign of the last day of the world, but would have delivered them over to one of the kingdoms to be chastised. DEMONSTRA-TIONS 21.6.[4]

16:61 Remember and Be Ashamed

REPENTANCE MEANS RECALLING SINS. ORIGEN: After receiving the price of my sins and being re-established, and the covenant made with me, then do I understand my evil deeds, and I am

---

[1]SC 352:336. [2]CCL 75:209. [3]OFP 104-5. [4]NPNF 2 13:394.

confounded, and within I punish myself. Homilies on Ezekiel 10.5.[5]

Prayer to Endure. Origen: Let us pray with
all our heart that God would grant us to fight for

truth to the very end of our mind and body.
Homilies on Ezekiel 10.5.[6]

---

[5]SC 352:346. [6]SC 352:346.

17:1-6 THE ALLEGORY OF THE TWO EAGLES PRESENTED

[1]*The word of the Lord came to me:* [2]*"Son of man, propound a riddle, and speak an allegory to
the house of Israel;* [3]*say, Thus says the Lord God: A great eagle with great wings and long pinions,
rich in plumage of many colors, came to Lebanon and took the top of the cedar;* [4]*he broke off the
topmost of its young twigs and carried it to a land of trade, and set it in a city of merchants.* [5]*Then
he took of the seed of the land and planted it in fertile soil; he placed it beside abundant waters. He
set it like a willow twig,* [6]*and it sprouted and became a low spreading vine, and its branches turned
toward him, and its roots remained where it stood. So it became a vine, and brought forth branches
and put forth foliage."*

Overview: The allegory of the two eagles is a
sign of the judgment of God and his people (Jerome, Chrysostom), which shows the church in
need of cleansing (Origen).

17:1 The Word to the Prophet

The Importance of Allegory. Jerome: To
no one is there any doubt that the prophet makes
known one thing in words as an allegory and a
parable but means something else, for even the
Savior spoke to the people in parables, which he
explained in secret to the apostles. Therefore we
must understand the allegory and the parable for
what they are. There are two eagles that are
placed before us in this part of the prophecy of
Ezekiel. Commentary on Ezekiel 5.17.1-6.[1]

17:2 The Allegory

The Meaning of the Allegory Important.
Chrysostom: [Ezekiel] calls the king of the
Babylonians an eagle and speaks of him as being
"great and long-winged"; and he calls him long-
extended and "full of claws," on account of the
multitude of his army, and the greatness of his
power and the swiftness of his invasion. For just
as the wings and claws of the eagle are his armor,
so are horses and soldiers to kings. Homilies
Concerning the Statues 19.9.[2]

17:3 Coming to Lebanon

The Church Is Cleansed of Evil. Origen:
He came to that Lebanon, which is the church,
where the offerings of God and the incense of his
prayers are celebrated, that great true evil, Neb-

---

[1]CCL 75:215-16. [2]NPNF 1 9:467*.

uchadnezzar, that is, the devil, and he sees it. Homilies on Ezekiel 11.5.[3]

17:6 The Low Spreading Vine

The Vine in All Its Fullness. Chrysostom: [Ezekiel] calls the city of Jerusalem a vine; but in saying that it stretched out its branches towards the eagle and that its roots were under him, he refers to the treaties and alliances made with him and that it cast itself on him. Homilies Concerning the Statues 19.9.[4]

The Vine Transplanted Did Not Last. Origen: As long as it was on holy ground, the vine was huge; but when it was taken to the land of sinners, it was made infirm and small. Homilies on Ezekiel 11.4.[5]

Safety Under the Protection of God. Jerome: Whoever has been under the wings of this sun [of justice and healing][6] who has said in the Gospel: how often would I have gathered your children together, as a hen gathers her young under her wings, but you would not! shall be safe from the devil hawk, safe under the great wings of that mighty eagle in Ezekiel, and all the wounds of his sins shall be healed. Homily 94 (On Easter Sunday).[8]

---

[3]SC 352:372. [4]NPNF 1 9:467*. [5]SC 352:368. [6]Mal 4:2. [7]Mt 23:37. [8]FC 57:253*.

17:7-21 THE ALLEGORY INTERPRETED

[7]*"But there was another great eagle with great wings and much plumage; and behold, this vine bent its roots toward him, and shot forth its branches toward him that he might water it. From the bed where it was planted* [8] *he transplanted it* [h] *to good soil by abundant waters, that it might bring forth branches, and bear fruit, and become a noble vine.* [9]*Say, Thus says the Lord God: Will it thrive? Will he not pull up its roots and cut off its branches,* [i] *so that all its fresh sprouting leaves wither? It will not take a strong arm or many people to pull it from its roots.* [10]*Behold, when it is transplanted, will it thrive? Will it not utterly wither when the east wind strikes it—wither away on the bed where it grew?"*

[11]*Then the word of the Lord came to me:* [12]*"Say now to the rebellious house, Do you not know what these things mean? Tell them, Behold, the king of Babylon came to Jerusalem, and took her king and her princes and brought them to him to Babylon.* [13]*And he took one of the seed royal and made a covenant with him, putting him under oath. (The chief men of the land he had taken away,* [14]*that the kingdom might be humble and not lift itself up, and that by keeping his covenant it might stand.)* [15]*But he rebelled against him by sending ambassadors to Egypt, that they might give him horses and a large army. Will he succeed? Can a man escape who does such things? Can he break the covenant and yet escape?* [16]*As I live, says the Lord God, surely in the place where the king dwells who made him king, whose oath he despised, and whose covenant with him he broke,*

in Babylon he shall die. ¹⁷*Pharaoh with his mighty army and great company will not help him in war, when mounds are cast up and siege walls built to cut off many lives.* ¹⁸*Because he despised the oath and broke the covenant, because he gave his hand and yet did all these things, he shall not escape.* ¹⁹*Therefore thus says the Lord* G<small>OD</small>*: As I live, surely my oath which he despised, and my covenant which he broke, I will requite upon his head.* ²⁰*I will spread my net over him, and he shall be taken in my snare, and I will bring him to Babylon and enter into judgment with him there for the treason he has committed against me.* ²¹*And all the pick^j of his troops shall fall by the sword, and the survivors shall be scattered to every wind; and you shall know that I, the* L<small>ORD</small>*, have spoken."*

h Cn: Heb *it was transplanted*   **i** Cn: Heb *fruit*   **j** Another reading is *fugitives*

OVERVIEW: The vine does not survive transplantation to new soil, and the punishment that this means must be borne with patience; in the end, righteousness can prevail, but the leaders of the church must be fully conscious of the weight of their responsibility (ORIGEN).

17:7-8 The Vine Taken to Good Soil

THE WEAKNESS OF THE TRANSPLANTED VINE. ORIGEN: Another crowd was taken by him, and it became a vine, less vigorous than it was when it was in the vineyard of God and on holy ground, where the sacrifices of God are celebrated, but it was transferred to Babylon as a weak vine. HOMILIES ON EZEKIEL 11.2.[1]

PUNISHMENT BORNE WITH PATIENCE. ORIGEN: One who was condemned by God does not escape his sentence and does not want to change the will of he who judges him, but he will bear it with all patience until God frees the one who he has condemned. HOMILIES ON EZEKIEL 11.2.[2]

REDEMPTION FOR ALL CREATURES. ORIGEN: When the association of such different natures is made in faith in Christ, the lion will no longer be impure, and all the animals called impure in the law of God will receive the purity of their former condition. HOMILIES ON EZEKIEL 11.3.[3]

17:12 Words to the Rebellious House

RIGHTEOUSNESS PREVAILS. ORIGEN: I am inclined to think that by the good quality of their conduct they increase yet more the agreeableness of the words of God, mixing the sweetness of the life with the sweet savor of the word. HOMILIES ON EZEKIEL 12.1.[4]

LEADERS OF THE CHURCH MUST BEWARE. ORIGEN: If we who appear to stand over the church have sinned and given place to the devil against the teaching of Paul when he says "do not give any place to the devil,"[5] in the same way the faults committed at Jerusalem mean that we provide Nebuchadnezzar with the chance to enter into the holy city and to take away those whom he chooses. HOMILIES ON EZEKIEL 12.2.[6]

17:13 A Covenant

THE COVENANT WITH GOD IS STRONG. ORIGEN: If you have the covenant with us in a blessing, Nebuchadnezzar cannot make a covenant with you. HOMILIES ON EZEKIEL 12.3.[7]

THE COVENANT CONTRASTED. ORIGEN: God makes covenant with us in a blessing; Nebuchadnezzar establishes his covenant in abuse. HOMILIES ON EZEKIEL 12.3.[8]

---

[1]SC 352:356. [2]SC 352:358. [3]SC 352:364. [4]SC 352:378. [5]Eph 4:27. [6]SC 352:382-84. [7]SC 352:386. [8]SC 352:386.

17:16 *The Covenant Broken*

THE COVENANT WITH GOD CONTRAVENES ALL OTHERS. ORIGEN: As holy Scripture tells us, God intends that the covenant with Israel is an abuse against Nebuchadnezzar. HOMILIES ON EZEKIEL 12.3.[9]

---

[9]SC 352:388.

17:22-24 THE GOODLY CEDAR
A TYPE OF THE MESSIAH

[22]*Thus says the Lord GOD: "I myself will take a sprig from the lofty top of the cedar, and will set it out; I will break off from the topmost of its young twigs a tender one, and I myself will plant it upon a high and lofty mountain;* [23]*on the mountain height of Israel will I plant it, that it may bring forth boughs and bear fruit, and become a noble cedar; and under it will dwell all kinds of beasts;*[k] *in the shade of its branches birds of every sort will nest.* [24]*And all the trees of the field shall know that I the LORD bring low the high tree, and make high the low tree, dry up the green tree, and make the dry tree flourish. I the LORD have spoken, and I will do it."*

k Gk: Heb lacks *all kinds of be*

OVERVIEW: God's judgments must be accepted for what they are, but the church is a spacious community nonetheless (ORIGEN); God's nature is to exalt and to humble (JEROME, THEODORET).

17:22 *The Cedar Sprig Planted on a High Mountain*

ACCEPTED OR REJECTED. ORIGEN: There is one who dishonors the judgment of God; there is another who honors it. HOMILIES ON EZEKIEL 12.4.[1]

PHARAOH CANNOT COME TO THE RESCUE. ORIGEN: To the one who has transgressed and has dishonored the judgment of God, Pharaoh cannot come to the rescue; he will die in the center of Babylon for his transgressions. HOMILIES ON EZEKIEL 12.4.[2]

17:23 *Planted to Grow and Bear Fruit*

LARGE IN EVERY WAY. ORIGEN: Consider the sublime grandeur of the church of Christ, to understand that according to the promise of God the word has been realized. . . . It will become a noble cedar; and under it will dwell all kinds of beasts; in the shade of its branches birds of every sort will nest. HOMILIES ON EZEKIEL 12.5.[3]

SPACE FOR REST. ORIGEN: Take the wings of the word of God, and you will be able to repose under this tree that has been planted over a high mountain. HOMILIES ON EZEKIEL 12.5.[4]

HUMILITY AND EXALTATION IN CHRIST. JEROME: The high tree humbled and the humble

---

[1]SC 352:392. [2]SC 352:392. [3]SC 352:394. [4]SC 352:394.

tree exalted refer to the passion of the Lord and Savior, "who, though he was in the form of God, did not count equality with God a theme to be grasped, but he emptied himself, taking the form of a servant,"[5] and after the resurrection, this very wood was afterwards raised high, which was fair and strong, and then made dry in death, and after reviving, received back its original strength. COMMENTARY ON EZEKIEL 5.17.22-24.[6]

GOD EXALTS AND HUMBLES. THEODORET OF CYR: He says, know that it is easy for me both to humble what is lofty and to raise up what is lowly; to make dry what is wet and to manifest what is dry to be in flower. COMMENTARY ON EZEKIEL 6.[7]

---

[5]Phil 2:6-7. [6]CCL 75:224. [7]PG 81:972.

18:1-4 THE SOUR GRAPES AND NEW LIFE

[1]*The word of the LORD came to me again:* [2]*"What do you mean by repeating this proverb concerning the land of Israel, 'The fathers have eaten sour grapes, and the children's teeth are set on edge'?* [3]*As I live, says the Lord GOD, this proverb shall no more be used by you in Israel.* [4]*Behold, all souls are mine; the soul of the father as well as the soul of the son is mine: the soul that sins shall die.*

OVERVIEW: Repentance is the key to a new relationship with God, which is wrought through Christ and made in baptism (AUGUSTINE, JEROME). It is our responsibilities that matter, not the good qualities—or the sins—of our ancestors (CHRYSOSTOM). There are three kinds of death, the death of sin, the mystical death of baptism and physical death (AMBROSE).

18:1-2 The Proverb of the Sour Grapes

THE JUSTICE OF GOD. JEROME: How good and just is the God of the law and the prophets, who keeps quiet and remains silent before the sins of the fathers and gives back to those who have not sinned! COMMENTARY ON EZEKIEL 6.18.1-2.[1]

REPENTANCE AND RESPONSIBILITY IN BAPTISM. AUGUSTINE: It was this new covenant that was prophesied about when it was said by Ezekiel that the children should not bear the iniquity of the parents, and that it should no longer be a proverb in Israel, "The fathers have eaten sour grapes, and the children's teeth are set on edge." Here lies the necessity that each person should be born again, that he might be freed from the sin in which he was born. For the sins committed afterwards can be cured by penitence, as we see is the case after baptism. ENCHIRIDION 46.[2]

REPENTANCE AND RESPONSIBILITY IN CHRIST. AUGUSTINE: For the last and supposedly strongest argument for your case, you refer to the prophetic testimony of Ezekiel, where we read that there will no longer be a proverb in which they say the parents have eaten sour grapes and the teeth of the children are on edge; the child will not die in the sin of his parent or the

---

[1]CCL 75:227. [2]EFHL 55-56*.

parent in the sin of his child, but the soul that sins shall die. You do not understand that this is the promise of the New Testament and of the other world. For the grace of the Redeemer ensured that he cancelled the paternal decree, so that each person should account for himself. AGAINST JULIAN 25.82.[3]

OUR SINS ARE WHAT MATTER. CHRYSOSTOM: It is not possible, if one person has sinned, for another to be punished. Besides, if we grant this, we shall assent to that other supposition as well, namely, that he committed sin before his birth. Therefore, just as by saying "neither has this man sinned," he did not mean that it is possible for anyone to sin before birth and be punished for this; so by saying "nor his parents" he did not imply that it is possible for anyone to be punished on account of his parents. Now, I say this because he removed this erroneous suspicion through Ezekiel. HOMILIES ON THE GOSPEL OF JOHN 56.[4]

18:4 The Soul That Sins Shall Die

DEATH AND THE FALL. AMBROSE: The soul dies to the Lord, not through natural infirmity but through the sickness caused by guilt. This type of death is not the release from this life but is the fall resulting from sin. ON HIS BROTHER SATYRUS 2.36.[5]

THREE KINDS OF DEATH. AMBROSE: There are three kinds of death. One is the death due to sin, concerning which it was written, the soul that sins shall itself die." Another death is the mystical, when someone dies to sin and lives to God;[6] concerning this the apostle likewise says, or we were buried with him by means of baptism into death. The third is the death by which we complete our lifespan with its functions—I mean the separation of the soul and body. Thus we perceive that the one death is an evil, if we die on account of sins, but the other, in which the deceased has been justified of sin, is a good, while the third

stands in between, for it seems good to the just and fearful to most people; although it gives release to all, it gives pleasure to few. DEATH AS A GOOD 2.3.[8]

THE INDIVIDUAL SINNER MATTERS. AUGUSTINE: The spiritual penalty always pertained only to the sinner. LETTER 1*.1.[9]

OUR OBLIGATIONS RESULT FROM OURSELVES. AUGUSTINE: This whole passage is so constructed as to show that bad children are not given relief because of good parents or good children oppressed because of bad parents. So having first established this absolutely true and rock-firm principle on our own account, we go on now to examine what our obligations are in our relations with others; and here we must be very careful to distinguish between the effect of salvation, which we must seek for ourselves, and the consideration that we must show to our neighbors. If you are good, you are good with your own goodness, not with someone else's. And yet through that goodness of yours with which you are good you also rejoice over another's goodness together with him, not by exchanging goodnesses but by exchanging love. SERMON 35.2.[10]

EVERYONE IS WEAK, INCLUDING OUR SOULS. JEROME: Show me a body that has never been sick or one that is sure of enjoying good health forever after sickness, and I will show you a soul that has never sinned. AGAINST THE PELAGIANS 3.11.[11]

BAPTISM MEANS A RADICAL NEW START. JEROME: The soul therefore that has not sinned shall live. Neither the virtues nor the vices of parents are imputed to their children. God takes account of us only from the time when we are born anew in Christ. LETTERS 60.8.[12]

---

[3]FC 35:393*. [4]FC 41:87*. [5]FC 22:212*. [6]Rom 6:11. [7]Rom 6:4. [8]FC 65:71*. [9]FC 81:11. [10]WSA 3 2:172. [11]FC 53:364. [12]NPNF 2 6:126.

18:5-9 THE RIGHTEOUS SHALL LIVE

⁵*"If a man is righteous and does what is lawful and right—* ⁶*if he does not eat upon the mountains or lift up his eyes to the idols of the house of Israel, does not defile his neighbor's wife or approach a woman in her time of impurity,* ⁷*does not oppress any one, but restores to the debtor his pledge, commits no robbery, gives his bread to the hungry and covers the naked with a garment,* ⁸*does not lend at interest or take any increase, withholds his hand from iniquity, executes true justice between man and man,* ⁹*walks in my statutes, and is careful to observe my ordinances[1]—he is righteous, he shall surely live, says the Lord God.*

l Gk: Heb *has kept my ordinances, to deal truly*

OVERVIEW: To be generous with food means living the life of the Beatitudes, and to be generous with clothing fulfills our baptismal life (JEROME). To hold fast under persecution means being strong in the face of a victory already won (VALERIAN).

18:7 Give Food and Clothing to the Needy

BREAD FOR THE HUNGRY. JEROME: This bread the just person gives to the hungry, of whom it is said in Scripture, blessed are those who hunger and thirst after righteousness, for they shall be satisfied.[1] COMMENTARY ON EZEKIEL 6.18.5-9.[2]

CLOTHING TO THE NAKED, IN BAPTISM. JEROME: Let us give the garment of Christ to those who are naked in faith and virtues, about which it is written, "as many are baptized into Christ put on Christ."[3] COMMENTARY ON EZEKIEL 6.18.5-9.[4]

18:9 Execute True Justice

THE VICTORY ALREADY WON. VALERIAN: Therefore, dearly beloved, let us shed our tears every day and ask this teacher of virtues to teach us to be devout to these profitable wounds. May he show us how to expose our breast in this warfare and sustain every onset of injury. It is not hard to enter a fight where you see that a victory has already been won. That which is taught by example quickly lodges in our minds. HOMILY 17.4.[5]

---

[1]Mt 5:6. [2]CCL 75:239. [3]Gal 3:27. [4]CCL 75:239. An allusion to the white baptismal garment. [5]FC 17:412.

[18:10-20 EACH GENERATION RESPONSIBLE FOR ITS OWN ACTIONS]

18:21-24 THE WICKED PERSON
WHO REPENTS SHALL LIVE

²¹But if a wicked man turns away from all his sins which he has committed and keeps all my statutes and does what is lawful and right, he shall surely live; he shall not die. ²²None of the transgressions which he has committed shall be remembered against him; for the righteousness which he has done he shall live. ²³Have I any pleasure in the death of the wicked, says the Lord God, and not rather that he should turn from his way and live? ²⁴But when a righteous man turns away from his righteousness and commits iniquity and does the same abominable things that the wicked man does, shall he live? None of the righteous deeds which he has done shall be remembered; for the treachery of which he is guilty and the sin he has committed, he shall die.

OVERVIEW: Repentance is about turning to God (TERTULLIAN), who calls us back to him (AUGUSTINE). Repentance is a gift, and it should happen now, without delay (CAESARIUS), for God's mercy is to be trusted (MARTIN), and sin destroys the soul (CYRIL OF JERUSALEM). The sins of which we repent are ours, not those of our parents (JEROME, THEODORET). God condemns the sins we have committed, not us (JEROME), which is why God wants us to repent (FASTIDIUS). The life of faith, however, means acknowledging evil for what it is (AUGUSTINE). Hence, the confession of our sins is an integral part of our life on earth (TERTULLIAN, CASSIODORUS, CHRYSOSTOM), since sins are committed by the righteous and the unrighteous alike (PACIAN, JEROME). Christ, the sinless one, delights in the conversion of sinners (CLEMENT OF ALEXANDRIA).

18:21 *The Wicked Person Turns from Sin*

REPENTANCE IS ABOUT TURNING. TERTULLIAN: Repentance, then, means life, since it is preferred to death. You must, as a sinner like myself —yes, and a lesser one than I, for I recognize my eminence in evil—lay hold on it and grip it fast, as one who is shipwrecked holds to a plank of salvation. It will buoy you up when you are plunged into a sea of sin and bear you safely to the haven of divine mercy. ON PENITENCE 4.[1]

SIN IS TERRIBLE. CYRIL OF JERUSALEM: Sin is a terrible thing, and the most grievous disease of the soul is iniquity, which corrodes the fiber of the soul and makes it liable to eternal fire. It is an evil freely chosen, the product of the will. CATECHETICAL LECTURES 2.1.[2]

GOD CALLS US BACK TO HIM. AUGUSTINE: Behold how God advises and arouses you so that you may be converted from your sins and be saved, though late. Behold how he urges one liable to death to live; how gently, how kindly he calls, not refusing his fatherly devotion even to sinners. He continues to call children those who have lost God their Father by their sins. ON THE CHRISTIAN LIFE 2.[3]

REPENTANCE POSSIBLE FOR ALL. AUGUSTINE: There are people who, as soon as they begin to think about the evil things they have done, assume that they can not be pardoned; and on the assumption that they can not be pardoned, they give their souls over to destruction from that moment. . . . They perish from despair, whether before they come to believe at all or whether they

---

[1]ACW 28:20*. [2]FC 61:96. [3]FC 16:13*.

are already Christians and have fallen by evil living into various sins and vicious forms of behavior. SERMON 87.10.[4]

REPENTANCE IS A GIFT. CAESARIUS OF ARLES: Since no one makes a fool of the Lord,[5] he deceives himself if having led a wicked life for a long time he arises to seek life when he is already half-dead. He should listen to the prophet say, "If the sinner turns away from his sins" —if he turns away, he says, not if he only talks about it—"he shall live because of the virtue he has practiced." Surely you have noticed that healing medicine of this kind must be asked with the lips, but it must be brought to completion by deeds. That gift of repentance that is received at the end of one's life should be believed to be profitable if it is accepted with a sublime intention, much crying and groaning, and is further enhanced by more abundant almsgiving. However, there must be as much piety on the part of sinners in healing the wounds as the intention of the mind was quick and active in doing evil. SERMON 209.1.[6]

REPENT NOW. CAESARIUS OF ARLES: A person who is always uncertain of his life is also swift to apply the remedy of his salvation. The same one who gave us assurance by the words, "On whatever day the sinner is converted, all his iniquities will be forgiven," also wanted to make us careful when he said, "Delay not to be converted to the Lord, and defer it not from day to day." SERMON 56.3.[7]

DO NOT DELAY. CAESARIUS OF ARLES: The person who believes that even if he does penance for his sins the divine mercy will not forgive him wrongly despairs, while one who defers the remedy of repentance to a much later day is presumptuous. Just as it is said to those who despair, "On whatever day the sinner is converted, all his iniquities will be forgotten," so it is said to the presumptuous, "Delay not to be converted to the Lord."[8] SERMON 64.4.[9]

DELAY IS IMPOSSIBLE. CASSIODORUS: Once the mind is lent brightness at the very beginning of good works and begins to recognize the truth, you are not to imagine that after sinning a delay ensues by reason of which it is enabled to be heard. EXPOSITIONS OF THE PSALMS 5.5.[10]

GOD'S MERCY NOT TO BE DOUBTED. MARTIN OF BRAGA: Do not doubt the mercy of God. Only perform in your heart your pact with God not to practice the worship of demons any more, or to worship anything except the God of heaven, or to commit homicide, or to be involved in adultery or fornication or theft or to swear falsely. And when you have promised God this with your whole heart and have not committed these sins again, hope confidently for pardon from God. . . . True repentance consists of a person not doing again the evils that he did but asking pardon for past sins and watching in the future not to fall into them again. REFORMING THE RUSTICS 17.[11]

OUR SINS ARE OURS ALONE. JEROME: The sins of the parents do not fall on the children, nor does a wicked parent burden a just child, nor are some punished for the crimes of others. One alone who was wrong and sinful before, if he afterwards becomes penitent and turns to better things, wipes out his former sins and is not judged by what he had done wrong, but he is received into my flock with a renewed virtue. COMMENTARY ON EZEKIEL 6.18.21-22.[12]

ALL SOULS ARE MINE. THEODORET OF CYR: I will not allow those punishments that the parents avoided to be repeated by their children, since I am the Lord of both of them and have the same care for all of them. For all souls are mine, and the soul that sins pays the penalty. Thus God teaches us forms of justice, and the way people can delight in life and be released by prayer and become free. COMMENTARY ON·EZEKIEL 6.18.[13]

---

[4]WSA 3 3:413. [5]Gal 6:7. [6]FC 66:90. [7]FC 31:280-81*. [8]Sir 5:7 (5:8 Vulg.). [9]FC 31:310-11*. [10]ACW 51:83. [11]FC 62:83. [12]CCL 75:245. [13]PG 81:972.

18:23 *The Living Repentant Sinner*

WE ARE NOT CONDEMNED. JEROME: It is the will of God "who desires all people to be saved and to come to the knowledge of the truth."[14] For everywhere that the purpose of God appears to be severe and stern, it is not the people but the sins that he condemns. COMMENTARY ON EZEKIEL 6.18.23.[15]

GOD ENCOURAGES US TO REPENT. FASTIDIUS: See, then, how God instructs and incites you, so that you may be converted from your sins, late though it is, and come to salvation. See how he exhorts you, doomed to death as you are, so that you may live; and with what sweetness and gentle compassion he cajoles you, so that he does not deny a father's love even to the sinner. ON THE CHRISTIAN LIFE.[16]

BE CONVERTED AND LIVE. AUGUSTINE: You have wished to die by sinning; he wishes you to live by being converted. O foolish, irreverent and ungrateful sinner, you do not yield in this respect to God, who wishes to have mercy on you, who prefers to save you because of his own goodness than to destroy you because of your sins. ON THE CHRISTIAN LIFE 2.[17]

SEEING EVIL FOR WHAT IT IS. AUGUSTINE: Dearly beloved, if you are good, you must put up with the bad; if you are bad, you must imitate the good. The fact is, on this threshing floor grains can degenerate into chaff, and again grains can be resurrected from chaff. This sort of thing happens every day, my dear brothers and sisters; this life is full of both painful and pleasant surprises. Every day people who seemed to be good fall away and perish; and again, ones who seemed to be bad are converted and live. "God," you see, "does not desire the death of the wicked but only that they may turn back and live." SERMON 223.2.[18]

CONFESSION ESSENTIAL. CASSIODORUS: One person prays to the Lord almost all his life, another is converted in middle age, another is saved at his life's end.... God with merciful patience awaits the hour of our conversion at any time, and so he bears with the guilty and awaits sinners with the words, "It is not my will that a sinner should die, but that he be converted and live." The only requirement is that in this life we confess all our sinning, for here we fail through human frailty. EXPOSITIONS OF THE PSALMS 55.10.[19]

GOD WANTS US TO REPENT. CHRYSOSTOM: If it had not been his will that they should hear and be saved, he ought to have been silent, not to have spoken in parables. But now by this very thing he stirs them up, even by speaking under a veil. HOMILIES ON THE GOSPEL OF MATTHEW 45.2.[20]

REPENTANCE MEANS WANTING TO END SINNING. CHRYSOSTOM: I mean, surely I seek nothing else than a mere end of their wickedness and a stop to their evil? Surely I look for no accounting of past deeds if I see them willing to change? Do I not cry aloud each day, "Surely I have no real wish for the death of the sinner as for his conversion and life"? Do I not take every means to snatch from destruction those ensnared in deceit? Surely, after all, if I see them changing I will not hesitate? ... Surely I do not bring you from nonbeing for the purpose of destroying you? It is not in vain that I prepared the kingdom and the countless good things beyond description, was it? Did I not also make the threat of hell for the purpose of encouraging everyone by this means also to hasten toward the kingdom? HOMILIES ON GENESIS 44.9.[21]

CHRIST WITHOUT SIN. CLEMENT OF ALEXANDRIA: He takes delight in the conversion of sinners, for he desires the conversion that follows their sins. Surely, he himself is the only sinless one. CHRIST THE EDUCATOR 3.12.93.[22]

---

[14]1 Tim 2:4. [15]CCL 75:245. [16]MFC 17:99. [17]FC 16:14*. [18]*WSA* 3 6:210. [19]ACW 52:35. [20]NPNF 1 10:285*. [21]FC 82:459. [22]FC 23:269-70.

PRAYER FOR FORGIVENESS. TERTULLIAN: A petition for pardon is a full confession; because one who begs for pardon fully admits his guilt. So, too, penitence is demonstrated as acceptable to God, who desires it rather than the death of a sinner. ON PRAYER 7.[23]

18:24 The Righteous Must Not Turn from Righteousness

THE RIGHTEOUS ARE TREATED STERNLY. CHRYSOSTOM: O such strictness toward the righteous! O such abundant forgiveness toward the sinner! He finds so many different means, without himself changing, to keep the righteous in check and forgive the sinner, by usefully dividing his rich goodness. And listen how. If he frightens the sinner who persists in sins, he brings him to desperation and to the exhaustion of hope. If he blesses the righteous, he weakens the intensity of his virtue and makes him neglect his zeal, since he considers himself already blessed. For this reason he is merciful to the sinner and frightens the righteous. HOMILIES ON REPENTANCE AND ALMSGIVING 7.2.5.[24]

SIN IS A PRESENT REALITY. PACIAN OF BARCELONA: Observe every one of the sins for which the Lord makes threats; you will at once see that they are current ones. But if someone's past righteousness is not beneficial to the righteous individual in the time of his sin, then neither will the sin that has been forsaken harm the wicked individual in the time of his righteousness. LETTER 3.16.2.[25]

AS EACH IS FOUND, SO EACH WILL BE JUDGED. JEROME: As a sinner who is now just is not harmed by his earlier offenses, so previous righteous deeds do not help a sinner who was once righteous; as each is found, so will it be judged in him. COMMENTARY ON EZEKIEL 6.18.24.[26]

---

[23]ANF 3:684*. [24]FC 96:90. [25]FC 99:57-58. [26]CCL 75:245.

18:25-29 THE WAY OF THE LORD IS JUST

[25]Yet you say, "The way of the Lord is not just." Hear now, O house of Israel: Is my way not just? Is it not your ways that are not just? [26]When a righteous man turns away from his righteousness and commits iniquity, he shall die for it; for the iniquity which he has committed he shall die. [27]Again, when a wicked man turns away from the wickedness he has committed and does what is lawful and right, he shall save his life. [28]Because he considered and turned away from all the transgressions which he had committed, he shall surely live, he shall not die. [29]Yet the house of Israel says, "The way of the Lord is not just." O house of Israel, are my ways not just? Is it not your ways that are not just?

OVERVIEW: The way of the Lord is the yoke of Christ, and it is up to us not to make it more burdensome than it need be through our sins (CAS-SIAN), since we have the opportunity to repent all the time (FULGENTIUS) and face the justice of God (CASSIODORUS, THEODORET).

18:25 *The Lord's Way Just*

TAKING THE YOKE OF CHRIST. JOHN CASSIAN: When we make the Lord's yoke heavy, with blasphemous spirit we accuse as harsh and rough either the yoke itself or Christ who imposes it. CONFERENCE 24.25.5.[1]

18:26 *Iniquity Means Death*

REPENTANCE MEANS TURNING AWAY. FULGENTIUS OF RUSPE: "When the wicked turn away from the wickedness they have committed and do what is lawful and right, they shall save their life. Because they considered and turned away from all the transgressions that they had committed, they shall surely live. They shall not die." Each statement is true because each is divine, whether it is that the just person when he will have turned away from his righteousness, all his righteous deeds will be consigned to oblivion, or whether it

is that the wicked person, when he will have been converted from wickedness to righteousness, will be saved, and all his wicked deeds will not be remembered. LETTER 7.10.[2]

18:28 *Repentance Means Living*

MERCY OFFERED TO ALL. CASSIODORUS: God's justice promises scourges to those without hope but mercy to those who hope in him. EXPOSITIONS OF THE PSALMS 31.10.[3]

GOD'S JUSTICE. THEODORET OF CYR: You see my just sentence and you dare to accuse me of injustice? You yourselves needed to be accused; you actually prefer injustice in the face of such an obvious example of justice by your own judge. COMMENTARY ON EZEKIEL 6.18.[4]

---

[1]ACW 57:847*. [2]FC 95:359*. [3]ACW 51:312*. [4]PG 81:977.

18:30-32 THE COMMANDMENT TO REPENT

[30]*Therefore I will judge you, O house of Israel, every one according to his ways, says the Lord GOD. Repent and turn from all your transgressions, lest iniquity be your ruin.*[o] [31]*Cast away from you all the transgressions which you have committed against me, and get yourselves a new heart and a new spirit! Why will you die, O house of Israel?* [32]*For I have no pleasure in the death of any one, says the Lord GOD; so turn, and live.*

o Or *so that they shall not be a stumbling block of iniquity to you*

OVERVIEW: Repentance is a challenge to Israel and leads to the promised land (JEROME); the new heart and new spirit means a new way of life (CYRIL OF JERUSALEM, PACHOMIUS). God had always intended that we should know repentance (EZNIK) and the healing power of forgiveness (BASIL, CAESARIUS), for confession is

a prayer that will always be answered (CASSIODORUS).

18:30 *Everyone Will Be Judged*

ISRAEL MUST REPENT. JEROME: This word is rightly directed against Israel, so that they might repent and leave behind their iniquities, their transgressions, with which they have sinned against God. COMMENTARY ON EZEKIEL 6.18.30-31.[1]

REPENTANCE LEADS TO THE PROMISED LAND. JEROME: These words show us that the mind must not fail to believe in the promised blessings and give way to despair; and the soul once marked out for perdition must not refuse to apply remedies on the ground that its wounds are past curing. LETTER 122.1.[2]

18:31 Cast Away All Transgressions

THE GOD OF THE NEW HEART. JEROME: "Get yourselves a new heart and a new spirit" means leaving behind the old age of the letter and living in the newness of the spirit. The new heart of Israel is to believe in him who before had denied them; the new heart is to forsake the idols of the Gentiles, to despise dead things and to believe in him who is "God of the living."[3] COMMENTARY ON EZEKIEL 6.18.31.[4]

A NEW HEART AND NEW SPIRIT. CYRIL OF JERUSALEM: "Make for yourselves a new heart and a new spirit" that you may become a subject of joy for the citizens of heaven. For if there is joy "over one sinner who repents,"[5] according to the Gospel, how much more will the salvation of so many souls gladden the blessed saints? You have entered on a good and glorious course: run the holy race in good earnest. CATECHETICAL LECTURES 1.1.[6]

BELIEVERS MUST LIVE. PACHOMIUS: Why are you dying? Do not go into the trap. These are the reminders given to the believers, that by walking in them and striving in the commandments they will do the works worthy of eternal life. LETTERS 3.9.[7]

18:32 Turn to the Lord and Live

WHAT REPENTANCE MEANS. JEROME: "I do not want you to die." He did not say "turn," unless those who were once with God and afterwards deserted his company and "live" through penitence, you who are dead through sin. Therefore Israel is believed to be dead because it does not turn back to its original state. COMMENTARY ON EZEKIEL 6.18.32.[8]

GOD'S PURPOSE. EZNIK OF KOLB: God knows everything beforehand. But there is that which he wills, and there is that which he does not. He willed to bring the flood, but it was not his will that by means of the flood humans and animals alike would be exterminated. He was brought to do what he did not will by the unworthy, arrogant couplings of the race. ON GOD 235.[9]

FORGIVENESS MEANS HEALING. BASIL THE GREAT: Remember the compassion of God, how he heals with olive oil and wine. Do not despair of salvation. Recall the memory of what has been written, how he that falls rises again, and he that is turned away turns again, he that has been smitten is healed, he that is caught by wild beasts escapes and he that confesses is not rejected. The Lord does not want the death of the sinner, but that he return and live. Do not be contemptuous like one who has fallen into the depths of sins. LETTER 44.[10]

TURNING TO THE MERCY OF GOD. CAESARIUS OF ARLES: As we shudder at the wounds of our sins as at deadly poisons, let us apply ourselves to almsgiving, prayer and fasting. Above all, by a charity that loves not only friends but even enemies, let us have recourse to the mercy of that heavenly physician to recover the health of our souls as if by spiritual remedies. For he said, "I take no pleasure in the death of the sinner but rather in the wicked person's conversion, that he may live."[11] SERMONS 150.5.[12]

---

[1]CCL 75:247. [2]NPNF 2 6:226*. [3]Mt 22:32. [4]CCL 75:247. [5]Lk 15:7. [6]FC 61:91*. [7]CS 47:56. [8]CCL 75:248. [9]EKOG 134*. [10]FC 13:114*. [11]Ezek 33:11. [12]FC 47:327*.

**CONFESSION MEANS ASKING FOR FORGIVE-
NESS.** CASSIODORUS: The prayer that frees us
from faults wins the heart of the judge and wipes
away sins; mercy cannot be withheld from the
one who asks for it, as humility fires us to pray
unceasingly for forgiveness. All this is achieved
by the devoted Lord, for he does not wish to condemn those whom he forewarns. EXPOSITIONS
OF PSALM 140.1.[13]

---

[13]ACW 53:393*.

[19:1-14 LAMENTATION FOR THE PRINCES OF ISRAEL]

20:1-26 ISRAEL'S IDOLATRY AND REBELLION

⁵*And say to them, Thus says the Lord GOD: On the day when I chose Israel, I swore to the seed
of the house of Jacob, making myself known to them in the land of Egypt, I swore to them, saying,
I am the LORD your God. ⁶On that day I swore to them that I would bring them out of the land of
Egypt into a land that I had searched out for them, a land flowing with milk and honey, the most
glorious of all lands. ⁷And I said to them, Cast away the detestable things your eyes feast on, every
one of you, and do not defile yourselves with the idols of Egypt; I am the LORD your God. ⁸But they
rebelled against me and would not listen to me; they did not every man cast away the detestable
things their eyes feasted on, nor did they forsake the idols of Egypt.*

*Then I thought I would pour out my wrath upon them and spend my anger against them in the
midst of the land of Egypt. ⁹But I acted for the sake of my name, that it should not be profaned in
the sight of the nations among whom they dwelt, in whose sight I made myself known to them in
bringing them out of the land of Egypt. ¹⁰So I led them out of the land of Egypt and brought them
into the wilderness. ¹¹I gave them my statutes and showed them my ordinances, by whose observance man shall live. ¹²Moreover I gave them my sabbaths, as a sign between me and them, that
they might know that I the LORD sanctify them. . . .*

²⁵*Moreover I gave them statutes that were not good and ordinances by which they could not
have life; ²⁶and I defiled them through their very gifts in making them offer by fire all their firstborn, that I might horrify them; I did it that they might know that I am the LORD.*

OVERVIEW: The infidelity of the people has
been occurring for a long time (CHRYSOSTOM).
The sabbath is given as a rest (AUGUSTINE),
and is for the people's benefit (CHRYSOSTOM,

AUGUSTINE). But the statutes of the Lord need to be changed, since they were made for an imperfect age (AMBROSE, JEROME, JOHN OF DAMASCUS), and the gospel requires change (JOHN CASSIAN, CHRYSOSTOM). God's statutes can still benefit the people by testing them (ORIGEN).

20:5 Infidelity

INFIDELITY LONG AGO. CHRYSOSTOM: Is it not true that from the beginning and long before today you lived with countless transgressions of the law? Did not the prophet Ezekiel accuse you ten thousand times when he brought in the two harlots, Oholah and Oholibah, and said, "You built a brothel in Egypt, you passionately loved barbarians, and you worshiped strange gods." DISCOURSES AGAINST JUDAIZING CHRISTIANS 6.2.5.[1]

20:12 The Sabbath Is Given

THE SABBATH'S PERFECT REST. AUGUSTINE: It is this truth that we shall realize perfectly when we shall be perfectly at rest and perfectly see that it is he who is God. CITY OF GOD 22.30.[2]

THE BENEFITS OF THE SABBATH. CHRYSOSTOM: For indeed the sabbath did at first confer many and great benefits; for instance, it made them gentle toward their household and humane; it taught them God's providence in the creation; as Ezekiel says, it trained them by degrees to abstain from wickedness and disposed them to regard the things of the Spirit. HOMILIES ON THE GOSPEL OF MATTHEW 39.3.[3]

20:25 Statutes That Were Not Good

GOD'S PRECEPTS ARE FOR OUR OWN GOOD. AUGUSTINE: But, why should I not say that the requirements of ancient ceremonies are not good because people are not justified by them; they are figures that foreshadow the grace, by which we are justified. . . . They are not bad, because they

were precepts of divine origin, adapted to times and people, although in this estimate I am supported by the prophetic statement in which God said that he had given to that people "statutes that were not good." It happens that he did not say that they were bad but only that they were not good: that is, such that with them, people become good; without them, they do not. I would like your kind sincerity to inform me whether any oriental saint who comes to Rome and fasts on Saturday—except the eve of Easter—is acting deceitfully. If we say that is wrong, we shall condemn the Roman church and also many places near it and others somewhat further away, where the same custom continues to be observed. LETTER 82.[4]

FOR AN IMPERFECT AGE. AMBROSE: He cannot impart perfect precepts to an imperfect age, because it cannot bear them. LETTER 68.[5]

THE DEMANDS OF THE GOSPEL. JOHN CASSIAN: Whoever lives in the light of gospel grace and overcomes evil not by resisting it but by putting up with it, not hesitating of his own will to offer his other cheek to the one who is striking his right; who gives his cloak as well to the one who wants to go to law against him for his coat, who loves his enemies and prays for those who slander him his person has put off the yoke of sin and broken its chains. For he does not live under the law, which does not destroy the seeds of sin. CONFERENCE 21.33.6-7.[6]

DOUBTFUL STATUTES NEED CHANGING. CHRYSOSTOM: To convince you that these laws contribute not to any virtue but were given to them as a sort of curb, providing them with an occasion of perpetual labor, hear what the prophet says concerning them: "I gave them statutes that were not good." What does "not good" mean? Statutes that did not contribute greatly

---

[1]FC 68:152*. [2]FC 24:510*. [3]NPNF 1 10:257*. [4]FC 12:400*. [5]FC 26:406. [6]ACW 57:746*.

toward virtue. Therefore he adds also, "and ordinances whereby they shall not live." HOMILIES ON I CORINTHIANS 7.9.[7]

IN THE END, BENEFICIAL. JEROME: [Israel] received statutes that were not good and commandments that were altogether evil whereby it should not live but should be punished through them. LETTER 79.10.[8]

TO BE CHANGED BY GOD. JOHN OF DAMASCUS: God finds fault with the commandments of the Old Testament, for he says, "I gave them statutes that were not good and ordinances by which they could not have life," because of their hardness of heart. ON DIVINE IMAGES 2.15.[9]

STATUTES GIVEN AS A TEST. ORIGEN: Having forgotten the benefits and marvels performed by God, they set up the head of a calf. For this reason, therefore, precepts are given to them by which they are tested. Hence it is that through the prophet Ezekiel the Lord says to them, "I gave you precepts and ordinances that were not good, by which you will not live." For when they were tested in the precepts of the Lord, they were not found faithful. HOMILIES ON EXODUS 7.2.[10]

THE TWO LEVELS OF MEANING. ORIGEN: We hold, then, that the law has a twofold sense—the one literal, the other spiritual—as has been shown by some before us. Of the first or literal sense it is said, not by us but by God, speaking in one of the prophets, that "the statutes are not good, and the judgments not good"; whereas, taken in a spiritual sense, the same prophet makes God say that "his statutes are good, and his judgments are good." AGAINST CELSUS 7.20.[11]

---

[7]NPNF 1 12:38*. [8]NPNF 2 6:168*. [9]JDDI 62*. [10]FC 71:302-3. [11]ANCL 23:443.

[20:27-31 ISRAEL'S FAITHLESSNESS]

20:32-39 GOD TO PURGE ISRAEL

[32]"*What is in your mind shall never happen—the thought, 'Let us be like the nations, like the tribes of the countries, and worship wood and stone.'*

[33] "*As I live, says the Lord GOD, surely with a mighty hand and an outstretched arm, and with wrath poured out, I will be king over you.* [34]*I will bring you out from the peoples and gather you out of the countries where you are scattered, with a mighty hand and an outstretched arm, and with wrath poured out;* [35]*and I will bring you into the wilderness of the peoples, and there I will enter into judgment with you face to face.* [36]*As I entered into judgment with your fathers in the wilderness of the land of Egypt, so I will enter into judgment with you, says the Lord GOD.* [37]*I will*

make you pass under the rod, and I will let you go in by number.[u] [38]*I will purge out the rebels from among you, and those who transgress against me; I will bring them out of the land where they sojourn, but they shall not enter the land of Israel. Then you will know that I am the* LORD.

[39]*As for you, O house of Israel, thus says the Lord* GOD: *Go serve every one of you his idols, now and hereafter, if you will not listen to me; but my holy name you shall no more profane with your gifts and your idols.*

u Gk :Heb *bring you into the bond of the covenant*

OVERVIEW: The new Passover will be a critical time, since it will separate those who are to be saved from those who will fall away (ORIGEN, TERTULLIAN, EUSEBIUS).

20:32 Let Us Be Like the Nations

THE NEW PASSOVER TO COME. ORIGEN: The first Passover belongs to the first people; the second Passover is ours. For we were "impure in soul,"[1] who "used to worship wood and stone" and "not knowing God, we used to serve those things that by nature were not gods."[2] HOMILIES ON EXODUS 7.4.[3]

20:34 Gathered from the Nations

SEPARATION A MARK OF FIDELITY. TERTULLIAN: He commands us to be completely separated from idolatry and have no close dealing with it, because even the earthly serpent sucks people into its jaws at a distance with its breath. THE CHAPLET 10.7.[4]

20:36 Judgment Will Come

FEW WILL SURVIVE. EUSEBIUS OF CAESAREA: Here is a clear witness that but few will come under God's staff and that this will be when the rest of Israel has fallen away from the promises. I have proved that the divine prophecies did not foretell good things to all the members of the Jewish race universally and indiscriminately whatever happened, to the evil and unholy and those who were the reverse, but to few of them and those easily numbered, in fact to those of them who believed in our Lord and Savior or those justified before his coming. I, therefore, consider that I have shown sufficiently that the divine promises were fulfilled not indiscriminately to all the Jews and that the oracles of the prophets are not more applicable to them than to those of the Gentiles who have received the Christ of God. PROOF OF THE GOSPEL 2.3.60*.[5]

---

[1]Num 9:10. [2]Gal 4:8. [3]FC 71:305-6. [4]FC 40:254. [5]POG 1:99*.

20:40-44 GOD TO SHOW MERCY ON THE OBEDIENT

[40]*For on my holy mountain, the mountain height of Israel, says the Lord* GOD, *there all the house of Israel, all of them, shall serve me in the land; there I will accept them, and there I will require your contributions and the choicest of your gifts, with all your sacred offerings.* [41]*As a*

pleasing odor I will accept you, when I bring you out from the peoples, and gather you out of the countries where you have been scattered; and I will manifest my holiness among you in the sight of the nations. ⁴²*And you shall know that I am the LORD, when I bring you into the land of Israel, the country which I swore to give to your fathers.* ⁴³*And there you shall remember your ways and all the doings with which you have polluted yourselves; and you shall loathe yourselves for all the evils that you have committed.* ⁴⁴*And you shall know that I am the LORD, when I deal with you for my name's sake, not according to your evil ways, nor according to your corrupt doings, O house of Israel, says the Lord GOD.*

OVERVIEW: Christ is our salvation (CYRIL OF ALEXANDRIA), for he removes us from the prison of darkness (TERTULLIAN), and the work is God's grace, not our good deeds (JOHN CASSIAN).

20:40 On the Holy Mountain

THE MEANS OF OUR SALVATION. CYRIL OF ALEXANDRIA: Admittedly the divine, because it is without a body, is untouchable and entirely intact, because the divine is beyond every creature, both visible and intelligible, and in nature it is incorporeal, immaculate, untouchable and incomprehensible. Since the only-begotten Word of God, having taken a body from the holy virgin, and, as I already said over and over again, having made it his own, offered himself in an odor of sweetness to God the Father as a spotless sacrifice, in this way it is asserted that he endured on our behalf what happened to his flesh. Everything that happened to flesh would rightly be attributed to him, sin alone excepted, for it is his own body. Accordingly, since God the Word became man, he remained impassible as God, but, because he necessarily made the things of his flesh his own, it is asserted that he endured what

is according to flesh, although he is without experience of suffering in so far as he is thought of as God. LETTER 50.11.[1]

20:41 A Pleasing Odor

WE ARE TAKEN OUT OF PRISON BY CHRIST. TERTULLIAN: Consider yourselves as having been transferred from prison to what we may call a place of safety. Darkness is there, but you are light; chains are there, but you are free before God. It breathes forth a foul smell, but you are an odor of sweetness. TO THE MARTYRS 2.4.[2]

20:43-44 Restoration

SALVATION THROUGH GOD'S GRACE ALONE. JOHN CASSIAN: We are taught in the very words of the Lord that everything is granted us by God when we are not always resisting and constantly unwilling and that the whole of our salvation must be ascribed not to our deserving works but to heavenly grace. CONFERENCE 13.18.3.[3]

---

[1]FC 76:217. [2]FC 40:20*. [3]ACW 57:490*.

[20:45–24:27 JUDGMENTS AGAINST ISRAEL AND JERUSALEM]

[25:1–27:36 JUDGMENTS AGAINST THE NATIONS]

28:1-10 THE PRIDE OF TYRE AND THE REASON FOR ITS RUIN

[1]The word of the LORD came to me: [2]"Son of man, say to the prince of Tyre, Thus says the Lord GOD:

"Because your heart is proud,
    and you have said, 'I am a god,
I sit in the seat of the gods,
    in the heart of the seas,'
yet you are but a man, and no god,
    though you consider yourself as wise as
    a god—
[3]you are indeed wiser than Daniel;
    no secret is hidden from you;
[4]by your wisdom and your understanding
    you have gotten wealth for yourself,
and have gathered gold and silver
    into your treasuries;
[5]by your great wisdom in trade
    you have increased your wealth,
    and your heart has become proud in your
    wealth—

[6]therefore thus says the Lord GOD:
"Because you consider yourself
    as wise as a god,
[7]therefore, behold, I will bring strangers
    upon you,
    the most terrible of the nations;
and they shall draw their swords against the
    beauty of your wisdom
    and defile your splendor.
[8]They shall thrust you down into the Pit,
    and you shall die the death of the slain
    in the heart of the seas.
[9]Will you still say, 'I am a god,'
    in the presence of those who slay you,
though you are but a man, and no god,
    in the hands of those who wound you?
[10]You shall die the death of the
    uncircumcised
    by the hand of foreigners;
    for I have spoken, says the Lord GOD."

OVERVIEW: The prince of Tyre represents corruption and evil (JEROME) and the ongoing conflict between good and evil (ORIGEN), in which Christ's divine nature is an essential feature (ATHANASIUS, EPHREM); for all that the devil rages in himself (THEODORET). No one can be wiser than Daniel and be without sin, because Daniel confessed his sins (AMBROSE, AUGUSTINE, JEROME).

28:2 A Proud Heart

THIS PASSAGE TO BE READ AND PREACHED. ORIGEN: The bishops have directed that the case of the prince of Tyre should be examined, to say something about merits and faults, and they have ordered also that I should return to the subject of Pharaoh, king of Egypt, on certain points. HOMILIES ON EZEKIEL 13.1.[1]

LIKENED TO A CORRUPT ROMAN GOVERNOR.
JEROME: If we want to regard the prince of Tyre having the same power as that public provincial authority that is entrusted him by God, let us look at the testimony: "I say, 'You are gods, sons of the Most High, all of you; nevertheless, you shall die like mortals, and fall like any prince.'"[2] For the provinces were handed over to them to be ruled, as judges, by the emperor; they besmeared his honor, as was recently the case with Heraclinus in Africa; they have been puffed up with the mind of a tyrant against the King and their Lord, so that, dispersed throughout the world, they assume for themselves the name of gods, gods that are really called idols and inflated with pride. They fall under the judgment of the devil, into the snare of which the Savior speaks in the Gospel, "I saw Satan fall like lightning from heaven."[3] COMMENTARY ON EZEKIEL 9.28.1-10.[4]

THE COSMIC CONFLICT OF GOOD AND EVIL.
ORIGEN: In the prophet Ezekiel the "prince of Tyre" is most plainly pictured as a certain spiritual power. When these, therefore, and other similar princes of this world, each having his own individual wisdom and formulating his own doctrines and peculiar opinions, saw our Lord and Savior promising and proclaiming that he had come into the world for the purpose of destroying all the doctrines (whatever they might be) of the "knowledge falsely so called,"[5] they immediately laid snares for him, not knowing who was concealed within him. For "the kings of the earth stood up, and the rulers were gathered together against the Lord and against his Christ."[6] But their snares became known, and the plots that they had contrived against the Son of God were understood when they "crucified the Lord of glory." Therefore the apostle says, "We speak a wisdom among the perfect; yet a wisdom not of

this world or of the rulers of this world, which are coming to naught . . . a wisdom that none of the rulers of this world knew. For had they known it, they would never have crucified the Lord of glory."[7] ON FIRST PRINCIPLES 3.3.2.[8]

SATAN DEFEATED BY CHRIST. EPHREM THE SYRIAN: Who then will pay the price for the shedding of the blood of him who came in human likeness, if not [Satan], who, clothing himself in a human form, betrayed him, not because he was able to condemn and betray him but because he wished to betray him? It was not [the Lord] who killed malice. It killed itself through its works. . . . If anyone shoots an arrow against his enemy that returns to strike him, he breaks the arrow and burns his bow. In the same way, Satan, seeing that the Son's death was victory for the world and that his cross freed created beings, entered into Judas, his [chosen] vessel, and the latter went and put a cord around his neck and choked himself. COMMENTARY ON TATIAN'S DIATESSARON 20.18.[9]

THE DEVIL MAKES HIMSELF GOD. THEODORET OF CYR: The devil has fallen into such madness and is excited in such a frenzy that he has called himself God, and he has persuaded people to offer worship to him instead. COMMENTARY ON EZEKIEL 11.28.[10]

28:3 *Wiser Than Daniel*

DANIEL'S BRAVERY. AMBROSE: Who would refuse the counsel of Daniel, of whom God said, "Who is wiser than Daniel?" How can people doubt about the minds of those to whom God has given such grace? By the counsel of Moses wars were brought to an end, and for his merit's sake food came from heaven and drink from the rock. How pure must have been the soul of Daniel to

---

[1]SC 352:400. [2]Ps 82:6-7 (81:6-7 LXX, Vulg.). [3]Lk 10:18. [4]CCL 75:388. Heraclinus was a notoriously bad Roman governor. [5]1 Tim 6:20. [6]Ps 2:2. [7]1 Cor 2:6-8. [8]OFP 224-25. [9]ECTD 302-3. [10]PG 81:1089.

soften the character of barbarians and to tame the lions! What temperance was his, what self-restraint in soul and body! Not unworthily did he become an object of admiration to all, when—and all people do admire this—though enjoying royal friendships, he looked not for gold or counted the honor given him as more precious than his faith. For he was willing to endure danger for the law of God rather than to be turned from his purpose in order to gain human favor. DUTIES OF THE CLERGY 2.11.57-58.[11]

WE ARE ALL SINNERS. AUGUSTINE: This is the reason, if I am not mistaken, why in the prophet Ezekiel a certain most haughty person is asked, "Are you then wiser than Daniel?" Nor on this point can that be possibly said that some contend for in opposition to the Lord's Prayer: "For although," they say, "that prayer was offered by the apostles, after they became holy and perfect and had no sin whatever, it was not on behalf of their own selves but for imperfect and still sinful people that they said, 'Forgive us our debts, as we also forgive our debtors.' They used the word *our*, they say, "in order to show that in one body are contained both those who still have sins and themselves, who were already altogether free from sin." Now this certainly cannot be said in the case of Daniel, who (as I suppose) foresaw as a prophet this presumptuous opinion when he said so often in his prayer, "We have sinned" . . . he expresses himself in language so distinct and precise . . . and wanted above all things to commend it to our notice: "My sins," says he, "and the sins of my people." Who can contradict such evidence as this, but one who is more pleased to defend what he thinks than to find out what he ought to think? ON THE MERITS AND FORGIVENESS OF SINS AND ON INFANT BAPTISM 2.13.10.[12]

EVEN DANIEL CONFESSES HIS SINS. AUGUSTINE: Can anyone claim to be without sin, when Daniel confesses his own sins? I mean, some proud person or other was asked through the prophet Ezekiel, "Are you wiser than Daniel?" Again, the prophet also placed this Daniel among the three holy men in whom God signifies the three sorts of human beings he is going to deliver when the great tribulation[13] comes on the human race. SERMON 397.1.[14]

DANIEL UNIQUE, BUT STILL A SINNER. AUGUSTINE: Could we be better than Daniel himself, concerning whom the Lord said to the prince of Tyre by the prophet Ezekiel: "Are you wiser than Daniel?" He is unique in being included among the three just men whom God says he will deliver, doubtless showing three special types of just people, when he says he will so deliver them as not to deliver their sons with them, but they only shall be delivered: namely, Noah, Daniel and Job.[15] LETTERS 111.[16]

WE ARE ALL IMPERFECT. JEROME: The same apostle writes that God alone is wise, although both Solomon and many other holy people are called wise, and it is said, according to the Hebrew, to the prince of Tyre, "You are wiser than Daniel." Therefore, just as he alone is called the light, immortal and wise, although they are many who are immortal, and who are lights and who are wise, so also the human perfection that proceeds not from nature but from grace shows that those who seem to be perfect are imperfect. AGAINST THE PELAGIANS 2.7.[17]

---

[11]NPNF 2 10:52*. [12]NPNF 1 5:49*. The Lord's Prayer figured prominently in patristic teaching. [13]Rev 7:14. [14]WSA 3 10:435*. [15]Ezek 14:14-16. [16]FC 18:248**. [17]FC 53:305-6*.

28:11-19 LAMENTATION

¹¹*Moreover the word of the* LORD *came to me:*
¹²*"Son of man, raise a lamentation over the king of Tyre, and say to him, Thus says the Lord* GOD:

> *"You were the signet of perfection,*[p]
>> *full of wisdom*
>> *and perfect in beauty.*
> ¹³*You were in Eden, the garden of God;*
>> *every precious stone was your covering,*
> *carnelian, topaz, and jasper,*
>> *chrysolite, beryl, and onyx,*
> *sapphire,*[q] *carbuncle, and emerald;*
>> *and wrought in gold were your settings*
>> *and your engravings.*[r]
> *On the day that you were created*
>> *they were prepared.*
> ¹⁴*With an anointed guardian cherub*
>> *I placed you;*[s]
>> *you were on the holy mountain of God;*
>> *in the midst of the stones of fire you*
>> *walked.*
> ¹⁵*You were blameless in your ways*
>> *from the day you were created,*
>> *till iniquity was found in you.*
> ¹⁶*In the abundance of your trade*
>> *you were filled with violence, and*
>> *you sinned;*
> *so I cast you as a profane thing from*
>> *the mountain of God,*
> *and the guardian cherub drove you out*
>> *from the midst of the stones of fire.*
> ¹⁷*Your heart was proud because of*
>> *your beauty;*
>> *you corrupted your wisdom for the sake*
>> *of your splendor.*
> *I cast you to the ground;*
>> *I exposed you before kings,*
>> *to feast their eyes on you.*
> ¹⁸*By the multitude of your iniquities,*
>> *in the unrighteousness of your trade*
>> *you profaned your sanctuaries;*
> *so I brought forth fire from the midst of you;*
>> *it consumed you,*
> *and I turned you to ashes upon the earth*
>> *in the sight of all who saw you.*
> ¹⁹*All who know you among the peoples*
>> *are appalled at you;*
> *you have come to a dreadful end*
>> *and shall be no more for ever."*

p Heb obscure q Or *lapis lazuli* r Heb uncertain s Heb uncertain

---

OVERVIEW: The cosmic conflict is played out in all its force (ORIGEN), highlighting the potential for good (JOHN CASSIAN) and the way different people respond (SALVIAN), but also taking into account the reality of the devil who is often involved in such a response (CYRIL OF JERUSALEM). The devil was originally adorned with the beauty of the angels (GREGORY THE GREAT), but then fell (JEROME) and freely chose to take up arms against God (JOHN OF DAMASCUS, TERTULLIAN), using the serpent's temptation in the garden of paradise as the first line of assualt (AMBROSE, AUGUSTINE, EPHREM). The devil freely chose this rebellion (ORIGEN). The cherub whhho was appointed as guardian on the holy mountain was Christ (APHRAHAT). He continues to guard his fledgling churches, although their days are numbered (JEROME), even as the devil continues his assualt seeking to destroy what God has built (SALVIAN, JEROME).

28:11 *The Word of the Lord to Ezekiel About Tyre*

THE COSMIC CONFLICT. ORIGEN: We now find in the prophet Ezekiel two prophecies addressed to the prince of Tyre, the first of which might appear, before one had heard the second, to be spoken of some man who was prince of the Tyrians. For the present, therefore, we shall take nothing from the first one. But since the second is most evidently of such a kind that it cannot possibly refer to a man but must be understood of some higher power that fell from higher places and was cast down to lower and worse ones, we shall conclude that as an illustration that most clearly proves that these opposing and wicked powers were not so formed and created by nature but came from better conditions and changed for the worse; and [we shall conclude] that the blessed powers also are not of such a nature as to be unable to admit qualities the opposite of their own, supposing one of them should desire to do so and should become negligent and fail to guard with the utmost caution the blessedness of his condition. For when he who is called "prince of Tyre" is said to have been "among the holy ones" and "without stain" and set "in the paradise of God," "adorned with a crown of honor and beauty," how, I ask, can we suppose such a being to have been inferior to any of the holy ones? He is described as having been "a crown of honor and beauty" and as having walked "in the paradise of God" "without stain." How then can anyone possibly suppose that such a being was not one of those holy and blessed powers that, dwelling as they do in a state of blessedness, we must believe are endowed with no other honor than this? . . . Who is there that, hearing such sayings as this, "You were a signet of likeness and a crown of honor in the delights of the paradise of God," or this, "from the time you were created with the cherubim, I placed you on the holy mount of God," could possibly weaken their meaning to such an extent as to suppose them spoken of a human being, even of a saint, not to mention the prince of Tyre? Or what "fiery stones" can he think of, "in the midst" of

which any person could have lived? Or who could be regarded as "stainless" from the very day he was created and yet at some later time could have acts of unrighteousness found in him and be said to be "cast forth into the earth"? This certainly indicates that the prophecy is spoken of one who, not being on the earth, was "cast forth into the earth," whose holy places also are said to be polluted. These statements, therefore, from the prophet Ezekiel concerning the prince of Tyre must relate, as we have shown, to an adverse power, and they prove in the clearest manner that this power was originally holy and blessed, and that he fell from this state of blessedness and was cast down into the earth "from the time that iniquity was found in him" and that his fallen condition was not due to his nature or creation. We consider, therefore, that these statements refer to some angel, to whom had been allotted the duty of supervising the Tyrian people, whose souls also were apparently committed to his care. But what Tyre, or what souls of Tyrians we ought to understand—whether it is the city that is situated in the territory of the province of Phoenicia or some other city of which the one we know on earth is a figure, and whether the souls are those of the actual Tyrians or of the inhabitants of that Tyre that we understand spiritually—there seems no need to inquire here. For we should appear to be investigating, in a casual manner matters whose importance and obscurity certainly demand a work and treatment of their own. ON FIRST PRINCIPLES 1.5.4.[1]

ALL THAT COULD HAVE BEEN PERFECT IS LOST. JOHN CASSIAN: The Lord speaks thus to Ezekiel about him: "Son of man, raise a complaint over the prince of Tyre, and say to him, thus says the Lord God, You were the sign of perfection, full of wisdom, perfect in beauty, in the delights of the paradise of God. Every precious stone was your covering—sardius, topaz and jasper, chrysolite and onyx and beryl, sapphire and carbuncle and emerald. Gold was the

---

[1]OFP 47-49.

work of your beauty, and your borings were prepared on the day that you were created. You were a cherub stretched out and protecting, and I placed you on the holy mountain of God; you walked in the midst of stones of fire. You were perfect in your ways from the day of your creation, until iniquity was found in you. In the multitude of your doings your inner parts were filled with iniquity, and you sinned. And I cast you down from the mountain of God, and I destroyed you in the midst of the stones of fire, O protecting cherub. In your beauty your heart was lifted up; in your beauty you lost your wisdom. I threw you down on the earth, and I set you before the face of kings so that they might behold you. In the multitude of your iniquities and in the iniquity of your actions you polluted your holiness. CONFERENCE 8.8.2.[2]

28:12-13 *Full of Wisdom and Beauty*

DIFFERENT METALS, DIFFERENT PEOPLES. SALVIAN THE PRESBYTER: The sacred word mentioned kinds of metals that were different among themselves. How are different metals fused together in the same furnace? It is because by the variety of metals there is meant the different kinds of humanity. Even silver, which is a metal of more noble material, is treated in the same fires because people have condemned the gifts of a more noble nature by their degenerate lives. THE GOVERNANCE OF GOD 7.14.[3]

THE REALITY OF THE DEVIL. CYRIL OF JERUSALEM: The chief author of sin, then, is the devil, the author of all evil. Not I but the Lord has said, "The devil sins from the beginning."[4] Before him no one sinned. Nor did he sin because by nature he was of necessity prone to sin—or else the responsibility for sin would reflect on him who created him in this way—but after being created good, he became a devil by his own free choice, receiving that name from his action. Though he was an archangel, he was afterwards called devil (slanderer) from his slandering, and though he

was once a good servant of God, he was afterwards rightly named Satan, for Satan is interpreted "the adversary." This is not my teaching but that of the inspired prophet Ezekiel. For taking up a lament against him, he says, "You were a seal of resemblance and crown of beauty; you were begotten in the paradise of God," and a little further on, "Blameless you were in your conduct from the day you were created until evil was found in you." CATECHETICAL LECTURES 2.4.[5]

ANGELS ARE MESSENGERS ONLY. GREGORY THE GREAT: We should notice that the nature of angels is not said to have been made in the likeness of God but as the seal of the likeness, since as its essential nature is finer, it is suggested that God's image is expressed with greater likeness in it. The prophet immediately adds, every precious stone was your covering, carnelian, topaz and jasper, chrysolite, onyx and beryl, sapphire, carbuncle and emerald. He gave the names of nine stones, since there are nine ranks of angels. The first angel was adorned and covered with these nine since when it was set ahead of the whole multitude of angels, it was more illustrious in comparison with them. Why have I briefly listed these choirs of steadfast angels, if I am not also to comment more specifically on their functions? In Greek, angels are "messengers," and archangels are the most important messengers. We should know too that the word *angel* is the name of a service, not of a nature. The holy spirits of our heavenly homeland are always indeed spirits, but they cannot always be called angels since they are only angels when some message is communicated by them. So the psalmist says, he makes his spirits angels,[6] as if to say plainly, he who always possesses them as spirits makes them angels when he wishes. Those that communicate relatively unimportant messages are called angels and those that communicate the most important are called archangels. That is why it was not just any angel, but the archangel Gabriel, that

---

[2]ACW 57:296. [3]FC 3:205*. [4]1 Jn 3:8. [5]FC 61:98. [6]Ps 104:4 (103:4 LXX, Vulg.).

was sent to the Virgin Mary.[7] It was right that a most important angel should come on this mission, to communicate the most important message of all. FORTY GOSPEL HOMILIES 34.[8]

THE FALL OF SATAN. JEROME: He fell, for his dwelling place was always in heaven. He is the one to whom the words of Ezekiel are addressed: "You were stamped with the seal of perfection." Notice exactly what the prophet says: "the seal of perfection." He did not say to the devil, you are the sign of perfection, but the seal of perfection. God had set his impression on you and made you like to himself, but you afterwards destroyed the resemblance. You were created in the image and likeness of God. HOMILIES ON THE PSALMS 14 (Ps 81).[9]

TOOK UP ARMS AGAINST GOD. JOHN OF DAMASCUS: One of the angel powers, the marshal of one host, bore in himself no trace of natural evil from his Maker's hand but had been created for good, yet by his own free and deliberate choice he turned aside from good to evil and was stirred up by madness to the desire to take up arms against his Lord God. BARLAAM AND JOSEPH 7.[10]

DEVIL CREATED GOOD BUT CHOSE EVIL. TERTULLIAN: It If you turn to the prophecy of Ezekiel, you will at once perceive that this angel was both by creation good and by choice corrupt. For he speaks of the devil there in the person of the prince of Tyre. AGAINST MARCION 2.10.[11]

THE SERPENT IS THE DEVIL. AMBROSE: It follows that the serpent in paradise was certainly not brought into being without the will of God. In the figure of the serpent we see the devil. That the devil existed even in paradise we are informed by the prophet Ezekiel, who in discussing the prince of Tyre says, "You are in Eden, the garden of God." The prince of Tyre stands for the devil. Shall we, therefore, accuse God because we cannot comprehend the treasures—with the excep-

tion of those that he has deigned to reveal—of his majesty and wisdom that lie hidden and concealed in Christ? Yet he did reveal to us the fact that the wickedness of the devil is fruitful for humanity's salvation. This would not be the devil's intention, but the Lord makes the wickedness of him who stands in opposition to us contribute something to our salvation. The wickedness of the devil has caused the virtue and patience of one holy man to shine in a clearer light. ON PARADISE 2.9.[12]

THE DEVIL ONCE FELL. AUGUSTINE: The Manichaeans do not understand that if the devil is evil by nature, there can be no question of sin at all. They have no reply to the witness of the prophets, for example, where Isaiah, representing the devil figuratively in the person of the prince of Babylon, asks, "How you are fallen from heaven, O Day Star, son of the dawn?"[13] or where Ezekiel says, "You were in Eden, the garden of God; every precious stone was your covering." These texts indicate that the devil was for a time without sin. CITY OF GOD 11.15.[14]

THE BEAUTY OF EDEN. EPHREM THE SYRIAN:
　　Blessed is the poor person
　　who gazes on that place;
　　riches are poured in profusion
　　outside and around it;
　　chalcedony and other gems
　　lie there cast out
　　to prevent their defiling
　　the glorious earth of paradise;
　　should someone place there
　　precious stones or beryls,
　　these would appear ugly and dull
　　compared with that dazzling land.
HYMNS ON PARADISE 7.4.[15]

THE FALL OF SATAN. JEROME: He who was nurtured in a paradise of delight as one of the twelve

---

[7]Lk 1:26-27. [8]CS 123:286-87. [9]FC 48:107*. [10]LCL 34:81*. [11]ANF 3:305**. [12]FC 42:291*. [13]Is 14:12. [14]FC 14:210. [15]HOP 120*.

precious stones was wounded and went down to hell from the mount of God. AGAINST JOVIN-IANUS 2.4.[16]

THE DELIBERATE CHOICE OF EVIL. ORIGEN: He had in himself the power of admitting either good or evil. Falling away from good, he turned with his whole mind to evil. There are other created beings who, while possessing the power to choose either, by the exercise of free will flee from evil and cleave to the good. ON FIRST PRINCIPLES 1.8.3.[17]

28:14 Guardianship of the Cherub

THE ANOINTING OF THE KING. APHRAHAT: For the king who was anointed with the holy oil was called a cherub. And he was overshadowing all his people. . . . They were sitting in the shadow of the king, while he was standing at their head. And when the crown of their head fell, they were without shade. And if anyone should say that this word is spoken concerning Christ, let him accept what I write for him without dispute, and he will be persuaded that it was said with reference to the king. DEMONSTRATIONS 5.9.[18]

28:16 Cast from the Mountain of the Lord

EVEN THE CHURCHES WILL PASS AWAY. JEROME: Lord, who shall sojourn in your tent?[19] . . . The tent seems to me to be the church of this world. Now the churches that you see are taber-nacles, for we are not here as permanent dwellers but rather as those about to migrate to another place. If "this world as we see it is passing away,"[20] and it says elsewhere that "heaven and earth will pass away,"[21] if, then, heaven and earth will pass away, how much more will the stones of the churches that we see also pass away? Now that is why churches are tabernacles, because we are going to migrate from them to the holy mountain of God. What is this holy mountain of God? It says in Ezekiel against the prince of Tyre, "You have been cut off as one slain from the mountain of God." HOMILIES ON THE PSALMS 5 (Ps 14).[22]

28:18 Destruction of Tyre

THE FIRE OF SIN. SALVIAN THE PRESBYTER: What is more true than this? The fire of sin went forth from the midst of their sin, a fire that devoured the good fortune of former times. THE GOVERNANCE OF GOD 7.14.[23]

THE WORK OF SATAN IN DESTRUCTION. JEROME: He polluted the sanctification that he had received when he walked on the mountain and moved around in the middle of the fiery stones. COMMENTARY ON EZEKIEL 9.28.11-19.[24]

---

[16]NPNF 2 6:391 [17]OFP 70*. [18]NPNF 2 13:355*. [19]Ps 15:1 (14:1 LXX, Vulg.). [20]1 Cor 7:31. [21]Mt 24:35. [22]FC 48:39. [23]FC 3:206*.

[28:20–32:32 PROPHECIES AGAINST SIDON AND EGYPT]

33:1-9 EZEKIEL AS ISRAEL'S WATCHMAN

¹*The word of the LORD came to me:* ²*"Son of man, speak to your people and say to them, If I bring the sword upon a land, and the people of the land take a man from among them, and make him their watchman;* ³*and if he sees the sword coming upon the land and blows the trumpet and warns the people;* ⁴*then if any one who hears the sound of the trumpet does not take warning, and the sword comes and takes him away, his blood shall be upon his own head.* ⁵*He heard the sound of the trumpet, and did not take warning; his blood shall be upon himself. But if he had taken warning, he would have saved his life.* ⁶*But if the watchman sees the sword coming and does not blow the trumpet, so that the people are not warned, and the sword comes, and takes any one of them; that man is taken away in his iniquity, but his blood I will require at the watchman's hand.*

⁷*"So you, son of man, I have made a watchman for the house of Israel; whenever you hear a word from my mouth, you shall give them warning from me.* ⁸*If I say to the wicked, O wicked man, you shall surely die, and you do not speak to warn the wicked to turn from his way, that wicked man shall die in his iniquity, but his blood I will require at your hand.* ⁹*But if you warn the wicked to turn from his way, and he does not turn from his way; he shall die in his iniquity, but you will have saved your life."*

OVERVIEW: There is a need for the prophet, the bishop or the presbyter to speak out (AUGUSTINE, CAESARIUS, GREGORY OF NAZIANZUS, JEROME, SYMEON THE NEW THEOLOGIAN, POSSIDIUS) and reprove the wicked (JOHN). Goodness results in peace; wickedness, in wars (THEODORET).

33:2 Speak to the People

THE PROPHET MUST SPEAK. AUGUSTINE: Do you see how dangerous it is to keep silent? He dies, and rightly dies; he dies in his own wickedness and sin; his own heedlessness kills him. Yes, the one who says "I live, says the Lord," would like to find a living shepherd. But since he has been heedless, not being warned by the one who was given charge and made a watchman for this very purpose of warning him, he will die justly, and the other will be justly condemned. . . . It is our business not to keep quiet; it is your business, even if we do keep quiet, to listen to the words of the shepherd from the holy Scriptures. SERMON 46.20.[1]

THE BURDEN OF MINISTRY. CAESARIUS OF ARLES: Mine is the burden that you just heard about when the prophet Ezekiel was read. It is not enough that the day itself admonishes us to reflect on the burden; in addition such a lesson was read to excite great fear in us, so we will think about what we are carrying. Unless the One who imposed the burden on us carried it with us, we fail. SERMON 231.2.[2]

THE RISKS OF SPEAKING OUT. GREGORY OF NAZIANZUS: How are we affected by Ezekiel, the beholder and expositor of the mighty mysteries and visions? By his injunction to the watchmen not to keep silence concerning vice and the sword impending over it, a course that would profit neither themselves nor the sinners, but rather to keep watch and forewarn and thus benefit at any rate those who gave warning, if not both those

---

[1]WSA 3 2:276. [2]FC 66:185*; CCL 104:915-16.

who spoke and those who heard. IN DEFENSE OF HIS FLIGHT TO PONTUS, ORATION 2.64.[3]

THE BLESSINGS OF TRUE PEACE. THEODORET OF CYR: These words teach that it is God who gives peace to people because of goodness and allows wars to happen because of the wickedness of people who bring disaster on themselves. COMMENTARY ON EZEKIEL 13.33.[4]

33:3 Sound the Trumpet

THE CHURCH LEADER'S RESPONSIBILITY. SYMEON THE NEW THEOLOGIAN: So it is necessary for you, the shepherd of Christ's sheep, to acquire, as we have said, every virtue of body and spirit. You are the head of the body of the church of Israel that is under your rule, so that the brothers may look to you as a good pattern and imprint on themselves those excellent and royal traits of character. May your trumpet never cease to resound! It should warn some of the sword that comes on the disobedient and stubborn, so that even if they ignore you, you may save your soul from the terrible wrath of God. DISCOURSES 18.15.[5]

33:6 Watchmen Must Blow the Trumpet

BISHOPS ARE TO REPROVE THE PEOPLE. AUGUSTINE: For this reason, overseers or rulers are set over the churches to reprimand sin, not to spare it. Nor is a person fully free from blame who is not in authority but who notices in those persons he meets in social life many faults he should censure and admonish. He is blameworthy if he fails to do this out of fear of hurting feelings or of losing such things as he may rightfully enjoy in his life but to which he is unduly attached. CITY OF GOD 1.9.[6]

33:7 A Watchman for the House of Israel

A KING, PROPHET, BISHOP OR PRESBYTER. JEROME: The watchman of the house of Israel can be understood as king or a prophet; the watch-

man of the church can be understood as to be the bishop or the presbyter who has been chosen by the people, in the reading of the Scriptures, recognizing and foreseeing what the future will hold, proclaiming to the people and correcting what is wrong. COMMENTARY ON EZEKIEL 10.33.1-9.[7]

AUGUSTINE A MODEL OF THE WATCHMAN. POSSIDIUS: In all this he thought of himself as a watchman set by the Lord over the house of Israel; he preached the word in season and out of season, convincing, exhorting, rebuking and teaching with unfailing patience[8] and taking special care to teach in turn those fitted for teaching others.[9] When asked by some to take a hand in their temporal concerns, he wrote letters to various persons for them, but he regarded this occupation as a kind of forced labor that took him away from more important things. His real delight was to speak of the things of God, whether in public addresses or at home in familiar converse with his brothers. LIFE OF AUGUSTINE 19.5-6.[10]

33:8 Warn the Wicked

THERE IS ALWAYS A SPECIAL NEED TO SPEAK OUT. JOHN OF DAMASCUS: Although it is best for us to be ever aware of our unworthiness and to confess our sins before God, nevertheless it is good and necessary to speak when the times demand it, for I see the church that God founded on the apostles and prophets, its cornerstone being Christ his Son, tossed on an angry sea, beaten by rushing waves, shaken and troubled by the assaults of evil spirits. Impious people seek to rend asunder the seamless robe of Christ and to cut his body in pieces: his body, which is the Word of God and the ancient tradition of the church. Therefore I think it unreasonable to keep silence and hold my tongue. ON DIVINE IMAGES 1.1.[11]

---

[3]NPNF 2 7:218*. [4]PG 81:1141. [5]SNTD 220*. [6]FC 8:32-33*. [7]CCL 75:468-69. [8]2 Tim 4:2. [9]2 Tim 2:2. [10]AS 1:86. [11]JDDI 13*.

33:10-19 THE WATCHMAN'S MESSAGE
OF RIGHTEOUSNESS

¹⁰And you, son of man, say to the house of Israel, Thus have you said: 'Our transgressions and our sins are upon us, and we waste away because of them; how then can we live?' ¹¹Say to them, As I live, says the Lord God, I have no pleasure in the death of the wicked, but that the wicked turn from his way and live; turn back, turn back from your evil ways; for why will you die, O house of Israel? ¹²And you, son of man, say to your people, The righteousness of the righteous shall not deliver him when he transgresses; and as for the wickedness of the wicked, he shall not fall by it when he turns from his wickedness; and the righteous shall not be able to live by his righteousness *when he sins. ¹³Though I say to the righteous that he shall surely live, yet if he trusts in his righteousness and commits iniquity, none of his righteous deeds shall be remembered; but in the iniquity that he has committed he shall die. ¹⁴Again, though I say to the wicked, 'You shall surely die,' yet if he turns from his sin and does what is lawful and right, ¹⁵if the wicked restores the pledge, gives back what he has taken by robbery, and walks in the statutes of life, committing no iniquity; he shall surely live, he shall not die. ¹⁶None of the sins that he has committed shall be remembered against him; he has done what is lawful and right, he shall surely live.*

¹⁷Yet your people say, 'The way of the Lord is not just'; when it is their own way that is not just. ¹⁸When the righteous turns from his righteousness, and commits iniquity, he shall die for it. ¹⁹And when the wicked turns from his wickedness, and does what is lawful and right, he shall live by it.

t Heb *by it*

OVERVIEW: The watchman's message is about the will to live (AUGUSTINE), the challenge to fight for Christ (BENEDICT), because God will not forsake us (CAESARIUS, JOHN CASSIAN, CHRYSOSTOM). Our repentance is a matter of rejoicing on God's part (CYPRIAN, GREGORY THE GREAT), but it is also about ourselves striving for a better way of life (JEROME), wrought through the salvation of Christ alone (PSEUDO-MACARIUS), which means that we must not despair of ourselves (PALLADIUS). Rather, as in the Lord's Prayer, we should confess our sins (TERTULLIAN), for confession always results in forgiveness (FULGENTIUS, JOHN OF DAMASCUS). All these demands must, however, make us thankful to God, and not angry with him (CYRIL OF ALEXANDRIA), since God's memory is large enough to encompass all of us (ISAAC OF NINEVEH). God does not intend for human beings to perish (LEO), but unconfessed sin leads to punishment (PACIAN, EZNIK).

33:11 *The Wicked Must Turn from Sin and Live*

THE WILL TO LIVE IS NECESSARY. AUGUSTINE: You though, standing there, having made no decision to put yourself right—let me speak like this as though to a single person. Whoever you are, you do not want to put yourself right; what are you promising yourself? SERMON 40.2.[1]

---

[1]WSA 3 2:221.

THE CALL TO FIGHT FOR CHRIST. BENEDICT: We must prepare our hearts and bodies for the battle of holy obedience to his instructions. What is not possible to us by nature, let us ask the Lord to supply by the help of his grace. RULE OF ST. BENEDICT, PROLOGUE 40-41.[2]

GOD NEVER ABANDONS US. CAESARIUS OF ARLES: Let your charity believe devoutly and firmly that God never abandons a person unless he is first deserted by him. Although a person may have committed serious sins once, twice and a third time, God still looks for him. SERMON 101.2.[3]

GOD'S LOVE FOR ALL. JOHN CASSIAN: How can it be thought without great sacrilege of him who does not want a single little one to perish that he does not wish all to be saved universally but only a few instead of all? CONFERENCE 13.7.2.[4]

THE CHALLENGES OF JUDGMENT. CHRYSOSTOM: How then is he good and merciful and full of loving kindness to humankind? Even here he is merciful, and he shows in these things the greatness of his lovingkindness. For he shows us these terrors, that through being constrained by them we may be awakened to the desire of the kingdom. HOMILIES ON 2 TIMOTHY 3.[5]

REPENTANCE REJOICES GOD. CYPRIAN: He who has thus satisfied God, who by repentance for his deed, who by shame for his sin has conceived more of both virtue and faith from the very sorrow for his lapsing, after being heard and aided by the Lord, will cause the church to rejoice, which he recently had saddened, and will merit not only the pardon of God but a crown. THE LAPSED 36.[6]

FORGIVENESS ENSURED. FULGENTIUS OF RUSPE: At whatever age a person will do true penance for his sins and change his life for the better under the illumination of God, he will not be deprived of the gift of forgiveness. To PETER ON THE FAITH 39.[7]

WE NEED TO STRIVE FOR THE BETTER THINGS. JEROME: Nothing makes God so angry as when people from despair of better things cleave to those which are worse; and indeed this despair in itself is a sign of unbelief. One who despairs of salvation can have no expectation of a judgment to come. LETTER 122.1.[8]

PARDON IS PROMISED. JEROME: Now this is what he actually is saying: you have entertained sin, I have pardoned you; you have done evil, I have forgiven you; you have not repented of your sins, I have excused you: did you also have to teach evil? What the Scripture implies is this: For three sins and for four, I shall not be angered against you, says the Lord. HOMILIES ON THE PSALMS 1.[9]

LIFE IS GIVEN TO THE PENITENT. JOHN OF DAMASCUS: For the wickedness of the wicked shall not hurt him in the day that he turns from his wickedness. If he acts righteously and walks in the statutes of life, he shall surely live; he shall not die. None of his sins that he committed shall be remembered against him. Because he has made the decree of righteousness, he shall live by it. BARLAAM AND JOSEPH 32.[10]

WE ARE NOT TO PERISH. LEO THE GREAT: As a result, dearly beloved, it was necessary (by the designs of a secret plan) for the unchangeable God (whose will cannot be separated from his goodness) to complete by a deeper mystery the first intentions of his love. It was necessary that human beings, tricked into sin by the devil's wickedness, should not perish in opposition to God's plan. SERMON 22.1.2.[11]

SALVATION THROUGH CHRIST. PSEUDO-MACARIUS: For this reason the Lord descended so that he might save sinners, raise up the dead

---

[2]RSB 165. [3]FC 47:99*. [4]ACW 57:472. [5]NPNF 1 13:485*. [6]FC 36:88*. [7]FC 95:85*. [8]NPNF 2 6:225*. [9]FC 48:5. [10]LCL 34:503*. [11]FC 93:81*.

and bring new life to those wounded by death and to enlighten those who lay in darkness. The Lord truly came and called us to be God's adopted children, to enter into a holy city, ever at peace, to possess a life that will endure forever, to share an incorruptible glory. Let us each strive to come to a good end after a good beginning. Let us persevere in poverty, in our pilgrimage, living in affliction and petitions to God without any shame as we continuously knock at the door. FIFTY SPIRITUAL HOMILIES 11.15.[12]

THE LORD REQUIRES REPENTANCE. PACIAN OF BARCELONA: You, I say, who are timid after being shameless, who are bashful after sinning! You who are not ashamed to sin but are ashamed to confess! You who with an evil conscience touch the holy things of God and do not fear the altar of the Lord! You who approach the hands of the priest and who come within the sight of the angels with the boldness of innocence! You who insult the divine patience! You who bring to God a polluted soul and a profane body, as if, because God is silent, he does not know! Hear what the Lord has done and then what he has said. ON PENITENTS 6.2.[13]

REPENTANCE PREVENTS DESPAIR. PALLADIUS OF HELENOPOLIS: Now therefore, Christians, since we know from the holy Scriptures and from divine revelations how great is the grace that God dispenses to those who truly run to him for refuge and who blot out their sins through repentance, and also how, according to his promise, he rewards them with good things and neither takes vengeance according to what is just nor bring on people a punishment for their sins, let us not be in despair of our lives. LAUSIAC HISTORY 2.44.[14]

WE NEED TO KEEP TRYING. TERTULLIAN: Come now, you tightrope walker, walking on a tightrope of purity and chastity and every sort of sexual asceticism, you who, on the slender cord of a discipline like this, far from the path of truth, advance with reluctant feet, balancing the flesh by the spirit, moderating your desires by the faith, guarding your eyes through fear, why do you watch your step so anxiously? ON PURITY 10.[15]

THE PRAYER FOR FORGIVENESS. TERTULLIAN: Having considered God's generosity, we pray next for his indulgence. For of what benefit is food if, in reality, we are bent on it like a bull on his victim? Our Lord knew that he alone was without sin.[16] Therefore he taught us to say in prayer, "Forgive us our trespasses." A prayer for pardon is an acknowledgment of sin, since one who asks for pardon confesses guilt. Thus, too, repentance is shown to be acceptable to God, because God wills this rather than the death of the sinner. ON PRAYER 7.1.[17]

ADAM'S SIN FOREKNOWN. EZNIK OF KOLB: He wished that Adam's transgression had not occurred. And because God knew beforehand the transgression, he commanded him beforehand not to eat of the fruit of the tree. And because he did not submit to the order, justly he was punished. ON GOD 235.[18]

33:12 The Righteous Still Transgress

WE MUST STRIVE FOR HEAVENLY GRACE. CYPRIAN: We must press on and persevere in the faith and virtue and in the consummation of heavenly and spiritual grace, that we may be able to arrive at the palm and the crown. EXHORTATION TO MARTYRDOM 5.8.[19]

LET US BE THANKFUL TO GOD. CYRIL OF ALEXANDRIA: When God offers us conversion on whatever day one may be willing to practice it, why do they not instead crown with grateful praises him who aids them, instead of foolishly and (we might say) contumaciously opposing him? For by so doing they bring condemnation on their own heads and call down on themselves

---

[12]*PMFSH* 97. [13]FC 99:77. [14]PHF 1:281*. [15]ACW 28:81*. [16]Cf. Jn 8:49. [17]FC 40:165. [18]EKOG 134. [19]FC 36:326. .

inevitable wrath. COMMENTARY ON LUKE 149.[20]

ENDS ARE MORE IMPORTANT THAN BEGIN-NINGS. JEROME: In the lives of Christians we look not to the beginnings but to the endings. Paul began badly but ended well. The start of Judas wins praise; his end is condemned because of his treachery. LETTER 54.6.[21]

33:13 Repentance Cancels Iniquity

BELIEVE IN GOD'S MERCY. GREGORY THE GREAT: If you are righteous, fear his wrath lest you slip; if you are a sinner, believe in his mercy so that you can arise. But see, we have already fallen, we are not strong enough to stand, we lie prostrate in our evil desires. He who created us to be upright still waits, and he appeals to us to rise. He opens up his heart of love and seeks to get us back to himself again through repentance. FORTY GOSPEL HOMILIES 34.[22]

33:14-15 The Wicked Must Repent

WE MUST LOOK TO THE DEMANDS OF GOD. JOHN CASSIAN: We are taught that we must not hold obstinately to our promises but with gentle mercy must soften threats that are made from some necessity. CONFERENCE 17.25.12.[23]

GOD'S MEMORY IS LARGE ENOUGH FOR US ALL. ISAAC OF NINEVEH: Remember God, that he too might always remember you; and when he has kept you in his memory and preserved you safe to the end, you will receive every blessing from him. Do not forget him, your mind being distracted with futile concerns, lest he forget you in the time of your warfare. When you enjoy abundance, be obedient to him, so that in the time of your afflictions you may have boldness before him through the heart's persevering prayer to him. ASCETICAL HOMILIES 5.[24]

33:18 The Righteous Must Not Commit Iniquity

WE MUST NOT DESPAIR. JEROME: All this shows that the sinner must not despair of salvation if he does penance, nor should the righteous person trust in his own righteousness if he lost through his own carelessness what he had laboriously sought. COMMENTARY ON EZEKIEL 10.33.10-20.[25]

---

[20]CGSL 593* [21]NPNF 2 6:104. [22]CS 123:294. [23]ACW 57:608. [24]AHSIS 48*. [25]CCL 75:472.

33:21-26 THE TIDINGS OF JERUSALEM'S FALL

[21]*In the twelfth year of our exile, in the tenth month, on the fifth day of the month, a man who had escaped from Jerusalem came to me and said, "The city has fallen."* [22]*Now the hand of the LORD had been upon me the evening before the fugitive came; and he had opened my mouth by the time the man came to me in the morning; so my mouth was opened, and I was no longer dumb.*

[23]*The word of the LORD came to me:* [24]*"Son of man, the inhabitants of these waste places in the land of Israel keep saying, 'Abraham was only one man, yet he got possession of the land; but we are many; the land is surely given us to possess.'* [25]*Therefore say to them, Thus says the Lord GOD: You*

eat flesh with the blood, and lift up your eyes to your idols, and shed blood; shall you then possess the land? [26]*You resort to the sword, you commit abominations and each of you defiles his neighbor's wife; shall you then possess the land?"*

OVERVIEW: The words of the prophet are spoken and are fulfilled, telling of Jerusalem's hopelessness (JEROME).

THE PROPHET SPEAKS. JEROME: The mouth of the prophet is opened when he is shown that what he had foretold has in fact happened, and he proclaims it with complete freedom. COMMENTARY ON EZEKIEL 10.33.21-22.[1]

THE HOPELESSNESS OF JERUSALEM. JEROME: Jerusalem is captured and the temple is destroyed, and the poor earth of which Jeremiah wrote was left behind in Jerusalem. Those who kept vines and tilled the land live in the ruins of burned city; when they ought to repent of the things that had brought about their captivity, they blind themselves with a false hope by saying, "Abraham was only one man, yet he got possession of the land." COMMENTARY ON EZEKIEL 10.33.23-33.[2]

33:26 You Will Not Possess the Land

THE HERETIC IN THE DESERT. JEROME: Every heretic lives in ruins and in the desert and thinks that he possesses the land of Israel. COMMENTARY ON EZEKIEL 10.33.23-33.[3]

---

[1]CCL 75:473. [2]CCL 75:475-76. [3]CCL 75:477.

[33:27-29 THE LAND OF ISRAEL DESOLATED]

[33:30-33 ISRAEL WILL LISTEN BUT NOT ACT]

34:1-10 INDICTMENT OF THE SHEPHERDS WHO FAIL TO CARE FOR THEIR SHEEP

[1]*The word of the LORD came to me:* [2]*"Son of man, prophesy against the shepherds of Israel, prophesy, and say to them, even to the shepherds, Thus says the Lord GOD: Ho, shepherds of Israel who have been feeding yourselves! Should not shepherds feed the sheep?* [3]*You eat the fat, you clothe yourselves with the wool, you slaughter the fatlings; but you do not feed the sheep.* [4]*The weak you have not*

strengthened, the sick you have not healed, the crippled you have not bound up, the strayed you have not brought back, the lost you have not sought, and with force and harshness you have ruled them. [5]So they were scattered, because there was no shepherd; and they became food for all the wild beasts. [6]My sheep were scattered, they wandered over all the mountains and on every high hill; my sheep were scattered over all the face of the earth, with none to search or seek for them.

[7]*"Therefore, you shepherds, hear the word of the LORD: [8]As I live, says the Lord GOD, because my sheep have become a prey, and my sheep have become food for all the wild beasts, since there was no shepherd; and because my shepherds have not searched for my sheep, but the shepherds have fed themselves, and have not fed my sheep; [9]therefore, you shepherds, hear the word of the LORD: [10]Thus says the Lord GOD, Behold, I am against the shepherds; and I will require my sheep at their hand, and put a stop to their feeding the sheep; no longer shall the shepherds feed themselves. I will rescue my sheep from their mouths, that they may not be food for them."*

OVERVIEW: There are shepherds of all kinds, in government and in the church (JEROME). They must care for the flocks (TERTULLIAN, SYMEON THE NEW THEOLOGIAN, BENEDICT), realizing the greatness of the responsibility given to them (AUGUSTINE), since they will be called to account for their service (APHRAHAT). Bishops are capable of being haughty and become bad shepherds (JEROME, THEODORET), but they must not be negligent (CYPRIAN, CAESARIUS, GREGORY THE GREAT). Rather, they should follow the example of the good Shepherd (CHRYSOSTOM, PACHOMIUS).

34:2 Prophesy Against the Shepherds

SHEPHERDS OF ALL KINDS. JEROME: This is directed at the shepherds of Israel, whom we must take to be kings and leaders, scribes and Pharisees and teachers of the Jewish people; and the gospel community, their bishops, presbyters and deacons, or if we interpret it mystically, the angels of the various churches, to whom John wrote in his Apocalypse and whose angels daily behold the face of God. COMMENTARY ON EZEKIEL II.34.1-31.[1]

THE SHEEP HAVE BEEN LOST. TERTULLIAN: Quite clearly he states that they have caused the sheep to be lost and to be devoured by the beasts of the field; nor, if they are abandoned, could they avoid being lost in death and devoured. But he does not say that they should be restored after they have been lost in death and devoured. ON PURITY 7.[2]

CHRISTIAN LEADERSHIP A HEAVY RESPONSIBILITY. AUGUSTINE: You see, we whom the Lord has deigned, thanks to no merits of ours, to set in this high station (about which a very strict account indeed has to be rendered) have two things about us that must be clearly distinguished: one, that we are Christians, the other, that we are placed in charge. Being Christians is for our sake; being in charge is for yours. It is to our advantage that we are Christians, only to yours that we are in charge. SERMON 46.2.[3]

SHEPHERDS WILL BE CALLED TO ACCOUNT. APHRAHAT: But when the great pastor, the chief of pastors, comes, he will call and visit his sheep and will take knowledge of his flock. And he will bring forward those pastors, and will extract an account from them and will condemn them for their deeds. And those who fed the sheep well, them the chief of pastors will cause to rejoice and to inherit life and rest. DEMONSTRATIONS 10.3.[4]

---

[1]CCL 75:484. [2]ACW 28:72. [3]WSA 3 2:263. [4]NPNF 2 13:384*.

34:3 *You Do Not Feed the Sheep*

BISHOPS CAN BE HAUGHTY. JEROME: They do not look for what has perished. They do not desire to save the lost, any more than to devour those who are in the churches. They govern them harshly and infuriatingly, behaving haughtily as is expected of them. They adorn the dignity of their office with their works and take on pride instead of humility. They think that they have assumed honor rather than the burden of their work, and whoever they see coming forward in the church preaching the word of God, they set out to oppress. COMMENTARY ON EZEKIEL 11.34.1-31.[5]

BAD SHEPHERDS SET A BAD EXAMPLE. AUGUSTINE: In the same way, everyone who leads a bad life for all those to see whom he has been put in charge of, as far as he is concerned is killing even the strong ones. Any who imitate him die; whoever does not imitate him lives. SERMON 46.9.[6]

INCREASE THE FLOCK. SYMEON THE NEW THEOLOGIAN: Hasten then to increase the flock of your master! Do not turn aside to relaxations or pleasures of the body or vilely squander the wool and the fat of Christ's sheep by hoarding up the goods of the monastery for your own benefit rather than of the brothers, so that you may enjoy yourself. Do nothing whatever, do not say anything for the sake of human glory, that does not pertain to the good of your monastery. DISCOURSES 18.17.[7]

34:4 *The Weak Not Strengthened*

SHEPHERDS MUST NOT BE NEGLIGENT. CYPRIAN: And since it is incumbent on us who seem to be in charge and in the place of shepherds to guard the flock, if we should be found negligent, what will be said to us was said to our predecessors who were such negligent leaders. LETTER 8.1.[8]

THE WOUNDED SHEEP MUST BE CARED FOR. CYPRIAN: If we scorn the repentance of those who have in some degree the assurance of a bearable conscience, immediately they are drawn by the devil's invitation into heresy or schism with their wife and children, whom they had kept unharmed. And it will be charged against us on judgment day that we have not cared for the wounded sheep and have lost many innocent ones because of one wounded. LETTER 55.15.[9]

THE FEEBLE NEED ATTENTION. AUGUSTINE: As regards the feeble it is to be feared that some trial may happen to him and break him. But the sick person is already ill with some kind of greed and prevented by some kind of greed from entering on the way of God, from submitting to the yoke of Christ. Think of people who want to lead a good life, who are already determined to lead a good life and are less capable of enduring evil, while they are quite ready to do good. But it is part of a Christian's strength not only to do what is good but also to put up with what is bad. SERMON 46.13.[10]

SHEPHERDS ARE PILOTS TOO. CAESARIUS OF ARLES: Since we have been appointed by the Lord to direct the ship of his church, let us with his help and the direction of the two Testaments so govern the ship of his church that we may not through some negligence turn aside either to the right or to the left but may without effort keep a straight course of life in the midst of the great dangers of this world. Just as any ship cannot gather earthly profits without many labors, so the ship of the church cannot obtain the gains and joy of the eternal homeland without many tribulations. For just as pilots of ships, if they fail to be alert because of an excessive desire for sleep or false sense of security and do not show the sailors what they should do, immediately suffer shipwreck, so unless the church's pilots with all vigilance teach, terrify, sometimes even censure and occasionally punish lightly, at times even threat-

---

[5]CCL 75:485. [6]WSA 3 2:268. [7]SNTD 222*. [8]FC 51:21. [9]FC 51:142. [10]WSA 3 2:271.

ening the day of judgment with severity and thus showing how to keep the straight path of eternal life, it is to be feared that they will receive judgment where they might have had a remedy. For this reason, with the inspiration and assistance of the Lord, let us endeavor as far as it lies in our power to inform by word and example the people entrusted to our care. SERMONS 1.19.[11]

WATCHFUL SHEPHERD. CHRYSOSTOM: Do you see a shepherd's vigilance? Do you see his heightened interest? What excuse could they have to whom rational flocks are entrusted but who are guilty of great negligence and day after day, in the prophet's words, slaughter some of them and look on without intending to take any care of others made the prey of wild beasts or the spoils of other people—even when the labor involved is slight and attention easy? It is a soul, after all, that is to be instructed; but that involves much labor for body and soul. HOMILIES ON GENESIS 57.32.[12]

CHRIST THE GOOD SHEPHERD. CHRYSOSTOM: Christ showed that he was different from those who neglect the flock when it is being preyed on by wolves, since he did not neglect them and even laid down his life for them so that the sheep might not perish. HOMILIES ON THE GOSPEL OF JOHN 60.[13]

SHEPHERDS MUST FEED THE FLOCK. AUGUSTINE: The shepherds who feed themselves and not the sheep are being told what they are diligent about and what they are negligent about. SERMON 46.3.[14]

LOOK OUT FOR THE STRONG. AUGUSTINE: If I do not worry about the one that strays and gets lost, even the one that is strong will think it is rather fun to stray and get lost. I do indeed desire outward gains, but I am more afraid of inner losses. SERMON 46.15.[15]

THE ABBOT'S CARE OF THE COMMUNITY. BENEDICT: It is the abbot's responsibility to have great concern and to act with all speed, discernment and diligence in order not to lose any of the sheep entrusted to him. He should realize that he has undertaken care of the sick, not tyranny over the healthy. RULE OF ST. BENEDICT 27.5-6.[16]

PASTORAL CARE BRINGS BACK THE CAST-AWAY. GREGORY THE GREAT: One who has been cast away is brought back when, after having fallen into sin, he is recalled to the state of righteousness by the influence of pastoral care; and the ligature binds a fracture when discipline subdues sin, lest the wound's bleeding leads to death if a tight bondage does not bind it up. Often, however, the fracture is made worse by an unskillful ligature, so that the lesion causes even greater pain from being bound up too tightly. PASTORAL CARE 2.6.[17]

34:5 The Sheep Scattered

MEDITATE ON THE GREAT SHEPHERD. PACHOMIUS: Let us struggle, my beloved, during these six days of the Passover, for they are given to us each year for the redemption of our souls, that we may spend them in the works of God. . . . He sent to us the great Shepherd of the sheep that were scattered, to gather us back into his holy fold. INSTRUCTIONS 2.1-2.[18]

34:6 The Sheep Wandered

HERETICS ARE SHEEP WHO HAVE WANDERED. AUGUSTINE: Pursuing all earthly objects, things that glitter obviously on the face of the earth, they love them, they set their hearts on them. They do not want to die, that their life may be hidden with Christ. . . . Not all heretics are to be found all over the face of the earth, but still heretics are to be found all over the face of the earth. Some here, others there, but there is no lack of them anywhere. SERMONS 46.18.[19]

---

[11]FC 31:22*. [12]FC 87:149. [13]FC 41:134-35*. [14]WSA 3 2:264. [15]WSA 3 2:272. [16]RSB 225. [17]ACW 11:66. [18]CS 47:47. [19]WSA 3

34:8 *The Lord Lives*

SHEPHERDS MUST LOOK TO CHRIST. AUGUSTINE: But which shepherds are dead? Those who seek their own advantage, not that of Jesus Christ. So will there be shepherds, and will they be found, who do not seek their own advantage but that of Jesus Christ? There certainly will be, and they will certainly be found; they are not lacking, and they won't be lacking. So let us see what the Lord has to say, who says he lives; whether he says he is going to take the sheep away from the bad shepherds, who feed themselves, not the sheep, and give them to good shepherds, who feed the sheep, not themselves. SERMONS 46.19.[20]

34:9-10 *The Lord Is Against the Shepherds*

THE SHEEP TAKEN AWAY. AUGUSTINE: Listen and learn, you sheep of God; from the bad shepherds God will require his sheep, and from their hands he will require their death. . . . So let us see, because that is what I had proposed to do, whether he takes the sheep away from the bad shepherds and gives them to good shepherds. SERMON 46.20-21.[21]

GOD WILL LOOK FOR THE SHEEP. JEROME: I myself will go to the shepherds and will seek out my flock from the hand of those who find it convenient to have a millstone placed around their neck. COMMENTARY ON EZEKIEL 11.34.1-31.[22]

THE END OF THE JEWISH PRIESTHOOD. THEODORET OF CYR: These words predict the end both of the kingdom of the Jews and the priesthood. I will free my flocks, he says, from those who look after them badly, who have steered them with no kind of providence but have only continued to devour them. Therefore through our Lord and Savior they are granted salvation. COMMENTARY ON EZEKIEL 13.34.[23]

---

[20]WSA 3 2:275. [21]WSA 3 2:276. [22]CCL 75:486. [23]PG 81:1153-56.

34:11-16 THE LORD IS THE SHEPHERD
OF THE SHEEP

[11]*For thus says the Lord GOD: Behold, I, I myself will search for my sheep, and will seek them out. [12]As a shepherd seeks out his flock when some of his sheep[v] have been scattered abroad, so will I seek out my sheep; and I will rescue them from all places where they have been scattered on a day of clouds and thick darkness. [13]And I will bring them out from the peoples, and gather them from the countries, and will bring them into their own land; and I will feed them on the mountains of Israel, by the fountains, and in all the inhabited places of the country. [14]I will feed them with good pasture, and upon the mountain heights of Israel shall be their pasture; there they shall lie down in good grazing land, and on fat pasture they shall feed on the mountains of Israel. [15]I myself will be the shepherd of my sheep, and I will make them lie down, says the Lord GOD. [16]I will seek the lost, and I will bring back the strayed, and I will bind up the crippled, and I will strengthen the weak,*

and the fat and the strong I will watch over;[w] I will feed them in justice.

v Cn: Heb *when he is among his sheep* **w** Gk Syr Vg: Heb *destroy*

OVERVIEW: The Shepherd stays out in any weather, determined to find his flock, feeding them on the rich pastures of the Scriptures (AUGUSTINE). Christ is the Shepherd (CLEMENT OF ALEXANDRIA) who will help us shepherd each other (GREGORY OF NAZIANZUS, CASSIODORUS, GREGORY THE GREAT), for even the shepherds require instruction (THEODORET) and should take care not to neglect their duties (BASIL).

34:11 The Lord Searches for the Sheep

SHEPHERDS DO NOT DESERT THE FLOCK. AUGUSTINE: Rain and fog, the errors of this world; a great darkness arising from human lusts, a thick fog covering the earth. And it is difficult for the sheep not to go astray in this fog. But the shepherd does not desert them. He seeks them, his piercing gaze penetrates the fog, the thick darkness of the clouds does not prevent him. SERMON 46.23.[1]

34:12 The Lord Seeks the Sheep

THE FLOCK CAN BE FOUND. AUGUSTINE: When it is difficult for them to be found, now I will find them. The fog is dense, the storm cloud thick; nothing escapes his eyes. SERMON 46.23.[2]

CHRIST IS SHEPHERD OF THE SHEPHERDS. GREGORY OF NAZIANZUS: He is shepherd to shepherds and a guide to guides: that we may feed his flock with knowledge, not with the instruments of a foolish shepherd. IN DEFENSE OF HIS FLIGHT TO PONTUS, ORATION 2.117.[3]

34:13 The Sheep to Be Gathered

THE SCRIPTURES ARE THE PASTURES. AUGUSTINE: He established the mountains of Israel, the authors of the divine Scriptures. Feed there, in

order to feed without a qualm. Whatever you hear from that source, let that taste good to you; anything from outside, spit it out. In order not to go astray in the fog, listen to the voice of the Shepherd. Gather yourselves to the mountains of holy Scripture. There you will find your heart's desire, there is nothing poisonous there, nothing unsuitable; they are the richest pastures. SERMON 46.24.[4]

ETERNAL FEEDING NOW. AUGUSTINE: There, life is wisdom, through which all these things come into being, both those that have been and those that will be. Yet, it is not made but is as it was, and thus it will be forever. Or rather, to have been in the past or to be in the future does not pertain to it, but simply to be, for it is eternal. To be in the past or to be in the future is not to be eternal. CONFESSIONS 9.24.[5]

34:14 I Will Feed Them

FEEDING ON CHRIST. AUGUSTINE: This is feeding Christ, this is feeding for Christ, this is feeding in Christ, not feeding oneself apart from Christ. There is not really a dearth of shepherds. SERMON 46.30.[6]

34:15 I Will Be Their Shepherd

LOOK TO THE MOUNTAINS FOR FEEDING. AUGUSTINE: Lift up your eyes to the mountains, by all means, from where help shall come to you—but pay attention to him saying, I myself will be the shepherd. SERMON 46.25.[7]

34:16 I Will Seek the Lost

---

[1]*WSA* 3 2:279. [2]*WSA* 3 2:279. [3]*NPNF* 2 7:227*. [4]*WSA* 3 2:279.
[5]*FC* 21:252. [6]*WSA* 3 2:283. [7]*WSA* 3 2:280.

THE PROMISE OF THE GOOD SHEPHERD.
CLEMENT OF ALEXANDRIA: This is the promise of him who is the good Shepherd. CHRIST THE EDUCATOR 1.9.84.[8]

BISHOPS HAVE TO TAKE GREAT CARE.
AUGUSTINE: The Lord did not say, "I will provide other good shepherds to do these things," but "I myself," he said, "will do them. I will commit my sheep to nobody else." You are all right, brothers; you are all right, you sheep. It is we bishops, it seems, who have got to worry, there being apparently not a single good shepherd. SERMON 46.26.[9]

SHEPHERDS NEED INSTRUCTION. THEODORET OF CYR: The words against the false shepherds have been hidden, as well as the prediction of God's attentiveness to come. He turns his words to the flocks and teaches the useless shepherds how not to fall back in any way in defending them. COMMENTARY ON EZEKIEL 13.34.[10]

GOD DOES NOT DESERT US. GREGORY THE GREAT: If we are negligent, does almighty God desert his sheep? No; he himself will pasture them, as he promised through the prophet. FORTY GOSPEL HOMILIES 19.[11]

WE CAN ALL SHEPHERD EACH OTHER. GREGORY THE GREAT: We must all of us strive zealously to make known to the church both the dreadfulness of the coming judgment and the kingdom of heaven's delight. Those who are not in a position to address a large assembly should instruct individuals, offering instruction in personal talks; they should try to serve those around them through simple encouragement. . . . You who are pastors, consider that you are pasturing God's flock. We often see a block of salt put out for animals to lick for their well-being. Priests among their people should be like blocks of salt. They should counsel everyone in their flocks in such a way that all those with whom they come in contact may be seasoned with eternal life as if

they had been sprinkled with salt. We who preach are not the salt of the earth unless we season the hearts of those who listen to us. We are really preaching to others if we ourselves do what we say, if we are pierced with God's love, if, since we cannot avoid sin, our tears wash away the stains on our life that come with each new day. We truly feel remorse when we take to heart the lives of our forebears in the faith so that we are diminished in our own eyes. Then do we truly feel remorse, when we attentively examine God's teachings and adopt for our own use what those we revere themselves used for theirs. And while we are moved to remorse on our own account, let us also take responsibility for the lives of those entrusted to our care. Our own bitter compunction should not divert us from concern for our neighbor. What good to love and strive to do good for our neighbor and abandon ourselves? We must realize that our passion for justice in the face of another's evil must never cause us to lose the virtue of gentleness. Priests must not be quick-tempered or rash; they must instead be temperate and thoughtful. We must support those we challenge and challenge those we support. If we neglect this, our work will lack either courage or gentleness. What shall we call the human soul but the food of the Lord? It is created to become nothing less than Christ's body and to bring about growth in the eternal church. We priests are to season this food. Cease to pray, cease to teach, and the salt loses its taste. FORTY GOSPEL HOMILIES 17.[12]

PASTORAL DUTIES OF SHEPHERDS. BASIL THE GREAT: If you are a shepherd, take care that none of your pastoral duties is neglected. And what are these duties? To bring back that which is lost, to bind up that which was broken, to heal that which is diseased. HOMILY ON THE WORDS "GIVE HEED TO THYSELF."[13]

---

[8]FC 23:75*. [9]WSA 3 2:280. [10]PG 81:1160. [11]CS 123:148. [12]BFG 100-101. [13]FC 9:437.

THE GRACE OF GOD WALKS AHEAD OF US.
CASSIODORUS: In every good deed we are anticipated by the Lord's grace. He deigns to inspire us to make us wish to entreat him. EXPOSI-TIONS OF THE PSALMS 118.10.[14]

---

[14]ACW 53:180-81.

34:17-24 THE LORD'S JUDGMENT BETWEEN SHEEP

[17]As for you, my flock, thus says the Lord GOD: Behold, I judge between sheep and sheep, rams and he-goats. [18]Is it not enough for you to feed on the good pasture, that you must tread down with your feet the rest of your pasture; and to drink of clear water, that you must foul the rest with your feet? [19]And must my sheep eat what you have trodden with your feet, and drink what you have fouled with your feet?

[20]Therefore, thus says the Lord GOD to them: Behold, I, I myself will judge between the fat sheep and the lean sheep. [21]Because you push with side and shoulder, and thrust at all the weak with your horns, till you have scattered them abroad, [22]I will save my flock, they shall no longer be a prey; and I will judge between sheep and sheep. [23]And I will set up over them one shepherd, my servant David, and he shall feed them: he shall feed them and be their shepherd. [24]And I, the LORD, will be their God, and my servant David shall be prince among them; I, the LORD, have spoken.

OVERVIEW: Scripture needs careful interpretation (ORIGEN), a ministry of discernment comparable to God's patience with his flock. This means that the good shepherds are reassured, whereas the bad have cause to be afraid (AUGUSTINE). The sustenance provided is not to be misused or squandered (JEROME, GREGORY THE GREAT); we must rely on God's mercy, not on our own efforts (AUGUSTINE), for Christ is the shepherd to come (ORIGEN, CHRYSOSTOM, AUGUSTINE).

34:17 I Judge Between Sheep

SCRIPTURE REQUIRES DISCERNMENT. ORIGEN: We who desire to be flocks of the shepherd must never try to escape from being fed even by the very things that seem to diverge from Scripture and are trampled on because of the discordance of what is said by those who neither want nor can use the nourishment that Scripture gives in all its fullness. HOMILIES ON EZEKIEL, PREFACE.[1]

THE JOY OF BEING GOD'S FLOCK. AUGUSTINE: If you really think, brothers, what a very great blessing it is to be God's flock, you must be filled even in the midst of these tears and troubles of ours with very great joy. SERMON 47.3.[2]

GOD'S PATIENCE WITH THE FLOCK. AUGUSTINE: What are he-goats doing here in God's

---

[1]PG 13:664. [2]WSA 3 2:299.

flock? In the same pastures, at the same springs, he-goats, though destined for the left hand, are mixing with those of the right hand, and those who are going to be separated are first tolerated. And this is to exercise the sheep in a patience after the likeness of God's own patience. SER-MON 47.6.[3]

THE GOOD REASSURED, THE BAD MADE AFRAID. AUGUSTINE: I am judging. What a relief, what reassurance! [The Lord] is judging; the good can be reassured. No opponent can corrupt their judge, no counselor twist him round their little finger or witness play fast and loose with him. But just as the good can be reassured, so to the same extent the bad should be afraid. He is not the sort of judge things can be kept hidden from. Do you imagine, after all, that God as judge is going to examine witnesses, to learn from them who you may be? How can he possibly be mistaken about who you may be, seeing that he knew what you were going to be? SERMON 47.7.[4]

34:18 Feed Them Properly

PASTURES TO EAT AND SPRINGS TO DRINK. AUGUSTINE: God's pastures are good, and God's springs are pure. We have them in the holy Scriptures. SERMON 47.9.[5]

USE ALL THE SUSTENANCE YOU ARE GIVEN. JEROME: Now he speaks to the sheep, that is, the people, and to the flock of either kind, that is, of sheep and she-goats but also to rams and he-goats who are leaders among flocks. To them he says, "Is it not enough for you to be fed for the good nourishment the Scriptures provide? But you crush under your feet what remains of your food, and when you have drunk the purest water that are the words of God, you disturb with your feet the waters that remain, so that my people chew food that is trodden on by you and drink water that has been disturbed by you." COMMENTARY ON EZEKIEL 11.34.1-31.[6]

CLEAR WATER IS BETTER TO DRINK. GREGORY THE GREAT: Evidently, the pastors drink water that is most clear, when with a right understanding they imbibe the streams of truth, whereas to foul the water with the feet is to corrupt the studies of holy meditation by an evil life. PASTORAL CARE 1.2.[7]

34:20 Judging Between All

WE ARE ALL SHEEP. AUGUSTINE: He makes no further mention of the he-goats. He mentioned them once, so that we would know they exist. He knows them well. After that he speaks as if all are sheep. SERMON 47.15.[8]

34:21-22 The Flock Will Be Saved

WE MUST RELY ON GOD'S MERCY. AUGUSTINE: If we lament the many sheep that are straying outside, woe to those whose shoulders and sides and horns have brought it about. It is only strong sheep who would do this. Who are the strong? Those who rely on their own righteousness. None but those who called themselves just divided the sheep and drove them outside. Shoulders bold at shoving, because they do not bear God's burden; evil sides, conspiracies of friends, companions in obstinacy; horns lifted up, high and mighty pride. Shove with sides and shoulders, flail with your horns, drive outside what you have not bought. Certainly this is your whole case, that you are just and others are unjust, and it was unfitting that the just should remain with the unjust, unfitting, that is to say, that the corn should remain among the weeds, unfitting that the sheep should feed among the goats until the shepherd should come who would make no mistake in separating them. SERMON 47.16.[9]

LOOK TO CHRIST FOR PROOF THAT THE GOSPEL IS TRUE. AUGUSTINE: Just as we must

---

[3]*WSA* 3 2:301. [4]*WSA* 3 2:303*. [5]*WSA* 3 2:304. [6]CCL 75:487. [7]ACW 11:24. [8]*WSA* 3 2:308. [9]*WSA* 3 2:309*.

abominate their injustice and cruelty, so we must praise the mercy of our Shepherd, who is truly our God; he will save his sheep. Perhaps, my brothers, he is doing this when we say this, doing it through the least of his servants, doing it perhaps through unworthy servants. Let him save his sheep; let them hear the voice of their Shepherd and follow him. Do not let them look for a proof of the church from the mouth of people. Let them look for it from the mouth of God, look for it from the mouth of Christ. Whoever he calls ungodly is ungodly, whoever he calls just is just, whoever he calls a sheep is a sheep, whoever he calls a goat is a goat. He himself is truth, let him speak, let the church be sought from him. Tell us, Lord, where is your church? SERMON 47.19.[10]

34:23 One Shepherd

THE SHEPHERD TO COME. CHRYSOSTOM: For both Ezekiel and other prophets besides speak of David as coming and rising again; not meaning him who was dead but those who were emulating his virtue. HOMILIES ON THE GOSPEL OF MATTHEW 2.6.[11]

THE CHRIST TO COME. ORIGEN: David also is called the Christ, as when Ezekiel prophesied to the shepherds and added, in the person of God, "I will raise up David my servant, who will shepherd them." For the patriarch David will not be raised up to shepherd the saints, but Christ. COMMENTARY ON THE GOSPEL OF JOHN 1.146.[12]

CHRIST IS THE ONE SHEPHERD. AUGUSTINE: You will readily understand, brothers, that it is a prophecy of Christ coming to people from the seed of David, if you realize the dates. This prophet Ezekiel lived in the time of the captivity, which resulted from the exile of the people to Babylonia. From the time of David to the time of the exile there are fourteen generations. SERMON 47.20.[13]

34:24 I Will Be Their God

THE UNITY OF GOD. AUGUSTINE: Pay close attention, brothers. Note the unity of the godhead, and yet the distribution of persons, in case we should say that he who is the Father is the Son, or that he who is the Son is the Father. SERMON 47.21.[14]

---

[10]WSA 3 2:313*. [11]NPNF 1 10:11. [12]FC 80:63. [13]WSA 3 2:314. [14]WSA 3 2:315.

34:25-31 THE LORD'S COVENANT OF PEACE

[25]I will make with them a covenant of peace and banish wild beasts from the land, so that they may dwell securely in the wilderness and sleep in the woods. [26]And I will make them and the places round about my hill a blessing; and I will send down the showers in their season; they shall be showers of blessing. [27]And the trees of the field shall yield their fruit, and the earth shall yield its increase, and they shall be secure in their land; and they shall know that I am the LORD, when I break the bars of their yoke, and deliver them from the hand of those who enslaved them. [28]They shall no more be a prey to the nations, nor shall the beasts of the land devour them; they shall

dwell securely, and none shall make them afraid. [29]*And I will provide for them prosperous*[x] *planta-tions so that they shall no more be consumed with hunger in the land, and no longer suffer the reproach of the nations.* [30]*And they shall know that I, the* LORD *their God, am with them, and that they, the house of Israel, are my people, says the Lord* GOD. [31]*And you are my sheep, the sheep of my pasture,*[y] *and I am your God, says the Lord* GOD.

x Gk Syr Old Latin: Heb *for renown*   y Gk Old Latin: Heb *pasture you are men*

OVERVIEW: The desert is a place of solitude, the conscience, where God can be found. The land will be irrigated properly, and people will live fruitful lives (AUGUSTINE). There will be no more violence, and the good Shepherd will come to feed those who are hungry for the Word of God (JEROME).

34:25 A Covenant in the Desert

SOLITUDE IN THE DESERT. AUGUSTINE: What is "in the desert"? In solitude. What is in soli-tude? Inside, in the conscience. It is a solitude indeed, because not only do no other human beings cross it, they do not even see it. Let us dwell there in hope, because we are not yet there in fact. After all, everything we have outside chops and changes with the storms and trials of the world. The desert is inside; that is where we should interrogate our faith. SERMON 47.23.[1]

34:26 A Place of Blessing

THE LAND WILL BE LOOKED AFTER. AUGUS-TINE: There is also, of course, the bad sort of thunder shower, that knocks down the house built on sand, that it is a great thing even for the house founded on the rock to stand up against. That is the thunder shower of temptation, bent on devastation, not on irrigation, of the earth. SERMON 47.24.[2]

34:27 Fruitful Trees

THOSE WHO HAVE FRUITFUL LIVES. AUGUS-TINE: [The fruitful trees are] in the plain, on level ground, not in rugged places, in a relatively easy life. Having things fairly easy in this life, with nothing steep or rugged, toilsome, difficult to cope with, this he calls the plain. Such is the life of many of the faithful in the church of God, who have their wives and husbands, children, families. They are like trees in the plain; they are not strong enough to climb anything steep or rugged. But only let them receive the shower; these trees too will give their fruit. SERMON 47.25.[3]

34:29 Prosperous Plantations

THOSE WHO CURSE WILL FALL. AUGUSTINE: The church has been raised up to such a pinnacle in the name of Christ that all who curse are now put to shame and dare not curse anymore. SERMON 47.28.[4]

NO MORE PILLAGE. JEROME: There will never be any more pillage among races filled with the devil, nor will the beasts of the earth devour those of whom we have spoken, but they will live faithfully and away from any terror. COMMEN-TARY ON EZEKIEL 11.34.1-31.[5]

34:30 They Will Know That God Is with Them

THE EFFECTS OF THE GOOD SHEPHERD. JEROME: A famine, a famine of hearing the Word of God, will never take place on the earth under a

---

[1]*WSA* 3 2:318*. [2]*WSA* 3 2:319*. [3]*WSA* 3 2:319*. [4]*WSA* 3 2:321*.
[5]*CCL* 75:489.

good shepherd descended from a famous stock, whose words are acclaimed by everyone and who sows peace on the earth. COMMENTARY ON EZEKIEL 11.34.1-31.[6]

34:31 You Are My Sheep

GOD LOOKS AFTER US. AUGUSTINE: O how blessed we are with such a possession and such a possessor! Because as well as him possessing us, we also possess him. He possesses us in order to tend us, and we possess him in order to tend him. But we tend him with worship as God, he tends us with cultivation as a field. SERMON 47.30.[7]

[6]CCL 75:490. [7]WSA 3 2:323.

[35:1-15 PROPHECY AGAINST EDOM]

36:1-15 JUDGMENT ON ISRAEL'S OPPRESSORS AND ISRAEL'S RETURN

[1]And you, son of man, prophesy to the mountains of Israel. . . . [5]Therefore thus says the Lord GOD: I speak in my hot jealousy against the rest of the nations, and against all Edom, who gave my land to themselves as a possession with wholehearted joy and utter contempt, that they might possess[b] it and plunder it. [6]Therefore prophesy concerning the land of Israel, and say to the mountains and hills, to the ravines and valleys, Thus says the Lord GOD: Behold, I speak in my jealous wrath, because you have suffered the reproach of the nations; [7]therefore thus says the Lord GOD: I swear that the nations that are round about you shall themselves suffer reproach.

[8]But you, O mountains of Israel, shall shoot forth your branches, and yield your fruit to my people Israel; for they will soon come home. [9]For behold, I am for you, and I will turn to you, and you shall be tilled and sown; [10]and I will multiply men upon you, the whole house of Israel, all of it; the cities shall be inhabited and the waste places rebuilt; [11]and I will multiply upon you man and beast; and they shall increase and be fruitful; and I will cause you to be inhabited as in your former times, and will do more good to you than ever before. Then you will know that I am the LORD. [12]

b One Ms: Heb drive out

OVERVIEW: God rebukes Israel's oppressors (GREGORY THE GREAT). The promise of new life results from God's nature, and the mountains are his ministers (JEROME). The blessings of the future are on his inheritance (JUSTIN MARTYR, THEODORET).

36:5 Possessing the Land to Plunder It

GOD'S REBUKE. GREGORY THE GREAT: Weighing these words carefully, we see that they were struck with severe rebuke, not because they merely rejoiced but because they rejoiced with the whole heart and mind. PASTORAL CARE 3.26.[1]

36:8 The Mountains Will Shoot Out Branches

THE PROMISE OF NEW LIFE. JEROME: In case this seems to be difficult I will come to you; I who have turned away from you will turn my face toward you, so that you may have the cultivation that you once had and that everything may be filled with seed. In this way there will be many people among you, and the cities that were once destroyed will be inhabited once again. COMMENTARY ON EZEKIEL 11.36.1-15.[2]

THE PROPHETS AND APOSTLES. JEROME: We say that the mountains of Israel, the prophets and the apostles, are those who hear the Word of God and are those to whom the devil is an enemy and against whom he scoffs. COMMENTARY ON EZEKIEL 11.36.1-15.[3]

THE JOY OF THE RETURNING PEOPLE. THEODORET OF CYR: I will strengthen the people's hope, and I will make steadfast their expectation of good things to come, and they will return and enjoy those fruits that are produced by you. COMMENTARY ON EZEKIEL 14.36.[4]

36:12 You Will Be Their Inheritance

GOD'S BLESSING ON HIS INHERITANCE. JUSTIN MARTYR: Since God blesses and calls this people Israel and announces aloud that it is his inheritance, why do you not feel compunction both for fooling yourselves by imagining that you alone are the people of Israel and for cursing those whom God has blessed? DIALOGUE WITH TRYPHO 123.[5]

---

[1]ACW 11:183. [2]CCL 75:499. [3]CCL 75:500. [4]PG 81:1177. [5]FC 6:339.

36:16-38 ISRAEL'S PUNISHMENT AND REGATHERING BY THE LORD

[16]The word of the LORD came to me: [17]"Son of man, when the house of Israel dwelt in their own land, they defiled it by their ways and their doings; their conduct before me was like the uncleanness of a woman in her impurity. [18]So I poured out my wrath upon them for the blood which they had shed in the land, for the idols with which they had defiled it. [19]I scattered them among the nations, and they were dispersed through the countries; in accordance with their conduct and their deeds I judged them. [20]But when they came to the nations, wherever they came, they profaned my holy name, in that men said of them, 'These are the people of the LORD, and yet they had to go out of his land.' [21]But I had concern for my holy name, which the house of Israel caused to be profaned among the nations to which they came.

²²"Therefore say to the house of Israel, Thus says the Lord GOD: It is not for your sake, O house of Israel, that I am about to act, but for the sake of my holy name, which you have profaned among the nations to which you came. ²³And I will vindicate the holiness of my great name, which has been profaned among the nations, and which you have profaned among them; and the nations will know that I am the LORD, says the Lord GOD, when through you I vindicate my holiness before their eyes. ²⁴For I will take you from the nations, and gather you from all the countries, and bring you into your own land. ²⁵I will sprinkle clean water upon you, and you shall be clean from all your uncleannesses, and from all your idols I will cleanse you. ²⁶A new heart I will give you, and a new spirit I will put within you; and I will take out of your flesh the heart of stone and give you a heart of flesh. ²⁷And I will put my spirit within you, and cause you to walk in my statutes and be careful to observe my ordinances. ²⁸You shall dwell in the land which I gave to your fathers; and you shall be my people, and I will be your God. ²⁹And I will deliver you from all your uncleannesses; and I will summon the grain and make it abundant and lay no famine upon you. ³⁰I will make the fruit of the tree and the increase of the field abundant, that you may never again suffer the disgrace of famine among the nations. ³¹Then you will remember your evil ways, and your deeds that were not good; and you will loathe yourselves for your iniquities and your abominable deeds. ³²It is not for your sake that I will act, says the Lord GOD; let that be known to you. Be ashamed and confounded for your ways, O house of Israel.

³³"Thus says the Lord GOD: On the day that I cleanse you from all your iniquities, I will cause the cities to be inhabited, and the waste places shall be rebuilt. ³⁴And the land that was desolate shall be tilled, instead of being the desolation that it was in the sight of all who passed by. ³⁵And they will say, 'This land that was desolate has become like the garden of Eden; and the waste and desolate and ruined cities are now inhabited and fortified.' ³⁶Then the nations that are left round about you shall know that I, the LORD, have rebuilt the ruined places, and replanted that which was desolate; I, the LORD, have spoken, and I will do it.

³⁷"Thus says the Lord GOD: This also I will let the house of Israel ask me to do for them: to increase their men like a flock. ³⁸Like the flock for sacrifices,ᶜ like the flock at Jerusalem during her appointed feasts, so shall the waste cities be filled with flocks of men. Then they will know that I am the LORD."

c Heb *flock of holy things*

OVERVIEW: The Holy Spirit is the source of all that we receive from God (AUGUSTINE). We must seek and not profane God's virtues (CHRYSOSTOM), for his faithfulness is known among us (CLEMENT OF ROME). This means a life of total and not partial commitment in baptism, wives as well as husbands (JEROME). At baptism, the bishop blesses the water before it is used (CYPRIAN). The promise of the future is of churches filled with returning exiles (JEROME) in search of the Lord (ISAAC). The new heart and the new spirit are gifts of God and will help us to use our free will to the good (AUGUSTINE, THEODORET), showing us how to act (FULGENTIUS) and softening our heart of stone (SAHDONA).

36:20 Israel Profaned God's Name

THE SOURCE OF ALL DIVINE LIFE. AUGUS-
TINE: All these sacraments may be possessed by
the evil person; but to have charity and be an evil
person is not possible. This therefore is the peculiar gift of the Spirit: he is the one and only fountain. To drink of it, God's Spirit calls you: God's
Spirit calls you to drink of himself. HOMILIES ON
I JOHN 7.6.[1]

**WE MUST BE HUMBLE AND NOT PROFANE
GOD.** CHRYSOSTOM: If we pursue virtue, let us
seek before all to gain for ourselves the approval
that comes from God alone, and let us take no
account of human praise. If we are lax, we should
be afraid and humble our thinking with the
thought of that judgment that cannot be bribed.
Let us tremble at the approach of that dread day
and the thought that our actions provoke blasphemy against God. BAPTISMAL INSTRUCTIONS
6.10.[2]

36:22 God's Holy Name Profaned

GOD'S HOLY NAME REACHES TO ALL. CHRY-
SOSTOM: Though you sigh only, though you weep
only, all these things he quickly snatches as an
occasion for saving you. HOMILIES ON THE GOS-
PEL OF MATTHEW 3.6.[3]

36:23 The Holiness of God's Name Vindicated

GOD'S HOLINESS KNOWN. CLEMENT OF ROME:
You brought into being the everlasting structure of the world by what you did. You, Lord,
made the earth. You who are faithful in all generations, righteous in judgment, marvelous
in strength and majesty, wise in creating, prudent in making creation endure, visibly good,
kind to those who trust in you. I CLEMENT
60.1.[4]

GOD'S HOLINESS WILL SAVE US. JEROME: All
these things the Lord will bestow, not because of
those who have perished as a result of their own

errors but because of his holy name. COMMEN-
TARY ON EZEKIEL 11.36.16-38.[5]

36:25 Clean Water Sprinkled

THE BLESSING OF THE BAPTISMAL WATER.
CYPRIAN: The water ought to be first cleansed
and sanctified by the bishop that it may be able to
wash away in its baptism the sins of the one who
is baptized. LETTER 70.1.[6]

NEW LIFE IN BAPTISM. JEROME: Careful consideration should be given to what a new heart
and a new spirit is given when the water has been
poured and sprinkled. COMMENTARY ON EZE-
KIEL 11.36.1-15.[7]

THE PURE WATER OF BAPTISM. THEODORET
OF CYR: He calls the pure water the water of
rebirth, because we who have been baptized have
received the forgiveness of our sins. COMMEN-
TARY ON EZEKIEL 14.36.[8]

SEE THE LORD. ISAAC OF NINEVEH: Seek the
Lord, O sinners, and be strengthened in your
thoughts because of hope. And seek his face through
repentance at all times. You will be sanctified by
the holiness of his presence, and you will be purified of your iniquity. ON ASCETICAL LIFE 5.76.[9]

36:26 A Heart of Flesh

**FREE WILL NEEDS GUIDANCE FROM GOD
ALONE.** AUGUSTINE: Free will is always present
in us, but it is not always good. For it is either
free of justice, while serving sin, and then it is
evil; or it is free of sin, while serving justice, and
then it is good. But the grace of God is always
good and brings about a good will in a person
who before was possessed of an evil will. It is by
this grace, too, that this same good will, once it

---

[1]LCC 8:315. [2]ACW 31:97*. [3]NPNF 1 10:18**. [4]LCC 1:71. [5]CCL
75:507. [6]FC 51:259*. An allusion to the baptismal liturgy, in which
the bishop was the normal presider. [7]CCL 75:506. [8]PG 81:1184.
[9]INAL 92.

begins to exist, is expanded and made so strong that it is able to fulfill whatever of God's commandments it wishes, whenever it does so with a strong and perfect will. ON GRACE AND FREE WILL 15.31.[10]

THE HEART OF FLESH GIVEN BY GRACE. AUGUSTINE: God by his grace takes away the stony heart[11] from unbelievers and forestalls merit in people of good will in such a way that their will is prepared by what goes before grace, but that grace is not given through some merit of human will. LETTER 217.[12]

THE HEART WILL INCLINE TO BETTER THINGS. THEODORET OF CYR: He means by these things a change of attitude. Your heart, he says, will incline to better things, no longer following your previous preference for what is worse. That "I will give" in no way damages free will, for by words and deeds and endless miracles, not only among them but in all races, so that they start to live piously; he persuades, he does not compel. And although he does not compel but persuades, he says that he has inclined their minds toward better things. COMMENTARY ON EZEKIEL 11.14.36.[13]

THE PURPOSE OF THE NEW HEART. FULGENTIUS OF RUSPE: God gives a new heart so that we may walk in his justifications, which are about beginning a good will. He also gives it so that we may observe and do his judgments, which are about doing good works. To MONIMUS 1.8.3.[14]

THE IMAGE OF CHRIST. ISAAC OF NINEVEH: The image of Christ is formed in us through the Spirit of wisdom and the revelation of the knowledge of him. ASCETICAL HOMILIES 37.[15]

THE SOFTENING OF THE HEART OF STONE. SAHDONA: The word of God is at the same time the seed and the water; and even though we have a heart like stone, it will be softened and split up by the water of the Spirit, so that it can bring

forth holy fruit that is pleasing to God. BOOK OF PERFECTION 53.[16]

THE NEW CHRISTIAN HEART. JEROME: We must consider the new heart and the new spirit that are given after the pouring and sprinkling of water. When a new heart and a new spirit are given, all hardness is taken away from the Jewish heart, which is compared with a heart of stone, and instead of a heart of stone there is a heart of flesh, soft and tender, which can receive the spirit of God within it and be written with the words of salvation. Then they will walk in the precepts of the Lord and will keep his judgments. COMMENTARY ON EZEKIEL 11.36.16-38.[17]

36:27 A New Spirit

THE NEW SPIRIT AND OUR GOOD DEEDS. AUGUSTINE: God promises that he will cause them to do those things that he commands to be done. Nor indeed does he here overlook the merits, but rather the evil deeds, of those to whom he shows that he will return good things for evil, by the very fact that he causes them to have good works from that point on, when he causes them to carry out the divine commands. PREDESTINATION OF THE SAINTS 11.22.[18]

THE WATERS OF TRUE TEACHING. JEROME: I will certainly not pour on them the waters of baptism but the waters of the teaching and the Word of God, and I will purify them of all their iniquities and from every single one of their idols and from the errors that they make in their hearts. COMMENTARY ON EZEKIEL 11.36.16-38.[19]

THE GIVING OF THE SPIRIT AND ITS EFFECTS. THEODORET OF CYR: These things did not happen before the coming of the Lord Christ. Since they had three prophets after the return to Jeru-

---

[10]FC 59:285*. [11]See also Ezek 11:19. [12]FC 32:94**. [13]PG 81:1184. [14]FC 95:198. [15]AHSIS 175. [16]CS 101:224. [17]CCL 75:506. [18]FC 86:244. [19]CCL 75:509.

salem, Haggai, Zechariah and Malachi, they were immediately deprived of the gift of prophecy. But after our God and Savior was made man and ascended into the heavens, and the Holy Spirit came on the holy apostles, through them grace was given not only to the Jews but also to all those from the peoples who came to faith. He calls a heart of stone one that is antagonistic and rebellious, and a heart of flesh, one that is compliant and obedient to what it is told, and is able to draw out the meaning of the divine writings ... this is the mark of a spirit of grace, which assists our free will and ensures that what has been said proceeds in due course. COMMENTARY ON EZEKIEL 14.36.[20]

36:31 Remember Your Evil Ways

PENITENTS MUST FEEL SHAME. JEROME: That

penitents may have their due it is enough for them to feel shame instead of all other punishment. AGAINST JOVINIANUS 2.31.[21]

36:38 Israel Will Flock to the Lord

THE CROWDS WILL FLOCK TO THE CHURCH. JEROME: Once again the prophetic word will encourage penitents to return to the churches and always seek the Lord and find him. The flocks of the Lord will thus be multiplied by the crowds who return, not of beasts of burden and wild animals, but flocks of people who are full of faith and reason, holy flocks, flocks of the city of Jerusalem. COMMENTARY ON EZEKIEL 11.36.16-38.[22]

---

[20]PG 81:1184. [21]NPNF 2 6: 412. [22]CCL 75:510.

37:1-14 THE VALLEY OF THE DRY BONES

The hand of the LORD was upon me, and he brought me out by the Spirit of the LORD, and set me down in the midst of the valley;[d] it was full of bones. [2]And he led me round among them; and behold, there were very many upon the valley;[d] and lo, they were very dry. [3]And he said to me, "Son of man, can these bones live?" And I answered, "O Lord GOD, thou knowest." [4]Again he said to me, "Prophesy to these bones, and say to them, O dry bones, hear the word of the LORD. [5]Thus says the Lord GOD to these bones: Behold, I will cause breath[e] to enter you, and you shall live. [6]And I will lay sinews upon you, and will cause flesh to come upon you, and cover you with skin, and put breath[e] in you, and you shall live; and you shall know that I am the LORD."

[7]So I prophesied as I was commanded; and as I prophesied, there was a noise, and behold, a rattling; and the bones came together, bone to its bone. [8]And as I looked, there were sinews on them, and flesh had come upon them, and skin had covered them; but there was no breath in them. [9]Then he said to me, "Prophesy to the breath, prophesy, son of man, and say to the breath,[f] Thus says the Lord GOD: Come from the four winds, O breath,[f] and breathe upon these slain, that they may live." [10]So I prophesied as he commanded me, and the breath came into them, and they lived,

and stood upon their feet, an exceedingly great host.

[11]*Then he said to me, "Son of man, these bones are the whole house of Israel. Behold, they say, 'Our bones are dried up, and our hope is lost; we are clean cut off.'* [12]*Therefore prophesy, and say to them, Thus says the Lord GOD: Behold, I will open your graves, and raise you from your graves, O my people; and I will bring you home into the land of Israel.* [13]*And you shall know that I am the LORD, when I open your graves, and raise you from your graves, O my people.* [14]*And I will put my Spirit within you, and you shall live, and I will place you in your own land; then you shall know that I, the LORD, have spoken, and I have done it, says the LORD."*

d Or *plain*   e Or *spirit*   f Or *wind* or *spirit*

OVERVIEW: The vision of the valley of the dry bones is a passage read regularly in the churches (JEROME) and foretells the resurrection (ORIGEN, GREGORY OF NYSSA, NOVATIAN, THEODORET) in the way that it reverses the order of nature (AMBROSE, CHRYSOSTOM), a process begun by the prophet uttering only one word (JEROME, APHRAHAT). The resurrection is central to the gospel (CYRIL OF JERUSALEM), in its movement from death to life (PAULINUS). The vision is also interpreted as a metaphor for caring for the weak (BASIL) or a prediction of future judgment (JUSTIN). The Spirit gives new life (JEROME, AMBROSE), shared in the celebration of the Eucharist, the memorial of the cross (JEROME).

THE MYSTERY OF THE RESURRECTION. ORIGEN: The mystery of the resurrection is great and difficult for many of us to understand. It is mentioned also in many other passages of the Scriptures and is proclaimed no less through these words in Ezekiel. COMMENTARY ON THE GOSPEL OF JOHN 10.233.[1]

THE DRAMA OF THE PROPHECY AND ITS PARADOXICAL MESSAGE. AMBROSE: In minute detail the holy prophet Ezekiel teaches and describes how strength will be restored to our dry bones, feeling return and motion added; how, with the return of sinews, the whole structure of the human body will grow strong, and how the driest bones will be clothed with restored flesh and the openings of the veins and the streams of the blood will be concealed by a veil of skin drawn tautly over them. At the very words of the prophet, as we read, the crop of human bodies seems to rise up again to life, and one may see the wide expanses of the fields sprouting with a novel kind of growth. ON HIS BROTHER SATYRUS 2.69.[2]

THE SPIRIT IS THE LAST TO RETURN. AMBROSE: Note how the prophet shows that there was hearing and movement in the bones before the Spirit of life was poured on them. For, above, both the dry bones are bidden to hear, as if they had the sense of hearing, and that on this each of them came to its own joint is pointed out by the words of the prophet. . . .

Great is the lovingkindness of the Lord, that the prophet is taken as a witness of the future resurrection, that we, too, might see it with his eyes. For all could not be taken as witnesses, but in that one all we are witnesses, for neither does lying come on a holy person or error on so great a prophet. ON HIS BROTHER SATYRUS 2.72-73.[3]

BY ONE WORD ONLY. APHRAHAT: But why, my beloved, was it that those dead did not rise because of the one word [spoken] through Ezekiel, and why was not their resurrection, both of bones and spirit, accomplished [through that one word]? For look! By one word the bones were fitted together, and by another the Spirit came. It was in order that full perfection might be left for

---

[1]FC 80:306. [2]FC 22:227. [3]NPNF 2 10:185.

our Lord Jesus Christ, who with one utterance and one word will raise up at the last day every human body. For it was not the word that was insufficient but its bearer was inferior. DEMONSTRATIONS 8.13.[4]

THE UNIQUE CHARACTER OF THIS VISION.

CHRYSOSTOM: There were at all events many wonderful and great prophets among ourselves who spoke many things about the future, and they in no way used to bid those who asked them to dig up the bones of the departed. Ezekiel standing near the bones themselves was not only not hindered by [the bones] but added flesh, and nerves and skin to them and brought them back to life again. DISCOURSE ON BLESSED BABYLAS 2.[5]

FAITH IN THE RESURRECTION IS FUNDAMENTAL.

CYRIL OF JERUSALEM: The hope of resurrection is the root of every kind of good work, for the expectation of reward braces the soul to productive toil. And whereas every worker is ready to sustain his toil if he can look forward to being repaid for his labors, where toil has no recompense the soul is soon discouraged and the body flags with it. A soldier who expects his share of the spoils is ready for war. But no one is prepared to die serving a king so undiscerning that he does not provide rewards for labors. In the same way, any soul that believes in resurrection takes care for itself, as is right, but any soul that disbelieves the resurrection abandons itself to destruction. A person who believes that the body survives to rise again is careful of this garment and does not soil it by fornicating. But a person who does not believe in the resurrection gives himself up to fornication, abusing his own body as if it were nothing to him.

A mighty message and teaching of the holy Catholic church is belief about the resurrection of the dead; mighty and most indispensable. While many deny it, the truth claims credence for it. Greeks deny it, Samaritans disbelieve, while heretics tear away the half. Truth never appears but in one shape, while contradiction assumes a hundred. CATECHETICAL LECTURES 18.1.[6]

EZEKIEL SAW THE RESURRECTION BEFORE HIM.

GREGORY OF NYSSA: Ezekiel, with prophetic spirit, has surpassed all time and space and with his power of prediction has stood at the very moment of the resurrection. Seeing the future as already present, he has brought it before our eyes in his description. ON THE SOUL AND THE RESURRECTION.[7]

THE WONDER OF THE RESURRECTION.

NOVATIAN: He will contemplate truly admirable souls that have been brought back from the grave to reanimate completely consumed bodies. ON THE SPECTACLES 10.2.[8]

FROM DEATH TO LIFE.

PAULINUS OF NOLA: If you are skeptical that ashes can be reassembled into bodies and souls restored to their vessels, Ezekiel will be your witness, for long ago the whole process of resurrection was revealed to him by the Lord. In his pages you will behold the dusty remains of people of old come to life over the entire region, bones scattered far and wide over the broad plain spontaneously hastening to fuse together when bidden, sprouting sinews from the innermost marrow and then drawing the skin over the flesh that had grown on them. Then the limbs are perfectly ordered more quickly than words can tell, and from the ancient dust stand forth people made new. POEM 31.311.[9]

THE VISION IS READ REGULARLY.

JEROME: The vision is a famous one and is celebrated by being read in all the churches of Christ. COMMENTARY ON EZEKIEL 11.37.1-14.[10]

THE NATURE OF THE VISION.

THEODORET OF CYR: Again this is the spirit of contemplation; he did not see these bodies that were shown to him with his eyes, but he had them revealed to him by

---

[4]NPNF 2 13:379*. [5]NPNF 1 9:142*. [6]LCC 4:178-79*. [7]FC 58:260. [8]FC 67:132. [9]ACW 40:319. [10]CCL 75:512. An allusion to the regular liturgical use of this passage, probably at Easter or Pentecost.

the Holy Spirit. COMMENTARY ON EZEKIEL 15.37.[11]

37:3 Speak to the Bones

EVEN DRY BONES CAN HEAR THE WORD OF GOD. JEROME: It is wonderful how he addresses the dry bones, bones that were able to hear the Word of God before they had nerves, flesh, skin and life-giving breath. COMMENTARY ON EZEKIEL 11.37.1-14.[12]

37:5 Breath Enters the Bones

THE WEAK ARE SUPPORTED BY THE STRONG. BASIL THE GREAT: There should . . . be certain bones of the inner person in which the bond of union and harmony of spiritual powers is collected. Just as the bones by their own firmness protect the tenderness of the flesh, so also in the church there are some who through their own constancy are able to carry the infirmities of the weak. And as the bones are joined to each other through articulations by sinews and fastenings that have grown on them, so also would be the bond of charity and peace, which achieves a certain natural junction and union of the spiritual bones in the church of God. HOMILIES ON THE PSALMS 16.13 (Ps 33).[13]

THE SPIRIT GIVES LIFE. JEROME: This is the resurrection of the dead, the Spirit breathing in, giving life that has entered the human bodies, and immediately they live and stand on their feet, which means the resurrection of the dead. COMMENTARY ON EZEKIEL 11.37.1-14.[14]

37:7-10 Ezekiel Prophesies

THE VISION PORTRAYS FUTURE JUDGMENT. JUSTIN MARTYR: The prophets have foretold two comings of Christ: the one, which already took place, was that of a dishonored and suffering man; the other coming will take place, as it is predicted, when he gloriously comes from heaven with his angelic army, when he also raises to life the bodies of all the people that ever were, cloaks the worthy with immortality and relegates the wicked, who will be subjected to pain for all eternity, into the eternal fire, together with the evil demons. We will now show how these things also have been predicted as yet to happen. Thus spoke the prophet Ezekiel, "And the bones came together, bone to its bone." FIRST APOLOGY 52.[15]

THE EYE GLORIFIED. ORIGEN: If there is some excellent glory in the eye, it is particularly in this: that either it is the leader of the body or it is not abandoned by the functions of the other members. I think this is what is taught to us through that vision of the prophet Ezekiel. HOMILIES ON LEVITICUS 7.2.9.[16]

THE BODIES COME BACK TO LIFE. THEODORET OF CYR: The proclamation, he says is made by me, by divine command. The bodies that were bound together came back to life, and they experienced a resurrection, and the multitude of those who rose again was not small. COMMENTARY ON EZEKIEL 15.37.[17]

37:14 God's Spirit Within You

THE TRUTH OF RESURRECTION BY GOD. AMBROSE: It is a prerogative of God to raise the dead. ON THE HOLY SPIRIT 3.19.149.[18]

THE WONDER OF RESURRECTION. AMBROSE: We notice here how the operations of the Spirit of life are again resumed; we know in what way the dead are raised from the opening tombs. And is it in truth a matter of wonder that the sepulchers of the dead are opened at the bidding of the Lord, when the whole earth from its utmost limits is shaken by one thunderclap, the sea overflows its bounds and again checks the course of

---

[11]PG 81:1189. [12]CCL 75:513. [13]FC 46:272*. [14]CCL 75:513. [15]FC 6:89*. [16]FC 83:137*. [17]PG 81:1192-93. [18]NPNF 2 10:156.

its waves? On His Brother Satyrus 2.76.[19]

The Eucharist Is the Memorial of the Cross. Jerome: We ourselves make the spiritual memorial that is fulfilled as a result of the cross of

the Lord and Savior. Commentary on Ezekiel 11.37.1-14.[20]

---

[19]NPNF 2 10:186. [20]CCL 75:516.

37:15-28 THE UNION OF THE TWO STICKS, ISRAEL AND JUDAH

[21]*Then say to them, Thus says the Lord God: Behold, I will take the people of Israel from the nations among which they have gone, and will gather them from all sides, and bring them to their own land;* [22]*and I will make them one nation in the land, upon the mountains of Israel; and one king shall be king over them all; and they shall be no longer two nations, and no longer divided into two kingdoms. . . .*

[27]*My dwelling place shall be with them; and I will be their God, and they shall be my people.*

Overview: The union of Israel and Judah is like the inseparable character of the Trinity and the joining together of heaven and earth (Cassiodorus), dwelling among us forever (Caesarius) and filling us with the being of the Christ (Cyril of Alexandria).

37:21 Israel Gathered

The Inseparable Trinity. Cassiodorus: So they are truly said to assemble together who hasten with devoted mind to believe in the inseparable Trinity, which is the one God. There follows too the happy change, so that the kingdoms of earth and heaven serve the Lord, and they are then all the more free since they are bound to their Maker in faithful service. Exposition of the Psalms 101.23.[1]

37:27 The Lord Will Dwell with Them

Christ Will Live Among Us Forever. Caesarius of Arles: If he has walked among us in this life, he will dwell among us in that other one: who lives and reigns for ever and ever. Sermon 217.4.[2]

Christ Fills Us with His Being. Cyril of Alexandria: To be made partakers of Christ, both intellectually and by our senses, fills us with every blessing. For he dwells in us, first, by the Holy Spirit, and we are his abode, according to that which was said of old by one of the holy prophets. Commentary on Luke 142.[3]

---

[1]ACW 53:14. [2]FC 66:124. [3]CGSL 568.

[38:1–39:29 THE PROPHECY AGAINST GOG]

40:1-5 THE NEW TEMPLE

¹*In the twenty-fifth year of our exile, at the beginning of the year, on the tenth day of the month, in the fourteenth year after the city was conquered, on that very day, the hand of the LORD was upon me,* ²*and brought me in the visions of God into the land of Israel, and set me down upon a very high mountain, on which was a structure like a city opposite me.*ᵖ ³*When he brought me there, behold, there was a man, whose appearance was like bronze, with a line of flax and a measuring reed in his hand; and he was standing in the gateway.* ⁴*And the man said to me, "Son of man, look with your eyes, and hear with your ears, and set your mind upon all that I shall show you, for you were brought here in order that I might show it to you; declare all that you see to the house of Israel."*

⁵*And behold, there was a wall all around the outside of the temple area, and the length of the measuring reed in the man's hand was six long cubits, each being a cubit and a handbreadth in length; so he measured the thickness of the wall, one reed; and the height, one reed.*

p Gk: Heb *on the south*

OVERVIEW: The vision is so mysterious that interpreters have to tread carefully (JEROME, GREGORY THE GREAT). The city is the church (GREGORY THE GREAT), in which there are different kinds of spiritual labors (ISAAC), the living stones being holy teachers. We must hear the word of God with the ears of the heart (GREGORY THE GREAT), aided by the master builder (JEROME); and the vision makes one aware of the difference between the active life and the contemplative (GREGORY THE GREAT).

40:1 The Hand of the Lord on Ezekiel

JEROME'S HESITATION. JEROME: Your prayers, daughter Eustochium, have conquered my fear in explaining the temple in Ezekiel, even my determination to be quiet on the matter, and so have the promises of the Lord when he says, "Ask and you will receive, seek and you will find, knock and the door will be open to you."[1] COMMENTARY ON EZEKIEL 3 PREFACE.[2]

THE GAP IN TIME. GREGORY THE GREAT: If [Ezekiel] told his first vision in the fifth year of the first captivity and describes this last vision as occurring in the twenty-fifth year, it is surely clear that he extended the space of his speech for twenty years until the account of his last vision. HOMILIES ON EZEKIEL 2.1.1.[3]

THE ALLEGORICAL INTERPRETATION'S IMPORTANCE. GREGORY THE GREAT: In holy Scripture those things that can be accepted

---

[1]Mt 7:7; Lk 11:9. [2]CCL 75:549. [3]HGE 158.

according to the history are very frequently to be understood spiritually so that faith in the truth of history is retained and spiritual understanding is derived from the mysteries of allegory. HOMILIES ON EZEKIEL 2.1.3.[4]

THE POWER OF REVELATION GIVEN. GREGORY THE GREAT: The hand expresses the virtue of power, but the visions express the actual revelation that he had received. The hand is surely in the visions, the virtue in the contemplation. HOMILIES ON EZEKIEL 2.1.3.[5]

40:2 Taken to a Mountain

THE HEIGHT FROM WHICH THE VISION IS SEEN. GREGORY THE GREAT: He who is said to be a mountain on the top of the mountain is here proclaimed as a very high mountain. HOMILIES ON EZEKIEL 2.1.4.[6]

THE CITY AS THE COMMUNION OF SAINTS. GREGORY THE GREAT: Clearly this city has here already its great building in the conduct of the saints. As in a building, stone carries stone because stone is placed on stone, and the stone that bears another is itself borne by a third. HOMILIES ON EZEKIEL 2.1.5.[7]

LOVE OF ONE ANOTHER. GREGORY THE GREAT: If I neglect to support you in your ways and you disdain to tolerate me in mine, from where does the building of charity rise between us, whom love of neighbor does not join in patience? HOMILIES ON EZEKIEL 2.1.5.[8]

THE SOUTH WIND IS THE SCRIPTURE. GREGORY THE GREAT: Those who are learned in holy scripture recall that the south wind is usually to be presented as a symbol of the holy Scripture. HOMILIES ON EZEKIEL 2.1.6.[9]

A DIFFERENT KIND OF SPIRITUAL LABOR. ISAAC OF NINEVEH: Ezekiel was taken away supernaturally by the action of revelation, and he came to Jerusalem; and in a divine revelation he beheld the renewal that was to come. It is the same with purity of soul. Some, going by the well-trodden road of the law through keeping the commandments in a life of many labors, enter into purity of soul by sweat and blood; and there are others who are granted purity of soul by the gift of grace. It is a marvelous thing that we are not permitted to ask in prayer for the purity that is granted us by grace and so to reject the active and laborious manner of life. EPISTLE TO ABBA SYMEON OF CAESAREA.[10]

40:3 The Man With the Measuring Rod

MEDITATION IS THE MEANS OF ENTRY. GREGORY THE GREAT: He enters the building of the heavenly city who meditates by imitating the ways of the good in holy church. HOMILIES ON EZEKIEL 2.1.7.[11]

THE SOUND OF THE INCARNATION. GREGORY THE GREAT: Why is it that his very incarnation is likened to sounding metal, except that by this same assumption of our humanity he resounded to all with the glory of his majesty? HOMILIES ON EZEKIEL 2.1.9.[12]

HOLY TEACHERS ARRANGE LIVING STONES. GREGORY THE GREAT: The translators of the Septuagint do not have a "line of flax" but a "builders' line." If in this verse we use their translation for exposition, what shall we take as builders but holy teachers who by speaking spiritual words arrange living stones, that is, the souls of the elect, into a heavenly building? Then whatever the early fathers, the prophets, the apostles, the successors of the apostles said, what was it but the arrangement of stones in this building of the saints, a building that is constructed daily? HOMILIES ON EZEKIEL 2.1.10.[13]

---

[4]HGE 159**. [5]HGE 159**. [6]HGE 160*. [7]HGE 161*. [8]HGE 161*. [9]HGE 161*. [10]*AHSIS* 429*. [11]HGE 162*. [12]HGE 164*. [13]HGE 164*.

FINE PREACHING. GREGORY THE GREAT: What must we understand by the line of flax if not fine, that is, spiritual, preaching? HOMILIES ON EZEKIEL 2.1.10.[14]

THE HEAVENLY BUILDING CONSTRUCTED CAREFULLY. GREGORY THE GREAT: By the inward stewardship of hidden judgment is led the line and measuring reed by which the one is dragged along and the other is left behind. The heavenly building is not constructed without pious and righteous scrutiny. HOMILIES ON EZEKIEL 2.1.13.[15]

SPIRITUAL PROGRESS. GREGORY THE GREAT: His eyes always gaze on his building because he unceasingly considers how much progress each is making in the virtues. HOMILIES ON EZEKIEL 2.1.16.[16]

HEARING THE WORD OF GOD. GREGORY THE GREAT: He who already stands at the door of his cave and hears the words of God in the ears of his heart must veil his face, because when we are led through heavenly grace to understanding of higher things, the more subtly we are lifted, the more often we should through humility restrain ourselves in our understanding, lest we try to be more wise than is right for us, but to be wise to the point of sobriety.[17] HOMILIES ON EZEKIEL 2.1.18.[18]

THE MEASURING LINE. JEROME: As far as the measuring line is concerned, these are the angels who minister at the command of God, or Moses and all the prophets and the apostles who built the city of God and the assistants or ministers at the will of the Lord. COMMENTARY ON EZEKIEL 12.40.1-4.[19]

THE MASTER BUILDER. JEROME: This man spoke to the prophet. In his hand was the measuring stick, and his face was like the sky, and he held in his hand a reed. The man who spoke to Ezekiel was a true master builder, whom Paul the apostle imitated, when he said, "like a skilled master builder I will lay the foundation."[20] COMMENTARY ON EZEKIEL 12.40.1-4.[21]

40:4 The Prophet Must Look at the Vision

THE PROPHET LOOKS SPIRITUALLY. JEROME: Not with the eyes of the flesh but with the spirit, not with the ears of the body but of the soul. COMMENTARY ON EZEKIEL 12.40.1-4.[22]

KEEP THE VISION IN YOUR MEMORY. JEROME: It is no use to see and hear, unless what you see and hear you place in the treasure of your memory. COMMENTARY ON EZEKIEL 12.40.1-4.[23]

GREGORY THE GREAT'S TENTATIVENESS. GREGORY THE GREAT: In case by any chance some people censure me in silent thought because I presume to discuss the profound mysteries of Ezekiel the prophet, which are untouched by the great interpreters, let them know with what mind I so do. HOMILIES ON EZEKIEL 2.2.1.[24]

THE BALANCE BETWEEN PRIDE AND WICKEDNESS. GREGORY THE GREAT: By wondrous stewardship the soul is balanced midpoint, so that it neither takes pride in its good deeds nor falls amid evil acts. HOMILIES ON EZEKIEL 2.2.3.[25]

40:5 The Wall Around the Outside of the Temple

THE WALL IS THE CHURCH. JEROME: We liken this to the church of Christ, and each day I can see it being built in the saints. COMMENTARY ON EZEKIEL 12.40.5-13.[26]

THE WALL IS THE INCARNATION. GREGORY THE GREAT: Very often in holy Scripture,

---

[14]HGE 165. [15]HGE 166-67. [16]HGE 168. [17]Rom 12:3. [18]HGE 170. Compare hearing with "the ear of the heart" with RSB prologue 1.18. [19]CCL 75:553. [20]1 Cor 3:10. [21]CCL 75:554. [22]CCL 75:554. [23]CCL 75:554. [24]HGE 170**. Theodoret of Cyr passes over this chapter rapidly, PG 81:1219-26. [25]HGE 172*. [26]CCL 75:557.

through the rampart of his protection, the incarnate Lord is himself used to being called a wall, as it is said of holy church through the prophet: a wall and a bulwark shall be set therein.[27] HOMILIES ON EZEKIEL 2.2.5.[28]

THE MEASURING REED. GREGORY THE GREAT: It is a measuring reed because by the hands of the scribes the life of the hearers is measured. HOMILIES ON EZEKIEL 2.2.7.[29]

ACTIVE AND CONTEMPLATIVE. GREGORY THE GREAT: The active life is signified by the six cubits and the contemplative by the hand breadth, because we complete the former by works, but even when we strive concerning the latter we hardly avail to attain too little. HOMI-LIES ON EZEKIEL 2.2.7.[30]

THE CONTEMPLATIVE LIFE IS LONG. GREGORY THE GREAT: The contemplative life, which is said to be as it were half an hour, is in Ezekiel the prophet not described as a cubit but a hand breadth. HOMILIES ON EZEKIEL 2.2.14.[31]

EVERYONE SPOKEN OF BY GOD. GREGORY THE GREAT: Almighty God, who is neither stretched by the great nor narrowed by the least, speaks in this way of the whole church at the same time as he speaks of a single soul. HOMILIES ON EZEKIEL 2.2.15.[32]

---

[27]Is 26:1. [28]HGE 173*. [29]HGE 174*. [30]HGE 174*. [31]HGE 178*. [32]HGE 178*.

40:6-16 THE OUTER COURT: THE EAST GATE

[6]Then he went into the gateway facing east, going up its steps, and measured the threshold of the gate, one reed deep;[q] [7]and the side rooms, one reed long, and one reed broad; and the space between the side rooms, five cubits; and the threshold of the gate by the vestibule of the gate at the inner end, one reed. [8]Then he measured the vestibule of the gateway, eight cubits; [9]and its jambs, two cubits; and the vestibule of the gate was at the inner end. [10]And there were three side rooms on either side of the east gate; the three were of the same size; and the jambs on either side were of the same size. [11]Then he measured the breadth of the opening of the gateway, ten cubits; and the breadth of the gateway, thirteen cubits. [12]There was a barrier before the side rooms, one cubit on either side; and the side rooms were six cubits on either side. [13]Then he measured the gate from the back[r] of the one side room to the back[r] of the other, a breadth of five and twenty cubits, from door to door. [14]He measured also the vestibule, twenty cubits; and round about the vestibule of the gateway was the court.[s] [15]From the front of the gate at the entrance to the end of the inner vestibule of the gate was fifty cubits. [16]And the gateway had windows round about, narrowing inwards into

their jambs in the side rooms, and likewise the vestibule had windows round about inside, and on the jambs were palm trees.

q Heb *deep, and one threshold, one reed deep* . r Compare Gk: Heb *roof* s Compare Gk: Heb *and he made the jambs sixty cubits, and to the jamb of the court was the gateway round about*

OVERVIEW: The entry into the temple reveals many mysteries. Entry itself is eternal life, and the preacher is a gate (GREGORY THE GREAT), for we must persevere in the life of faith (JEROME), spurred on by hope and charity. To interpret involves moving from history into allegory, with the aid of the Old and New Testaments (GREGORY THE GREAT).

40:6 The Threshold Measured

THE PREACHER IS A GATE OF ENTRY. GREGORY THE GREAT: Each preacher can be understood under the name "gate" because whoever opens for us the door of the heavenly kingdom through his speech is a gate. HOMILIES ON EZEKIEL 2.3.2.[1]

VIRTUES ARE THE STEPS THROUGH THE GATE. GREGORY THE GREAT: We must not be surprised if the steps are from virtue to virtue, when each very virtue is, as it were, increased by certain steps and thereby led through increases of merits to the heights. HOMILIES ON EZEKIEL 2.3.4.[2]

THE THRESHOLD IS THE EARTHLY ANCESTRY OF JESUS. GREGORY THE GREAT: If the gate is the Lord, who is the threshold of this gate but those ancient ancestors from whose ancestry the Lord deigned to be incarnate? HOMILIES ON EZEKIEL 2.3.7.[3]

UNDERSTANDING HOLY THINGS. JEROME: The apostle Paul, wanting the Ephesians to understand the more holy things, prayed for them to be filled with the wisdom and love of the Lord; being so rooted, they might be able to know and understand the breadth and length

and height and depth of the riches of God.[4] COMMENTARY ON EZEKIEL 12.40.5-13.[5]

40:7 The Threshold of the Gate

EXPECTATION AND LOVE. GREGORY THE GREAT: Truly the length pertains to the longsuffering of expectation and the breadth to the amplitude of charity. HOMILIES ON EZEKIEL 2.3.11.[6]

40:8 The Vestibule of the Gateway

THE TEN COMMANDMENTS. JEROME: Ten is a perfect number and comprises the Decalogue. COMMENTARY ON EZEKIEL 12.40.5-13.[7]

THROUGH HISTORY TO ALLEGORY. GREGORY THE GREAT: The outer threshold of holy Scripture is history, and the inner is allegory. Scripture leads through history to allegory, as if we come from the threshold that is outside to that which is inside. HOMILIES ON EZEKIEL 2.3.18.[8]

THE ACTIVE AND THE CONTEMPLATIVE. GREGORY THE GREAT: If the gate in this passage is interpreted as being each preacher, the outer threshold in the gate is the active life, but the inner is the contemplative. HOMILIES ON EZEKIEL 2.3.23.[9]

40:9 The Gateway Jambs

ETERNAL LIFE CONCEIVED IN HOPE. GREGORY THE GREAT: What then is meant by the inner porch but the breadth of eternal life, which now

---

[1]HGE 180*. [2]HGE 181**. [3]HGE 182*. [4]See Eph 3:17-19. [5]CCL 75:560-61. [6]HGE 184. [7]CCL 75:563. [8]HGE 188-89*. [9]HGE 192-93*.

in the limits of our present life is only conceived in the mind through hope? HOMILIES ON EZEKIEL 2.4.1.[10]

LOVE OF GOD AND NEIGHBOR. GREGORY THE GREAT: The front of the gate measures two cubits because whoever is zealous to preserve the love of God and of his neighbor himself arrives at the court of eternity. HOMILIES ON EZEKIEL 2.4.3.[11]

40:10 Rooms on Either Side of the East Gate

HEARTS INFLAMED BY GOD. GREGORY THE GREAT: The chambers beside the eastward way are the hearts of those inflamed with love for God. HOMILIES ON EZEKIEL 2.4.4.[12]

THE OLD AND THE NEW TESTAMENTS. GREGORY THE GREAT: The measure of the front is on both parts, because our fathers, coming either before from the Old, or now from the New Testament, agree in one faith in the Mediator [Christ]. HOMILIES ON EZEKIEL 2.4.8.[13]

40:11 Measuring the Opening of the Gateway

THE TRINITY FULFILLS THE DECALOGUE. GREGORY THE GREAT: So with grace supervening through the New Testament, every faithful people knows the one God to be the Trinity, and by their recognition of him they have fulfilled the virtue of the Decalogue. HOMILIES ON EZEKIEL 2.4.11.[14]

FAITH GOES BEFORE CHARITY. GREGORY THE GREAT: As we have often said, the chambers are the hearts of the elect burning with love for almighty God. What is expressed by the border before the chambers if not faith? For if this is not first held it does not attain to spiritual love. So charity does not precede faith but faith charity. No one can love what he has not believed. HOMILIES ON EZEKIEL 2.4.13.[15]

40:13 Measuring the Gate from the Back

CONTEMPLATION AND WORKS. GREGORY THE GREAT: Certain faithful so love almighty God that they are both perfect in works and suspended in contemplation. HOMILIES ON EZEKIEL 2.5.1.[16]

PROGRESS TOWARD HUMILITY. GREGORY THE GREAT: Some things are closed so that when we do not understand them and recognize the weakness of our blindness, we may advance to humility rather than to intelligence. HOMILIES ON EZEKIEL 2.5.4.[17]

THE HEAVENLY LIFE. GREGORY THE GREAT: We are still on the way, we hear many reports of that heavenly country, we already understand some through reason and the spirit and reverence others without comprehending them. HOMILIES ON EZEKIEL 2.5.4.[18]

LOVE SPILLS OVER INTO WORKS. GREGORY THE GREAT: What you have already learned from holy Scripture, and how much you secretly love your neighbor, you demonstrate in the breadth of your good works. HOMILIES ON EZEKIEL 2.5.5.[19]

DOING GOOD. GREGORY THE GREAT: Let the breadth be great from the roof of the chamber to the roof of the gate. This means that from the secrets of charity on our neighbor's behalf to the point of humility of knowledge, we may always do good—insofar as we understand and can for the sake of God. HOMILIES ON EZEKIEL 2.5.6.[20]

ENTRY TO HEAVEN. GREGORY THE GREAT: The gate can also be understood as the very entry to the heavenly kingdom. HOMILIES ON EZEKIEL 2.5.7.[21]

FAITH AND WALKING IN FAITH. GREGORY THE GREAT: In the knowledge of almighty God our first door is faith and the second his appearance

---

[10]HGE 193*. [11]HGE 194*. [12]HGE 196*. [13]HGE 198. [14]HGE 200. [15]HGE 201. [16]HGE 205*. [17]HGE 206*. [18]HGE 206*. [19]HGE 207*. [20]HGE 208**. [21]HGE 208*.

to which we attain by walking in faith. For in this life we enter the latter so that we may later be led to the former. HOMILIES ON EZEKIEL 2.5.8.[22]

WONDER AT CREATION. GREGORY THE GREAT: Why should we who perceive the footprints of his virtue even among his creatures wonder so much at the power of the Creator? HOMILIES ON EZEKIEL 2.5.10.[23]

40:14 Measuring the Vestibule

THE BURDEN IS LIGHT. GREGORY THE GREAT: The spiritual tasks we impose on an unaccustomed spirit are hard. Yet the burden of God is light when we have begun to bear it so that even persecution pleases us through our love of him. Every affliction for his sake comes in sweetness of mind, for the holy apostles too rejoiced when they endured the whip for the Lord. HOMILIES ON EZEKIEL 2.5.13.[24]

HEAVENLY HOPE SETS THE EARTHLY IN CONTEXT. GREGORY THE GREAT: The hope for the heavenly strengthens the mind lest it be shaken by the turbulence of earthly tumults. HOMILIES ON EZEKIEL 2.5.14.[25]

40:15 From the Front of the Gate to the Inner Vestibule

THE RESURRECTION BRINGS US CLOSE TO GOD. JEROME: The first day of the eight is the day of the resurrection, and it leads us to the entrance of the temple, for when we have done everything and repented of the sins we have committed, then we are brought close to God. COMMENTARY ON EZEKIEL 12.40.5-13.[26]

HOPE LEADS US ON. GREGORY THE GREAT: This space signified our hope, which leads the mind to the porch of the inner gate when it seeks eternal rest. HOMILIES ON EZEKIEL 2.5.16.[27]

FAITH, CHARITY AND HOPE. GREGORY THE GREAT: Let faith be held in the gate that leads to understanding, charity in the court that stretches the mind to love, hope in the place that is described by fifty cubits, because by yearning and sighs it leads the spirit to the hidden joys of peace. HOMILIES ON EZEKIEL 2.5.16.[28]

A PROPER ESTIMATION OF OURSELVES. GREGORY THE GREAT: Let no one reckon that he has the gift of the true light as his own, because he thinks he is superior. It is often the case that another to whom he does not attribute any good gift is richer. HOMILIES ON EZEKIEL 2.5.19.[29]

---

[22]HGE 209. [23]HGE 210**. [24]HGE 212*. [25]HGE 213*. [26]CCL 75:567. [27]HGE 214*. [28]HGE 214. [29]HGE 215.

40:17-23 THE THIRTY CHAMBERS, THE PAVEMENT AND THE NORTH GATE

[17]*Then he brought me into the outer court; and behold, there were chambers and a pavement, round about the court; thirty chambers fronted on the pavement.* [18]*And the pavement ran along the side of the gates, corresponding to the length of the gates; this was the lower pavement.* [19]*Then he*

measured the distance from the inner front of the lower gate to the outer front of the inner court, a hundred cubits.

Then he went before me to the north, [20]*and behold, there was a gate[u] which faced toward the north, belonging to the outer court. He measured its length and its breadth.* [21]*Its side rooms, three on either side, and its jambs and its vestibule were of the same size as those of the first gate; its length was fifty cubits, and its breadth twenty-five cubits.* [22]*And its windows, its vestibule, and its palm trees were of the same size as those of the gate which faced toward the east; and seven steps led up to it; and its vestibule was on the inside.* [23]*And opposite the gate on the north, as on the east, was a gate to the inner court; and he measured from gate to gate, a hundred cubits.*

t Compare Gk: Heb *from before*   u Gk: Heb *a hundred cubits on the east and on the north.* [20]*And the gate*

OVERVIEW: The pavement is there to prevent the sinner going forward without repenting (JEROME), and the treasure chambers are the teachers, who must be schooled in the active life as well as the contemplative, which are themselves expressed in the Decalogue. We must be aware of the darkness of sin, which has been left behind, just as we must be aware, too, of the very different vocations that co-exist in this spiritual building: married couples, celibates and preachers (GREGORY THE GREAT). The fifty cubits are the fifty days of Easter, the foundation of the Christian faith (JEROME) and the path of faith that is open to any penitent (GREGORY THE GREAT).

40:17 Chambers and a Pavement

THE PAVEMENT TO STOP SINNERS SOILING THE ENTRANCE. JEROME: The pavement is spread wide with stone, to stop the footsteps of the sinners who live there being made dirty with mire and earth and dust. COMMENTARY ON EZEKIEL 12.40.17-19.[1]

TREASURE CHAMBERS AS THE KNOWLEDGE OF TEACHERS. GREGORY THE GREAT: What is meant by these treasure chambers if not the knowledge of the teachers? HOMILIES ON EZEKIEL 2.6.1.[2]

TREASURE CHAMBERS DEFINED. GREGORY THE GREAT: Those who contain within themselves true riches are rightly called treasure chambers. HOMILIES ON EZEKIEL 2.6.2.[3]

THE ACTIVE AND THE CONTEMPLATIVE UNITED IN THE DECALOGUE. GREGORY THE GREAT: The number ten is always taken to mean perfection because the custody of the law is contained within ten precepts. The active and the contemplative life are simultaneously united in the commandments of the Decalogue because the observance of love of God and love of neighbor are enjoined in them. HOMILIES ON EZEKIEL 2.6.5.[4]

40:18 The Pavement Along the Sides of the Gates

THE DEEDS AND WORDS OF PREACHERS. GREGORY THE GREAT: If we ponder the deeds and words of our preachers that we read, we recognize the height to which the gates will rise. HOMILIES ON EZEKIEL 2.6.9.[5]

THE AUTHORSHIP OF 2 PETER DEFENDED. GREGORY THE GREAT: There were some who said that the second epistle of Peter, in which the letters of Paul were praised, was not written by him. But if they had been willing to ponder the words of this same epistle, they could have had a far different perception. HOMILIES ON EZEKIEL 2.6.11.[6]

---

[1]CCL 75:570. [2]HGE 217. [3]HGE 218*. [4]HGE 219. [5]HGE 221*.
[6]HGE 222*.

PREACHERS LIKE CLOUDS. GREGORY THE GREAT: The holy preachers are rightly called clouds because they rain with words and flash with miracles. They are also said to fly like clouds because when living on earth they were above the earth through all that they did. HOMILIES ON EZEKIEL 2.6.15.[7]

40:19 The Distance from the Lower Gate to the Inner Court

FAITH LEADS TO CONTEMPLATION. GREGORY THE GREAT: If in these words we take the gate to be the door through which we enter into knowledge of the Lord, the lower gate is faith and the inner court is surely contemplation. HOMILIES ON EZEKIEL 2.6.16.[8]

THE DARKNESS OF SIN. GREGORY THE GREAT: Let us recall the darkness from which we came, so that we may give thanks for the light that we have received. No one understands divine mercy who is not mindful of his own wretchedness. HOMILIES ON EZEKIEL 2.6.21.[9]

40:20 The North Gate of the Outer Court

ONE GATE IS FAITH. GREGORY THE GREAT: When the prophet spoke at length about a single gate, faith is rightly understood because the faith of all the elect is one. When other gates are mentioned, the mouths of the preachers may be understood, where the true life is recognized, and through which lies ascent to the knowledge of spiritual mysteries. HOMILIES ON EZEKIEL 2.7.1.[10]

PREACHING OPENS OUR LIVES. GREGORY THE GREAT: The gate looks northward when each preacher examines the life of a sinner and opens to him the inner life through the word of preaching. HOMILIES ON EZEKIEL 2.7.2.[11]

CHAMBERS IN THE SAME BUILDING. GREGORY THE GREAT: There are three orders of those who lead virtuous lives, that is, good spouses, celibates and preachers. Some who are married strive in love for the heavenly kingdom, but others in hope of eternal joy torment their flesh, flee all earthly activities and disdain to be involved in the care of this age. Others again despise earthly goods and proclaim the heavenly joys that they know. What are all these but chambers in the spiritual building, in whose thoughts and meditation the soul is joined to her heavenly groom? HOMILIES ON EZEKIEL 2.7.3.[12]

LIFE AS A WITNESS TO FAITH. GREGORY THE GREAT: This gate also has a front because there are in the life of the preacher open works that are seen. HOMILIES ON EZEKIEL 2.7.3.[13]

40:21 Side Rooms, Jambs and Vestibules

THE CURTAINS ARE THE SAINTS. GREGORY THE GREAT: The curtains of the tabernacle are all the saints who contribute with various colors of virtues to the adornment of holy church. HOMILIES ON EZEKIEL 2.7.4.[14]

THE FIFTY DAYS OF EASTER. JEROME: After seven weeks, there are fifty days designated for eternal respite, stretching from the day of the resurrection to the kingdom of heaven, in which there is true respite. COMMENTARY ON EZEKIEL 12.40.20-23.[15]

40:22 Windows and Steps

CONTEMPLATION, HUMILITY AND GOOD DEEDS. GREGORY THE GREAT: We need to note that the gate looking northward is said to have all the features that the gate to the east has, that is, windows of contemplation, a porch of humility and engravings of good deeds. HOMILIES ON EZEKIEL 2.7.6.[16]

---

[7]HGE 225*. [8]HGE 225. [9]HGE 227*. [10]HGE 231*. [11]HGE 231*. [12]HGE 232*. [13]HGE 232. [14]HGE 233*. [15]CCL 75:573-74. [16]HGE 234.

THE SEVEN GIFTS OF THE HOLY SPIRIT.
GREGORY THE GREAT: The gate is approached by
seven steps because the entrance of the heavenly
life is opened to us through the sevenfold grace of
the Holy Spirit. HOMILIES ON EZEKIEL 2.7.7.[17]

THE PORCH AS FAITH. GREGORY THE GREAT: It
is also possible to understand the porch as faith.
For it is before the steps and the gate, because
we come first to faith and afterward,
via the steps of spiritual gifts, we enter the
door of the heavenly life. HOMILIES ON EZEKIEL
2.7.9.[18]

**REPENTANCE LEADS TO THE HEAVENLY KING-
DOM.** GREGORY THE GREAT: The inner gate does
not only face the gate of the east but also that of
the north: the joys of the inner court are opened
to those who remain in innocence, but they are
also opened to condemned sinners by their repentance of their sins. They then recognize the
unspeakable mystery of the heavenly kingdom, by
recognizing them they thirst for them, by thirst-
ing for them they hasten and by hastening they
arrive. HOMILIES ON EZEKIEL 2.7.10.[19]

40:23 The Gate to the Inner Court

THE GATE IS OPEN TO THE PENITENT. GREG-
ORY THE GREAT: We must observe that in the
spiritual building one entrance lies open to the
east, another to the north and another to the
south. Just as the cold of the north denotes sinners, so the southern way stands for the fervent
in spirit who, kindled by the heat of the Holy
Spirit, grow up in virtues as in the noonday light.
Then let the gate lie open to the east so that those
who, after the beginning of heat and light, have
relapsed in the coldness and darkness of their sins
may through the work of penitence return to pardon and recognize what is the true rejoicing on
inward recompense. Let the gate lie open to the
south so that those who burn in virtues with holy
desires may daily penetrate the mysteries of
inward joy with spiritual understanding. HOMI-
LIES ON EZEKIEL 2.7.13.[20]

TRAVEL LIGHT. GREGORY THE GREAT: We strive
the more freely towards the kingdom because, as
it were, we travel light. HOMILIES ON EZEKIEL
2.7.18.[21]

DESIRE GOES BEYOND NECESSITY. GREGORY
THE GREAT: Desire seeks more than need. HOMI-
LIES ON EZEKIEL 2.7.19.[22]

THE PREACHER'S INNER LIFE. GREGORY THE
GREAT: The excellent preacher has a palm on this
side and on that, because abundance does not
lead him astray to pride, nor does need lead him
to avarice. HOMILIES ON EZEKIEL 2.7.16.[23]

---

[17]HGE 234. [18]HGE 235 [19]HGE 236*. [20]HGE 238-39*. [21]HGE
242. [22]HGE 242. [23]HGE 241**.

40:24-48 THE SOUTH GATE, THE TABLES, THE CHAMBERS AND THE VESTIBULE

[24]*And he led me toward the south, and behold, there was a gate on the south; and he measured
its jambs and its vestibule; they had the same size as the others.* [25]*And there were windows round
about in it and in its vestibule, like the windows of the others; its length was fifty cubits, and its*

breadth twenty-five cubits. ^{26}And there were seven steps leading up to it, and its vestibule was on the inside; and it had palm trees on its jambs, one on either side. ^{27}And there was a gate on the south of the inner court; and he measured from gate to gate toward the south, a hundred cubits.

^{28}Then he brought me to the inner court by the south gate, and he measured the south gate; it was of the same size as the others. ^{29}Its side rooms, its jambs, and its vestibule were of the same size as the others; and there were windows round about in it and in its vestibule; its length was fifty cubits, and its breadth twenty-five cubits. ^{30}And there were vestibules round about, twenty-five cubits long and five cubits broad. ^{31}Its vestibule faced the outer court, and palm trees were on its jambs, and its stairway had eight steps.

^{32}Then he brought me to the inner court on the east side, and he measured the gate; it was of the same size as the others. ^{33}Its side rooms, its jambs, and its vestibule were of the same size as the others; and there were windows round about in it and in its vestibule; its length was fifty cubits, and its breadth twenty-five cubits. ^{34}Its vestibule faced the outer court, and it had palm trees on its jambs, one on either side; and its stairway had eight steps.

^{35}Then he brought me to the north gate, and he measured it; it had the same size as the others. ^{36}Its side rooms, its jambs, and its vestibule were of the same size as the others;^{v} and it had windows round about; its length was fifty cubits, and its breadth twenty-five cubits. ^{37}Its vestibule^w faced the outer court, and it had palm trees on its jambs, one on either side; and its stairway had eight steps.

^{38}There was a chamber with its door in the vestibule of the gate,^{x} where the burnt offering was to be washed. ^{39}And in the vestibule of the gate were two tables on either side, on which the burnt offering and the sin offering and the guilt offering were to be slaughtered. ^{40}And on the outside of the vestibule^y at the entrance of the north gate were two tables; and on the other side of the vestibule of the gate were two tables. ^{41}Four tables were on the inside, and four tables on the outside of the side of the gate, eight tables, on which the sacrifices were to be slaughtered. ^{42}And there were also four tables of hewn stone for the burnt offering, a cubit and a half long, and a cubit and a half broad, and one cubit high, on which the instruments were to be laid with which the burnt offerings and the sacrifices were slaughtered. ^{43}And hooks, a handbreadth long, were fastened round about within. And on the tables the flesh of the offering was to be laid.

^{44}Then he brought me from without into the inner court, and behold, there were two chambers^z in the inner court, one^a at the side of the north gate facing south, the other at the side of the south^b gate facing north. ^{45}And he said to me, This chamber which faces south is for the priests who have charge of the temple, ^{46}and the chamber which faces north is for the priests who have charge of the altar; these are the sons of Zadok, who alone among the sons of Levi may come near to the LORD to minister to him. ^{47}And he measured the court, a hundred cubits long, and a hundred cubits broad, foursquare; and the altar was in front of the temple.

^{48}Then he brought me to the vestibule of the temple and measured the jambs of the vestibule, five cubits on either side; and the breadth of the gate was fourteen cubits; and the sidewalls of the gate were three cubits^c on either side.

v One Ms Compare verses 29 and 33: Heb lacks *were of the same size as the others*   w Gk Vg Compare verses 26, 31, 34: Heb *jambs*   x Cn: Heb *at the jambs of the gates*   y Cn: Heb *to him who goes up*   z Gk: Heb *and from without to the inner gate were chambers for singers*   a Gk: Heb *which*   b Gk: Heb *east*   c Gk: Heb *and the breadth of the gate was three cubits*

Overview: The life of the gospel lies before those who enter the temple precincts (Jerome), and the journey is not without its demands. The gates are interpreted variously, but the preacher is at the forefront (Gregory the Great). The eight steps are the mystery of the gospel (Jerome), in which repentance is always needed and a fresh offering can be made, the heart of our faith being love of God and neighbor. The life of the preacher needs constant attention, including the way hard truths are tempered by gentleness. The gospel life is costly, as the martyrs knew (Gregory the Great). The three cubits on the sidewalls of the gate of the vestibule are the Trinity, in whose name we are baptized (Jerome).

40:27 The Gate on the South of the Inner Court

The Gospel Lies Ahead. Jerome: He goes through the gate so that he reaches good ground and the grace of the gospel. Commentary on Ezekiel 12.40.24-31.[1]

The Ascent Can Be Demanding. Gregory the Great: The gates of the spiritual building have seven steps because they proclaim to their hearers fear of the Lord, godliness and knowledge, fortitude and counsel, understanding and wisdom. But when they require the renunciation of all things, when they warn that nothing in this world is to be loved and nothing retained through fondness, when they advocate concentration on the contemplation of the heavenly kingdom and rejoicing in its mysteries, they add a step and pass over to inner truths. Homilies on Ezekiel 2.8.4.[2]

40:28 The Inner Court by the South Gate

The Hearts of Good Hearers Are Humble. Gregory the Great: The porches are flat because the hearts of good hearers are humble. They are long because they persevered in the longsuffering of hope. Homilies on Ezekiel 2.8.11.[3]

Different Interpretations of the Gates. Gregory the Great: The east gate may also stand for the Lord, the south for Judea and the north for the converted Gentiles. Homilies on Ezekiel 2.8.13.[4]

The Words and Works of Preachers. Gregory the Great: The forefronts of the gates are the words and works of the preachers whereby we recognize them outside as they live inwardly. Then there is a door for every treasure chamber at the forefronts of the gates because each teacher opens the understanding in the heart of the hearer in the words and deeds of the Fathers. Homilies on Ezekiel 2.8.14.[5]

40:32 The Inner Court on the East Side

The Mystery of the Gospel. Jerome: We reach the top by eight steps, for what satisfies the number eight for us is the mystery of the gospel; even though we once regarded Christ from a human point of view, we regard him in this way no longer, which is understood to be according to the flesh. Commentary on Ezekiel 12.40.32-34.[6]

40:38 In the Chamber in the Vestibule

The Old and New Testaments. Jerome: These are the living stones in which the walls of the Old and New Testaments are contained, for the number four indicates the mysteries of the

---

[1]CCL 75:577. [2]HGE 247*. [3]HGE 251. [4]HGE 252*. [5]HGE 253*. [6]CCL 75:580.

Gospels. COMMENTARY ON EZEKIEL 12.40.35-43.[7]

A NEW OFFERING. GREGORY THE GREAT: Whenever we realize that an element of malice or perverse love is mingled with our good works, let us return to tears, let us wash the whole burnt offering. HOMILIES ON EZEKIEL 2.8.17.[8]

40:39 The Two Tables in the Vestibule

HOLY PREACHERS ARE THE GATES. GREGORY THE GREAT: It is possible to understand holy preachers under the name of gates, so that the porch of the gate is the people. When they accept the words of preaching with a humble mind, tables for sacrifice are constructed in them through their virtues. HOMILIES ON EZEKIEL 2.9.2.[9]

LOVE OF GOD AND NEIGHBOR. GREGORY THE GREAT: The inner gate has in the great multitude of the faithful two sides, the love of God and the love of neighbor. HOMILIES ON EZEKIEL 2.9.2.[10]

SIN AND TRESPASS DISTINGUISHED. GREGORY THE GREAT: There is this difference between a sin and a trespass: a sin is to do wrong, but a trespass is to fail to do the good that is diligently to be maintained. HOMILIES ON EZEKIEL 2.9.3.[11]

THE SQUARE STONES. GREGORY THE GREAT: What are we to understand as the square stones in this passage but all the saints whose life knew how to stand bravely in prosperity and adversity? HOMILIES ON EZEKIEL 2.9.5.[12]

40:42 Four Tables for the Burnt Offering

THE FOUR GOSPELS. GREGORY THE GREAT: Our gate has four tables in the inner porch because holy church [was instructed by the preaching of four Evangelists through whose teaching the heart learned to ascend to love of almighty God and to offer its thoughts to him in sacrifice. Two of them are said to be on this side

and two on that, because two Evangelists bore witness to what they saw concerning the Lord, and two reported what they learned by listening to their seniors. Surely there are four tables in the inner porch, this which we plainly see, because holy church] received for the instruction of the faithful peoples four orders of rulers whom Paul enumerates by the gift of the almighty Lord, saying, "He gave some, apostles; some, prophets; some, evangelists; and some, pastors and teachers."[13] HOMILIES ON EZEKIEL 2.9.6.[14]

THE LOVE OF THE SAINTS. GREGORY THE GREAT: The tables have a width of one and a half cubits, because the hearts of the saints are spread in breadth of charity for the neighbor whom they love and see, and they measure one cubit. HOMILIES ON EZEKIEL 2.9.10.[15]

THE SOULS OF THE FAITHFUL. GREGORY THE GREAT: What are the souls of the faithful if not holy vessels that catch the words of piety, so that the whole burnt offering of life and prayer may be sacrificed from their minds. HOMILIES ON EZEKIEL 2.9.12.[16]

THE TEACHING OF THE PREACHERS. GREGORY THE GREAT: The borders of the tables measure one hand breadth because the hand is extended in the palm, and the holy fathers and the teachers preach those things in which the works of the hearers are extended. HOMILIES ON EZEKIEL 2.9.13.[17]

THE INNER LIFE OF THE PREACHER. GREGORY THE GREAT: The borders of the tables are bent inward when the teachers are silent in thought and recall what they say and closely examine themselves as to whether they practice what they

---

[7]CCL 75:582. [8]HGE 255. [9]HGE 259*. [10]HGE 259*. [11]HGE 260*. [12]HGE 261*. [13]Eph 4:11. [14]HGE 262*. The bracketed portion indicates a possible later edition; see SC 360:440. [15]HGE 264*. [16]HGE 265*. [17]HGE 266*.

preach. HOMILIES ON EZEKIEL 2.9.15.[18]

MIX DEMAND WITH WARMTH. GREGORY THE GREAT: Apparent harshness but charity in mind is to be shown to the wicked, for a vigorous appearance can coerce the wrongdoer, and the preservation of charity does not lose the reward of meekness. HOMILIES ON EZEKIEL 2.9.18.[19]

40:43 Offerings Laid on the Tables

THE MINISTRY OF FORGIVENESS INVOLVES CAREFUL DISCERNMENT. GREGORY THE GREAT: This is indeed the office of discipline, so that it knows how prudently to punish sins as well as how piously to remit them. But those who do not possess the spirit of discernment remit the sins so that they do not correct them or strike in such a way that they pretend to correct them but do not actually remit them. Therefore let the teacher who must speak of the control of discipline know that he is a table of God, and let him bend his lip inward so that what he says in preaching he may vigilantly practice beneath the spirit of discernment. HOMILIES ON EZEKIEL 2.9.20.[20]

40:44 The Two Chambers in the Inner Court

THE ANGELIC CHOIR. JEROME: The inner court is set in the side of the gate that looked north and south and east so that singers of the Lord and those who are engaged in the task of angels will always remember and recognize the divine mysteries of each place carefully. COMMENTARY ON EZEKIEL 12.40.44-49.[21]

40:45 The Chamber Is for the Priests

THE TEMPORAL AND ETERNAL LIVES OF THE CHURCH. GREGORY THE GREAT: Holy church has two lives, the one that it leads temporally, the other that it receives for eternity, the one in which it labors on earth, the other in which it is rewarded in heaven, the one in which it earns rewards, the other truly in which it rejoices in the receipt thereof, and in each life it offers sacrifices. HOMILIES ON EZEKIEL 2.10.4.[22]

40:46 The Priests Who Have Charge of the Altar

THE PRIESTS GUARD THE CHURCH. GREGORY THE GREAT: The priests who guard the temple of God are those who by praying, preaching and keeping watch with spiritual actions defend holy church from the incursions of evil spirits, from the persuasion of the wicked and from the errors of heretics. HOMILIES ON EZEKIEL 2.10.12.[23]

40:47 The Court Measured

THE FAITHFUL ARE THE TEMPLE. GREGORY THE GREAT: What is the temple if not the faithful people? HOMILIES ON EZEKIEL 2.10.19.[24]

40:48 The Vestibule of the Temple

THE TRINITY. JEROME: Be careful, reader, to understand the number three to refer to the mystery of the Trinity, which is the gate of those who go to God. The Father is in the Son, and the Son is in the Father, and the Holy Spirit is in each, which is the number three, and there is one gate for those who after baptism in the Trinity arrive at salvation. COMMENTARY ON EZEKIEL 12.40.44-49.[25]

---

[18]HGE 267*. [19]HGE 270*. [20]HGE 272**. [21]CCL 75:585*. [22]HGE 276. [23]HGE 280*. By "priest" Gregory means bishop. [24]HGE 284. [25]CCL 75:586.

[41:1–42:20 FURTHER MEASUREMENTS OF THE TEMPLE]

43:1-12 THE GLORY ENTERS THE TEMPLE, AND THE MESSAGE IS GIVEN

¹*Afterward he brought me to the gate, the gate facing east. *²*And behold, the glory of the God of Israel came from the east; and the sound of his coming was like the sound of many waters; and the earth shone with his glory. *³*And*ᵍ *the vision I saw was like the vision which I had seen when he came to destroy the city, and*ʰ *like the vision which I had seen by the river Chebar; and I fell upon my face. *⁴*As the glory of the LORD entered the temple by the gate facing east, *⁵*the Spirit lifted me up, and brought me into the inner court; and behold, the glory of the LORD filled the temple.*

⁶*While the man was standing beside me, I heard one speaking to me out of the temple; *⁷*and he said to me, "Son of man, this is the place of my throne and the place of the soles of my feet, where I will dwell in the midst of the people of Israel for ever. And the house of Israel shall no more defile my holy name, neither they, nor their kings, by their harlotry, and by the dead bodies*ⁱ *of their kings, *⁸*by setting their threshold by my threshold and their doorposts beside my doorposts, with only a wall between me and them. They have defiled my holy name by their abominations which they have committed, so I have consumed them in my anger. *⁹*Now let them put away their idolatry and the dead bodies*ⁱ *of their kings far from me, and I will dwell in their midst for ever.*

¹⁰*"And you, son of man, describe to the house of Israel the temple and its appearance and plan,*ʲ *that they may be ashamed of their iniquities. *¹¹*And if they are ashamed of all that they have done, portray*ᵏ *the temple, its arrangement, its exits and its entrances, and its whole form; and make known to them all its ordinances and all its laws; and write it down in their sight, so that they may observe and perform all its laws*ˡ *and all its ordinances. *¹²*This is the law of the temple: the whole territory round about upon the top of the mountain shall be most holy. Behold, this is the law of the temple."*

g Gk: Heb *And like the vision* h Syr: Heb *and the visions* i Or *the monuments* j Gk: Heb *the temple that they may measure the pattern* k Gk: Heb *the form of* l Compare Gk: Heb *its whole form*

OVERVIEW: Beholding the glory of God makes us new, just as we shall be at the second coming of Christ (JEROME). The man standing by is like the archangel Michael (THEODORET). The eucharistic altar stands apart, as does the altar of sacrifice in the temple; the church will last forever (JEROME).

43:1-2 *The Glory*

BEHOLDING GOD RE-CREATES US. JEROME: When his face is revealed and we contemplate the glory of God, we are reformed in the image of the Creator. COMMENTARY ON EZEKIEL 13.43.1-9.[1]

THE SECOND COMING OF CHRIST. JEROME: The earth shone with his glory, which really takes place at the coming of Christ, when the sound of the apostles goes forth on the whole earth and their words to the ends of the earth. COMMENTARY ON EZEKIEL 13.43.1-9.[2]

43:5 Ezekiel Raised after Seeing the Glory

THE VOICE SPEAKS TO AN OVERWHELMED PROPHET. JEROME: Immediately the Spirit raised me up, for I myself was lying and not able to go any further, and he led me to the inner courtyard, for I had fallen outside. And behold, I who had earlier glimpsed the glory of the God of Israel coming from the east, now saw the house of the Lord filled with his glory, and I heard a voice speaking as someone speaking to me from inside the house. COMMENTARY ON EZEKIEL 13.43.1-9.[3]

43:6 The Man Standing Beside the Prophet

THE MAN IS LIKE THE ARCHANGEL MICHAEL. THEODORET OF CYR: He showed me that there was an angel who measured the building, and he showed me these things; and he was very like Michael, who was given the responsibility of looking after the people. COMMENTARY ON EZEKIEL 16.43.[4]

43:8 The Dividing Wall

THE EUCHARISTIC TABLE. JEROME: There is a wall between me and them, so that a very short wall divides the sacrifices of the priests and the place for the mystery of the body and blood of Christ. COMMENTARY ON EZEKIEL 13.43.1-9.[5]

43:9 The Lord Will Dwell Among Them Forever

THE CHURCH LASTS FOREVER. JEROME: He did not dwell for a short time as in the synagogue, but forever, as is shown in the church of Christ. COMMENTARY ON EZEKIEL 13.43.1-9.[6]

43:11 All the Temple's Ordinances and Laws

THE CHURCH OF CHRIST. JEROME: For the house and the law of all the teachings of God and the city that is built on top of the mountain are to be believed from what is written; a city on a hill cannot be hid, and there is a river whose streams make glad the city of God,[7] which clearly refers to the church of God. COMMENTARY ON EZEKIEL 13.43.10-12.[8]

---

[1]CCL 75:623. [2]CCL 75:623. [3]CCL 75:624. [4]PG 81:1228. [5]CCL 75:626. An allusion to church architecture of the time. [6]CCL 75:626. [7]Ps 46:4 (45:5 LXX, Vulg.). [8]CCL 75:629.

[43:13-17 THE DIMENSIONS OF THE ALTAR]

[43:18-27 THE ORDINANCES OF THE ALTAR]

44:1-3 THE EAST GATE AND THE PRINCE

¹Then he brought me back to the outer gate of the sanctuary, which faces east; and it was shut. ²And he° said to me, "This gate shall remain shut; it shall not be opened, and no one shall enter by it; for the LORD, the God of Israel, has entered by it; therefore it shall remain shut. ³Only the prince may sit in it to eat bread before the LORD; he shall enter by way of the vestibule of the gate, and shall go out by the same way."

o Cn: Heb *the* LORD

OVERVIEW: The east gate is closed, which means the importance of the right interpretation of the Scriptures, the Old and New Testaments, as revealed by Christ (ORIGEN), but it also may mean the womb of the Virgin Mary (JEROME, THEODORET, AMBROSE, RUFINUS, CYRIL OF ALEXANDRIA, JOHN OF DAMASCUS). The bread consumed before the Lord is eaten by Christ the Savior, like the daily bread we pray for in the Lord's Prayer (ORIGEN).

44:2 The Outer Gate of the Sanctuary

THE LORD COMES AND GOES. ORIGEN: The Lord God, maker of the universe, enters and departs through one gate, made from sensible material and always closed. HOMILIES ON EZEKIEL 14.1.[1]

THE KEY OF KNOWLEDGE. ORIGEN: There is a key of knowledge to open what is closed. HOMILIES ON EZEKIEL 14.2.[2]

THE KEY OF INTERPRETATION. ORIGEN: Even though my God has not come, the law was closed, the prophetic word closed, the text of the Old Testament veiled. HOMILIES ON EZEKIEL 14.2.[3]

THE FULL REVELATION. JEROME: Before the Savior took a human body and humbled himself, the law and the prophets and all knowledge of Scriptures were closed, and so paradise was as

well. COMMENTARY ON EZEKIEL 13.44.1-3.[4]

THE CLOSED DOOR. JEROME: Some people nobly understand the Virgin Mary as the door that is closed, who before and after birth remained a virgin, through which only the Lord God of Israel enters. COMMENTARY ON EZEKIEL 13.44.1-3.[5]

THE WOMB OF THE VIRGIN. THEODORET OF CYR: It is very likely that these words refer to the womb of the Virgin, through which no one enters and from which no one departs other than the only one who is the Lord. COMMENTARY ON EZEKIEL 16.44.[6]

MARY IS THE CLOSED GATE. AMBROSE: What is that gate of the sanctuary, that outer gate facing the east and remaining closed? Is not Mary the gate through whom the Redeemer entered this world? LETTER 44.[7]

ONLY THE SAVIOR OPENS THE GATE OF THE SCRIPTURES. JEROME: Could it be possible that in that entrance there were both seven steps and eight? Just notice what he says: the east gate, the gate from which the light enters—our Lord and Savior. There is indeed a gate, and no one enters it except the high priest. And what does holy

---

[1]SC 352:434. [2]SC 352:436. [3]SC 352:438. [4]CCL 75:644. [5]CCL 75:646. [6]PG 81:1233. [7]FC 26:227*.

Scripture say about it? "This gate is to remain closed"; it is not opened, moreover, except to the priest. Even so the Covenant, both Old and New, has always been closed; it has not been opened except to the Savior.... One gate, then, has both seven steps and eight. In the Old Testament, for example, the divine mysteries point to the Gospels, and in the New Testament back to the law. HOMILIES ON THE PSALMS 19 (Ps 89).[8]

THE VIRGIN BIRTH. CYRIL OF ALEXANDRIA: The word was made flesh without sexual intercourse, being conceived altogether without seed; then he was born without injury to her virginity. COMMENTARY ON LUKE 1.[9]

44:3 Only the Prince May Eat Bread Before the Lord

JESUS CHRIST IS THE ONE WHO EATS THE BREAD. ORIGEN: As the priest does not eat his food in the house or in any other place, except in the Holy of Holies, so does my Savior eat the bread, and no one can eat with him. HOMILIES ON EZEKIEL 14.3.[10]

THE DAILY BREAD FOR WHICH WE PRAY. ORIGEN: Each one of us asks for "daily bread" and when asking for "daily bread" does not receive either the same bread or the same measure. So without ceasing, thanks to pure prayers and a clean conscience, in the works of justice, we eat daily bread. And if anyone is less pure, he eats the daily bread in another way. HOMILIES ON EZEKIEL 14.3.[11]

THE TWO NATURES OF CHRIST. JEROME: So great is the goodness and compassion of our sovereign that when he alone sits in the door that is closed and eats in the presence of the Lord, he wants to have more companions to share with him at table.... For he alone eats bread before the Lord: he separated from the substance all creatures because he himself has the divine nature. He goes in and out of the same door of the forecourt. COMMENTARY ON EZEKIEL 13.44.1-3.[12]

THE VIRGIN MARY IS THE EAST GATE. JEROME: Christ himself is a virgin, and his mother is also a virgin; though she is his mother, she is a virgin still. For Jesus has entered in through the closed doors, and in his tomb—a new one hewn out of the hardest rock—no one is laid either before him or after him.... Mary is the east gate, spoken of by the prophet Ezekiel, always shut and always shining and either concealing or revealing the Holy of Holies. LETTER 48.21.[13]

THE CONCEPTION AND BIRTH OF THE SON OF GOD. JOHN OF DAMASCUS: Without seed the Son of God was conceived of the Holy Spirit, and in the Virgin's womb he formed for himself a fleshly body, animate with a reasonable and intelligent soul. From it [he came] forth in one substance but in two natures, perfect God and perfect man. It preserved undefiled, even after birth, the virginity of her that bore him. Being made of like passions with ourselves in all things, yet without sin, he took our infirmities and bore our sicknesses. For, since by sin death entered into the world, he who was to redeem the world had to be without sin, and not by sin subject to death. BARLAAM AND JOSEPH 7.[14]

THE VIRGIN'S WOMB. RUFINUS OF AQUILEIA: What could be said with such evident reference to the inviolate preservation of the Virgin's condition? That gate of virginity was closed: through it he came forth from the Virgin's womb into this world; and the virginity was preserved inviolate, and the gate of the Virgin remained closed for ever. Therefore the Holy Spirit is spoken of as the creator of the Lord's flesh and of his temple. COMMENTARY ON THE APOSTLES' CREED 9.[15]

---

[8]FC 48:151-52*. [9]CGSL 48. [10]SC 352:442. [11]SC 352:442. The Lord's Prayer figured frequently in patristic writings, including a lengthy treatise by Origen (see ACW 19:65-140). [12]CCL 75:646. [13]NPNF 2 6:78*. [14]LCL 34:91-93*. [15]NPNF 2 3:547*.

[44:4-8 EXCLUSION OF THE UNCIRCUMCISED AND THE IDOLATROUS LEVITES]

44:9-14 THE MINISTRY OF THE LEVITES IN THE TEMPLE

⁹*Therefore^t thus says the Lord GOD: No foreigner, uncircumcised in heart and flesh, of all the foreigners who are among the people of Israel, shall enter my sanctuary. ¹⁰But the Levites who went far from me, going astray from me after their idols when Israel went astray, shall bear their punishment. ¹¹They shall be ministers in my sanctuary, having oversight at the gates of the temple, and serving in the temple; they shall slay the burnt offering and the sacrifice for the people, and they shall attend on the people, to serve them. ¹²Because they ministered to them before their idols and became a stumbling block of iniquity to the house of Israel, therefore I have sworn concerning them, says the Lord GOD, that they shall bear their punishment. ¹³They shall not come near to me, to serve me as priest, nor come near any of my sacred things and the things that are most sacred; but they shall bear their shame, because of the abominations which they have committed. ¹⁴Yet I will appoint them to keep charge of the temple, to do all its service and all that is to be done in it.*

t Gk: Heb *for you*

OVERVIEW: The faith must be kept in all its purity, as if we were circumcised (ORIGEN), and the church is to be purified (JEROME), just as prayer can reach a point of self-forgetful purity (ISAAC). The clergy can sin, with serious results (GREGORY THE GREAT).

44:9 No Foreigners Allowed in the Sanctuary

THE CIRCUMCISED ARE THOSE WHO KEEP THE PURE FAITH. ORIGEN: He is uncircumcised in heart who holds heretical views in his mind and arranges blasphemous assertions against knowledge of Christ in his heart. But he is circumcised in heart who guards the pure faith in sincerity of conscience, about whom it can be said, "Blessed are the pure in heart, for they shall see God."[1] HOMILIES ON GENESIS 3.6.[2]

PURE PRAYER. ISAAC OF NINEVEH: When the mind is longingly involved with one of these stirrings—this depends on the urgency of the matter at the time of supplication and is the result of great eagerness—the gaze of its stirring is drawn by the eye of faith inside the veil of the heart, and the entries of the soul are fenced off, keeping out alien thoughts, which are called "strangers," who are not permitted by the law to enter inside the tent of witness. This is what they describe as "an acceptable sacrifice of the heart" and "pure prayer." Prayer's boundaries reach this point: afterwards it is not to be named prayer. MYSTICAL TREATISES 22.[3]

---

[1]Mt 5:8. [2]FC 71:98. [3]CS 101:256*.

44:10-14 *The Levites Shall Be Punished*

THE CHURCH IS TO BE PURIFIED. JEROME:
How is it that in the book of Ezekiel, where a
description is given of the future church and
of the heavenly Jerusalem, the priests who have
sinned are degraded to the rank of sacristans
and doorkeepers, and although they are in the
temple of God, that is, on the right hand,
they are not among the rams but among the
poorest of the sheep? AGAINST JOVINIANUS
2.28.[4]

44:12 *God's Decision Concerning the Levites*

CLERICAL SINS SERIOUS IN CONSEQUENCE.
GREGORY THE GREAT: No one does more harm in
the church than he who has the title or rank of
holiness and acts in an evil way. No one presumes
to take to task such a delinquent. The offense
serves as an example and has far-reaching consequences when the sinner is honored out of the
respect paid to his rank. PASTORAL CARE 1.2.[5]

---

[4]NPNF 2 6:409. [5]ACW 11:24*.

44:15-31 THE SERVICE OF THE LEVITICAL SONS OF ZADOK

[15]But the Levitical priests, the sons of Zadok, who kept the charge of my sanctuary when the
people of Israel went astray from me, shall come near to me to minister to me; and they shall
attend on me to offer me the fat and the blood, says the Lord GOD; [16]they shall enter my sanctuary,
and they shall approach my table, to minister to me, and they shall keep my charge. [17]When they
enter the gates of the inner court, they shall wear linen garments; they shall have nothing of wool
on them, while they minister at the gates of the inner court, and within. [18]They shall have linen
turbans upon their heads, and linen breeches upon their loins; they shall not gird themselves with
anything that causes sweat. [19]And when they go out into the outer court to the people, they shall
put off the garments in which they have been ministering, and lay them in the holy chambers; and
they shall put on other garments, lest they communicate holiness to the people with their garments.
[20]They shall not shave their heads or let their locks grow long; they shall only trim the hair of their
heads.

OVERVIEW: The ministry of the church requires
special vestments for the celebration of the liturgy, as well as proper limits placed on worldly
cares (GREGORY THE GREAT).

44:17, 19 *Linen Garments Worn for Temple Duty*

DIFFERENT CLOTHING FOR THE LITURGY.
GREGORY THE GREAT: Woolen garments are
thicker. When the priest approaches the holy
ministry, when through compunction he enters
within, he must be vested in a finer understanding, as with a linen garment. But when he goes
outside to the people, he has to lay aside the gar-

ments in which he had ministered within and appear to the people dressed in other clothing, because if he restrains himself in the rigor of his compunction, if he perseveres in the solemnity that he held at the time of prayer, he does not admit to accept the words of external things. And what is the flock to do about necessities if their shepherd refuses to hear and ponder what this present time requires? Therefore a priest who goes out before the people puts on thicker garments in order to compose the habit of his mind for the benefit of his children, even to bear earthly cares. Think, I ask you, dearest brothers, how much toil there is for the watchman, both to extend his heart to the sublime and suddenly to recall it to the depths, and to refine the spirit in the heights of inward understanding and because of the exterior causes of his neighbors, so to speak, suddenly thicken in contemplation. HOMILIES ON EZEKIEL 1.11.28.[1]

44:20 Their Hair Allowed to Grow

THE LIMITS REQUIRED ON EXTERNAL MATTERS. GREGORY THE GREAT: They are rightly called priests who preside over the faithful to provide them guidance in sacred matters. The hairs on the head are the thoughts about exterior matters. When these grow insensibly above the brain, they denote the cares of this life, which sometimes arise unseasonably for lack of observation and issue forth as if we are unconscious of them. Since, then, all who are placed over others should have a care of external things, but without being excessively occupied with them, priests are rightly forbidden to shave the head or let the hair grow long. This means that they may not wholly discard all consideration for the flesh on behalf of the lives of their subjects nor again allow it to engross them too much. PASTORAL CARE 2.7.[2]

---

[1]HGE 141*. [2]ACW 11:74*.

[45:1-9 THE ALLOTMENT OF THE LAND]

[45:13–46:24 THE REGULATION OF OFFERINGS]

47:1-12 THE RIVER FLOWING THROUGH THE TEMPLE

[1]*Then he brought me back to the door of the temple; and behold, water was issuing from below the threshold of the temple toward the east (for the temple faced east); and the water was flowing*

down from below the south end of the threshold of the temple, south of the altar. ²Then he brought me out by way of the north gate, and led me round on the outside to the outer gate, that faces toward the east;ʰ and the water was coming out on the south side.

³Going on eastward with a line in his hand, the man measured a thousand cubits, and then led me through the water; and it was ankle-deep. ⁴Again he measured a thousand, and led me through the water; and it was knee-deep. Again he measured a thousand, and led me through the water; and it was up to the loins. ⁵Again he measured a thousand, and it was a river that I could not pass through, for the water had risen; it was deep enough to swim in, a river that could not be passed through. ⁶And he said to me, "Son of man, have you seen this?"

Then he led me back along the bank of the river. ⁷As I went back, I saw upon the bank of the river very many trees on the one side and on the other. ⁸And he said to me, "This water flows toward the eastern region and goes down into the Arabah; and when it enters the stagnant waters of the sea,ⁱ the water will become fresh. ⁹And wherever the riverʲ goes every living creature which swarms will live, and there will be very many fish; for this water goes there, that the waters of the seaᵏ may become fresh; so everything will live where the river goes. ¹⁰Fishermen will stand beside the sea; from En-gedi to En-eglaim it will be a place for the spreading of nets; its fish will be of very many kinds, like the fish of the Great Sea. ¹¹But its swamps and marshes will not become fresh; they are to be left for salt. ¹²And on the banks, on both sides of the river, there will grow all kinds of trees for food. Their leaves will not wither nor their fruit fail, but they will bear fresh fruit every month, because the water for them flows from the sanctuary. Their fruit will be for food, and their leaves for healing."

h Heb obscure   i Compare Syr: Heb *into the sea to the sea those that were made to issue forth*   j Gk Syr Vg Tg: Heb *two rivers*   k Compare Syr: Heb lacks *the waters of the sea*

OVERVIEW: The waters flowing from the temple are the teaching of the church (JEROME), the waters of baptism (EPISTLE OF BARNABAS), waters that are made sweet by Christ's entry into them at his baptism, which grants forgiveness (JEROME, THEODORET) and overflowing spiritual nourishment (PSEUDO-DIONYSIUS). The prophet enters the water, a sign of our spiritual journey (ISAAC) and the capacity of the apostolic teaching to irrigate the most arid soul (JEROME). Christ meets the fishermen by the sea, transforming their work (EPHREM); the abundance of fruit represents the proper interpretation of the Scriptures (JEROME).

47:1-3 Water Flowing from the Threshold of the Temple

THE TEACHING OF THE CHURCH. JEROME: The waters that flow forth from the threshold of the temple refer to the teaching of the church. . . . We can understand water up to the ankles as meaning first the human sins that are forgiven us who enter the waters of the Lord; they show the saving grace of baptism and are the beginnings of our progress. COMMENTARY ON EZEKIEL 14.47.1-5.[1]

THE WATERS OF BAPTISM. EPISTLE OF BARNABAS: This means that we go down into the water full of sins and foulness, and we come up bearing fruit in our hearts, fear and hope in Jesus in the Spirit. EPISTLE OF BARNABAS 11.11.[2]

THE SAVIOR SWEETENS THE WATERS OF BAPTISM. JEROME: From the temple of the Lord, that

[1]CCL 75:707, 709. [2]FC 1:210.

is, from his bosom, the Savior came forth and sweetened the Dead Sea and the bitter waters. HOMILIES ON THE PSALMS 10 (Ps 76).[3]

SPIRITUAL FEEDING IN ABUNDANCE. PSEUDO-DIONYSIUS: The rivers of fire signify those divine channels that are forever dispensing their generous and unchecked flow and nourishing with their life-giving fruitfulness. CELESTIAL HIERARCHY 15.9.[4]

FORGIVENESS THROUGH BAPTISM. JEROME: When the world falls into sin, nothing but a flood of waters can cleanse it again. LETTER 69.6.[5]

CLEANSED BY WATER AND THE SPIRIT. THEODORET OF CYR: Thoroughly instructed in sacrificial matters, after he learned that sacrifices have to be offered for sins in a figurative manner, the prophet was taught that two expiations of souls were made through water and spirit. COMMENTARY ON EZEKIEL 16.47.[6]

47:3 Ankle Deep

THE SPIRITUAL JOURNEY. ISAAC OF NINEVEH: After these things, the intellect comes to behold what in Ezekiel the prophet is indicated by the appearance of the torrent. This depicts the figure of the three stages of soul that draw near to things divine, and beyond the third there is no passage. The beginning of all these things is a good purpose directed toward God, the many labors of stillness and the straightforwardness that is born of prolonged separation from the world. ASCETICAL HOMILIES 18.[7]

47:8 The Prophet Goes into the Waters

THE TEACHING OF THE APOSTLES. JEROME: We said a little time ago that the waters signify either the grace of baptism or the teaching of the gospel. If these waters go out from the threshold of the temple of the Lord and carry the teaching of the apostles, they have the power to make piles of gravel, sterile and infertile as they are, bear fruit, and they can irrigate every plain and every desert. COMMENTARY ON EZEKIEL 14.47.6-12.[8]

47:10 Fishermen Beside the Sea

CHRIST THE FISHERMAN. EPHREM THE SYRIAN: He was baptized and came up who draws all things into his net. Out of the stream from which Simon caught fish came the fisher of men, and he took him. With the cross, which catches all robbers, he caught that robber up into life. The living by his death emptied hell; he unloosed it and let entire multitudes fly away from it. HYMNS ON THE NATIVITY 3.[9]

47:12 All Kinds of Fruit

FRUITFUL INTERPRETATION OF SCRIPTURE. JEROME: Their fruit for food and their leaves for healing mean the mysteries of the divine books, of which one refers to the letter, the other to the spirit, so that we can understand simple words among their leaves and the meaning that truly lies in their fruitful stock. COMMENTARY ON EZEKIEL 14.47.6-12.[10]

---

[3]FC 48:76*. [4]PDCW 189-90. [5]NPNF 2 6:145. [6]PG 81:1240. [7]AHSIS 96-97*. [8]CCL 75:714. [9]NPNF 2 13:230*. [10]CCL 75:718.

[47:13-48:35 HOW THE LAND SHALL BE DIVIDED]

Introduction to Daniel

To guide the reader into the early church's reading of the book of Daniel, we offer at the outset a brief review of the history of the text used by the early church as well as broad remarks on the use and interpretation of the book of Daniel. This biblical book entered into the life of the Christian community at a very early stage. Allusions to Daniel appear in the words of Jesus, and they continue to surface in canonical and noncanonical texts from the earliest phase of the development of the Christian movement. From early on, for the fathers of the church, it played an important role not only in anchoring the church's confidence in the messianic status of Christ but also in offering narratives of heroic faith that proved important sources of strength and consolation. But before we begin unearthing the treasures of the church's reading, we need to turn to the rather vexing question of just what text the church fathers had before them.

The Text of the Book of Daniel

The text of the Old Testament used by the early church was almost without exception the Greek translation known as the Septuagint (LXX) or Old Greek.[1] This translation had been produced in Alexandria around 270 B.C. Over time, other translations were offered, but this particular text was favored in large part because of the story of its origins. The earliest recording of the translation (in the *Letter of Aristeas*, 130 B.C.) describes the process in scholarly terms, employing the Greek phrase *antiballein*, meaning to harmonize or collate the efforts of the seventy-two translators who had been called together to produce the Greek text from the Hebrew. No reference is made to any sort of divine intervention guiding the outcome. The story is changed, however, in the work of the Jewish philosopher Philo. Writing just after the beginning of the common era, Philo introduces divine inspiration: "they [the secluded translators] became as it were possessed and under inspiration, wrote, not each scribe something different, but the same word for word as though dictated to each by an invisible prompter."[2] The claim for divine guidance was accepted by early Christian writers, and even more richly elaborated tales of its creation can be found in the works of Pseudo-Justin and Irenaeus, among others. As a result, this Greek translation was almost universally hailed as the authoritative text of the Old Testament for early Christian readers and interpreters.

The widespread acceptance of the divine origin of the Alexandrian Septuagint did not, however, shield it from criticism or prohibit other versions from appearing. By the mid-first century A.D., at least two other Greek versions of the Hebrew Scriptures had found their way into the stream of sacred literature, one probably originating in Palestine (Proto-Lucianic recension) and the other in Babylonia (Proto-Theodotionic or *kaige* recension). By the mid-second century, three other versions had been produced.

The book of Daniel proved early on the exception to the rule in terms of Christian dependence on the Septuagint. For example, New Testament citations of Daniel at a number of points (e.g., Rev 9:20 and Dan

---

[1]See the full discussion of the textual history in J. Collins, *A Commentary on Daniel* (Minneapolis: Fortress, 1993), 2-24.
[2]*De Vita Mosis* 2:37, cited in J. Braverman, *Jerome's Commentary on Daniel* (Washington, D.C.: Catholic Biblical Association of America, 1978), 16.

5:23; Rev 10:5-6 and Dan 12:7; Heb 11:33 and Dan 6:22) are at variance with the Septuagint. The New Testament writers appear to have access to a Greek version that was very similar to that used to create the version known as Theodotion.[3] This tendency to replace the Septuagint with a form of the Theodotion version continued to be the case in early Christian texts for reasons that are not entirely clear. Indeed, by the end of the fourth century Theodotion Daniel had universally been put into place over the Septuagint, as Jerome records, noting his own ignorance as to the reasons for this shift in use. "The churches of the Lord Savior do not read the prophet Daniel according to Seventy Interpreters, but use the edition of Theodosius; why this happened, I do not know. . . . But this much I can affirm: [the Septuagint] differs a great deal from the truth [*veritas hebraica*] and for good reason was rejected."[4]

Both Theodotion Daniel and the Septuagint contain material that was excluded from the Jewish canon, perhaps as early as the end of the first century A.D. The additions do appear in the Latin Vulgate and in the sixth-century Codex Ambrosianus and are considered sacred text by the Roman Catholic Church, which has given them the status of deuterocanonical. These "additions to Daniel" include the "Prayer of Azariah and the Hymn of the Three Jews" (Dan 3:24-90) and the narratives of Susanna and Bel and the Dragon (Dan 13 and 14 in Roman Catholic editions).

The recent recovery of manuscripts with portions of Daniel among the Dead Sea Scrolls has suggested that the text employed by the Jewish scribes who created the Hebrew/Aramaic text of Daniel (known as the Masoretic text or MT) was itself based on an ancient textual tradition that in the main is very close to the Septuagint version.[5] The Masoretic text and the Septuagint diverge most significantly in their rendering of the end of Daniel 3, wherein the Septuagint and Theodotion Daniel included the Prayer of Azariah and the Song of the Three Children (both of which were likely inserted by a later translator/redactor) and Daniel 4-6. Recent studies of Daniel 4-6 have argued that they are based on a *Vorlage* that differed from that used for other parts of the Septuagint.[6]

The Syriac interpretive tradition depended on two texts, known as the Peshitta and the Syro-Hexapla. The Peshitta was a Syriac rendering of one or more Hebrew/Aramaic texts, whereas the Syro-Hexapla is based on a Greek text. The Peshitta does include the additions to Daniel 3 and to Daniel 12 (Bel and the Serpent). The Peshitta was the standard version of the Nestorian and Jacobite churches and from the seventh century on the standard text of the Maronite church. The Peshitta also served as the Bible for the Melkite church until the Middle Ages.[7]

---

[3]Tim McClay's study of the Greek versions of Daniel (*The Old Greek and the Versions of Daniel* [Atlanta: Scholars Press, 1996]) argues that Theodotion Daniel had access to a version of Daniel distinct from that used by the Old Greek translator as well as that used in the creation of the Old Greek.

[4]CCL 75A:774-75; cf. JCD 17-18.

[5]In this regard, Collins (*Daniel*, 3) remarked, "On the whole, the Qumran discoveries provide powerful evidence of the antiquity of the textual tradition of the MT." It should also be noted that the correspondence between the proto-MT and the LXX is based on the Old Greek text known as papyrus 967, which Joseph Ziegler (*Susanna, Daniel, Bel et Draco* [Göttingen: Vandenhoeck & Ruprecht, 1954]), among others, has argued is most faithful witness to the original OG text.

[6]See McLay's remarks (*The Old Greek and the Versions of Daniel*, 9-10) and the extensive bibliography cited there. See also R. Albertz, *Das Gott Des Daniel* (Stuttgart: Katholisches Bibelwerk, 1988), who argues that Daniel 4-6 come from a different translator.

[7]See the discussion in Matthias Henze, *The Madness of King Nebuchadnezzar* (Leiden: E. J. Brill, 1999), 143-47; for a detailed study of the Peshitta of Daniel, see R. A. Taylor, *The Peshitta of Daniel* (Leiden: E. J. Brill, 1994).

Authorship and Prominent Themes

Authorship. Early Christian interpreters of the book of Daniel assumed that the third-person narrative sections (Dan 1-6) as well as the visions of the latter part of the book of Daniel were the work of a single Jewish author born during the time of Jeremiah and living in exile in Babylonia. This assumption received a powerful challenge in the work of the late third-century pagan philosopher Porphyry.[8] Porphyry's attack on the Christians, entitled *Against the Christians,* included an argument that the book of Daniel had been written in the time of Antiochus Epiphanes and "did not so much say what was yet to happen as he narrated past events."[9] Porphyry well understood the force of such a claim. Early Christian authors had on many occasions linked the truth of the Christian religion to the prophetic texts they read as foreseeing the birth and ministry of Christ and the rise of the church. Justin Martyr in his *First Apology* claimed, "We do not trust in mere hearsay but are forced to believe those who prophesied these things before they happened, because we actually see things that have happened and are happening as was predicted. This will, as we think, be the greatest and surest demonstration for you too" (*First Apology* 30).[10] So also Jerome asserts the power of prophecy for convicting even the pagan: "For it is from prophecy that we convince gainsaying pagans. 'Who is Christ?' says the pagan. To whom we reply, 'He whom the prophets foretold.' 'What prophets?' he asks. We quote Isaiah, Daniel, Jeremiah and other holy prophets: we tell him that they came along before Christ . . . and they foretold his coming" (*Commentary on John* 35).[11] As Jerome notes, Daniel had figured prominently in this argument, and in particular, the third and seventh chapters of Daniel were frequently cited by early Christian authors as proof that Jesus' birth and work were foreseen in a prophetic sense. "I wish to stress in my preface this fact, that none of the prophets has so clearly spoken concerning Christ as has this prophet Daniel. For not only did he assert that he would come, a prediction common to other prophets as well, but also he set forth the very time at which he would come."[12] Furthermore, historical events in Palestine in the first century provided striking actualization of the prophecy. "Moreover, he [Daniel] went through the various kings in order, stated the actual number of years involved and announced beforehand the clearest signs of events to come. And because Porphyry saw that all these things had been fulfilled and could not deny that they had taken place, he overcame this evidence of historical accuracy by taking refuge in this evasion concerning antichrist at the end of the world was actually fulfilled in the reign of Antiochus Epiphanes, because of certain similarities to things which took place at his time."[13]

The effect of Porphyry's argument was to force Christian interpreters of Daniel to make explicit the claim that the book of Daniel was written in the time of the Babylonian exile and to secure that claim with substantive arguments. In fact, several fourth-century Christian authors made it their business to counter the claims of Porphyry. As Jerome noted in the prologue to his commentary on Daniel, Methodius, Eusebius of Caesarea and Apollinarius had all replied to Porphyry. Indeed, despite a disclaimer ("But inasmuch it is not our purpose to make answer to the false accusations of an adversary") it is quite evident that

---

[8]P. Casey, "Porphyry and the Origin of the Book of Daniel," *Journal of Theological Studies* n.s. 27 (1976): 15-33.
[9]Porphyry's remarks on the book of Daniel are contained in Jerome's *Commentary on Daniel.*
[10]FC 6:66.
[11]NPNF 1 7:206.
[12]JCD 15.
[13]JCD 15.

Jerome's *Commentary on Daniel* is written in large part as a rebuttal to Porphyry.

A closely related issue was that of the status of the person of Daniel. The text itself identifies Daniel as a wise man (Dan 1:3-5; 2:48-49) and as one "much beloved "(by God; Dan 9:23) but never applies the title *nabi* ("prophet") to Daniel. This did not prevent a presumption and indeed an assertion of the claim that Daniel was a prophet at least as early as the writing of the texts of Qumran and repeated in Josephus and carried forth into the work of early Christian interpreters, such as Hippolytus: "The prophet [Daniel] having thus instructed us with all exactness as to the certainty of the things that are to be, broke off from his present subject and passed again to the kingdom of the Persians and Greeks, recounting to us another vision which took place and was fulfilled in its proper time; in order that by establishing our belief in this, he might be able to present us to God as believers well versed in the things that are to be" (*Commentary on Daniel* 2.7).[14] The shift from simply assuming Daniel's status as prophet to incorporating an argument for this claim into the exegesis arose because of a change in the Jewish position on the status of Daniel that moved the book of Daniel from the Prophets and into the Writings. While it is difficult to establish with precision at what point this change was enacted, it is recorded in the Babylonian Talmud perhaps as early as the fifth century A.D. It was one thing for a pagan like Porphyry to challenge the reading of Daniel as prophetic; it was quite another for Jewish interpreters to rob Daniel of his prophetic role. Christian interpreters of the Bible have always been acutely aware (acknowledged or otherwise) that they were claiming a text that continued to be treated as sacred and read and interpreted by a thriving Jewish community alongside and sometimes in opposition to their own reading. Theodoret of Cyr's *Commentary on Daniel* is the most obvious case of composing an interpretation to meet the challenge posed by the Jewish claims on the text. In his prologue to his commentary on Daniel, Theodoret announced that he had taken up the task once more of offering an interpretation of this Scripture to prove the Jews were wrong in moving Daniel to the Writings. "We endeavor to interpret this prophecy that is before us, unlike others who scorn it or make no attempt . . . this prepares us for the folly and shamelessness of the Jews, that others avoid, as we reveal that which is predicted and make it clear. For into the far reaches of shamelessness they [the Jews] have gone as they have segregated him [Daniel] from the chorus of the prophets and withheld from it [the book of Daniel] the very title 'prophecy'" (*Commentary on Daniel, prefatio*).[15]

Prominent Themes. These arguments over the author and his status point to two important dimensions of the history of the interpretation of Daniel. First, it meant that the interpretation was often couched in terms that have an eye to the apologetic dimension of the exegesis. That is, the interpretation incorporates the text from Daniel into the larger argument for the veracity of the Christian religion and anticipates and at times explicitly responds to adversarial claims.

Second, it meant that the weight of the interest in Daniel falls on the side of unpacking the elements of the text that have a predictive or eschatological dimension. Parts of Daniel 3 along with Daniel 7-12 receive the lion's share of attention by early Christian interpreters. This body of interpretation also naturally harbors the most divergent moments in the interpretation as early Christian readers wrestled over the historical referents for the symbolic figures (e.g., "the fourth beast," Dan 7:23) and numbers (e.g., "seventy weeks,"

---

[14]ANF 5:179.
[15]PG 81:1257, 1268.

Dan 9:24). In this regard, one can detect a pattern in the interpretation of Daniel from its inclusion in the texts (chiefly pre-second century) that warned of an imminent final conflict and rescue of the faithful to a reading that located the events foreseen in a time frame that extended into the distant future or, as in the case of Origen, were allegorized into timeless realities.

Aside from the predictive and eschatological, Daniel also offered an opportunity for paraenetic (practical, ethical teaching) reflections. Daniel and his companions' behavior in the courts of kings of Babylon was taken over as exemplary, and the rewards for such behavior were emphasized as that which is given to the faithful. Daniel and his companions make evident the power of prayer as well as the rewards of fasting and the rejection of the practices and foods of the unfaithful or unrepentant. "I come again to Daniel and his brothers, preferring as they did a diet of vegetables and the beverage of water to the royal dishes and decanters and even in such a state they were found 'more handsome' (lest any be concerned on the question of his feeble body, to boot), besides being spiritually cultured as well. So God gave to the young men knowledge and understanding in every kind of literature, and to Daniel in every word and in dreams and in all sorts of wisdom. And indeed this wisdom was to make him wise in this very thing—namely, the means by which the understanding of mysteries was to be obtained from God" (Tertullian *On Fasting* 9). Moreover, the early Christian literature on martyrdom wove Daniel and his companions' survival of the fiery furnace in Daniel 3 into its promises of sure salvation for the martyr. Origen's *Exhortation to Martyrdom*, for example, refers frequently to Daniel and his three companions as models for Christian martyrs. "Among those martyrs we find in his *Exhortation to Martyrdom* are Abel, Abraham, Daniel and his three companions, along with the Maccabean martyrs, the prophets and apostles."[16]

The fourth chapter of Daniel gave rise to a rich interpretive tradition especially among Syriac interpreters. The madness of King Nebuchadnezzar and his eventual restoration to his kingship was utilized for extensive and at times quite divergent reflections on divine punishment and penance. The majority of Christian exegetes would point to Nebuchadnezzar's "exile" as a paradigmatic act of contrition, while a minority would read the text as expressive of God's great anger at the king's hubris. In terms of the latter, the great Syrian exegete Aphrahat offered an extended reflection that conflated elements of Daniel 4 and Daniel 7 to produce an image of a series of transformations ending finally in the king as humbled and thus restored.

> While the king was like the head of gold, men served him as a king.... But when his heart exalted itself, and he did not know that the power was given to him from heaven, the yoke of iron was broken from the neck of men. And he went out with the beasts, and instead of the heart of a king there was given him a heart of a lion. And when he exalted himself over the beasts, the lion's heart was taken away from him, and the heart of a bird was given to him.... And when he realized that the Most High has authority over the kingdom of man, to give it to whom he wants, then he gave praise like a man.[17]

One final paraenetic element of note occurs in Cyprian, where Cyprian utilized Daniel's exhortation to Nebuchadnezzar to "practice righteousness" (Dan 4:27) as the basis for almsgiving (*On Works and Alms* 5).[18]

---

[16]See Origen, *Exhortation to Martyrdom* 50, 14, 33, 23-26, etc.
[17]Aphrahat *Demonstrations* 5.16; NPNF 2 13:358**.
[18]ANF 5:477.

The book of Daniel also played a role in the development of various positions on the work and person of Christ, especially in the earliest phases of that development. The references to "the Son of man" (LXX) in Daniel 7 and Daniel 9 were particularly important in this regard. In several places in the Gospels, Jesus uses *ho huios tou anthrōpou* as a self-designation. Whether these references should be read as originating with the historical Jesus or with the later communities' adaptation of the text in Daniel to the death and resurrection of Jesus is disputed, as is the precise meaning of the phrase when it is employed in the New Testament. The majority of scholarship suggests three options: a future, apocalyptic Son of man; the suffering, resurrected Son of man; or the present, authoritative Son of man.[19] Analysis of these texts has made clear that not all can be considered as allusions to the "son of man" introduced in Daniel 7. The early Christian interpretations of Daniel 7 will emphasize the first of the two options stressing the connection of the Danielic vision with Jesus' resurrection, his everlasting kingdom and his expected return to establish that kingdom. Justin Martyr's remarks in his *Dialogue with Trypho* are a good example.

> For we call him Helper and Redeemer, the power of whose name even the demons do fear; and at this day, when they are exorcised in the name of Jesus Christ, crucified under Pontius Pilate, governor of Judea, they are overcome. And thus it is manifest to all that his Father has given him so great power, by virtue of which demons are subdued to his name, and to the dispensation of his suffering. But if so great a power is shown to have followed and to be still following the dispensation of his suffering, how great shall that be which shall follow his glorious advent. For he shall come on the clouds as the Son of man, so Daniel foretold, and his angels shall come with him.[20]

The Commentary Tradition

The book of Daniel is a complex scriptural text as it joins historical narrative to dreams and visions that are laced with highly symbolic images. Such a rich text naturally spawned an equally rich body of interpretation. Moreover, the appearance of references to Daniel in the words of Jesus and in New Testament writings as well as its early and critical role in early Christian apologetics insured its place among early Christian exegetes.

Full commentaries on the book of Daniel (commentaries that cover the chapters in order and comment on essentially all verses) were composed in Greek by Hippolytus (202), Origen, Theodore of Mopsuestia (c. 400), Cyril of Alexandria (c. 420), Theodoret of Cyr (433) and Polychronius (c. 430), in Latin by Jerome (407), and in Syriac by Ephrem the Syrian (c. 370) and Isho'dad of Merv (fl. c. 850). Only those of Theodoret and Jerome survive in full, although we have a large part of the work of Hippolytus. A full commentary attributed to Ephrem exists, but its authenticity is disputed.[21] A full commentary attributed to John Chrysostom is clearly not the work of the Antiochene preacher but from the pen of a later, anonymous writer. It is to the commentaries that we now turn to hear the voice of the church as it weaves the book of Daniel into the lives of Christians.

C. Thomas McCollough

---

[19]See the essay by A. Y. Collins in J. Collins, *A Commentary on the Book of Daniel*, 90-116.
[20]ANF 1:209.
[21]Though similarities exist between the commentary and Ephrem's thought, the commentary was most likely composed by someone schooled in the Syriac exegetical tradition. For further discussion see Phil J. Botha, "The Reception of Daniel Chapter 2 in the Commentary Ascribed to Ephrem the Syrian Church Father," *Acta Patristica et Byzantina* 17 (2006): 119-43.

DANIEL

1:1-2 NEBUCHADNEZZAR'S CAPTURE OF JERUSALEM AND THE EXILE

¹In the third year of the reign of Jehoiakim king of Judah, Nebuchadnezzar king of Babylon came to Jerusalem and besieged it. ²And the Lord gave Jehoiakim king of Judah into his hand, with some of the vessels of the house of God; and he brought them to the land of Shinar, to the house of his god, and placed the vessels in the treasury of his god.

OVERVIEW: Similar to other prophets, Daniel begins his prophecy by giving the reader a historical setting (THEODORET). The exile referred to in Daniel is that begun under King Jehoiakim, who should not be confused with the king named Jehoiachin who appears in the prophecy of Ezekiel. The land to which the vessels of the temple are transferred is the same as that where earlier the people tried to build a tower to heaven and where a confusion of tongues erupted and so the place was called Babylon. In the telling of the capture of Jerusalem, Scripture makes evident that God is in control of the course of history (HIPPOLYTUS, JEROME).

1:1 The Third Year of Jehoiakim's Reign

PROPHECY AND HISTORY. THEODORET OF CYR: Naturally, at the outset, the king who ruled is revealed and the year made clear, when the capture first occurred. And so by calling to mind the king that reigned at that point, he [Daniel] demonstrates . . . that he is a prophet. For other prophets begin in the very same way. COMMENTARY ON DANIEL 1.1.[1]

1:2 The Will of the Lord

GOD "GAVE" FOR CORRECTION. HIPPOLYTUS: These words, "and the Lord gave," are written that no one, in reading the introduction to the book, may attribute their capture to the strength of the captors and the slackness of their chief. And it is well said "with part,"[2] for the deportation was for the correction, not the ruin, of the whole nation, that there might be no misapplication of the cause. SCHOLIA ON DANIEL 1.2.[3]

GOD'S WILL. JEROME: The fact that Jehoiakim is recorded to have been given over shows that it was not a victory for the might of his enemies but rather it was of the will of the Lord. COMMENTARY ON DANIEL 1.2.[4]

THE VESSELS ARE GOD'S TRUTHS. JEROME: At the same time, it should be noted, by way of a spiritual interpretation, that the king of Babylon was not able to transport all of the vessels of God and place them in the idol house that he had built himself, but only a part of the vessels of God's

¹PG 81:1268; WGRW 7:17. ²LXX variant: "And the Lord gave into his hand Joakim king of Judah, and part of the vessels of the house of God." ³ANF 5:185*. ⁴JCD 19; CCL 75A:777.

house. For if you go through all of the works of the philosophers, you will necessarily find in them some portion of the vessels of God. For example, you will find in Plato that God is fashioner of the universe. . . . But because the philosophers combine truth with error and corrupt the good of nature with many evils, for that reason

they are recorded to have captured only a portion of the vessels of God's house, and not all of them in their completeness and perfection. COMMENTARY ON DANIEL 1.2.[5]

[5]JCD 20*; CCL 75A:778.

1:3-7 DANIEL AND HIS COMPANIONS ARE SUMMONED BY THE KING

[3]*Then the king commanded Ashpenaz, his chief eunuch, to bring some of the people of Israel, both of the royal family and of the nobility,* [4]*youths without blemish, handsome and skilful in all wisdom, endowed with knowledge, understanding learning, and competent to serve in the king's palace, and to teach them the letters and language of the Chaldeans.* [5]*The king assigned them a daily portion of the rich food which the king ate, and of the wine which he drank. They were to be educated for three years, and at the end of that time they were to stand before the king.* [6]*Among these were Daniel, Hananiah, Misha-el, and Azariah of the tribe of Judah.* [7]*And the chief of the eunuchs gave them names: Daniel he called Belteshazzar, Hananiah he called Shadrach, Misha-el he called Meshach, and Azariah he called Abednego.*

OVERVIEW: At first, the king summons from the Israelite captives the most important and the most handsome, foolishly assuming these are important marks of human character. In fact, those who are ultimately summoned before the king are not elites, and so the Scripture sets before us the lesson of humility (THEODORET). The Hebrew names are changed, as God had allowed at other times because of sojourning in a foreign land or to signal a critical moment or event (JEROME).

1:3-4 The Royal Family and the Nobility

THE KING'S FOOLISH VALUES. THEODORET OF CYR: And so the God of all makes evident the foolishness, infirmity and loathsome ways of the world in order to put to shame its power and wis-

dom. People who care for bodily things and seek beauty, greatness and great bodily strength know nothing of divine wisdom but rather only a false and artificial sort of eloquence. And thus is the distance between humanity and God. The false pretense of the king is shown as he wished not only the other captives be servants but also that they be descendents from kings. Now all this happened just as Isaiah had predicted to Hezekiah . . . : "And some of your own sons will become slaves, yes eunuchs, in the palace of the king of Babylon."[1] COMMENTARY ON DANIEL 1.3-4.[2]

RULERS. JEROME: Instead of *Ashpenaz* ("Asphanez") I found *Abriesdri* written in the Vul-

[1]Is 39:7. [2]PG 81:1273; WGRW 7:23.

gate edition.[3] For the word *phorlhommin*, which Theodotion uses, the Septuagint and Aquila translated "the chosen ones," whereas Symmachus rendered "Parthians," understanding it as the name of a nation instead of a common noun. This is in disagreement with the Hebrew edition as it is accurately read; I have translated it as "rulers," especially because it is preceded by the words "of the royal seed." From this passage the Hebrews think that Daniel, Hananiah, Mishael and Azariah were eunuchs, thus fulfilling that prophecy that is spoken by Isaiah regarding Hezekiah: "And they shall take of your seed and make eunuchs of them in the house of the king of Babylon."[4] If, however, they were of the royal seed, there is no doubt but what they were of the line of David. COMMENTARY ON DANIEL 1.3-4.[5]

1:4 Language of the Chaldeans

ABRAHAM A CHALDEAN. JEROME: Philo supposes that Chaldee is the same thing as the Hebrew language, because Abraham came from the Chaldeans. But if we accept this, we must ask how the Hebrew youths could now be bidden to be taught a language that they already knew; unless, perchance, we should say, as some believe, that Abraham was acquainted with two languages. COMMENTARY ON DANIEL 1.4.[6]

1:5-6 The King Assigned a Daily Portion

OF HUMBLE ORIGINS. THEODORET OF CYR: So here he informs us of the king's generosity in providing them with nourishment that was not of an ordinary kind fit for captives and slaves; instead,

he gave orders for them to share in the king's table. Shortly afterward he mentions their self-control and sound values, not indulging in self-glorification but proposing a beneficial lesson to those prepared to accept benefit. It is possible to see also the moderation in his thinking: after mentioning above that the king ordered young men of royal birth to be chosen, fair to behold and of becoming stature, and citing at this point the persons' names, he simply referred to the tribe of Judah and concealed their royal connections. COMMENTARY ON DANIEL 1.5-6.[7]

1:7 The Chief Eunuch Gave Them Names

GOD'S HAND EVIDENT. JEROME: It is not only the overseer or master of the eunuchs (as others have rendered it, the chief eunuch) who changed the names of saints, but also Pharaoh called Joseph in Egypt *Zaphenathpaneah*,[8] for neither of them wished to have Jewish names in the land of captivity. Wherefore the prophet says in the psalm, "How shall we sing the Lord's song in a strange land?"[9] Furthermore, the Lord himself changes names benignly, and on the basis of events imposes names of special significance, so as to call Abram Abraham, and Sarai Sarah.[10] Also in the Gospel, the former Simon received the name of Peter,[11] and the sons of Zebedee are called "sons of thunder." COMMENTARY ON DANIEL 1.7.[12]

---

[3]The Vulgate is the Latin translation of the Septuagint. [4]Is 39:7. [5]JCD 20*; CCL 75A:778-79. [6]JCD 21; CCL 75A:779. [7]WGRW 7:25. [8]Gen 41:45. [9]Ps 137:4 (136:4 LXX). [10]Gen 17:5, 15. [11]Mk 3:16. [12]JCD 21; CCL 75A:780.

1:8-21 REJECTION OF THE KING'S FOOD

[8]*But Daniel resolved that he would not defile himself with the king's rich food, or with the wine which he drank; therefore he asked the chief of the eunuchs to allow him not to defile himself.* [9]*And God gave Daniel favor and compassion in the sight of the chief of the eunuchs;* [10]*and the chief of the eunuchs said to Daniel, "I fear lest my lord the king, who appointed your food and your drink, should see that you were in poorer condition than the youths who are of your own age. So you would endanger my head with the king."* [11]*Then Daniel said to the steward whom the chief of the eunuchs had appointed over Daniel, Hananiah, Misha-el, and Azariah,* [12]*"Test your servants for ten days; let us be given vegetables to eat and water to drink.* [13]*Then let our appearance and the appearance of the youths who eat the king's rich food be observed by you, and according to what you see deal with your servants."* [14]*So he hearkened to them in this matter, and tested them for ten days.* [15]*At the end of ten days it was seen that they were better in appearance and fatter in flesh than all the youths who ate the king's rich food.* [16]*So the steward took away their rich food and the wine they were to drink, and gave them vegetables.*

[17]*As for these four youths, God gave them learning and skill in all letters and wisdom; and Daniel had understanding in all visions and dreams.* [18]*At the end of the time, when the king had commanded that they should be brought in, the chief of the eunuchs brought them in before Nebuchadnezzar.* [19]*And the king spoke with them, and among them all none was found like Daniel, Hananiah, Misha-el, and Azariah; therefore they stood before the king.* [20]*And in every matter of wisdom and understanding concerning which the king inquired of them, he found them ten times better than all the magicians and enchanters that were in all his kingdom.* [21]*And Daniel continued until the first year of King Cyrus.*

OVERVIEW: Captives in a strange land, Daniel and his companions were not seduced by the customs of the land, rejecting meat offered to idols (HIPPOLYTUS, JEROME). The favor shown to Daniel was due to the mercy of God and not the benevolence of the king's servants (JEROME). Bodily and spiritual flourishing stems from the exercise of self-control, not indulgence (THEODORET, LEANDER, TERTULLIAN). Some prophets were wise men before they became prophets (ORIGEN). The youths were given knowledge and learning in secular literature (JEROME). Gifted with understanding, Daniel perceived clearly what others perceived only dimly (JEROME).

1:8 Daniel's Resolve

NOT SEDUCED. HIPPOLYTUS: Daniel kept the covenant of the fathers and did not transgress the law given by Moses but feared the God proclaimed by him. These, though captives in a strange land, were not seduced by delicate meats, nor were they slaves to the pleasures of wine, nor were they caught by the bait of princely glory. SCHOLIA ON DANIEL 1.8.[1]

THE YOUTHS REJECT THE KING'S FOOD. THEODORET OF CYR: For those who love God do not seek after the God of all in just one place, but even in the midst of this misfortune they wor-

---

[1]ANF 5:185*.

shiped as if in the house of the Creator. In that place there are many wondrous moments to be found. For having been reared on the teachings of the Jews and having learned the customary service to God, they now were dwelling in a foreign land and were being forced into slavery exactly at the prime of their life. They were forced to abide under the foreign customs. But having seen the Babylonians offer defiled meat to the idols and the polluted libations at the temple, they took heed and, neglecting their own safety, rejected the king's banquet, beseeching the chief eunuch to allow them to be excused from partaking of the king's food. COMMENTARY ON DANIEL 1.8.[2]

1:9 God Gave Daniel Favor

THE MERCY OF GOD. JEROME: He who was taken into captivity on account of the sins of his ancestors received an immediate reward for the measure of his own virtue. For he had purposed in his heart that he would not be defiled by food from the king's table and preferred humble fare to royal delicacies; therefore, by the bountiful favor of the Lord, he received favor and compassion in the sight of the prince of the eunuchs. By this we may understand that if ever under pressing circumstances holy people are loved by unbelievers, it is a matter of the mercy of God, not of the goodness of perverted people. COMMENTARY ON DANIEL 1.9.[3]

1:10 Endangering the Eunuch with the King

FEAR COMES FROM A SENSUAL ORIENTATION. THEODORET OF CYR: This pointless objection of the eunuch was cowardly. He [the eunuch] was a man whose spirit did not know grace but took pleasure in his own sensuality. Of this man and human morality, take heed as there is the opinion that sumptuous feeding on nutritious foods provides for the body nourishment enough for it to flourish. In fact, it is not with such indulgence that you should chance your life, for it was with a small portion and by way of self-control that

they [Daniel and his friends] flourished. COMMENTARY ON DANIEL 1.10.[4]

1:12 Testing for Ten Days

LEARN TEMPERANCE FROM THE ANCIENTS. LEANDER OF SEVILLE: A fish is caught by being enticed by a hook. A bird falls into a net while trying to get food. Animals that are tough by nature's endowment fall into a pit from the desire to eat, and what nature does not soften, food deceives. Therefore, learn temperance and parsimony from the prayer and the examples of ancients: from prayer, because the Lord says, "Lest your hearts be overburdened with self-indulgence and drunkenness";[5] from examples, because David was unwilling to drink the water he wanted, since he recognized the danger of being responsible for another's blood;[6] because Daniel scorned the feasts of kings and lived on vegetables. What you possess in common with your companions should be acceptable to you, and you should not cause others to be intemperate; also, do not become a cause for scandal to those to whom you wish to set an example by encouragement and by proof of a good life. THE TRAINING OF NUNS 13.[7]

THE VALUE OF PARTIAL FASTS. TERTULLIAN: The exception of certain kinds from use as food is a partial fast.... Daniel and his companions, preferring as they did a diet of vegetables and the beverage of water to the royal dishes and decanters, were found "more handsome" ... and in addition were more spiritually cultured. For God gave to the young men knowledge and understanding in every kind of literature, and to Daniel in every word, and in dreams and in every kind of wisdom; which [wisdom] was to make him wise in this very thing also, namely, by what means the recognition of mysteries was to be obtained from God. ON FASTING 9.[8]

---

[2]PG 81:1276; WGRW 7:25. [3]JCD 22*; CCL 75A:781. [4]PG 81:1277; WGRW 7:27. [5]Lk 21:34. [6]2 Sam 23:14-17. [7]FC 62:208*. [8]ANF 4:107*.

1:17 God Gave Them Learning

PROPHET OF GOD. ORIGEN: In regard to the prophets among the Jews, some of them were wise men before they became divinely inspired prophets, while others became wise by the illumination that their minds received when divinely inspired. They were selected by divine providence to receive the divine Spirit and to be the depositaries of his holy oracles, on the ground of their leading a life of almost unapproachable excellence, intrepid, noble, unmoved by danger or death. AGAINST CELSUS 7.7.[9]

EYES OF UNDERSTANDING. JEROME: Note that God is said to have given the holy youths knowledge and learning in secular literature, in every book and branch of wisdom. Symmachus rendered this by "grammatical art," implying that they understood everything they read, and by the Spirit of God they could make a judgment concerning the lore of the Chaldeans. But Daniel had an outstanding gift over and above the three youths, in that he could astutely discern the significance of visions and dreams in which things to come are shown forth by means of certain symbols and mysteries. Therefore that which others saw only in a shadowy appearance he could perceive clearly with the eyes of his understanding. COMMENTARY ON DANIEL 1.17.[10]

1:18 At the End of the Time

COMPLETED DAYS. JEROME: By the "completed days" understand the period of three years that the king had appointed, so that after they had been nourished and trained for three years, they should then stand in the presence of the king. COMMENTARY ON DANIEL 1.18.[11]

1:20 Soothsayers and Magicians

VULGATE TRANSLATION. JEROME: For "soothsayers" and "magicians" the Vulgate edition of the Septuagint translated "sophists" and "philosophers"—terms to be understood not in the sense of the philosophy and sophistic erudition that Greek learning holds forth but rather in the sense of the lore of a barbarian people, which the Chaldeans pursue as philosophy even to this day. COMMENTARY ON DANIEL 1.20.[12]

---

[9]ANF 4:613*. [10]JCD 22*; CCL 75A:781-82. [11]JCD 22-23. [12]JCD 23.

2:1-16 NEBUCHADNEZZAR HAS A DREAM

[1]In the second year of the reign of Nebuchadnezzar, Nebuchadnezzar had dreams; and his spirit was troubled, and his sleep left him. [2]Then the king commanded that the magicians, the enchanters, the sorcerers, and the Chaldeans be summoned, to tell the king his dreams. So they came in and stood before the king. [3]And the king said to them, "I had a dream, and my spirit is troubled to know the dream." [4]Then the Chaldeans said to the king,[a] "O king, live for ever! Tell your servants the dream, and we will show the interpretation." [5]The king answered the Chaldeans, "The word from me is sure: if you do not make known to me the dream and its interpretation, you shall be torn limb from limb, and your houses shall be laid in ruins. [6]But if you show the dream and its

interpretation, you shall receive from me gifts and rewards and great honor. Therefore show me the dream and its interpretation." [7]*They answered a second time, "Let the king tell his servants the dream, and we will show its interpretation."* [8]*The king answered, "I know with certainty that you are trying to gain time, because you see that the word from me is sure* [9]*that if you do not make the dream known to me, there is but one sentence for you. You have agreed to speak lying and corrupt words before me till the times change. Therefore tell me the dream, and I shall know that you can show me its interpretation."* [10]*The Chaldeans answered the king, "There is not a man on earth who can meet the king's demand; for no great and powerful king has asked such a thing of any magician or enchanter or Chaldean.* [11]*The thing that the king asks is difficult, and none can show it to the king except the gods, whose dwelling is not with flesh."*

[12]*Because of this the king was angry and very furious, and commanded that all the wise men of Babylon be destroyed.* [13]*So the decree went forth that the wise men were to be slain, and they sought Daniel and his companions, to slay them.* [14]*Then Daniel replied with prudence and discretion to Ari-och, the captain of the king's guard, who had gone out to slay the wise men of Babylon;* [15]*he said to Ari-och, the king's captain, "Why is the decree of the king so severe?" Then Ari-och made the matter known to Daniel.* [16]*And Daniel went in and besought the king to appoint him a time, that he might show to the king the interpretation.*

a Heb adds *in Aramaic*, indicating that the text from this point to the end of chapter 7 is in Aramaic

---

OVERVIEW: In making reference to the precise time when Nebuchadnezzar's dream occurred, Daniel places himself in the company of the great prophets. Nebuchadnezzar's bewilderment over the dream that troubled him so deeply is a sign of the divine origin of the dream (JEROME). The failure of the king's counselors as interpreters of the dream makes evident that these mysteries of God cannot be accessed or interpreted by people who think of earthly things. The heavenly mysteries are revealed only to those like Joseph, Daniel and the other prophets (and "in our time, the monks") (THEODORET), that is, to those who seek heavenly things (HIP-POLYTUS). There are two types of dreams: those from the devil and those from God. God uses dreams to pour forth his bountiful grace on all of humankind (TERTULLIAN). The Spirit of prophecy does not affect everyone in the same way (AUGUSTINE).

2:1 In the Second Year of Nebuchadnezzar's Reign

A MARK OF TRUE PROPHECY. THEODORET OF CYR: We learned earlier that at the beginning of his [Nebuchadnezzar's] reign, he advanced with the army to Judea in the third year of the reign of Joachim.... So most blessed Daniel, recalling the first year after the capture of the Jews, ... now adds, "in the second year of his reign, Nebuchadnezzar has a dream." He [Daniel] added this not without reason but that we should know the time with precision. This is like the divine ways of the prophets, noting the facts related to the kings, a sure reference to the number of years. COMMENTARY ON DANIEL 2.1.[1]

THE KING IS USED BY GOD. JEROME: The impious king beheld a dream concerning things to come, in order that he might give glory to God after the holy man interpreted what he had seen and that great consolation might be afforded the captive [Jews] and those who still served God in their captive state. We read this same thing in the

---

[1]PG 81:1284-85; WGRW 7:35.

case of Pharaoh, not because Pharaoh and Neb-uchadnezzar deserved to behold visions but in order that Joseph and Daniel might appear as deserving of preference over all other people because of their gift of interpretation. Commentary on Daniel 1.2.18.[2]

The Spirit of Prophecy. Augustine: The Spirit of prophecy does not affect everyone in the same way. The Spirit's infusion in some people confers images of things; others are granted the mental fruit of understanding; others are given both by inspiration; and still others know nothing. But the Spirit works through the infusion in two ways. The first way comes during sleep, and not only to saints, but even Pharoah and King Nebuchadnezzar saw what neither of them was able to understand but both of them were able to see. The second way is through demonstration in ecstasy (which some Latins translate as "trembling"—astonishingly idiosyncratic, but close in meaning nonetheless), where the mind is separated from the bodily senses so that the human spirit, which is assumed by the divine Spirit, might be free of perceiving and intuiting ideas, as, for instance, when it was shown to Daniel what he had not understood, and to Peter, the sheet let down from heaven by its four corners, who only later recognized what this vision represented.[3] One way is through the mental fruit of understanding, when the significance and relevance of the things demonstrated through images is revealed, which is a more certain prophecy, for the apostle calls such prophecy "greater,"[4] as Joseph deserved to understand but Pharaoh only to see, and as Daniel explained to the king that he saw but did not know. On Various Questions to Simplician 2.1.1.[5]

God Uses Dreams to Pour Grace on Humankind. Tertullian: There is a type of dream that comes from God, since he has promised to pour out the grace of the Holy Spirit on all flesh and has ordained that his sons and hand-maidens shall utter prophecies and dream dreams. Such dreams may be compared with the grace of God as being honest, holy, prophetic, inspired, edifying and inducing to virtue. Their bountiful nature causes them to overflow even to the unbelievers since God with divine impartiality causes the rain to fall and the sun to shine on just and unjust alike. On the Soul 47.[6]

2:2 Tell the King His Dreams

The Dream Is Hidden. Hippolytus: The vision was concealed from the king for this purpose: that he who was chosen by God [i.e., Daniel] might be shown to be a prophet. For when things concealed from some are revealed by another, he who tells them is of necessity shown to be a prophet. Scholia on Daniel 2.5.[7]

Foolishness Compared with Wisdom. Theodoret of Cyr: The providential plan is unveiled to the wise. The dream was made known to the prophet and so making evident that which he willed to be accomplished, that in turn [the prophet's] good and saving counsel would be readily received. The king was frightened by the dream, and yet he also feared that he would forget the dream. That which the God of all foreknows is made known to those who are faithful, as is likewise the foolishness of the king. For surely it is foolish to ask others to recall the dream. Commentary on Daniel 2.2.[8]

2:3 We Will Interpret the Dream

Human Wisdom Inadequate. Theodoret of Cyr: And having summoned them, they were given the request by that one whom they serve, and foolishly they promised. For human wisdom is incapable of knowing the divine mysteries without assistance from above. Commentary on Daniel 2.3-4.[9]

---

[2]CCL 75A:783; JCD 24. [3]See Acts 10:9-20. [4]1 Cor 14:5. [5]CCL 44:58-59. [6]ANF 3:225-26**. [7]ANF 5:186*. [8]PG 81:1285; WGRW 7:35. [9]PG 81:1285; WGRW 7:35.

2:8 A Corrupt Statement

FALSE INTERPRETATION. THEODORET OF CYR: While the demand in these words was high-handed and insane, the accusation was very true: You want to learn what the dream was, he is saying, so as to hatch in common some false interpretation and trick me as usual, using the lapse in time as an advantage and waiting for the moment of fulfillment. COMMENTARY ON DANIEL 2.8-9.[10]

2:11 The King Asks a Difficult Thing

UNJUST REQUEST. THEODORET OF CYR: The Chaldeans responded, Wherefore it is not possible to know precisely what you [the king] thought. What is humanly possible, they said, you may require from us, but not that which is beyond our nature. You who govern the greatest of all kingdoms must act justly in the governance of that kingdom and require from your subjects that which is possible. That which is now requested is by no mean just. Such knowledge does not belong to human beings. COMMENTARY ON DANIEL 2.11.[11]

IT IS IN GOD'S POWER TO KNOW THE FUTURE. JEROME: The magi confess, along with the soothsayers—and all secular learning concurs—that foreknowledge of the future lies not in human province but in God's. By this test it is proved that the prophets who proclaimed things to come spoke by the Spirit of God. COMMENTARY ON DANIEL 1.2.11.[12]

POSSIBLE FOR GOD. HIPPOLYTUS: [The magi] said that it was impossible for a human being to tell what the king asked. So, God showed them that what is impossible with people is possible with God. SCHOLIA ON DANIEL 2.10.[13]

2:12-16 All the Wise Men to Be Destroyed

ARIOCH, THE CHIEF EXECUTIONER. HIPPOLYTUS: In effect, Arioch was the head cook, and as the cook slays all animals and cooks them, so here he has a similar occupation. For the rulers of the world slay people, butchering them like brute beasts. SCHOLIA ON DANIEL 2.14.[14]

---

[10]WGRW 7:37. [11]PG81:1288; WGRW 7:37. [12]CCL 75A:785; JCD 25-26. [13]ANF 5:186**. [14]ANF 5:186**.

2:17-30 DANIEL PRAYS FOR AND RECEIVES THE INTERPRETATION

[17]Then Daniel went to his house and made the matter known to Hananiah, Misha-el, and Azariah, his companions, [18]and told them to seek mercy of the God of heaven concerning this mystery, so that Daniel and his companions might not perish with the rest of the wise men of Babylon. [19]Then the mystery was revealed to Daniel in a vision of the night. Then Daniel blessed the God of heaven. [20]Daniel said:

"Blessed be the name of God for ever and ever,
    to whom belong wisdom and might.
[21]He changes times and seasons;

he removes kings and sets up kings;
he gives wisdom to the wise
   and knowledge to those who have understanding;
²²he reveals deep and mysterious things;
   he knows what is in the darkness,
   and the light dwells with him.
²³To thee, O God of my fathers,
   I give thanks and praise,
for thou hast given me wisdom and strength,
   and hast now made known to me what we asked of thee,
   for thou hast made known to us the king's matter."

²⁴Therefore Daniel went in to Ari-och, whom the king had appointed to destroy the wise men of Babylon; he went and said thus to him, "Do not destroy the wise men of Babylon; bring me in before the king, and I will show the king the interpretation."

²⁵Then Ari-och brought in Daniel before the king in haste, and said thus to him: "I have found among the exiles from Judah a man who can make known to the king the interpretation." ²⁶The king said to Daniel, whose name was Belteshazzar, "Are you able to make known to me the dream that I have seen and its interpretation?" ²⁷Daniel answered the king, "No wise men, enchanters, magicians, or astrologers can show to the king the mystery which the king has asked, ²⁸but there is a God in heaven who reveals mysteries, and he has made known to King Nebuchadnezzar what will be in the latter days. Your dream and the visions of your head as you lay in bed are these: ²⁹To you, O king, as you lay in bed came thoughts of what would be hereafter, and he who reveals mysteries made known to you what is to be. ³⁰But as for me, not because of any wisdom that I have more than all the living has this mystery been revealed to me, but in order that the interpretation may be made known to the king, and that you may know the thoughts of your mind."

OVERVIEW: Daniel is an example of the injunction to pray in secret (CHROMATIUS). Trusting not in their own wisdom, Daniel and his companions trust the One who rules over all to reveal the meaning of the dream (THEODORET). It is by the will of God that kings and empires succeed one another. Daniel invokes imagery of darkness and light to describe God's revelation of the deep and secret matters. Darkness signifies ignorance, and light signifies knowledge and learning (JEROME). The divine nature is omniscient and omnipotent but does not will all it has the power to accomplish (JOHN OF DAMASCUS). The Son is the true light because he makes known the Father (CHROMATIUS). Daniel appears before Nebuchadnezzar to reveal

the meaning of his dream. The source of Daniel's interpretation is not human will but divine (CHRYSOSTOM, HIPPOLYTUS). Daniel was endowed with both the gift of seeing the sign and that of understanding the sign (AUGUSTINE). Dreams arise from a number of sources; therefore the faithful must be reluctant to put trust in them (GREGORY THE GREAT). Wealth and earthly power are gifts of God, but they are not spiritual gifts (ORIGEN).

2:18 Seeking the Mercy of God

EXAMPLES OF PRAYING IN SECRET. CHROMATIUS OF AQUILEIA: We find in the books of Kings the very holy woman Hannah fulfilling the precepts of this Gospel teaching. For while praying without uttering a sound, in her heart and in the sight of God she poured out her desire in her prayers. She was immediately found worthy to be heard by the Lord.[1] In the same way the Lord granted to Daniel, who always prayed in secret with three servants, to understand the interpretations of his dream and the secrets of revelation. Cornelius too, not yet instructed in the gospel, prayed secretly and faithfully in his room and was found worthy to hear the voice of the angel speaking.[2] TRACTATE ON MATTHEW 27.1.4-5.[3]

PRAYER REVEALED THE DREAM'S MEANING. THEODORET OF CYR: Truly, much that is true is found in the midst of the lies. Those who seek God are the friends of truth, while those who depend on human reason alone are wicked and in all they say and do attempt to seduce people. But the friends of truth adhere to nothing apart from that which comes from on high. They call on the One who rules over all, taking heed to depend on prayer, standing steadfast, not distressed, not at this moment or in this place, but standing against the onslaught of human reason. And through the testimony of blessed Daniel, we see the beloved youth given straightaway the revelation concerning the dream, not because of his calculations but simply because it was proper time to hand over to the one who prays. He alone was of great courage, but at the same time his companions jointly took up the prayer. For none had abandoned the hope. COMMENTARY ON DANIEL 2.17-18.[4]

THE WORK OF THE SPIRIT. GREGORY THE GREAT: What a skillful workman the Spirit is! There is no question of delay in learning. It no sooner touches the mind in regard to anything it chooses than it teaches; its very touch is teaching. It changes a human mind in a moment to enlighten it; suddenly what it was no longer is, suddenly it is what it was not. FORTY GOSPEL HOMILIES 30.[5]

2:20 Blessing the Name of God

HYMN OF GRATITUDE. THEODORET OF CYR: In everything he reveals his gratitude, not only composing the hymn but also making the discovery of the dream the theme of the composition. It is proper, he is saying, constantly to sing praises of God, who is eternal and everlasting, fount of wisdom and understanding as he is, governing everything correctly and beneficently. COMMENTARY ON DANIEL 2.19-22.[6]

DANIEL BLESSES THE MIGHTY NAME OF GOD. JEROME: Let us not marvel, therefore, whenever we see kings and empires succeed one another, for it is by the will of God that they are governed, altered and terminated. And the situations of individuals are well known to him who founded all things. He often permits wicked kings to arise that they may in their wickedness punish the wicked. At the same time, by indirect suggestion and general remarks, he prepares the reader for the fact that the dream Nebuchadnezzar saw was concerned with the change and succession of empires. COMMENTARY ON DANIEL 2.21.[7]

GOD'S OMNISCIENCE. JOHN OF DAMASCUS: Further, the divine nature has the property of penetrating all things without mixing with them and of being itself impenetrable by anything else. Moreover, there is the property of knowing all things with a simple knowledge and seeing all things simply with his divine, all-surveying, immaterial eye, the things of the present, and the things of the past and the things of the future before they come into being. The divine nature is also sinless, and can cast sin out and bring salvation. And all that it wills, it can accomplish, but it does not will all it could accomplish. For it could destroy the universe, but it does not will so to do. ORTHODOX FAITH 1.14.[8]

---

[1] 1 Sam 1:13-17. [2] Acts 10:1-4. [3] CCL 9A:325-26. [4] PG 81:1292; WGRW 7:41. [5] CS 123:245. [6] WGRW 7:41. [7] JCD 27; CCL 75A:787. [8] NPNF 2 9:17.

2:21 Deposing and Setting Up Kings

GIFTS OF GOD. ORIGEN: Many other things may also be called gifts of God, such as riches and bodily strength, physical beauty and earthly power. These things are also given by God, as Daniel says: "He deposes kings and sets up kings," but they are not spiritual gifts. COMMENTARY ON THE EPISTLE TO THE ROMANS 1.12.[9]

BESTOWING WISDOM. JEROME: One to whom God makes profound revelations and who can say, "O the depth of the riches of the knowledge and wisdom of God," he it is who by the indwelling of the Spirit probes even into the deep things of God and digs the deepest of wells in the depths of his soul. COMMENTARY ON DANIEL 2.22.[10]

2:22 Light Dwells with God

GOD BRINGS LIGHT TO THE DARKNESS. JEROME: The darkness signifies ignorance, and the light signifies knowledge and learning. Therefore as wrong cannot hide God away, so also he is encompassed and surrounded by right. We may also interpret these words to mean that all the dark mysteries and deep things [concerning God].... This is similar to that which is read in the Psalms, "Dark waters in the clouds of the sky."[11] For one who ascends to the heights and forsakes the things of earth, and like the birds themselves seek after the most rarified atmosphere and everything ethereal, he becomes like a cloud to which the truth of God penetrates and that habitually showers rain on the saints. COMMENTARY ON DANIEL 2.22.[12]

THE SON WITH THE FATHER. CHROMATIUS OF AQUILEIA: Concerning the light Daniel noted, "It reveals the profound and hidden things, knowing those things that are in the darkness and the light is with it," that is, the Son with the Father, for even as the Father is light, so too is the Son light. And David also speaks in the psalm: "In your light shall we see light,"[13] for the Father is seen in the Son, as the Lord tells us in the Gospel: "Who sees me, sees the Father."[14] From the true light, indeed, the true light proceeded, and from the invisible the visible. TRACTATE ON MATTHEW 15.1.[15]

ACKNOWLEDGING THE SOURCE OF UNDERSTANDING. THEODORET OF CYR: Such is the life of the devout, acknowledging that God is the source of understanding. He was the One who met Daniel's needs at the right moment and assured him a safe harbor. And after being well supplied with that which was the best, Daniel did not prove forgetful of the gifts but sang praises in response to his holy benefactor. COMMENTARY ON DANIEL 2.23.[16]

2:24-30 Daniel Appears Before Nebuchadnezzar

DANIEL RESCUED THE WISE MEN OF BABYLON. CHRYSOSTOM: Let us not then be looking open-mouthed toward others. For it is true, the prayers of the saints have the greatest power, on condition, however, of our repentance and change. Since even Moses, who had rescued his own brother and six hundred thousand men from the wrath that was then coming on them from God, had no power to deliver his sister.[17] ... And Samuel was not able to save Saul from the wrath from above, yet he oftentimes preserved the Israelites. ... And Daniel saved the barbarians from slaughter, but he did not deliver the Jews from their captivity. ... So on the one hand, if we are careless, we shall not be able to obtain salvation, no, not even by the help of others; if, on the other hand, we are watchful, we shall be able to do this by ourselves, and by ourselves rather than by others. Yes, for God is more willing to give his grace to us than to others for us, that we, by our zeal to avoid his wrath, may both

---

[9]FC 103:82**. [10]JCD 27*; CCL 75A:788. [11]Ps 18:11 (17:11 LXX). [12]JCD 27-28*; CCL 75A:788-89. [13]Ps 36:9 (35:9 LXX). [14]Jn 14:9. [15]CCL 9A:259. [16]PG 81:1293; WGRW 7:43. [17]Exod 32; Num 12:10.

enjoy a deep trust in him and become better people. HOMILIES ON THE GOSPEL OF MATTHEW 5.7.[18]

THE GLORIFICATION OF GOD.

CHRYSOSTOM: For nothing is so advantageous and so likely to pacify the hearers as to say nothing about one's self of an honorable nature, but on the contrary, to forestall all suspicion of wishing to do so. And, in truth, much more did they [the apostles] increase their glory by despising glory and showing that what had just taken place was not a human act but a divine work; and that it was their part to join with the beholders in admiration rather than to receive it from them. . . . In the same manner also did the ancient fathers, for instance, Daniel, say, "Not because of any wisdom I have more than all the living has this mystery been revealed to me." . . . And again Joseph, "Do not interpretations belong to God?"[19] HOMILIES ON THE ACTS OF THE APOSTLES 30.[20]

DREAMS ARISE FOR A VARIETY OF REASONS.

GREGORY THE GREAT: "To you, O king, as you lay in bed came thoughts of what would be hereafter, and he who reveals mysteries made known to you what is to be." And a little later, "You, O king, saw, and behold, a great image." . . . Daniel, therefore, in reverently indicating that the dream was to be fulfilled and in telling from what thoughts it arose, shows clearly that dreams often rise from our thoughts and from revelation. Seeing, then, that dreams may arise from such a variety of causes, one ought to be very reluctant to put one's faith in them, since it is hard to tell from what source they come. . . . If the mind is not on its guard against these, it will be entangled in countless vanities by the master of deceit, who is clever enough to foretell many things that are true in order finally to capture the soul by but one falsehood. This happened recently to one of our people who believed strongly in dreams. In one of them he was promised a long life. After collecting a large sum of money to last him for many years, he died suddenly, leaving all of his wealth behind untouched, without having so much as a single good work to

take with him. DIALOGUE 4.50.5-6.[21]

DANIEL'S APPEARANCE INVOKES TRUE BELIEF.

HIPPOLYTUS: For the king, on making himself master of the land of Egypt, and taking hold of Judea and carrying off the people, thought on his bed what should come after these things. He who knows the secrets of all and searches the thoughts of the hearts revealed to him by means of the image the things that were to be. But he hid from the king the vision, in order that the counsels of God might not be interpreted by the wise men of Babylon but that by the blessed Daniel, as a prophet of God, things kept secret from all might be made manifest. SCHOLIA ON DANIEL 2.29.[22]

VISIONS ARE MANIFESTED TO THE SPIRIT.

AUGUSTINE: The one who interprets what another has seen is more a prophet than the one who had seen. . . . Less a prophet is he who . . . sees in spirit only the signs of the things signified, and a greater prophet is he who is granted only an understanding of images. But the greatest prophet is he who is endowed with both gifts, namely, that of seeing in spirit the symbolic likeness of corporeal objects and that of understanding them with the vital power of the mind. Such a one was Daniel. His preeminence was tested and established when he not only told the dream he had had but also explained the meaning of it. For the corporeal images themselves were produced in his spirit, and an understanding of them was revealed in his mind. I am using the word *spirit*, therefore, in the sense in which Paul uses it, where he distinguishes it from the mind: "I will pray with the spirit, but I will pray with the mind also."[23] Here he implies that signs of things are formed in the spirit and that an understanding of the signs shines forth in the mind. ON THE LITERAL INTERPRETATION OF GENESIS 12.9.20[24]

---

[18]NPNF 1 10:34-35*. [19]Gen 40:8. [20]NPNF 1 11:190**. [21]SC 265:174-76. [22]ANF 5:186*. [23]1 Cor 14:15. [24]ACW 42:189-90.

2:31-45 THE DREAM AND ITS INTERPRETATION

[31]You saw, O king, and behold, a great image. This image, mighty and of exceeding brightness, stood before you, and its appearance was frightening. [32]The head of this image was of fine gold, its breast and arms of silver, its belly and thighs of bronze, [33]its legs of iron, its feet partly of iron and partly of clay. [34]As you looked, a stone was cut out by no human hand, and it smote the image on its feet of iron and clay, and broke them in pieces; [35]then the iron, the clay, the bronze, the silver, and the gold, all together were broken in pieces, and became like the chaff of the summer threshing floors; and the wind carried them away, so that not a trace of them could be found. But the stone that struck the image became a great mountain and filled the whole earth.

[36]This was the dream; now we will tell the king its interpretation. [37]You, O king, the king of kings, to whom the God of heaven has given the kingdom, the power, and the might, and the glory, [38]and into whose hand he has given, wherever they dwell, the sons of men, the beasts of the field, and the birds of the air, making you rule over them all—you are the head of gold. [39]After you shall arise another kingdom inferior to you, and yet a third kingdom of bronze, which shall rule over all the earth. [40]And there shall be a fourth kingdom, strong as iron, because iron breaks to pieces and shatters all things; and like iron which crushes, it shall break and crush all these. [41]And as you saw the feet and toes partly of potter's clay and partly of iron, it shall be a divided kingdom; but some of the firmness of iron shall be in it, just as you saw iron mixed with the miry clay. [42]And as the toes of the feet were partly iron and partly clay, so the kingdom shall be partly strong and partly brittle. [43]As you saw the iron mixed with miry clay, so they will mix with one another in marriage,[b] but they will not hold together, just as iron does not mix with clay. [44]And in the days of those kings the God of heaven will set up a kingdom which shall never be destroyed, nor shall its sovereignty be left to another people. It shall break in pieces all these kingdoms and bring them to an end, and it shall stand for ever; [45]just as you saw that a stone was cut from a mountain by no human hand, and that it broke in pieces the iron, the bronze, the clay, the silver, and the gold. A great God has made known to the king what shall be hereafter. The dream is certain, and its interpretation sure.

b Aramaic by the seed of men

OVERVIEW: Daniel's piety is rewarded with the ability to reveal and interpret the dream of the king (PSEUDO-CLEMENT). The precious substances from which the dream's image are composed and that are ultimately shattered teach humility as they remind us of the fleeting nature of the earth and its elements (EUSEBIUS). Daniel reveals that the elements stand for kingdoms that will follow one another ending with Alexander and the Hellenistic kings that followed (EPHREM) or the Roman Empire, whose strength is indicated by iron but whose ultimate demise is indicated by its being merged with clay (JEROME, HIPPOLYTUS, APHRAHAT). The stone cut from the mountain foretells the advent of Christ (GREGORY OF NYSSA). The stone that grows into a mountain foretells the triumph of the church over all temporal powers (AUGUSTINE). The shattering of the image tells of the second advent and the final triumph of the righteous (THEODORET, IRENAEUS, IGNATIUS).

2:31 A Great Image

TRUTH REVEALED THROUGH INTELLIGENCE.
PSEUDO-CLEMENT: It is made known that the devout as well as the impious see visions and dreams, as can be proved from Scripture. . . . Nebuchadnezzar, who worshiped images and ordered those who worshiped God to be cast into fire, saw a dream extending over the whole age of the world. . . . Thus, we cannot infer with absolute certainty that the one who has seen visions and dreams and apparitions is undoubtedly devout. For in the case of the devout person, the truth gushes up natural and pure in his mind, not worked through dreams but granted to the good through intelligence. PSEUDO-CLEMENTINE HOMILIES 17.[1]

THE END OF HUMAN KINGDOMS. EUSEBIUS OF CAESAREA: And it was fitting that the king, who prized the substances deemed precious among people, gold, and silver, and brass and iron, should identify these substances as the kingdoms that held sovereignty at different times in the life of humankind; but that the prophet should describe these same kingdoms under the likeness of beasts, in accordance with the manner of their rule.[2] And again, the king—who was puffed up, so it appears, in his own conceit and prided himself on the power of his ancestors—is shown the vicissitude to which affairs are subject and the end destined for all the kingdoms of the earth. This is done in order to teach him humility and understand that there is nothing lasting among people but only that which is appointed the end of all things—the kingdom of God. PROOF OF THE GOSPEL 15.1.[3]

2:32 The Prized Metals

GOLD, THE MOST PRECIOUS METAL. JEROME: "You are the head of gold," he says. By this statement it is clear that the first empire, the Babylonian, is compared with the most precious metal,

gold. COMMENTARY ON DANIEL 2.31-35.[4]

BABYLONIAN SOVEREIGNTY. HIPPOLYTUS: For the image shown at that time to Nebuchadnezzar furnished a type of the whole world. In these times, the Babylonians were sovereign over all, and these were the golden head of the image. SCHOLIA ON DANIEL 2.31.[5]

BABYLON IS A GOLDEN CUP. APHRAHAT: As Daniel said, "You are the head of gold." And why was he called the head of gold? Was it not because the word of Jeremiah was fulfilled in him? For Jeremiah said, "Babylon is a golden cup in the hand of the Lord that makes all the earth to drink of its wine."[6] And also Babylon was called the head of all kingdoms, as it is written, "Babylon was the head of the kingdom of Nimrod."[7] DEMONSTRATIONS 5.11.[8]

THE PERSIANS AND MEDES. JEROME: That is to say [arms of silver], the empire of the Medes and Persians, which bears a resemblance to silver, being inferior to the preceding empire and superior to that which is to follow. COMMENTARY ON DANIEL 2.31-35.[9]

PERSIANS REIGNED FOR 245 YEARS. HIPPOLYTUS: And then, after [the Babylonians], the Persians held the supremacy for 245 years, and they were represented by the silver. SCHOLIA ON DANIEL 2.31.[10]

SILVER IS INFERIOR TO GOLD. APHRAHAT: This signified a kingdom that was inferior to it; namely, Darius the Mede [king of Persia]. For he put the kingdom on the scales, and the kingdom of the house of Nimrod was weighed and found wanting. And because it was wanting, Darius received it. Because of this he [Daniel] said "another kingdom inferior to you." And because it

---

[1]ANF 8:323. [2]Rev 13. [3]GCS 6:494. [4]JCD 31*; CCL 75A:794. [5]ANF 5:186. [6]Jer 51:7. [7]Cf. Gen 10:8-10. [8]NPNF 2 13:356*. [9]JCD 32; CCL 75A:794. [10]ANF 5:186.

was inferior, the children of Media did not rule in all the earth. DEMONSTRATIONS 5.12.[11]

TWO PEOPLES. THEODORET OF CYR: The second element, silver, signifies the Persian kingdom and the Medes. Cyrus, by way of his own success and marriage, created from the Medes the kingdom of Persia. . . . He speaks of a chest and arms to show that he knows there were two peoples, each limb a founder, that are joined together. COMMENTARY ON DANIEL 2.31-33.[12]

THE KINGDOM FOUNDED BY ALEXANDER. JEROME: This [thighs of bronze] signifies the Alexandrian empire, and that of the Macedonians and of Alexander's successors. Now this is properly termed brazen, for among all the metals, bronze possesses an outstanding resonance and a clear ring, and the blast of a brazen trumpet is heard far and wide, so that it signifies not only fame and power of the empire but also the eloquence of the Greek language. COMMENTARY ON DANIEL 2.39.[13]

THE MACEDONIAN'S REIGN. HIPPOLYTUS: Then the Greeks had the supremacy, beginning with Alexander the Macedonian, for three hundred years, so that they were brass. SCHOLIA ON DANIEL 2.31.[14]

CHILDREN OF JAPHET. APHRAHAT: This is the kingdom of the children of Javan, who are children of Japhet.[15] For the children of Javan came against the kingdom of their brothers. For Madai and Javan are sons of Japhet. But Madai was foolish and incapable of governing the kingdom, until Javan, his brother, came, who was wise and cunning, to destroy the kingdoms. For Alexander, son of Philip, ruled in all the earth. DEMONSTRATIONS 5.12.[16]

2:33 Legs of Iron, Toes of Clay

THE ROMAN EMPIRE. JEROME: Now the fourth empire, which clearly refers to the Romans, is the iron empire that breaks in pieces and overcomes all others. But its feet and toes are partly iron and partly of earthenware, a fact clearly revealed at the present moment. For just as there was at the first nothing stronger or hardier than the Roman realm, so also in these last days there is nothing more feeble, since we require the assistance of barbarian tribes both in our civil wars and against foreign nations. COMMENTARY ON DANIEL 2.40.[17]

TOES OF CLAY AND IRON. HIPPOLYTUS: After [the Greeks] came the Romans, who were the iron. Then we have the toes of clay and iron to signify the democracies that were subsequently to rise, partitioned among the ten toes of the image, in which iron shall be mixed with clay. SCHOLIA ON DANIEL 2.31.[18]

ALEXANDER. EPHREM THE SYRIAN: The iron is Alexander, the conqueror of all nations. Indeed, as iron submits all bodies, so he broke the forces of all princes and kings, and subjected their authorities. And the toes . . . these are the ten Hellenistic kings which originated from Alexander's empire: some of them were strong and powerful like iron; others were weak and humble. And even though they tried to settle peace and friendship among them with mutual marriages, they were never able to reach an agreement nor to stay firm in their decisions. COMMENTARY ON DANIEL 2.40.[19]

2:34 A Stone

THE STONE CUT FROM THE MOUNTAIN. AUGUSTINE: We know that the stone cut from the mountain without hands is Christ, who came from the kingdom of the Jews without human father: the stone that shattered all the kingdoms of the earth, all the tyrannies of idols and devils; the stone that grew and became a great mountain and filled the whole world. HOMILIES ON 1 JOHN 1.12.[20]

---

[11]NPNF 2 13:356*. [12]PG 81:1297; WGRW 7:49. [13]JCD 32; CCL 75A:794. [14]ANF 5:186. [15]Gen 10:2. [16]NPNF 2 13:356-57*. [17]JCD 32; CCL 75A:794-95. [18]ANF 5:186. [19]ESOO 2:207. [20]NPNF 1 7:467**.

CHRIST IS THE STONE. GREGORY OF NYSSA: What is the stone . . . but Christ? For of him Isaiah says, "And I am laying in Zion for a foundation, a costly stone, precious, elect"[21]; and Daniel likewise, "A stone was cut out but not by hand," that is, Christ was born without a man. ON THE BAPTISM OF CHRIST.[22]

2:35 A Great Mountain

THE MOUNTAIN VEILED TO HERETICS. AUGUSTINE: It talks of a mountain, and the mountain is veiled to the party of Donatus. . . . The holy Daniel saw a vision and wrote down what he saw, and he said that he had seen a stone hewn out of a mountain without hands. It is Christ, coming from the nations of the Jews, which was also a mountain, you see, because it has the kingdom. . . . What is the mountain over which the heretics stumbled? Listen to Daniel again: "And that stone grew and became a great mountain, such that it filled all the face of the earth." How right the psalm is to say to Christ the Lord as he rises again, "Be exalted over the heavens, O God, and let your glory be over the whole earth."[23] What is your glory over the whole earth? Over the whole earth is your church, over the whole earth your bride. SERMON 147A.4.[24]

THE MOUNTAIN IS THE CHURCH. AUGUSTINE: "His holy hill"[25] is his holy church. It is that mountain which, according to Daniel's vision, grew from a very small stone till it overtook the kingdoms of the earth and grew to such a size that it "filled the face of the earth." EXPLANATIONS OF THE PSALMS 43.4.[26]

DANIEL FORETELLS THE RESURRECTION. IRENAEUS: Therefore, God who is great showed future things by Daniel and confirmed them by his Son; and Christ is the stone that is cut out without hands, who shall destroy temporal kingdoms and introduce an eternal one, which is the resurrection of the just. AGAINST HERESIES 5.26.2.[27]

2:44 A Kingdom That Will Not Be Destroyed

KINGDOM OF HEAVEN. THEODORET OF CYR: Clearly, this teaches about that which will occur at the end, that is, the coming of the kingdom of heaven that is without end. For the kingdom of iron having been brought alongside the weaker element and the composite vessel having been wrought, then shall appear "the stone cut without hand." . . . The stone that was cut without hands and grew into a great mountain and fills the whole earth is the second advent, and it will strike against the feet of the vessel . . . and all kingdoms will be destroyed and delivered up to oblivion, and the kingdom without end will be established. COMMENTARY ON DANIEL 2.44-45.[28]

THE KINGDOM OF THE SON. IGNATIUS OF ANTIOCH: He, being begotten by the Father before the beginning of time, was God the Word, the only-begotten Son, and remains the same forever; for "of his kingdom there shall be no end," says Daniel the prophet. Let us all therefore love one another in harmony, and let no one look on his neighbor according to the flesh, but in Christ Jesus. Let nothing exist among you that may divide you; but be united with your bishop, being through him subject to God in Christ. EPISTLE TO THE MAGNESIANS 6.[29]

---

[21]Is 28:16. [22]NPNF 2 5:521*. [23]Ps 57:11 (56:12 LXX); 108:5 (107:6 LXX). [24]WSA 3 4:454**. [25]Ps 3:4 (3:5 LXX). [26]NPNF 1 8:139*. [27]ANF 1:555*. [28]PG 81:1308-1309; WGRW 7:59-63. [29]ANF 1:61*.

2:46-49 THE KING HONORS DANIEL
AND THE COMPANIONS

⁴⁶*Then King Nebuchadnezzar fell upon his face, and did homage to Daniel, and commanded that an offering and incense be offered up to him.* ⁴⁷*The king said to Daniel, "Truly, your God is God of gods and Lord of kings, and a revealer of mysteries, for you have been able to reveal this mystery."* ⁴⁸*Then the king gave Daniel high honors and many great gifts, and made him ruler over the whole province of Babylon, and chief prefect over all the wise men of Babylon.* ⁴⁹*Daniel made request of the king, and he appointed Shadrach, Meshach, and Abednego over the affairs of the province of Babylon; but Daniel remained at the king's court.*

OVERVIEW: In Babylon, the captives became more glorious than their captors. The usefulness and greatness of prophecy becomes evident in the fact that through it Nebuchadnezzar was introduced and instructed in the faith. The captor is transformed (CHRYSOSTOM). Daniel, a prophet of God, displays his love for God and his neighbor in his actions (THEODORET).

2:46 Homage to Daniel

DEVOTION TO GOD OVERCOMES FEAR. CHRYSOSTOM: The people who were in Babylon say this: being there, I will remember you. Therefore, let us also, as being in Babylon, [do the same]. For although we are not sitting among warlike foes, yet we are among "enemies." For some indeed were captives but did not feel their captivity, as Daniel, as the three children; who, even while they were in captivity became in that very country more glorious even than the king who had made them captive. . . . Do you see how great is virtue? When they were in actual captivity, he waited on them as masters. He therefore was the captive, rather than they. . . . Do you see that the really splendid things are those that relate to God, whereas human things are a shadow? . . . Let us fear God, beloved, let us fear [him]: even should we be in captivity, we are more glorious than all people. Let the fear of

God be present with us, and nothing will bring us grief, even though they speak of poverty, or of disease, or of captivity, or of slavery or of any other grievous thing. In fact, even these very things will themselves work together for us the other way. These men were captives, and the king worshiped them. Paul was a tent maker, and they sacrificed to him as a god. ON THE EPISTLE TO THE HEBREWS, HOMILY 26.6-7.[1]

2:47 Your God Is God of Gods

THE POWER OF PROPHECY. CHRYSOSTOM: Prophecy is both free from reproach among the unbelievers and has very great credit and usefulness. For none will say in regard to prophesying, "they are mad," nor will anyone deride them that prophesy, but, on the contrary, they will be astonished at and admire them. . . . So also, Nebuchadnezzar worshiped God. . . . Observe the might of prophecy, how it changed that savage one and allowed him to be instructed and introduced him to faith. HOMILIES ON 1 CORINTHIANS 36.3.[2]

GOD'S POWER TRANSFORMS THE CAPTOR. CHRYSOSTOM: The king here does not say, "What must I do to be saved?" but the teaching is more obvious in his case than any language whatever.

---

[1]NPNF 1 14:485*. [2]NPNF 1 12:217-218*.

He immediately becomes a proclaimer; he does not need to be instructed like the jailor.[3] The king proclaims God and confesses God's power. . . . And what then followed? Not one single jailor but many are taught by way of the king's writings, by way of the mere observance of the facts. . . . How great the force of praises that are sung in the midst of tribulation. HOMILIES ON EPHESIANS 8.[4]

2:48 The King Honored Daniel

DANIEL'S SIMILARITY TO JOSEPH. THEODORET OF CYR: This is itself divine guidance. It is most fitting that the subjects benefit from the piety of the ruler: so also at one point God had done the same with Joseph. . . . He sent a man before them; Joseph was sold as a slave.[5] COMMENTARY ON DANIEL 2.48.[6]

2:49 Daniel's Request of the King

DANIEL'S LOVE OF GOD. THEODORET OF CYR: Truly this holy prophet loved God with all his heart, all his soul, all his strength, all his power. And having loved so fervently, he genuinely trusted, and he believed deeply, expecting that help would come from him. And it was as he had expected. And so also one is taught about the love of a neighbor, as it happened that the companions were also accepted. "For all the ancient Scriptures were written for our instruction and that through fortitude and the encouragement of the Scriptures we may have faith in Jesus Christ,"[7] who is the glory for the Father with the Holy Spirit world without end. Amen. COMMENTARY ON DANIEL 2.49.[8]

---

[3]Acts 16:25-40. [4]NPNF 1 13:93*. [5]See Gen 45:5. [6]PG 81:1312; WGRW 7:65. [7]Rom 15:4-5. [8]PG 81:1313; WGRW 7:67*.

3:1-11 THE KING ERECTS A GOLDEN IMAGE

[1]King Nebuchadnezzar made an image of gold, whose height was sixty cubits and its breadth six cubits. He set it up on the plain of Dura, in the province of Babylon. [2]Then King Nebuchadnezzar sent to assemble the satraps, the prefects, and the governors, the counselors, the treasurers, the justices, the magistrates, and all the officials of the provinces to come to the dedication of the image which King Nebuchadnezzar had set up. [3]Then the satraps, the prefects, and the governors, the counselors, the treasurers, the justices, the magistrates, and all the officials of the provinces, were assembled for the dedication of the image that King Nebuchadnezzar had set up; and they stood before the image that Nebuchadnezzar had set up. [4]And the herald proclaimed aloud, "You are commanded, O peoples, nations, and languages, [5]that when you hear the sound of the horn, pipe, lyre, trigon, harp, bagpipe, and every kind of music, you are to fall down and worship the golden image that King Nebuchadnezzar has set up; [6]and whoever does not fall down and worship shall immediately be cast into a burning fiery furnace." [7]Therefore, as soon as all the peoples heard the sound of the horn, pipe, lyre, trigon, harp, bagpipe, and every kind of music, all the peoples, nations, and languages fell down and

worshiped the golden image which King Nebuchadnezzar had set up.

[8]*Therefore at that time certain Chaldeans came forward and maliciously accused the Jews.* [9]*They said to King Nebuchadnezzar, "O king, live for ever!* [10]*You, O king, have made a decree, that every man who hears the sound of the horn, pipe, lyre, trigon, harp, bagpipe, and every kind of music, shall fall down and worship the golden image;* [11]*and whoever does not fall down and worship shall be cast into a burning fiery furnace."*

OVERVIEW: God, through Daniel, had been gracious to the king and led him to true piety, but the king was weak and turned back to impiety (THEODORET). Those in power are called on initially to worship the golden image because those with power are more easily manipulated to act wrongfully (JEROME). Ultimately, God's hand can be seen in this act as those that are gathered become an audience to God's power. The command to worship at the sound of music combines both elements of the enemy of true piety: pleasure and fear (CHRYSOSTOM).

3:1 The King's Idol

HUMANS ARE VAIN AND WEAK. THEODORET OF CYR: Our Lord is good and loves humankind, so the creator and ruler desires "all to be saved and to know the truth"[1] and "does not seek the death of the wicked but that they should turn and live."[2] Indeed, for that reason he died for our salvation. So truly he [the king] acts like a fool; being enslaved to arrogance, he derives no benefit from the divine remedy, but like the one who lives with illness, he rejects the cure from those who practice medicine. Thus, the awful disease tends to grow day by day. Such a man is this boastful king, who the God of all bestowed on him kindness without bounds, applying the cure for countless transgressions and acts of impiety. So also God revealed that the bringing of peace is fragile and passing, as he held aloft the ones made captive by war and who bore by compulsion the yoke of slavery. They shined splendidly and steadfastly and were admired for the wisdom of their prophecy. And thereby the God of all was indeed confessed to be the true God. But after a short time, the king came back into his true nature, just "as a dog returns to his vomit."[3] COMMENTARY ON DANIEL 3.1.[4]

3:2 The King Summons His Administrators

THOSE GIVEN POWER ARE MORE EASILY MANIPULATED. JEROME: It is the higher ranks that stand in the greater peril, and those who occupy the loftier position are the more sudden in their fall. The princes are assembled to worship the statue in order that through their princes the nations also might be attracted to error. For those who possess riches and power are all the more easily overthrown because of their apprehension of being bereft of them. But after the magistrates are led astray, the subject populace perishes through the evil example of their superiors. COMMENTARY ON DANIEL 3.2.[5]

GOD ORCHESTRATES THE SUMMONS. CHRYSOSTOM: The enemy prepares the theater, and the king himself collects the spectators and prepares the lists; a theater too, not of chance persons or of some private individuals but of all those who were honorable and in authority, so that their testimony may be worthy of credit with the multitude. They had come summoned for one thing; but they all departed having beheld another thing. They came in order to worship the image; and they departed, having derided the image and struck with wonder at the power of God through the signs that had taken place with respect to these young men. HOMILIES CONCERNING THE STATUES 4.8.[6]

---

[1]1 Tim 2:4. [2]Ezek 18:23, 32. [3]Prov 26:11. [4]PG 81:1313-16; WGRW 7:67-69. [5]JCD 35-36; CCL 75A:798. [6]NPNF 1 9:368*.

3:4 The Herald Commands Worship of the Image

INSTRUMENTS OF THE ENEMY OF PIETY.
CHRYSOSTOM: See how the struggles are so difficult, how irresistible is the snare, how deep the valley, and a precipice on either hand. But be not afraid. By whatever means the enemy increases his machinations, so much the more does he make evident the courage of the young men. For this reason is there this symphony of so many musicians; for this reason the burning furnace; in order that both pleasure and fear might attack the souls of those gathered. . . . Thus was fear as well as pleasure present; the one entering to assault the soul by way of the ears, the other by the eyes. But the noble character of these youths was not by any such means to be conquered. HOMILIES CONCERNING THE STATUES 4.8.[7]

THE ENEMY CANNOT PERSUADE THE SAINTS

TO WORSHIP IDOLS. ORIGEN: And we know that once we have been persuaded by Jesus to abandon idols and the atheism of worshiping many gods, the enemy cannot persuade us to commit idolatry, though he tries to force us. That is why he empowers those over whom he has authority to do such things. . . .

It is not just of old that Nebuchadnezzar's image of gold was set up or only then that he threatened Ananias, Azarias and Misael that he would throw them into the burning fiery furnace unless they worshiped it. Even now Nebuchadnezzar says the same thing to us, the true Hebrews in exile from our homeland. But as for us, let us imitate those holy men so that we may experience the heavenly dew that quenches every fire that arises in us and cools our governing mind. EXHORTATION TO MARTYRDOM 32-33.[8]

---

[7]NPNF 1 9:368*. [8]OSW 63.

3:12-23 THE KING CASTS THE THREE INTO THE FURNACE

[12]"There are certain Jews whom you have appointed over the affairs of the province of Babylon: Shadrach, Meshach, and Abednego. These men, O king, pay no heed to you; they do not serve your gods or worship the golden image which you have set up."

[13]Then Nebuchadnezzar in furious rage commanded that Shadrach, Meshach, and Abednego be brought. Then they brought these men before the king. [14]Nebuchadnezzar said to them, "Is it true, O Shadrach, Meshach, and Abednego, that you do not serve my gods or worship the golden image which I have set up? [15]Now if you are ready when you hear the sound of the horn, pipe, lyre, trigon, harp, bagpipe, and every kind of music, to fall down and worship the image which I have made, well and good; but if you do not worship, you shall immediately be cast into a burning fiery furnace; and who is the god that will deliver you out of my hands?"

[16]Shadrach, Meshach, and Abednego answered the king, "O Nebuchadnezzar, we have no need to answer you in this matter. [17]If it be so, our God whom we serve is able to deliver us from the

burning fiery furnace; and he will deliver us out of your hand, O king.[c] [18]But if not, be it known to you, O king, that we will not serve your gods or worship the golden image which you have set up."

[19]*Then Nebuchadnezzar was full of fury, and the expression of his face was changed against Shadrach, Meshach, and Abednego. He ordered the furnace heated seven times more than it was wont to be heated. [20]And he ordered certain mighty men of his army to bind Shadrach, Meshach, and Abednego, and to cast them into the burning fiery furnace. [21]Then these men were bound in their mantles,[d] their tunics,[d] their hats, and their other garments, and they were cast into the burning fiery furnace. [22]Because the king's order was strict and the furnace very hot, the flame of the fire slew those men who took up Shadrach, Meshach, and Abednego. [23]And these three men, Shadrach, Meshach, and Abednego, fell bound into the burning fiery furnace.*

c Or Behold, our God . . . king. Or If our God is able to deliver us, he will deliver us from the burning fiery furnace and out of your hand, O king   d The meaning of the Aramaic word is uncertain

OVERVIEW: The accusation of refusal to worship the idol is ironically a tribute to the young Jews' piety. As righteous people, these young men are not afraid to stand against the crowd or the powerful ruler (CHRYSOSTOM). They do not fear the possibility of death, for the Holy Spirit leads them to focus on the world above rather than this world (HIPPOLYTUS). The young men wisely do not answer the king's question directly (ROMANUS). Their determined refusal to obey the king (i.e., a refusal to engage in idolatry) makes clear the limits of Christian obedience to political rulers (TERTULLIAN). The young men display an unconditional devotion to God as they confess their love of God whether they are saved from the furnace or not (JEROME, THEODORET). In their words of confession and commitment to God, they win the crown of victory that is finally placed on their heads in the midst of the fiery furnace (CHRYSOSTOM).

The close friendship of the young men is an example of the power of friendship to sustain one even in the face of such a horrific threat (AMBROSE). The young men do not throw themselves into the furnace, making clear that taking one's own life is not given biblical warrant (AUGUSTINE). The fire of the furnace shows good judgment as it consumes the unbelievers who throw the children into the furnace rather than the devout children (HIPPOLYTUS). God allows the unbelievers to be consumed by the fire to make it clear that the children's survival is no mere trick or illusion (ISHO'DAD). Like all true servants of the Lord, the children do not show fear in the face of even the most severe threat to their lives and their happiness (MARTYRDOM OF POLYCARP, AMBROSE).

3:12 The Jews Are Accused of Not Worshiping the Image

REFUSAL TO WORSHIP THE LIFELESS IMAGE.
ROMANUS MELODUS:
When in Babylon an image had been made,
　　And everyone against his will worshiped
　　　the lifeless things as though it were alive,
Then, as Scripture tells, three youths,
　　Having received in their hearts divine
　　　guidance, did not leave the straight path,
For they considered the madness of many as
　　a path that leads astray.
　　And so the steadfast young men did not follow
　　　it.
But, advancing on the straight road, always
　　toward the truth,
　　They mocked the trickery of the Persians,
Or rather, the sainted boys mourned and
　　lamented,
　　For a righteous person does not rejoice over
　　　the destruction of another but with groans
　　　　prays:

"Hasten, Merciful One; and in compassion
  come quickly
To our aid, since you are able to do what you
  will."
Kontakion on the Three Children 2.[1]

Testimony to Their Courage and Piety.
Chrysostom: Consider along with me the wickedness of those who were their accusers, and how maliciously and bitterly they brought the accusation! . . . They did not merely mention the nation, but they also bring to mind their [the Jews'] honorable positions, that they may inflame the wrath of the king. It is almost as if they had said, "These slaves, these captives, who are without a city, you have made rulers over us. But they show contempt for such an honor and treat insolently the one who has given them this honor!" They go on then to say, "The Jews whom you have set over the province of Babylon do not obey or serve your gods." The accusation becomes their greatest praise; and the crimes imputed, their encomium; a testimony that is unassailable as it is brought forward by their enemies. Homilies Concerning the Statues 4.8.[2]

3:13 The King Commands Their Presence

The Righteous Young Men Are Not Frightened. Chrysostom: Then the youths alone are led into the midst; in order that from this also the conquest may become even more illustrious, they alone conquering and being proclaimed victors among so vast a multitude. This courage would not have been so surprising if they had acted courageously at the outset, when no one had fallen prostrate. But the greatest and most astonishing fact was that the multitude of those who fell down neither made them frightened nor made them weak. They did not say to themselves such things as many often do, "If we were first, and the only persons to worship the image, this would have been a sin; but if we do this with so many persons, who will not make allowance? Who will not think us worthy of defense?" But

nothing of this sort did they say or think when they beheld the shapes of so many princes. . . . What does the king do at this point? He commands that they should be brought into the midst, so that he may make them scared in every way. But nothing dismayed them, neither the wrath of the king, nor their being left alone in the midst of so many, nor the sight of the fire, nor the sound of the trumpet nor the whole multitude looking wrathfully at them; for deriding all these things, as if they were about to be cast into a cool fountain of water, they entered the furnace uttering that blessed sentence, "We will not serve your gods." . . . I have told you this history with good reason that you may learn that whether it is the wrath of a king, or the violence of soldiers, or the envy of enemies, or captivity, or destitution, or fire, or furnace or ten thousand terrors, nothing will work to shame or terrify a righteous person. Homilies Concerning the Statues 4.8-9.[3]

Led by the Holy Spirit. Hippolytus: Behold the Holy Spirit as it is manifest in the martyrs' eloquent speech, comforting them and consoling them and encouraging them to disregard death. . . . A person deprived of the Holy Spirit would be frightened and hide in fear, taking precautions against this death. . . . He is terrified as he stands before the blade, panicked at the idea of torment and seeing only the world below. This man is consoled with the life below, as he prefers to have a wife and the love of his children and to see only wealth. This man, who does not possess the power of heaven, readily is lost. Thus, whoever is close to the Word hears the command of the King and Lord of the sky: "Whoever does not take up his cross and follow me is not worthy of me, and whoever does not give up all of his possessions will not become my disciple."[4] Commentary on Daniel 2.21.1-3.[5]

3:15 Who Is the God Who Will Deliver You?

---

[1]KRBM 2:137. [2]NPNF 1 9:368*. [3]NPNF 1 9:368-69**. [4]Mt 10:38; Lk 14:33. [5]SC 14:156.

The Only Fear Should Be of Offending God. Chrysostom: But I say all this now, and select all the histories that contain trials and tribulations and the wrath of kings and their evil designs, in order that we may fear nothing except offending God. For then also was there a furnace burning; yet they derided it but feared sin. For they knew that if they were consumed in the fire, they should suffer nothing that was to be dreaded, but if they were guilty of impiety, they should undergo the extremes of misery. It is the greatest punishment to commit sin, though we may remain unpunished; . . . it is the greatest honor and repose to live virtuously, though we may be punished. Homilies Concerning the Statues 6.14.[6]

3:16 No Need to Answer

Do Not Reply to a Fool. Romanus Melodus:

When they heard these words, the young people
    Laughed at the great vanity of the king.
However, lest he consider himself to be very wise,
    The wise youths raised their eyes and said:
"O Nebuchadnezzar, king of Babylon,
We have no need to talk this over with them,[7]
For no one answers you if you say foolish things,
    For thus it is written in the Scripture:
'Do not give reply to a fool that is of similar
    kind.'[8]
    Therefore, we have chosen to keep silent, and
        we pray in silence:
    'Hasten, Merciful One, and in compassion
        come quickly
    To our aid, since you are able to do what you
        will.'"
Kontakion on the Three Children 12.[9]

The Limits of Obedience. Tertullian: In terms of the honors due to king or emperor, we have a clear ruling to be subject in all obedience, according to the apostle's command, to magistrates and princes and those in authority,[10] but this obedience must be within the bounds of

Christian discipline. That is, it is proper so long as we keep ourselves free of idolatry. It was for this reason that the familiar example of the three friends occurred before our time. Obedient in other respects to King Nebuchadnezzar, they most firmly refused to honor his image, and by this they proved that to extend the honor proper to a mortal beyond its due limits until it resembles the grandeur of God is idolatry. Daniel, in the same way, subjected himself to Darius in all points and performed his duty as long as it did not imperil his religion. To avoid that, Daniel showed no more fear of the king's lions than they had shown of the king's fires. On Idolatry 15.[11]

Nothing Compares with the Fire of Judgment. Jerome: Let us turn our thoughts to the three boys in the fiery furnace in Babylonia, and listen to what they say when Nebuchadnezzar summons them before him and compels them to worship Bel. What is their answer to Nebuchadnezzar? "King, there is no need to defend ourselves." . . . Look at their faith! We believe, it says, that he is able to save us; but if it should be that our sins prevent him, we still believe in him who will not deliver us. We do not believe in this life but in the future life; nor do we believe in him in order to escape burning here but in order to escape passing from this fire into another fire. Go ahead, then, prepare your furnace; this heat, this fire, is our purgation. Happy is he whose help is the God of Jacob! Homilies on the Psalms 55 (Psalm 145).[12]

The Young Men Showed No Fear. Chrysostom: Observe that they [the young men] by a special dispensation are ignorant of the future, for if they had foreknown, there would have been nothing wonderful in their doing what they did. For what marvel is it if, when they had a guarantee of safety, they defied all terrors? Then God indeed would have been glorified in that he was

---

[6]NPNF 1 9:387**. [7]"Them" refers to their accusers, the Chaldeans. [8]Prov 26:4. [9]KRBM 2:141. [10]Rom 13:7; 1 Pet 2:13. [11]ANF 3:71**. [12]FC 48:394*.

able to deliver them from the furnace, but they would not have been wondered at, inasmuch as they would not have cast themselves into dangers. For this reason, he caused them to be ignorant of the future that he might glorify them the more. And as they cautioned the king that he was not to condemn God of weakness though they might be burned, so God accomplished both purposes: manifesting his own power and making even more obvious the zeal of the children. . . . And so they entered into the fire; manifesting all courage and gentleness and doing nothing for reward or for compensation or return. . . . We also have already our compensation, for indeed we have it in that we have been given the full knowledge of him, being made members of Christ. HOMILIES ON 1 CORINTHIANS 28.6.[13]

THE YOUNG MEN'S RESPONSE WON THEM THE CROWN OF VICTORY. CHRYSOSTOM: The reason why I admire those youths and pronounce them blessed and enviable is not because they trampled on the flame and vanquished the force of the fire but because they were bound and cast into the furnace and delivered to the fire for the sake of true doctrine. For this was the whole of their triumph, and the wreath of victory was placed on their brows as soon as they were cast into the furnace. And yet, even before this momentous event, the wreath was woven for them. It was from the moment that they uttered those words as they spoke with such boldness and forthrightness to the king when they were brought into his presence. "We have no need to answer you concerning these things." . . . After the utterance of these words, I proclaimed them conquerors; after these words, grasping the prize of victory, they hastened on to the glorious crown of martyrdom, following up the confession that they made through their words with the confession made through their deeds. NONE CAN HARM HIM WHO DOES NOT INJURE HIMSELF 17.[14]

SUSTAINED BY FRIENDSHIP. AMBROSE: Preserve then, my sons, that friendship you have begun with your brothers, for nothing in the world is more beautiful than that. It is indeed a comfort in this life to have one to whom you can open your ear, with whom you can share secrets and to whom you can entrust the secrets of your heart. It is a comfort to have a trusty person by your side who will rejoice with you in prosperity, sympathize in troubles, encourage in persecution. What good friends those Hebrew children were whom the flames of the fiery furnace did not separate from the love of each other! DUTIES OF THE CLERGY 3.22.131.[15]

THE YOUNG MEN DID NOT SEEK TO BE KILLED. AUGUSTINE: Examine the divine Scriptures, and scrutinize them as closely as you can and see whether this [killing oneself] was ever done by any of the good and faithful souls, even though they suffered great trials at the hands of those who were trying to drive them to eternal destruction, not to eternal life. . . . I have heard that you said the apostle Paul meant that this was lawful when he said, "If I should deliver my body to be burned."[16] . . . But notice carefully and understand in what sense Scripture says that anyone should deliver his body to be burned: not, certainly, that he should jump into the fire when harassed by a pursuing enemy but that, when a choice is offered him of either doing wrong or suffering wrong, he chooses not to do wrong rather than not to suffer wrong. In this case, he delivers his body not to the power of the slayer, as those three men did who were being forced to adore the golden statue and who were threatened by the one who was forcing them with the furnace of burning fire if they did not do it. They refused to adore the idol, but they did not cast themselves into the fire. LETTER 173.[17]

NO FEAR OF DANGER. MARTYRDOM OF POLYCARP: So they did not nail him but tied him. Then he, placing his hands behind him and being bound

---

[13]NPNF 1 12:104*. [14]NPNF 1 9:283*. [15]NPNF 2 10:88. [16]1 Cor 13:3. [17]FC 30:76-77*.

to the stake, like a noble ram out of a great flock for an offering, a burnt sacrifice made ready and acceptable to God, looking up to heaven said, "O Lord God Almighty, the Father of the beloved and blessed Son Jesus Christ, through whom we have received the knowledge of you, the God of angels and powers and of all creation and of the whole race of the righteous, who live in your presence." ... When he had offered up the Amen and finished his prayer, the firemen lighted the fire. And, a mighty flame flashing forth, we to whom it was given to see a marvel, yes, we were preserved that we might relate to the rest what happened.

The fire, making the appearance of a vault, like the sail of a vessel filled by the wind, made a wall round about the body of the martyr; and it was there in the midst, not like flesh burning but like [a loaf in the oven or like] gold and silver refined in a furnace. For we perceived such a fragrant smell, as if it were the wafted odor of frankincense or some other precious spice. So at length the lawless men, seeing that his body could not be consumed by the fire, ordered an executioner to go up to him and stab him with a dagger. And when he had done this, there came forth [a dove and] a quantity of blood, so that it extinguished the fire; and all the multitude marveled that there should be so great a difference between the unbelievers and the elect. MARTYRDOM OF POLYCARP 14-16.[18]

3:18 But If Not . . .

SERVICE TO GOD ONLY. THEODORET OF CYR: Far from serving our Lord for payment, we are motivated by affection and longing, and at the same time we prefer the service of our God to everything. Hence, instead of asking for relief from the troubles unconditionally, we embrace the Lord's planning and providence; and without knowledge of what will be of benefit, we leave the helm to the pilot, no matter what he wishes, understanding clearly that he is able to free us from the threatened evils. Whether he wishes to do so, we do not know; but we leave it to him,

wise governor as he is, and accept his verdict, confident that it is to our benefit. Whether he rescues us or not, therefore, we shun worship of your statue and your gods. COMMENTARY ON DANIEL 3.18.[19]

3:22 The Flames Consume the King's Mighty Men

THE FIRE RECOGNIZES THE WICKED. HIPPOLYTUS: The fire exploded outward. . . . See how even the fire appears intelligent, as if it recognized and punished the guilty. For it did not touch the servants of God, but it consumed the unbelieving and impious Chaldeans. SCHOLIA ON DANIEL 3.47.[20]

THE RESCUE OF THE VIRTUOUS IS NO ILLUSION. ISHO'DAD OF MERV: The flames killed because the slanderers, being carried away by their joy, approached the furnace to observe the burning of their [victims], but through divine intervention they were consumed by the heat of the furnace. So also, in order that the king and the Babylonians might not think that because of a hallucination or illusion those youths made the fire harmless, God caused many of those who had gathered around the furnace to be consumed while the youths felt just like the king in his bedroom. COMMENTARY ON DANIEL 3.22.[21]

3:23 The Three Young Men Fall into the Fiery Furnace

THE CHILDREN FACE DANGER WITHOUT FEAR. AMBROSE: It happens that one may witness merit and virtue made manifest even in captivity. For Jeremiah was not less happy in captivity, nor was Daniel, nor Esdras, nor were Anania and Azaria and Misael less happy than if they had not fallen into captivity. They entered into captivity in such a way that they brought to their people both present consolations in captiv-

---

[18]AF¹ 113-14. [19]WGRW 7:75-77. [20]ANF 5:188*. [21]CSCO 328:106.

ity and the hope of escaping it. It falls to the one who has been perfected to sustain nature's common lot with courageous spirit, to bring it to better things and not to give way before those experiences that most people consider fearful and frightening. Instead, like a brave soldier, one must withstand onslaughts of the most severe calamities and undergo conflicts; like a pilot of foresight, he must steer his ship in the storm, and as he meets the mounting waves, he must avoid shipwreck by plowing through such waters rather than by turning away from them. . . . He is not weak in regard to wrongs done to his own or anxious about the burial of his body, for he knows that heaven is its due. . . . The one who is perfected is such that he wished to do good to all people and desires that no evil befall anyone; but if something happens beyond his wish, he loses nothing of his own happiness. Jacob and the Happy Life 8.36.[22]

---

[22]FC 65:142-43*.

3:24-25 FOUR IN THE FIERY FURNACE

[24]*Then King Nebuchadnezzar was astonished and rose up in haste. He said to his counselors, "Did we not cast three men bound into the fire?" They answered the king, "True, O king."* [25]*He answered, "But I see four men loose, walking in the midst of the fire, and they are not hurt; and the appearance of the fourth is like a son of the gods."*

OVERVIEW: The virtuous know God in their hearts while the wicked are brought to God by way of spectacular deeds and dreams (Pseudo-Clement). The Father is invisible, but the Son appears to humankind in various ways (Irenaeus). The ability to recognize the Son of God is a gift given by God (Hippolytus). The presence of the angel in the flames foreshadows the descent of Christ to rescue souls from the fires of hell (Jerome).

3:25 Four Men Walking in the Fire

The Wicked Are Led to God Through Visions. Pseudo-Clement: Nebuchadnezzar, having ordered the three men to be cast into fire, saw a fourth when he looked into the furnace and said, "I see the fourth as the Son of God." He was impious and yet saw apparitions, visions and dreams. Thus, we cannot infer with absolute certainty that the one who has seen visions and dreams and apparitions is truly impious. To be sure, for the devout person, the truth gushes up natural and pure in his mind, and not by way of dreams. Pseudo-Clementine Homilies 17.[1]

The Son of God Appears in Different Forms. Irenaeus: It is manifest [in Scripture] that the Father is indeed invisible, of whom also the Lord said, "No one has seen God at any time."[2] But his Word, as he willed it and for the benefit of those who saw, did show the Father's brightness and explained his will. . . . He

---

[1]ANF 8:323*. [2]Jn 1:18.

---

appeared to those who saw him not in one figure or in one character but according to the reasons and purposes that he wanted to achieve, as we see written in Daniel. He was seen with those who were around Ananias, Azarias and Misael as present with them in the furnace of fire, in the burning, and preserving them from [the effects of] fire: "And the appearance of the fourth," it is said, "was like the Son of God." At another time [he is represented as] "a stone cut out of the mountain without hands"[3] and as destroying all temporal kingdoms . . . and as himself filling all the earth. Then too he is the same being beheld as the Son of man coming in the clouds of heaven and drawing near to the Ancient of Days.[4] AGAINST HERESIES 4.20.11.[5]

THE KING WITNESSES TO THE PRESENCE OF THE SON OF GOD. HIPPOLYTUS: Tell me, Nebuchadnezzar, when did you see the Son of God, that you should confess that this is the Son of God? And who stirred your heart, that you should utter such a phrase? And with what eyes were you able to look into this light? And why was this manifest to you alone and to none of the satraps around you? Thus it is written, "The heart of a king is in the hand of God," and of God is here, whereby the Word stirred his heart, so that he might recognize him in the furnace and

glorify him. And this idea of ours is not without good ground . . . the Scripture showed beforehand that the Gentiles would recognize him incarnate, whom, while not incarnate, Nebuchadnezzar saw and recognized of old in the furnace and acknowledged to be the Son of God. SCHOLIA ON DANIEL 3.92[25].[6]

AN ANGEL WHO FORESHADOWS THE PRESENCE OF CHRIST. JEROME: As for the fourth man, which he asserts to be like the son of God . . . I do not know how an ungodly king could have merited a vision of the Son of God. For that reason . . . we are to think of angels here, who after all are very frequently called gods as well as sons of God. So much for the story itself. But as for its typical significance, this angel of the Son of God foreshadows our Lord Jesus Christ, who descended into the furnace of hell, in which the souls of both sinners and of the righteous are imprisoned, in order that he might without suffering any scorching by fire or injury to his person deliver those who were held imprisoned by chains of death. COMMENTARY ON DANIEL 3.92 [25].[7]

---

[3]Dan 2:45. [4]Dan 7:13-14. [5]ANF 1:491*. [6]ANF 5:188*. [7]JCD 43-44*.

3:26-27 THE YOUNG MEN ARE UNHARMED

[26]*Then Nebuchadnezzar came near to the door of the burning fiery furnace and said, "Shadrach, Meshach, and Abednego, servants of the Most High God, come forth, and come here!" Then Shadrach, Meshach, and Abednego came out from the fire.* [27]*And the satraps, the prefects, the governors, and the king's counselors gathered together and saw that the fire had not had any power over the bodies of those men; the hair of their heads was not singed, their mantles[d] were not harmed, and no smell of fire had come upon them.*

d The meaning of the Aramaic word is uncertain

OVERVIEW: The three young men are unharmed by the fire because they trust that God will be present in times of trouble (AUGUSTINE). As God was present to turn back the flames of the furnace, so also God will be present to those who seek to resist the temptations of this world (SYMEON). The three show they are servants of God, and for that they are rewarded (CHRYSOSTOM). God's preservation of the three young men foreshadows the resurrection of the body (TERTULLIAN). As God displays his ability to turn back the destruction wrought by flames, so also God is capable of creating a body that will not be destroyed by death (AUGUSTINE). Even the clothes of the young men are not burned by the fire: such is the reach of God's providential care for those who worship him (NOVATIAN).

3:26 Come Forth!

TRUST IN GOD. AUGUSTINE: Let faith be yours, and God will be with you in your trouble. There are waves on the sea, and you are tossed about in your cabin, because Christ sleeps.... If you allow faith to sleep in your heart, Christ is, you might say, sleeping with you in your ship. Because Christ dwells in you through faith, when you begin to be tossed about, awake Christ from his sleep. Awaken your faith, and you shall be assured he will not desert you. You may think that you are forsaken, because he does not rescue you at the very moment you desire. But did he not deliver the three children from the fire? EXPLANATIONS OF THE PSALMS 91.19.[1]

THE LORD DELIVERS. AUGUSTINE: The flame could not approach or hurt the innocent and righteous children praising God, and he delivered them out of the fire. Some might say, "Truly, those who are righteous are those that are heard," as it is written, "The righteous cried, and the Lord heard them and delivered them out of their troubles."[2] But I have cried, and he does not deliver me; either I am not righteous, or I do not do the things that he commands me to do or per-haps he just does not see me. Fear not: do what he commands you, and if he does not deliver you in bodily form, he will deliver you spiritually.... He delivered Peter when the angel came to him when he was in prison and said, "Arise, and go forth,"[3] and suddenly his chains were released, and he followed the angel, and he delivered him. Had Peter, then, lost his righteousness when he did not deliver him from the cross? Did he not deliver him then? Even then God delivered him. ... When God first delivered Peter, how many times did he suffer afterwards? So in the end, God sent him where he could suffer no evil. EXPLANATIONS OF THE PSALMS 34.21.[4]

THE FLAMES OF PASSION. SYMEON THE NEW THEOLOGIAN: When a person has abandoned the world, it seems to him that he is living in a remote desert, full of wild beasts. He is filled with unutterable fear and indescribable trembling and cries to God like Jonah from the whale, from the sea of this life, or like Daniel from the pit of the lions and the fierce passions or like the three children from the burning furnace and the flames of innate desire.... The Lord hears him and delivers him from the abyss of ignorance and the love of this world.... He delivers him, as he delivered Daniel, from the pit of desire and evil thoughts that rise up to devour the souls of people. Against the attacks of the fires of passion that consume and destroy the soul, pushing and pulling it into evil acts, he guards it from burning and sprinkles it with the dew of the Holy Spirit as he did with the three Israelites. THE PRACTICAL AND THEOLOGICAL CHAPTERS 1.76.[5]

SERVANTS OF THE MOST HIGH GOD. CHRYSOSTOM: "You servants of the most high God, come forth and come here!" How are they to come forth, O king? Did you not cast them into the fire bound? But because they sang praises to God, they were saved. The fire reverenced their

---

[1]NPNF 1 8:452*. [2]Ps 34:17 (33:16b-17 LXX). [3]Acts 12:7. [4]NPNF 1 8:77**. [5]CS 41:54*.

readiness to suffer, and afterwards it reverenced that wonderful song and their hymns of praise. By what title do you then call them? As I noted earlier, "You servants of the most high God." Yes, to the servants of God all things are possible; for if some, who are the servants of people, have, just so, power and authority . . . much more have the servants of God. He called them by the name most delightful to them; he knew that by this means he flattered them most; for indeed, if it was in order to continue to be servants of God that they entered into the fire, there could be no sound more delightful to them than this. Had he called them kings, had he called them lords of the world, yet he would not have brought them joy as when he called them "servants of the most high God." HOMILIES ON EPHESIANS 8.[6]

3:27 The Fire Lacked Power

THE SAFETY OF THE YOUNG MEN FORESHADOWS THE RESURRECTION. TERTULLIAN: "God shall wipe away all tears from their eyes, and there shall be no more death"[7] and therefore no more corruption, it being chased away by incorruption, even as death is by immortality. . . . That the raiment and shoes of the children of Israel remained unworn and fresh for the space of forty years . . . that the fires of Babylon injured neither the cloaks nor the trousers of the three young men . . . that Jonah was swallowed by the monster of the deep, in whose belly whole ships were devoured and after three days was vomited out safe and sound—to what faith do these notable facts bear witness, if not to that which ought to inspire in us the belief that they are proofs . . . of our own future integrity and perfect resurrection? . . . They are written that we may believe both that the Lord is more powerful than all natural laws about the body, and that he shows himself the preserver of the flesh the more emphatically, in that he has preserved for the body even its very clothes and shoes. ON THE RESURRECTION OF THE FLESH 58.[8]

THE INCORRUPTION OF RESURRECTION BODIES. AUGUSTINE: Human weakness uses its acquaintance with things experienced to measure divine works that are beyond its experience and thinks it has made a keen observation when it says, "If there is flame, it is hot; if it is hot, it burns; if it burns, then it burned the bodies of the three men thrown into the fiery furnace by the wicked king." If then even those who might not understand the idea of divine works still believe that a miracle was wrought on these three men, why should we then not believe that he who prevented those bodies from being consumed by the fire also prevented his body from being consumed by fire or famine or disease or old age or any other of the forces by which corruption usually breaks down human bodies? But if anyone says that incorruption against the fire was not added to the flesh of the three men, but that the power of the destruction was taken away from the fire itself, why do we fear that he who took away the ability of the fire to destroy not make flesh that could not be destroyed? . . . The divine power is able to remove whatever qualities he wills from that visible and palpable nature of bodies, while some qualities remain unchanged; so he is able to add unwearying strength to mortal members, preserving the characteristic marks of their form, even when they have died because of the corruption of mortality, so that the mortal appearance is there but wasting disease is absent; motion is there, but fatigue is not; the ability to eat is there, but the necessity of hunger is not. LETTER 205.[9]

GOD'S PROVIDENTIAL CARE KNOWS NO BOUNDS. NOVATIAN: The Father's care and providence neither allowed the garments of the Israelites to perish nor the worthless shoes on their feet to wear out;[10] nor, finally, did he permit the wide trousers of the captive young men to be burned. And this is not without reason, for if he who contains all things embraces all things (all

---

[6]NPNF 1 13:93*. [7]Rev 21:4. [8]ANF 3:590-91*. [9]FC 32:10-11*. [10]Deut 8:4.

things, however, and the whole sum are made up of individual parts), then it follows logically that his care will be bestowed on every individual part because his providence extends to the whole,

whatever it be. On the Trinity 8.6.[11]

[11]FC 67:40*.

3:28-30 THE KING PROCLAIMS THE POWER OF GOD

[28]*Nebuchadnezzar said, "Blessed be the God of Shadrach, Meshach, and Abednego, who has sent his angel and delivered his servants, who trusted in him, and set at nought the king's command, and yielded up their bodies rather than serve and worship any god except their own God. [29]Therefore I make a decree: Any people, nation, or language that speaks anything against the God of Shadrach, Meshach, and Abednego shall be torn limb from limb, and their houses laid in ruins; for there is no other god who is able to deliver in this way." [30]Then the king promoted Shadrach, Meshach, and Abednego in the province of Babylon.*

Overview: The episode of the fiery furnace confirms that God wills that he should be known by all (Ambrose). The transformation of a king who persecutes the righteous to a king who acknowledges and supports the worshipers of the true God foreshadows a world ruled by righteous rulers (Augustine). As the king is astonished at the power of God to turn back the threat of death, so also God astonishes us with Jesus' power over death. The king recognizes not only the power of God but also the extraordinary virtue of the three young men (Chrysostom). The rescue of the three led the king to proclaim the majesty of God to all the nations as the coming of Christ leads all the nations to glorify God (Romanus, Aphrahat).

3:28-30 Blessed Be God

God Wills to Be Known by All. Ambrose: This is our faith. Thus did God will that he should be known by all, thus believed the three children [of the fiery furnace] who did not feel the fire into which they were cast, which destroyed and burned up the unbelievers while it fell harmless as a dew upon the faithful. The flames kindled by others became cold, seeing that the torment has justly lost its power in conflict with faith. For with them there was one in the form of an angel, comforting them, to the end that in number of the Trinity one supreme power might be praised. God was praised; the Father of God was seen in God's angel and holy and spiritual grace in the children. On the Christian Faith 1.4.33.[1]

The Conversion of the Roman World Foreshadowed. Augustine: If past events in the prophetic books serve as a figure of future ones, in the king named Nebuchadnezzar two periods were foreshadowed: that during the time of the apostles and the present one in which

[1]NPNF 2 10:206*.

Christ is now living. For in the times of the apostles and martyrs that part was fulfilled that was foreshadowed when the king forced devout and upright men to adore an idol and when they refused had them thrown into a fire. Now, however, that part is fulfilled that was prefigured in the same king when he was converted to the true God and decreed for his realm that whoever blasphemed the God of Shadrach, Meshach and Abednego should suffer due penalties. Therefore, the first part of the king's reign signified the earlier periods of impious kings, when Christians suffered instead of the impious, but the latter part of that king's reign signified the period of later faithful kings under whom the impious suffered instead of the Christians. LETTER 93.[2]

YOUR GOD IS IN TRUTH GOD. ROMANUS MELODUS:

"In spite of myself, then, I revere the God of the
     Hebrews,
     And I command all the people in my land to
          join in praising him.
'Come, then, holy children, come forth from the
     furnace,
     For I am convinced that your God is in truth
          God.'" (Nebuchadnezzar)
These things happened in Babylon as the
     Scriptures says,
     At a time when those who had provoked
          God's anger were in captivity.
Therefore, my brothers, see to it that you do not
     grieve
     The Master and be given over to the enemy,
For we make him sad if we deny him,
     And if we do not hasten to his temples,
     and if we do not sing to him everywhere,
     "Hasten, Merciful One, and in compassion
          come quickly
     To our aid, since you are able to do what you
          will."
KONTAKION ON THE THREE CHILDREN 30.[3]

FORESHADOWING CHRIST'S VICTORY OVER DEATH. CHRYSOSTOM: "Blessed be God who has

sent his angel." . . . For how can it be otherwise than astonishing for the emperor of the world, with so many arms around him, and legions, and generals, and viceroys, and consuls and land and sea subject to his sway, to be despised by captive children; for the bound to overcome the binder and conquer all that army? Neither was there any power in the king and his company to do what they would, no, not even with the furnaces for an ally. But they who were naked, and slaves, and strangers and few (for what number could be more contemptible than three?), being in chains, vanquished an innumerable army. For already now was death despised, since Christ was henceforth about to sojourn in the world. And as when the sun is on the point of rising, even before his rays appear the light of the day grows bright; so also when the Sun of righteousness was about to come, death henceforth began to withdraw himself. What could be more splendid than that theater? What more conspicuous than that victory? HOMILIES ON 1 CORINTHIANS 18.5.[4]

AN EXTRAORDINARY DISPLAY OF VIRTUE.

CHRYSOSTOM: Contemplate with me how he [the king] at first proclaims the Arbiter of the contest: "Blessed be God." . . . This he proclaims as regards the power of God. He speaks also of the virtue of the combatants: "Because they trusted in him." . . . Could anything equal the virtue of this? Before this, when they said, "We will not serve your gods," he was inflamed more fiercely than the very furnace; but now, when by their deeds they had taught him this, he was so far from being indignant that he praised and admired them for not having obeyed him! So good a thing is virtue that it has even its enemies themselves to applaud and admire it! These young men had fought and conquered, but the vanquished party gave thanks that the sight of the fire had not terrified them but that the hope in their Lord had comforted them. . . . For this reason he both applauds those who had despised him, and pass-

---

[2]FC 18:65*. [3]KRBM 2:149. [4]NPNF 1 12:103*.

ing by so many governors, kings and princes, those who had obeyed him, he stands in admiration of the three captives and slaves who derided his tyranny! For they did these things not for the sake of contention but for the love of wisdom; not of defiance but of devotion; not being puffed up with pride but on fire with zeal. For great indeed is the blessing of a hope in God. HOMILIES CONCERNING THE STATUES 6.13.[5]

3:29 The King Issues a Decree

THE NATIONS GLORIFY GOD. APHRAHAT: Hananiah and his brothers worshiped not the image of the king of Babylon; and Jesus restrained the nations from the worship of dead images. Because of Hananiah and his brothers, the nations and languages glorified the God who had delivered them from the fire; and because of Jesus, the nations and all languages shall glorify God who delivered his Son, so that he saw no corruption. On the garments of Hananiah and his brothers the fire had no power; and on the bodies of the righteous, who have believed in Jesus, the fire shall have no power in the end. DEMONSTRATIONS 21.19.[6]

---

[5]NPNF 1 9:387*. [6]NPNF 2 13:400*.

4:1-3 THE KING'S LETTER

[1e]King Nebuchadnezzar to all peoples, nations, and languages, that dwell in all the earth: Peace be multiplied to you! [2]It has seemed good to me to show the signs and wonders that the Most High God has wrought toward me.
[3]How great are his signs,
    how mighty his wonders!
His kingdom is an everlasting kingdom,
    and his dominion is from generation to generation.

e Ch 3:31 in Aramaic

OVERVIEW: The children's miraculous survival in the furnace flames enlightens the king to God's power, and he in turn sends forth the message of God's power and glory to enlighten all the nations (CHRYSOSTOM). The king acknowledges that God is the ultimate source of all power and glory (CYRIL OF JERUSALEM).

4:1 Pleased to Recount

THE KING PROCLAIMS THE MESSAGE OF

GOD'S GLORY. CHRYSOSTOM: Observe the piety of the children: they showed no indignation, no anger, no gainsaying, but they came forth . . . as though they were going forth from heaven itself. . . . And what the prophet says of the sun, that "he is as a bridegroom going out of his chamber,"[1] so one could also say such a thing of them. But though he [the sun] goes forth [like the bridegroom], yet did they come out with even more

---

[1]Ps 19:5 (18:6 LXX).

glory than he, for he indeed goes forth to enlighten the world with natural light, they to enlighten the world in a different way, I mean, spiritually. For because of them the king immediately issued a decree, "The signs and wonders that the most high God has worked for me I am pleased to recount." . . . So they went forth, shedding a yet more glorious radiance, beaming indeed in that very region, even more so by way of the king's writings, being diffused over the world and thus dispelling the darkness that everywhere prevails. HOMILIES ON EPHESIANS 8.[2]

4:3 An Everlasting Kingdom

GOD AS THE SOURCE OF POWER. CYRIL OF

JERUSALEM: Nothing is excluded from the dominion of God, for Scripture says of him, "All things serve you."[3] God, then, rules over all things, and in his forbearance he endures even murderers and robbers and fornicators, having determined a fixed time for requiting each, that they who, granted a long reprieve, remain impenitent may suffer the greater condemnation. There are kings . . . who reign on earth, yet not without power from on high. This, of old, Nebuchadnezzar knew from experience when he said, "his kingdom is an everlasting kingdom." CATECHETICAL LECTURES 8.5.[4]

---

[2]NPNF 1 13:93*. [3]Ps 119:91 (118:91 LXX). [4]FC 61:182*.

4:4-9 THE KING SUMMONS DANIEL TO INTERPRET ANOTHER DREAM

[4f]I, Nebuchadnezzar, was at ease in my house and prospering in my palace. [5]I had a dream which made me afraid; as I lay in bed the fancies and the visions of my head alarmed me. [6]Therefore I made a decree that all the wise men of Babylon should be brought before me, that they might make known to me the interpretation of the dream. [7]Then the magicians, the enchanters, the Chaldeans, and the astrologers came in; and I told them the dream, but they could not make known to me its interpretation. [8]At last Daniel came in before me—he who was named Belteshazzar after the name of my god, and in whom is the spirit of the holy gods—and I told him the dream, saying,[9] "O Belteshazzar, chief of the magicians, because I know that the spirit of the holy gods[g] is in you and that no mystery is difficult for you, here is[h] the dream which I saw; tell me its interpretation."

f Ch 4:1 in Aramaic g Or Spirit of the holy God h Cn: Aramaic visions of

---

OVERVIEW: The dream, and its subsequent interpretation, clearly refers to Nebuchadnezzar. The clarity of the narrative does not lend itself to a spiritual interpretation, in which the figure of Nebuchadnezzar is a type of Satan (JEROME). The theme of the letter is that nothing can happen without God permitting it (THEODORET). The indwelling Spirit enlightens (CYRIL OF JERU-

SALEM) and purifies the soul (BASIL).

4:4 Nebuchadnezzar in His Palace

THE BIBLE CLEARLY SPEAKS OF THE KING.
JEROME: The narrative is clear indeed and
requires but little interpretation. Because he displeased God, Nebuchadnezzar was turned into a
madman and dwelled for seven years among the
brute beasts and fed on the roots of herbs. Afterwards, by the mercy of God, he was restored to
his throne and praised and glorified the King of
heaven.... But there are some who claim to
understand by the figure of Nebuchadnezzar the
hostile power that the Lord speaks of in the Gospel, saying, "I behold Satan falling from heaven
like lightning."[1] ... These authorities assert that
it was absolutely impossible for a man who was
reared in luxury to subsist on hay for seven years
and so dwell among wild beasts for seven years
without being mangled by them. Also they ask
how the imperial authority could have been kept
waiting for a mere madman and how so mighty a
kingdom could have gone without a king for so
long a period.... And so they pose all of these
questions and offer as their reply the proposition
that since the episode does not stand up as genuine history, the figure of Nebuchadnezzar represents the devil. To this position we make not the
slightest concession; otherwise everything we
read in Scripture may appear to be imperfect representations and mere fables. For once people
have lost their reason, who would not perceive
them to lead their existence like brutish animals
in the open fields and forest regions ... what is so
remarkable about the execution of such a divine
judgment as this for the manifestation of God's
power and the humbling of the pride of kings?
COMMENTARY ON DANIEL 4.1.[4].[2]

THE LETTER'S THEME. THEODORET OF CYR:
Nebuchadnezzar was in control of the whole of
Asia, had brought Egypt under his control and had
subjugated the Ethiopians living near Egypt. Nevertheless he treated his subjects very harshly and

had reached such a state of arrogance as to think
that he was greater and more powerful than not
only the so-called gods but even the true God....
[But] nothing of what was done by him would
have happened without God's permitting it and
wanting to call to account for impiety those who
had suffered this from him. Hence he was right to
add, "Surely an axe will not be glorified apart from
the one wielding it? Or the saw exalted apart from
the one pulling it? Likewise for anyone holding rod
or staff." As it is impossible, he is saying, for axe or
saw or rod to move of itself (each of these operat-
ing when someone chooses to move them by using
their hand), so too you did what you did, when my
providence allowed you, on account of the lawlessness of the victims. So do not think you achieved
this by your own wisdom and power. If, however,
you are not prepared to learn this lesson in a sensible fashion and put an end to your lofty arrogance,
you will learn by experience that this is the way
things are.... [So] God struck that arrogant mind
that had dreamed of preternatural things with
insanity and dementia. Then, when he became
wildly enraged, he caused him to be driven out and
live in the desert for a long time. He next caused
him to gain an appreciation of the fate that had
befallen him; after all, it was impossible for one
who lacked all sense and feeling to reap any benefit. Thus, after refusing to do so, that fellow
acknowledged the rapid changes in his life, wept
and wailed for his own stupidity and confessed
God's kingdom to be without succession, lasting
for all ages. Learning this from experience, he once
more through God's ineffable loving kindness
returned to his own kingdom. In the belief, however, that it would be an injustice to all people if he
were to conceal God's providence, he recounted in
a letter to all his subjects throughout the world his

---

[1]Lk 10:18. [2]JCD 46-47. It is unclear who Jerome has in mind as the
purveyor of this interpretation. Often in the commentary Jerome is
countering the claims of Porphyry, but here it is not apparently the
case. As Matthias Henze has pointed out (*The Madness of King Nebuchadnezzar* [Leiden: E. J. Brill, 1999], Jewish interpreters of Daniel 4
had tended to interpret the king in exile and punishment as symbolic
of the devil.

former prosperity and the misfortune that befell him, then the repentance by which he won the Lord over. While this is the theme of the letter, then, I developed it at length, in my wish . . . to make clear the care of the God of all for everyone. COMMENTARY ON DANIEL 4.1.[3]

THE HEIGHT OF GOOD FORTUNE. THEODORET OF CYR: It was not without purpose that he cited his own name: it was to confirm his name in word; since he was very famous as having control of everyone throughout Asia, Egypt and Ethiopia, he cited his name at the beginning as sufficient confirmation of what was said. He meant, I was at the height of good fortune and surrounded continually with countless good things. COMMENTARY ON DANIEL 4.7-8.[4]

4:6-7 The Wise Men of Babylon

NARRATIVE DETAILS PROVIDED FOR COMPARISON. THEODORET OF CYR: He did not give these details casually: it was in parallel so as to make clear to everyone the prophet's wisdom by comparison—hence his listing the nationalities of the wise men of Babylon so as to highlight the fact that whereas they understood absolutely nothing, he was illuminated by the divine Spirit. COMMENTARY ON DANIEL 4.7-8.[5]

4:8 The Spirit Empowers Daniel

INTERPRETING THE DREAM. CYRIL OF JERUSALEM: The spirit filled the soul of Daniel with wisdom. . . . Even Nebuchadnezzar recognized that the Holy Spirit was in Daniel. . . . One thing he said was true and one was false. That he had the spirit was true, but he was not the chief of the magicians. He was no magician, but he was wise by the Holy Spirit. . . . You see the power of the Holy Spirit; they who had seen the vision do not understand, while they who had not seen it understand and interpret

it. CATECHETICAL LECTURES 16.31.[6]

THE INDWELLING OF THE SPIRIT PURIFIES THE SELF. BASIL THE GREAT: We are not capable of glorifying God on our own; only in the Spirit is this made possible. In him we are able to thank God for the blessings we have received. To the extent that we are purified from evil, each receives a smaller or larger portion of the Spirit's help that each may offer the sacrifice of praise to God. If we offer glory to God, in the Spirit, we mean that the Spirit enables us to fulfill the requirements of true religion. . . . The words of Paul are appropriate: "I think I have the Spirit of God."[7] . . . Likewise it is said concerning Daniel, "the Holy Spirit of God is in you." ON THE HOLY SPIRIT 63.[8]

4:9 Tell Its Interpretation

PHYSICIAN OF THE SOUL. THEODORET OF CYR: Good fortune often causes the general run of people to forget their benefactors, whereas it is necessity that recalls to mind those who have treated us well; and while the person in good health does not keep in mind the physician's competence, on falling ill he or she remembers having that complaint before and returning to good health thanks to such and such a physician. So too Nebuchadnezzar: when he consigned those holy people to the fire, he did not remember Daniel's favor; but when he later had a dream and felt alarm in his soul, he remembered Daniel's wisdom and his recall and interpretation of the previous dream. Hence he said he had God's Spirit and was capable of interpreting every mystery, and he requested him to make clear to him this dream as well, obscure as it was. COMMENTARY ON DANIEL 4.9-10.[9]

---

[3]WGRW 7:101-11*. [4]WGRW 7:113. [5]WGRW 7:115. [6]FC 64:94-95. [7]1 Cor 7:40. [8]OHS 96-97*. [9]WGRW 7:115.

4:10-18 THE KING TELLS OF HIS DREAM OF A TREE

¹⁰*The visions of my head as I lay in bed were these: I saw, and behold, a tree in the midst of the earth; and its height was great.* ¹¹*The tree grew and became strong, and its top reached to heaven, and it was visible to the end of the whole earth.* ¹²*Its leaves were fair and its fruit abundant, and in it was food for all. The beasts of the field found shade under it, and the birds of the air dwelt in its branches, and all flesh was fed from it.*

¹³*I saw in the visions of my head as I lay in bed, and behold, a watcher, a holy one, came down from heaven.* ¹⁴*He cried aloud and said thus, "Hew down the tree and cut off its branches, strip off its leaves and scatter its fruit; let the beasts flee from under it and the birds from its branches.* ¹⁵*But leave the stump of its roots in the earth, bound with a band of iron and bronze, amid the tender grass of the field. Let him be wet with the dew of heaven; let his lot be with the beasts in the grass of the earth;* ¹⁶*let his mind be changed from a man's, and let a beast's mind be given to him; and let seven times pass over him.* ¹⁷*The sentence is by the decree of the watchers, the decision by the word of the holy ones, to the end that the living may know that the Most High rules the kingdom of men, and gives it to whom he will, and sets over it the lowliest of men."*

OVERVIEW: The king's dream is filled with symbols of his arrogance, for which he will be punished (Isho'dad). Christ calls on us to follow in the way of humility and so avoid the punishment that the haughty suffer (Jerome). The watchers, angels (Theodoret), teach from on high those who follow the will of God (Isaac).

4:10 A Tree in the Middle of the Earth

The King Symbolized by the Tree. Theodoret of Cyr: By the tree blessed Daniel said [Nebuchadnezzar] personally was depicted, and he said its height reached to heaven to suggest not the real tree but his thoughts and imaginings. . . . His [conceited attitude] is the reason he sees the height of the tree reaching to heaven; but since, so to say, he even had control of the whole world, he sees the tree trunk—that is, the extent of its breadth—expanding as far as the ends of the earth. COMMENTARY ON DANIEL 4.10-11.[1]

Many Symbols of the King's Arrogance. Isho'dad of Merv: "Its top," that is, of the tree, is his thoughts and the pride of his spirit. "Its foliage" is his army. "Its fruits" are his nobles. "The animals of the fields and the birds" are the nations and kingdoms that he has subdued. "From it all living beings were fed" are because the silver and gold that were for the benefit of people were coined by his mint. "A holy watcher" is one of the spiritual beings. "Its branches" is his dominion. "Its stumps and roots" is said because his sovereignty will last until his return. "With bands[2] of iron and bronze in the grass of the field" are the words because when he is in the desert and feeds on vegetables, his sovereignty will stay with him in this manner, like something bound with iron and bronze. COMMENTARY ON DANIEL 4.11-15.[3]

---

[1]WGRW 7:117. [2]The plural is used by Isho'dad, but the Peshitta has the singular. [3]CSCO 328:107.

4:12 Food for All

FOLIAGE. THEODORET OF CYR: By "foliage" he refers to the visible splendor in apparel, throne, palace, warriors bearing shields and javelins, and foot soldiers, and by "fruit" to the tribute offered from all quarters. COMMENTARY ON DANIEL 4.12.[4]

UNDER HIS AUTHORITY. THEODORET OF CYR: Barbarians lived a wild life, whereas more reasonable and civilized people, rapid and uplifted in their thinking, continued to pass their life under his authority. COMMENTARY ON DANIEL 4.12.[5]

4:13 A Watcher

AN ANGEL. THEODORET OF CYR: By *eir*[6] he refers to the watcher, the meaning in Greek. By watcher he means an angel, thus bringing out its bodiless form: what is clad in a body is subject to sleeping, whereas what is rid of a body is superior to the need for sleeping. So he means, I saw an angel, bodiless in nature, who descended from heaven. COMMENTARY ON DANIEL 4.13.[7]

THE WATCHERS TEACH FROM ON HIGH. ISAAC OF NINEVEH: One who passes the night with thought of him makes of God a housemate; and one who earnestly desires the will of God will find the watchers on high to be his teachers. ON ASCETICAL LIFE 5.14.[8]

4:17 The Most High Rules

THERE IS ONE GOD. THEODORET OF CYR: This is what the angel means, that the fate of the tree will come to pass for this purpose, for everyone to know through this that there is one God, Lord and King, who appoints kings on the earth and entrusts the kingdom to whomever he wishes. In fact, to bring out his own authority, he appoints as king the one who is at one time the most insignificant and thought to be of no value and makes those of greatest rank obey him. COMMENTARY ON DANIEL 4.17.[9]

THE KING EXALTS HIMSELF. JEROME: It is not only of Nebuchadnezzar, king of the Chaldeans, but also of all impious people that the prophet says, "I beheld the impious man highly exalted and lifted up like the cedars of Lebanon."[10] Such people are lifted up not by the greatness of their virtues but by their own pride; and for that reason they are cut down and fall into ruin. Therefore it is good to follow the teaching of our Lord in the Gospel: "Learn from me, for I am meek and lowly in heart."[11] COMMENTARY ON DANIEL 4.7[10].[12]

---

[4]WGRW 7:117. [5]WGRW 7:117. [6]*Eir* is the Hebrew form cited by Theodotion. Though commonly adopted in the Qumranic literature, it is used only once in the Old Testament to refer to an angel. See Alexander Di Lella, "Daniel," *NJBC*, 443. [7]WGRW 7:117-19. [8]INAL 82-83*. [9]WGRW 7:119-21. [10]Ps 37:35 (36:35 LXX). [11]Mt 11:29. [12]JCD 49*.

4:19-23 DANIEL HESITATES TO INTERPRET THE DREAM

[19]Then Daniel, whose name was Belteshazzar, was dismayed for a moment, and his thoughts alarmed him. The king said, "Belteshazzar, let not the dream or the interpretation alarm you." Belteshazzar answered, "My lord, may the dream be for those who hate you and its interpretation

for your enemies! [20]*The tree you saw, which grew and became strong, so that its top reached to heaven, and it was visible to the end of the whole earth;* [21]*whose leaves were fair and its fruit abundant, and in which was food for all; under which beasts of the field found shade, and in whose branches the birds of the air dwelt—*[22]*it is you, O king, who have grown and become strong. Your greatness has grown and reaches to heaven, and your dominion to the ends of the earth.* [23]*And whereas the king saw a watcher, a holy one, coming down from heaven and saying, 'Hew down the tree and destroy it, but leave the stump of its roots in the earth, bound with a band of iron and bronze, in the tender grass of the field; and let him be wet with the dew of heaven; and let his lot be with the beasts of the field, till seven times pass over him.' "*

OVERVIEW: Knowing that the king's dream anticipates the king's punishment, Daniel is hesitant, not because of fear but out of respect for the king (EPHREM). Daniel prefaces his interpretation with a reminder of what great power the king has accumulated (JEROME, THEODORET).

4:19 May the Dream Be for Those Who Hate You

DANIEL DOES NOT FEAR THE KING. EPHREM THE SYRIAN: Daniel did not speak these words ("may the dream be for those who hate you") . . . because he feared the majesty of the king or in order to flatter him and his fortune but either to show respect for the king and the worship of the vessels in the temple or for that general edict through which he [the king] repressed those who wanted to scorn the divine name in their actions or words. COMMENTARY ON DANIEL 4.19.[1]

DANIEL AVOIDS A DIRECT INSULT. JEROME: Daniel silently understood that the dream was directed against the king . . . and he felt sorry for the man who had conferred on him the greatest of honor. And to avoid all appearance of taunting the king or appearing as an enemy, he only told him what he [Daniel] understood of the matter

after he had begged to be excused. . . . He explained the truth without insulting the king; so as to avoid appearing to charge the king with sinful pride, he explains [human] power as in itself presumptuous. COMMENTARY ON DANIEL 4.16[19]-17[20].[2]

4:20 The Tree

DANIEL'S WISDOM IN SPEECH. THEODORET OF CYR: Daniel's wisdom is worth admiring: he did not say simply, the big tree, but *grown* to great size and strength—in other words, instead of being great from the beginning, you became great gradually, and instead of having strength from the outset, you gradually acquired it. Hence he goes further, "Because you have grown great and strong, your greatness has increased, you reach to heaven and your lordship to the ends of the earth." It was very fitting and appropriate for him to relate these things to heaven and earth: he said his lordship had reached the ends of the earth, that is, his authority, whereas it was not yet his lordship that had reached to heaven but his imaginings. COMMENTARY ON DANIEL 4.20-22.[3]

---

[1]ESOO 2:208. [2]JCD 50. [3]WGRW 7:121-23.

4:24-27 DANIEL TELLS OF THE KING'S FALL AND THE POWER OF PENANCE

[24]This is the interpretation, O king: It is a decree of the Most High, which has come upon my lord the king, [25]that you shall be driven from among men, and your dwelling shall be with the beasts of the field; you shall be made to eat grass like an ox, and you shall be wet with the dew of heaven, and seven times shall pass over you, till you know that the Most High rules the kingdom of men, and gives it to whom he will. [26]And as it was commanded to leave the stump of the roots of the tree, your kingdom shall be sure for you from the time that you know that Heaven rules. [27]Therefore, O king, let my counsel be acceptable to you; break off your sins by practicing righteousness, and your iniquities by showing mercy to the oppressed, that there may perhaps be a lengthening of your tranquillity.

OVERVIEW: Although it appeared that the king had cleansed himself of pride by way of his edict regarding the one God, the dream makes evident that God will judge us not only by our actions but also by our thoughts (GREGORY THE GREAT). Daniel warns of the punishment that might befall the king but also offers advice on how to avoid such punishment (CYPRIAN). God has taught us many ways to find repentance, and almsgiving is one of those (CHRYSOSTOM). By giving alms, the king, though a sinner, may be brought into the kingdom of God (AUGUSTINE). Almsgiving is the "mother of that love" that defines what it means to be a Christian (CHRYSOSTOM). This is not a matter of God changing God's mind but showing that God will commute a sentence as long as there are acts of mercy (JEROME, THEODORET).

4:24 A Decree of the Lord

GOD JUDGES OUR THOUGHTS AND ACTIONS.
GREGORY THE GREAT: Often, when there are ample resources at hand and things can be done that subjects admire just because they are done, the mind has proud thoughts and provokes the anger of the judge, though no overt acts are committed. For he who judges is within; what is judged is within. When, therefore, we transgress

in the heart, people do not know what we are engaged on, but the judge is the witness of our sin. The king of Babylon, for instance, was not guilty of pride merely when he came to utter proud words, for from the mouth of the prophet [Daniel] he heard the sentence of reprobation before he had given vent to his pride. He had, indeed, already cleansed himself of the sin of his guilty pride, when he proclaimed to all his subject peoples the omnipotent God whom he found he had offended. . . . For the strict judge first sees invisibly what he afterwards reprehends by open chastisement. Wherefore, too, the judge turned him into an irrational animal. PASTORAL CARE 1.4.[1]

APPROPRIATE TITLE. THEODORET OF CYR: At this point it is possible to learn the value of the apostolic teaching, "Let every person be subject to the governing authorities";[2] blessed Daniel, note, calls the impious king "lord" and, influenced by the norm of authority, he adopts the appropriate titles, and he gives a glimpse of the truth of the dream, distressing though it is. COMMENTARY ON DANIEL 4.23-24.[3]

---

[1]ACW 11:28-29*. [2]Rom 13:1. [3]WGRW 7:123.

4:25 Seven Times Will Pass

THREE AND A HALF YEARS. THEODORET OF CYR: Now, while some commentators claimed the "seven times" are seven years,[4] others said three and a half. The divine Scripture, in fact, divides the year not into four seasons but into two more generic parts, winter and summer; so seven divisions of that kind amount to three and a half years. You will spend such a length of time in misfortune. COMMENTARY ON DANIEL 4.25.[5]

LEARN FROM EXPERIENCE. THEODORET OF CYR: God will take from you even human reason and will make you resemble the beasts so that you may learn from experience what is human and what is God, what is human fortune and what is divine kingship, and the fact that it is impossible to attain it unless God wishes. COMMENTARY ON DANIEL 4.25.[6]

4:26 Showing Mercy to the Oppressed

SATISFACTION OF SIN BY ALMSGIVING. CYPRIAN: The remedies for propitiating God have been given in the words of God; divine instructions have taught that God is satisfied by just works, that sins are cleansed by the merits of mercy. . . . The Holy Spirit declares in the Psalms, saying, "Blessed is the one who thinks of the needy and the poor; the Lord will save him in the evil day."[7] Mindful of these teachings, Daniel, when king Nebuchadnezzar, being frightened by an unfavorable dream, was worried, gave a remedy for averting evils by obtaining divine help. . . . When the king did not obey him, he suffered the misfortunes and trouble that he had seen, which he might have escaped and avoided, if he had redeemed his sins by almsgiving. The angel Raphael also testifies likewise and urges that almsgiving be practiced freely and generously, saying, "Prayer is good with fasting and alms, for alms delivers from death, and it purges away sin."[8] He shows that our prayers and fasting are of less avail, unless they are aided by almsgiving. The angel reveals and manifests and certifies that our petitions become effective by almsgiving, that life is redeemed from dangers by almsgiving, that souls are delivered from death by almsgiving. WORKS AND ALMSGIVING 5.[9]

REPENTANCE AND ALMSGIVING. CHRYSOSTOM: Do you wish that I should speak of the ways of repentance? They are many and various and different, and all lead to heaven . . . a fourth way is almsgiving. For Daniel said to Nebuchadnezzar, when he had come to all kinds of evil and had entered on all impiety, "O king, let my counsel be acceptable to you." . . . What could be compared with this act of compassion? After countless sins, after so many transgressions, he is promised that he will be reconciled with him whom he has had conflict with if only he will show kindness to his own fellow servants. . . . So we have shown you five ways to repentance: first the condemnation of sins, next the forgiveness of our neighbor's sins, third that which comes of prayer, fourth that which comes of almsgiving, fifth that which comes of humility. Do not then be lazy, but walk in this day by day. CONCERNING THE POWER OF DEMONS, HOMILY 2.6.[10]

ALMSGIVING AND CHARITY. AUGUSTINE: It is written, as I reminded you a short while ago, "O king, let my counsel be acceptable to you." . . . And there are many other teachings in the divine writings that show how much almsgiving and deeds of charity avail for extinguishing and wiping out sins. Accordingly, to those whom he is going to condemn—no, first, on the contrary to those whom he is going to reward with crowns, he is going to impute nothing but their acts of charity, as though to say, "It would be difficult, if I examined you closely, and weighed you in the balance and thoroughly scrutinized your deeds, for me not to find reasons to condemn you; but,

---

[4]Only Hippolytus provides this interpretation. [5]WGRW 7:123. [6]WGRW 7:123. [7]Ps 41:1 (40:2 LXX). [8]Tob 12:8-9. [9]FC 36:231-32**. [10]NPNF 1 9:190*.

'Go into the kingdom; for I was hungry and you gave me to eat.'[11] So you are not going into the kingdom because you never sinned, but because you redeemed your sins with alms deeds." SERMON 389.5.[12]

ALMSGIVING IS THE MOTHER OF LOVE. CHRYSOSTOM: Do you not see that when the prophet [Daniel] gave that excellent advice to Nebuchadnezzar, he did not merely consider the poor; but what? . . . Give up your wealth not that others may be fed but that you may escape punishment. And Christ says, "Go and sell what you possess, and give it to the poor . . . and come follow me."[13] . . . Virginity and fasting and lying on the ground are more difficult than this, but nothing is so strong and powerful to extinguish the fire of our sins as almsgiving. It is greater than all other virtues. It places the lover of it by the side of the king, and justly. . . . Almsgiving extends to all and embraces the members of Christ, and actions that extend their effects to many are far greater than those that are confined to one. Almsgiving is the mother of love, of that love which is the characteristic of Christianity, which is greater than all miracles by which the disciples of Christ are made plain. It is the medicine of our sins, the cleansing of the filth of our souls, the ladder fixed to heaven; it binds together the body of Christ. HOMILIES ON TITUS 6.[14]

GOD IS ANGERED AT PEOPLE'S SINS. JEROME: Since [Daniel] had previously announced the sentence of God, which of course cannot be altered, how could he exhort the king to deeds of charity and acts of mercy toward the poor? This difficulty is easily solved by reference to the example of King Hezekiah, who Isaiah had said was going to die; and again, to the example of the Ninevites, to whom it was said, "Yet forty days, and Nineveh shall be destroyed."[15] And yet the sentence of God was changed in response to the prayers of Hezekiah and the city of Nineveh, not by any means of the ineffectualness of the judgment itself but because of the conversion of those who merited pardon. . . . For after all, God is not angered at people but at their sins; and when no sins inhere in a person, God by no means inflicts a punishment that has been commuted. In other words, let us say that Nebuchadnezzar performed deeds of mercy toward the poor in accordance with Daniel's advice, and for that reason the execution of the sentence against him was delayed for twelve months. But because he afterwards while walking about in his palace at Babylon said boastingly, "Is not this great Babylon, which I have built by my mighty power as a royal residence and for the glory of my majesty?" therefore he lost the virtue of his charitableness by reason of the wickedness of his pride. COMMENTARY ON DANIEL 4.26, 27.[16]

REMEDY SUITED TO THE WOUND. THEODORET OF CYR: Having foretold the future in this way, [Daniel] offers exhortation and excellent advice and applies a remedy suited to the wound . . . "compassion for the poor." In this he implies the insatiable cruelty with which [Nebuchadnezzar] treated his subjects. Do you wish, he asks, to receive lovingkindness? Give evidence of it to those who share the same nature as you; this is the way you will persuade the judge to cancel his threat and leave it unfulfilled. COMMENTARY ON DANIEL 4.26, 27.[17]

---

[11]Mt 25:34-35. [12]*WSA* 3 10:409-10*. [13]Mt 19:21. [14]NPNF 1 13:542*. [15]Jon 3:4. [16]JCD 51-52. [17]WGRW 7:125.

4:28-33 PRIDE AND PUNISHMENT

²⁸*All this came upon King Nebuchadnezzar.* ²⁹*At the end of twelve months he was walking on the roof of the royal palace of Babylon,* ³⁰*and the king said, "Is not this great Babylon, which I have built by my mighty power as a royal residence and for the glory of my majesty?"* ³¹*While the words were still in the king's mouth, there fell a voice from heaven, "O King Nebuchadnezzar, to you it is spoken: The kingdom has departed from you,* ³²*and you shall be driven from among men, and your dwelling shall be with the beasts of the field; and you shall be made to eat grass like an ox; and seven times shall pass over you, until you have learned that the Most High rules the kingdom of men and gives it to whom he will."* ³³*Immediately the word was fulfilled upon Nebuchadnezzar. He was driven from among men, and ate grass like an ox, and his body was wet with the dew of heaven till his hair grew as long as eagles' feathers, and his nails were like birds' claws.*

OVERVIEW: The threat of prophecy reaches its factual conclusion after Nebuchadnezzar failed to repent (THEODORET). The king's sin is immediately punished to make it evident that he had been rewarded for acts of charity (JEROME). While the king was insolent, God had shown only patience and compassion (EPHREM). The king is made into a beast and all that was dear to him is taken away thus making quite evident that the king is finally dependent on God. Nebuchadnezzar's declining appearance suggests the condition of divine neglect (THEODORET).

4:29 After Twelve Months

FAILED TO REPENT. THEODORET OF CYR: The text then conveys also the span of divine longsuffering: after the passage of twelve months the threat in the prophecy reached its factual conclusion. Though given such a length of time to repent, he failed to meet the deadline for repentance; it would be of him that blessed Paul spoke, "Do you despise the riches of his kindness, forbearance and longsuffering? Are you unaware that the kindness of God leads you to repentance? In your hard and impenitent heart, however, you are storing up wrath for yourselves on the day of wrath, revelation and right judgment by God,

who will render to everyone according to each one's works: eternal life to those who by perseverance in good works seek glory and honor and immortality, while anger and wrath will come to those who in self-seeking do not obey the truth but obey iniquity. There will be tribulation and distress for every person guilty of evildoing."[1] COMMENTARY ON DANIEL 4.27.[2]

4:30 By My Power

THE KING'S ARROGANCE. JEROME: His arrogant boasting is immediately punished by the Lord. The execution of the sentence is not delayed, lest mercy toward the poor seem to have not profited him at all. But as soon as he has spoken in pride, Nebuchadnezzar immediately loses the kingdom that had been reserved for him on account of his works of charity. COMMENTARY ON DANIEL 4.28-29 [31-32].[3]

GOD'S PATIENCE IGNORED. EPHREM THE SYRIAN: Then the king became even more insolent, even as God was patient and had shown magnanimity by endeavoring to lead him to repentance. And as he walked on the terrace of the royal

---

[1]Rom 2:4-9. [2]WGRW 7:125. [3]JCD 52*.

house and looked around over his fortune, he said, "Where became of all those sad omens by which the saint had meant to frighten me? I certainly rule Babylon, which I made magnificent." COMMENTARY ON DANIEL 4.30.[4]

4:31 The Kingdom Has Departed

NEBUCHADNEZZAR DEPRIVED OF HIS KINGDOM. THEODORET OF CYR: Since he dreamed of going up to heaven, he received the verdict from there; and since he was not satisfied with the palace here below, and instead at the same time he insanely hankered after one on high, he was deprived of the one here below; in his wish to snatch heaven he was driven also from earth. COMMENTARY ON DANIEL 4.31.[5]

4:33 Hair As Long As Eagles' Feathers

CONDITION OF NEGLECT. THEODORET OF CYR: By all this it suggested his condition of neglect and carelessness: bereft of divine providence, he was not even a recipient of care from his own—wife, children and family; instead, like a wild animal he kept frequenting uninhabited places, filling his stomach with the food of brute beasts. COMMENTARY ON DANIEL 4.33.[6]

---

[4]ESOO 2:209. [5]WGRW 7:127. [6]WGRW 7:127-29.

4:34-37 NEBUCHADNEZZAR'S SANITY RESTORED

[34]At the end of the days I, Nebuchadnezzar, lifted my eyes to heaven, and my reason returned to me, and I blessed the Most High, and praised and honored him who lives for ever;
    for his dominion is an everlasting dominion,
        and his kingdom endures from generation to generation;
    [35]all the inhabitants of the earth are accounted as nothing;
        and he does according to his will in the host of heaven
        and among the inhabitants of the earth;
    and none can stay his hand
        or say to him, "What doest thou?"
[36]At the same time my reason returned to me; and for the glory of my kingdom, my majesty and splendor returned to me. My counselors and my lords sought me, and I was established in my kingdom, and still more greatness was added to me. [37]Now I, Nebuchadnezzar, praise and extol and honor the King of heaven; for all his works are right and his ways are just; and those who walk in pride he is able to abase.

OVERVIEW: Nebuchadnezzar regained his former intelligence and returned to his senses (JEROME, EPHREM). He then praised and glorified God. In contrast to the living, eternal God, human beings are "nothing," that is, insignificant. Nebuchadnezzar returned to his throne and was accepted back by his nobility (THEODORET). Nebuchadnezzar recognized that God's action was justified and that his humiliation was a result of his self-exaltation (JEROME).

4:34 Eyes Raised to Heaven

REGAINED SANITY. JEROME: Had he not raised his eyes toward heaven, he would not have regained his former intelligence. Moreover, when he says that his intelligence returned to him, he shows that he had lost, not his outward appearance, but only his mind. COMMENTARY ON DANIEL 4.31 [34].[1]

MASTER OF HIS OWN MIND. EPHREM THE SYRIAN: "My reason returned to me," that is, I was made again master of my own mind, and certainly returned to my senses. "I blessed the Most High, who does what he wills," that is, who with his divinity and will rules and administrates not only the affairs of human beings, whom he fashioned from clay, but also those of the spiritual powers, whom he placed in heaven. COMMENTARY ON DANIEL 4.34.[2]

4:35 God Is Sovereign Over All

THE IMPERMANENCE OF HUMAN NATURE. THEODORET OF CYR: Up to the present I [Nebuchadnezzar] thought myself very great and elevated, whereas now I know clearly that all human nature is nothing compared with God. Having sought a term for insignificance and not found one suitable, he used "nothing," which gives a sufficient clue to the instability and impermanence of nature; while calling God "Most High, Lord, living and eternal king," he spoke of all human beings as "nothing." In similar fashion also blessed Isaiah in comparing the divine nature with the idols focused on human nature: "If all the nations are like a drop from a bucket, and are accounted as a turn of the scale and will be accounted as spittle, while Lebanon is not sufficient for burning, and all its animals not sufficient for a burnt offering, and all the nations are nothing and were reckoned as nothing in compar-

ison with him, to what will you compare the Lord? and with what analogy compare him?"[3] COMMENTARY ON DANIEL 4.35.[4]

HAPPILY ACCEPTING GOD'S SOVEREIGNTY. THEODORET OF CYR: He says, "There is no one who will oppose his hand or say to him, 'Why did you do that?'" to bring out the invincibility of God's power. One must accept gladly what is done by him, whether it is pleasing or distressing: resisting or criticizing what is wisely ordained by him is a rash endeavor. COMMENTARY ON DANIEL 4.35.[5]

4:36 Reason Returned

RECOGNIZED BY GRACE. THEODORET OF CYR: Squalid and dirty, in all likelihood, unkempt and with nails grown long, he washed away the dirt, and thanks to divine grace he was recognized as the person who previously had administered the mighty kingdom. "My rulers and my nobility sought me out": they put aside their hatred and adopted a friendly attitude toward me. COMMENTARY ON DANIEL 4.36.[6]

4:37 God Is Just

PUNISHMENT JUSTIFIED. EPHREM THE SYRIAN: Through that punishment, which he inflicted on me, [God] showed that he gives back to each one his properties with justice and impartiality and humiliates those who walk in arrogance; and as he mortified me, who was too full of myself and behaved arrogantly, so he will break the audacity of people similar to me with similar consideration. COMMENTARY ON DANIEL 4.37.[7]

HUMILIATION LED TO HUMILITY. JEROME: Nebuchadnezzar understood the reason why he had suffered in seven years' punishment, and for that reason he humbled himself, since he had

---

[1]JCD 53. [2]ESOO 2:210. [3]Is 40:15-18. [4]WGRW 7:129-31. [5]WGRW 7:131. [6]WGRW 7:131. [7]ESOO 2:210.

exalted himself against God. COMMENTARY ON DANIEL 4.34 [37].[8]

DIVINE WISDOM AND GOVERNANCE. THEODORET OF CYR: Having had experience of misfortune and then being rid of it, I sing the praises of the one who to my advantage brought on me one

condition and the other in his great wisdom. I know he is the King of heaven and Lord of all, acting in truth, governing everything justly and capable of humbling those behaving haughtily. COMMENTARY ON DANIEL 4.37.[9]

---

[8]JCD 54. [9]WGRW 7:131-33.

5:1-9 HANDWRITING ON THE WALL

[1]*King Belshazzar made a great feast for a thousand of his lords, and drank wine in front of the thousand.*
[2]*Belshazzar, when he tasted the wine, commanded that the vessels of gold and of silver which Nebuchadnezzar his father had taken out of the temple in Jerusalem be brought, that the king and his lords, his wives, and his concubines might drink from them.* [3]*Then they brought in the golden and silver vessels[j] which had been taken out of the temple, the house of God in Jerusalem; and the king and his lords, his wives, and his concubines drank from them.* [4]*They drank wine, and praised the gods of gold and silver, bronze, iron, wood, and stone.*
[5]*Immediately the fingers of a man's hand appeared and wrote on the plaster of the wall of the king's palace, opposite the lampstand; and the king saw the hand as it wrote.* [6]*Then the king's color changed, and his thoughts alarmed him; his limbs gave way, and his knees knocked together.* [7]*The king cried aloud to bring in the enchanters, the Chaldeans, and the astrologers. The king said to the wise men of Babylon, "Whoever reads this writing, and shows me its interpretation, shall be clothed with purple, and have a chain of gold about his neck, and shall be the third ruler in the kingdom."* [8]*Then all the king's wise men came in, but they could not read the writing or make known to the king the interpretation.* [9]*Then King Belshazzar was greatly alarmed, and his color changed; and his lords were perplexed.*

j Theodotion Vg: Aramaic *golden vessels*

OVERVIEW: Belshazzar was a descendent of Nebuchadnezzar, but not his son. Jewish interpreters suggest that the banquet was arranged to mock the Jewish expectation of release from captivity as predicted by Jeremiah (JEROME). Belshazzar ordered the misuse of the vessels after he had become intoxicated (ISHO'DAD, EPHREM, THEODORET). The punishment of Belshazzar's

misuse of consecrated objects teaches that objects dedicated to God should be treated with reverence (ISAAC, JOHN OF DAMASCUS). The hand appeared immediately in order that Belshazzar might recognize his impending punishment was due to blasphemy (JEROME). The purple garment and gold necklaces he offers are mere ornaments (TERTULLIAN).

5:1 King Belshazzar

DESCENDENT OF NEBUCHADNEZZAR. JEROME: "Belshazzar the king made a great feast for his one thousand nobles; and each one drank in the order of his age." It should be known that this man was not the son of Nebuchadnezzar, as readers commonly imagine; but according to Berosus, who wrote the history of the Chaldeans, and also Josephus, who follows Berosus, after Nebuchadnezzar's reign of forty-three years, a son named Evil-merodach succeeded to his throne. It was concerning this king that Jeremiah wrote that in the first year of his reign he raised the head of Jehoiachin, king of Judah, and took him out of his prison.[1] Josephus likewise reports that after the death of Evil-merodach, his son[2] Neriglissar succeeded to his father's throne; after whom in turn came his son Labosordach.[3] On the latter's death, his son, Belshazzar,[4] obtained the kingdom, and it is of him that the Scripture now makes mention. After he had been killed by Darius, king of the Medes, who was the maternal uncle of Cyrus, king of the Persians, the empire of the Chaldeans was destroyed by Cyrus the Persian. It was these two kingdoms[5] that Isaiah in chapter 21 addresses as a charioteer of a vehicle drawn by a camel and an ass. Indeed, Xenophon also writes the same thing in connection with the childhood of Cyrus the Great; likewise Pompeius Trogus and many others who have written up the history of the barbarians. Some authorities think that this Darius was the Astyages mentioned in the Greek writings, while others think it was Astyages' son, and that he was called by the other name among the barbarians. "And each one of the princes who had been invited drank in the order of his own age." Or else, as other translators have rendered it, "The king himself was drinking in the presence of all the princes whom he had invited." COMMENTARY ON DANIEL 5.1.[6]

COMPOSING PROPHECY. THEODORET OF CYR: This man was the son of Nebuchadnezzar but did not directly succeed him. . . . After Neb-

uchadnezzar, then, Evil-merodach ruled, and after him Belshazzar.[7] The most divine Daniel, however, omitted mention of the former man, since he was composing not history pure and simple but prophecy—hence his not recording everything done by Nebuchadnezzar, either, but only those things of which mention was required with a view to bringing benefit. So since also in the time of Belshazzar God gave evidence of a wonderful miracle capable of instilling reverence and dread not only in the people of that time but also in those of any later time and of leading them to the true religion, he did not think it right to conceal in silence such a great act of kindness, judging it instead a holy thing to put it in writing and leave for everyone a record of the teaching. COMMENTARY ON DANIEL 5.1.[8]

5:2-3 He Tasted the Wine

MOCKING GOD'S PROMISE. JEROME: The Hebrews hand down some such story as this: that up until the seventieth year, on which Jeremiah had said that the captivity of the Jewish people would be released, Belshazzar had esteemed God's promise to be of no effect; therefore he turned the failure of the promise into an occasion of joy and arranged a great banquet, scoffing somewhat at the expectation of the Jews and at the vessels of the temple of God. Punishment, however, immediately ensued. And as to the fact that the author calls Nebuchadnezzar the father of Belshazzar, he does not make any mistake in the eyes of those who are acquainted with the holy Scripture's manner of speaking, for in the Scripture all progenitors and ancestors are called fathers. This factor also should be borne in mind, that he was not sober when he did these things, but rather when he was intoxicated and forgetful of the punishment that had come on his progeni-

---

[1]Jer 52:31. [2]Actually his brother-in-law. [3]The cuneiform spelling is *Labashi-Marduk.* [4]Jerome is not aware of Belshazzar's father, Nabonidus. [5]The Median and the Persian. [6]JCD 55. [7]Theodoret's kingly succession omits a number of names from Jerome's list. [8]WGRW 7:133-35.

tor, Nebuchadnezzar. Commentary on Daniel 5.2.[9]

Tasting Wine. Isho'dad of Merv: The words "at the taste[10] of the wine, [Belshazzar] said," that is, after he became drunk and unreasonable as a consequence of tasting wine. Commentary on Daniel 5.2.[11]

Vessels. Ephrem the Syrian: "Under the influence of wine, he commanded that they bring the vessels" from the sanctuary and did not hesitate in showing them to his lords and concubines and other guests, as he intended to use them for a profane symposium. His father had taken those vessels from the temple of Jerusalem, when Nebuchadnezzar had conquered the city and had destroyed it; nonetheless he had set them in a decent place and had preserved them with holy devotion. [Belshazzar] went beyond any limit. Commentary on Daniel 5.1.[12]

Used like Ordinary Vessels. Theodoret of Cyr: In other words, intoxication confused his thinking, and intemperance gave rise to this insane action against God: the vessels consecrated to the worship of God, which his father Nebuchadnezzar had seized when God surrendered them but had honored in the way he thought fit and had kept from human use, this man presumed to use like ordinary vessels, not only giving the order but giving effect to the order. Commentary on Daniel 5.2.[13]

Consecrated Vessels. Isaac of Nineveh: God showed that his true servants and friends are those who walk before him in fear and reverence and do his will, since virtuous deeds and purity of conscience are things holy [and beloved] of God. But when people repudiate paths, the Lord repudiates them, casts them away from his face and takes from them his grace. For why was the sentence against Belshazzar issued so swiftly and why did it strike him down, as it were, by the form of a hand? Was it not because he acted with

audacity toward the untouchable vessels of offering that he seized from Jerusalem, drinking out of them, both he and his concubines? In the same manner, those who have consecrated their members to God but are audacious as to use them once more for worldly deeds, the same perish, being smitten by an invisible blow. Ascetical Homilies 10.[14]

Treatment of Sacred Objects. John of Damascus: The third kind of relative worship we give to objects dedicated to God, such as the holy Gospel and other books, for they have been written for our instruction, on whom the end of the ages has come.[15] Obviously, patens, chalices, censers, candlesticks and altars should all receive respect. Remember how Belshazzar made his people serve wine in sacred vessels and how God brought his kingdom to an end. On Divine Images 3.35.[16]

Unchaste Eyes. Jerome: Therefore I summon you before God and Jesus Christ and his elect angels to guard that which you have received, not readily exposing to the public gaze the vessels of the Lord's temple.... Unchaste eyes see nothing correctly. They fail to appreciate the beauty of the soul and only value that of the body. Hezekiah showed God's treasure to the Assyrians,[17] who ought never to have seen what they were sure to covet. The consequence was that Judea was torn by continual wars and that the very first things carried away to Babylon were these vessels of the Lord. We find Belshazzar at his feast and among his concubines (vice always glories in defiling what is noble) drinking out of these sacred cups. Letter 22.23.[18]

5:4 Gods of Gold and Silver

Misuse of God's Property. Jerome: As they

---

[9]JCD 56. [10]This is the reading of the Peshitta. [11]CSCO 328:110. [12]ESOO 2:210. [13]WGRW 7:137. [14]AHSIS 75-76*. [15]1 Cor 10:11. [16]JDDI 86-87. [17]2 Kings 20:12-13. [18]NPNF 2 6:31*.

drank from golden vessels, they were praising gods of wood and of stone. As long as the vessels had been in the idol temple of Babylon, God was not moved to wrath, for they had evidently consecrated the property of God to divine worship, even though they did so in accordance with their own depraved views of religion. But after they defiled holy things for the use of people, their punishment followed on the heels of their sacrilege. Moreover, they were praising their own gods and scoffing at the God of the Jews, on the ground that they were drinking from his vessels because of the victory their own gods had bestowed on them. COMMENTARY ON DANIEL 5.4.[19]

5:5 A Hand Writes

PUNISHMENT RECOGNIZED. JEROME: He puts it nicely when he says, "At that same hour," just as we earlier read concerning Nebuchadnezzar, "While the saying was yet in the king's mouth." This was in order that the offender might recognize that his punishment was not inflicted on him for any other reason but his blasphemy. COMMENTARY ON DANIEL 5.5.[20]

A LESSON ON DIVINE NATURE. THEODORET OF CYR: Since, you see, he had sung the praises of the idols, deprived as they were of any power to move, and had scorned the God of all, the Lord of all gives him a lesson in his invisible and incorporeal nature by letting him see only fingers writing, the purpose being to instruct him that he would not even see them were it not that he personally had provided the occasion of need. COMMENTARY ON DANIEL 5.5.[21]

5:7 The King Cried Out

HE FOLLOWED THE ANCIENT ERROR OF HIS FAMILY. JEROME: Forgetting about the experiences of Nebuchadnezzar, he was following after the ancient and ingrained error of his family, so that instead of summoning a prophet of God he

summons the magicians and Chaldeans and soothsayers. COMMENTARY ON DANIEL 5.7.[22]

GARMENTS OF PURPLE. TERTULLIAN: Now we have to consider the mere ornaments and trappings of office. Each has its proper dress for daily and for ceremonial use. In Egypt and Babylon, the purple robe and gold necklaces were marks of rank, just as provincial priests have their golden wreaths and their robes of state. . . . But there was a difference in the obligation. They were conferred on men who earned the king's friendship, simply as a mark of honor. . . . Purple as such, then, was not yet a mark of high office among the barbarians, but of free birth. Joseph, who had been a slave, and Daniel, who had changed his status by captivity, attained citizenship of Egypt or Babylon by means of the garments that indicated free birth among the barbarians. ON IDOLATRY 18.[23]

THIRD IN RANK. JEROME: That means either that he is to be third in rank after the king, or else one of the three princes of the realm—for we elsewhere read of the *tristatai*.[24] COMMENTARY ON DANIEL 5.7.[25]

5:9 Belshazzar Was Alarmed

PUNISHMENT WITHHELD FOR THE BENEFIT OF OTHERS. THEODORET OF CYR: From this it is clear that the Lord was concerned for the welfare of the others and did not take the king's life on the spot, instead giving a glimpse of the writer's fingers. But having startled him by this and instilled fear, he caused the wise men of the Chaldeans to be summoned and showed up their falsity and weakness while producing the need for Daniel's wisdom so as through his tongue to accredit him and benefit the others, and with this happening to inflict punishment at that stage on the impious king. COMMENTARY ON DANIEL 5.9.[26]

---

[19]JCD 56*. [20]JCD 57. [21]WGRW 7:139. [22]JCD 58. [23]LCC 5:103. [24]A *tristates* is one who stands next in rank to the king and queen (i.e., a vizier). [25]JCD 58. [26]WGRW 7:139-41.

5:10-31 DANIEL INTERPRETS THE DREAM

[10]*The queen, because of the words of the king and his lords, came into the banqueting hall; and the queen said, "O king, live for ever! Let not your thoughts alarm you or your color change.* [11]*There is in your kingdom a man in whom is the spirit of the holy gods.*[k] *In the days of your father light and understanding and wisdom, like the wisdom of the gods, were found in him, and King Nebuchadnezzar, your father, made him chief of the magicians, enchanters, Chaldeans, and astrologers,*[l] [12]*because an excellent spirit, knowledge, and understanding to interpret dreams, explain riddles, and solve problems were found in this Daniel, whom the king named Belteshazzar. Now let Daniel be called, and he will show the interpretation."*

[13]*Then Daniel was brought in before the king. The king said to Daniel, "You are that Daniel, one of the exiles of Judah, whom the king my father brought from Judah.* [14]*I have heard of you that the spirit of the holy gods*[k] *is in you, and that light and understanding and excellent wisdom are found in you.* [15]*Now the wise men, the enchanters, have been brought in before me to read this writing and make known to me its interpretation; but they could not show the interpretation of the matter.* [16]*But I have heard that you can give interpretations and solve problems. Now if you can read the writing and make known to me its interpretation, you shall be clothed with purple, and have a chain of gold about your neck, and shall be the third ruler in the kingdom."*

[17]*Then Daniel answered before the king, "Let your gifts be for yourself, and give your rewards to another; nevertheless I will read the writing to the king and make known to him the interpretation.* [18]*O king, the Most High God gave Nebuchadnezzar your father kingship and greatness and glory and majesty;* [19]*and because of the greatness that he gave him, all peoples, nations, and languages trembled and feared before him; whom he would he slew, and whom he would he kept alive; whom he would he raised up, and whom he would he put down.* [20]*But when his heart was lifted up and his spirit was hardened so that he dealt proudly, he was deposed from his kingly throne, and his glory was taken from him;* [21]*he was driven from among men, and his mind was made like that of a beast, and his dwelling was with the wild asses; he was fed grass like an ox, and his body was wet with the dew of heaven, until he knew that the Most High God rules the kingdom of men, and sets over it whom he will.* [22]*And you his son, Belshazzar, have not humbled your heart, though you knew all this,* [23]*but you have lifted up yourself against the Lord of heaven; and the vessels of his house have been brought in before you, and you and your lords, your wives, and your concubines have drunk wine from them; and you have praised the gods of silver and gold, of bronze, iron, wood, and stone, which do not see or hear or know, but the God in whose hand is your breath, and whose are all your ways, you have not honored.*

[24]*"Then from his presence the hand was sent, and this writing was inscribed.* [25]*And this is the writing that was inscribed: MENE, MENE, TEKEL, and PARSIN.* [26]*This is the interpretation of the matter: MENE, God has numbered the days of your kingdom and brought it to an end;*

27TEKEL, you have been weighed in the balances and found wanting; 28PERES, your kingdom is divided and given to the Medes and Persians."

29Then Belshazzar commanded, and Daniel was clothed with purple, a chain of gold was put about his neck, and proclamation was made concerning him, that he should be the third ruler in the kingdom.

30That very night Belshazzar the Chaldean king was slain. 31And Darius the Mede received the kingdom, being about sixty-two years old.

k Or *Spirit of the holy God*   l Aramaic repeats *the king your father*

OVERVIEW: The queen was not the king's wife but his mother (THEODORET, ORIGEN) or his grandmother (Josephus via JEROME). The queen recognized the praiseworthy character of Daniel (JEROME) and the grace of the Holy Spirit that was with him (THEODORET, AMBROSE). Nebuchadnezzar is an example of God giving gifts to unworthy persons in order that they might benefit others (CHRYSOSTOM). He is put forth by Daniel in order to teach the justice of God and to teach the king his imminent punishment is because of his pride (JEROME). In his pride, the king believed that he was superior to the Lord of heaven (EPHREM). The inscription announced that God had numbered the days of his kingdom and brought it to an end. God also had taken hold of the king in order to weigh him on the scales of judgment. Belshazzar would not die from natural causes but be killed, and his kingdom would be divided among the Medes and the Persians (JEROME). The king honored Daniel, not for his distressing interpretation, but in order to dispel his ruin by honoring a prophet extremely pleasing to God (JEROME, EPHREM).

5:10 The Queen

THE QUEEN KNOWS MORE THAN THE KING.
JEROME: Josephus says she was Belshazzar's grandmother, whereas Origen says she was his mother. She therefore knew about previous events of which the king was ignorant. So much for Porphyry's far-fetched [interpretation], who fancies that she was the king's wife and makes fun

of the fact that she knows more than her husband does. COMMENTARY ON DANIEL 5.10.[1]

THE QUEEN WAS HIS MOTHER. THEODORET of CYR: "Amid the king's and his nobles' words the queen entered the banqueting hall," that is, with them pondering what should be done and various people making various suggestions under pressure of fear, the queen entered. Now, in my view, this lady was his mother: the wives were attending the banquet along with the concubines, and drinking from the gold and silver vessels was himself and his nobles, his wives—that is, his spouses—and his concubines, partners of his not by law but in lust. Now, this lady entered after the hubbub, and being old she probably was not a party at that stage to the drunkenness and antics or dancing. COMMENTARY ON DANIEL 5.10.[2]

A CUSTOMARY GREETING. THEODORET OF CYR: This was probably an introduction offered at that time to kings by their subjects; even to this day this custom prevails. COMMENTARY ON DANIEL 5.10.[3]

5:11 To Have Enlightenment

DANIEL'S GREAT VIRTUE. JEROME: All the authorities except Symmachus, who adheres to the Chaldean original, render "the spirit of God." "And in the days of your father, wisdom and knowledge were found in him." . . . She calls

---

[1]JCD 58. [2]WGRW 7:141. [3]WGRW 7:141.

Nebuchadnezzar his father, according to the custom of the Scriptures, even though, as we remarked before, he was actually his great-grandfather. But Daniel's godly manner of life even among the barbarians is worthy of our imitation, for the very grandmother or mother of the king extolled him with such words of praise because of the greatness of his virtues. COMMENTARY ON DANIEL 5.10 [11].[4]

ALERTNESS. THEODORET OF CYR: Now, by "alertness" she referred to vigilance of soul, and by "understanding" to a grasp of hidden things and an insight into what escaped many. "Your father King Nebuchadnezzar," she went on, "made him chief of magicians, soothsayers, astrologers, and fortune tellers," adding the reason, "because an extraordinary spirit was in him," that is, he has the surpassing grace of the Spirit. COMMENTARY ON DANIEL 5.11.[5]

5:12 Found in Daniel

A RECEPTACLE OF THE DIVINE SPIRIT. THEODORET OF CYR: Daniel, having become a receptacle of the divine Spirit, gives wise advice on everything, makes intelligent utterances on everything, clarifies riddles in dreams, removes the obscurity from what is hidden in some obscurity and by setting free what is held in bondage in secret recesses, as it were. COMMENTARY ON DANIEL 5.12.[6]

5:14 Spirit of the Gods

HOLY SPIRIT. AMBROSE: And lest any one should perhaps think that, as the Scripture says, "God raised up the Holy Spirit of a young youth," the spirit in him was that of a person, not the Holy Spirit, let him read farther on, and he will find that Daniel received the Holy Spirit and therefore prophesied. Lastly, too, the king advanced him because he had the grace of the Spirit. For he speaks thus: "Daniel, you are able, forasmuch as the Holy Spirit of God is in you."

And farther on it is written: "And Daniel was set over them, because an excellent Spirit was in him."[7] OF THE HOLY SPIRIT 3.6.43.[8]

5:17 Let Your Gifts Be to Yourself

THE HUMILITY OF DANIEL. CHRYSOSTOM: Why then, you ask, being so humble did Daniel not repel either the adoration that was paid him by the king or the offerings? This I will not say, for it is sufficient for me simply to mention the question, and the rest I leave to you, that at least in this way I may stir up your thoughts. . . . For that [Daniel] did not do this out of arrogance is evident from his saying, "your gifts be to yourself." ON THE EPISTLES TO THE HEBREWS, HOMILY 26.8-9.[9]

DANIEL'S EXAMPLE. JEROME: We should follow the example of a man like Daniel, who despised the honor and gifts of a king and who without any reward even in that early day followed the Gospel injunction: "Freely have you received, freely give."[10] And besides, when one is announcing sad tidings, it is unbecoming for him willingly to accept gifts. COMMENTARY ON DANIEL 5.11 [17].[11]

5:18 The Most High Gave Greatness

GRACE AND THE UNWORTHY. CHRYSOSTOM: And in the Old Testament it may be found, in that grace many times came on unworthy persons that it might do good to others. . . . Nebuchadnezzar was very full of iniquity; yet to him [Daniel] revealed what was to follow after many generations. And again to the son of this last, though surpassing his father in iniquity, he signified the things to come, ordering a marvelous and great dispensation. Accordingly because then also the beginnings of the gospel were taking place, and it was requisite that the manifestation of its power should be abundant, many even of the

---

[4]JCD 58-59*. [5]WGRW 7:141-43. [6]WGRW 7:143. [7]Dan 6:3. [8]NPNF 2 10:141*. [9]NPNF 1 14:486*. [10]Mt 10:8. [11]JCD 59.

unworthy used to receive gifts. However, from those miracles no gain accrued to them; rather, they are punished even more. HOMILIES ON THE GOSPEL OF MATTHEW 24.2.[12]

FEAR OF THE KING DIVINELY ORDAINED.

THEODORET OF CYR: Do not think it was by relying on his own strength that your father subjected the whole world and brought under one kingdom the countless races of the nations speaking various tongues. It was, in fact, the Lord of all, maker of everything, wise governor of all things, who gave him the kingdom, and it was as a result of the divine decree that fear of your father possessed his subjects. COMMENTARY ON DANIEL 5.18-19.[13]

5:19 All Trembled and Feared

THE JUSTICE OF GOD. JEROME: Thus [Daniel]

sets forth the example of the king's great-grandfather, in order to teach him the justice of God and make it clear that his great-grandson too was to suffer similar treatment because of his pride. Now if Nebuchadnezzar killed whomever he would and struck to death whomever he wished to; if he set on high those whom he would and brought low whomever he wished to, there is certainly no divine providence or scriptural injunction behind these honors and slayings, these acts of promotion and humiliation. But rather, such things ensue from the will of the people who do the slaying and promoting to honor and all the rest. If this is the case, the question arises as to how we are to understand the Scripture: "The heart of a king reposes in the hand of God; he will incline it in whatever direction he wishes."[14] Perhaps we might say that every saint is a king, for sin does not reign in his mortal body, and his heart therefore is kept safe, for he is in God's hand.[15] And whatever has once come into the hand of God the Father, according to the Gospel, no one is able to take it away. And whoever is taken away, it is understood that he never was in God's hand at all. COMMENTARY ON DANIEL 5.19.[16]

5:20 Deposed from the Throne

DEPRIVED OF ALL HONOR. THEODORET OF

CYR: "He was deposed from the throne of his kingdom: just as he elevated those he wanted and humbled those he wanted," doing so not altogether by a right decision, so the King and Lord of all gave your father the kingdom as he wanted, but on perceiving him giving vent to an overweening sense of his own importance, running the kingdom in an arrogant and conceited manner, a victim of haughtiness, he deprived him of the royal throne and stripped him of the honor paid him by everyone. Instead of divesting him only of the kingdom, however, he drove him also from normal association, gave him over to insanity and derangement and caused him to live with wild asses and savage beasts, taking on the life of the animals whose ferocity he had imitated. COMMENTARY ON DANIEL 5.20.[17]

5:22 You Have Not Humbled Yourself

GOD RESISTS THE PROUD. JEROME: Because

your great-grandfather, he says, lifted up his heart and hardened his spirit in pride, he therefore was put down from his royal throne and his glory was taken away, and so on.[18] Therefore in your case also, because you knew these things about your relative and understood that God resists the proud and gives grace to the humble, you should not have lifted up your heart against the ruler of heaven and scoffed at his majesty and perpetrated the deeds that you did. COMMENTARY ON DANIEL 5.22-23.[19]

5:23 Exalting Oneself Over God

ARROGANCE AND LUXURY. EPHREM THE SYR-

IAN: "You have exalted yourself against God." . . . Certainly, he says, you were brought to such madness that you placed yourself above God and

---

[12]NPNF 1 10:168*. [13]WGRW 7:145. [14]Prov 21:1. [15]Rom 6:12-14. [16]JCD 59. [17]WGRW 7:145-47. [18]Dan 4:33. [19]JCD 60*.

overcame your father in arrogance and luxury. Indeed, [Nebuchadnezzar] thought that nobody among humankind was equal to him, but you believed that the Lord of heaven was inferior to you. COMMENTARY ON DANIEL 5.16.[20]

THE KING'S HEART ELEVATED. THEODORET OF CYR: He did well to instruct those present to worship not visible things but their Creator and Lord. At the same time he also convicts the king of conceit and teaches him that the highest heaven has for its creator the unseen God. You, he is saying, made your heart more elevated not than heaven but than the God of heaven, the Lord of all creation; if you were not guilty of such awful conceit, you would not have ordered the vessels of his house to be brought in. COMMENTARY ON DANIEL 5.23.[21]

THE SOURCE OF ALL LIFE. THEODORET OF CYR: Now, [Daniel] did well and showed much wisdom in putting in parallel the idols and the God of all with a view to the benefit felt by the hearers; after emphasizing that the former neither see nor hear, instead of proceeding to say in regard to the God of all that he sees and hears and knows, he cited the more powerful fact of all, your life and your ways are in his hand, since providing life to others and in turn removing it at will is more important than having life. He brought out, then, that while the idols are deprived of life and all sensation, the Lord God of all is the source of all life and both gives it and takes it, governing as he wills. Nevertheless, [Daniel] is saying, despite his being of this stature, so great, with power of life and death, appointing kings and removing them, you not only did not sing his praises but rather even persisted in your drunken behavior, making fun of vessels dedicated to him. COMMENTARY ON DANIEL 5.23.[22]

5:24 The Writing That Was Inscribed

INTERPRETING THE INSCRIPTION. JEROME: The inscription of these three words on the wall

simply meant "Mane, Thecel, Phares"; the first of which sounds forth the idea of "number," and the second "a weighing out" and the third "removal." And so there was a need not only for reading the inscription but also for interpreting what had been read, in order that it might be understood what these words were announcing. That is to say, that God had numbered [Belshazzar's] kingdom and brought it to an end and that he had seized hold on him to weigh him in his judgment scales, and the sword would slay him before he should meet a natural death; and his empire would be divided among the Medes and Persians. COMMENTARY ON DANIEL 5.25-28.[23]

5:26 This Is the Interpretation

THE DREAM'S INTERPRETATION. THEODORET OF CYR: By "interpretation," he refers to the meaning. "Mane: God has measured your kingdom and brought it to an end," that is, he has seen you are unworthy of kingship, and he decided to leave you bereft of it. "Thekel: he was weighed in the balance and found wanting." In this the prophet taught not only him but also us the lesson that nothing goes unweighed by God; instead, mercy and longsuffering are shown to people according to a certain measure and weight. Since, then, [Daniel] is saying, you exceeded the limit of lovingkindness, receive the divine sentence. "Phares: your kingdom has been divided and has been given to the Medes and Persians." COMMENTARY ON DANIEL 5.25-28.[24]

5:29 Daniel Was Honored

HONORING THE PROPHET. JEROME: Or else, it might be construed as having authority over a third part of the kingdom. At any rate, he received the royal insignia of necklace and purple, with the result that he appeared more notable to Darius, who was to be the successor in the royal

---

[20]ESOO 2:211. [21]WGRW 7:147. [22]WGRW 7:149. [23]JCD 60*. [24]WGRW 7:149-51*.

power, and all the more honorable because of his notability. Nor was it strange that Belshazzar should have paid the promised reward on hearing sad tidings. For either he supposed that his predictions would take place in the distant future, or else he hoped he would obtain mercy by honoring the prophet of God. And if he did not obtain this reward, it was because his sacrilege toward God outweighed the honor he accorded to [a] man. COMMENTARY ON DANIEL 5.29.[25]

DANIEL HONORED FOR HIS OWN SAKE.

EPHREM THE SYRIAN: The vain king did not do that in order to give honor to Daniel for those sad omens, which he had announced to him by interpreting the writing, but he tried to catch his benevolence, as if he had understood that Daniel was extremely pleasing to God, and therefore he hoped that he would have dispelled his ruin, which the hand sent from above had signed, and Daniel himself had announced, through his intercession. But Belshazzar's efforts were pointless: on that very night Belshazzar was killed and Babylon was destroyed, and was affected by every misfortune from the Medes and the Persians, as the prophets had already foretold a long time before, and the kingdom of the Chaldeans passed to the Medes, after Darius, king of the Persians and the Medes, had assumed power. COMMENTARY ON DANIEL 5.29.[26]

5:30 The King Was Killed

NO PARDON. THEODORET OF CYR: Now, it is necessary to inquire why on earth the God of all corrected Nebuchadnezzar and in turn restored him to his kingdom but forthwith deprived this man of both kingdom and life. On consideration, then, we find, first, that Nebuchadnezzar had not observed another person paying the penalty for impiety, and hence God's just sentence granted him pardon, whereas this other man, though observing his father's heavy penalty, gained noth-

ing from it. The just judge was therefore within his rights in confining punishment of the former to a specified time, whereas he granted the latter no pardon. In particular, God foresees all future events and thus knows them clearly as if already in the past; so he knew ahead of time the repentance of the former and arranged for his fate accordingly, whereas he knew ahead of time the latter's incorrigible impiety and put a stop to the increase in impiety with death. COMMENTARY ON DANIEL 5.28.[27]

5:31 Darius the Mede

DARIUS BECOMES RULER OF BABYLON.

JEROME: Josephus writes in his tenth book of the Jewish Antiquities that when Babylon had been laid under siege by the Medes and Persians, that is, by Darius and Cyrus, Belshazzar, king of Babylon, fell into such forgetfulness of his own situation as to put on his celebrated banquet and drink from the vessels of the temple, and even while he was besieged he found leisure for banqueting. From this circumstance the historical account could arise, that he was captured and slaughtered on the same night, while everyone was either terrified by fear of the vision and its interpretation or else taken up with festivity and drunken banqueting. As for the fact that while Cyrus, king of the Persians, was the victor, and Darius was only king of the Medes, it was Darius who was recorded to have succeeded to the throne of Babylon; this was an arrangement occasioned by factors of age, family relationship and the territory ruled over. By this I mean that Darius was sixty-two years old and that, according to what we read, the kingdom of the Medes was more sizable than that of the Persians, and being Cyrus's uncle, he naturally had a prior claim and ought to have been accounted as successor to the rule of Babylon. COMMENTARY ON DANIEL 5.30-31.[28]

---

[25]JCD 61. [26]ESOO 2:212. [27]WGRW 7:151. [28]JCD 61.

6:1-9 THE SATRAPS' SCHEME

¹It pleased Darius to set over the kingdom a hundred and twenty satraps, to be throughout the whole kingdom; ²and over them three presidents, of whom Daniel was one, to whom these satraps should give account, so that the king might suffer no loss. ³Then this Daniel became distinguished above all the other presidents and satraps, because an excellent spirit was in him; and the king planned to set him over the whole kingdom. ⁴Then the presidents and the satraps sought to find a ground for complaint against Daniel with regard to the kingdom; but they could find no ground for complaint or any fault, because he was faithful, and no error or fault was found in him. ⁵Then these men said, "We shall not find any ground for complaint against this Daniel unless we find it in connection with the law of his God."

⁶Then these presidents and satraps came by agreement^m to the king and said to him, "O King Darius, live for ever! ⁷All the presidents of the kingdom, the prefects and the satraps, the counselors and the governors are agreed that the king should establish an ordinance and enforce an interdict, that whoever makes petition to any god or man for thirty days, except to you, O king, shall be cast into the den of lions. ⁸Now, O king, establish the interdict and sign the document, so that it cannot be changed, according to the law of the Medes and the Persians, which cannot be revoked." ⁹Therefore King Darius signed the document and interdict.

m Or thronging

OVERVIEW: The chronological confusion of referring to Daniel in the court of Darius the Mede and then back in the court of Belshazzar, the Babylonian, is clarified by realizing Daniel 6 brings to an end the historical moments in Daniel's life (JEROME). As the Babylonians had employed trickery in having the golden statue erected, so now the Medes attempt to use trickery to destroy Daniel (ISHO'DAD, EPHREM). Daniel is again shown to have the Holy Spirit indwelling and thereby commands respect (AMBROSE, THEODORET).

6:1 Darius

CHRONOLOGICAL INCONSISTENCY. JEROME: Hence we see that when Babylon was overthrown, Darius returned to his own kingdom in Media and brought Daniel along with him the same honorable capacity to which he had been promoted by Belshazzar. . . . But as for the fact

that a nonchronological order is followed, so that some history is narrated in the reign of Darius before material is given for Belshazzar's reign, whereas we are subsequently to read that he was put to death by Darius, it seems to me that the anachronism results from the fact that the author has brought all the historical portions together in immediate sequence. COMMENTARY ON DANIEL 6.1.[1]

TRICKERY UTILIZED TO DESTROY DANIEL. ISHO'DAD OF MERV: We need to take notice that previously the Babylonians, that is, their princes, had used trickery in their jealousy of Daniel to destroy Daniel and his companions and had persuaded Nebuchadnezzar to build the golden statue and to order that it alone be worshiped by those under his authority. So, too, now the

[1]JCD 63.

Medes use trickery in the elaboration of the edict and decree in order to destroy Daniel. COMMENTARY ON DANIEL 6.4.[2]

THE INDWELLING HOLY SPIRIT EMPOWERED DANIEL. AMBROSE: Daniel received the Holy Spirit and therefore prophesied. So, too, the king promoted him because he had the grace of the Spirit. For the king spoke in this regard, "I have heard of you that the Spirit of the holy God is in you."[3] And farther on it is written, "Then Daniel became distinguished above all the other presidents and satraps, because an excellent spirit was in him." And the spirit of Moses also was shared by those who were to be judges.[4] ON THE HOLY SPIRIT 3.6.43.[5]

6:2 Three Presidents

VICEROYS. THEODORET OF CYR: Normally, in fact, those entrusted with kingship or any other rule confide least in the people closest to their predecessors; but Daniel enjoyed the same trust from all, receiving equal privileges and being entrusted with the same governance—hence, of course, his becoming one of the three supervisors under Darius. Now, by "supervisors" I think there is reference to what are now called viceroys, and by "satraps" to the governors of the nations, Daniel being one of the supervisors. COMMENTARY ON DANIEL 6.1-2.[6]

6:3 An Excellent Spirit

THE GRACE OF WISDOM. THEODORET OF CYR: [Daniel] had received from God a greater and more abundant grace. Now, from this we learn that to those also who are entrusted with conduct of earthly affairs, even if unsympathetic to religion, a grace of wisdom is given from God for their management of those they rule. Blessed Daniel implied as much in saying, "Because there was an extraordinary spirit in him," that is, he had received the grace in keeping with his religious sentiments. COMMENTARY ON DANIEL 6.3.[7]

6:4 No Ground for Complaint

ABOVE SUSPICION. JEROME: I myself would simply interpret this as meaning that they were unable to discover any pretext of accusation against him in any matter in which he had injured the king, for the simple reason that he was a faithful man and no suspicion of blame was discoverable in him. Instead of "suspicion" Theodotion and Aquila have rendered "offense" (*amblakema*), which is *essaitha* in Chaldean. And when I asked a Jew for the meaning of this word, he replied that the basic significance of it was "snare," and we may render it as a "lure" or *sphalma*, that is, a "mistake." Furthermore, Euripides in his *Medea* equates the word *amplakiai* ["offenses"] (spelling it with a *p* instead of a *b*) to *hamartiai*, that is to say, "sins." COMMENTARY ON DANIEL 6.1.[8]

6:6 The Rulers Came to the King

SURREPTITIOUS. JEROME: It was well said that they "went surreptitiously," for they did not come right out with what they were aiming at but contrived their plot against a private enemy on the pretext of honoring the king. COMMENTARY ON DANIEL 6.6.[9]

6:7 Establishing an Ordinance

ENVY. THEODORET OF CYR: Nothing is more repugnant than envy: it pressured them into committing impiety and caused an impious decree to be published forbidding those intent on offering prayers to God; they prevented not only themselves from doing it but also all others subject to royal control.... In surrendering their mind's eye to envy, they did not understand that the king could not supply everything to petitioners, like health, life, fathering children, abundance of rain and anything else that we receive when we ask it

---

[2]CSCO 328:107. [3]Dan 5:14. [4]Num 11:25. [5]NPNF 2 10:141. [6]WGRW 7:159. [7]WGRW 7:159. [8]JCD 64-65. [9]JCD 65.

of God. Losing their senses, however, they ascribed to the king what belongs to God and persuaded the foolish king to reach the same verdict and ratify their request. COMMENTARY ON DANIEL 6.6-9.[10]

6:8 It Cannot Be Changed

THE LAW OF THE MEDES AND PERSIANS.
EPHREM THE SYRIAN: Darius, as he loved quietness and inactivity and found work and business unpleasing, left the care of the empire to his prefects, and for this reason the Scripture adds, he set over the kingdom satraps, that is, 120 governors. And over them he placed three presidents, including Daniel. Then they asked him to set an interdict according to the law of the Medes and Persians. Indeed, among the Persians and the

Medes, a law stated that when the king had set a certain rule, it was not permitted to rescind it. So the satraps asked the king for this kind of firm and immutable decree; and they were certain that the king would have not rescinded such a decree in order to save Daniel. It is likely that Daniel was not present in the hall of justice on that day, when the king argued from morning till evening with his satraps in order to save Daniel. If he had been present, he would have immediately confessed that he had prayed [to God], and after the confession of the crime the trial would have not been extended until evening. COMMENTARY ON DANIEL 6.1-15.[11]

---

[10]WGRW 7:161-63*. [11]ESOO 2:212.

6:10-18 DANIEL IN THE LIONS' DEN

[10]*When Daniel knew that the document had been signed, he went to his house where he had windows in his upper chamber open toward Jerusalem; and he got down upon his knees three times a day and prayed and gave thanks before his God, as he had done previously.* [11]*Then these men came by agreement*[m] *and found Daniel making petition and supplication before his God.* [12]*Then they came near and said before the king, concerning the interdict, "O king! Did you not sign an interdict, that any man who makes petition to any god or man within thirty days except to you, O king, shall be cast into the den of lions?" The king answered, "The thing stands fast, according to the law of the Medes and Persians, which cannot be revoked."* [13]*Then they answered before the king, "That Daniel, who is one of the exiles from Judah, pays no heed to you, O king, or the interdict you have signed, but makes his petition three times a day."*

[14]*Then the king, when he heard these words, was much distressed, and set his mind to deliver Daniel; and he labored till the sun went down to rescue him.* [15]*Then these men came by agreement*[m] *to the king, and said to the king, "Know, O king, that it is a law of the Medes and Persians that no interdict or ordinance which the king establishes can be changed."*

[16]*Then the king commanded, and Daniel was brought and cast into the den of lions. The king said to Daniel, "May your God, whom you serve continually, deliver you!"* [17]*And a stone was*

brought and laid upon the mouth of the den, and the king sealed it with his own signet and with the signet of his lords, that nothing might be changed concerning Daniel. [18]*Then the king went to his palace, and spent the night fasting; no diversions were brought to him, and sleep fled from him.*

m Or *thronging*

OVERVIEW: Daniel prayed towards Jerusalem, according to Solomon's instruction (JEROME, THEODORET, PETER CHRYSOLOGUS). He prayed three times a day, which corresponds to the church's tradition (JOHN CASSIAN, DIDACHE, ORIGEN). Though Daniel did not pray in an obscure spot, he also did not rashly expose himself to danger. His accusers referred to Daniel as an exile as a way of showing contempt. Envy, not race or religion, was the motivation behind the conspiracy against Daniel. Though bound by his own law, Darius sought to rescue Daniel by ingenuity (JEROME), but it is God who delivers (CLEMENT OF ROME, IGNATIUS, APOSTOLIC CONSTITUTIONS). Darius sealed the pit for Daniel's protection and to prevent fraudulent rumors (EPHREM).

6:10 Daniel Prayed to God

DANIEL'S COURAGE. THEODORET OF CYR: Note how much this verse implied in a few words in mentioning the piety and courage of blessed Daniel. First, when Daniel learned that the decision has been reached, "he went into his house" —that is, when he got news of the passing of the law, he had great scorn for it and continued openly doing the opposite. It next mentions a further detail that reveals his courage: the windows were open, it says—in other words, he said his prayers not in secret but openly, with everyone watching, not for vainglory but in scorn for the impiety of the law. COMMENTARY ON DANIEL 6.10.[1]

UPPER ROOMS. JEROME: We must quickly draw from our memory and bring together from all of holy Scripture all the passages where we have read of *domata*, which means in Latin either "walled enclosures" (*menia*) or "beds" or "sun terraces," and also the references to *anogaia*, that is,

"upper rooms." For after all, our Lord celebrated the Passover in an upper room,[2] and in the Acts of the Apostles the Holy Spirit came on the 120 souls of believers while they were in an upper room.[3] And so Daniel in this case, despising the king's commands and reposing his confidence in God, does not offer his prayers in some obscure spot but in a lofty place, and he opens up his windows toward Jerusalem, from whence he looked for the peace [of God]. He prays, moreover, according to God's behest and according to what Solomon had said when he admonished the people that they should pray in the direction of the temple. Furthermore, there are three times in the day when we should bow our knees to God, and the tradition of the church understands them to be the third hour, the sixth hour and the ninth hour [i.e., 9:00 a.m., noon and 3:00 p.m.]. Last, it was at the third hour that the Holy Spirit descended on the apostles. It was at the sixth hour that Peter, purposing to eat, ascended to the upper room for prayer.[4] It was at the ninth hour that Peter and John were on their way to the temple.[5] COMMENTARY ON DANIEL 6.10.[6]

FACING JERUSALEM. THEODORET OF CYR: When blessed Daniel in Babylon prayed, he opened the windows facing Jerusalem, not under the impression that God was confined there but from his knowledge that the divine manifestation occurred there. COMMENTARY ON PSALM 28.2.[7]

SOLOMON'S PRAYER. THEODORET OF CYR: He did this not only to provoke his accusers but also to fulfill an ancient law: when Solomon built that famous temple and celebrated the festival of con-

---

[1]WGRW 7:163. [2]Mk 14:13-25. [3]Acts 2:1-4. [4]Acts 10:9. [5]Acts 3:1. [6]JCD 65-66*. [7]FC 101:179.

secration, he prayed a prayer of supplication for divine grace and implored that the temple be filled with it, adding this in addition to other things, "If you surrender your people to their foes, and they take them as captives to a land distant or near, and they have a change of heart in the land where they are transported and pray to you in their exile in the words, We sinned, we did wrong, we broke the law, and they turn back to you with their whole heart and with their whole soul in the land of their foes where you transferred them, and they pray to you toward their land which you gave their ancestors, and the city that you chose and the house that I built to your name, may you hearken from heaven, forthwith from your dwelling place, and forgive their sins by which they have sinned against you and all the transgressions they have committed against you, and show them pity before their captors."[8] Instructed in this, Daniel faced Jerusalem in praying. Commentary on Daniel 6.10.[9]

The Holy Spirit Descended at the Third Hour. John Cassian: And so in the monasteries of Palestine and Mesopotamia and all the East the services of the above-mentioned hours are ended each day with three psalms apiece, so that constant prayers may be offered to God at the appointed times, and yet, the spiritual duties being completed with due moderation, the necessary offices of work may not be in any way interfered with: for at these three seasons we know that Daniel the prophet also poured forth his prayers to God day by day in his chamber with the windows open. Nor is it without good reasons that these times are more particularly assigned to religious offices, since at them what completed the promises and summed up our salvation was fulfilled. For we can show that at the third hour the Holy Spirit, who had been of old promised by the prophets, descended in the first instance on the apostles assembled together for prayer. Institutes 3.3.[10]

Three Times a Day. Didache: Do not pray as the hypocrites; but as the Lord commanded in his Gospel,[11] thus pray: Our Father in heaven, hallowed be your name. Your kingdom come. Your will be done, as in heaven, so on earth. Give us today our daily [needful] bread, and forgive us our debt as we also forgive our debtors. And bring us not into temptation, but deliver us from the evil one (or, evil); for yours is the power and the glory forever. Three times a day thus pray. Didache 8.[12]

Meriting Freedom. Peter Chrysologus: The psalmist instructs us to allot three periods a day to God when he says, "At evening, at morning and at midday I shall speak what I have to say, and you will hearken to my voice."[13] For those three periods while Daniel diligently beseeched God, not only did they obtain foreknowledge of the future, but he also merited the freedom of his people held captive for so long. Sermon 21.6.[14]

6:11 Daniel Found Making a Petition

Daniel Did Not Seek Persecution. Jerome: From this passage we learn that we are not to expose ourselves rashly to danger, but so far as it lies in our power, we are to avoid the plots of our enemies. And so in Daniel's case, he did not contravene the king's authority in a public square or out in the street but rather in a private place, in order that he might not neglect the commands of the one true God almighty. Commentary on Daniel 6.11.[15]

6:13 An Exile Prays to His God

Mere Captive. Jerome: In order to magnify the dishonor involved in this contempt, they speak of the man who showed this contempt for the king's commands as a mere captive. Commentary on Daniel 6.13.[16]

---

[8]See 1 Kings 8:46-50; 2 Chron 6:36-39. [9]WGRW 7:163-65. [10]NPNF 2 11:213. [11]Mt 6:5, 9-13. [12]ANF 7:379*. [13]Ps 55:17 (54:18 LXX). [14]FC 109:94-95*. [15]JCD 66. [16]JCD 66.

PRAYER. ORIGEN: And he prays "constantly" (deeds of virtue or fulfilling the commandments are included as part of prayer) who unites prayer with the deeds required and right deeds with prayer. For the only way we can accept the command to "pray constantly"[17] as referring to a real possibility is by saying that the entire life of the saint taken as a whole is a single great prayer. What is customarily called prayer is, then, a part of this prayer. Now prayer in the ordinary sense ought to be made no less than three times each day. This is evident in the story of Daniel, who prayed three times each day when such great peril had been devised for him. ON PRAYER 12.2.[18]

6:14 Darius Determined to Save Daniel

THE KING ATTEMPTS TO DELIVER DANIEL. JEROME: He realized that he had been tripped up by his own reply to their question and that envy was the motive of their plot. And so to avoid the appearance of acting against his own law, he wanted to deliver Daniel from danger by ingenuity and strategy rather than by exerting his royal authority. And so earnestly did he labor and strive that he would not accept any food, absolute monarch though he was, even until sunset. And as for the plotters, so firmly did they persist in their evil purpose that no consideration of the king's personal desire or of the damage he would sustain had any effect on them. COMMENTARY ON DANIEL 6.14.[19]

6:15 Established Ordinances

ROYAL COMMANDS CANNOT BE NULLIFIED. JEROME: Just as the king understood that the princes were making their accusation out of motives of envy, so also they for their part understood what the king's purpose was, namely, that he wished to rescue Daniel from imminent death. And so they allege that according to the law of the Medes and Persians, the commands of a king cannot be nullified. COMMENTARY ON DANIEL 6.15.[20]

UNDER PRESSURE. THEODORET OF CYR: You do not have the authority to overturn what you have prescribed, the laws of Medes and Persians ordering that the laws passed by the previous king be fulfilled. Under pressure both from the compelling logic of the words and from the number of the accusers, the king surrendered blessed Daniel to the lions. COMMENTARY ON DANIEL 6.15.[21]

6:16 May Your God . . . Deliver You

THE DEFENDER AND PROTECTOR. CLEMENT OF ROME: For what shall we say? Was Daniel cast into the den of lions by those who feared God? Were Ananias and Azarias and Mishael shut up in a furnace of fire by those who observed the great and glorious worship of the Most High? Far from us be such a thought! Who, then, were they that did such things? The hateful, and those full of all wickedness, were roused to such a pitch of fury that they inflicted torture on those who served God with a holy and blameless purpose [of heart], not knowing that the Most High is the defender and protector of all such as with a pure conscience venerate his all-excellent name. . . . But they who with confidence endured [these things] are now heirs of glory and honor and have been exalted and made illustrious by God in their memorial for ever and ever. 1 CLEMENT 45.[22]

SPARED LIKE DANIEL. IGNATIUS OF ANTIOCH: From Syria even to Rome I fight with beasts: not that I am devoured by brute beasts, for these, as you know, by the will of God, spared Daniel, but by beasts in the shape of people, in whom the merciless wild beast himself lies hid and pricks and wounds me day by day. But none of these hardships "move me, neither count I my life dear unto myself,"[23] in such a way as to love it better than the Lord. Wherefore I am prepared for [encountering] fire, wild beasts, the sword or the cross, so that only I may see Christ my Savior and

---

[17]1 Thess 5:17. [18]OSW 104*. [19]JCD 67. [20]JCD 67. [21]WGRW 7:165. [22]ANF 1:17*. [23]Acts 20:24.

God, who died for me. I therefore, a prisoner of Christ, who is driven along by land and sea, exhort you: "stand fast in the faith,"[24] and be steadfast, "for the just shall live by faith";[25] be unwavering, for "the Lord causes those to dwell in a house that are of one and the same character." EPISTLE TO THE TARSIANS I.[26]

A PRAYER. APOSTOLIC CONSTITUTIONS: Lord, who fulfilled your promises made by the prophets, and had mercy on Zion and compassion on Jerusalem, by exalting the throne of David, your servant . . . by the birth of Christ, who was born of his seed according to the flesh, of a virgin alone; please, O Lord God, accept the prayers that proceed from the lips of your people which are of the Gentiles, which call on you in truth, as you accepted the gifts of the righteous in their generations. In the first place you respected the sacrifice of Abel . . . of Ezra at the return;[27] of Daniel in the den of lions; of Jonah in the whale's belly.[28] CONSTITUTIONS OF THE HOLY APOSTLES 7.37.[29]

DELIVER BY GOD'S POWER. APOSTOLIC CONSTITUTIONS: Let not, therefore, any one that works signs and wonders judge any one of the faithful who is not granted the same: for the gifts of God that are bestowed by him through Christ are various; and one person receives one gift and another another. . . . For neither did the wise Daniel, who was delivered from the mouths of the lions, nor the three children, who were delivered from the furnace of fire, despise the rest of their fellow Israelites: for they knew that they had not escaped these terrible miseries by their own might but by the power of God did they both work miracles and were delivered from miseries. Wherefore let none of you exalt himself against his brother, though he is a prophet or though he is a worker of miracles. CONSTITUTIONS OF THE HOLY APOSTLES 8.1.[30]

6:17 Sealed with the King's Signet

THE PIT SEALED FOR DANIEL'S PROTECTION. JEROME: He sealed with his ring the rock by which the opening of the pit was shut up, so that the enemies of Daniel might not make any attempt to harm him. For he had entrusted him to the power of God, and although not worried about lions, he was fearful of men. He also sealed it with the ring of his nobles, in order to avoid all ground for suspicion so far as they were concerned. COMMENTARY ON DANIEL 6.17.[31]

SEALED TO PREVENT RUMORS OF FRAUD. EPHREM THE SYRIAN: Certainly it had been decided by Darius to save Daniel from the present danger with any possible means; therefore he sealed the entrance of the den with his own signet and invited the satraps to do the same. This had to be done for two reasons: first, in order that [the satraps] might not steal there without being seen and, after rolling off the lid, might kill him; second, in order that they might not spread among the people the rumor that some fraud had been used inside the den. COMMENTARY ON DANIEL 6.17.[32]

6:18 The King Went to His House

HUMANITY AND COWARDICE. THEODORET OF CYR: Each of these details testifies both to his humanity and to his cowardice: a mark of his humanity was his refusing to partake of food or let his eyes rest in sleep, instead staying awake in grief for the unjust punishment of Daniel; it was a mark of cowardice that he was not so affected as to counter the accusers and invoke his royal authority and power to save the wronged. COMMENTARY ON DANIEL 6.18.[33]

---

[24]1 Cor 16:13. [25]Hab 2:4; Gal 3:11. [26]ANF 1:107*. [27]Ezra 8. [28]Jon 2. [29]ANF 7:474-75*. [30]ANF 7:480*. [31]JCD 67-68. [32]ESOO 2:213. [33]WGRW 7:167.

6:19-28 DANIEL SAVED FROM THE LIONS

[19]Then, at break of day, the king arose and went in haste to the den of lions. [20]When he came near to the den where Daniel was, he cried out in a tone of anguish and said to Daniel, "O Daniel, servant of the living God, has your God, whom you serve continually, been able to deliver you from the lions?" [21]Then Daniel said to the king, "O king, live for ever! [22]My God sent his angel and shut the lions' mouths, and they have not hurt me, because I was found blameless before him; and also before you, O king, I have done no wrong." [23]Then the king was exceedingly glad, and commanded that Daniel be taken up out of the den. So Daniel was taken up out of the den, and no kind of hurt was found upon him, beause he had trusted in his God. [24]And the king commanded, and those men who had accused Daniel were brought and cast into the den of lions—they, their children, and their wives; and before they reached the bottom of the den the lions overpowered them and broke all their bones in pieces.

[25]Then King Darius wrote to all the peoples, nations, and languages that dwell in all the earth: "Peace be multiplied to you. [26]I make a decree, that in all my royal dominion men tremble and fear before the God of Daniel,

for he is the living God,
enduring for ever;
his kingdom shall never be destroyed,
and his dominion shall be to the end.
[27]He delivers and rescues,
he works signs and wonders
in heaven and on earth,
he who has saved Daniel
from the power of the lions."
[28]So this Daniel prospered during the reign of Darius and the reign of Cyrus the Persian.

OVERVIEW: Darius's faith led him to seal the lions' den the night before and to return early the next morning, while it was still dark (THEODORET), to see if Daniel was still alive (JEROME, EPHREM). Faith stopped the mouth of lions (CYRIL OF JERUSALEM). Daniel did not despair, believing that adversity was permitted by God (CHRYSOSTOM). Daniel's persecutors were ashamed when Daniel came out of the lions' den, just as those who had crucified Jesus were ashamed (APHRAHAT). Daniel's rescue resulted in Darius's proclamation of the only God (CYPRIAN).

6:19 At Daybreak

STILL DARK. THEODORET OF CYR: "King Darius rose early at daybreak," that is, while it was still dark, around dawn, so that there was even need of lamps (the meaning of "at daybreak"). COMMENTARY ON DANIEL 6.19.[1]

DRY CISTERN. JEROME: The term "pit" (*lacus*) implies a really deep depression, or dry cistern, in

[1]WGRW 7:167.

which the lions were fed. And so he proceeded hastily to the pit at the break of dawn, believing that Daniel was alive. COMMENTARY ON DANIEL 6.19.[2]

DARIUS RETURNED BECAUSE OF FAITH. EPHREM THE SYRIAN: The same faith, which on the previous evening had led Darius to seal the entrance of the den, brought him again to that place, as if he would have seen Daniel still alive. COMMENTARY ON DANIEL 6.19.[3]

6:20 Darius Cried Out

TEARS. JEROME: By his tears he showed his inner emotion, and forgetting his royal dignity, the conqueror ran to his captive, the master to his servant. COMMENTARY ON DANIEL 6.20.[4]

THE LIVING GOD. THEODORET OF CYR: Each of these phrases shows the religious spirit of the king, who complimented Daniel on his piety: first, he calls him not his own servant but God's; next, he calls Daniel's God "living;" then, in praise of his piety, "whom you serve with constancy," that is, you were not prevented from worship under pressure of the law. The question "Was he able to rescue you from the lions' mouth?" means, "Was it his will to render you impervious against the lions?" After all, he would not have referred to God as powerless after calling him "living." COMMENTARY ON DANIEL 6.19-20.[5]

6:23 Daniel Had Trusted in God

ACCOMPLISHED BY FAITH. CHRYSOSTOM: "Stopped the mouths of lions, quenched raging fire and escaped the edge of the sword."[6] See how they were in death itself, Daniel encompassed by the lions, the three children abiding in the furnace, the Israelites, Abraham, Isaac, Jacob, in diverse temptations; and yet not even so did they despair. For this is faith. When things are turning out adversely, then we ought to believe nothing

adverse is done but all things in due order. ON THE EPISTLE TO THE HEBREWS, HOMILY 27.4.[7]

FAITH ENLIGHTENS CONSCIENCE. CYRIL OF JERUSALEM: The lesson that was read today invites you to the true faith, by setting before you the way in which you also must please God. It affirms that "without faith it is impossible to please him." For when will an individual resolve to serve God, unless he believes that "he is a giver of reward"? When will a young woman choose a virgin life, or a young man live soberly, if they do not believe that for chastity there is "a crown that does not fade away"?[8] Faith is an eye that enlightens every conscience and imparts understanding. The prophet says, "And if you do not believe, you shall not understand."[9] Faith "stops the mouth of lions," as in Daniel's case, for Scripture says concerning him, "Daniel was brought up out of the den and was found to be hurt in no way, because he believed in his God." CATECHETICAL LECTURES 5.4.[10]

6:24 Those Who Had Accused Daniel

HIS ACCUSERS WERE ASHAMED. APHRAHAT: Daniel also was persecuted as Jesus was persecuted. . . . Daniel they cast into the pit of lions, and he was delivered and came up out of its midst uninjured; and Jesus they sent down into the pit of the abode of the dead, and he ascended, and death had not dominion over him. Concerning Daniel they expected that when he had fallen into the pit he would not come up again; and concerning Jesus they said, "Since he has fallen, he shall not rise again."[11] From [harming] Daniel the mouths of the ravenous and destructive lions were closed; and from [harming] Jesus was closed the mouth of death, [though] ravenous and destructive of [living] forms. They sealed the pit of Daniel and guarded it with diligence; and they

[2]JCD 68. [3]ESOO 2:213. [4]JCD 68. [5]WGRW 7:167-69. [6]Heb 11:33-34. [7]NPNF 1 14:488*. [8]1 Pet 5:4. [9]Is 7:9 LXX. [10]NPNF 2 7:29-30*. [11]Ps 41:8 (40:9 LXX).

guarded the grave of Jesus with diligence, as they said, "Set guards to watch at the tomb."[12] When Daniel came up, his accusers were ashamed; and when Jesus rose, all they who had crucified him were ashamed. DEMONSTRATIONS 21.18.[13]

PUNISHMENT EQUAL TO OFFENSE. EPHREM THE SYRIAN: Since a simple punishment was not sufficient for those culprits, in order to balance the offense they had brought against a righteous man, after being condemned to the same punishment, they were thrown to the beasts together with their wives and children. COMMENTARY ON DANIEL 6.24.[14]

6:26 Fear Before the God of Daniel

FOUNDATION OF HOPE. CYPRIAN: The foundation and strength of hope and faith is fear. In Psalm 111: "The fear of the Lord is the beginning of wisdom."[15] Of the same thing in the Wisdom of Solomon,[16] ... in the Proverbs,[17] ... in Isaiah,[18] ... in Genesis,[19] ... and in Psalm 2,[20] ... Then Darius the king wrote, "To all peoples, tribes and languages that are in my kingdom, peace be to you from my face. I decree and ordain that all those who are in my kingdom shall fear and tremble before the Most High God whom Daniel serves." To QUIRINIUS: TESTIMONIES AGAINST THE JEWS 3.20.[21]

6:27 God Works Signs and Wonders

SIGNS PROCLAIM THE ONLY GOD. JEROME: The reason why signs are performed amid barbarian peoples through the agency of God's servants is that the worship and religion of the only God may be proclaimed. COMMENTARY ON DANIEL 6.25-27.[22]

6:28 The Reign of Darius

DANIEL TRANSFERRED TO MEDIA. JEROME: And so the statement that we read above at the end of the first vision, "And Daniel lived until the first year of King Cyrus," is not to be understood as defining the span of his life. In view of the fact that we read in the last vision, "In the third year of Cyrus, king of the Persians, a word was revealed to Daniel, whose surname was Belteshazzar"; this is what is meant, that up to the first year of King Cyrus, who destroyed the empire of the Chaldeans, Daniel continued in power in Chaldea, but afterwards he was transferred to Media by Darius. COMMENTARY ON DANIEL 6.28.[23]

---

[12]Mt 27:64. [13]NPNF 2 13:399*. [14]ESOO 2:213. [15]Ps 111:10 (110:10 LXX). [16]Sir 1:14. [17]Prov 28:14. [18]Is 66:2. [19]Gen 22:11-12. [20]Ps 2:11. [21]ANF 5:539-41*. [22]JCD 69. [23]JCD 69-70.

7:1-8 THE VISION OF THE FOUR BEASTS

[1]In the first year of Belshazzar king of Babylon, Daniel had a dream and visions of his head as he lay in his bed. Then he wrote down the dream, and told the sum of the matter. [2]Daniel said, "I saw in my vision by night, and behold, the four winds of heaven were stirring up the great sea. [3]And four great beasts came up out of the sea, different from one another. [4]The first was like a lion

and had eagles' wings. Then as I looked its wings were plucked off, and it was lifted up from the ground and made to stand upon two feet like a man; and the mind of a man was given to it. ⁵And behold, another beast, a second one, like a bear. It was raised up on one side; it had three ribs in its mouth between its teeth; and it was told, 'Arise, devour much flesh.' ⁶After this I looked, and lo, another, like a leopard, with four wings of a bird on its back; and the beast had four heads; and dominion was given to it. ⁷After this I saw in the night visions, and behold, a fourth beast, terrible and dreadful and exceedingly strong; and it had great iron teeth; it devoured and broke in pieces, and stamped the residue with its feet. It was different from all the beasts that were before it; and it had ten horns. ⁸I considered the horns, and behold, there came up among them another horn, a little one, before which three of the first horns were plucked up by the roots; and behold, in this horn were eyes like the eyes of a man, and a mouth speaking great things."

OVERVIEW: Daniel records his dream for posterity (JEROME). These visions, revealed by the Spirit, demonstrate that Daniel was a prophet not only to his contemporaries but also to future generations (HIPPOLYTUS). His vision of the four winds of heaven may represent angelic powers, while earth represents sin, and the four beasts are symbolic of the four kingdoms (JEROME, HIPPOLYTUS). There are two different streams of interpretation of the four kingdoms: the Syriac minority (EPHREM, ISHO'DAD) versus the rest who constitute the majority (HIPPOLYTUS, CYRIL OF JERUSALEM, CHRYSOSTOM, THEODORET, JEROME). All interpreters agree that the image of the lioness refers to the Babylonian Empire, but they diverge on which kingdoms are signified by the final three beasts. Hippolytus, Jerome, Chrysostom and Theodoret interpret the imagery as follows: the second beast (bear) refers to the Persian kingdom, the third beast (leopard) refers to the Macedonian kingdom, and the fourth beast refers to the Roman Empire. Ephrem and Isho'dad interpret the imagery in the following manner: the second beast refers to the Median kingdom, the third beast refers to the Persian kingdom, and the fourth beast refers to Macedonian kingdom. The ten horns refer to the ten kings up to Antiochus (JEROME). Among the ten horns appears a little one, which is the antichrist (HIPPOLYTUS). The little horn with human eyes is a man of sin in whom Satan resides

(JEROME). The fourth beast looks different from the others due to its horns, and the three horns represent Egypt, Libya and Ethiopia (HIPPOLYTUS). The antichrist is the persecutor of the Jews (EPHREM). Antiochus Epiphanes is the little horn (ISHO'DAD). David has prophesied about God's inheritance being defiled by the Gentiles (APHRAHAT).

7:1 Daniel's Dream and Visions

THE RECORD OF VISIONS PRESERVED FOR POSTERITY. JEROME: In the passages now before us, an account is given of various visions that were beheld on particular occasions and of which only the prophet was aware and which therefore lacked any importance as signs or revelations so far as the barbarian nations were concerned. But they were written down only so a record of the things beheld might be preserved for posterity. COMMENTARY ON DANIEL 7.1.[1]

DANIEL'S PROPHECY. THEODORET OF CYR: Up to these words the blessed Daniel has written his prophecy more in the style of a historian. First, remember at the beginning he related what happened to those captured in war, and he adds how God, the author of all, was greatly

---

[1]JCD 71.

concerned about these matters. Then he tells how Nebuchadnezzar paid the penalty for his cruelty and arrogance and then how Belshazzar suffered for his disrespectful use of the sacred vessels. Once the latter had been killed by a divine blow and his empire handed over to the Medes, Daniel went on to write those things that happened to himself and to Darius and explained how it was that Darius favored him, what sorts of plots Daniel had to endure at the hands of the generals and satraps, and how he was delivered from their hands by divine aid. Having expounded these things in a historian's fashion, now Daniel begins to expound those predictions that he had learned through revelations. First he sets forth the revelation of the four beasts, quite similar to the dream of Nebuchadnezzar. However, Daniel sees the fourfold content manifested in only one image, while Nebuchadnezzar saw four beasts ascending from the one sea. But lest anyone think that we are forced to say the same things again, let us turn to interpret the individual elements of the prophecy, where this truth will be openly demonstrated. COMMENTARY ON DANIEL 7.1.[2]

7:2 Four Winds of Heaven

ANGELIC POWERS. JEROME: The four winds of heaven I supposed to have been angelic powers to whom the principalities have been committed.[3] ... The sea signifies this world[4] and the present age, overwhelmed with salty and bitter waves, in accordance with the Lord's own interpretation of the dragnet cast into the sea.[5] COMMENTARY ON DANIEL 7.2-3.[6]

SUDDEN CHANGE. THEODORET OF CYR: For his part, Nebuchadnezzar sees the image, drawing a lesson in the futility of things of this life and the fact that they are appearances, as the divine apostle asserts, and not realities, there is nothing lasting or stable in them, everything fluid and failing and fading.[7] Daniel, [by contrast], is gazing at a sea, gaining a lesson in the haze of the present

life. After all, when a prisoner of war is compelled to see a foreign land, he fittingly learns to recognize the storms and tempests of life. And since the king too was haughty because of his silver, bronze and iron, he is given the mysteries concerning the kingdoms through a statue composed of the very same materials.[8] In this way he perceives the successions of kings and is admonished lest he be removed because of a kingdom liable to swift and sudden change. . . .

He calls life "the sea" since it has those countless and great storms; he calls the changes of regimes "winds," since they act against the very onslaught. For just as the streams rush to the north whenever the south wind blows and the wind is driven southward again when the north wind stirs up the sea, so when the Assyrians obtained dominion over the whole world, they drew all their conquered people to their land; but when the kingdom was handed over to the Persians, there was also a confluence of their subjects to the Persians. And when the Macedonians in turn obtained the scepter, all brought to them twice the usual tribute, except for those to whom they had been previously obedient. And when the Romans acquired command over all nations, everyone rushed to the west and thought nothing of the Macedonians. And the Macedonians themselves were counted now as one of the conquered nations. Quite appropriately then he compares the changes of the wind with the changes of regimes, since the winds drive sailors now this way, now that way. Therefore, he mentioned the four winds, since there were four successions of kingdoms. But he teaches us in what manner the beasts differ among themselves. COMMENTARY ON DANIEL 7.2-3.[9]

7:3 Four Great Beasts

FOUR KINGDOMS. JEROME: But as for the four

---

[2] PG 81:1412; cf. WGRW 7:173-74. [3] See Isho'dad, CSCO 328:112. [4] See Ephrem *Commentary on Daniel 7:2-3*, ESOO 2:213-14. [5] Mt 13:47-48. [6] JCD 71-72. [7] See 1 Cor 7:31. [8] Dan 2:31-45. [9] WGRW 7:175-77**.

beasts who came up out of the sea and were differentiated from one another, we may identify them from the angel's discourse. "These four great beasts," he says, "are four kingdoms that shall rise up from the earth." And as for the winds that strove in the great sea, they are called winds of heaven because each one of the angels does for his realm the duty entrusted to him. This too should be noted, that the fierceness and cruelty of the kingdoms concerned are indicated by the term "beasts." COMMENTARY ON DANIEL 7.2-3.[10]

TYPES AND IMAGES. HIPPOLYTUS: As various beasts then were shown to the blessed Daniel, and these were different from each other, we should understand that the truth of the narrative deals not with certain beasts but, under the type and image of different beasts, exhibits the kingdoms that have risen in this world in power over the race of humankind. For by the great sea he means the whole world. SCHOLIA ON DANIEL 7.3.[11]

FEARFUL KINGDOMS. THEODORET OF CYR: But the prophet, full of disdain for these various metals, sees "four beasts." From those four beasts he understands that those four formidable kingdoms, which will strike fear into all people, will at last have an end, but there will be only one kingdom that will remain for all time without any end, namely, the kingdom that God has prepared for his saints.[12] COMMENTARY ON DANIEL 7.2-3.[13]

7:4 The First Beast

NEBUCHADNEZZAR. HIPPOLYTUS: Now since these things, spoken as they are with a mystical meaning, may seem to some hard to understand, we shall keep back nothing fitted to impart an intelligent apprehension of them to those who are possessed of a sound mind. He said, then, that a "lioness came up from the sea," and by that he meant the kingdom of the Babylonians in the

world, which also was the head of gold on the image. In saying that it "had wings as of an eagle," he meant that Nebuchadnezzar the king was lifted up and was exalted against God. Then he says "the wings were plucked," that is to say, his glory was destroyed; for he was driven out of his kingdom. And the words "a man's heart was given to it, and it was made to stand on the feet as a man," refer to the fact that he repented and recognized himself to be only a man and gave the glory to God. ON THE ANTICHRIST 23.[14]

THE BABYLONIAN EMPIRE. JEROME: The kingdom of the Babylonians was not called a lion but a lioness,[15] on account of its brutality and cruelty, or else because of its luxurious, lust-serving manner of life. For writers on the natural history of beasts assert that lionesses are fiercer than lions, especially if they are nursing their cubs, and constantly are passionate in their desire for sexual relations. And as for the fact that she possessed eagle's wings, this indicates the pride of the all-powerful kingdom, the ruler of which declares in Isaiah, "Above the stars of heaven I will place my throne, and I shall be like unto the Most High."[16] Therefore he is told, "Though you are borne on high like an eagle, from there I will drag you down."[17] Moreover, just as the lion occupies kingly rank among beasts, so also the eagle among the birds. But it should also be said that the eagle enjoys a long span of life and that the kingdom of Assyrians had held sway for many generations. And as for the fact that the wings of the lioness or eagle were torn away, this signifies the other kingdoms over which it had ruled and soared about in the world. COMMENTARY ON DANIEL 7.4.[18]

THE BOUNDARIES OF NATURE. THEODORET OF CYR: This passage Daniel places the strongest of the beasts in the first kingdom; he does not imply that the first beast possessed greater

---

[10]JCD 72. [11]ANF 5:188. [12]See Dan 2:44. [13]PG 81:1413. [14]ANF 5:209. [15]LXX variant. [16]Is 14:13. [17]Obad 4. [18]JCD 72-73.

might but only that it was nobler. Nonetheless, he saw "those wings plucked out," that is, abandoned by all the people who had been subjected to it and deprived of its earlier power. He says, "and it was removed from the earth," that is, it ceased to reign. "And it stood on the feet of a man," that is, it turned out to be equal to those who had been subjected to it. "And the heart of a man was given to it." Experience teaches us to think about human matters, and it teaches us not to go beyond the boundaries of nature with the thoughts of our minds. Because they had been afflicted with the disease of haughtiness and boundless arrogance when they had held the helm of state, Isaiah said, "God will stir up the prince of the Assyrians against their great mind."[19] Experience rightly teaches them to think about human matters, when they see that fortunes change and that happiness is slippery and transient. They will come to learn who they are and so acquire a human heart. Thus Daniel speaks about the things that pertain to the first beast. COMMENTARY ON DANIEL 7.4.[20]

THE EAGLE REPRESENTS THE BABYLONIANS. EPHREM THE SYRIAN: This beast obviously represents the kingdom of the Babylonians. The present vision of Daniel perfectly fits in with the already mentioned dream of Nebuchadnezzar, who saw a statue, and it forms a single and same prophecy with it. Indeed, as the Babylonian kingdom, in that dream, was compared with gold, which is the noblest among metals, here it is described as a lion, which is the strongest of all beasts, and an eagle, which is of the highest perniciousness among birds. COMMENTARY ON DANIEL 7.4.[21]

7:5 A Bear

THE PERSIAN KINGDOM. JEROME: The second beast resembling a bear is the same as that of which we read in the vision of the statue, "His chest and arms were of silver."[22] In the former case the comparison was based on the hardness

of the metal, in this case on the ferocity of the bear. For the Persian kingdom followed a rigorous and frugal manner of life after the manner of the Spartans, and that too to such an extent that they used to use salt and nasturtium cress in their relish.[23] COMMENTARY ON DANIEL 7.5.[24]

CRUELTY. THEODORET OF CYR: Here he indicates the Persian kingdom, which he states to have been like a bear because of the cruelty and savageness of the punishments it meted out. For the Persians were the cruelest of all the barbarians when it came to punishing. They would rip out the very hearts of offenders, or they would contrive long tortures in which they would sever the guilty limb by limb. They were always inflicting a harsh death on whomever they punished. COMMENTARY ON DANIEL 7.5.[25]

THE SYMBOLS OF THE KINGDOM OF DARIUS. EPHREM THE SYRIAN: These are the symbols of the kingdom of Darius, king of the Medes. As in the statue of Nebuchadnezzar the Mede empire had been foreshadowed under the aspect of silver, which is a viler metal than gold, so in this dream it is indicated by the image of the bear, which is less agile than the lion. In addition he says that "the beast was raised up on one side," because Darius received a kingdom that was confined within the limits of his power and was never extended to that greatness, which the previous kingdom of Nebuchadnezzar had reached by including all the surrounding regions. COMMENTARY ON DANIEL 7.5.[26]

THREE NATIONS. HIPPOLYTUS: The three nations he calls three ribs. The meaning, therefore, is this: that beast had the dominion, and these others under it were the Medes, Assyrians and Babylonians. SCHOLIA ON DANIEL 7.5.[27]

---

[19]Is 10:12. [20]PG 81:1413-16. [21]ESOO 2:214. [22]Dan 2:32. [23]Jerome cites "The Education or Training" of Cyrus as the factual basis for this comment. [24]JCD 73-74. [25]PG 81:1416; cf. WGRW 7:179. [26]ESOO 2:214. [27]ANF 5:189.

KINGDOMS OF BABYLONIANS, MEDES AND PERSIANS.

JEROME: But as for the three rows or ranks that were in his mouth and between his teeth, one authority has interpreted this to mean that allusion was made to the fact that the Persian kingdom was divided up among three princes, just as we read in the sections dealing with Belshazzar and with Darius that there were three princes who were in charge of the 120 satraps. . . . Therefore the three rows in the mouth of the Persian kingdom of the Babylonians, the Medes and the Persians, all of which were reduced to a single realm. COMMENTARY ON DANIEL 7.5.[28]

THE EAST, THE NORTH AND THE SOUTH.

THEODORET OF CYR: The Persians ruled three parts of the world: the east, the north and the south. Cyrus . . . brought into submission all the east, as far as the Hellespont. His son subdued Egypt and made the Ethiopians subject to him. Darius[29] . . . acquired the realm of the nomadic Scythians, to whom it had been destined to inhabit the northern realms. And Xerxes the son of Darius tried to join Europe under his rule. But he was defeated by the Athenians in a naval battle and had to return home in shame. He realized that the defeat had been caused by his insatiable greed. Therefore Daniel says, "Three wings were in its mouth." Some manuscripts read "ribs," but it really does not make any difference. Whether three ribs or three wings are placed in its mouth, it teaches that the Persian Empire harvested the fruits of three parts of the world and took tribute from everywhere. And he rightly stated "in its mouth" to show the tribute that would be paid by all to it. COMMENTARY ON DANIEL 7.5.[30]

AHASUERUS ORDERED THE KILLING OF THE JEWS.

JEROME: And as for the information, "devour flesh in abundance," this refers to the time when in the reign of the Ahasuerus, whom the Septuagint calls Artaxerxes, the order was given, at the suggestion of Haman the Agagite, that all the Jews be slaughtered on a single day.[31]

And very properly, instead of saying, "He was devouring them" the account specifies, "Thus they spoke to him." This shows that the matter was only attempted and was by no means ever carried out. COMMENTARY ON DANIEL 7.5.[32]

7:6 The Third Beast

THE MACEDONIANS.

HIPPOLYTUS: In mentioning the leopard, he means the kingdom of the Greeks, over whom Alexander of Macedon was king. And he likened them to a leopard, because they were quick and inventive in thought and bitter in heart, just as that animal is many-colored in appearance and quick in wounding and in drinking human blood. SCHOLIA ON DANIEL 7.6.[33]

THE BRONZE OF THE STATUE AND THE IMAGE OF THE LEOPARD.

EPHREM THE SYRIAN: These words concern the kingdom of the Persians. Indeed, what in the statue of Nebuchadnezzar had been indicated under the aspect of bronze, a very hard metal, here is seen under the image of the leopard, an extremely agile and harmful beast. [The beast] is also provided with four wings and four heads. This is because it brought its dominion to the four winds of heaven. "And dominion was given to it": this is a reference to the multitude of peoples to be submitted. This passage must be compared with the prophecy of Isaiah: "He will strip kings of their robes, etc."[34] In that same prophet we can read these words said about Cyrus to Cyrus by God. COMMENTARY ON DANIEL 7.6.[35]

THE SWIFTNESS OF ALEXANDER'S VICTORIES.

JEROME: "And it had four wings." There was never, after all, any victory won more quickly than Alexander's, for he traversed all the way from Illyricum and the Adriatic Sea to the Indian

---

[28]JCD 74. [29]The son of Hystaspes. [30]PG 81:1416-17; WGRW 7:179-81. [31]Esther 3. [32]JCD 74-75. [33]ANF 5:189*. [34]Is 45:1. [35]ESOO 2:214.

Ocean and the Ganges River, not merely fighting battles but winning decisive victories; and in six years he subjugated to his rule a portion of Europe and all of Asia. COMMENTARY ON DANIEL 7.6.[36]

FOUR HEADS AS FOUR DIVIDED KINGDOMS AFTER ALEXANDER. THEODORET OF CYR: The "four heads" refer to the division of the empire that took place after Alexander. Four kings were established instead of one. The rulership of Egypt was entrusted to Ptolemy, son of Lagos; the realm of the Orient was granted to Seleucus; Antigonus acquired Asia; and Antipater Macedonia (although some historians say that Alexander's brother, Philip, also known as Aridaeus) acquired Macedonia. The "four heads" then allude to the four kingdoms that arose after Alexander, and the "four wings" allude to the principate of Alexander itself, who conquered the four parts of the world. Moreover, Daniel said that "power was given to the beast," because it had obtained those very things that earlier kings had not obtained. Nonetheless, also that kingdom, which was superior to all others, came to an end. COMMENTARY ON DANIEL 7.6.[37]

FOUR GENERALS. JEROME: And by the four heads reference is made to his generals . . . Ptolemy, Seleucus, Philip and Antigonus. "And power was given to it" shows that the empire did not result from Alexander's bravery but from the will of God. COMMENTARY ON DANIEL 7.6.[38]

7:7 The Fourth Beast

THE ROMAN EMPIRE. HIPPOLYTUS: That there has arisen no other kingdom after that of the Greeks except that which stands sovereign at present is manifest to all. This one has iron teeth, because it subdues and reduces all by its strength, just as iron does. And the rest it did tread with its feet, for there is no other kingdom remaining after this one, but from it will spring ten horns. SCHOLIA ON DANIEL 7.7.[39]

THE FOURTH EMPIRE. JEROME: The fourth empire is the Roman Empire, which now occupies the entire world. . . . The Hebrews believe that the beast that is here not named is the one spoken of in the Psalms: "A boar from the forest laid her waste, and a strange wild animal consumed her."[40] Instead of this the Hebrews read, "All the beasts of the field have torn her." While they are all included in the one empire of the Romans, we recognize at the same time those kingdoms that were previously separate. And as for the next statement . . . "devouring and crushing and pounding all the rest to pieces under his feet," this signifies that all nations have either been slain by the Romans or else have been subjected to tribute and servitude. COMMENTARY ON DANIEL 7.7.[41]

THE FOURTH BEAST. THEODORET OF CYR: He calls the Roman Empire "the fourth beast," but he does not give it a name because the Roman state was forged together from very many nations and so acquired mastery over the whole world. First it was governed by kings, then by the people, then by the aristocracy, and at last it returned to the first mode of government, monarchy. He states that this beast is "fearsome and very awe-inspiring," because this was the mightiest kingdom of all the other kingdoms. And in the statue that Nebuchadnezzar saw, he put down the fourth metal as iron. Just as iron crushes and breaks everything, so this empire would crush and break everything. COMMENTARY ON DANIEL 7.7.[42]

IRON TEETH. CHRYSOSTOM: Then he tells that the fourth beast would arrive in all sorts of different ways and nothing could be compared with it, it was so different. But at last it conquered all the other kingdoms. The other empires all got their strength from the speed by which they conquered, but this beast would have its strength in

---

[36]JCD 75. [37]PG 81:1417; WGRW 7:181, 183. [38]JCD 75. [39]ANF 5:189. [40]Ps 80:13 (79:14 LXX). [41]JCD 75-76. [42]PG 81:1420; cf. WGRW 7:183.

its teeth, made of iron. "And he trampled the rest with his feet." He understands many wars. Commentary on Daniel 7.[43]

The Children of Shem, the Children of Esau. Aphrahat: Now the fourth beast has swallowed up the third. And this third consists of the children of Japhet, and the fourth consists of the children of Shem, for they are the children of Esau. When Daniel saw the vision of the four beasts, he saw first the children of Ham, the seed of Nimrod, which the Babylonians are; and second, the Persians and Medes, who are the children of Japhet; and third, the Greeks, the brothers of the Medes; and fourth, the children of Shem, which the children of Esau are. For a confederacy was formed between the children of Japhet and the children of Shem. Then the government was taken away from the children of Japhet, the younger, and was given to Shem, the elder; and to this day it continues and will continue for ever. But when the time of the consummation of the dominion of the children of Shem shall have come, the ruler, who came forth from the children of Judah, shall receive the kingdom, when he shall come in his second advent. Demonstrations 5.10.[44]

Alexander. Ephrem the Syrian: This is Alexander, king of the Greeks, and the prophet says that he is similar to iron, which is the hardest among metals. He adds that the beast is armed with iron teeth, and with this symbol he indicates Alexander's powerful armies, which nearly subdued all kings. Then he adds that it was seen while devouring or trampling all that came its way, while destroying everything. With these words he predicted that Alexander would have attacked the vastness of almost all provinces, would have robbed their inhabitants and would have abandoned their fields and estates to his soldiers for pillage and destruction, so that it seemed that he had squeezed the entire world and all its precious things under a press and had offered all this to his soldiers in order that they

might trample it. Commentary on Daniel 7.7.[45]

Antichrist Shall Appear Suddenly in the Ten Horns. Hippolytus: As the prophet said already of the leopard, that the beast had four heads and that was fulfilled, and Alexander's kingdom was divided into four principalities, so also now we ought to look for the ten horns that are to spring from it, when the time of the beast shall be fulfilled, and the little horn, which is antichrist, shall appear suddenly in their midst, and righteousness shall be banished from the earth, and the whole world shall reach its consummation. So we ought not to anticipate the counsel of God but exercise patience and prayer that we do not fall on such times. We should not, however, refuse to believe that these things will come to pass. For if the things that the prophets predicted in former times have not been realized, then we need not look for these things. But if those former things did happen in their proper seasons, as was foretold, these things also shall certainly be fulfilled. Scholia on Daniel 7.7.[46]

Ten Succeeding Kings. Jerome: Porphyry[47] assigned the last two beasts, that of the Macedonians and that of the Romans, to the one realm of the Macedonians and divided them up as follows. He claimed that the leopard was Alexander himself and that the beast that was dissimilar to the others represented the four successors of Alexander, and then he enumerates ten kings up to the time of Antiochus, surnamed Epiphanes, and who were very cruel. And he did not assign the kings themselves to separate kingdoms, for example, Macedon, Syria, Asia or Egypt, but rather he made out the various kingdoms a single realm consisting of a series. This he did of course in order that the

---

[43]PG 56:230. [44]NPNF 2 13:356*. [45]ESOO 2:214-15. [46]ANF 5:189*. [47]Porphyry (c. 232-c. 305) was a prominent critic of Christians and Christian methods of biblical interpretation. In book 12 of his fifteen-volume work *Against the Christians*, Porphyry argues, on the basis of a historical interpretation of Daniel, that Daniel was not to be interpreted as a messianic prophecy.

words which were written: "a mouth uttering overweening boasts" might be considered as spoken about Antiochus instead of about antichrist. COMMENTARY ON DANIEL 7.7.[48]

7:8 Considering the Horns

THIS BEAST DIFFERS FROM THE OTHERS. HIPPOLYTUS: That is to say, I looked intently at the beast and was astonished at everything about it, but especially at the number of the horns. For the appearance of this beast differed from that of the other beasts in kind. SCHOLIA ON DANIEL 7.8.[49]

THE SON OF PERDITION. JEROME: We should therefore concur with the traditional interpretation of all the commentators of the Christian church, that at the end of the world, when the Roman Empire is to be destroyed, there shall be ten kings who will partition the Roman world among themselves. Then an insignificant eleventh king will arise, who will overcome three of the ten kings, that is, the king of Egypt, the king of [North] Africa and the king of Ethiopia, as we shall show more clearly in our later discussion. Then, after they have been slain, the seven other kings also will bow their necks to the victor. "And behold," he continues, "there were eyes similar to human eyes in that horn." Let us not follow the opinion of some commentators and suppose him to be either the devil or some demon, but rather, one of the human race, in whom Satan will wholly take up his residence in bodily form". . . and a mouth uttering overweening boasts. . . ."[50] For this is the man of sin, the son of perdition, and that also to such a degree that he dares to sit in the temple of God, making himself out to be like God. COMMENTARY ON DANIEL 7.8.[51]

THE ANTICHRIST ARISES AND PREVAILS. THEODORET OF CYR: Here he alludes to the antichrist, who arises among the ten horns, and he states that the antichrist will pluck out root and all three horns before himself. This means that he will overpower three kings of the ten who would reign at that time. And he calls it a "little" horn, as it was born from the little tribe of the Jews. However, he also calls it "eminent" since he would be noble. By its "eyes" he refers to its prudence and astuteness, by which he will deceive many. And yet he speaks of its "mouth speaking great things," which refers to its arrogance and haughtiness. COMMENTARY ON DANIEL 7.7-8.[52]

CONQUERED ONLY BY GOD. CHRYSOSTOM: Who are the ten kings? What is the little horn? I say that the antichrist will appear among a certain number of kings. "And in that horn were eyes like the eyes of a human and a mouth boasting great things." What greater boast can be said with that mouth than this thing that is said, "He will place himself above everything that is called God or divine, so much so that he will sit in the temple of God"?[53] Do not marvel if he has the eyes of a human, even if he speaks such things. He is a person. Why does the horn appear to be little and not big in the beginning? It will grow after this time and will rule certain kingdoms. Why? No kingdom will conquer this king, but God will abolish and destroy him. COMMENTARY ON DANIEL 7.[54]

ANTIOCHUS THE PERSECUTOR OF THE JEWS. EPHREM THE SYRIAN: This is Antiochus, the persecutor of the Jews, who sprang up in the midst of the ten kings and grew up. And this last horn, he says, "after three of the earlier horns were plucked by the roots, spoke arrogantly." Since there is here a hint of the fall of the previous three horns, it must be referred to the grandchildren and successors of the three past kings. Indeed the arrogant words, which this small horn spoke, are the insults and blasphemies thrown against God. COMMENTARY ON DANIEL 7.8.[55]

[48]JCD 76-77*. [49]ANF 5:189. [50]See 2 Thess 2. [51]JCD 77*. [52]PG 81:1420-21; WGRW 7:185. [53]2 Thess 2:4. [54]PG 56:230. [55]ESOO 2:215. See also Isho'dad Commentary on Daniel (CSCO 328:113) and Araphrat Demonstrations 5.20 (NPNF 2 13:359).

The Metaphors. Chrysostom: When scripture wishes to expound on the kingdoms, it uses the metaphor of beasts. A kingdom is an incorporeal object; therefore, some type of body has to be ascribed to it. And was it not fitting to describe kingdoms as beasts? Most certainly. For since the qualities of those kingdoms exist chiefly in those beasts, so he found them useful. He wished to show fierce arrogance and luxury, and he made use of a lioness. He wished to show slowness, and he made use of a bear. He wished to show speed and briskness and such as would overthrow all empires by its wars; thus he introduced a leopard. Look how earlier he had seen a beautiful sea, which represented the whole earth. For the world is filled with so many tumults and is stirred up in the same way that the sea is stirred up, although the sea is filled with fish, not humans. Christ even declares this to be the case, namely, that the present life is the sea, when he says, "The kingdom of heaven is like a dragnet thrown into the sea, which brings together fish of every kind."[56] "And behold," Daniel says, "the four winds of the heavens rushed on the great sea." He declares that those beasts then went forth from there, and so he shows the swiftness of divine providence. For when we talk about speed, we introduce the figure of the winds. Daniel says that the winds rushed on the sea and the beasts emerged from the sea, for our leaders partake of our nature. So he often calls a king "a lion," wishing to show its royal dignity and yet its feral nature. Or he does so because that wind is an easterly one, this wind is a northerly one, and yet another is a southerly one. It is as if someone had said, "He overturns the sea; the winds from the sky have stirred it up." Commentary on Daniel 7.7.[57]

---

[56]Mt 13:47. [57]PG 56:229.

7:9-12 THE DIVINE JUDGMENT

⁹As I looked,
>   thrones were placed
>   and one that was ancient of days took his seat;
>   his raiment was white as snow,
>   and the hair of his head like pure wool;
>   his throne was fiery flames,
>   its wheels were burning fire.
¹⁰A stream of fire issued
>   and came forth from before him;
>   a thousand thousands served him,
>   and ten thousand times ten thousand stood before him;
>   the court sat in judgment,
>   and the books were opened.
¹¹I looked then because of the sound of the great words which the horn was speaking. And as I

looked, the beast was slain, and its body destroyed and given over to be burned with fire. [12]*As for the rest of the beasts, their dominion was taken away, but their lives were prolonged for a season and a time.*

OVERVIEW: God, who is incorporeal and without form, makes use of visions whenever he wills (THEODORET); therefore, it is appropriate to interpret this vision symbolically (CHRYSOSTOM, THEODORET). The Ancient of Days is the Father (HIPPOLYTUS). The title "Ancient of Days" teaches the eternity of God (CASSIODORUS, THEODORET). The thrones set in place indicate divine judgment (JEROME, CHRYSOSTOM, EPHREM). The divine judgment is made when the Ancient of the Days takes his seat among the thrones (GREGORY OF NAZIANZUS, AMBROSE). His hair, described as pure wool, is a sign of forgiveness of sins (ORIGEN, CYRIL OF JERUSALEM). God's power is declared through the symbols of the throne, river and wheels (THEODORET). The phrase "thousands on thousands" was not employed to indicate a specific number of attendants but to indicate a multitude too great for human computation (JEROME). Those attending upon the Lord are true priests (GREGORY OF NYSSA) and empowered by the Holy Spirit to serve (BASIL). The books of judgment opened at the sitting of the court contain the memory of deeds of each person (THEODORET). God does not need books, but the prophet employs human imagery to illustrate the rigorous examination on which the judgments of God are based (ISHO'DAD).

The divine judgment descends for the humbling of the proud (JEROME). Each earthly kingdom is given a time to rule followed by the destruction it deserves (THEODORET). After the fourth empire is destroyed, it will not be replaced with an earthly empire but by the abode of the saints (JEROME).

7:9 The Ancient of Days

THE THRONES. CHRYSOSTOM: Are they not the thrones concerning which our Lord said, "You

will sit on twelve thrones"?[1] . . . Beloved, do not imagine God as having anything like a body, and do not think that God, who is boundless, can be confined to a throne. For if "in his hands are the boundaries of the earth," and if "he erected the mountains," and if "all the nations are reckoned as spittle in his sight" and if "all things are as dust before him,"[2] as he himself says, what place would be able to enclose him altogether at one time? What shall we say? The state of affairs cannot be exactly as it is described; God is not confined to a throne. If he was wearing clothing, how would fire not consume it? And why is that one called the Ancient of Days, when he existed before all ages? In what way can he even be said to be ancient, since the Scripture says, "You are always the same."[3] Why then is he called ancient, when it is written, "And your years will not come to an end?" And what would be the garment to be cast around a boundless and incorporeal being? For it says, "There is no end to his greatness."[4] And again, "If I ascend into heaven, you are there; if I descend into hell, you are there."[5] How then can he be restrained by human clothing and yet not consume it? But truly the prophet was able to see and read many other things of this type. How were his hairs not burned with fire? COMMENTARY ON DANIEL 7.[6]

GOD IS WITHOUT FORM. THEODORET OF CYR: It is fitting for us to know that God is incorporeal, simple and without form and that he admits of no circumscription. Although it pertains to his nature not to be able to be circumscribed, very often to help us he makes use of visions, whenever he wills. And one can see that he appears to Abraham in one way, to Moses in another and to

---

[1]Mt 19:28. [2]Is 40:12, 15. [3]Ps 102:27 (101:28 LXX). [4]Ps 145:3 (144:3 LXX). [5]Ps 139:8 (138:8 LXX). [6]PG 56:231-32.

Isaiah in yet another; likewise, he showed Ezekiel still a different appearance. Therefore, whenever you see the variety of revelation, do not think that God has many forms, but rather listen to God as he speaks through the prophet Hosea: "I multiplied the visions, and I was proclaimed in parables in the warnings of the prophets."[7] He said, "I adopted likenesses," not I appeared. He fashions in a vision however it suits him. So too blessed Ezekiel, when he had at length pondered on him whom he had seen to consist of gold and fire, added as he narrated the vision, "These things are an image of the glory of the Lord."[8] And he did not say that he had seen the Lord or even the Lord's glory but rather something resembling the glory of the Lord. COMMENTARY ON DANIEL 7.9-10.[9]

ALONE ON HIS THRONE. JEROME: And so the many thrones that Daniel saw seem to me to be what John called the twenty-four thrones. And the Ancient of Days is the one who, according to John, sits alone on his throne. Likewise the Son of man, who came to the Ancient of Days, is the same as he who, according to John, is called the lion of the tribe of Judah,[10] the root of David and the titles of that sort. I imagine that these thrones are the ones of which the apostle Paul says, "Whether thrones or dominions. . . ."[11] And in the Gospel we read, "You yourselves shall sit upon twelve thrones, judging the twelve tribes of Israel."[12] And God is called the one who sits and who is the Ancient of Days, in order that his character as eternal judge might be indicated. COMMENTARY ON DANIEL 7.9.[13]

LET HIM BE STANDING FOR YOU. AMBROSE: Let him then be standing for you that you may not be afraid of him sitting; for when sitting he judges, as Daniel says, "the thrones were placed, and the books were opened, and the Ancient of Days did sit." But in Psalm 81 [82] it is written, "God stood in the congregation of gods and decides among the gods."[14] So then when he sits he judges, when he stands he decides, and he judges concerning the imperfect but decides among the gods. Let him stand for you as a defender, as a good shepherd, lest the fierce wolves assault you. LETTER 63.6.[15]

NO HIDING FROM FINAL JUDGMENT. BASIL THE GREAT: Remember the vision of Daniel and how he brings the judgment before us . . . clearly disclosing in the hearing of all, angels and human beings, things good and evil, things done openly and in secret, deeds, words and thoughts all at once. What then must those people be who have lived wicked lives? Where then shall that soul hide that in the sight of all these spectators shall suddenly be revealed in its fullness of shame? With what kind of body shall it sustain those endless and unbearable pangs . . . without end? There is no release after death; no device, no means of coming forth from the chastisement of pain. LETTER 46.5.[16]

THE TITLE IS SYMBOLIC. CHRYSOSTOM: Let us strive with our minds to understand, beloved, for it is no small matter that we are discussing. He says, "Thrones were set, and the Ancient of Days was seated." Who is he? When you heard about a bear, you did not think about a bear; when you heard about a lioness, you did not perceive that animal but rather kingdoms; and when you heard about the sea, you did not perceive a sea but rather the world. Each time you thought of something else as being present in those images. That is also the case now. What is an Ancient of Days? He is similar to an old man. Now this old man takes shape for the purposes for which he appears. And here he shows that old men must be entrusted with rendering judgment. For just as when you hear the word *throne*, you do not understand it to mean a mere chair—for who would lay hold of such a base and vulgar meaning, when God seems fully armed here and bloodthirsty

---

[7]Hos 12:10. [8]Ezek 1:28. [9]PG 81:1421; WGRW 7:187. [10]Rev 5:5. [11]Col 1:16. [12]Mt 19:28. [13]JCD 78*. [14]Ps 82:1 (81:1 LXX). [15]NPNF 2 10:457*. [16]NPNF 2 8:151*.

there?—so he wishes this to mean that it is a time for judgment. "His clothing was white as snow." Why? It is not only a time of judgment but also retribution. All those must stand before him because "his judgment will go forth like the light."[17] COMMENTARY ON DANIEL 7.[18]

THE FATHER OF CHRIST. HIPPOLYTUS: The Ancient of Days is, for Daniel, nothing more than the Lord, God and Master of all, the Father of Christ himself. COMMENTARY ON DANIEL.[19]

"ANCIENT" MEANS HIGHEST GLORY. CHRYSOSTOM: And again, "The Ancient of Days sat," here again, taking the term "ancient" as among those laudatory expressions that confer highest glory. Elsewhere the Scripture takes the term "old" in the sense of blame; for seeing that the things are of various aspects as being composed of many parts, it uses the same words both in a good and an evil import, not according to the same shade of meaning. HOMILIES ON 1 CORINTHIANS 15.10.[20]

OLD MEANS ETERNAL. CASSIODORUS: By "things of old" he means things eternal, confined neither beginning nor end; as we read in Daniel: "Thrones were placed, and the Old of Days sat." EXPOSITIONS OF THE PSALM 138.5.[21]

THE HAIR IS WHITE LIKE WOOL. ORIGEN: Next they come to Libnah,[22] which means "whitewashing." I know that in some respects whitewashing has a pejorative connotation, as when we speak of a "whitewashed wall"[23] and "whitewashed tombs."[24] But this whitewashing is that concerning which the prophet says, "You will wash me, and I shall be whiter than snow."[25] And again Isaiah says, "Though your sins are like scarlet, I will whiten them like snow and will make them white like wool."[26] Again in the psalm, "They were whitened with snow in Zalmon."[27] And the hair of the Ancient of Days is said to be dazzling, white, that is, white like wool. So then, this whitewashing must be understood to come

from the radiance of the true light and to descend from the brightness of heavenly visions. HOMILIES ON NUMBERS 27.12.[28]

WOOL SYMBOLIZES THE FORGIVENESS OF SINS. CYRIL OF JERUSALEM: This is spoken anthropomorphically. And its spiritual sense is that he is the king of those who are not defiled with sins. For God says, "Your sins shall be as white as snow and shall be as wool."[29] Wool is the emblem of forgiveness of sins, as also of innocence. CATECHETICAL LECTURES 15.19-21.[30]

BLAMELESS AND HOLY. THEODORET OF CYR: Daniel contemplates his pure hair and his splendid garb, altogether blameless and holy. Daniel had already learned not only his divine nature but also those things that can be understood about it, namely, his righteousness, providence, care and judgment. When he sees "a horn using haughty words" and plotting countless treacheries against the worshipers of God, Daniel understands through the purity that glistens everywhere that God is not neglecting his people, but out of his ineffable governance of history he is permitting the horn to dare such things. COMMENTARY ON DANIEL 7.9-10.[31]

THE ANCIENT OF DAYS TAKES HIS SEAT. GREGORY OF NAZIANZUS: When the thrones are set and the Ancient of Days takes his seat, and the books are opened, and the fiery stream comes forth, and the light before him and the darkness prepared . . . they that have done good shall go into the resurrection of life, now hid in Christ and to be manifested hereafter with him, and they that have done evil, into the resurrection of judgment, to which they who have not believed have been condemned already by the word that judges them. Some will be welcomed by the

---

[17]Hos 6:5. [18]PG 56:231. [19]JECS 7 1:141; GCS 1:212. [20]NPNF 1 12:87. [21]ACW 53:374. [22]Num 33:20. [23]Acts 23:3. [24]Mt 23:27. [25]Ps 51:7 (50:9 LXX). [26]Is 1:18. [27]Ps 68:14 (67:15 LXX). [28]OSW 263. [29]Is 1:18. [30]LCC 4:162-63*. [31]PG 81:1424; cf. WGRW 7:187.

unspeakable light and the vision of the holy and royal Trinity, which now shines on them with greater brilliancy and purity and unites itself wholly to the whole soul, in which solely and beyond all else I take it that the kingdom of heaven consists. The others, among other torments, but above and before them all must endure the being outcast from God and the shame of conscience that has no limit. ON HIS FATHER'S SILENCE, ORATION 16.9.[32]

THE VISION REVEALS GOD'S NATURE. THEODORET OF CYR: Through the throne, wheels and river God's nature is revealed as secure and liable to no reproach; and through the word *ancient* his eternity, wisdom and clemency is told. COMMENTARY ON DANIEL 7.10.[33]

7:10 A Stream of Fire

GOD IS LIKE A STREAM OF FIRE. ORIGEN: But as it is in the mockery that Celsus says we speak of "God coming down like a torturer bearing fire" and thus compels us unseasonably to investigate words of deeper meaning, we shall make a few remarks, sufficient to enable our hearers to form an idea of the defense that disposes of the ridicule of Celsus against us, and then we shall turn to what follows. The divine word says that our God is "a consuming fire" and that "he draws rivers of fire before him"; no, that he even enters in as "a refiner's fire and as a fuller's herb,"[34] to purify his own people. But when he is said to be a "consuming fire," we inquire what are the things that are appropriate to be consumed by God. And we assert that they are wickedness and the works that result from it and that, being figuratively called "wood, hay, stubble,"[35] God consumes as a fire. The wicked person, accordingly, is said to build up on the previously laid foundation of reason, "wood and hay and stubble." . . . And, in like manner, "rivers of fire" are said to be before God, who will thoroughly cleanse away the evil that is intermingled throughout the whole soul. AGAINST CELSUS 4.13.[36]

A RIVER OF FIRE WINDS BEFORE HIS FACE. CHRYSOSTOM: He who is now despised, the same will then be our judge; think ever on him and the river of fire: "For a river of fire" we read, "winds before his face"; for it is impossible for one who has been delivered over by him to the fire to expect any end of his punishment. But the unseemly pleasures of this life do not differ from shadows and dreams; for before the deed of sin is completed, the conditions of pleasure are extinguished, and the punishments for these have no limit. And the sweetness lasts for a little while, but the pain is everlasting. LETTER TO THE FALLEN THEODORE 2.3.[37]

7:10 A Thousand Thousands

THE GREAT NUMBER OF THE SERVANTS OF GOD. JEROME: This was not intended to be a specific number for the servants of God but only indicates a multitude too great for human computation. COMMENTARY ON DANIEL 7.9.[38]

THEY ARE ALL MINISTERING SPIRITS. ORIGEN: And to him to whom we offer firstfruits we also send up our prayers, "having a great high priest who has passed into the heavens, Jesus the Son of God," and "we hold fast this profession" as long as we live; for we find God and his only-begotten Son, manifested to us in Jesus, to be gracious and kind to us. And if we would wish to have besides a great number of beings who shall ever prove friendly to us, we are taught that "thousand thousands stood before him, and ten thousand times ten thousand ministered to him." And these, regarding all as their relations and friends who imitate their piety toward God and in prayer call on him with sincerity, work along with them for their salvation, appear to them, deem it their office and duty to attend to them, and as if by common agreement they visit with all manner of kindness and deliverance those who

---

[32]NPNF 2 7:250*. [33]PG 81:1424; cf. WGRW 7:187. [34]Mal 3:2. [35]1 Cor 3:12. [36]ANF 4:502*. [37]NPNF 1 9:114*. [38]JCD 79.

pray to God, to whom they themselves also pray. "For they are all ministering spirits, sent forth to minister for those who shall be heirs of salvation."[39] AGAINST CELSUS 8.34.[40]

A THOUSAND THOUSANDS STOOD BEFORE HIM. GREGORY OF NYSSA: If this all seems little in your eyes, to be crucified with Christ, to present yourself a sacrifice to God, to become a priest to the most high God, to make yourself worthy of the vision of the Almighty, what higher blessings than these can we imagine for you, if indeed you make light of the consequences of these as well? And the consequence of being crucified with Christ is that we shall live with him, and be glorified with him and reign with him; and the consequence of presenting ourselves to God is that we shall be changed from the rank of human nature and human dignity to that of angels; for so speaks Daniel, that "thousand thousands stood before him." He too who has taken his share in the true priesthood and placed himself beside the great high priest remains altogether himself a priest forever, prevented for eternity from remaining any more in death. ON VIRGINITY 24.[41]

GLORIOUS HARMONY OF THE HIGHEST HEAVENS. BASIL THE GREAT: Do "thousand thousand" of angels stand before him, and "ten thousand times ten thousand" ministering spirits? They are blamelessly doing their proper work by the power of the Spirit. All the glorious and unspeakable harmony of the highest heavens in the service of God and in the mutual concord of the celestial powers can therefore be preserved only by the direction of the gradually perfected by increase and advance, but they are perfect from the moment of the creation, there is in creation the presence of the Holy Spirit, who confers on them the grace that flows from him for the completion and perfection of their essence. ON THE HOLY SPIRIT 16.38.[42]

TEN THOUSAND TIMES TEN THOUSAND. CYRIL OF JERUSALEM: "The Son of man," it is

written, "shall come in his glory, and all the angels with him."[43] Note, my friend, before how many you will come to be judged. Every race of humankind will be present then. Think therefore of the numbers of imperial citizens. Think what the barbarian nations amount to. Take the numbers now living and those who have died in the last hundred years. Think how many have been buried in the last thousand years. Think of all the human race from Adam till today. It is a vast multitude, and yet by comparison it is nothing much, for the angels are more numerous. They are the "ninety and nine" sheep,[44] while the human race is the lone one. For we must suppose that the multitude of inhabitants is everywhere in proportion to the space. Now the whole earth's surface is like a point when compared with the heaven above it. And the heaven that wraps the earth around is inhabited by a multitude proportioned to its extent. And the heavens of heavens contain a multitude beyond computation. Scripture says, "Thousand thousands ministered to him, and ten thousand times ten thousand stood before him." That does not mean that those who were all there were but that the prophet could find no expression to convey more than that. At that day of judgment there will be present God the Father of all, with Jesus Christ enthroned beside him, and the Holy Spirit present with them. The angel trumpet will summon us before them, bringing our deeds with us. CATECHETICAL LECTURES 15.24.[45]

TWO BOOKS. JEROME: The consciences of humankind and the deeds of individuals that partake of either character, whether good or bad, are disclosed to all. One of the books is the good book of which we often read, namely, the book of the living. The other is the evil book that is held in the hand of the accuser, who is the fiend and avenger of whom we read in Revelation: "The accuser of

---

[39]Heb 1:14. [40]ANF 4:652*. [41]NPNF 2 5:371. [42]NPNF 2 8:24-25. [43]Mt 25:31. [44]Mt 18:12. [45]LCC 4:163-65*.

our brothers."[46] This is the earthly book of which the prophet says, "Let them be written on earth."[47] Commentary on Daniel 7.10.[48]

God Judges with Equity. Isho'dad of Merv: "The books were opened," not because God needs books, but the prophet is speaking in human terms, according to the style of Scriptures, which speak materially with material beings; in addition, he says that in order to show the rigorous examination, on which the judgments of God are based, that [God] judges with equity and forbearance. Commentary on Daniel 7.10.[49]

Memory of Deeds. Theodoret of Cyr: That is to say, he affixed the rest of the time to be a time of judgment, and he unfolded the memory of all the deeds done by each and every person. He calls the memory about each person "the books." But if someone thinks that this refers to the promise of the Lord made to his apostles, "Twelve thrones will be placed, and you will sit down and judge the twelve tribes of Israel,"[50] he would not be far off the mark, inasmuch as the promise of the truth has no part in a lie. Commentary on Daniel 7.9-10.[51]

7:11 The Horn and the Beast

Arrogant Words. Jerome: The judgment of God descends for the humbling of pride. Hence the Roman Empire also will be destroyed, because [it is] the horn [that] was uttering the lofty words. Commentary on Daniel 7.11.[52]

All the Kingdoms Are to Be Destroyed. Jerome: In the one empire of the Romans, all the kingdoms at once are to be destroyed, because of the blasphemy of the antichrist. And the [succeeding] empire shall not be an earthly empire at all, but it is simply the abode of the saints, which is spoken of here, and the advent of the conquering Son of God. Commentary on Daniel 7.11.[53]

The Fourth Beast Destroyed. Theodoret of Cyr: Because of the madness of that beast, he says that it was judged, and the fourth kingdom was destroyed, "and the body of the beast was given over for the fire to consume." We ought to take note that he did not simply say "the beast was handed over" but "the body of the beast" was handed over for the fire to consume. Since he portrays every kingdom through a beast, and in every kingdom some are pupils of godliness and others are servants of wickedness (the former being commonly called "spiritual," the latter "carnal," in accordance with the usage of the divine Scripture), he rightly said that the beast was not handed over to be burned but the body of the beast, that is, the cruder sorts of people and those who are fleshly and those who do not think spiritually at all. Commentary on Daniel 7.11.[54]

7:12 The Rest of the Beasts

The Beasts Punished. Theodoret of Cyr: The dominion of the other beasts had fallen, although they had spent a period of many years ruling; to each kingdom there was a certain definite time given to rule. When these things have taken place, since all the other kingdoms had been destroyed earlier, also those who were in the fourth kingdom were handed over to the punishment by fire, as they well deserved. Commentary on Daniel 7.12.[55]

Medes, Persians and Chaldeans. Ephrem the Syrian: This refers to the kingdoms of the Medes, Persians and Chaldeans. "But their lives were prolonged for a season and a time," that is, the kings of the nations mentioned above would have not been completely powerless. Commentary on Daniel 7.12.[56]

---

[46]Rev 12:10. [47]Jer 17:13. [48]JCD 79. [49]CSCO 328:113. [50]Mt 19:28. [51]PG 81:1424; cf. WGRW 7:187-89. [52]JCD 79. [53]JCD 80. [54]PG 81:1424. [55]PG 81:1425; cf. WGRW 7:189. [56]ESOO 2:215.

7:13-14 THE DIVINE JUDGMENT: THE SON OF MAN

¹³*I saw in the night visions,*
    and behold, with the clouds of heaven
        there came one like a son of man,
    and he came to the Ancient of Days
        and was presented before him.
¹⁴*And to him was given dominion*
    and glory and kingdom,

that all peoples, nations, and languages
    should serve him;
his dominion is an everlasting dominion,
    which shall not pass away,
and his kingdom one
    that shall not be destroyed.

OVERVIEW: There are two advents of the Lord our Savior (HIPPOLYTUS, TERTULLIAN). Christ's kingdom has no end, and his dominion has eternity (RUFINUS, HILARY OF POITIERS). His second advent is full of glory (CYRIL OF JERUSALEM, JUSTIN MARTYR, THEODORET). The Son of man is the Son of God taking on human flesh (JEROME), who was in heaven from the beginning (EUSEBIUS, HIPPOLYTUS), coming to judge and forgive sins (TERTULLIAN) with the clouds, where God manifests himself (CHRYSOSTOM). The prophecy is about the Lord and fulfilled in him (EPHREM), who is called the Son of man because he was naturally begotten as Son (CYRIL OF JERUSALEM), brought forth by God (JUSTIN MARTYR), as described in the apostle's statement (JEROME). The Ancient of Days does not become old by times and days, and his appearance is proof that the Father appeared to the prophets (AUGUSTINE). The stone that destroys the iron legs and the Son of man are the same reference (HIPPOLYTUS). Though one like a son of man is said to be the Maccabees, in truth it refers to Christ (ISHO'DAD, JEROME). The Son is the first-begotten of God and a new Adam, numbered among the dead and overcoming death by death (HIPPOLYTUS). His kingdom lasts forever, and humankind in it is like angels (TERTULLIAN). The whole earth will worship him (CHRYSOSTOM).

THE FIRST AND SECOND ADVENT OF THE

LORD. HIPPOLYTUS: For as two advents of our Lord and Savior are indicated in the Scriptures, the one being his first advent in the flesh, which took place without honor by reason of his being made nothing, as Isaiah spoke of him previously, saying, "We saw him, and he had no form or beauty."[1] . . . But his second advent is announced as glorious, when he shall come from heaven with the host of angels and the glory of his Father, as the prophet said, "You shall see the King in glory,"[2] and, "I saw one like the Son of man coming with the clouds of heaven; and he came to the Ancient of Days" . . . and he was brought to him. And there were given him dominion and honor and glory. ON THE ANTICHRIST 44.[3]

THE SON OF MAN IN THE ETERNAL KINGDOM OF THE AGES. HILARY OF POITIERS: Glance over the whole course of time, and realize in what guise he appeared to Joshua the son of Nun, a prophet bearing his name, or to Isaiah, who relates that he saw him, as the gospel also bears witness, or to Ezekiel, who was admitted even to knowledge of the resurrection, or to Daniel, who confesses the Son of man in the eternal kingdom of the ages, or to all the rest to whom he presented himself in the form of various created beings, for the ways of God and for the works of

---

[1]Is 53:2. [2]See Is 33:17. [3]ANF 5:213*.

God, that is to say, to teach us to know God and to profit our eternal state. Why does this method, expressly designed for human salvation, bring about at the present time such an impious attack on his eternal birth? The creation, of which you speak, dates from the commencement of the ages; but his birth is without end and before the ages. Maintain this by all means: we are doing violence to words, if a prophet, or the Lord, or an apostle or any oracle whatever has described by the name of creation the birth of his eternal divinity. In all these manifestations God, who is a consuming fire, is present, as created, in such a manner that he could lay aside the created form by the same power by which he assumed it, being able to destroy again that which had come into existence merely that it might be looked on. ON THE TRINITY 12.47.[4]

CHRIST'S SECOND COMING. CYRIL OF JERUSALEM: What we proclaim is not one single coming of Christ but a second as well, much fairer than the first. For the first presented a demonstration of longsuffering, but the second wears the crown of the kingdom of God. Most things about our Lord Jesus Christ are twofold. His birth is twofold, once of God before the ages, and once of the Virgin in the end of the ages. Twice he comes down, once all unseen like dew on a fleece, and a second time still future and manifest. When first he came, he was swaddled in a manger. When next he comes, he will "clothe himself with light as with a garment."[5] At his first coming "he endured the cross, despising the shame";[6] at his second, he comes surrounded with glory and escorted by hosts of angels. We do not therefore simply rest on Christ's first coming, by itself, but let us look forward also to his second. . . . The Savior comes again, but not to be judged again, for he will pass judgment on those who passed judgment on him, and he who previously kept silence as they judged him now reminds those lawless people who did their outrageous deeds to him on the cross and says, "these things you have done, and I kept silent."[7]

He adapted himself when he came then and taught humankind by persuasion, but this time it is they who will be forced to bow to his rule, whether they will or not. CATECHETICAL LECTURES 15.1.[8]

HIS SECOND GLORIOUS ADVENT. JUSTIN MARTYR: If such power is shown to have accompanied and still now accompanies his passion, just think how great shall be his power at his glorious advent! For, as Daniel foretold, he shall come on the clouds as the Son of man, accompanied by his angels. DIALOGUE WITH TRYPHO 31.[9]

CHRIST'S SECOND COMING FORETOLD. THEODORET OF CYR: The blessed Daniel openly teaches what our Lord says in the Gospels: "You will see the Son of man coming on the clouds of heaven with his angels";[10] and the blessed apostle, "For the Lord will descend from heaven with a shout, with the voice of an archangel and with the trumpet of God, and the dead shall rise immortal. And we who remain alive will be snatched in the clouds to meet the Lord in the air. And so we will be with the Lord forever."[11] Daniel foretells the second coming of the Savior. He openly calls him the "Son of man" because of that nature that he has assumed. He says that he is "coming on the clouds," as he himself promised, so that he can show his power. He says that he "receives honor, dominion and the kingdom" from the Ancient of Days, although he is a human being. In Psalm 2 blessed David says this about the person of the Lord: "The Lord said to me, 'You are my Son; today I have begotten you. Ask me, and I will give you the nations as your inheritance and the ends of the earth as your possession.'"[12] Blessed Daniel states the very same thing: "All peoples, tribes and languages will serve him." And he shows that his reign will be without end: "His power will be an eternal

---

[4]NPNF 2 9:230-31*. [5]Ps 104:2 (103:2 LXX). [6]Heb 12:2. [7]Ps 50:21 (49:21 LXX). [8]LCC 4:147-48*. [9]FC 6:192-93*. [10]Mt 24:30. [11]1 Thess 4:16-17. [12]Ps 2:7-8.

power, which will not pass away, and his kingdom will not be destroyed." So he adds, when he writes down this revelation. COMMENTARY ON DANIEL 7.13-14.[13]

DANIEL'S VISION REFERS TO OUR SAVIOR.
EUSEBIUS OF CAESAREA: For instance, Daniel the prophet, under the influence of the divine Spirit, seeing his kingdom at the end of time, was inspired thus to describe the divine vision in language fitted to human comprehension. . . . It is clear that these words can refer to no one else than to our Savior, the Word who was in the beginning with God, and who was called the Son of man because of his final appearance in the flesh. ECCLESIASTICAL HISTORY 1.2.[14]

7:13 The Son of Man

INCARNATION. JUSTIN MARTYR: Does not Daniel allude to this very truth when he says that he who received the eternal kingdom is "as a Son of man"? The words "as a Son of man" indicate that he would become man and appear as such but that he would not be born of a human seed. Daniel states the same truth figuratively when he call Christ "a stone cut out without hands,"[15] for, to affirm that he was cut out without hands signifies that he was not the product of human activity but of the will of God, the Father of all, who brought him forth. DIALOGUE WITH TRYPHO 76.[16]

THE SON OF MAN AS THE ROCK NOW INCARNATE. JEROME: He who was described in the dream of Nebuchadnezzar as a rock cut without hands, which also grew to be a large mountain and smashed the earthenware, the iron, the bronze, the silver and the gold, is now introduced as the very person of the Son of man, so as to indicate in the case of the Son of God how he took on himself human flesh. [This is] according to the statement that we read in the Acts of the Apostles: "You men of Galilee, why do you stand gazing up toward heaven? This

Jesus who has been taken up from you into heaven shall so come in the same way as you have seen him going into heaven."[17] COMMENTARY ON DANIEL 7.13-14.[18]

THE WORD UNINCARNATE. HIPPOLYTUS: Who was in heaven but the Word unincarnate, who was dispatched to show that he was on earth and was also in heaven? For he was Word, he was Spirit, he was Power. The same took to himself the name common and current among humankind and was called from the beginning the Son of man on account of what he was to be, although he was not yet man, as Daniel testifies when he says, "I saw, and behold, one like the Son of man came on the clouds of heaven." Rightly, then, did he say that he who was in heaven was called from the beginning by this name, the Word of God, as being that from the beginning. AGAINST NOETUS 4.[19]

TO JUDGE. CYRIL OF JERUSALEM: He is called Christ, not for any unction from human hands but from the Father's, as having been anointed for eternal high priesthood on behalf of humanity. He is called the dead, not as having gone to "join the majority," like all souls in Hades, but as the one "free among the dead."[20] He is called Son of man, not as it is said of each one of us that we sprang from earth, but in the context of his "coming in the clouds of heaven" to judge both the living and the dead.[21] He is called Lord, not in the catachrestic[22] sense in which the title is given to people, but as possessing lordship by right of nature and forever. He is called Jesus because the name fits him, and he has that appellation in view of the saving medicine he brings. He is called Son, not meaning that God promoted him to that dignity but that he was naturally begotten as Son. CATECHETICAL LECTURES 10.4.[23]

---

[13]PG 81:1425. [14]NPNF 2 1:85*. [15]Dan 2:34. [16]FC 6:268*. [17]Acts 1:11. [18]JCD 80*. [19]ANF 5:225*. [20]Rev 1:18; Ps 88:5 (87:5 LXX). [21]Jn 5:25-27. [22]The misapplication of a word or phrase. [23]LCC 4:132-33*.

The Power of Judging. Tertullian: He revealed to Daniel himself expressly as "the Son of man, coming in the clouds of heaven" as a judge, as also the Scripture shows. What I have advanced might have been sufficient concerning the designation in the prophecy of the Son of man. But the Scripture offers me further information, even in the interpretation of the Lord himself. The Jews, who looked at him as merely man, were not yet sure that he was God also, as being likewise the Son of God. They rightly enough said that a man could not forgive sins, but God alone. Why did he not, following up their point, answer them, that he had power to remit sins, inasmuch as, when he mentioned the Son of man, he also named a human being? Because he wanted, by help of the very designation Son of man from the book of Daniel, so to induce them to reflect as to show them that he who remitted sins was God and man—that only the Son of man, indeed, in the prophecy of Daniel, who had obtained the power of judging, and thereby, of course, of forgiving sins likewise (for he who judges also absolves); so that, when once that objection of theirs was shattered to pieces by their recollection of Scripture, they might the more easily acknowledge him to be the Son of man himself by his actual forgiveness of sins. Against Marcion 4.10.[24]

The Father Giving, and the Son Receiving, an Eternal Kingdom. Augustine: I do not know in what manner these people understand that the Ancient of Days appeared to Daniel, from whom the Son of man, which he deigned to be for our sakes, is understood to have received the kingdom; namely, from him who says to him in the Psalms, "You are my son; this day have I begotten you; ask of me, and I shall give you the nations for your inheritance"[25] and who has "put all things under his feet."[26] If, however, both the Father giving the kingdom and the Son receiving it appeared to Daniel in bodily form, how can those people say that the Father never appeared to the prophets, and, therefore, that he only ought to be understood to be invisible whom no one has seen or can see? For Daniel has told us thus. . . . Behold the Father giving and the Son receiving an eternal kingdom; and both are in the sight of him who prophesies, in a visible form. On the Trinity 2.18.33.[27]

Equal with God. Jerome: All that is said here concerning his being brought before almighty God and receiving authority and honor and royal power is to be understood in the light of the apostle's statement: "Who, although he was in the form of God, thought it not robbery to be equal with God; but he emptied himself, taking the form of a servant, being made in the likeness of humankind, and was found in his condition to be as a man. He humbled himself, becoming obedient unto death, even to the death of the cross."[28] And if the sect of the Arians were willing to give heed to all Scripture with a reverent mind, they would never direct against the Son of God the denigration that he is not on an equality with God. Commentary on Daniel 7.13-14.[29]

7:14 His Dominion

Who Breaks the Little Horn to Pieces? Jerome: Let Porphyry answer the query of whom out of all humankind this language might apply to, or who this person might be who was so powerful as to break and smash to pieces the little horn, whom he interprets to be Antiochus? If he replies that the princes of Antiochus were defeated by Judas Maccabeus, then he must explain how Judas could be said to come with the clouds of heaven like to the Son of man and to be brought to the Ancient of Days, and how it could be said that authority and royal power were bestowed on him, and that all peoples and tribes and language groups served him and that his power is eternal and not terminated by any conclusion. Commentary on Daniel 7.13-14.[30]

---

[24]ANF 3:359*. [25]Ps 2:7-8. [26]Ps 8:6 (8:7 LXX). [27]NPNF 1 3:53*. [28]Phil 2:6-8. [29]JCD 80*. [30]JCD 80-81*.

THE FIRST-BEGOTTEN OF GOD. HIPPOLYTUS: The Father, having put all things in subjection to his own Son, both things in heaven and things on earth, showed him forth by all as the first-begotten of God, in order that, along with the Father, he might be approved the Son of God before angels and be manifested as the Lord also of angels. SCHOLIA ON DANIEL 7.14.[31]

THE WHOLE WORLD WILL SERVE HIM. CHRYSOSTOM: What, I ask, is more obvious than these words? "And all the peoples, tribes and tongues will serve him." See how he embraced every nation of the world. See how he took the judge's seat and power. Lest you should think that this is temporary, he says, "These things will not pass away, and his kingdom will not perish" but will stay and remain. But if you doubt, you can be persuaded by considering the matter. Do you see the equality of honor he has with the Father? Since the Son appeared after the Father, he says that the Son came with the clouds. But it is clear from the very clouds that he had existed before then, if indeed he came on them. "And honor was conferred on him," namely, the power that he had. "And the peoples, tribes and tongues will serve him." Indeed, he had dominion previously, but then he will take that dominion that he had obtained. For just as you understand the hair of the Father and the other aspects of the vision, so you must understand this part of the vision. When you hear "it was given" and other similar things, you will not think in human terms about the Son or think lowly of him. For though you saw an old man, you did not think that he was an old man, so also you must think about the other things. Do not seek crystal clarity among the prophets, where you will find instead shadows and riddles, just as you do not seek constant light in a thunderbolt. Instead, it suffices if light appears for just a bit. COMMENTARY ON DANIEL 7.7.[32]

---

[31]ANF 5:189. [32]PG 56:232-33.

7:15-18 THE INTERPRETATION OF THE VISION

[15]*As for me, Daniel, my spirit within me was anxious and the visions of my head alarmed me.* [16]*I approached one of those who stood there and asked him the truth concerning all this. So he told me, and made known to me the interpretation of the things.* [17]*"These four great beasts are four kings who shall arise out of the earth.* [18]*But the saints of the Most High shall receive the kingdom, and possess the kingdom for ever, for ever and ever."*

OVERVIEW: It was understandable that Daniel was shaken considering what he perceived (CHRYSOSTOM). The four beasts indicate four empires (EPHREM), which are earthly (JEROME). The multitudes of attendants stand in the heavenly court to assist in the divine judgment (THEODORET). The heavenly kingdom will begin when the four earthly empires run through their course (HIPPOLYTUS). The four kingdoms are counted to be nothing (THEODORET). Only the kingdom of the saints can remain forever (JEROME), which is the promise of eternal blessedness from God (AUGUSTINE). Daniel's prophecy of the kingdom of the saints is based on the merit of the New Testament (AUGUSTINE).

7:15 Daniel Alarmed by the Visions

VISIBLY SHAKEN. CHRYSOSTOM: Quite understandably, given what things he had seen. He is the first and only one to see the Father and the Son as in a vision. . . . When the advent of our Lord was soon drawing near, quite appropriately marvelous visions also appeared. COMMENTARY ON DANIEL 7.7.[1]

7:16 An Angel Interprets

ASSISTANTS. THEODORET OF CYR: Just as in human courts some of the subjects assist in carrying the dreadful judgment before themselves, while others come and go, bearing the responses of the tribunal, so in that most dreadful judgment Daniel sees ten thousand assistants and a thousand thousands to whom the task of service was given. When he had drawn near, he asked what was the interpretation of this revelation, and he was told the truth by one of those who stood by to assist. COMMENTARY ON DANIEL 7.16.[2]

7:17 Interpretation of the Four Beasts

THE SECRET MEANING DISCLOSED BY AN ANGEL. EPHREM THE SYRIAN: The secret meaning of that vision had been disclosed to him by the angel, and the expression "four beasts" indicated the four empires: the Babylonian, which flourished at that time, the Mede, the Persian and the Greek. But the power, he says, would have been transferred, at a certain time, from these kingdoms to the holy ones of the Most High because of the mystery hidden in many righteous people of his people and in the holy ones of the Most High, and he predicts that they would have reigned forever. COMMENTARY ON DANIEL 7.16.[3]

THE FOUR KINGDOMS ARE EARTHLY. JEROME: The four kingdoms of which we have spoken above were earthly in character. "For everything that is of the earth shall return to earth."[4] But the saints shall never possess an earthly kingdom, but only a heavenly. Away, then, with the fable about a millennium! COMMENTARY ON DANIEL 7.17-18.[5]

7:18 The Saints Will Receive the Kingdom

THE TIME TO BEGIN THE HEAVENLY KINGDOM. HIPPOLYTUS: For when the three beasts have finished their course and been removed and the one still stands in vigor—if this one, too, is removed, then finally earthly things [shall] end and heavenly things begin. The indissoluble and everlasting kingdom of the saints may be brought to view and the heavenly King manifested to all, no longer in figure, like one seen in vision or revealed in a pillar of cloud on the top of a mountain but amid the powers and armies of angels, as God incarnate and man, Son of God and Son of man—coming from heaven as the world's judge. SCHOLIA ON DANIEL 7.17.[6]

THE KINGDOMS COUNT FOR NOTHING. THEODORET OF CYR: These kingdoms will be wiped out and the true, eternal kingdom will be handed over to the saints of the Almighty. Thus, while waiting for that eternal kingdom, count the kingdoms of this present age to be as nothing, which will soon enough come to their end. COMMENTARY ON DANIEL 7.17-18.[7]

CAN AN EARTHLY KINGDOM REMAIN FOREVER? JEROME: "And possess the kingdom forever." . . . If this is taken to refer to the Maccabees, the advocate of this position should explain how the kingdom of the Maccabees is of a perpetual character. COMMENTARY ON DANIEL 7.17-18.[8]

---

[1]PG 56:233. [2]PG 81:1428; cf. WGRW 7:193. [3]ESOO 2:216. [4]Eccles 3:20. [5]JCD 81. [6]ANF 5:189*. [7]PG 81:1428; cf. WGRW 7:193. [8]JCD 81.

THE PROMISE OF ETERNAL BLESSEDNESS TO THE SAINTS. AUGUSTINE: Just as God's promise made to Abraham is already visibly fulfilled in Christ, so other promises made to the seed of Abraham will be no less certainly fulfilled. The promise to Abraham was that "all the nations of the earth will be blessed in your seed."[9] It is one of many such promises. Some of the prophecies concerning Abraham's seed say, "The dead shall rise again. . . . There shall be a new heaven and a new earth, and the former things will not be remembered, and they will not come on the earth, but they will be glad and rejoice forever in these things. For see, I shall make Jerusalem a rejoicing and my people joy. And I will rejoice in Jerusalem and joy in my people, and the voice of weeping will be heard in it no more."[10] Then there are the promises made to and through another prophet, saying, "At that time your people will be saved, everyone that will be found written in the book. And every one of those who sleep in the dust of the earth shall awaken, some to everlasting life and others to reproach and everlasting confusion. . . . But the saints of the most high God will take the kingdom, and they will possess the kingdom forever and ever . . . whose kingdom is an everlasting kingdom."[11] CITY OF GOD 22.3.[12]

THE VALUE OF THE NEW TESTAMENT FORETOLD. AUGUSTINE: But then there had not yet risen the prophet Daniel to say, "The saints shall receive the kingdom of the Most High." For by these words he foretold the merit not of the Old but of the New Testament. In the same manner did the same prophets foretell that Christ himself would come, in whose blood the New Testament was consecrated. PROCEEDINGS OF PELAGIANS 14.[13]

---

[9]Gen 22:18. [10]Is 26:19; 65:17-19. [11]See Dan 12:1-2; 7:27. [12]FC 24:420*. [13]NPNF 1 5:189.

7:19-28 THE FOURTH BEAST

[19]*Then I desired to know the truth concerning the fourth beast, which was different from all the rest, exceedingly terrible, with its teeth of iron and claws of bronze; and which devoured and broke in pieces, and stamped the residue with its feet;* [20]*and concerning the ten horns that were on its head, and the other horn which came up and before which three of them fell, the horn which had eyes and a mouth that spoke great things, and which seemed greater than its fellows.* [21]*As I looked, this horn made war with the saints, and prevailed over them,* [22]*until the Ancient of Days came, and judgment was given for the saints of the Most High, and the time came when the saints received the kingdom.*

[23]*Thus he said: 'As for the fourth beast,*
there shall be a fourth kingdom on earth,
which shall be different from all the
kingdoms,
and it shall devour the whole earth,
and trample it down, and break it
to pieces.
[24]*As for the ten horns,*

out of this kingdom
> ten kings shall arise,
> and another shall arise after them;
he shall be different from the former ones,
> and shall put down three kings.
²⁵He shall speak words against the
> Most High,
> and shall wear out the saints of the
> Most High,
> and shall think to change the times and
> the law;
and they shall be given into his hand
> for a time, two times, and half a time.
²⁶But the court shall sit in judgment,
> and his dominion shall be taken away,

to be consumed and destroyed to the end.
²⁷And the kingdom and the dominion
> and the greatness of the kingdoms under
> the whole heaven
> shall be given to the people of the saints
> of the Most High;
their kingdom shall be an everlasting
> kingdom,
> and all dominions shall serve and
> obey them.'
²⁸"Here is the end of the matter. As for me,
> Daniel, my thoughts greatly alarmed me,
> and my color changed; but I kept the
> matter in my mind.

OVERVIEW: The two different interpretation streams continue through this section. Most commentators—Hippolytus, Jerome, Cyril of Jerusalem, Theodoret—argue that the fourth kingdom refers to the Roman Empire. The little horn, the antichrist, will be a future king of the fourth kingdom. He will gain his position by subverting the three kings of Egypt, Libya and Ethiopia (HIPPOLYTUS) and by sorcery (CYRIL OF JERUSALEM). This king will ruthlessly attack the saints for three and a half years (JEROME, ISHO'DAD, THEODORET). After this period of tribulation, the holy people of God will receive the kingdom. This will be the end of all things, when all earthly kingdoms fail and the eternal kingdom is handed over to the people of God (THEODORET). Since the kingdom was not given to the saints after the death of Antiochus, the fourth kingdom cannot refer to the Macedonian kingdom. The minority stream—Ephrem, Isho'dad—interpret the fourth beast to signify the Macedonian kingdom. As a result the little horn signifies Antiochus. He will prevent the priests from performing their duties and abolish the traditional festivals (EPHREM). In his arrogance, Antiochus will command the people to abandon their

gods and worship him (ISHO'DAD). This period will last three and one half years (EPHREM, ISHO'DAD). Antiochus' unexpected demise is divine judgment (EPHREM, APHRAHAT). The kingdom, which will be given to the saints, will last forever (IGNATIUS), and the Ancient of Days will prevail (EZNIK).

7:19 The Truth About the Fourth Beast

THE FOURTH KINGDOM AND ANTICHRIST.
HIPPOLYTUS: It is to the fourth kingdom, of which we have already spoken, that he here refers: that kingdom, than which no greater kingdom of like nature has arisen on the earth, from which also ten horns are to spring and to be apportioned among ten crowns. And amid these another little horn shall rise, which is that of the antichrist. And it shall pluck by the roots the three others before it; that it is to say, he shall subvert the three kings of Egypt, Libya and Ethiopia, with the view of acquiring for himself universal dominion. And after conquering the remaining seven horns, he will at last begin, inflated by a strange and wicked spirit, to stir up war against the saints and to persecute all every-

where, with the aim of being glorified by all and being worshiped as God. SCHOLIA ON DANIEL 7.19.[1]

THE OTHER HORN IS ANTIOCHUS. EPHREM THE SYRIAN: "Then I desired to know the truth concerning the fourth beast and the other horn," which was seen while attacking and harshly afflicting the holy ones with his arms. This is Antiochus, who, as the angel reveals, would have made war and submitted the holy ones and the priests and the righteous ones. COMMENTARY ON DANIEL 7.19.[2]

CLAWS OF BRONZE. THEODORET OF CYR: Take note of the iron teeth and the bronze claws that are mentioned. The kingdom of the Romans took tribute from all nations; thus he says that it had iron teeth. And since many of those who had started out in the Macedonian kingdom were enlisted into its soldiery, and since claws serve the same function for a beast that soldiers do for an empire, he rightly speaks of Rome's bronze claws, just as he called the third kingdom a bronze kingdom. COMMENTARY ON DANIEL 7.19.[3]

7:20 The Ten Horns and the Other Horn

THE LITTLE HORN IS GREATER THAN THE OTHERS. THEODORET OF CYR: It is not surprising that he said previously that the horn was little, but here he says that its appearance "was greater than the rest." But one does need to pay close attention to the things that are being said. For when he saw the horn being born, he called it "little," since it arose from a little nation, that is, the nation of the Jews, and obtained meanwhile a small kingdom. However, after it had uprooted and pulled up three greater horns, he quite deservedly calls its appearance "greater than the rest." COMMENTARY ON DANIEL 7.20.[4]

7:21 The Tenth Horn Fighting Against the Saints

ANTICHRIST'S RUTHLESSNESS TOWARD THE SAINTS. CYRIL OF JERUSALEM: Paul says further, "who opposes and exalts himself above all that is called god or that is worshiped,"[5] that is, above every divinity, so that antichrist will be the bitter foe of the idolatrous cults. He continues, "so that he sits in the temple of God." What temple is that? Paul says it is the destroyed temple of the Jews. For God forbid that it should be that temple of God in which we are! Why should I suggest such a thing? Lest you should think me complacent about us Christians. For if antichrist will come to the Jews as messiah and seek worship from the Jews, he will show great zeal for the temple so as to deceive them the more, hinting that he is that man of the house of David destined to rebuild the temple erected by Solomon. Antichrist will come at such a time as there shall not be left of the temple of the Jews "one stone on another," to quote the sentence pronounced by the Savior. For it is not until all the stones are overthrown, whether by the decay of age or through being pulled down for building material or in consequence of this or that other happening, and I do not mean merely the stones of the outer walls but the floor of the inner temple where the cherubim were, that antichrist will come "with all signs and lying wonders" treating all the idols with disdain, at first adopting a show of being humane but later displaying his ruthlessness, especially toward the holy people of God. For it says, "I beheld, and the same horn made war with the saints," and in another Scripture it says, "And there shall be a time of trouble, such as never was since there was a nation even to that same time."[6] Antichrist is the terrible wild beast, the great dragon unconquerable by people and ready to swallow them up. CATECHETICAL LECTURES 15.15.[7]

7:22 The Ancient of Days Prevails

---

[1]ANF 5:190. [2]ESOO 2:216. [3]PG 81:1428; cf. WGRW 7:193-95. [4]PG 81:1429; cf. WGRW 7:195. [5]2 Thess 2:4. [6]Dan 12:1. [7]LCC 4:158-60*.

THE ANCIENT OF DAYS COMES. HIPPOLYTUS: At length the Judge of judges and the King of kings comes from heaven, who shall subvert the whole dominion and power of the adversary and shall consume all with the eternal fire of punishment. But to his servants, and prophets, and martyrs and to all who fear him, he will give an everlasting kingdom; that is, they shall possess the endless enjoyment of good. SCHOLIA ON DANIEL 7.22.[8]

GOD'S LOVE FOR HUMANITY REVEALED. EZNIK OF KOLB: And [God] himself would appear like an old man, sometimes like a youth, for one or another manifestation of providence, having taken the form for a cherished man.[9] And in this way by [God's] own appearances and those of his servants as well, he would make clear the excess of love that he possessed for humanity. ON GOD 118.[10]

7:23-24 The Fourth Kingdom and the Ten Horns

THE FOURTH KINGDOM AND ITS TEN HORNS. CYRIL OF JERUSALEM: These doctrines are not the fruit of ingenuity but are derived from the sacred Scriptures read in the church, particularly as gathered out of the prophecy of Daniel, in today's lection, and according to the interpretation given by the archangel Gabriel, who spoke as follows, "the fourth beast shall be the fourth kingdom on earth, which shall surpass all kingdoms." Ecclesiastical commentators have traditionally taken this kingdom to be the Roman Empire.... Further on Gabriel continues his interpreting and says, "And the ten horns out of this kingdom are ten kings that shall arise; and another king shall rise up after them, and he shall surpass in wickedness all who were before him" (not merely the ten kings, you note, but all kings that ever were) "and he shall subdue three kings" (clearly out of the ten that preceded him; and he had reduced three of the ten to powerlessness; it is equally clear that he will reign as the eighth king) "and he will

speak great words against the Most High." Antichrist is a blasphemer and flouter of all law. He will not succeed to the empire but will usurp it by means of sorcery. CATECHETICAL LECTURES 15.13.[11]

PARABLE AND EXPERIENCE. THEODORET OF CYR: These things were once taught people through riddles, but we ourselves have learned these very things by experience. We see the fulfillment of the prophecy; we behold daily that tributes are exacted, poverty oppresses many people, and other such things happen. COMMENTARY ON DANIEL 7.23.[12]

7:25 He Shall Speak Words Against the Most High

CHANGING THE WAY OF LIFE. THEODORET OF CYR: And he will think that he will be able to overturn completely their godliness, which will be flourishing at that time. Daniel alludes to this when he says, "He will change the times and the law," that is, the way of life prevailing at the time. Then he adds, "And it will be given over to his hand." That is, divine providence will permit these things. And he goes on to show the time of the deformity caused by those evils: "The poor will certainly not be handed over to oblivion forever, and the patience of the poor will not perish forever."[13] COMMENTARY ON DANIEL 7.25.[14]

THE ARROGANCE OF THE ANTICHRIST. JEROME: The antichrist will wage war against the saints and will overcome them; and he shall exalt himself to such a height of arrogance as to attempt changing the very laws of God and the sacred rites as well. He will also lift himself up against all that is called God, subjecting all religion to his own authority. COMMENTARY ON DANIEL 7.25.[15]

---

[8]ANF 5:190. [9]See Dan 9:23; 10:11. [10]EKOG 89-90*. [11]LCC 4:157-58. [12]PG 81:1429; cf. WGRW 7:195. [13]Ps 9:18 (9:19 LXX). [14]PG 81:1432; cf. WGRW 7:199-201. [15]JCD 81.

HE WILL WEAR OUT THE HOLY ONES.
EPHREM THE SYRIAN: He will prevent the priests from performing their duties and holy service. "And [he] shall attempt to change the sacred seasons and the law," which means he shall attempt to delete the holy laws of God and to abolish the traditional festivals and Neomenias.[16] COMMENTARY ON DANIEL 7.25.[17]

TIME OF THE TRIBULATION OF THE SAINTS.
JEROME: "Time" is equivalent to "year." The word *times*, according to the idiom of the Hebrews (who also possess the dual number), represents "two years." The half a year signifies "six months." During this period the saints are to be given over to the power of the antichrist. . . . In the final vision we shall assert the inappropriateness of this period to Antiochus. COMMENTARY ON DANIEL 7.25.[18]

7:26 The Heavenly Court Set Up for Judgment

ANTIOCHUS WILL BE PUNISHED AND DESTROYED. EPHREM THE SYRIAN: "Then the court shall sit in judgment" in order to revenge the tribulations of the holy ones and of the righteous ones, who preserved the law of the Most High, and in order to punish and destroy Antiochus, the little horn, by whom the Zealots of the house of Jacob had been afflicted and vexed. And that accursed man died of an immediate death, whereas those, who were righteous, received an everlasting power and empire. COMMENTARY ON DANIEL 7.26.[19]

THE JUDGMENT OF ANTIOCHUS. APHRAHAT: For the judgment came on Antiochus, a judgment from heaven; and he became sick with a grievous and evil sickness, and on account of the smell of him as he rotted, no one could approach him, for worms were crawling and falling from him and eating his flesh because he oppressed the "worm Jacob."[20] And his flesh rotted in his lifetime, because he caused the dead bodies of the sons of Jerusalem to rot and they were not buried. And he became defiled in his own eyes, because he had defiled the sanctuary of God. And he prayed and was not heard,[21] because he did not hearken to the groanings of the righteous whom he killed. For he wrote a letter and sent it to the Jews and called them "my friends," but God had not mercy on him. He died in his torment. DEMONSTRATIONS 5.20.[22]

PAUL ALSO REFERS TO THE JUDGMENT. THEODORET OF CYR: The blessed Paul also teaches more clearly to . . . the Thessalonians, and through them he teaches all lovers of godliness. He says that we should not think that the enemy of truth will appear now, for first the error of the idols, which now holds people in check, must be wiped out and the preaching of the gospel disseminated, then, and only then, will the lawless person be revealed . . . and overthrown.[23] COMMENTARY ON DANIEL 7.26.[24]

7:27 The Kingdom of the Saints

AN EVERLASTING KINGDOM. CYRIL OF JERUSALEM: Take, also, another like expression. "For until this day . . . when Moses is read, the veil is on their hearts."[25] Does "until this day" mean "up to the time that Paul wrote the words and no longer"? Does it not mean until this present day and indeed to the very end? And if Paul should say, "For we come as far as you also in preaching the gospel of Christ, having hope, when your faith is increased, to preach the gospel in the regions beyond you,"[26] you can see clearly that the phrase "as far as" sets no limit but indicates what lies beyond. With what meaning, therefore, ought you to recall the words "till he has put all enemies"? Just the same as in another saying of Paul, "But exhort each other daily, while it is called today,"[27] this clearly means

---

[16]Feasts of the New Moon. [17]ESOO 2:216; cf. CSCO 328:114. [18]JCD 81-82. [19]ESOO 2:216. [20]Is 41:14. [21]2 Macc 9:13-28. [22]NPNF 2 13:359*. [23]2 Thess 2:8. [24]PG 81:1432-33; cf. WGRW 199. [25]2 Cor 3:14-15. [26]2 Cor 10:14-16. [27]Heb 3:13.

for all time. For as we must not talk of a beginning of the days of Christ, so never suffer anyone to speak of an end of his kingdom. For Scripture says, "his kingdom is an everlasting kingdom." CATE-CHETICAL LECTURES 15.32.[28]

NOT APPLICABLE TO MACCABEAN SUCCES-SION. THEODORET OF CYR: In other words, this is the end of the end of all affairs of this life, all the empires of earth coming to a close and the eternal kingdom being given to the holy ones of the Most High, with those in charge obeying and devotedly serving him, since his kingdom is eternal and does not come to an end. . . . This cannot be applied to the Maccabees; instead of being entrusted with kingship, they led troops and conquered and met a rapid end. COMMENTARY ON DANIEL 7.27-28.[29]

LOVE ONE ANOTHER. IGNATIUS OF ANTIOCH: He, being begotten by the Father before the beginning of time, was God the Word, the only-begotten Son, and he remains the same forever; for "of his kingdom there shall be no end," says Daniel the prophet. Let us all therefore love one another in harmony, and let no one look on his neighbor according to the flesh, but in Christ

Jesus. Let nothing exist among you that may divide you; but be united with your bishop, being through him subject to God in Christ. EPISTLE TO THE MAGNESIANS 6.[30]

7:28 The End of the Matter

THE INTERPRETATION OF THE VISION. EPHREM THE SYRIAN: Daniel adds, "Here the account ends," that is, the interpretation of the vision. "As for me, my thoughts greatly terrified me, and my face turned pale," because of the sad news of the afflictions, which the little horn will impose on my people and priests. "But I kept the matter in my mind," so that I might not sadden my listeners with such a bad omen. COMMENTARY ON DANIEL 7.28.[31]

THE CHALDEAN AND SYRIAC LANGUAGES. JEROME: Up to this point the book of Daniel was written in the Chaldean and Syriac languages. All the rest that follows up to the very end of the volume we read in Hebrew. COMMENTARY ON DANIEL 7.28.[32]

---

[28]LCC 4:166-67*. [29]WGRN 7:20-23*. [30]ANF 1:61*. [31]ESOO 2:216. [32]JCD 82*.

8:1-8 VISION OF THE RAM AND THE GOAT

[1]In the third year of the reign of King Belshazzar a vision appeared to me, Daniel, after that which appeared to me at the first. [2]And I saw in the vision; and when I saw, I was in Susa the capital, which is in the province of Elam; and I saw in the vision, and I was at the river Ulai. [3]I raised my eyes and saw, and behold, a ram standing on the bank of the river. It had two horns; and both horns were high, but one was higher than the other, and the higher one came up last. [4]I saw the ram charging westward and northward and southward; no beast could stand before him, and there was no one who could rescue from his power; he did as he pleased and magnified himself.

[5]As I was considering, behold, a he-goat came from the west across the face of the whole earth,

without touching the ground; and the goat had a conspicuous horn between his eyes. [6]*He came to the ram with the two horns, which I had seen standing on the bank of the river, and he ran at him in his mighty wrath.* [7]*I saw him come close to the ram, and he was enraged against him and struck the ram and broke his two horns; and the ram had no power to stand before him, but he cast him down to the ground and trampled upon him; and there was no one who could rescue the ram from his power.* [8]*Then the he-goat magnified himself exceedingly; but when he was strong, the great horn was broken, and instead of it there came up four conspicuous horns toward the four winds of heaven.*

OVERVIEW: Daniel's second vision is dated two years after his first. In the vision, Daniel is transported to Susa, the chief city of the Elamites (JEROME). Textual variants make it difficult to ascertain if he was standing near the gate above the river Ulai or by the Ulai canal. Both variants are found in the interpretative tradition (JEROME, ISHO'DAD). In either case, Daniel observes a ram, signifying the Persian Empire or the Persian king Darius, with two horns, signifying his rule over the Medes and the Persians (EPHREM). Theodoret interprets the horns as representative of the two bloodlines among the Persian kings (THEODORET). The longer of the two horns makes reference to the superior military power of the Persians (JEROME). In the vision, Daniel observes the ram charging in various directions, signifying the expansion of the Medo-Persian Empire (CHRYSOSTOM). Next, he observes a goat charging the ram and breaking its two horns. The goat represents Alexander of Macedonia and his military defeat of Darius and the Medes and the Persians—the two horns (APHRAHAT, ISHO'DAD). Alexander, after his defeat of Darius, extended the empire of the Greeks (EPHREM). Alexander died childless at the age of thirty-two. His kingdom was divided between four individuals: Ptolemy, Philip (Alexander's half-brother), Seleucus Nicator and Antigonus (JEROME).

8:1 In the Third Year

TWO YEARS AFTER THE PREVIOUS VISION. JEROME: This vision came two years after the pre-

vious revelation, for the latter was beheld in the first year of Belshazzar, whereas this was beheld in the third year. And so he informs us, "after that which I had seen at the first." COMMENTARY ON DANIEL 8.1.[1]

DATING THE VISION. THEODORET OF CYR: Now, it is not without purpose that he indicates the time: it is to inform us that long before these things happened, he received foreknowledge of them from the God of all. COMMENTARY ON DANIEL 8.1.[2]

8:2 In the Vision

THE VISION WAS A DREAM. THEODORET OF CYR: "I saw in a vision" means I was not awake, nor did I see it during the day: the God of all showed it to me in a dream. COMMENTARY ON DANIEL 8.2.[3]

SUSA THE CHIEF CITY OF THE REGION OF THE ELAMITES. JEROME: We may render, as Symmachus has translated it, "in the city of Elam," from which of course the region took its name, just as the Babylonians were named from Babylon. So also the Elamites were thus named from Elam, in consequence of which the Septuagint translates it "the region of Elamais." And Susis [that is, Susa] is the chief city of the region of the Elamites. COMMENTARY ON DANIEL 8.2.[4]

NEAR THE ULAI CANAL. JEROME: Instead of this

---

[1]JCD 83. [2]WGRW 7:205. [3]WGRW 7:205. [4]JCD 83.

Aquila translated "over the Ubal of Ulai"; Theodotion rendered "above Ubal"; the Septuagint "above the gate of Ulai." But it should be understood that Ulai is the name of a place, or else of a gate, just as there was in Troy a gate called the *Skaia* ("Western"), and among the Romans there is one called *Carmentalis*. In each case the name has originated from special circumstances. COMMENTARY ON DANIEL 8.2.[5]

THE GATE OPENS ON THE RIVER ULAI.

ISHO'DAD OF MERV: That is, before the vestibule and the gate where the river Ulai passed, that is, the gate that opens on the river Ulai. COMMENTARY ON DANIEL 8.2.[6]

8:3 A Ram

THE PERSIAN EMPIRE. THEODORET OF CYR:
He sees the Persian Empire in the form of a ram since it was flush with wealth and had a great abundance of resources. COMMENTARY ON DANIEL 8.3.[7]

DARIUS THE PERSIAN IS THE RAM. EPHREM
THE SYRIAN: He signifies Darius the Persian by saying "it had two horns," as Darius ruled the Medes and the Persians. "Both horns were long, but one was longer than the other": this is referred to the Persians, whose power was superior to that of the Medes and rose to a higher level. "And the longer one came up second": this is said because the Persians, after the Medes, would have obtained the rule over the world. COMMENTARY ON DANIEL 8.3.[8]

CYRUS IS THE HIGHER HORN. JEROME: He
calls Darius, Cyrus's uncle, a ram. He reigned over the Medes after his father, Astyages. And the one horn, which was higher than the other and growing still larger, signified Cyrus, who succeeded his maternal grandfather, Astyages, and reigned over the Medes and Persians along with his uncle, Darius, whom the Greeks called Cyaxeres. COMMENTARY ON DANIEL 8.3.[9]

TWO BLOOD LINES. THEODORET OF CYR: He
perceived two horns on the ram because Cyrus was the first to reign over it and transmitted the empire only to his sons; when his son Cambyses died, soothsayers held power for a few months, but shortly afterwards Darius son of Hystaspes, who passed the empire on to his offspring and theirs up to the last Darius, whose empire Alexander the Macedonian took over after slaying him. So by the two horns he means two races of kings, seeing both to be tall, but the second taller than the first. COMMENTARY ON DANIEL 8.3.[10]

8:4 The Ram Charging

PERSIA'S MILITARY DOMINANCE. CHRYSOS-
TOM: He was speaking of the Persian power and dominion that overran the whole earth. DISCOURSES AGAINST JUDAIZING CHRISTIANS 5.7.2.[11]

DARIUS'S WEALTH AND POWER. JEROME: Not
that he saw the ram itself, that is, the ram of Cyrus or Darius, but rather the ram of the same kingdom as theirs, that is, the second Darius, who was the last king of the Persian power and who was overcome by the king of the Macedonians, Alexander the son of Philip. And as to the fact that Darius was a very powerful and wealthy king, both the Greek and the Latin and the barbarian historical accounts so relate. COMMENTARY ON DANIEL 8.4.[12]

OTHER KINGDOMS. THEODORET OF CYR: By
"beasts" he refers again to the other kingdoms individually, Syria, Cilicia, Arabia, Egypt, calling them "beasts" on account of their being fearsome to those they ruled. So no kingdom, he is saying, could resist that empire charging to the north, south and west, nor could any human being liberate anyone from that power. Yet for all its appear-

---

[5]JCD 83. [6]CSCO 328:114. [7]WGRW 7:205. [8]ESOO 2:217. [9]JCD 84. [10]WGRW 7:205-7. [11]FC 68:121. [12]JCD 84.

ance it met its end. COMMENTARY ON DANIEL 8.4.[13]

8:5 A He-Goat

GABRIEL EXPLAINS THE PROPHET'S VISION.
JEROME: So that no one will think that I am attaching a private interpretation to this, let us simply repeat the words of Gabriel as he explained the prophet's vision. He said, "The ram you saw with two horns is the king of the Medes and Persians." This was, of course, Darius the son of Astyages, in whose reign the kingdom of the Medes and Persians was destroyed. "There was in addition a he-goat, who was coming from the west," and because of his extraordinary speed he appeared not to touch the ground. This was Alexander, the king of the Greeks, who after the overthrow of Thebes took up arms against the Persians. Commencing the conflict at the Granicus River, he conquered the generals of Darius and finally smashed against the ram himself and broke in pieces his two horns, the Medes and the Persians. Casting him beneath his feet, he subjected both horns to his own authority. COMMENTARY ON DANIEL 8.5.[14]

FLEETNESS OF FOOT. THEODORET OF CYR: The dream's riddle here suggested the Macedonian Empire, calling it a "goat" because of its speed and fleetness of foot, a goat being faster than a ram. He said it came from the southwest: since it had previously subjugated Egypt, it thus advanced into the land of the Persians, conquering Darius in Cilicia, and from there traversing Syria, Phoenicia and Palestine, taking some of the cities by surrender, securing others by force. It then also gained possession of that empire, occupied the Persians and destroyed the greater part of their power. COMMENTARY ON DANIEL 8.5.[15]

THE SHREWDNESS OF ALEXANDER. THEODORET OF CYR: By the "one horn visible," in the sense of famous and illustrious, he refers to Alexander; he says the horn was growing between its eyes on account of the shrewdness, intelligence and sagacity of Alexander's thinking. COMMENTARY ON DANIEL 8.5.[16]

8:7 Two Horns Broken

ALEXANDER DEFEATED THE MEDES AND THE PERSIANS. APHRAHAT: Again the ram was lifted up and exalted, and it pushed with its horns toward the west, and toward the north and toward the south, and it humbled many beasts. And they could not stand before him, until the he-goat came from the west and struck the ram and broke his horns and humbled the ram completely. But the ram was the king of Media and Persia, that is, Darius; and the he-goat was Alexander, the son of Philip, the Macedonian. . . . And the he-goat of the goats came up from the region of the Greeks and exalted himself against the ram, and he struck him and broke both his horns, the greater and the lesser. And why did he say that he broke both his horns? Clearly because he humbled both the kingdoms that he ruled; the lesser, that of the Medes, and the greater, that of the Persians. But when Alexander the Greek came, he killed Darius, king of Media and Persia. DEMONSTRATIONS 5.5.[17]

THE HORNS REPRESENT TWO POWERS.
ISHO'DAD OF MERV: The words "breaking its two horns," that is, the two powers, which Darius possessed, as the kingdom was subjected to two races, since the Medes and Persians were indicated together. In the same manner Cyrus, who was the first to rule, was a Mede on his mother's side and a Persian on his father's side. As their first king was called a Persian and a Mede, so the peoples, who were under his dominion, were indicated with the same names, because these two territories made a single kingdom. COMMENTARY ON DANIEL 8.7.[18]

---

[13]WGRW 7:207. [14]JCD 84-85. [15]WGRW 7:207-9. [16]WGRW 7:209. [17]NPNF 2 13:354*. [18]CSCO 328:115.

8:8 *The Great Horn Was Broken*

Alexander Died Without Children.
Ephrem the Syrian: After the defeat of Darius,
Alexander extended the empire of the Greeks in
every direction and made it firm with strong garrisons. In the meantime "the great horn was broken," that is, Alexander died, "and in its place
there came up four horns." Indeed, since Alexander had died without children, he left his
divided monarchy to his friends Seleucus, Demetrius, Philip and Ptolemy. Commentary on
Daniel 8.8.[19]

Common Fate. Theodoret of Cyr: Despite
that great conquest, Alexander met the common
fate of humankind. Commentary on Daniel
8.8.[20]

**The Empire Was Divided Among Four
Generals.** Jerome: When Alexander died in
Babylon at the age of thirty-two, his four generals
rose up in his place and divided his empire among
themselves. For Ptolemy, the son of Lagos, seized
Egypt; the Philip who was also called Aridaeus
(variant: Arius), the (half-) brother of Alexander
took over Macedonia; Seleucus Nicator took over
Syria, Babylonia and all the kingdoms of the East;
and Antigonus ruled over Asia Minor. . . . "And a
long time afterward" there shall arise "a king of
Syria who shall be of shameless countenance and
shall understand [evil] counsels," even Antiochus
Epiphanies, the son of the Seleucus who was also
called Philopator. Commentary on Daniel 8.5.[21]

The Succession of Alexander. Theodoret of Cyr: By "four horns" he hints at the
four kings who succeeded Alexander at the one
time: Ptolemy son of Lagus took control of
Egypt; Seleucus Nicanor got possession of
Babylon and the other parts bordering on Syria;
Antigonus was in charge of Asia; Antipater,
Macedonia—or, as some historians think, Philip,
who is also called Arrhideus, brother of Alexander. Commentary on Daniel 8.8.[22]

---

[19]ESOO 2:217.   [20]WGRW 7:209.   [21]JCD 85.   [22]WGRW 7:209-11.

8:9-14 THE OVERTHROW OF THE SANCTUARY

[9]*Out of one of them came forth a little horn, which grew exceedingly great toward the south,
toward the east, and toward the glorious land.* [10]*It grew great, even to the host of heaven; and some
of the host of the stars it cast down to the ground, and trampled upon them.* [11]*It magnified itself,
even up to the Prince of the host; and the continual burnt offering was taken away from him, and
the place of his sanctuary was overthrown.* [12]*And the host was given over to it together with the
continual burnt offering through transgression;[n] and truth was cast down to the ground, and the
horn acted and prospered.* [13]*Then I heard a holy one speaking; and another holy one said to the
one that spoke, "For how long is the vision concerning the continual burnt offering, the transgression that makes desolate, and the giving over of the sanctuary and host to be trampled under foot?"[o]*
[14]*And he said to him,[p] "For two thousand and three hundred evenings and mornings; then the
sanctuary shall be restored to its rightful state."*

n Heb obscure   **o** Heb obscure   **p** Theodotion Gk Syr Vg: Heb *me*

OVERVIEW: Antiochus Epiphanes, from the family of the Seleucid kingdom, is signified by the little horn (EPHREM). He will torture Jerusalem for 1,290 days (CHRYSOSTOM). Antiochus waged war to the south against Egypt, to the East against Persia and toward the glorious land, against Judea and Jerusalem (JEROME). The stars refer to the Maccabees (ISHO'DAD). He exalted himself against God and persecuted his saints (JEROME). He killed thousands of the inhabitants of Jerusalem, pillaged the temple, abolished the twice daily sacrifice offered in the temple and built an altar to Zeus (THEODORET, ISHO'DAD). An angel asks another angel, how long the holy things of God will be given over to the immoral (JEROME, EPHREM), and the angelic reply is interpreted to be 2,300 days, which corresponds to the times, time and half time mentioned previously in Daniel 7:25 (EPHREM).

8:9 A Little Horn

ANTIOCHUS. EPHREM THE SYRIAN: This is Antiochus, who was born from the family of Seleucus Nicanor. "It grew great toward the south and toward the east." Antiochus extended his empire especially in these two parts of the world. COMMENTARY ON DANIEL 8.9.[1]

WAR WOULD COME ON ISRAEL. CHRYSOSTOM: As Josephus told the story, Daniel saw a smaller horn rise up from these, and it grew strong. God, who showed Daniel the vision, was telling him that war would come on his nation, that Jerusalem would be taken by storm, the temple would be pillaged, the sacrifices would be hindered and cut short, and this would last for 1,290 days. DISCOURSES AGAINST JUDAIZING CHRISTIANS 5.8.7.[2]

ANTIOCHUS WAGED WAR AGAINST EGYPT AND JUDEA. JEROME: After he had been a hostage in Rome and had without the knowledge of the Senate obtained rule by treachery, Antiochus fought with Ptolemy Philometor, that is, "against the South" and against Egypt; and then again "against the East" and against those who were fomenting revolution in Persia. At the last he fought against the Jews and captured Judea, entering into Jerusalem and setting up in the temple of God the statue of Jupiter Olympius[3] . . . "and against the power of heaven," that is, against the children of Israel, who were protected by the assistance of angels. He pushed his arrogance to such an extreme that he subjected the majority of the saints to the worship of idols, as if he would tread the very stars beneath his feet. And thus it came to pass that he held the south and the east, that is, Egypt and Persia, under his sway. COMMENTARY ON DANIEL 8.9.[4]

A CONCISE HISTORY. THEODORET OF CYR: The first and second books of the Maccabees inform us of this more clearly, and the historian Josephus made a precise record of it, and we shall outline concisely the facts about him. When the Jews of the high-priestly family rebelled against the high priest of the time, those anxious for the position went to Antiochus and persuaded him to change the Jewish way of life to the Greek and to build a gymnasium in the city. When this happened, devout people were in mourning at seeing the blatant violation of the laws, while the remaining throng had no qualms about trampling on the divine law and treating with contempt the commandment about circumcision. When the uprising became more serious, Antiochus arrived and put to death most of the devout, and he had the audacity even to enter the precincts of the temple; after entering he sacked the whole temple, appropriating to himself the treasures, all the offerings, cups and bowls and vessels, the golden table, the golden censer, the lampstands made of gold, and in short all the instruments of divine worship. In addition to this he built in God's temple an altar to Zeus, filled the whole city with idols and obliged everyone to sacrifice, while he himself sacrificed a pig on the divine altar and named the

---

[1]ESOO 2:217. [2]FC 68:128. [3]Jupiter was the highest deity of the ancient Romans, corresponding with Zeus in the Greek tradition. [4]JCD 85.

temple after Zeus of Olympus. COMMENTARY ON DANIEL 8.10.[5]

8:10 The Host of Heaven

THE PRIESTLY ORDER. EPHREM THE SYRIAN: He signifies here the priestly order, which he compares with the host of heaven. "It threw down to the earth some of the host and some of the stars and trampled on them." Here he prophesies about the sons of Semona and the allies killed by Antiochus. COMMENTARY ON DANIEL 8.10.[6]

THE MACCABEES. ISHO'DAD OF MERV: "The host of heaven" and "the stars and princes of the host": he recalls in this way Onias and Eleazar and those of the house of the Maccabees.[7] He calls them "stars" because of the brightness and beauty of the fear of God, by alluding to the words "I will make your offspring as numerous as the stars of heaven."[8] COMMENTARY ON DANIEL 8.10-11.[9]

STARS. THEODORET OF CYR: Most of the people by transgressing God's law quickly fell away from heavenly things, and they were trampled down by this tyrant to their own destruction. He referred to them as stars on account of the fame and splendor of their piety, hinting also at the promise to Abraham, "I shall make your offspring like the stars of heaven."[10] COMMENTARY ON DANIEL 8.10.[11]

8:11 The Horn Magnified Itself

ANTIOCHUS LIFTED HIMSELF UP AGAINST GOD. JEROME: This means that [Antiochus] lifted himself up against God and persecuted his saints. He even took away the *endelekhismos* or "continual offering," which was customarily sacrificed in the morning and at evening, and he prevailed to the casting down of the "place of his sanctuary." And he did not do this by his own prowess but only "on account of the sins of the people." And thus it came to pass that truth was prostrated on the ground, and as the worship of

idols flourished, the religion of God suffered an eclipse. COMMENTARY ON DANIEL 8.11-12.[12]

PERFORMED IN THE GREEK MANNER. THEODORET OF CYR: Then he foretells with greater clarity the audacity that would be committed by Antiochus. "On account of him sacrifice was disrupted by transgression": he did not permit the sacrifices prescribed by law to be made, requiring instead that they be performed in the Greek manner. COMMENTARY ON DANIEL 8.11.[13]

THE SACRIFICES WERE ABOLISHED. ISHO'DAD OF MERV: "The host was given over," so that "the regular burnt offering" that is, the sacrifices and offerings, were abolished and removed from their place. They were called so, because they had been established since the days of Moses and had continued constantly, or because the Jews offered sacrifices in the morning and in the evening; and they came to an end as a consequence of the intervention of that criminal. "The place of his sanctuary," that is, he destroyed, scattered and overturned the vessels and adornments of the house of the Lord. COMMENTARY ON DANIEL 8.11.[14]

8:12 Truth Cast Down

AN ALTAR WAS BUILT TO ZEUS IN THE TEMPLE. ISHO'DAD OF MERV: "The sanctuary[15] was cast to the ground." Indeed, when Antiochus gets into Jerusalem and kills forty thousand [inhabitants] and rapes the women, he then enters the temple, destroys the candlestick, breaks the table of the breads of the presence and all the vessels of the sanctuary, builds an altar to Zeus inside the temple, which he calls "temple of Zeus," and offers a pig to him. He gets into the treasury, where he steals eighteen hundred golden talents and the vessels of the

---

[5]WGRW 7:211-13. [6]ESOO 2:217. [7]See 2 Macc 4:30-35; 6:18-31. [8]Gen 22:17. [9]CSCO 328:115-16. [10]Gen 22:17. [11]WGRW 7:213. [12]JCD 85-86*. [13]WGRW 7:213-15. [14]CSCO 328:116. [15]This is the reading of the Peshitta.

cult. When he departs from [the city], he leaves behind some immoral men in order to overturn the prescriptions and laws of the righteous. COMMENTARY ON DANIEL 8.12.[16]

8:13 A Holy One Speaking

HOW LONG? THEODORET OF CYR: The word *phelmouni* means "a person" in Greek; Syriac, which is close to Hebrew, also confirms this. So blessed Daniel is saying, I heard one holy one asking another holy one. Clearly he is witnessing angels conversing and wanting to learn how long is the period of the offenses of impiety and lawlessness, the devastation of the temple, the illicit and loathsome sacrifice and the oppression of the people. COMMENTARY ON DANIEL 8.13.[17]

THE NAME OF THE ANGEL. ISHO'DAD OF MERV: *Plūmni*:[18] interior. This name is given to the angel on the basis of his actions and the place that he occupies; it indicates the one who is in the inside and close to the Judge and who knows the secrets and the events that are about to happen. It is a Hebrew term. COMMENTARY ON DANIEL 8.13.[19]

AN IMAGE OF JUPITER IN THE TEMPLE. JEROME: One angel asks another angel for how long a period the temple is by the judgment of God to be desolated under the rule of Antiochus, king of Syria, and how long the image of Jupiter is to stand in God's temple (according to his additional statement: ". . . and the sanctuary and the

strength be trodden under foot?"). COMMENTARY ON DANIEL 8.13.[20]

ANTICHRIST. JEROME: Most of our commentators refer this passage to the antichrist and hold that what occurred under Antiochus was only by way of a type that shall be fulfilled under antichrist. COMMENTARY ON DANIEL 8.14.[21]

8:14 Evenings and Mornings

THE PERIOD OF TRANSGRESSION. THEODORET OF CYR: By "evening" he referred to the beginning of the calamities and by "morning" to the end of the calamities, since night and darkness are figures of distress. From the present time, the beginning of the troubles, to the end, he is saying, the period is of that length [twenty-three hundred evenings and mornings]. COMMENTARY ON DANIEL 8.14.[22]

TIMES, TIMES AND HALF TIME. EPHREM THE SYRIAN: The intention of the angel who asked the question was to learn for how long the holy things would be given into the hands of immoral people. To him the angel who interprets the vision says, "For two thousand three hundred days," to which "the times, time and half time"[23] mentioned above correspond. COMMENTARY ON DANIEL 8.14.[24]

---

[16]CSCO 328:116. [17]WGRW 7:215. [18]This is the word used in the Peshitta for "to the one that spoke." [19]CSCO 328:116. [20]JCD 86. [21]JCD 87*. [22]WGRW 7:215. [23]Dan 7:25. [24]ESOO 2:218.

8:15-27 GABRIEL INTERPRETS THE VISION

¹⁵When I, Daniel, had seen the vision, I sought to understand it; and behold, there stood before me one having the appearance of a man. ¹⁶And I heard a man's voice between the banks of the Ulai, and it called, "Gabriel, make this man understand the vision." ¹⁷So he came near where I stood; and when he came, I was frightened and fell upon my face. But he said to me, "Understand, O son of man, that the vision is for the time of the end."

¹⁸As he was speaking to me, I fell into a deep sleep with my face to the ground; but he touched me and set me on my feet. ¹⁹He said, "Behold, I will make known to you what shall be at the latter end of the indignation; for it pertains to the appointed time of the end. ²⁰As for the ram which you saw with the two horns, these are the kings of Media and Persia. ²¹And the he-goat*q* is the king of Greece; and the great horn between his eyes is the first king. ²²As for the horn that was broken, in place of which four others arose, four kingdoms shall arise from his*r* nation, but not with his power. ²³And at the latter end of their rule, when the transgressors have reached their full measure, a king of bold countenance, one who understands riddles, shall arise. ²⁴His power shall be great,*s* and he shall cause fearful destruction, and shall succeed in what he does, and destroy mighty men and the people of the saints. ²⁵By his cunning he shall make deceit prosper under his hand, and in his own mind he shall magnify himself. Without warning he shall destroy many; and he shall even rise up against the Prince of princes; but, by no human hand, he shall be broken. ²⁶The vision of the evenings and the mornings which has been told is true; but seal up the vision, for it pertains to many days hence."

²⁷And I, Daniel, was overcome and lay sick for some days; then I rose and went about the king's business; but I was appalled by the vision and did not understand it.

q Or *shaggy he-goat*   r Theodotion Gk Vg: Heb *the*   s Theodotion and Beatty papyrus of Gk: Heb repeats *but not with his power* from verse 22

OVERVIEW: Daniel did not comprehend what he had seen and sought to understand it. Angels may appear as if human beings but are not by nature (JEROME). An angel, identified as Daniel's guardian angel (EPHREM) or the archangel Michael, asked Gabriel to interpret the vision. The revealing of the angelic name, Gabriel, serves to illustrate the fact that the only true remedy is to be found in God (JEROME). Daniel was frightened by the brightness of the angel and bowed down to him in veneration but not adoration (JOHN OF DAMASCUS). Daniel is the first person to be referred to in scripture as "son of man" (ORIGEN). Gabriel explains the rise of Darius, Alexander and Antiochus. The ruthless acts of Antiochus, whose rise to power was facilitated by cunning and deceit, are spelled out by Gabriel (EPHREM). Gabriel commands that the vision be sealed to illustrate the hidden character of the things spoken and their incomprehensibility prior to their fulfillment (THEODORET, ANDREW). The vision remained indecipherable to Daniel, who responded in the only manner open to him: he marveled at the vision and resigned everything to God's omniscience (JEROME).

8:15 Daniel Seeks Understanding

DANIEL FAILED TO UNDERSTAND THE VISION. JEROME: He beheld the vision by way of a picture or likeness, and he failed to understand it. Consequently, not everyone who sees comprehends what he has seen; it is just as if we read the holy Scripture with our eyes and do not understand it with our heart. COMMENTARY ON DANIEL 8.15.[1]

ANGELS RESEMBLE HUMANS IN APPEARANCE. JEROME: Angels, after all, are not actually humankind by nature, but they resemble humankind in appearance. For example, three persons appeared as human beings to Abraham at the oak of Mamre,[2] and yet they certainly were not human beings, for one of them was worshiped as the Lord. And so the Savior also stated in the Gospel: "Abraham beheld my day; he beheld it and rejoiced."[3] COMMENTARY ON DANIEL 8.15.[4]

8:16 A Man's Voice

THE LORD. THEODORET OF CYR: I heard someone else as well using a human voice and bidding the one standing near me, whom he called Gabriel, to interpret the riddle of the revelation to me. It is possible from what was said to come to the conclusion that the one giving the orders was the Lord. COMMENTARY ON DANIEL 8.16.[5]

GABRIEL TO INTERPRET THE VISION. EPHREM THE SYRIAN: The guardian angel of Daniel, who never parted from him, asked the angel Gabriel, who was now by him, now by all the other saints in everything concerning visions, to explain to Daniel his dream. COMMENTARY ON DANIEL 8.15.[6]

GABRIEL. JEROME: The Jews claim that this man who directed Gabriel to explain the vision to Daniel was Michael. Quite appropriately it was Gabriel, who has been put in charge of battles, to whom this duty was assigned, inasmuch as the vision had to do with battles and contests between kings and even between kingdoms themselves. For Gabriel is translated into our language as "the strength of, or the mighty one of, God." And so at that time also when the Lord was about to be born and to declare war against the demons and to triumph over the world, Gabriel

came to Zacharias and to Mary.[7] And then we read in the Psalms concerning the Lord in his triumph: "Who is this king of glory? The Lord strong and mighty, the Lord mighty in battle; he is the King of glory."[8] . . . Of course the significance of the name indicates the fact that the only true remedy is to be found in God.[9] COMMENTARY ON DANIEL 8.16-17.[10]

8:17 Daniel Became Frightened

THE BRILLIANCE OF GABRIEL. EPHREM THE SYRIAN: "And I became frightened," being struck by the excessive brightness of this angel. COMMENTARY ON DANIEL 8.17.[11]

ADORATION AND VENERATION DIFFER. JOHN OF DAMASCUS: Joshua, the son of Nun,[12] and Daniel bowed in veneration before an angel of God, but they did not adore him. For adoration is one thing, and that which is offered in order to honor something of great excellence is another. ON DIVINE IMAGES 1.8.[13]

IMAGE AND LIKENESS. ORIGEN: The first definite person we find named in Scripture "son of man" is, speaking at the moment from memory, Daniel. And after him, Ezekiel. They were prophets in the captivity, so far as our researches go in the undisputed books that pass currently as inspired, there is no one named by this title. . . . It was, as we think, because the people of captivity were sinners that Daniel alone, to their reproach, because they preserved the dignity of human nature, made according to the image and the likeness, was addressed as the son of man. As much may be said also of Ezekiel. For the name "man" was first given to him who was made by God according to his image and likeness, so that he would be man in the true sense. SELECTIONS IN PSALMS.[14]

---

[1]JCD 87. [2]Gen 18. [3]Jn 8:56. [4]JCD 87. [5]WGRW 7:217. [6]ESOO 2:218. [7]Lk 1:11, 26-28. [8]Ps 24:8, 10 (23:8, 10 LXX). [9]The Hebrew word for "mighty" is *gibbôr*, from the root of which comes the *gabri-* of Gabriel. [10]JCD 88. [11]ESOO 2:218. [12]Josh 1:1. [13]JDDI 19. [14]SCHO 39*.

FAR IN THE FUTURE. THEODORET OF CYR: Do not think that these things come to fulfillment in the present age; they will happen after a great number of years. When the set time has run its course, then each of them will reach its fulfillment. COMMENTARY ON DANIEL 8.17.[15]

8:18 Gabriel Set Daniel on His Feet

GABRIEL CONSOLES DANIEL. THEODORET OF CYR: Perceiving me prostrate with fear, he first set me upright, then consoled me by making known why he had come, to inform me in my anxiety of the future and what in turn would overtake my people as a result of God's wrath. Then, in his wish to allay the fear besetting me, he mentioned that this would happen after a time and interpreted to me the meaning of each of the things I had seen. COMMENTARY ON DANIEL 8.18-19.[16]

8:20 The Two Horns Interpreted

GABRIEL INTERPRETS THE HORNS. EPHREM THE SYRIAN: "As for the ram that you saw with the two horns, this is the king[17] of the Medes and the Persians." [Gabriel] alludes to Darius. "The two horns" signify the two kingdoms, the Persian and the Mede. "The male goat is the king of Greece": Alexander. "And the great horn between his eyes" signifies his highest power and his exceedingly extended empire all over the world. "After the horn was broken, four kingdoms arose from it": the monarchy of Alexander, after his death, will be diminished and divided into parts assigned to his friends Seleucus, Philip, Demetrius and Ptolemy. COMMENTARY ON DANIEL 8.20.[18]

8:22 Four Other Horns Arose

THE DIVISION OF THE KINGDOM. THEODORET OF CYR: After [Alexander's] death his empire will be divided into four kingdoms, but though those reigning over them are four, they will not succeed in achieving what he achieved but will be seen to be much inferior to his strength. COMMENTARY ON DANIEL 8.22.[19]

8:23 At the End of Their Rule

THE JEWS ABANDONED THE LAW. EPHREM THE SYRIAN: When the Jews begin to abandon the law and faith of God and to estrange themselves, the grandchildren of Seleucus Nicator will invade the last part of their kingdom. "A king of bold countenance shall arise": this is Antiochus, who is able to understand riddles, is cunning and is ready to weave intrigues and to prepare his domination by means of his intelligence. COMMENTARY ON DANIEL 8.23.[20]

8:24 A Powerful King

THE PROSPERITY OF THE WICKED. THEODORET OF CYR: Nothing will be an obstacle to him; instead, he will do what he wishes. Of such people blessed David says in exhortation, "Do not vie with the one who prospers in his way, with the one who commits lawlessness":[21] it often happens that people living a godless and lawless life prosper considerably in their lawless pursuits. COMMENTARY ON DANIEL 8.24-25.[22]

8:25 By His Cunning

ANTIOCHUS TAKES JERUSALEM THROUGH FRAUDULENCE. EPHREM THE SYRIAN: [Gabriel] says this because [Antiochus] got into the city through fraudulence, polluted the precious vessels of the temple and committed pillages and demolished the walls. "Without warning he shall destroy many": he killed forty thousand Jews and captured just as many. "And he shall even rise up against the Prince of princes": either because Antiochus would have attacked God with curses and blasphemies or because he would have violated the temple of God

---

[15]WGRW 7:217. [16]WGRW 7:217. [17]This is the reading of the Peshitta as well as of the LXX. [18]ESOO 2:219 [19]WGRW 7:219. [20]ESOO 2:219. [21]Ps 37:7 (36:7 LXX). [22]WGRW 7:219. ²

and would have destroyed the holy vessels. COMMENTARY ON DANIEL 8.25.[23]

8:26 Seal Up the Vision

THE PROPHETIC EVENTS REMAIN HIDDEN. JEROME: Having explained the vision that we have examined above to the best of our ability, the angel Gabriel adds at the end, "You, therefore, seal up the vision, because it shall come to pass after many days." By the mention of a seal, he showed that the things spoken were of a hidden character and not accessible to the ears of the multitude or susceptible of comprehension prior to their actual fulfillment by the events themselves. COMMENTARY ON DANIEL 8.26.[24]

THE OBSCURITY OF PROPHECY. THEODORET OF CYR: "Seal up the vision because it will be in many days time," that is, leave it obscure for many people; I have made it clear to you in your longing before the event. COMMENTARY ON DANIEL 8.26.[25]

EXPLAINED BY EXPERIENCE. ANDREW OF CAESAREA: "Seal up what the seven thunders have said, and after these things write."[26] This shows that what is now undisclosed is to be explained through experience and the course of the events themselves. And from the heavenly voice the Evangelist learned that the voices are to be imprinted on the mind, but that the final understanding and the clear interpretation of them is reserved for the last times. Also Daniel learned that such words are to be sealed and locked away. COMMENTARY ON THE APOCALYPSE 10.4.[27]

8:27 Daniel Languished

DANIEL'S RESPONSE IS IN CHARACTER WITH HIS GODLINESS. JEROME: This is the same thing as we read in Genesis about Abraham, for after he had heard the Lord speaking to him, he averred that he was but dust and ashes.[28] And so Daniel states that he languished as a reaction to the hor-

ror of the vision and suffered illness. And after he had risen from his sickbed, he says he performed the tasks assigned to him by the king, rendering to all people all that was due them and bearing in mind the Gospel principle: "Render to Caesar the things that are Caesar's and to God the things that are God's."[29] COMMENTARY ON DANIEL 8.27.[30]

DANIEL CONTINUED THE KING'S WORK. THEODORET OF CYR: On learning the troubles that would overtake the people in due course, I became so unwell as to fall a victim to illness. Yet despite being thus indisposed, I managed the work entrusted to me by the king, with no one aware of the cause of the sickness. He was in the habit of saying along with blessed Paul, "Who is weak, and I am not weak? Who is made to stumble, and I am not indignant?"[31] and "Weeping with those who weep, rejoicing with those who rejoice,"[32] and "If one limb suffers, all the limbs suffer together."[33] This man felt the same way, and he had this affection for his fellow slaves; and on learning of the calamities to overtake his fellow slaves many generations later, he kept weeping and wailing. He had a precise knowledge that he personally would not experience those things but would instead be freed from the present life before long. COMMENTARY ON DANIEL 8.27.[34]

GABRIEL'S INTERPRETATION DID NOT GIVE SPECIFIC INFORMATION. JEROME: If there was no one who could interpret it, how was it that the angel interpreted it in the previous passage? What he means is that he had heard mention of kings and did not know what their names were; he learned of things to come, but he was tossed about with uncertainty as to what time they would come to pass. And so he did the only thing he could do: he marveled at the vision and resigned everything to God's omniscience. COMMENTARY ON DANIEL 8.27.[35]

---

[23]ESOO 2:219. [24]JCD 89. [25]WGRW 7:221. [26]Rev 10:4. [27]MTS 1 Supp 1:107-8. [28]Gen 18:27. [29]Lk 20:25. [30]JCD 89. [31]2 Cor 11:29. [32]Rom 12:15. [33]1 Cor 12:26. [34]WGRW 7:221-23. [35]JCD 89.

9:1-19 DANIEL PRAYS FOR HIS PEOPLE

[1]In the first year of Darius the son of Ahasu-erus, by birth a Mede, who became king over the realm of the Chaldeans— [2]in the first year of his reign, I, Daniel, perceived in the books the number of years which, according to the word of the LORD to Jeremiah the prophet, must pass before the end of the desolations of Jerusalem, namely, seventy years.

[3]Then I turned my face to the Lord God, seeking him by prayer and supplications with fasting and sackcloth and ashes. [4]I prayed to the LORD my God and made confession, saying, "O Lord, the great and terrible God, who keeps covenant and steadfast love with those who love him and keep his commandments, [5]we have sinned and done wrong and acted wickedly and rebelled, turning aside from thy commandments and ordinances; [6]we have not listened to thy servants the prophets, who spoke in thy name to our kings, our princes, and our fathers, and to all the people of the land. [7]To thee, O Lord, belongs righteousness, but to us confusion of face, as at this day, to the men of Judah, to the inhabitants of Jerusalem, and to all Israel, those that are near and those that are far away, in all the lands to which thou hast driven them, because of the treachery which they have committed against thee. [8]To us, O Lord, belongs confusion of face, to our kings, to our princes, and to our fathers, because we have sinned against thee. [9]To the Lord our God belong mercy and forgiveness; because we have rebelled against him, [10]and have not obeyed the voice of the LORD our God by following his laws, which he set before us by his servants the prophets. [11]All Israel has transgressed thy law and turned aside, refusing to obey thy voice. And the curse and oath which are written in the law of Moses the servant of God have been poured out upon us, because we have sinned against him. [12]He has confirmed his words, which he spoke against us and against our rulers who ruled us, by bringing upon us a great calamity; for under the whole heaven there has not been done the like of what has been done against Jerusalem. [13]As it is written in the law of Moses, all this calamity has come upon us, yet we have not entreated the favor of the LORD our God, turning from our iniquities and giving heed to thy truth. [14]Therefore the LORD has kept ready the calamity and has brought it upon us; for the LORD our God is righteous in all the works which he has done, and we have not obeyed his voice. [15]And now, O Lord our God, who didst bring thy people out of the land of Egypt with a mighty hand, and hast made thee a name, as at this day, we have sinned, we have done wickedly. [16]O Lord, according to all thy righteous acts, let thy anger and thy wrath turn away from thy city Jerusalem, thy holy hill; because for our sins, and for the iniquities of our fathers, Jerusalem and thy people have become a byword among all who are round about us. [17]Now therefore, O our God, hearken to the prayer of thy servant and to his supplications, and for thy own sake, O Lord,[i] cause thy face to shine upon thy sanctuary, which is desolate. [18]O my God, incline thy ear and hear; open thy eyes and behold our desolations, and the city which is called by thy name; for we do not present our supplications before thee on the ground of our righteousness, but on the ground of thy great mercy. [19]O LORD, hear; O LORD, forgive; O LORD,

give heed and act; delay not, for thy own sake, O my God, because thy city and thy people are called by thy name."

t Theodotion Vg Compare Syr: Heb *for the Lord's sake*

OVERVIEW: Daniel refers to Darius, who conquered the Chaldeans and Babylonians with Cyrus (JEROME). Though he is called Darius the Mede, only one of his parents was a descendent of the Mede line (THEODORET). Daniel prays at the appropriate time (ISHO'DAD) and humbly lest he offend God (JEROME). Daniel counts years not from the time of his own capture but from that of the captivity of Israel. Jeremiah has prophesied seventy years for the captivity of Israel (CHRYSOSTOM). God keeps his promises to the faithful (JEROME, BEDE).

Daniel takes the corporate sin as his responsibility (JEROME, THEODORET) and supplicates God to forgive his people (CYPRIAN). Daniel is despondent about the coming troubles caused by his people's trespasses (TERTULLIAN, CHRYSOSTOM). Daniel's repentance for his people shows the justice of the divine punishment (THEODORET). Divine judgment is followed by God's mercy (JEROME). Once one sins against God, the curse written in the law of Moses befalls him (THEODORET, EPHREM). Daniel's people are so obdurate that they are far from God's truth and forgiveness (JEROME). God's chastening is a sign for discipline, so Daniel appeals to God for divine clemency (JEROME). God's reactions are described in anthropomorphic language (JEROME).

9:1 Darius Son of Ahasuerus

CONFUSIONS REGARDING THE NAME DARIUS.
JEROME: This is the Darius who in cooperation with Cyrus conquered the Chaldeans and Babylonians. We are not to think of that other Darius in the second year of whose reign the temple was built (as Porphyry supposes in making out a late date for Daniel); nor are we to think of the Darius who was vanquished by Alexander, the king of the Macedonians. He therefore adds the name of

his father and also refers to his victory, inasmuch as he was the first of the race of the Medes to overthrow the kingdom of the Chaldeans. He does this to avoid any mistake in the reading that might arise from the similarity of the name. COMMENTARY ON DANIEL 9.1-2.[1]

DARIUS FROM THE RACE OF THE MEDES.
THEODORET OF CYR: We must distinguish between the reign of Darius son of Ahasuerus and that of Darius the Persian. In this way, the things that are now being read will harmonize with the things that were spoken earlier. He did not simply introduce Darius as Darius the Mede but rather as one "from the race of the Medes." Now, as it is clear, he was not a Mede on both sides of his family, that is, on his father's and mother's side. At the same time he ruled over the kingdom of the Chaldeans, when Belshazzar was killed in the middle of the night by a divine intervention after his godless act. According to my research, this Darius seems to have reigned for a very brief time. COMMENTARY ON DANIEL 9.1-2.[2]

9:2 Seventy Years

THE COUNTING OF THE SEVENTY YEARS.
BEDE: Darius, the son of Astyages, who destroyed the Babylonian Empire with the help of his kinsmen Cyrus, was sixty-two years old when he attacked Babylon. He is called by another name by the Greeks. He took the prophet Daniel and led him into the middle of his court and feted him with every honor. Daniel himself made mention of this Darius: "In the first year of Darius . . . ." In his chronology, Eusebius counts thirty years from the destruction of Jerusalem to the beginning of the reign of Cyrus, king of the Persians. Julius

---

[1]JCD 90. [2]PG 81:1456.

Africanus, however, counts seventy years. More-over, Jerome has this to say in his exposition of the prophet Daniel: "The Hebrews pass on a story of this sort up until the seventieth year, when Jeremiah had said that the captivity of the Jews would come to an end. Zechariah also speaks about this at the beginning of his book." BOOK ON THE MEANING OF TIME 66.[3]

DANIEL PRAYS ONLY AT THE APPOINTED TIME. ISHO'DAD OF MERV: When the time fixed for the captivity is completed, Daniel begins to pray for the return; indeed, he had not dared to pray [to that purpose] before that moment, in order not to press God needlessly and in order not to hear the word that had been addressed to Jeremiah: "Do not pray for this people, and do not intercede with me, for I will not hear you."[4] But after seeing that the sentence had been exe-cuted, he prays with fasting and sackcloth and ashes. At the same time he thought that the Jews might stay a longer time in captivity because of their sins, according to the fact that God had added thirty years to the Jews in Egypt and had reduced [the time for repentance con-ceded] to the generation of Noah of twenty years and of fifty in the case of the house of Ephrem. Moreover, it is not at the beginning of their fault that the sinners ask questions of the judge but after the punishment. COMMENTARY ON DANIEL 9.2.[5]

DANIEL AVOIDS CARELESSNESS. JEROME: Jere-miah had predicted seventy years for the desola-tion of the temple,[6] at the end of which the people would again return to Judea and build the temple and the city of Jerusalem. However, this fact did not render Daniel careless but rather encouraged him to pray that God might through his suppli-cations fulfill that which he had graciously promised. Thus he avoided the danger that care-lessness might result in pride, and pride cause offense to the Lord. Accordingly we read in Gene-sis that prior to the deluge, 120 years were ap-pointed for humankind to come to repentance;[7]

and as they refused to repent even within so long an interval of time as a hundred years, God did not wait for the remaining twenty years to be ful-filled but brought on the punishment earlier that he had threatened for a later time.[8] So also Jere-miah is told, on account of the hardness of the heart of the Jewish people: "Pray not for this peo-ple, for I will not hearken to you."[9] Samuel also was told, "How long will you mourn over Saul? I also have rejected him."[10] And so it was with sack-cloth and ashes that Daniel requested God to ful-fill what he had promised, not because Daniel lacked faith concerning the future, but because he would rather avoid the danger that a feeling of security might produce carelessness, for careless-ness in turn might produce an offense to God. COMMENTARY ON DANIEL 9.2.[11]

9:3 Daniel Prays and Fasts

THE EFFECT OF DANIEL'S PRAYER AND FAST-ING. TERTULLIAN: Nor is it merely a change of nature, or aversion of perils or obliteration of sins but likewise the recognition of mysteries that fasts will merit from God. Look at Daniel's exam-ple. . . . In the first year of King Darius, when, after careful and repeated meditation on the times predicted by Jeremiah, he set his face to God in fasts and sackcloth and ashes. An angel was sent to him and immediately stated this had been the cause of the divine honor; he said, "I came to show you, wretched as you are," namely, because he had been fasting. ON FASTING 7.[12]

---

[3]Cetedoc 2320.66.627. [4]Jer 7:16; cf. Chrysostom "Orations on the Jews," PG 48:891. [5]CSCO 328:118. [6]Jer 29:10. [7]Gen 6:3. [8]This deduction seems to have been based on the fact that Genesis 5:32 mentions that Noah was 500 years old when he had begotten Ham, Shem and Japheth, and therefore was still the same age when God appointed the 120 years (Gen 6:3). Since the flood dried up in the year when Noah was 601 (Gen 8:13), therefore the waiting period could not have been more than 100 years. Yet it could also have been that the age given in Genesis 5:32 was the age when, within the 120-year period, Noah's family was complete, the youngest son being born within that period and being old enough to be married by the time the flood occurred. [9]Jer 7:16. [10]1 Sam 16:1. [11]JCD 90-91**. [12]ANF

DANIEL HUMBLES HIMSELF. CHRYSOSTOM: What will you say, Daniel? You are among the good; you enjoy honor before God and people; why do you concern yourself with the others? But Moses also acted the same way. And what does he say? "He asked for the things that were due with fasting, sackcloth and ashes." Why did he do that, if what he was asking was due the Israelites? He did it so that he might not make them unworthy of this. For there is no compulsion that can be applied to God; he is above all laws. He did this "to seek in prayer and petition." COMMENTARY ON DANIEL 9.[13]

9:4 The Lord Keeps Covenant

KEEPING HIS COVENANT. THEODORET OF CYR: [Daniel] calls [God] "great and wonderful" for his ability to do great and wonderful things. Godly people, after all, are accustomed to apply divine names on the basis of benefits conferred. He spoke of his "keeping covenant and mercy with those who love him" in recalling the promises to Abraham, Isaac and Jacob. Being very precise in his prayer, he mentions that he does not keep it with anyone but with "those who love him and keep his commandments;" if someone transgresses your commands, he renders himself unworthy of the promises. COMMENTARY ON DANIEL 9.4.[14]

GOD'S PROMISES ARE TRUTHFUL. JEROME: It is not therefore the case that what God promises will come to pass without further ado, but rather he fulfills his promises toward those who keep his commandments. COMMENTARY ON DANIEL 9.4.[15]

9:5-6 God's People Have Sinned

DANIEL CONFESSES IN HUMILITY. CYPRIAN: Although Daniel has already received manifold grace due to his faith and innocence and although he has received quite a reputation before the Lord in regard to his virtues and praises, he strives

with fasting to be worthy of God; he puts on sackcloth and ashes and makes confession with tears. THE LAPSED 31.[16]

GOD'S CONSTANT CARE. THEODORET OF CYR: Then to bring out God's constant care for them and the people's great insensitivity, [Daniel] went on, "We have not hearkened to your servants the prophets, who kept speaking in your name to our kings, to our rulers, to our fathers and to the whole people of the land." Your grace did not cease watching over us and speaking through the prophets, at one time to kings and rulers, at another to priests and teachers, referring to them as fathers, and on many occasions to the whole people. Yet even when this happened, we continued to contradict you. COMMENTARY ON DANIEL 9.6.[17]

9:7 Confusion

DANIEL CONFESSES THE CORPORATE SINS. THEODORET OF CYR: Lord, the things done by you proclaim your righteousness. But we are ashamed because of our great transgression and denounced for our own ingratitude. No harm comes to you because of our godlessness, but we have reaped the fruit of these seeds. He speaks in a pitiable fashion. Daniel both accuses his kin and associates himself with their trespasses. COMMENTARY ON DANIEL 9.7.[18]

CONFUSION HAS OVERWHELMED US. EPHREM THE SYRIAN: "Yours is the victory, O Lord, in this case,"[19] because you foresaw our many sins and threatened those about to sin with many curses, keeping your watch lest we might sin. Righteousness is on your side, O Lord, because no evil will besiege us that was not announced to us beforehand. So now confusion

---

[13]PG 56:238. [14]WGRW 7:229*. [15]JCD 91*. [16]Cetedoc 0042.31.618. [17]WGRW 7:231. [18]PG 81:1461. [19]This passage is not in the Peshitta and must belong to another version of the Syriac Bible employed by Ephrem.

has overwhelmed us everywhere, and we are dispersed in every place. COMMENTARY ON DANIEL 9.7.[20]

9:8 We Have Sinned

DANIEL REPENTS FOR HIS PEOPLE. CHRYSOSTOM: Daniel was despondent and in pain. It was not merely the present troubles alone that bothered him but also the troubles to come, since he had not yet been allowed to learn those things through his prophetic eyes. When he saw that the Jews had not yet been freed from their earlier servitude, he was compelled to see another captivity falling on them, and he saw the city that had not yet been rebuilt being captured again. He saw the temple defiled by sacrifices and made desolate and the Holy of Holies overturned. To STAGIRIUS 1-3.[21]

DANIEL'S CONFESSION DRAWS COMPASSION. THEODORET OF CYR: Each of these would be enough to turn the most savage person to tears, not to mention what it would do to the gentle and humane individual. Through these words he shows that not only the lowest and unnoticed of the people had been filled with shame but also the kings themselves and the princes and the priests—the latter he called "fathers." Then, to show the justice of the punishment, he added, "because we sinned against you." COMMENTARY ON DANIEL 9.8.[22]

9:9 Mercy Belongs to the Lord

GOD IS MERCIFUL AND JUST. JEROME: Concerning the same God of whom [Daniel] had previously said, "To you, O Lord, belongs justice," he now says (since the Lord is not only just but also merciful): "To you belongs mercy." He says this in order that he might call on the judge to show mercy, after his sentence has been imposed. COMMENTARY ON DANIEL 9.8.[23]

9:11 The Curse

WE CAN TAKE ONLY A DROPLET OF GOD'S FURY. JEROME: That is, you have not poured out on us all your wrath, for we should not have been able to bear it, but you have poured forth a mere droplet of your fury, in order that we might return to you once we have been enmeshed in your snare. . . . In Deuteronomy, we read the curses and blessings of the Lord,[24] which were afterwards uttered in Mount Gerizim and Ebal on the righteous and on the sinners. COMMENTARY ON DANIEL 9.11.[25]

CURSES COME WITH SINNING. THEODORET OF CYR: If some had sinned while others had been diligent keepers of your laws, they would not have awaited this misfortune. But since their transgression was common to all and had been undertaken by all, Daniel quite reasonably says, "The curse has fallen on. . . ." By "oath" he refers to the one made in Deuteronomy: "I will raise my hand to heaven and I will swear by my right hand and I will say, 'As I live forever, I will sharpen my sword like lightning, and my hand of judgment will be stretched out, and I will avenge. . . .'" And a little before this he says, "I said, 'I will scatter them and make the memory of them to cease from among humankind.'"[26] He is describing the curse that was uttered by the six tribes that were on Mount Ebal.[27] So he is saying that the oath and curse that had been spoken in the law of Moses is actualized with us. COMMENTARY ON DANIEL 9.10-11.[28]

9:13 Not Seeking the Lord's Favor

THEY DID NOT TURN TO GOD. JEROME: Their stubbornness was so great that even in the midst of their toils they would not entreat God, and even if they had entreated him, it would not have been a genuine entreaty, because they had not turned back from their iniquities. Yet to consider

---

[20]ESOO 2:220. [21]PG 47:486-87. [22]PG 81:1461. [23]JCD 91-92. [24]Deut 27:11–28:19; cf. Ephrem *Commentary on Daniel* 9.10-11. [25]JCD 92*. [26]Deut 32:40-42, 26. [27]See Deut 27:13. [28]PG 81:1461-64.

the truth of God is equivalent to turning back from iniquity. Commentary on Daniel 9.13.[29]

9:14 God Is Righteous

A Sign of Divine Watchfulness. Jerome: Whenever we are rebuked because of our sins, God is keeping watch over us and visiting us with discipline. But whenever we are left alone by God and we do not suffer judgment but are unworthy of the Lord's rebuke, then he is said to slumber. And so we read in the Psalms as well: "The Lord has risen up as one who was slumbering or as a man out of a drunken sleep."[30] For our wickedness and iniquity inflames God with wine, and whenever it is rebuked in our case, God is said to be keeping careful watch and to be rising up out of his drowsy sleep, in order that we who are drunken with sin may be made to pay careful heed to righteousness. Commentary on Daniel 9.14.[31]

9:15 O Lord Our God

Memory of Divine Kindness. Jerome: Daniel remembers God's ancient kindness in order that he may appeal to him for a similar act of clemency. Commentary on Daniel 9.15.[32]

God's People Need Mercy. Ephrem the Syrian: "And now, O Lord our God, who brought your people out of the land of Egypt, let your anger and wrath, we pray, turn away from Jerusalem," that is, "You made, O Lord, your name renowned everywhere when you divided the sea and submerged the Egyptians into the water, and now, since your people are banished because of their sins and wander through every land in exile, draw near to us and have mercy on your holy mountain and your city Jerusalem, which have become a disgrace among all our neighbors." Commentary on Daniel 9.16.[33]

9:18 Daniel's Supplication

God Is Referred to in Human Language. Jerome: This appeal is couched in anthropomorphic language, with the implication that whenever our prayers are heard, God seems to incline his ear; and whenever God deigns to have regard to us, he appears to open his eyes; but whenever he turns his face away, we appear to be unworthy of attention either from his eyes or his ears. Commentary on Daniel 9.18.[34]

---

[29]JCD 92*. [30]Ps 78:65 (77:65 LXX). [31]JCD 92*. [32]JCD 92. [33]ESOO 2:220. [34]JCD 93*.

9:20-27 DANIEL'S CONFESSION AND GABRIEL'S INTERPRETATION

[20]*While I was speaking and praying, confessing my sin and the sin of my people Israel, and presenting my supplication before the Lord my God for the holy hill of my God;* [21]*while I was speaking in prayer, the man Gabriel, whom I had seen in the vision at the first, came to me in swift flight at the time of the evening sacrifice.* [22]*He came^u and he said to me, "O Daniel, I have now come out to give you wisdom and understanding.* [23]*At the beginning of your supplications a word went forth, and I have come to tell it to you, for you are greatly beloved; therefore consider the word and understand the vision.*

²⁴*"Seventy weeks of years are decreed concerning your people and your holy city, to finish the transgression, to put an end to sin, and to atone for iniquity, to bring in everlasting righteousness, to seal both vision and prophet, and to anoint a most holy place.*^v ²⁵*Know therefore and understand that from the going forth of the word to restore and build Jerusalem to the coming of an anointed one, a prince, there shall be seven weeks. Then for sixty-two weeks it shall be built again with squares and moat, but in a troubled time.* ²⁶*And after the sixty-two weeks, an anointed one shall be cut off, and shall have nothing; and the people of the prince who is to come shall destroy the city and the sanctuary. Its*^w *end shall come with a flood, and to the end there shall be war; desolations are decreed.* ²⁷*And he shall make a strong covenant with many for one week; and for half of the week he shall cause sacrifice and offering to cease; and upon the wing of abominations shall come one who makes desolate, until the decreed end is poured out on the desolator."*

u Gk Syr: Heb *made to understand*   v Or *thing* or *one*   w Or *his*

OVERVIEW: Daniel humbles himself to obtain pardon from God for his people (JEROME). The prayer of fasting is richer during the evening (TERTULLIAN). The commissions of Gabriel are evidence of the one and the same God (IRENAEUS). The law of God is given through the angels (AUGUSTINE). Gabriel is an angel of good news (JULIAN), whose name means the "might of God" (ISIDORE).

The particular words he uses are the key to understanding the vision (EPHREM). Daniel is worthy of God's love so that divine secret is revealed to him (JEROME). The holy city and the temple will be restored for seventy weeks (QUODVULTDEUS, EPHREM, ISHO'DAD). Seventy weeks symbolize 490 years counting from the release from Babylonian captivity (ISHO'DAD).

Daniel's prophecy is about the Christ (TERTULLIAN, BASIL, QUODVULTDEUS) and is fulfilled at the first coming of our Lord (PRIMASIUS, AUGUSTINE). Christ is the Holy of Holies (THEODORET, ISHO'DAD). The prophecy of the last week of the seventy has been fulfilled in history (BEDE). Daniel prophesies things to happen instead of those having already happened (PSEUDO-HEGESIPPUS). No greater disaster has ever happened to the Jews and the city of Jerusalem than the one predicted by Daniel (EUSEBIUS). The abomination of desolation refers to the imperial symbol of

Rome placed in the temple (EPHREM, ISHO'DAD).

9:21 Gabriel Comes to Daniel

DANIEL SEES GABRIEL WHILE FASTING. TERTULLIAN: This was the evening fast, which offers a richer prayer to God, since it takes place with fasting during the evening. ON FASTING 10.[1]

THE ARCHANGEL OF THE ONE AND THE SAME GOD. IRENAEUS: This passage reveals to us . . . that there is one and the same God the Father, who was declared by the prophets but made manifest by Christ. The Lord confirmed those things Daniel prophesied about the end, when our Lord said, "When you see the abomination of desolation that was told by Daniel the prophet." The angel Gabriel explained the visions to Daniel. This Gabriel is both the archangel of the Creator (*Demiurge*) and the one who proclaimed to Mary the coming and incarnation of Christ. Thus, most clearly, it must be one and the same God who sent the prophets and who sent forth his Son and called us to recognize him.[2] AGAINST HERESIES 5.25.5.[3]

---

[1]ANF 4:109**. [2]Irenaeus employs the figure of the archangel Gabriel to argue against the Gnostic assertion that the creator God of the Old Testament, referred to as the Demiurge, is not the same as the God of the New Testament, the Father of Jesus. [3]ANF 1:554**.

GABRIEL COMES AS THE VIRTUOUS ONE.
JEROME: The effect of his prayer was considerable, and the promise of God was fulfilled that says, "While you are yet speaking, see, I am at hand."[4] And Gabriel appears not as an angel or archangel but as a person (*vir*), a term used to indicate the quality of virtue rather than specifying his gender. . . . It is stated that he flew, because he had made his appearance as a human being. It is said that it was at the time of the evening sacrifice, in order to show that the prophet's prayer had persisted from the morning sacrifice even to the evening sacrifice and that God for that reason directed his mercy toward him. COMMENTARY ON DANIEL 9.21.[5]

GOD SPEAKS THROUGH THE ANGELS. AUGUSTINE: Let them read that Daniel says, "And behold, the man Gabriel." But why do we delay to shut up their mouths with another most evident and weighty proof, where no angel is mentioned individually or humankind in the plural, but rather the angels in their entirety are mentioned, namely, when it is said that through the angels not just any old word was spoken, but the law itself was given? Certainly, none of the faithful doubts that God gave Moses the law so that the people of Israel might be made subject to it, but nonetheless the law was given through angels. Thus Stephen says, "You received the law proclaimed by angels, and yet you do not keep it."[6] What is more evident than this? What is stronger and with such authority? The law was given to that people in the proclamations of the angels, but the coming of our Lord Jesus Christ was arranged and foretold through the law. Christ himself, the Word of God, was in a marvelous and indescribable manner in the angels, in whose proclamation the law was given. Thus he says in the Gospel, "If you believed Moses, you would believe me also, for he wrote about me." Therefore, the Lord was speaking then through the angels; through the angels the Son of God, the one who would be the mediator between God and humankind,

arranged his coming from the seed of Abraham so that he could find those who would receive him and confess themselves guilty, inasmuch as their failure to keep the law had made them transgressors. ON THE TRINITY 3.10.[7]

ANGEL OF GLAD TIDINGS. JULIAN OF TOLEDO: As is clear to all, Daniel himself gave the name of the very angel in the book of his prophecy, when he learned from the angel those mysteries of the weeks that would take place concerning the birth of Christ. . . . According to the Gospel, the wonderful name of the very angel was found to have been given again in these times, for the same angel told Zechariah, "I am Gabriel and I stand before God." ON THE CONFIRMATION OF THE SIXTH AGE 2.1.[8]

THE "MIGHT OF GOD." ISIDORE OF SEVILLE: Gabriel is translated from Hebrew into our tongue as "might of God." Wherever God's power or might is shown, Gabriel is sent. Therefore, also at that time, when the Lord was about to be born and triumph over the world, Gabriel came to Mary and announced him who had humbly agreed to come to defeat the powers of the air. ETYMOLOGIES 7.5.[9]

9:22 Gabriel Offers Wisdom and Understanding

GABRIEL COMES FROM GOD. JEROME: The vision was so obscure that the prophet needed the angel's teaching. . . . "Daniel, I have now come out to give you wisdom and understanding." That is, I have been sent to you and have come forth, not from the presence of God in the sense of departing from him but only in the sense of coming to you. COMMENTARY ON DANIEL 9.22.[10]

9:23 Consider and Understand

---

[4]Is 58:9. [5]JCD 93*. [6]Acts 7:53. [7]Cetedoc 0329.50.3.10.146. [8]Cetedoc 1260.2.1.14. [9]Cetedoc 1186.7.5.10. [10]JCD 94*.

Daniel Is Worthy of God's Love. Jerome: That is, at the time when you did begin to ask God, you did immediately obtain his mercy, and his decision was put forth. I have therefore been sent to explain to you the things of which you are ignorant, inasmuch as you are a man of desires, that is to say, a lovable man, worthy of God's love—even as Solomon was called *Idida* (variant: *Jedida*) or "man of desires." I have been sent because you are worthy, in recompense for your affection for God, to be told the secret counsels of God and to have a knowledge of things to come. Commentary on Daniel 9.23.[11]

Contemplate the Vision. Ephrem the Syrian: "So consider the word, which I will speak,"[12] that is, investigate and weigh carefully the meaning and the strength of the proposed vision; and in those things that I am about to tell you about it, contemplate a sort of expressed image of the future events. Commentary on Daniel 9.23.[13]

Pay Careful Attention. Theodoret of Cyr: The Lord . . . sent me to convey the future to you. For your part, give precise attention to what is said; what will be said is too profound for a human being (the meaning of "understand what is in the vision"), that is, what will be said in riddles, and requires of you precise attention for grasping it. Now, riddles occur when divine realities are spoken and written, the purpose being to prevent what is revealed to the holy ones becoming clear to everyone; after all, familiarity breeds contempt. Commentary on Daniel 9.22-23.[14]

9:24 Seventy Weeks

Various Interpretations. Jerome: I realize that this question has been argued over in various ways by people of greatest learning, and each of them has expressed his views according to the capacity of his own genius. And so . . . I shall . . . leave it to the reader's judgment as to whose explanation ought to be followed. Commentary on Daniel 9.24-27.[15]

Mystery of the Seventy Weeks. Quodvultdeus: As the end of the seventy-year period was drawing near, during which Jerusalem would be left desolate, as the Lord had foretold through the prophet Jeremiah, Daniel poured forth his prayer. . . . The archangel Gabriel came to his aid and told him about the mysteries that would take place. There would be seventy brief weeks among his people and in the holy city so that sin could end and trespasses be sealed up and unrighteousness ended and eternal righteousness brought in. Also the visions of the prophets would end, and the Holy of Holies would be anointed. From the time that this word went out in reply and Jerusalem would be built up would be seven weeks; until Christ, the prince, would come, sixty-two weeks. The Book of Promises and Predictions of God 2.35.[16]

A Time of Quietness for the People. Ephrem the Syrian: This means that there will be quietness for your people, so that the transgressions may be finished and the sins expiated through the seventy years of the bondage in Babylon may end, as well as all the crimes of the children of Israel. Again "to finish the transgression, to put an end to sin": here he also hints at the transgressions and sins of the Gentiles, which will happen in the end of the seventy weeks. "And to atone for iniquity": and this began from the baptism of John; "to bring everlasting righteousness": and soon Christ will appear, the Author of justice, who had been announced by the prophets before the centuries, and he will justify then sinners. "To seal both vision and prophet": certainly Christ fulfilled all the oracles of the prophets with his advent, passion and death, and he showed that they were true

---

[11]JCD 94*. [12]This reading is not in the Peshitta and must belong to another version of the Syriac Bible employed by Ephrem. [13]ESOO 2:221. [14]WGRW 7:239. [15]JCD 95. [16]Cl. 0413.2.35.28.

through facts. "And to anoint a most holy one": from the conclusion of this prophecy you will learn this: he endowed the holy ones with holiness. COMMENTARY ON DANIEL 9.24.[17]

CHRIST THE HOLY OF HOLIES. THEODORET OF CYR: Daniel . . . teaches that God decided that a period of 490 years should be allotted to Jerusalem to enjoy divine gifts as usual until it committed that sacrilegious and fearsome crime—I mean, the crucifixion of the Savior, who is known as Holy of Holies for his being the fount of holiness; he is anointed in his humanity by the Holy Spirit, and seals and confirms the ancient prophecies by fulfilling everything foretold by them and grants forgiveness of sins to those who believe in him. COMMENTARY ON DANIEL 9.24.[18]

ALL THE PREDICTIONS ARE FULFILLED IN CHRIST. ISHO'DAD OF MERV: The words "seventy weeks will linger,"[19] that is, until the destruction caused by the Romans. In fact, even though, in the meantime, they are sometimes afflicted, they will not be abandoned completely. Seventy weeks make 490 years; they are calculated from the time when they will come back from Babylon and will begin to build the temple to the year when the Romans will make war against them after the ascension of our Lord. COMMENTARY ON DANIEL 9.24.[20]

9:25 A Prince

THE COMING OF THE MESSIAH. BASIL OF SELEUCIA: Since there is much testimony from the writings of the Law and the Prophets concerning the coming of the Savior, so that the Jews cannot deny it, the more thoughtful among them admit that he will come but say that he has not yet come. We have deemed it fitting, therefore, to offer this proof from the discourse of the archangel Gabriel as he spoke precisely of the times to the prophet Daniel in the vision that came to him. . . . When the times were fulfilled in the days of Augustus, the foretold Christ came to his peo-

ple, was crucified and fulfilled all the things written about him through the holy angels and prophets. Thus, even if they do not blush on hearing the testimony of the archangel, let them cease from their vain waiting for the Messiah. Since the prophet Daniel was one of those longing to see the coming of the Messiah, our Lord himself says about him and the others, "Many prophets and just people longed to see those things that you see, but they did not see them, and to hear those things that you hear but did not hear them."[21] HOMILY 38.1.[22]

ANOINTED LEADER. THEODORET OF CYR: Now, it gave Christ a second name as leader. . . . He is our leader in his humanity as "the firstborn of all creation,"[23] that is, a new creation: "If anyone is in Christ, there is a new creation"[24]—and as firstborn from the dead, so as to have, as Paul says, "first place in everything."[25] Hence holy Gabriel called him "Christ the leader." To him from the rebuilding of Jerusalem, therefore, are "seven weeks and sixty-two weeks." COMMENTARY ON DANIEL 9.25.[26]

9:26 Sixty-two Weeks

DANIEL PREDICTS THE COMING OF CHRIST. TERTULLIAN: Now you hesitate to believe what we have stated, although you see that these things have happened. Therefore we ought to seek again the times that were foretold, both as pertaining to the birth and suffering of Christ and the removal of the city Jerusalem, that is, its destruction. Daniel says that the holy city and its sanctuary will be removed when the prince comes and that its pinnacle would be utterly destroyed. The times for the coming of the Christ must be sought again, as we found out in Daniel. When we have made a reckoning of these things, we will prove that he had already come, based on the

---

[17]*ESOO* 2:221 [18]WGRW 7:245**. [19]This is the reading of the Peshitta. [20]CSCO 328:118. [21]Lk 10:24. [22]PG 85:400. [23]Col 1:15. [24]2 Cor 5:17. [25]Col 1:18. [26]WGRW 7:247-49.

chronology that had been foretold, the signs that accompanied him, his works and the events that followed him, which would take place after his coming, as had been foretold, so that we might believe that all these predictions had been fulfilled. Daniel had thus foretold about him, so that he showed when and where he would free the nations and in what year after his passion the holy city would be removed. AN ANSWER TO THE JEWS 8.[27]

SEVENTY AND SIXTY-TWO WEEKS. PRIMASIUS: This is what [Daniel] says when he talks about the seventy weeks: "Seventy weeks will be for the rebuilding of Jerusalem and sixty-two weeks until Christ the prince. After the sixty-two weeks the Christ will be killed, and he will have nothing. And a people with their leader will come and destroy the city and the sanctuary." A little later: "He will confirm a covenant with many for a week, and in the middle of the week the offering and sacrifice will fail, and there will be an abomination of desolation." Since these things must be understood to refer to Christ's first coming, in which those things were done and also received their outcome, nonetheless that portion after the division of the weeks (which he had distributed in a rather secret manner of heavenly inspiration, first making mention of seven, then sixty-two, finally one, which he also divided into two parts), that is, the final week is aptly applied to the end of the first coming of Christ and to the beginning of his second coming. To state it more clearly, I think that it necessarily must apply to both comings in an interpretation that applies harmoniously to both. For after seven and sixty-two weeks the Christ would come and be killed, and he would reprove those who killed him, just as it was said that the same people will not be his. And as for his confirming a covenant with many during one week, one would rightly understand that all the words of the Old Testament and the actions that foretold by type the Christ's coming have been fulfilled by the truth of his presence, who is the end of the law. Nonetheless, I think

that the intention of this week most aptly pertains to the end of the world, since I hear soon thereafter, "And in half a week offering and sacrifice will come to an end." COMMENTARY ON THE APOCALYPSE 3.11.[28]

THE LAW COMES TO AN END. ISHO'DAD OF MERV: Theodoret interprets ("the king who will come") as the foreign kingship and the unlawful doctrine.[29] Others say, "With the king who will come," meaning with the Christ who will come. Instead of the words "the anointed one shall be killed," the Jews [say foolishly], "The oil[30] shall be cut off." Therefore, since there is no oil, and the oil of the anointment does not flow anymore, and it stops and does not proceed anymore, there was nobody to anoint with it both the kings and the priests according to the rule observed since Moses and afterwards. It was necessary that the law come to an end, because without priesthood and without the anointment of all that was anointed under the law, the law itself could not survive anymore. In the same manner, with what will your "anointed prince" be anointed, as there is no oil or ointment? "Its end shall come with a flood" and with destruction just like in the deluge of the generations of Noah. COMMENTARY ON DANIEL 9.26.[31]

9:27 For One Week

THE PERIOD AFTER THE PASSION. BEDE: Christ was killed not immediately after the sixty-two weeks but at the end of the seventieth week. As far as we can figure out, [Daniel] separates this last week from the others, for he was going to say more about this week. Christ was crucified in that week. . . . The events that follow—the fact that a people and their general would destroy the city and the sanctuary and that its end would be devastation and after the end of the war desolation would be decreed for it—these events do not

---

[2]Cetedoc 0033.8.1.9. [28]Cetedoc 0873.3.11.120 [*]. [29]See Theodoret, PG 81:1481. [30]This reading is attested only in certain manuscripts. [31]CSCO 328:120.

pertain to the seventy weeks. It had foretold that those weeks extend up to the leadership of the Christ, but still the Scriptures, after foretelling his coming and passion, wanted to show what would take place thereafter to the people who refused to welcome him. He says that Titus would come with the Roman people, who in the fortieth year after the passion of our Lord destroyed the city and the temple so that not even one rock remained on top of another. But having given a taste of these things in anticipation, he soon returns to expounding the week that he had glossed over. "He will confirm a covenant with many during one week," that is, in that last week in which John the Baptist, our Lord and the apostles converted many to the faith. "And in the middle of the week offering and sacrifice will come to an end." The middle of this week was the fifteenth year of Tiberias Caesar, when at the baptism of Christ the purification brought by the sacrifices began to grow obsolete, as far as the faithful were concerned. Again that which follows, "In the temple there will be an abomination of desolation, and the desolation will remain until the consummation and the end," has a view to the era that follows. The history of past generations and the events of our own times confirm the truthfulness of this prophecy. THE RECKONING OF TIME 9.[32]

THE ABOMINATION OF DESOLATION. PSEUDO-HEGESIPPUS: But what else did Daniel proclaim? He was prophesying not that which had already been done but that which would take place. What is the abomination of desolation that he proclaimed would take place when the Romans came, unless it is those things that now threaten? What is the oracle that we often mention as hav-

ing been declared by the most high God, that the city will perish down to its foundation, when their own prince will have been killed at the hands of his fellow tribe members, unless it is that which we now see being fulfilled? And perhaps because it did not please them to keep the temple unstained by innocent blood, it pleases God to purify it by fire. ON THE JEWISH WAR BY JOSEPHUS FLAVIUS 5.2.[33]

CHRIST REMOVES THE ABOMINATION.
EPHREM THE SYRIAN: Certainly this end of the Jews will be by no means similar to their transmigration to Egypt or Babylon; in fact they were dismissed from there after four hundred years, and from here after seventy. This ruin fixed by the decree of God the judge will remain immutable to the end. He shall make a strong covenant with many: Christ will make the Testament holy and firm through one week and half a week, until he removes the victim and the sacrifice. He is the one who set the victim and the sacrifice but who also abolishes them. In their place shall be an abomination that desolates: the Romans,[34] after submitting Judea to their power, placed the eagle, symbol of their emperor, in the temple. And this is what we read: "So when you see the desolating sacrilege standing in the holy place, as was spoken by the prophet Daniel."[35] Until the decreed end is poured out on desolation, that is, until the full execution of the divine decrees, the city will be given to oblivion and will lie destroyed and abandoned. COMMENTARY ON DANIEL 9.27.[36]

---

[32]Cetedoc 2320.9.61. [33]Cetedoc 0190A.5.2.372.27. [34]Theodoret and Isho'dad also refer to this occasion of Pilate's desecration of the temple. [35]Mt 24:15. [36]ESOO 2:222.

10:1-9 DANIEL TO RECEIVE ANOTHER VISION

¹*In the third year of Cyrus king of Persia a word was revealed to Daniel, who was named Belteshazzar. And the word was true, and it was a great conflict. And he understood the word and had understanding of the vision.*

²*In those days I, Daniel, was mourning for three weeks. *³*I ate no delicacies, no meat or wine entered my mouth, nor did I anoint myself at all, for the full three weeks. *⁴*On the twenty-fourth day of the first month, as I was standing on the bank of the great river, that is, the Tigris, *⁵*I lifted up my eyes and looked, and behold, a man clothed in linen, whose loins were girded with gold of Uphaz. *⁶*His body was like beryl, his face like the appearance of lightning, his eyes like flaming torches, his arms and legs like the gleam of burnished bronze, and the sound of his words like the noise of a multitude. *⁷*And I, Daniel, alone saw the vision, for the men who were with me did not see the vision, but a great trembling fell upon them, and they fled to hide themselves. *⁸*So I was left alone and saw this great vision, and no strength was left in me; my radiant appearance was fearfully changed, and I retained no strength. *⁹*Then I heard the sound of his words; and when I heard the sound of his words, I fell on my face in deep sleep with my face to the ground.*

OVERVIEW: At the end of Chapter One, the text concludes, "Daniel continued [in the king's court] until the first year of King Cyrus," which seems to contradict the opening sentence of Chapter Ten, "In the third year of Cyrus king of Persia a word was revealed to Daniel." Theodoret suggests that some commentators argue that this discrepancy was due to a scribal error, but he argues that the correct number is the third year (THEODORET, ISHO'DAD). Jerome does not offer a solution but presents two possible readings. Daniel mourns on behalf of his people for their indocility to return to their homeland (ISHO'DAD, THEODORET) by fasting in the sense of our Lord's teaching (EPHREM). Daniel humbles himself and secures divine favor (TERTULLIAN). He fasts in hope that the Israelites might be delivered from Babylon (EPHREM). Daniel demonstrates that fasting prepares the humble for receiving a vision (AMMONIUS) and strengthens his intercession (JEROME). As commanded, Daniel does not celebrate the Passover while in exile (THEODORET).

Daniel lifts up his eyes in order to perceive a vision. Hippolytus suggests that Daniel sees the Lord, while others identify the person in the vision as an angel. The angel in the vision is clothed in linen with a belt of pure gold. The word *baddim* is a transliteration of the Hebrew rendered by the Septuagint translators as "fine linen" (JEROME). The belt around his waist is described as being made of pure gold (AMMONIUS, JEROME). Daniel is awed at the sight of the angel and falls prostrate (CYRIL OF JERUSALEM). His companions, on the other hand, flee in fright (HIPPOLYTUS, THEODORET).

10:1 *In the Third Year of Cyrus*

TIME OF THE EVENT. ISHO'DAD OF MERV: It is evident that Daniel lived up to the third year [of Cyrus] and beyond, even though at the beginning of the book we read "until the first year of the king Cyrus."[1] COMMENTARY ON DANIEL 10.1.[2]

---

[1]Dan 1:21. [2]CSCO 328:121.

DANIEL SURVIVED UNTIL CYRUS. THEODORET OF CYR: To some it seems that Daniel is mistaken about the time and the one writing the book from the beginning puts "in the third year" instead of "in the first year." And the proof of this is that the blessed Daniel says right after the beginning of the prophecy, "And Daniel continued until year one of King Cyrus."[3] For if the prophet had lived only up until the first year of Cyrus' reign, the critic says, how could he have seen the revelation in the third year? Now I think that the former does not indicate the stated time nor does "the first year of Cyrus' reign" mark the end of blessed Daniel's life. For he does not say "until the first year of Cyrus the king" but "for year one." As it appears to me, he intends to instruct those encountering the prophetic book that he survived until Cyrus, king of the Persians, who set free those Jewish captives. COMMENTARY ON DANIEL 10.1.[4]

TWO POSSIBLE SOLUTIONS. JEROME: And how is it that we read at the end of the first vision, "And Daniel lived until the first year of Cyrus the king"?[5] Well then, we understand that he enjoyed his former high position among the Chaldeans and was clothed in purple and fine linen right up until the first year of King Cyrus, when Cyrus overthrew the Chaldeans, and afterwards Daniel commenced service under Darius, the son of Ahasuerus of the Median line, who reigned over the kingdom of the Chaldeans. Or else, indeed, that Darius had already died in whose first year Daniel had learned of the mystery of the seventy weeks, and he is now relating that he beheld these things in the third year of King Cyrus. COMMENTARY ON DANIEL 10.1.[6]

TRUTHFULNESS AND POWER OF THE VISION. THEODORET OF CYR: Quite suitably he calls it "a word" and "a vision." He saw holy angels; he also heard them conversing and from them learned accurately the things that would happen. And he says that the word was "true" so that all might receive the things about to be spoken without any

doubts. COMMENTARY ON DANIEL 10.1.[7]

THE MEANING OF STRENGTH. JEROME: "And it was a true word and great strength" refers either to the strength of the God who was going to perform these things or to the strength of the prophet who would comprehend them. COMMENTARY ON DANIEL 10.1.[8]

10:2 Daniel Mourns

DANIEL MOURNS FOR HIS PEOPLE'S INIQUITY. THEODORET OF CYR: We must seek the source of his grief. . . . Although the king permitted all who wanted their freedom and permission to return [to their homeland and rebuild the temple], most had built homes in Babylon and were held back by their bond to these houses and, thinking lightly of the chance to return, preferred a foreign land to their own. Only the lovers of godliness and guardians of the ancestral laws despised their possessions in Babylon and preferred their desolate homeland and its kingdom. Then the following fact also wrought a great pain for blessed Daniel: when he saw the trustworthiness of the divine promise and the kindness and benevolence of the king—and the stubborn and ungovernable nature of the people—he was very despondent in his soul, and he spent his time grieving. . . . He spent three weeks fasting. COMMENTARY ON DANIEL 10.2-3.[9]

DANIEL'S MOURNING. EPHREM THE SYRIAN: He says that the mourning had been protracted "for three weeks," because he had fasted for all that space of time. He calls fasting "mourning" in the same sense used by our Lord, when he defended himself and his disciples from the detractions of the Pharisees. When the disciples were reproached by the Pharisees because they were not fasting, the Lord answered, "The wed-

---

[3]Dan 1:21. [4]PG 81:1488; cf. WGRW 7:261-63. [5]Dan 1:21. [6]JCD 111. [7]PG 81:1488; cf. WGRW 7:263. [8]JCD 111. [9]PG 81:1489; cf. WGRW 7:263-65.

ding guests cannot mourn," that is, fast, "as long as the bridegroom is with them, can they"?[10] COMMENTARY ON DANIEL 10.1-2.[11]

10:3 Daniel Ate No Delicacies

DISCIPLINE OF THE BODY AND SPIRITUAL VISIONS. TERTULLIAN: This abstinence Daniel used in order to please God by humiliation, and not for the purpose of producing a sensibility and wisdom for his soul previous to receiving communication by dreams and visions, as if it were not rather to effect such action in an ecstatic state. This "sobriety" . . . will have nothing to do with exciting ecstasy but will rather serve to recommend its being wrought by God. ON THE SOUL 48.[12]

FASTING AND PRAYER. AMMONIUS OF ALEXANDRIA: The prophet teaches us that fasting is a great virtue and so too is affliction with prayer. Through these things sometimes a person is deemed worthy even of visions. FRAGMENTS ON DANIEL 10.3.[13]

SIGNIFICANCE OF BREAD. THEODORET OF CYR: Daniel paid no attention to his body in these days either by anointing the outside or [by taking] food within. Quite well and usefully he has added the descriptor desirable not to meat but to bread. For bread is the most necessary food of all; the wealthy enjoy meat, but the poor as well as the rich enjoy bread. Therefore, he called it "the desirable bread," on the grounds that is a most common food and most desired of all food. COMMENTARY ON DANIEL 10.2-3.[14]

ABSTINENCE. JEROME: By this example we are taught to abstain from the pleasanter types of food (I think that the term "desirable bread" is that inclusive) during a period of fasting, and that we neither eat flesh nor drink wine and specially that we desire no anointing with ointments. This custom is maintained among those in Persia and India even to this day, that they use ointment as a

substitute for baths. Also, Daniel afflicted his soul for three consecutive weeks so that his intercession might not appear cursory or casual. COMMENTARY ON DANIEL 10.2-3.[15]

10:4 Daniel Stands by the Tigris

NO PASSOVER CELEBRATION IN EXILE. THEODORET OF CYR: On the fourteenth day of the first month at evening the divine law commanded them to celebrate the Passover, but blessed Daniel maintained his fast until the twenty-fourth day. . . . Daniel did not celebrate the Passover in obedience to the law, which expressly commands Israel to celebrate the three feast days in the place which the Lord God chose. Those Jews who dared to celebrate these festivals in a foreign land would have been transgressing this command. COMMENTARY ON DANIEL 10.4.[16]

10:5 Daniel Lifted His Eyes

PREPAREDNESS FOR A VISION. JEROME: We must lift up our eyes if we are to be able to discern a mystical vision. COMMENTARY ON DANIEL 10.5.[17]

DANIEL SEES THE SON OF GOD. HIPPOLYTUS: In the first vision he says, "Behold, the angel Gabriel [was] sent."[18] Here, however, it is not so; he sees the Lord, not yet indeed as perfect man but with the appearance and form of man, as he says: "And, behold, a man clothed in linen." For in being clothed in a various-colored coat, he indicated mystically[19] the variety of the graces of our calling. For the priestly coat was made up of different colors, as various nations waited for Christ's coming, in order that we might be made up (as one body) of many colors. COMMENTARY ON DANIEL 2.24.[20]

---

[10]Mt 9:15. [11]ESOO 2:223. [12]ANF 3:226*. [13]PG 85:1377. [14]PG 81:1492. [15]JCD 111*. [16]PG 81:1492; cf. WGRW 7:267. [17]JCD 112. [18]See Dan 8:16; 9:21. [19]In the text, μυστηριων ("of mysteries"), for which μυστηριωδων or μυστικως ("mystically") is proposed. [20]ANF 5:182.

THE MAN'S CLOTHING. JEROME: Instead of "linen," as Aquila rendered it, Theodotion simply puts *baddim* [a transcription of the Hebrew word], whereas the Septuagint renders it as *byssus* ["fine linen"] and Symmachus as *exaireta* ["choice vestments"], that is, "distinguished clothing" (*praecipua*). And instead of what we have rendered as, "Behold, a man," on the basis of the Hebrew text, Symmachus puts, "One like to a man," for he was not actually a man but only had the appearance of one. COMMENTARY ON DANIEL 10.5.[21]

SYMBOLISM OF UPHAZ. HIPPOLYTUS: Now the word Uphaz, which is a word transferred from Hebrew to Greek, denotes pure gold. COMMENTARY ON DANIEL 2.25.[22]

THE ROBE CHRIST WEARS. AMMONIUS OF ALEXANDRIA: [The Hebrew word] *baddim* means an intricately woven cloak, just as believers, whom Christ wears as a robe, are eminent in the weave of virtues. God puts on the faithful and girds them with the precious and pure gospel so that they might believe in the resurrection. For Orphaz means "pure." FRAGMENTS ON DANIEL 10.5.[23]

10:6 His Appearance

THE SOUNDING VOICE OF THE ANGEL. THEODORET OF CYR: He says, "And his body was like *Tharseis*" instead of "it resembled purified gold brought from Tharseis," for refined gold was brought to Solomon from there. "And his face was like the appearance of lightning." He says that a radiance resembling light shone from his face. "And his eyes were like lamps of fire and his arms and legs like the sight of burnished bronze and the sound of his words like the sound of a crowd." He says that he has eyes emitting fire and arms resembling the finest bronze. You would think that he had heard a multitude speaking. COMMENTARY ON DANIEL 10.5-6.[24]

THE ANALOGY OF THE GEM. JEROME: For "chrysolite," one of the twelve gems inserted in the oracular breastplate of the high priest, the Hebrew has *tarshish*, a word that Theodotion and Symmachus simply left unchanged in transcription. But the Septuagint called it "the sea," according to the usage in the Psalms: "With a violent gale you dash the ships of Tharsis in pieces," that is, "the ships of the sea."[25] Jonah, also, was desirous of fleeing not to Tarsus, the Cilician city (as most people suppose), substituting one letter for another, not to some region in India (as Josephus imagines), but simply out to the high seas in general.[26] COMMENTARY ON DANIEL 10.6.[27]

10:7 Daniel Alone Saw the Vision

DANIEL IS AWED AT THE SIGHT OF THE ANGEL. CYRIL OF JERUSALEM: What would you do then? That he who came for our salvation should become a minister of destruction because people could not bear him? Or that he should suit his grace to our measure? Daniel could not bear the vision of an angel, and were you capable of the sight of the Lord of angels? Gabriel appeared, and Daniel fell down; and of what nature or in what guise was he that appeared? His countenance was like lightning, not like the sun, "and his eyes as lamps of fire," not as a furnace of fire. "And the voice of his words [was] as the voice of a multitude," not as the voice of twelve legions of angels; nevertheless the prophet fell down. . . . If an angel appearing took away the prophet's strength, would the appearance of God have allowed him to breathe? . . . So then after trial had shown our weakness, the Lord assumed that which people required: for since people required to hear from one of like countenance, the Savior took on him the nature of like affections, that people might

---

[21]JCD 112*. [22]ANF 5:182*; cf. JCD 112. [23]PG 85:1377. [24]PG 81:1492-93; cf. WGRW 7:267-69. [25]Ps 48:7 (47:8 LXX). [26]Jon 1:3. [27]JCD 113*.

be the more easily instructed. Catechetical Lectures 12.14.[28]

Only Daniel Is Worthy to See the Vision. Hippolytus: Also at that time there were many who stood alongside Daniel, but they did not see the vision, for they were not worthy. Commentary on Daniel 4.38.3.[29]

Daniel's Companions Flee in Fright. Theodoret of Cyr: But perhaps someone would say, "Why then did they flee, if they did not see the vision?" Most likely this fact is what filled them all the more with dread, for since they saw no one and yet heard a great voice, they likely all ran away in fright. Then he calls their astonishment not only cowardice but also the inability to see. These events resemble the things that happened to Paul on the road near Damascus. There

he too saw a light that flashed around him. His companions saw nothing but only heard a voice.[30] And then his companions likewise fled from the divine prophet when they heard only the voice, while he remained there alone. Commentary on Daniel 10.7.[31]

10:8 Daniel Worn Down by the Vision

Only the Faithful Can See. Ammonius of Alexandria: "I was left alone." The unbelievers do not know Christ and flee, while the faithful will see him, since they are illuminated by him, even as faithful Daniel was. Fragments on Daniel 10.8.[32]

---

[28]NPNF 2 7:75*. [29]SC 14:340. [30]Acts 9:3-7. [31]PG 81:1493; cf. WGRW 7:269. [32]PG 85:1377.

10:10-21 THE REVELATION: THE CELESTIAL CONFLICT AMONG ANGELS

[10]*And behold, a hand touched me and set me trembling on my hands and knees.* [11]*And he said to me, "O Daniel, man greatly beloved, give heed to the words that I speak to you, and stand upright, for now I have been sent to you." While he was speaking this word to me, I stood up trembling.* [12]*Then he said to me, "Fear not, Daniel, for from the first day that you set your mind to understand and humbled yourself before your God, your words have been heard, and I have come because of your words.* [13]*The prince of the kingdom of Persia withstood me twenty-one days; but Michael, one of the chief princes, came to help me, so I left him there with the prince of the kingdom of Persia[x]* [14]*and came to make you understand what is to befall your people in the latter days. For the vision is for days yet to come."*

[15]*When he had spoken to me according to these words, I turned my face toward the ground and was dumb.* [16]*And behold, one in the likeness of the sons of men touched my lips; then I opened my mouth and spoke. I said to him who stood before me, "O my lord, by reason of the vision pains have come upon me, and I retain no strength.* [17]*How can my lord's servant talk with my lord? For now no strength remains in me, and no breath is left in me."*

^{18}*Again one having the appearance of a man touched me and strengthened me.* ^{19}*And he said,* *"O man greatly beloved, fear not, peace be with you; be strong and of good courage." And when he spoke to me, I was strengthened and said, "Let my lord speak, for you have strengthened me."* ^{20}*Then he said, "Do you know why I have come to you? But now I will return to fight against the prince of Persia; and when I am through with him, lo, the prince of Greece will come.* ^{21}*But I will tell you what is inscribed in the book of truth: there is none who contends by my side against these except Michael, your prince."*

x Theodotion Compare Gk: Heb *I was left there with the kings of Persia*

OVERVIEW: The angel appearing to Daniel assumes a human form in order not to terrify him (JEROME). He instructs Daniel to listen carefully to the mysteries to be revealed (EPHREM). Daniel desires wisdom and understanding (AUGUSTINE, JEROME); the angel prophesies through the Holy Spirit (BASIL). The prayer of the righteous is effective (THEODORET). Daniel's prayer leads the angel to prepare for the people a salvation plan (EPHREM) that allows them to return (AMMONIUS). Daniel's praying in faithfulness and patience drives the angel to plead for him to God (JEROME). His fasting through the Passover (CHRYSOSTOM) awakened a divine response (THEODORET).

Each nation has its own guardian angel (THEODORET); Michael is assigned to Israel (HIPPOLYTUS, PSEUDO-DIONYSIUS), who comes to help in time (EPHREM). The princes of the earthly powers represent the powers from above (CHRYSOSTOM, THEODORET, ORIGEN). The prince of Persia resists releasing the captive nation of Israel (JEROME), for he is delighted in the presence of Israel in Persia and hopes to convert Persia with Israel's piety for God (EPHREM). Gabriel comes and interprets to Daniel the situation in which the princes of the nations hostile to God are in conflict with him and Michael (JOHN CASSIAN). The things that happen to Israel at the end of the world are what concern Daniel (JEROME). Daniel's restoration by the one like a son of man is symbolic of our being strengthened by the Lord in the resurrection of life (HIPPOLYTUS). The one like a son of man is the incarnation of the Only Begotten (AMMO-

NIUS). The "lord" Daniel addresses is an honorific usage rather than a reference to God (THEODORET). The Word is the force of revival (HIPPOLYTUS) and the source of strength (AMMONIUS). The touch of the one like a son of man frees Daniel of terror and enables him to receive divine secrets (JEROME).

The prince of Greece knows what is to happen to Alexander the ruler of the world (AMMONIUS), who slays Darius and overthrows the kingdoms of the Persians and of the Medes so that the prince of Greece overcomes that of Persia (JEROME).

10:10 *Daniel Restored by a Touch*

CHRIST'S UPHOLDING HUMANITY. AMMONIUS OF ALEXANDRIA: The hand indicates partial knowledge of the truth of the gospel. For Christ is the one who will raise the whole human race. FRAGMENTS ON DANIEL 10.10.[1]

THE ANGEL ASSUMES A HUMAN FORM. JEROME: The angel appeared in the form of a man and laid his hand on the human prophet as he lay upon the ground, in order that he might not be terrified, beholding a form similar to his own. COMMENTARY ON DANIEL 10.10.[2]

10:11 *The Angel Speaks to Daniel*

DANIEL DESIRES WISDOM. AUGUSTINE: Daniel was called by the angel "a man of desires." What

---

[1]PG 85:1377. [2]JCD 113*.

were those desires of his, but ardent longings for the beauty of wisdom? Because in his youth he had trampled on lust, as a prisoner he had crushed the pride of kings, when shut in close he had shut the mouths of lions. SERMON 391.5.[3]

MAN OF DESIRE. JEROME: It was fitting that [Daniel] was addressed as a man of desires, for by dint of urgent prayer and affliction of body and the discipline of severe fasting he desired to learn of the future and to be informed of the secret counsels of God. Instead of "man of desires," Symmachus rendered it as "desirable man." The term is apt, for every saint possesses a beauty of soul and is beloved by God. COMMENTARY ON DANIEL 10.11.[4]

REVELATION COMES THROUGH THE HOLY SPIRIT. BASIL THE GREAT: I indeed maintain that even Gabriel[5] in no other way foretells events to come than by the foreknowledge of the Spirit, by reason of the fact that one of the boons distributed by the Spirit is prophecy. And whence did he who was ordained to announce the mysteries of the vision to the man of desires[6] derive the wisdom whereby he was enabled to teach hidden things, if not from the Holy Spirit? The revelation of mysteries is indeed the peculiar function of the Spirit, as it is written, "God has revealed them to us by his Spirit."[7] ON THE HOLY SPIRIT 16.38.[8]

DANIEL IS INSTRUCTED TO STAY ALERT. EPHREM THE SYRIAN: "Daniel, pay attention," . . . that is, learn and weigh carefully the mysteries of those things whose results you asked with constant prayer and with three weeks of mourning and fast. COMMENTARY ON DANIEL 10.9-11.[9]

10:12 Fear Not

THE FIRST DAY. EPHREM THE SYRIAN: "From the first day," that is, from that day when you began to fast, being inflamed by the desire to learn those things that you asked, so that you persevered in praying and supplicating before your God. "Your words have been heard, and I have come because of your words": your prayers led me, as well, to prepare a plan for the salvation of your people according to your vows. COMMENTARY ON DANIEL 10.12.[10]

DANIEL PRAYS WITH PATIENCE AND FAITH. JEROME: On the twenty-fourth day of the first month, that is, of Nisan, after three weeks or twenty-one days had elapsed, he beheld this vision. And he heard from the angel that on the very first day he had begun to pray and to afflict himself before God; his words had been heard and granted. The question arises, why, if he had been heard, was the angel not sent to him right away? Well, by reason of the delay an opportunity was afforded him of praying to the Lord at greater length, so that in proportion as his earnest desire was intensified, he might deserve to hear more than he would otherwise. And as for the angel's statement, "And I have come in response to your words," his meaning is this: After you began to invoke God's mercy by good works and tearful supplication and fasting, then I for my part embraced the opportunity of entering in before God and praying for you. COMMENTARY ON DANIEL 10.12.[11]

10:13 The Prince of Persia

THE ONE RULING OVER THE KING. THEODORET OF CYR: He does not simply say "prince of the Persians" but "prince of the kingdom of the Persians." He means to say "the one entrusted to rule over the very king of the Persians." COMMENTARY ON DANIEL 10.13-14.[12]

NOT HUMANS BUT POWERS. ORIGEN: Accordingly we find in the holy Scriptures that there are rulers over individual nations, as for instance, we

[3]WSA 3 10:419. [4]JCD 113*. [5]Lk 1:19. [6]"Man greatly beloved" (RSV, Dan 10:11). [7]1 Cor 2:10. [8]NPNF 2 8:24*. [9]ESOO 2:223. [10]ESOO 2:224. [11]JCD 113-14*. [12]PG 81:1497-1500; cf. WGRW 7:275.

read in Daniel of a certain "prince of the kingdom of the Persians" and another "prince of the kingdom of the Greeks," who, as is clearly shown by the sense of the passage itself, are not humans but powers.[13] ON FIRST PRINCIPLES 3.3.2.[14]

EVEN IN CONFLICT, EACH NATION HAS ITS OWN GUARDIAN ANGEL. THEODORET OF CYR: Moses teaches us these things more distinctly: "For when the Most High allotted the nations, as he scattered the sons of Adam, he appointed the boundaries of the nations according to the numbers of the angels."[15] And in the holy Gospels our Lord says to the apostles, "See that you do not despise one of these little ones, because their angels daily see the face of my Father in heaven."[16] ... We learn then from these passages that each of the angels is entrusted with our care, to guard and protect us and to ward off the wicked demon's plots, but the archangels are entrusted with authority over the nations.... And blessed Daniel agrees with them, for he also speaks of the prince of the kingdom of the Persians [and] ... the prince of the Greeks, and [he] calls the prince of Israel Michael.

Why then [does] the prince of the Persian kingdom seem to oppose the advocate of God's people? After all, it is clear to everyone that the nature of the angels is better than the passions by which we are gripped, and their nature is full of holiness. The fact that they unquestionably obey the wishes of God can be learned throughout Scripture. How then does the prince of the kingdom of the Persians seem to oppose the care of the Israelites? ... For the prince of the Persians and the prince of Greeks, that is, those who have been entrusted with the protection and care of these nations, inasmuch as they are fondly disposed toward those in their care and see the transgression of Israel, were displeased to see the Israelites enjoying more consideration.[17] They did not know the mystery that had been hidden in God, who made all things. After the incarnation of our Savior, as Paul says, "The manifold wisdom of God was made known to the rulers and

authorities through the church."[18] Therefore, since they did not know this mystery and they saw God's great providence for Israel, those who had been entrusted with the care for the other nations were displeased to see that after the law, the prophets and such teaching and care, the Israelites behaved worse and were inflamed by more evil than the nations who were shepherded by them. COMMENTARY ON DANIEL 10.13.[19]

MICHAEL IS THE PRINCE OF THE JEWS. PSEUDO-DIONYSIUS: Michael is called the ruler of the Jewish people, and other angels are described as rulers of other nations, for the Most High has established the boundaries of the nations by the number of his angels.... Michael presides over the government in order to make clear that Israel, like the other nations, was assigned to one of the angels, to recognize through him the one universal ruling source. For there is only one Providence over all the world, a suprabeing transcending all power visible and invisible; and over every nation there are presiding angels entrusted with the task of raising up toward that divine Providence, as their own source, everyone willing to follow, as far as possible. CELESTIAL HIERARCHY 9.2-4.[20]

TWENTY-ONE DAYS. THEODORET OF CYR: This means "I spent all these days persuading him how the Israelites were justifiably worthy of this attention. And Michael, one of the chief princes, joined in advocating with me." COMMENTARY ON DANIEL 10.13.[21]

THE IDENTITY OF THE PRINCE OF PERSIA. JEROME: In my opinion this was the angel to whose charge Persia was committed, in accor-

[13]See Ezek 28. [14]OFP 224*. [15]Deut 32:8 LXX; cf. Chrysostom, PG 56:242. [16]See Mt 18:10. [17]See also Ephrem *Commentary on Daniel* 10.13. Ephrem suggests that the angels fought each other in a friendly way. The prince of Persia attempted to prevent the return of the Jews because he hoped the presence of the Jewish people would guide the Persian nation to God. [18]Eph 3:9-10. [19]PG 81:1496-97; cf. WGRW 7:271-73. [20]PDCW 171-73. [21]PG 81:1497; cf. WGRW 7:275.

dance with what we read in Deuteronomy.[22] These are the princes of whom Paul also says, "We speak forth among the perfect a wisdom that none of the princes of this world knew. For if they had known it, they would have never have crucified the Lord of glory."[23] And so the prince of the Persians offered resistance, acting on behalf of the province entrusted to him, in order that the entire captive nation might not be released. And it may well be that although the prophet was graciously heard by God from the day when he set his heart to understand, the angel was nevertheless not sent to proclaim to him God's gracious decision, for the reason that the prince of Persia opposed him for twenty-one days, enumerating the sins of the Jewish people as a ground for their justly being kept in captivity and as proof that they ought not to be released. COMMENTARY ON DANIEL 10.13.[24]

HOSTILE POWERS. JOHN CASSIAN: There is no doubt whatsoever that the prince of the kingdom of the Persians was the adversary power that befriended the Persian nation, which was hostile to the people of God. And he stood in the way of the benefit that he saw the archangel was going to procure in response to the request that the prophet had made of the Lord, being envious lest the angel's salutary consolation come to Daniel too quickly and lest he comfort the people of God over which the archangel Gabriel had been sent. CONFERENCE 8.13.2.[25]

10:14 A Vision of the Latter Days

THE ANGEL COMES TO GIVE DANIEL UNDERSTANDING. AUGUSTINE: The Greek version has a more concise expression for "give me understanding," *sunetison me*, expressing "give understanding" by the single word *sunetison*, which the Latin cannot do; as if one could not say, "Heal me," and it were necessary to say, "Give me health," as it is here said, "Give me understanding"; or "Make me whole," as here it may be said, "Make me intelligent." This indeed an angel could do, for he said

to Daniel, "I come to give you understanding"; and this word is in the Greek, as it is here also, *sunetisai se*; as if the Latin translator were to render *therapeusai se by sanitatem dare tibi*. For the Latin interpreter would not make a circumlocution by saying, to give you understanding, if, as we say from health, "to heal you," so one could say from intellect, "to intellectuate you." But if an angel could do this, what reason is there that this man should pray that this be done for him by God? Is it because God had commanded the angel to do it? Just so: for Christ is understood to have given this command to the angel.[26] EXPLANATIONS OF THE PSALMS 119.73.[27]

DANIEL FOREKNOWS THE FUTURE OF HIS PEOPLE. JEROME: The very petition that Daniel had requested is the thing that he deserves to hear from God, namely, what is going to happen to the people of Israel, not in the near future but in the last days, that is, at the end of the world. COMMENTARY ON DANIEL 10.14.[28]

10:16 Pains from the Vision[29]

DANIEL IS STRENGTHENED BY AN INVISIBLE BEING. HIPPOLYTUS: "While I was in this position," he continues, "I was strengthened beyond my hope. For one unseen touched me, and immediately my weakness was removed, and I was restored to my former strength." For whenever all the strength of our life and its glory pass from us, then are we strengthened by Christ, who stretches forth his hand and raises the living from among the dead, and as it were from Hades itself, to the resurrection of life. SCHOLIA ON DANIEL 10.16.[30]

DANIEL FORESEES THE INCARNATION. AMMONIUS OF ALEXANDRIA: "Like the Son of man." He foresees the incarnation of the Only Begotten and

---

[22]Deut 32:8 LXX. [23]1 Cor 2:6, 8. [24]JCD 114. [25]ACW 57:299. [26]Dan 8:15-16 . [27]NPNF 1 8:572*. [28]JCD 115. [29]LXX: "O my lord, at the sight of you my bowels were turned within them." [30]ANF 5:190.

calls him the Son of man, the one who was to be born of holy Mary and made human. "And my insides churned." Since life is compared with a wheel, the one who lives among the saints, that is, the soul being directed in this life, ought to leave behind the evils here below and ought to bring up good things, that is, good deeds, from the earthly realm to the sublime and heavenly. FRAGMENTS ON DANIEL 10.16.[31]

THE INCOMPREHENSIBILITY OF GOD. CHRYSOSTOM: Let those Anomoeans[32] listen who, out of curiosity, are investigating into the essence of the Lord of angels. Daniel, to whom the eyes of the lions showed reverence,[33] Daniel, who had a more than human power in his human body, could not endure the presence of his fellow servant but lay on the ground before the angel[34] and could not breathe. For he said, "My bowels were turned within me at what I saw, and no breath was left in me." But these Anomoeans, who are so far removed from the virtue of that just man, profess to know with all exactness the highest and first of essences, the very essence of God, who has created myriads of these angels. And yet Daniel did not have the strength to look on a single one of them. AGAINST THE ANOMOEANS 3.23.[35]

GLORIFIED IS THE VISION OF GOD. JEROME: Theodotion interprets it this way, in accordance with what we read in Psalm 102 [Vulgate]: "Bless the Lord, O my soul, and all that is within me, bless his holy name."[36] For our inward nature must direct its gaze without, before we deserve to behold a vision of God; and when we actually have beheld a vision of God, then our inward nature is converted within us and we become wholly of the number of those concerning whom it is written in another psalm: "All the glory of the daughter of kings is within, in golden borders." COMMENTARY ON DANIEL 10.16.[37]

10:17 My Lord

THE ONE WHO APPEARS TO DANIEL IS NOT

THE LORD. THEODORET OF CYR: Let no one think that the one who appeared to Daniel was the Lord because Daniel addressed him as "lord." For Daniel at the end of the vision said, "He stretched out his hand to the heaven and swore by the living God,"[38] confessing candidly thereby his servitude to the Lord. Daniel called him "lord" not as if he were God, but rather paying him the customary honor. For when we too converse with humans of more honorable rank, we typically use this salutation, just as also blessed Abraham did when he saw the angels appearing as men and conversed with them as with men: "I ask you, my lord, if I have found favor in your sight, do not pass by your servant." And blessed Rebecca spoke to the servant of blessed Abraham, "Drink, my lord, and I will give water to your camels."[39] Accordingly, also this word *lord* does not altogether indicate God. And we will learn this more clearly from the end, as long as we hold to this train of argument. COMMENTARY ON DANIEL 10.16-17.[40]

10:18 Daniel Is Strengthened

GOD IS THE SOURCE OF STRENGTH. AMMONIUS OF ALEXANDRIA: When the strength of our life fails and we leave behind all earthly glory, so that we are no longer strong in it, then we receive the power from God, as Christ stretches out his hand upon us and says, "Be bold and strong." FRAGMENTS ON DANIEL 10.19.[41]

A HEART FREE OF FEAR. JEROME: For unless the angel had reassured him by touching him like a son of man, so that his heart was freed of terror, he would not have been able to hearken to God's secrets. COMMENTARY ON DANIEL 10.19.[42]

THE ANGEL ENCOURAGES DANIEL. THEO-

---

[31]PG 85:1380. [32]Those of the post-Nicene era who considered Jesus, the Son, to be unlike (*anomoios*) God, the Father. [33]Dan 6:23 LXX. [34]Dan 10:8-9. [35]FC 72:105. [36]Ps 103:1 (102:1 LXX). [37]JCD 115. [38]See Dan 12:7. [39]Gen 24:46. [40]PG 81:1500. [41]PG 85:1380. [42]JCD 115.

doret of Cyr: He meant, "Do not be in distress at all; for I did not come to harm you but to make known to you what you desired to know. Cast off your fear, be brave, and be strong." And the deed followed word. Commentary on Daniel 10.18-19.[43]

10:20 The Prince of Persia

The Guardian Angel of Each Nation Knows. Ammonius of Alexandria: Each nation has a guardian angel over them, so that they may not be harmed by the demons. . . . Therefore, the prince of the Greeks was also in the presence of God so that he himself heard the prophecies that were spoken concerning Alexander and those after him who would rule the world. Fragments on Daniel 10.20.[44]

10:20 The Prince of Greece

Macedonian Succession. Jerome: "For as I was coming away, the prince of the Greeks appeared and entered."[45] He means, "I myself was departing from God's presence in order to announce to you the events that are to befall your people in the last days; and yet I am still not secure, since the prince of the Persians stands to plead against the granting of your petitions and the acceptance of my advocacy on your behalf. And behold, the prince of the Greeks, or Macedonians, had just come, and he entered in before God's presence to lodge accusation against the prince of the Medes and Persians, in order that the kingdom of the Macedonians might succeed in their place." Truly marvelous are the secret counsels of God, for it indeed came to pass that after the Jewish people had been freed from captivity, Alexander, king of the Macedonians, slew Darius and overthrew the kingdom of the Persians and Medes, so that the prince of the Greeks did overcome the prince of the Persians. Commentary on Daniel 10.20.[46]

10:21 What Is Inscribed

Relating What Was Foretold. Jerome: "Nevertheless I will relate to you what has been set down in the Scripture of truth." That is the order that the words follow: The fulfillment is still in doubt. For even though you do beseech the Lord and I present your prayers to him, yet the prince of the Persians takes his stand on the opposite side and is unwilling that your people be freed from captivity. But because the prince of the Greeks has come and in the meanwhile is contending against the prince of the Persians, and also because I have Michael there as my assistant, I shall, during their mutual conflict, report to you the coming events that God has foretold to me and has asked me to relate to you. Commentary on Daniel 10.21.[47]

Human Will. Ephrem the Syrian: The angel reported these events, so that Daniel might know that there were not many among the Jews who asked God for their return, nor did the angels approve Daniel's vow, nor was everything you requested, Daniel, accepted by the angels, in order that the freedom of human will not be restricted. Commentary on Daniel 10.21.[48]

Petitioning God. Jerome: He implies, I am that angel who presents your prayers to God, and I have no other helper in petitioning God on your behalf except the archangel Michael, to whose charge the Jewish nation has been entrusted. Commentary on Daniel 10.21.[49]

Michael Wages War and Gabriel Interprets Dreams. Theodoret of Cyr: He says in effect, "Why then do I speak of one or two, the prince of the Persians or that of the Greeks? For none of the heavenly powers wishes your people to obtain anything good, manifestly because of their great lawlessness. Only Michael so desires, who was entrusted with the care of your people." He used the expression "to wage war" instead of

---

[43]PG 81:1500-1501. [44]PG 85:1380. [45]LXX. [46]JCD 115-16. [47]JCD 116*. [48]ESOO 2:226. [49]JCD 116.

"to argue and persuade," since he wished to show the just irritation of his opponent at the people and his own good will on their behalf. It is likely that the angel who is doing the debating is the holy Gabriel, for this angel had already inter-preted the other dreams for him. COMMENTARY ON DANIEL 10.20-21.[50]

---

[50]PG 81:1501; WGRW 7:277.

11:1-4 FOUR PERSIAN KINGS

[1]*And as for me, in the first year of Darius the Mede, I stood up to confirm and strengthen him.*

[2]*And now I will show you the truth. Behold, three more kings shall arise in Persia; and a fourth shall be far richer than all of them; and when he has become strong through his riches, he shall stir up all against the kingdom of Greece.* [3]*Then a mighty king shall arise, who shall rule with great dominion and do according to his will.* [4]*And when he has arisen, his kingdom shall be broken and divided toward the four winds of heaven, but not to his posterity, nor according to the dominion with which he ruled; for his kingdom shall be plucked up and go to others besides these.*

OVERVIEW: Who is speaking? Some suggest the angel Gabriel (THEODORET, ISHO'DAD, EPHREM); others suggest it is Daniel who is speaking. Historians record at least ten Persian monarchs who ruled after Cyrus, a record that conflicts with the prophetic text, which records only four. Neither account is incorrect. Prophecy was not concerned with preserving historical details but only in summarizing the most important parts (JEROME). The identity of the four kings is as follows: Cambyses, Smerdis (or the Magi), Darius and Xerxes (JEROME, THEODORET). Other interpreters identify the three kings as the kings who were named Darius. The fourth king was Darius, who was defeated by Alexander (ISHO'DAD). Alexander's great kingdom was soon to be divided into four parts (THEODORET, HIP-POLYTUS, EPHREM). Though the kingdom was divided into four parts, the author does not spend much time on the ruler of Asia Minor or Macedonia but only on those kingdoms that were the source of much harm to the Jewish people (THEODORET).

11:1 The First Year of Cyrus[1]

THE ANGEL RISES UP FOR ISRAEL. THEO-DORET OF CYR: [The divine angel says,] As soon as Cyrus came to the throne and the end of captivity had been reached, I took my place until I had secured release and liberation for the people. COMMENTARY ON DANIEL 11.1.[2]

DANIEL SPEAKS. JEROME: Daniel implies, "From the first year of the reign of Darius, who overthrew the Chaldeans and delivered me from the hand of my enemies to the extent of his ability . . . I for my part stood before God, and I besought God's mercy on him, in view of the man's love for me, in order that either he or his king-

---

[1]LXX; the MT says Darius, not Cyrus. [2]WGRW 7:277.

dom might be strengthened and confirmed. And since I persevered in my prayer, I was answered by God and given to understand the following information." COMMENTARY ON DANIEL 11.1.[3]

11:2 More Kings Shall Rise

REQUEST FOR REVELATION. JEROME: "Now I shall proclaim the truth to you." This means, "because you desired to know what will happen to the kings of Persia, listen to the order of events and hear the answer to your request." COMMENTARY ON DANIEL 11.2.[4]

FOUR KINGS. JEROME: [Gabriel] states that four kings shall arise in Persia after Cyrus, namely, Cambyses, the son of Cyrus; and the Magus named Smerdis, who married Pantaptes, the daughter of Cambyses. Then, when he was slain by seven magi and Darius had succeeded to his throne, the same Pantaptes married Darius and by him gave birth to Xerxes,[5] who became a most powerful and wealthy king, and led an innumerable host against Greece and performed those deeds that are related by the Greek historians. For in the archonship of Callias he destroyed Athens by fire, and about that same time he waged the war at Thermopylae and the naval battle at Salamis. It was in his time that Sophocles and Euripides[6] became famous and Themistocles fled in exile to Persia, where he died as a result of drinking the blood of a bull. And so that writer[7] is in error who records Darius as the fourth king, who was defeated by Alexander, for he was not the fourth king but the fourteenth king of the Persians after Cyrus. It was in the seventh year of his rule that Alexander defeated and killed him. Moreover it should be observed that after he has specified four kings of Persia after Cyrus, Daniel omits the nine others and passes right on to Alexander. For the spirit of prophecy was not concerned about preserving historical detail but in summarizing only the most important matters. COMMENTARY ON DANIEL 11.2.[8]

THE PERSIAN KINGS. ISHO'DAD OF MERV: After Cyrus, who reigned first, there were numerous kings in Persia until those three. But the angel indicates by "three kings" those who were called with the name Darius, because there were only three kings who had the same name Darius. And by revealing through whom the kingdom of the Persians would have ceased, he says, "The fourth shall be far richer than all of them," that is, Darius, who became more powerful than all his predecessors; "and when he has become strong," this Darius, he means, "in his homeland,"[9] in power and riches, "he shall stir up," that is, he will cause Alexander, of the house of the Greeks, to march against him. COMMENTARY ON DANIEL 11.2.[10]

11:3 A Mighty King

THE RISE OF ALEXANDER. ISHO'DAD OF MERV: "And [Alexander] shall arise," he says, "and will kill [Darius] and will take action as he pleases,"[11] and nobody will rise against him. This Darius, son of Arshak, was the tenth king after Cyrus, and in his sixth year Alexander marches against him and kills him. Alexander, when he came to Jerusalem, enters the temple, worships God and honors the temple with many gifts. COMMENTARY ON DANIEL 11.3.[12]

11:4 The Kingdom Will Be Broken

ALEXANDER'S KINGDOM DIVIDED. THEODORET OF CYR: When, as we have already mentioned, Alexander joined together the whole known world, so to speak, into his kingdom and then suffered the fate common to all humankind,

---

[3]JCD 118. [4]JCD 118*. [5]Theodoret also identifies Xerxes, son of Darius, as the fourth king. [6]It could be in Sophocles' time, but Euripides had not yet written his first play; see Gleason L. Archer, JCD 119. [7]Archer believes Jerome is referring to Tertullian. [8]JCD 118-19. [9]This is the reading of the Peshitta (CSCO 328:123). [10]CSCO 328:123. [11]This reading is not in the Peshitta and must belong to a different Syriac Bible employed by Isho'dad (CSCO 328:124). [12]CSCO 328:124.

the kingdom was divided into four parts. COMMENTARY ON DANIEL 11.3-4.[13]

NO HEIRS. EPHREM THE SYRIAN: Understand this as referring to Alexander, who was certain that his last day was not close and therefore did not have children, who could be the heirs of his reign, and left it to his friends after dividing it into four parts. COMMENTARY ON DANIEL 11.3.[14]

ADDITIONAL PIECES. JEROME: Besides the four kingdoms of Macedonia, Asia Minor, Syria and Egypt, the kingdom of the Macedonians was torn asunder among other rulers of less prominence and among petty kings. The reference here is to Perdiccas and Craterus and Lysimachus, for Cappadocia, Armenia, Bithynia, Heracleia, Bosphorus and various other provinces withdrew themselves from the Macedonian power and set up various kings for themselves. COMMENTARY ON DANIEL 11.3-4.[15]

TWO KINGS. THEODORET OF CYR: He does not spend much time on the ruler of Asia Minor or Macedonia, especially since no grief befell the Jews through them. He mentions only the two through whom the Jews would be tested with grievous misfortunes. These are the king of Egypt and the one entrusted with the rule of the nations that lay to the east. The latter held palaces in both Antioch and Babylon. COMMENTARY ON DANIEL 11.3-4.[16]

---

[14]ESOO 2:226. [15]JCD 120. [16]PG 81:1504; cf. WGRW 7:281.

11:5-9 WAR BETWEEN THE KINGDOMS OF THE SOUTH AND NORTH

[5]*Then the king of the south shall be strong, but one of his princes shall be stronger than he and his dominion shall be a great dominion. [6]After some years they shall make an alliance, and the daughter of the king of the south shall come to the king of the north to make peace; but she shall not retain the strength of her arm, and he and his offspring shall not endure; but she shall be given up, and her attendants, her child, and he who got possession of[y] her.*

[7]*In those times a branch[z] from her roots shall arise in his place; he shall come against the army and enter the fortress of the king of the north, and he shall deal with them and shall prevail. [8]He shall also carry off to Egypt their gods with their molten images and with their precious vessels of silver and of gold; and for some years he shall refrain from attacking the king of the north. [9]Then the latter shall come into the realm of the king of the south but shall return into his own land.*

y Or *supported*   Gk: Heb *from a branch*

OVERVIEW: The reference to the king of the South is to Ptolemy (323-285 B.C.), the son of Lago. Ptolemy's son, Ptolemy Philadelphus (285- 246 B.C.), is the prince described in Daniel 11:5. The first king of the north was Seleucus Nicator. The Seleucid king was followed by Antiochus So-tor and then Antiochus II Theos (261-246 B.C.). Ptolemy Philadelphus gave his daughter Berenice in marriage (c. 250 B.C.) to Antiochus Theos (JEROME). This marriage lasted for only a few years. Antiochus was poisoned by his former wife, Laodice, and Berenice, her son, and her entourage were then murdered. Theodoret continues his timeline and argues that the reference to the king of the south in Daniel 11:6 refers to Ptolemy Epiphanes, son of Ptolemy Philopator, and the reference to the king of the north refers to Antiochus the Great (223-187 B.C.). After the death of Antiochus, Berenice's brother, Ptolemy Euergetes, ascended to the throne. He then attacked the king of the north, Selecucus Callinicus (son of Laodice), and seized Syria. Euergetes returned to Egypt with vast amounts of wealth and left the cities to be reoccupied by the Seleucid king (JEROME). An alternative reading is offered by Theodoret: citing Josephus, he argues that the king of the south is Ptolemy Philopator (221-203 B.C.) and "prince" refers to his general Scopas. The Ptolemy rulers, Philopator and his son Epiphanes, enjoyed successive victories over Antiochus the Great. Not long afterwards Antiochus defeated the Ptolemy general Scopas and reoccupied cities in Palestine and Samaria.

11:5 A Strong King from the South

TWO PTOLEMIES; THE SEPTUAGINT TRANSLATED. JEROME: The reference is to Ptolemy, son of Lagos, who was the first to become king in Egypt and was a very clever, mighty and wealthy man. . . . [During his reign] he acquired Caria and many islands, cities and districts unnecessary to detail at this time. But no further notice is taken of the other kingdoms, Macedonia and Asia Minor, because Judea lay in a midway position and was held now by one group of kings and now by another. And it is not the purpose of holy Scripture to cover external history apart from the Jews but only that which is linked up with the nation of Israel.

"One of the great princes shall prevail." . . .

The person mentioned is Ptolemy Philadelphus, the second king of Egypt. . . . It was in his reign that the seventy translators are said to have translated the holy Scripture into Greek.[1] . . . Philadelphus is reported to have possessed such great power as to surpass his father, Ptolemy. For history relates that he possessed 200,000 infantrymen, 20,000 cavalry and even 2,000 chariots and 400 elephants, which he was the first to import from Ethiopia. He also had 1,500 war galleys of the type now known as Liburnian, and 1,000 others for the transporting of military provisions. COMMENTARY ON DANIEL 11.5.[2]

JOSEPHUS ON PTOLEMY. THEODORET OF CYR: He is talking about Ptolemy Philopator,[3] who was not satisfied with the kingdom of Egypt but who added also Phoenicia, Samaria and Judea. When he says, "one of his princes will grow strong," he is talking about Scopas, whom also Josephus the Hebrew historian mentions. Scopas was an outstanding general and placed under Ptolemy's power many of the nations that were outside of the kingdom of Ptolemy. He speaks of this one enigmatically: "And he will rule with much power beyond his authority," that is, he will rule over many nations beyond the realm that had been allotted to him. COMMENTARY ON DANIEL 11.5.[4]

11:6 Making an Alliance

THE FAILED MARRIAGE OF BERENICE. JEROME: And so after many years of war, Ptolemy Philadelphus[5] wished to be done with this bitter struggle, and so he gave his daughter, named Berenice, in marriage to Antiochus Theos,[6] who had already had a wife named Laodice. . . . As for Antiochus, even though he had said he would regard Berenice as his royal consort and keep Laodice in the status of a concubine, he was

---

[1]The Septuagint. [2]JCD 120-21. [3]Ptolemy IV Philopator (221-203 B.C.). [4]PG 81:1505; WGRW 7:283. [5]Ptolemy Philadelphus (285-246 B.C.). [6]Antiochus II Theos (261-246 B.C.).

finally prevailed on by his love for Laodice to restore her to the status of queen, along with her children. But she was fearful that her husband might in his fickleness restore Berenice to favor once more, and so she had him put to death by her servants with the use of poison. And she handed over Berenice and the son . . . and then set up her elder son, Seleucus Callinicus, as king in his father's place. And so this is the matter referred to in this passage, namely, that after many years Ptolemy Philadelphus and Antiochus Theos would conclude a friendship, and the daughter of the king of the south, that is, Ptolemy, would go to the king of the north, that is, Antiochus, in order to cement friendly relations between her father and her husband. And the text says that she will not be able to gain her end, nor shall her posterity remain on the throne of Syria, but instead both Berenice and the men who had escorted her there shall be put to death. And also the king, Antiochus, who had strengthened her, that is, through whom she could have obtained the mastery, was killed by his wife's poison. COMMENTARY ON DANIEL 11.6.[7]

THE SUCCESSION OF PTOLEMIES. THEODORET OF CYR: After Ptolemy Philpator died, his son Ptolemy (surnamed Epiphanes) reigned. That is what he means, "After his years, they will make an alliance." And he explains how they will make an alliance. By the king of the north he means Antiochus—not Antiochus Epiphanes but Antiochus the Great, who was the father of Antiochus Epiphanes. It was Antiochus the Great who was the contemporary with those Ptolemies. COMMENTARY ON DANIEL 11.6.[8]

MARRIAGE AND WEALTH. THEODORET OF CYR: But the marriage will not suffice to bring about an alliance. She will be returned to the one who had given her through those who brought her, along with the things that had been presented by her (for he says, "the one supporting her during those times"). Wealth was what had accomplished the strong and desired marriage. COMMENTARY ON DANIEL 11.6.[9]

11:7 A Branch Arises

PTOLEMY EUERGETES. JEROME: After the murder of Berenice and the death of her father, her brother, named Ptolemy Euergetes, succeeded to the throne as the third of his dynasty, being in fact an offshoot of the same plant and a bud of the same root as she was, inasmuch as he was her brother. He came up with a great army and advanced into the province of the king of the north, that is, Seleucus Callinicus, who together with his mother, Laodice, was ruling in Syria. He abused them, and he seized Syria, Cilicia, the remoter regions beyond the Euphrates and nearly all of Asia as well. And then, when he heard that a rebellion was afoot in Egypt, he ravaged the kingdom of Seleucus and carried off as booty forty thousand talents of silver and precious vessels and images of the gods to the amount of two and a half thousand. . . . Euergetes retained possession of Syria, but he handed over Cilicia to his friend, Antiochus, that he might govern it, and the provinces beyond the Euphrates he handed over to Xanthippus, another general. COMMENTARY ON DANIEL 11.7-9.[10]

---

[7]JCD 121-22*. [8]PG 81:1505-8; cf. WGRW 7:283-85. [9]PG 81:1508; cf. WGRW 7:285. [10]JCD 122-23*.

11:10-19 SOUTH AND NORTH
CONTINUE TO FIGHT

^{10}His sons shall wage war and assemble a multitude of great forces, which shall come on and overflow and pass through, and again shall carry the war as far as his fortress. ^{11}Then the king of the south, moved with anger, shall come out and fight with the king of the north; and he shall raise a great multitude, but it shall be given into his hand. ^{12}And when the multitude is taken, his heart shall be exalted, and he shall cast down tens of thousands, but he shall not prevail. ^{13}For the king of the north shall again raise a multitude, greater than the former; and after some years^a he shall come on with a great army and abundant supplies.

^{14}In those times many shall rise against the king of the south; and the men of violence among your own people shall lift themselves up in order to fulfil the vision; but they shall fail. ^{15}Then the king of the north shall come and throw up siegeworks, and take a well-fortified city. And the forces of the south shall not stand, or even his picked troops, for there shall be no strength to stand. ^{16}But he who comes against him shall do according to his own will, and none shall stand before him; and he shall stand in the glorious land, and all of it shall be in his power. ^{17}He shall set his face to come with the strength of his whole kingdom, and he shall bring terms of peace^b and perform them. He shall give him the daughter of women to destroy the kingdom;^{c} but it shall not stand or be to his advantage. ^{18}Afterward he shall turn his face to the coastlands, and shall take many of them; but a commander shall put an end to his insolence; indeed^d he shall turn his insolence back upon him. ^{19}Then he shall turn his face back toward the fortresses of his own land; but he shall stumble and fall, and shall not be found.

a Heb *at the end of the times years*   b Gk: Heb *upright ones*   c Heb *her* or *it*   d Heb obscure

OVERVIEW: Seleucus III (226-223 B.C.) and his brother Antiochus III (223-187 B.C.), called the Great, took up arms against Ptolemy Philopator. Antiochus III assumed the throne on the death of Seleucus III. Antiochus the Great obtained possession of Syria and lost it again to Ptolemy Philopator.[1] After the death of Ptolemy Philopator in 204, Antiochus the Great aligned with King Philip of Macedon and engaged the forces of Ptolemy Epiphanes (204-180 B.C.), the six-year-old son of Ptolemy Philopator (THEODORET, HIPPOLYTUS). Antiochus briefly gained control of Palestine but soon was pushed out by the Ptolemy commander Scopas. During the conflict, Judea was divided into factions, one favoring Antiochus and another favoring Ptolemy. Soon afterward Antiochus the Great engaged and defeated Scopas near the sources of the Jordan.[2] Antiochus attempted to gain control of Egypt through a marriage of his daughter, Cleopatra, to Ptolemy Epiphanes. His plan did not come to fruition as Cleopatra inclined herself to her husband and not her father. Antiochus turned his attention toward Asia Minor with some success but later was opposed by Scipio and his Roman forces. The Ro-

[1]The fourth Syrian war (221-217 B.C.).   [2]Antiochus's defeat of the Egyptian forces ended a century of Ptolemic rule of Israel.

man forces defeated Antiochus the Great, and he surrendered in disgrace (JEROME).

11:10 His Sons Will Assemble

SELEUCID INFIGHTING. JEROME: After the flight and death of Seleucus Callinicus, his two sons, Seleucus surnamed Ceraunus, and Antiochus, who was called the Great, were provoked by a hope of victory and of avenging their father, and so they assembled an army against Ptolemy Philopator.... When the elder brother, Seleucus, was slain in Phrygia ... through the treachery of Nicator and Apaturius, the army that was in Syria summoned his brother, Antiochus the Great, from Babylon to assume the throne. And so this is the reason why the present passage states that the two sons were provoked and assembled a multitude of very sizable armies. But it implies that Antiochus the Great came by himself from Babylon to Syria, which at the time was held by Ptolemy Philopator.... And after he had ... obtained possession of Syria (which had already been held by a succession of Egyptian kings), he became so emboldened by his contempt for Philopator's luxurious manner of life and for the magical arts that he was said to employ that he took the initiative in attempting an invasion of Egypt itself. COMMENTARY ON DANIEL 11.10.[3]

11:11 The King of the South

PTOLEMY PHILOPATOR DEFEATS ANTIOCHUS THE GREAT. JEROME: The Ptolemy Philopator, having lost Syria, gathered together a very great multitude and launched an invasion against Antiochus the Great, the king of the north, at the region where Egypt borders on the province of Judea. For owing to the nature of the region, this locality lies partly to the south and partly to the north. If we speak of Judea, it lies to the north of Egypt and to the south of Syria. And so when he had joined battle near the town of Raphia at the gateway of Egypt, Antiochus lost his entire army

and was almost captured as he fled through the desert. And after he had conceded the loss of Syria, the conflict was finally brought to an end on the basis of a treaty and certain conditions of peace.

And this is what the Scripture means here by the statement that Ptolemy Philopator "shall cast down many thousands" and yet shall not prevail. For he was unable to capture his adversary. COMMENTARY ON DANIEL 11.11-12.[4]

11:13 Raising a Multitude

ANTIOCHUS THE GREAT MAKES AGREEMENT WITH PHILIP OF MACEDON. JEROME: This indicates that Antiochus the Great, who despised Ptolemy Philopator, assembled a huge army from the upper regions of Babylon. And since Ptolemy Philopator was now dead, Antiochus broke his treaty and set his army in motion against Philopator's four-year-old son—Epiphanes....

Moreover Philip, king of Macedon, and Antiochus the Great made peace with each other and engaged in a common struggle against Ptolemy Epiphanes, on the understanding that each of them should annex to his own dominion those cities of Ptolemy that lay nearest to them. And so this is what is referred to in this passage, which says that many shall rise up against the king of the south, that is, Ptolemy , who was then a mere child. COMMENTARY ON DANIEL 11.13-14.[5]

HEBREW IDIOM. THEODORET OF CYR: He will lead again an army greater than the earlier one and will set out against Egypt, and he will do this near the end of his own reign. That is what is meant by the sentence "at the end of the seasons he will make his entrance with great power and with much wealth." This doubling is a Hebraism; he wished to say that he would make a great entrance. This is the idiom of both the Hebrews

---

[1]The fourth Syrian war (221-217 B.C.). [2]Antiochus's defeat of the Egyptian forces ended a century of Ptolemic rule of Israel. [3]JCD 123-24. [4]JCD 124. [5]JCD 124-25*.

and the Arameans, for they are accustomed to say, "entering he entered" and "departing he departed" and "eating he eats," and so forth. The translators were rather accurate and followed Hebrew usage. COMMENTARY ON DANIEL 11.13.[6]

11:14 Men of Violence

A JEWISH TEMPLE BUILT IN EGYPT. JEROME: During the conflict between Antiochus the Great and the generals of Ptolemy, Judea, which lay between them, was rent into contrary factions, the one group favoring Antiochus and the other favoring Ptolemy. Finally the high priest, Onias, fled to Egypt, taking a large number of Jews along with him. . . . He received the region known as Heliopolis, and by a grant of the king, he erected a temple in Egypt like the temple of the Jews, and it remained standing up until the reign of Vespasian, over a period of 250 years. . . . So countless multitudes of Jews fled to Egypt on the occasion of Onias's pontificate. . . .

This is the matter referred to in this passage: "The sons of the transgressors of your people," who forsook the law of the Lord and wished to offer blood sacrifices to God in another place than what he had commanded. They would be lifted up in pride and would boast that they were fulfilling the vision, that is, the thing that the Lord had enjoined. But they shall fall to ruin, for both temple and city shall be afterwards destroyed. And while Antiochus held Judea, a leader of the Ptolemaic party called Scopas Aetholus was sent against Antiochus, and after a bold campaign he took Judea. COMMENTARY ON DANIEL 11.13-14.[7]

11:15 Building Siegeworks

ANTIOCHUS OVERCOMES SCOPAS. JEROME: Purposing to retake Judea and the many cities of Syria, Antiochus joined battle with Scopas, Ptolemy's general, near the sources of the Jordan near where the city now called Paneas was founded, and he put him to flight and besieged

him in Sidon together with ten thousand of his soldiers. In order to free him, Ptolemy dispatched the famous generals Eropus, Menocles and Damoxenus. Yet he was unable to lift the siege, and finally Scopas, overcome by famine, had to surrender and was sent away with his associates, despoiled of all he had. And as for the statement "he shall cast up a mound," this indicates that Antiochus is going to besiege the garrison of Scopas in the citadel of Jerusalem for a long time, while the Jews add their exertions as well. And he is going to capture other cities that had formerly been held by the Ptolemaic faction in Syria, Cilicia and Lycia.[8] COMMENTARY ON DANIEL 11.15-16.[9]

SUCCESSES OF ANTIOCHUS III. HIPPOLYTUS: "And a king shall stand up and shall enter into the fortress of the king of Egypt."[10] For Antiochus became king of Syria. He held the sovereignty in the 107th year of the kingdom of the Greeks. And in those same times indeed he made war against Ptolemy king of Egypt, and conquered him and won the power. On returning from Egypt he went up to Jerusalem, in the 103rd year, and carrying off with him all the treasures of the Lord's house, he marched to Antioch. COMMENTARY ON DANIEL 2.30-31.[11]

11:16 The Beautiful Land

THE GLORIOUS LAND. JEROME: The term "glorious land," or, as the Septuagint interprets it, "the land of desire" (that is, in which God takes pleasure) signifies Judea, and particularly Jerusalem, to which Antiochus pursued those men of Scopas's party who had been honorably received there. Instead of the phrase "glorious land," as Aquila rendered it, Theodotion simply puts the

---

[6]PG 81:1509-12; WGRW 7:289. [7]JCD 125-26*. [8]Variant reading: Lydia (JCD 126). [9]JCD 126. [10]The wording resembles Daniel 11:7, but there the Egyptian king enters the northern king's fortress. Hippolytus reverses that image by utilizing the events of Daniel 11:15-16, where a Seleucid king attacks Egypt, and "none shall stand before him." [11]ANF 5:183.

Hebrew word itself, *Sabin;* instead of that Symmachus translated it "land of bravery." COMMENTARY ON DANIEL 10.15-16.[12]

11:17 *His Kingdom Will Not Stand*

ANTIOCHUS GIVES HIS DAUGHTER TO PTOLEMY. JEROME: "That she may overthrow him."[13] That is to say, the intention is to overthrow him, that is, Ptolemy, either to overthrow him, that is, Ptolemy, or else to overthrow it, that is, his kingdom. Antiochus not only wished to take possession of Syria, Cilicia and Lycia and the other provinces that had belonged to Ptolemy's party but also to extend his empire to Egypt. He therefore used the good offices of Eucles of Rhodes to betroth his daughter, Cleopatra, to young Ptolemy in the seventh year of this reign; and in his thirteenth year she was given to him in marriage, professedly endowed with all of Coele-Syria[14] and Judea as her marriage portion. By pleonasm she is called a daughter of women, just as the poet says, "Thus she spoke with her mouth. . . . And with these ears did I drink in her voice."[15] COMMENTARY ON DANIEL 11.17-19.[16]

11:18 *To the Coastlands*

THE ROMANS PUSH BACK ANTIOCHUS. JEROME: He was unable to take possession of Egypt, because Ptolemy Epiphanes and his generals detected the stratagem and followed a cau-

tious policy. And besides, Cleopatra inclined more to her husband's side than to her father's. And so he turned his attention to Asia Minor, and by carrying on naval warfare against a large number of islands, he seized Rhodes, Samos, Colophon,[17] Phocea and many other islands. But he was opposed by Lucius Scipio Nasica and his brother, Publius Scipio Africanus, who had vanquished Hannibal. . . . Antiochus was vanquished and commanded to confine his rule to the other side of the Taurus range. And so he took refuge in Apamia and Susa and advanced to the easternmost cities of his realm. And during a war against the Elymaeans he was destroyed together with his entire army.

And so this is what the Scripture refers to in this passage, when it states that he would capture many islands, and yet because of the Roman conqueror he would lose the kingdom of Asia; and that the disgrace he had inflicted would come back on his own head; and that in the end he would flee from Asia Minor and return to the empire of his own land and would then stumble and fall, so that his place would not be found. COMMENTARY ON DANIEL 11.17-19.[18]

---

[12]JCD 126-27. [13]Jerome's text differs both from MT and from most LXX manuscripts at this point, which do not mention any intention of overthrowing, although the LXX says "she shall not be with him." [14]"Hollow Syria," the southwestern region divided by the Great Rift Valley. [15]JCD says the second line is from Virgil's *Aeneid* 4.359, but the first is unknown (127). [16]JCD 127. [17]Variant: Colophonia and Bocla. [18]JCD 127-28.

11:20-28 ANTIOCHUS EPIPHANES

[20]*Then shall arise in his place one who shall send an exactor of tribute through the glory of the kingdom; but within a few days he shall be broken, neither in anger nor in battle.* [21]*In his place shall arise a contemptible person to whom royal majesty has not been given; he shall come in without warning and obtain the kingdom by flatteries.* [22]*Armies shall be utterly swept away before him*

and broken, and the prince of the covenant also. [23] *And from the time that an alliance is made with him he shall act deceitfully; and he shall become strong with a small people.* [24] *Without warning he shall come into the richest parts[e] of the province; and he shall do what neither his fathers nor his fathers' fathers have done, scattering among them plunder, spoil, and goods. He shall devise plans against strongholds, but only for a time.* [25] *And he shall stir up his power and his courage against the king of the south with a great army; and the king of the south shall wage war with an exceedingly great and mighty army; but he shall not stand, for plots shall be devised against him.* [26] *Even those who eat his rich food shall be his undoing; his army shall be swept away, and many shall fall down slain.* [27] *And as for the two kings, their minds shall be bent on mischief; they shall speak lies at the same table, but to no avail; for the end is yet to be at the time appointed.* [28] *And he shall return to his land with great substance, but his heart shall be set against the holy covenant. And he shall work his will, and return to his own land.*

e Or *among the richest men*

OVERVIEW: The one who will arise in his place is Seleucus Philopator, the son of Antiochus, who ruled over Syria for a short period and died without ever fighting a single battle (JEROME). Or it can refer to Antiochus Epiphanes, who succeeded his brother Seleucus Philopator on his death (THEODORET). Most commentators agree that the person called contemptible in Daniel 11:21 is Antiochus Epiphanes and that the "prince of the covenant" refers to the high priest Onias (THEODORET), though some argue that "prince" refers to Judas Maccabeus or possibly Ptolemy. Jerome argues that this section refers not to Antiochus Epiphanes but to the antichrist who appears at the end of the world. Consequently, Porphyry and others, who offer a historical interpretation of the text, are incorrect. Before leaving Egypt, Antiochus made a peace treaty and ate with his nephew Ptolemy, but peace was not secured (THEODORET). On his return, Antiochus's heart was against the covenant, that is, he looted the Jewish temple (JEROME).

11:20-21 Arising in His Place

SELEUCUS PHILOPATOR. JEROME: The reference is to the Seleucus surnamed Philopator, the son of Antiochus the Great, who during his reign performed no deeds worthy of Syria or of his father but perished ingloriously without fighting a single battle. Porphyry, however, claims that it was not this Seleucus who is referred to, but rather Ptolemy Epiphanes, who contrived a plot against Seleucus and prepared an army to fight against him, with the result that Seleucus was poisoned by his own generals. They did this because when someone asked Seleucus where he was going to get the financial resources for the great enterprises he was planning, he answered that his financial resources consisted in his friends. When this remark was publicly noised abroad, the generals became apprehensive that he would deprive them of their property and for that reason did him to death by nefarious means.

Yet how could Ptolemy be said to rise up in the place of Antiochus the Great, since he did nothing of the sort? This is especially improbable since the Septuagint translated, "And there shall stand up a plant from his root," that is, "of his issue and seed," who should deal a severe blow to the prestige of the empire; "and within a few days he shall be destroyed without wrath or battle." The Hebrews claim that it is Trypho who was intended by the man who was most vile and unworthy of kingly honor, for as the boy king's guardian he seized the throne for himself. COMMENTARY ON DANIEL 11.20.[1]

ANTIOCHUS EPIPHANES. THEODORET OF CYR: He is talking about Antiochus Epiphanes, who on his return from Rome succeeded his brother Seleucus. Seleucus (called Philopator) succeeded Antiochus the Great, since he was his son. When Seleucus died, Antiochus Epiphanes received the throne. He says about the latter, "From his root kingship will sprout, and he will put aside his readiness." That is to say, he will imitate his father's power and will be adequate to lay hold of the kingdom readied by his father. COMMENTARY ON DANIEL 11.20.[2]

PREVAILING THROUGH GUILE AND DECEIT. THEODORET OF CYR: He was in fact not glorious, seeming instead to be an insignificant figure, because he was kept under guard in Rome. "And he will return, and he will gain mastery over a kingdom by his cunning." But, nonetheless, especially since he had been brought down to nothing, he will come with great advantage and a very large army, and he will overpower the kingdom with deceit as its helper, and he will use gross deceit all the more. The blessed Daniel saw this fact also in the second vision, and he heard holy Gabriel saying, "Guile is in his hand, and he will become arrogant in his heart. He will destroy many, and he will prevail as many are destroyed."[3] Thus, he says here words to the same effect: "He will gain mastery over a kingdom by his cunning." COMMENTARY ON DANIEL 11.21.[4]

ANTIOCHUS A TYPE OF THE ANTICHRIST. JEROME: Up to this point the historical order has been followed, and there has been no point of controversy between Porphyry and those of our side. But the rest of the text from here on to the end of the book he interprets as applying to the person of the Antiochus who was surnamed Epiphanes. . . . But those of our persuasion believe all these things are spoken prophetically of the antichrist who is to arise in the end time.

But this factor appears to them as a difficulty for our view, namely, the question as to why the prophetic discourse should abruptly cease mention of these great kings and shift from Seleucus to the end of the world. The answer is that in the earlier historical account where mention was made of the Persian kings, only four kings of Persia were presented, following after Cyrus, and many who came in between were simply skipped over, so as to come quickly to Alexander, king of the Macedonians. We hold that it is the practice of Scripture not to relate all details completely but only to set forth what seems of major importance. Those of our school insist also that since many of the details that we are subsequently to read and explain are appropriate to the person of Antiochus, he is to be regarded as a type of the antichrist, and those things that happened to him in a preliminary way are to be completely fulfilled in the case of the antichrist. COMMENTARY ON DANIEL 11.24.[5]

11:22 Armies Swept Away

THE EGYPTIANS. THEODORET OF CYR: Here again he hinted at the empire of the Egyptians, that though they too were very powerful, destroying their adversaries like an inundation, and rendering them totally undone, they themselves would be subject to an inundation from him and would be crushed—and not they alone but "the prince of the covenant as well." COMMENTARY ON DANIEL 11.22.[6]

11:23 An Alliance Is Made

REVOLT AGAINST THE HIGH PRIEST. THEODORET OF CYR: Here he foretells the revolt against Onias the high priest by Joshua, also called Jason, and by Onias, son of Menelaus. The former, Jason, had recourse to Antiochus and

---

[1]JCD 128-29. [2]PG 81:1513-16; WGRW 7:293. [3]Dan 8:25. [4]PG 81:1516; WGRW 7:295. [5]JCD 129*. [6]WGRW 7:295.

threw his own brother out from the high priest-hood. Menelaus, who was commissioned to bring tributes and gold to Antiochus, appointed himself high priest and drove out Jason. . . . COMMENTARY ON DANIEL 11.23.[7]

11:24 Scattering Plunder

ANTIOCHUS ACTS CONTRARY TO PREVIOUS KINGS. THEODORET OF CYR: Although all his fathers and forefathers had honored the Jewish nation, he does everything to the contrary. He steals, plunders and enslaves—and bestows all these things on his troops. "And he shall make plans against Egypt, and yet only until a certain time." That is to say, he will not rule for long. COMMENTARY ON DANIEL 11.24.[8]

PORPHYRY'S POSITION SUMMARIZED. JEROME: Not only does the text say that Antiochus Epiphanes conquered Ptolemy by fraud but also the prince of the covenant, that is, Judas Maccabeus, he overcame by treachery. Or else this is what is referred to, that after he had secured peace with Ptolemy and had become the prince of the covenant; he afterwards devised a plot against him.

Now the Ptolemy meant here was Ptolemy Philometor, the son of Antiochus's sister, Cleopatra; and so Antiochus was his maternal uncle. . . . After Ptolemy's generals were defeated by Antiochus's forces, Antiochus showed leniency towards the boy, and making a pretense of friendship, he went up to Memphis and there received the crown after the Egyptian manner. Declaring that he was looking out for the lad's interests, he subjected all Egypt to himself with only a small force of men, and he entered into rich and prosperous cities. And so he did things that his father had never done, nor his fathers' fathers. For none of the kings of Syria had ever laid Egypt waste after this fashion and scattered all their wealth. Moreover, he was so shrewd that he even overcame by his deceit the well-laid plans of those who were the boy king's generals. This is the line of interpretation that Porphyry followed, pursu-ing the lead of Sutorius with much redundancy. COMMENTARY ON DANIEL 11.24.[9]

JEROME'S INTERPRETATION. JEROME: But the scholars of our viewpoint have made a better and more correct interpretation, stating that the deeds are to be performed by the antichrist at the end of the world. It is he who is destined to arise from a small nation, that is, from the Jewish people, and he shall be so lowly and despised that kingly honor will not be granted him. But by means of intrigue and deception he shall secure the government, and by him shall the arms of the fighting nation of Rome be overcome and broken. He is to effect this result by pretending to be the prince of the covenant, that is, of the law and testament of God. And he shall enter into the richest of cities and shall do what his fathers never did, nor his fathers' fathers. For none of the Jews except the antichrist has ever ruled over the whole world. And he shall form a design against the firmest resolves of the saints and shall do everything [he wishes] for a time, for as long as God's will shall have permitted him to do these things. COMMENTARY ON DANIEL 11.24.[10]

11:25 Power and Courage

ANTIOCHUS ASSAULTS EGYPT. THEODORET OF CYR: The first book of the Maccabees relates this assault on Egypt: "Antiochus came to Egypt with a mighty host and with chariots, elephants, horses and a great expedition and battled against Ptolemy, king of Egypt. Ptolemy fled, and many of his soldiers were wounded and fell. Antiochus captured the fortresses of Egypt and plundered Egypt."[11] COMMENTARY ON DANIEL 11.25.[12]

THE CONQUEROR IS THE ANTICHRIST. JEROME: Porphyry interprets this as applying to

---

[7]PG 81:1516; cf. WGRW 7:295. [8]PG 81:1517; cf. WGRW 7:297. [9]JCD 130-31*. [10]JCD 131*. [11]1 Macc 1:17-19. [12]PG 81:1520; cf. WGRW 7:297.

Antiochus. . . . But those of our view with greater plausibility interpret all this as applying to the antichrist, for he is to be born of the Jewish people and come from Babylon, and he is first of all going to vanquish the king of Egypt, who is one of the three horns of which we have already spoken earlier. COMMENTARY ON DANIEL 11.25-26.[13]

11:27 At the Same Table

ANTIOCHUS CONQUERS EGYPT. JEROME: There is no doubt but what Antiochus did conclude a peace with Ptolemy and ate at the same table with him and devised plots against him, yet without attaining any success thereby, since he did not obtain his kingdom but was driven out by Ptolemy's soldiers. But it cannot be proved from this set of facts that the statement of this Scripture was ever fulfilled by past history, namely, that there were two kings whose hearts were deceitful and who inflicted evil on each other. Actually, Ptolemy was a mere child of tender years and was taken in by Antiochus's fraud; how then could he have plotted evil against him? And so our party insists that all these things refer to the antichrist and to the king of Egypt whom he has for the first time overcome. COMMENTARY ON DANIEL 11.27-30.[14]

THE WOUND OF FRIENDSHIP. THEODORET OF CYR: As the historian Josephus teaches us, the Romans learned about this army of his and commanded him to depart from Egypt. Then he made a peace treaty and shared a table with Ptolemy. The angel who addressed Daniel explained the festering wound underlying the friendship when he said, "Their hearts will turn to evil, and they will speak lies at the same table and will not set it right." That is, the peace will not be secured: "Because the end will be at the appointed time." That is, once this time has passed, they will engage again and march out in battle array. COMMENTARY ON DANIEL 11.27.[15]

11:28 A Heart Set Against the Covenant

ANTIOCHUS LOOTS THE TEMPLE. JEROME: Both the Greek and the Roman historians relate that after Antiochus has been expelled from Egypt and had gone back once more, he came to Judea, that is, against the holy covenant, and that he despoiled the temple and removed a huge amount of gold; and then, having stationed a garrison in the citadel, he returned to his own land. COMMENTARY ON DANIEL 11.27-30.[16]

THE KING WILL SET HIS HEART AGAINST THE COVENANT. THEODORET OF CYR: But nonetheless he will then return to his own kingdom with much wealth and great abundance. "And his heart will be against the holy covenant." At last, he will have one endeavor, namely, to destroy the law given by God to the Jews. Because he desires this, he puts his plans into effect. "And he will act and return to his land." The book of the Maccabees and the history of Josephus explain this.[17] COMMENTARY ON DANIEL 11.28.[18]

---

[13]JCD 132*. [14]JCD 132*. [15]PG 81:1520; WGRW 7:299. [16]JCD 132-33. [17]On his return, Antiochus brutally suppressed his political opposition in Jerusalem by killing eighty thousand people in three days. With the assistance of Menelaus, he entered the temple and removed a number of holy vessels. See 2 Macc 5:11-17. [18]PG 81:1520; WGRW 7:299.

11:29-39 ANTIOCHUS' SECOND CAMPAIGN AGAINST EGYPT

²⁹At the time appointed he shall return and come into the south; but it shall not be this time as it was before. ³⁰For ships of Kittim shall come against him, and he shall be afraid and withdraw, and shall turn back and be enraged and take action against the holy covenant. He shall turn back and give heed to those who forsake the holy covenant. ³¹Forces from him shall appear and profane the temple and fortress, and shall take away the continual burnt offering. And they shall set up the abomination that makes desolate. ³²He shall seduce with flattery those who violate the covenant; but the people who know their God shall stand firm and take action. ³³And those among the people who are wise shall make many understand, though they shall fall by sword and flame, by captivity and plunder, for some days. ³⁴When they fall, they shall receive a little help. And many shall join themselves to them with flattery; ³⁵and some of those who are wise shall fall, to refine and to cleanse them^f and to make them white, until the time of the end, for it is yet for the time appointed.

³⁶And the king shall do according to his will; he shall exalt himself and magnify himself above every god, and shall speak astonishing things against the God of gods. He shall prosper till the indignation is accomplished; for what is determined shall be done. ³⁷He shall give no heed to the gods of his fathers, or to the one beloved by women; he shall not give heed to any other god, for he shall magnify himself above all. ³⁸He shall honor the god of fortresses instead of these; a god whom his fathers did not know he shall honor with gold and silver, with precious stones and costly gifts. ³⁹He shall deal with the strongest fortresses by the help of a foreign god; those who acknowledge him he shall magnify with honor. He shall make them rulers over many and shall divide the land for a price.

f Gk: Heb *among them*

OVERVIEW: The phrase "appointed time" refers to the time suitable for war (THEODORET). Two years after he looted the temple and suppressed the rebellion, Antiochus attacked Egypt for a second time. His second attack ended when Roman officials ordered his withdrawal. On his return, he again brutally vented his anger on God's people in Jerusalem. These events foreshadow the antichrist, who is to persecute Christians. Consequently, many interpreters argued that Nero was the antichrist because of his vicious attacks against Christians. Theodoret, citing 2 Maccabees, suggests that Daniel 11:31 refers to two separate events that followed two years after An-

tiochus's brutal suppression of Jerusalem (alluded to in Dan 11:28): the first was the sending of Apollonius to inflict even more punishment on the inhabitants of Jerusalem. The second was the arrival of an Athenian senator who actively suppressed Jewish religious practices and erected an altar to Zeus in the temple—the desolating abomination. Jerome, citing these same events, argues that these events serve only as a type of the antichrist, who is the subject of the vision. The Jews understood this passage not in terms of Antiochus Epiphanes or the antichrist but the Romans, specifically relating to Titus's destruction of the temple (JEROME, ATHANASIUS). The wise are those who would rather suffer death than forsake the divine law (THEODORET). The phrases "strong take action" and "a little help" refers to Mattathias and his sons (CHRYSOSTOM, THEODORET). The wise ones who fall will be punished as an example to all (ISHO'DAD). In Daniel 11:35-36, the prophetic text transitions from the type, Antiochus, to the archetype, the antichrist. As a result, the remainder of the passage is to be interpreted in light of the archetype, the antichrist (THEODORET, JEROME). He honors himself above the gods of his ancestors (VICTORINUS, HIPPOLYTUS).

11:29 At the Appointed Time

THE DEFEATED ONE WILL RETURN. THEODORET OF CYR: "And he will return at his appointed time," that is, he will not conquer and prevail in the same manner as before, but he will return in defeat. The phrase "at his appointed time" indicates the time suitable for warfare. COMMENTARY ON DANIEL 11.29.[1]

11:30 Ships of Kittim

ROME FORCES ANTIOCHUS OUT OF EGYPT. JEROME: And then two years later[2] he gathered an army against Ptolemy and came to the south. And while he was besieging his two nephews . . . at Alexandria, some Roman envoys arrived on the scene, one of whom was Marcus Popilius Laenas. And when he had found Antiochus standing on the shore and had conveyed the senatorial decree to him by which he was ordered to withdraw from those who were friends of the Roman people and to content himself with his own domain, and then Antiochus delayed his reply in order to consult with his friends.

But Laenas is said to have made a circle in the sand with the staff that he held in his hand and to have drawn it around the king, saying, "The senate and people of Rome give order for you to make answer in this very spot as to what your decision is." At these words Antiochus was greatly alarmed and said, "If this is the good pleasure of the senate and people of Rome, then I must withdraw." And so he immediately set his army in motion. But he is said to have been dealt a heavy blow, not that he was killed but that he lost all of his proud prestige. COMMENTARY ON DANIEL 11.27-30.[3]

THE ANTICHRIST FIGHTS AGAINST THE COVENANT. JEROME: As for the antichrist, there is no question but what he is going to fight against the holy covenant, and when he first makes war against the king of Egypt, he shall immediately be frightened off by the assistance of the Romans. But these events were typically prefigured under Antiochus Epiphanes, so that this abominable king who persecuted God's people foreshadows the antichrist, who is to persecute the people of Christ. And so there are many of our viewpoint who think that Domitius Nero[4] was the antichrist because of his outstanding savagery and depravity. COMMENTARY ON DANIEL 11.27-30.[5]

FURIOUS AGAINST THE HOLY COVENANT. THEODORET OF CYR: "And those who arrive from Kittim will come to him, and they will be brought low." He will ally himself with many Cypriots[6] and other islanders (Kition to the present day is the main city of Cyprus); then he will set out against Egypt but return defeated and humiliated. "And he will return and become angry at the holy covenant." He will spew forth against the holy covenant all his anger that came about because of his defeat. And he will show this anger in action, for he says, "and he will act." At his second coming he will slaughter many, and he will make a treaty with those who had abandoned the holy covenant. He will accomplish every plan of the transgressors, that is, those who wish to deny that they are Jews and who wish instead to act as

---

[1]PG 81:1520; WGRW 7:299. [2]After he looted the temple in Jerusalem. [3]JCD 133. [4]"Domitius was the name of Nero's father, Ahenobarbus" (JCD 133). [5]JCD 133*. [6]Theodoret here refers to the original application of Hebrew *Kittim* to Cypriots. See WGRW 7:299.

Greeks. COMMENTARY ON DANIEL 11.30.[7]

ANTIOCHUS COMES IN ANGER AGAINST THE TEMPLE. JEROME: We read of these matters at greater length in the exploits of the Maccabees,[8] where we learn that after the Romans expelled him from Egypt, he came in anger against the covenant of the sanctuary and was welcomed by those who had forsaken the law of God and taken part in the religious rites of the Gentiles. But this is to be more amply fulfilled under the antichrist, for he shall become angered at the covenant of God and devise plans against those whom he wishes to forsake the law of God. And so Aquila has rendered it in a more significant way: "And he shall devise plans to have the compact of the sanctuary abandoned." COMMENTARY ON DANIEL 11.27-30.[9]

11:31 The Sacrifice Halted

ANTIOCHUS, THE ANTICHRIST OR THE ROMANS? JEROME: But those of the other[10] claim that the persons mentioned are those who were sent by Antiochus two years after he had plundered the temple in order to exact tribute from the Jews and to eliminate the worship of God, setting up an image of Jupiter Olympius in the temple at Jerusalem and statues of Antiochus himself. These are described as the abomination of desolation, having been set up when the burnt offering and continual sacrifice were taken away. But we on our side contend that all these things took place in a preliminary way as a mere type of the antichrist, who is destined to seat himself in the temple of God and make himself out to be as God.

The Jews, however, would have us understand these things as referring not to Antiochus Epiphanes or the antichrist but to the Romans, of whom it was earlier stated, "And war galleys shall come," whether Italian or Roman, "and he shall be humbled." Considerably later, says the text, a king, Vespasian, shall emerge from the Romans themselves, who had come to Ptolemy's assis-

tance and threatened Antiochus. It is his arms or descendants who would rise up, namely, his son, Titus, who with his army would defile the sanctuary and remove the continual sacrifice and devote the temple to permanent desolation. By the terms *siim* (*Siyyim*) and *chethim* (*Kittiym*), which we have rendered as "galleys" and "Romans," the Jews would have us understand "Italians" and "Romans." COMMENTARY ON DANIEL 11.31.[11]

APOLLONIUS AND THE ATHENIAN SENATOR. THEODORET OF CYR: He calls the generals who assist him his "arms," since after the manner of arms they fulfill the commands of the king. Therefore, he will send some to profane the sanctuary of the kingdom, that is, the temple dedicated to almighty God. He will erect an altar to an idol inside of it; he refers to it as the "desolating abomination." The second book of the Maccabees teaches us this when it says, "And about this time Antiochus sent a second expedition to Egypt."[12] . . . Then he relates how the slaughter proceeded against all his comrades. The dead were numbered at eighty thousand. Shortly thereafter he says again, "Since Antiochus had a hostile disposition against the Jews, he sent the most loathsome Apollonius with an army of twenty thousand against two thousand and ordered them to slaughter everyone in every company they met."[13] And a little later he says again, "Soon thereafter the king sent an Athenian senator to compel the Jews to depart from their ancestral laws and not to conduct themselves any longer by the laws of God but to defile the temple in Jerusalem and to swear by Olympian Zeus."[14] COMMENTARY ON DANIEL 11.31.[15]

THE HOLY PLACE IS LAID WASTE. CHRYSOSTOM: Daniel then went on to show that Antiochus destroyed the Jewish commonwealth and way of

---

[7]PG 81:1520; cf. WGRW 7:299-301. [8]1 Macc 1. [9]JCD 133-34*. [10]Porphyry et al. [11]JCD 134*. [12]2 Macc 5:1. [13]2 Macc 5:24. [14]2 Macc 6:1-2. [15]PG 81:1521; cf. WGRW 7:299-301.

life when he said, And through him the sacrifice was disordered by transgression. DISCOURSES AGAINST JUDAIZING CHRISTIANS 5.7.4.[16]

ROMAN DESTRUCTION OF JERUSALEM. ATHANASIUS: "[Jesus] breathed on the disciples and said to them, 'Receive the Holy Spirit.'"[17] As soon as these things were done, everything was finished. The altar was broken, and the veil of the temple was torn from top to bottom. And although the city was not yet sacked and destroyed, the abomination of desolation was soon to rest on the temple and the city. The consummation of the ancient ceremonies was at hand. FESTAL LETTERS 1.8.[18]

11:32 Standing Strong

THE TIME OF THE MACCABEES. CHRYSOSTOM: He means the events in the time of the Maccabees: Judas, Simon and John. DISCOURSES AGAINST JUDAIZING CHRISTIANS 5.7.5.[19]

MATTATHIAS RESISTS THE DECREE. THEODORET OF CYR: He speaks enigmatically here about those around the blessed Mattathias, who was the first to oppose the decrees of Antiochus and to seek solitude with his sons; he took the field with few soldiers and prevailed against Antiochus's generals. COMMENTARY ON DANIEL 11.32.[20]

HEARTS GROW COLD. JEROME: This will take place in the time of the antichrist, when the love of many shall wax cold. It is concerning these people that our Lord says in the Gospel, "Do you think that the Son of man, when he comes, will find faith on the earth?"[21] COMMENTARY ON DANIEL 11.32.[22]

11:33 The Wise Will Make Many Understand

PREFERRING DEATH TO THE LIFE OF GODLESSNESS. THEODORET OF CYR: Those who properly use the knowledge supplied by God will utterly despise that fellow's laws and will prefer death for the divine law to a life of godlessness. To suggest as much, he went on, "they will fall to the sword" . . . the impious one employed all kinds of different punishments in an attempt to move the godly, inflicting them untimely death and as it were robbing them of the remainder of their life. COMMENTARY ON DANIEL 11.33.[23]

KEEPING THE LAW. JEROME: The books of Maccabees relate the great sufferings the Jews endured at the hands of Antiochus, and they stand as a testimony of their triumph; for they endured fire and sword, slavery and rapine and even the ultimate penalty of death itself for the sake of guarding the law of God. But let no one doubt that these things are going to happen under the antichrist, when many shall resist his authority and flee away in various directions. The Jews, of course, interpret these things as taking place at the destruction of the temple, which took place under Vespasian and Titus, and they claim that there were very many of their nation who knew their Lord and were slain for keeping his law. COMMENTARY ON DANIEL 11.33.[24]

11:34 A Little Help

THE DEATHS OF TWO MACCABEES. JEROME: Porphyry thinks that the "little help" was Mattathias of the village of Modin, for he rebelled against the generals of Antiochus and attempted to preserve the worship of the true God.[25] He says he is called a little help because Mattathias was slain in battle; and later on his son Judas, who was called Maccabeus, also fell in the struggle. . . .

Our writers, however, would have it understood that the small help shall arise under the reign of the antichrist, for the saints shall gather together to resist him. . . .

---

[16]FC 68:122. [17]Jn 20:22. [18]NPNF 2 4:509**. [19]FC 68:122-23. [20]PG 81:1521; cf. WGRW 7:303. [21]Lk 18:8. [22]JCD 135*. [23]WGRW 7:303.[24]JCD 135*. [25]1 Macc 2.

Some of the Jews understand these things as applying to the princes Severus and Antoninus, who esteemed the Jews very highly. But others understand the emperor Julian as the one referred to; for after they were oppressed by Gaius Caesar and had steadfastly endured such suffering in the afflictions of their captivity, Julian rose up as one who pretended love for the Jews, promising that he would even offer sacrifice in their temple. They were to enjoy a little help from him, and a great number of Gentiles were to join themselves to their party, although falsely and insincerely. For it was only for the sake of their own idolatrous religion. COMMENTARY ON DANIEL 11.34-35.[26]

11:35 Those Who Are Wise Shall Fall

THE PURGING OF THE WISE. CHRYSOSTOM: Daniel gave the reason why God permitted them to be involved in such trials. What is the reason? "To purge them, to choose them and to make them white until the time of the end" . . . so as to cleanse them and to show who among them was genuine and approved. DISCOURSES AGAINST JUDAIZING CHRISTIANS 5.7.6.[27]

SEPARATING THE FALSE FROM THE TRUE. THEODORET OF CYR: Many of those who seem to be godly will turn to the other direction. "So that they may be refined." . . . These things will not harm the people of this time; they will learn not to have confidence in their previous successes. . . . For the vicissitudes in the situation will purify them as if by fire and test them and will separate the false from the tried and true. . . . These things take place partly in the present life, but in the time to come a complete testing of the people will occur. Once he said these things concerning Antiochus Epiphanes, he changes the remainder of the passage from the type to the archetype. COMMENTARY ON DANIEL 11.35.[28]

THE PRIESTS PUNISHED. ISHO'DAD OF MERV: When the priests, who give scandal, that is, the wise ones with regard to evil . . . are overturned and fall, they will become a furnace of testing before everybody's eyes, and it will be recognized that because of their evil actions punishment has come over them and more evils are forthcoming. "And may understand until the time of the end,"[29] that is, everybody will consider and understand, with regard to the evils that will befall them, that they come according to justice until the time of the end, because evilness has "still an interval" to gain its successes. COMMENTARY ON DANIEL 11.35.[30]

11:36 The King Will Prosper

HIS SUCCESS IS SHORT-LIVED. THEODORET OF CYR: Antiochus will enjoy success, but not forever: "until his wrath has been spent," that is, until he kindles and draws out God's exceedingly great wrath. He calls the retribution God inflicts "his wrath," for the divine nature has no passion. COMMENTARY ON DANIEL 11.36.[31]

THE JEWS ON THE ANTICHRIST. JEROME: As another has translated it, "for in him shall be the consummation." The Jews believe that this passage has reference to the antichrist, alleging that after the small help of Julian a king is going to rise up who shall do according to his own will, and shall lift himself up against all that is called god and shall speak arrogant words against the God of gods. He shall act in such a way as to sit in the temple of God and shall make himself out to be God, and his will shall be prospered until the wrath of God is fulfilled, for in him the consummation will take place. We too understand this to refer to the antichrist. COMMENTARY ON DANIEL 11.36.[32]

11:37 Giving No Heed

---

[26]JCD 135-36*. See also Theodoret, WGRW 7:303, and Hippolytus, ANF 5:183. [27]FC 68:123. [28]PG 81:1524. [29]This is the reading of the Peshitta (CSCO 328:128). [30]CSCO 328:128-29. [31]PG 81:1525; cf. WGRW 7:307. [32]JCD 136*.

ANTIOCHUS REVERED THE GODS OF HIS FATHERS. THEODORET OF CYR: But we find that Antiochus filled Jerusalem and all Judea with altars dedicated to idols and sacrificed to Zeus in the temple of God and called the temple in Jerusalem after Olympian Zeus and the temple on Mount Gerizim after Zeus Xenios. How, then, could it be said that this so superstitious man, this man so entranced by idols, "will not hearken to the gods of his fathers"? Antiochus spent all his time doing the opposite of the antichrist: he revered his fathers' gods, while he rejected the God worshiped by the Jews. These prophecies do not fit Antiochus in the least, but rather the archetype of Antiochus, of whom Antiochus was a type and a foreshadowing, who will vie to outdo all the kings before him in his ungodliness. COMMENTARY ON DANIEL 11.37.[33]

11:37 Beloved by Women[34]

PUBLIC LEWDNESS. JEROME: If we read it as *apo koinou*,[35] "and he shall have no knowledge concerning a lust for women," then it is more easily applied to the antichrist; that is, that he will assume a pretense of chastity in order to deceive many. But if we read it in this fashion, "And occupied with lust for women," understanding . . . "he shall be," then it is more appropriate to the character of Antiochus. For he is said to have been an egregious voluptuary and to have become such a disgrace to the dignity of kingship through his lewdness and seductions that he publicly had intercourse with actresses and harlots and satisfied his sexual passions in the presence of the people. COMMENTARY ON DANIEL 11.37-39.[36]

NO RESPECT TO THE GODS. VICTORINUS OF PETOVIUM: Because he will use another name, he will undertake another life, so that they might welcome him as if he were Christ. For Daniel says that he will not acknowledge the desire of women—because he himself is most filthy—and he will not recognize the god of his fathers. That is, he will not be able to seduce the people to circumcision, unless he is an avenger of the law. At last he will force the saints to nothing other than accepting circumcision, if he will be able to seduce them. COMMENTARY ON THE APOCALYPSE 13.3.[37]

11:38 God of Fortresses

ANTIOCHUS GLORIFIES AN UNKNOWN GOD. HIPPOLYTUS: He has no regard for every god of his fathers or the desire of women, and he has no regard for every god, because he magnifies himself over them all. And he will also glorify the god Mazoeim in his place, a god whom his fathers did not know, and he will glory in gold and silver and precious stone. COMMENTARY ON DANIEL 4.48.2.[38]

GOD MIGHTY AND STRONG. THEODORET OF CYR: Whereas all his ancestors acknowledged their natural limitations and did not presume to name themselves as god over all things, he gives himself the title God mighty and strong (the sense of *Maozeim*)—hence his putting "in his place," meaning himself. COMMENTARY ON DANIEL 11.38.[39]

11:39 Parceling Out the Land

MAOZEIM. JEROME: In regard to the statement "And he shall take measures to fortify Maozeim," . . . Theodotion has interpreted as follows: "And he shall conduct these affairs so as to fortify garrisons with a strange god, and with them he shall manifest and increase glory; and he shall cause them to bear rule over many and divide up the land as a free gift." COMMENTARY ON DANIEL 11.37-39.[40]

---

[33]PG 81:1525-28; cf. WGRW 7:307. [34]LXX: "nor the desire of women." [35]"The use of a common word in two different clauses" (JCD 138). [36]JCD 138*. [37]CSEL 49:120. [38]TLG 2115.030, 4.48.2.5-10. [39]WGRW 7:309. Robert Hill comments, "The Greek versions simply transliterate the Hebrew for '[god] of Fortresses,' a probable reference to the Roman god Jupiter Capitolinus, equivalent to Olympian Zeus. Unaware of this, Theodoret rationalizes, encouraged by the connotation of divinity in the name Epiphanes." [40]JCD 138.

THE ANTICHRIST WILL DECEIVE THE LAND.
THEODORET OF CYR: He says that he will raise
temples for himself and adorn them with silver,
gold and precious stones and subject many people
to them; that is, he will subject the many people
who have been deceived by his signs or who have
been weakened by his punishments. But he will
also "divide the land in exchange for gifts," that is,
he will bestow the largest portion of the land on
those who have obediently chosen to be godless.
COMMENTARY ON DANIEL 11.39.[41]

[41]PG 81:1528; WGRW 7:309.

11:40-45 THE APOCALYPSE

[40]*At the time of the end the king of the south shall attack[g] him; but the king of the north shall
rush upon him like a whirlwind, with chariots and horsemen, and with many ships; and he shall
come into countries and shall overflow and pass through.* [41]*He shall come into the glorious land.
And tens of thousands shall fall, but these shall be delivered out of his hand: Edom and Moab and
the main part of the Ammonites.* [42]*He shall stretch out his hand against the countries, and the land
of Egypt shall not escape.* [43]*He shall become ruler of the treasures of gold and of silver, and all the
precious things of Egypt; and the Libyans and the Ethiopians shall follow in his train.* [44]*But tidings
from the east and the north shall alarm him, and he shall go forth with great fury to exterminate
and utterly destroy many.* [45]*And he shall pitch his palatial tents between the sea and the glorious
holy mountain; yet he shall come to his end, with none to help him.*

g Heb *thrust at*

OVERVIEW: The reference to Libya is understood by most commentators to refer to North
Africa (JEROME). The prophecy concerning the
king's control of the treasuries (EPHREM) of the
Libyans and the Ethiopians was not fulfilled
during the life of Antiochus (THEODORET, JE-
ROME). The final chapter of this vision should
therefore be interpreted as relating to the antichrist and interpreted in light of the previous vision of the little horn uprooting the three horns.
Therefore the three horns must refer to Egypt,
Ethiopia and Libya (THEODORET, JEROME). The
antichrist will subject these three countries and
then will attack regions in the north, killing
many. He will then make his way to the area of
Jerusalem. On the Mount of Olives, the site of
the Lord's ascension, the antichrist will perish
(JEROME, ISHO'DAD).

11:40 At the End Time

PROPHECY REFERRING TO THE ANTICHRIST.
THEODORET OF CYR: We have often said that the
ten horns that appeared on the fourth beast represent ten kings who would reign at the same
time at the end of the Roman Empire. From these
kings the king of the south will wage war against
this one, who is called the king of the north. "For
from the north he will set ablaze all troubles
against the inhabitants of the land."[1] Antiochus,

[1]Jer 1:14.

who happened to be a type of the antichrist, also was called the king of the north. When the king of the south engages him in fight, he will march out against him with a multitude and with strong forces both on land and on sea and acquire the victory. The Lord in the holy Gospels foretold these wars: "Nation will rise against nation and kingdom against kingdom. And there will be famines, plagues and earthquakes in various places. But all these things are the beginnings of the birth pangs."[2] Now that we have seen that the prediction of the Lord corresponds with this prophecy, we will be able to understand the verses before us. COMMENTARY ON DANIEL 11.40.[3]

11:41-43 Invasion of the Glorious Land

ANTIOCHUS STEALS TEMPLE FURNISHINGS. EPHREM THE SYRIAN: Antiochus will assail Judea, will occupy Jerusalem, will rush into the secret places of the sanctuary, will destroy the sacred objects of God, will break the vessels and will take away the golden altar, the candlestick and the table. COMMENTARY ON DANIEL 11.41.[4]

ARABIA UNTOUCHED. JEROME: They say that in his haste to fight Ptolemy, the king of the south, Antiochus left untouched the Idumeans, Moabites and Ammonites, who dwelt to the side of Judea, lest he should make Ptolemy the stronger by engaging in some other campaign. The antichrist also is going to leave Idumea, Moab and the children of Ammon (i.e., Arabia) untouched, for the saints are to flee there to the deserts. COMMENTARY ON DANIEL 11.40-41.[5]

LIBYA UNDERSTOOD AS NORTH AFRICA. JEROME: "Power over all the precious things of Egypt." We read that Antiochus partially accomplished this. But as for the added detail, "He shall pass through the Libyans and the Ethiopians," our school insists that this is more appropriate to the antichrist. For Antiochus never held Libya, which most writers understand to be North Africa, or Ethiopia; unless, of course, his capture

of Egypt involved the harassment of those provinces of Egypt that lay in the same general region as Ethiopia and that lay as distant neighbors to it, on the other side of the deserts. Hence there is no assertion of his conquering them, but only the statement that he passed through the Libyans and the Ethiopians. COMMENTARY ON DANIEL 11.42-43.[6]

THE THREE HORNS AND THEIR REPRESENTATIONS. THEODORET OF CYR: These things do not fit at all with Antiochus. He never gained power over Libya or Ethiopia, or even Egypt itself. He was ordered by the Romans to leave, which he did. Therefore, the three horns that the little horn uprooted must refer to these three nations. The antichrist will destroy three great nations [Egypt, Ethiopia and Libya] governed by three kings, and he will subject them to himself. COMMENTARY ON DANIEL 11.42-43.[7]

11:44 Tidings from the East

DECREE OF THE ROMANS. THEODORET OF CYR: This does not apply to Antiochus either. I mean that the disturbances did not drive him out of Egypt, but rather the decree of the Romans, which came from the west, not from the east. But as far as the antichrist is concerned, the prophecy says that once he takes Egypt, Libya and Ethiopia and subjugates them to himself, he will return, because he will be troubled by a certain rumor, and he will come in great anger "to curse and to obliterate many." This is a hendiadys: "to obliterate" is to be stripped naked of godliness, and "to curse" is to declare that godliness is foreign to oneself. COMMENTARY ON DANIEL 11.44.[8]

RUMORS OF WAR. JEROME: We explain the final chapter of this vision as relating to the antichrist and stating that during his war against

---

[2]Mt 24:7-8. [3]PG 81:1529; cf. WGRW 7:309-11. [4]ESOO 2:231. [5]JCD 140*. [6]JCD 140*. [7]PG 81:1532; cf. WGRW 7:313. [8]PG 81:1532; cf. WGRW 7:313.

the Egyptians, Libyans and Ethiopians, in which he shall smash three of the ten horns, he is going to hear that war has been stirred up against him in the regions of the north and east. Then he shall come with a great host to crush and kill many people, and he shall pitch his tent in Apedno near Nicopolis, which was formerly called Emmaus, at the beginning of the mountainous region in Judea. Finally he shall make his way thence to go up to the Mount of Olives and ascend to the area of Jerusalem. . . . Then he shall come to the summit of the Mount of Olives, the spot from which the Lord ascended to heaven, and it is here the antichrist will per-

ish. COMMENTARY ON DANIEL 11.44-45.[9]

11:45 Between the Sea and the Mountain

PITCHING HIS TENT MEANS DEATH.

ISHO'DAD OF MERV: "He shall pitch his palatial tents in a plain,[10] between the sea of Soph and the mountain," where Moses ascended; "he shall pitch his tent there," that is, he will die there. COMMENTARY ON DANIEL 11.45.[11]

---

[9]JCD 142**. [10]This is the reading of the Peshitta (CSCO 328:130). [11]CSCO 328:130.

12:1-4 THE GENERAL RESURRECTION

[1]At that time shall arise Michael, the great prince who has charge of your people. And there shall be a time of trouble, such as never has been since there was a nation till that time; but at that time your people shall be delivered, every one whose name shall be found written in the book. [2]And many of those who sleep in the dust of the earth shall awake, some to everlasting life, and some to shame and everlasting contempt. [3]And those who are wise shall shine like the brightness of the firmament; and those who turn many to righteousness, like the stars for ever and ever. [4]But you, Daniel, shut up the words, and seal the book, until the time of the end. Many shall run to and fro, and knowledge shall increase.

OVERVIEW: Michael (traditionally considered an archangel) is described as a prince (PSEUDO-DIONYSIUS; CASSIODORUS). The people of God will face a time of great anguish, which corresponds to Antiochus' return from Egypt. Some early commentators saw two periods of anguish, one corresponding to the abomination of destruction, the period of persecution by Antiochus, and second, the abomination of desolation, which refers to the period of tribulation that will take place during the time of the antichrist (HIPPOLYTUS). Those delivered are those whose names are

written in the book, that is, those who are known by God to be his people (AUGUSTINE). The "book" then refers to the knowledge of God (THEODORET). The phrase "many shall wake" refers to the resurrection of the body (JOHN OF DAMASCUS; METHODIUS; HIPPOLYTUS). Since the Maccabees clearly died, Daniel's prophecy refers to the final judgment (JEROME, THEODORET). At the final judgment, those who believe in the true Life will enter into everlasting life; those who are attached to the antichrist to shame (HIPPOLYTUS, BASIL). At the resurrection, differing bodies will be conferred on those who are destined for glory and those for punishment (CYRIL OF JERUSALEM, THEODORET, LACTANTIUS, APOSTOLIC CONSTITUTIONS). The wise—teachers, apostles, martyrs, ascetics, and priests—as in a mirror will shine like the stars (JEROME, AMBROSE, PACHOMIUS, IRENAEUS). These words of testimony are sealed with a seal of obscurity (JEROME, THEODORET, ISHO'DAD). The seal of obscurity is removed for believers by the grace of the Holy Spirit and the incarnation of the Son (THEODORET). Finally, the knowledge from which Scripture was originally composed never ceases to multiply (BEDE).

12:1 *Michael and the Resurrection*

WHO IS MICHAEL? PSEUDO-DIONYSIUS: The revealing rank of principalities, archangels and angels presides among themselves over the human hierarchies, in order that the uplifting and return toward God and the communion and union might occur according to proper order.... Michael is called the ruler of the Jewish people, and other angels are described as rulers of other nations, for "the Most High has established the boundaries of the nations by the number of his angels."[1] CELESTIAL HIERARCHY 9.2.[2]

PRINCES ARE ANGELS. CASSIODORUS: The devil is also called a prince, as in the Gospel passage, "Behold, the prince of this world comes, and in me he will not find anything."[3] Likewise a good angel is called a prince, as we read in Daniel: "Michael your prince." So they are saying that the hope of humankind must rest in neither wicked nor good angels but in the Lord alone. Even if we love the good angels for the devotion they bestow on us, we praise the Lord's blessing that they manifest. EXPOSITIONS OF THE PSALMS 117.9.[4]

DESTRUCTION VERSUS DESOLATION. HIPPOLYTUS: Daniel foretold two abominations, one of destruction, the other of desolation. What is the abomination of destruction other than that which

Antiochus erected during his time? And what is the abomination of desolation other than that which will generally take place when the antichrist comes? COMMENTARY ON DANIEL 4.54.1.[5]

END-TIME TRIBULATIONS. HIPPOLYTUS: "There shall be a time of trouble." For at that time there shall be great trouble, such as has not been from the foundation of the world, when some in one way, and others in another, shall be sent through every city and country to destroy the faithful; and the saints shall travel forth from the west to the east and shall be driven in persecution from the east to the south, while others shall conceal themselves in the mountains and caves. And the abomination shall war against them everywhere, and shall cut them off by sea and by land by his decree and shall endeavor by every means to destroy them out of the world. SCHOLIA ON DANIEL 12.1.[6]

THE LORD KNOWS HIS OWN. AUGUSTINE: "And the sheep hear his voice, and he calls his own sheep by name." For he has their names written in the book of life.[7] "He calls his own sheep by name."[8] Because of this the apostle says, "The Lord knows who are his."[9] "And he leads them out. And when he has led out his own sheep, he goes before them, and the sheep follow him because they know his voice.[10] TRACTATES ON THE GOSPEL OF JOHN 45.6.3.[11]

KNOWLEDGE OF GOD. THEODORET OF CYR: That is, those worthy of salvation, who obeyed the preaching of Elijah, the ones whom he foreknew from the first and the very beginning. He calls the knowledge of God "the book." COMMENTARY ON DANIEL 12.1.[12]

12:2 *The General Resurrection*

---

[1]Deut 32:8 LXX has "angels of God"; the MT has "sons of God." [2]PDCW 171. [3]Jn 14:30. [4]ACW 53:166. [5]TLG 2115.30.4.54.1.1-4. [6]ANF 5:190. [7]See Phil 4:3; Rev 3:5; 13:8. [8]Jn 10:3. [9]2 Tim 2:19. [10]Jn 10:4. [11]FC 88:191*. [12]PG 81:1536; cf. WGRW 7:317.

"MANY" AND "ALL" DO NOT CONTRADICT.

AUGUSTINE: Nor is there any real contradiction between John's "all who are in the tombs"[13] and Daniel's "many" in place of "all." As an illustration of this, notice how, in one place, God said to Abraham, "I have made you the father of many nations"[14] and in another, "In your descendants all the nations of the earth shall be blessed."[15] CITY OF GOD 20.23.[16]

A PHYSICAL RESURRECTION.

METHODIUS: It is the flesh that dies; the soul is immortal. So then, if the soul is immortal and the body is a corpse, those who say that there is a resurrection, but not of the flesh, deny any resurrection; because it is not that which remains standing but that which has fallen and been laid down that is to be set up, according to what was written: "Does not he who falls rise again, and he who turns aside return?"[17] Since flesh was made to border on incorruption and corruption, being itself neither the one nor the other, and was overcome by corruption . . . and delivered over to death through disobedience, God did not leave it to corruption, to be triumphed over . . . but, after conquering death by the resurrection, he delivered it again to incorruption . . . "For this corruptible must put on incorruption."[18] ON THE RESURRECTION 1.12-13.[19]

BODIES SLEEP IN THE DUST.

JOHN OF DAMASCUS: "Many shall awake" means the resurrection of their bodies, for I do not suppose that anyone would speak of souls sleeping in the dust of the earth. . . . The Lord, too, has clearly shown in the holy Gospels that there is a resurrection of the body, for "they that are in the graves," he says, "shall hear the voice of the Son of God. And they that have done good things shall come forth to the resurrection of life; but they that have done evil, to the resurrection of judgment."[20] Now, no person in his right mind would ever say that it was the souls that were in the graves. ORTHODOX FAITH 4.27.[21]

RADIANT BODIES.

HIPPOLYTUS: Who are the ones sleeping in "the tombs of the earth" but the bodies of those people who will receive their own souls back and rise from the dead? Some will rise "to the resurrection of life," receiving pure, transparent and radiant bodies "like the brilliance of the firmament." Others will arise "to the resurrection of judgment," receiving bodies suitable to everlasting punishment. COMMENTARY ON DANIEL 4.56.2.[22]

FINAL JUDGMENT FOR ALL.

THEODORET OF CYR: Let those who try to apply these things to Antiochus tell us who was resurrected in his day—with some obtaining eternal life and others reaping the fruit of reproach and eternal shame. And if someone should say that the Maccabees are referred to by these words, inasmuch as they went out from the caves, he would incur rather much laughter, for the same people will have to be found to be both lovers of godliness and workers of iniquity, for the prophecy says, "Many of those sleeping in the tombs of the earth will rise, some to everlasting life and others to reproach and everlasting shame." Therefore, if someone should apply these words to the Maccabees, they will say that the Maccabees themselves were both evil and good or that some of them were good and others evil. But this is impossible to find, for their whole company was godly. Moreover, "eternal life" does not fit them as far as the present life is concerned, since they all were killed and departed from this life. Then let us leave behind those old wives' tales and learn about the common resurrection of the dead and the judgment that will take place after the resurrection. Some will receive eternal life, and others will be scorned and reproached forever. COMMENTARY ON DANIEL 12.2.[23]

SHAME.

BASIL THE GREAT: To all who reason rightly, the heaviest of punishments is shame. We also have learned this in the case of the judgment,

---

[13]Jn 5:28. [14]Gen 17:5. [15]Gen 22:18. [16]FC 24:316. [17]Jer 8:4. [18]1 Cor 15:53. [19]ANF 6:367-68*. [20]Jn 5:28-29. [21]FC 37:403; cf. NPNF 2 9:100. [22]TLG 2115.030, 4.56.2.1-7. [23]PG 81:1536; cf. WGRW 7:317-19.

when "some" shall rise "to everlasting life and some to everlasting shame and contempt." LETTER 260.4, TO OPTIMUS THE BISHOP.[24]

APOSTATE PRIESTS PUNISHED. ISHO'DAD OF MERV: "And many of those who sleep in the dust of the earth shall awake," that is, many of those who lie among afflictions and are prostrated by their misfortunes, that is, the Maccabees—"some to everlasting life," that is, their patience and justice will make them rejoice in the life in the two worlds, and, in addition, it will make them illustrious through a precious memory in all the centuries after those, in which they lived—"and some to destruction and the opprobrium of their fellow citizens,"[25] that is, the impious and scandalous priests will be given to punishment because of their crimes, and they will leave an evil and accursed name to their fellow citizens forever. COMMENTARY ON DANIEL 12.2.[26]

THERE WILL BE JUST REWARDS. LACTANTIUS: This sentiment set forth by Cicero . . . "if the soul will be in a state of vigor without the body, it is a divine life; and if it is without perception, assuredly that is not bad," is clever . . . but false. For the sacred writings teach that the soul is not annihilated but that it is either rewarded according to its righteousness or eternally punished according to its crimes. DIVINE INSTITUTES 3.19.[27]

OUR CHOICE CREATES HELL. JOHN OF DAMASCUS: The dead shall rise again, and they that are in the graves shall awake. They that have kept the commandments of Christ and have departed this life in the true faith shall inherit eternal life; and they that have died in their sins and have turned aside from the right faith shall go away into eternal punishment. Do not believe that there is any true being or kingdom of evil or suppose that it is without beginning, or self-originated or born of God—forget such an absurdity! But believe rather that it is the work of us and the devil, come on us through our inattentiveness, because we were endowed with free will, and we made our

choice, of deliberate purpose, whether it be good or evil. BARLAAM AND JOSEPH 19.164-65.[28]

SEPARATED FROM CORRUPTION. METHODIUS: Man [humanity], though he was not made mortal and corruptible, dies, and his soul is separated from his body, in order that his transgression might be destroyed by death, being unable to live after he was dead. Thus, with sin dead and destroyed, he can rise again in immortality and sing a hymn of praise to God who saves his children from death by means of death. SYMPOSIUM, OR BANQUET OF THE TEN VIRGINS 9.2.[29]

12:3 The Wise Shall Shine

ALL WILL BE JUDGED. APOSTOLIC CONSTITUTIONS: Gabriel speaks to Daniel. . . . Therefore the most holy Gabriel foretold that the saints should shine like the stars: for his sacred name did witness to them, that they might understand the truth. Nor is a resurrection only declared for the martyrs but for all people, righteous and unrighteous, godly and ungodly, that every one may receive according to his desert. For God, says the Scripture, "will bring every work to judgment."[30] CONSTITUTIONS OF THE HOLY APOSTLES 5.7.[31]

FLORESCENCE IS A FORETASTE. CYRIL OF JERUSALEM: This body shall rise, but it will not abide in its present condition but as an eternal body. No longer will it, as now, need nourishment for life or stairs for its ascent, for it will become spiritual, a marvelous thing, beggaring description. "Then shall the just," it is said, "shine forth like the sun and the moon and like the splendor of the firmament."[32] God, foreknowing human unbelief, has given to the smallest worms to emit from their bodies beams of light in the summer, that

---

[24]NPNF 2 8:298*. [25]This is the reading of the Peshitta (CSCO 328:131). [26]CSCO 328:131. [27]ANF 7:90. [28]LCL 34:279. [29]ACW 27:135*. [30]Eccles 12:14. [31]ANF 7:440*. [32]Combining Mt 13:43 and Dan 12:3.

natural fluorescence might be a parable of what we expect. . . . He who makes the worm shine luminously will much more illumine the just person. Therefore we shall rise again, all with eternal bodies, though not all with like bodies. A just person will receive a heavenly body, to dwell worthily with the angels, whereas the sinner will receive an eternal body and so never be consumed, though it burn eternally in fire. CATECHETICAL LECTURES 18.18-19.[33]

DIFFERING GLORIES. THEODORET OF CYR: "And the wise will shine. . . ." And the Lord says in the holy Gospels, "Then the righteous will shine like the sun."[34] "And from their many righteous deeds, they will shine like the stars forever and ever." The most upright above all will be compared with the brightness of the firmament and with the light of the sun itself. Those who are less than these (that is what he means by the word "many") will imitate the luster of the stars, sending down this light forever. So also Paul distinguished the ranks of the godly: "The glory of the sun is one kind, the glory of the moon another, and the glory of the stars yet another, for star differs from star in glory."[35] COMMENTARY ON DANIEL 12.3.[36]

NATURALISTIC EXPLANATION IS FOOLISH. JEROME: Porphyry argues this was written with reference to Antiochus, for after he had invaded Persia, he left his army with Lysias, who was in charge of Antioch and Phoenicia, for the purpose of warring against the Jews and destroying their city of Jerusalem. . . . Porphyry contends that the tribulation was such as had never previously occurred . . . [but after] the generals of Antiochus had been slain and Antiochus himself had died in Persia, the people of Israel experienced salvation, even all who had been written down in the book of God, that is, those who defended the law with great bravery. Contrasted with them were those who proved to be transgressors of the law and sided with the party of Antiochus.

Then it was, he asserts, that these guardians of the law, who had been, as it were, slumbering in the dust of the earth and were cumbered with a load of afflictions and even hidden away in the tombs of wretchedness, rose up once more from the dust of the earth to a victory unhoped for, and lifted up their heads, rising up to everlasting life, even as the transgressors rose up to everlasting disgrace. But those masters and teachers who possessed a knowledge of the law shall shine like the heaven, and those who have exhorted the more backward peoples to observe the rites of God shall blaze forth after the fashion of the stars for all eternity. He also adduces the historical account concerning the Maccabees, in which it is said that many Jews under the leadership of Mattathias and Judas Maccabeus fled to the desert and hid in caves and holes in the rocks and came forth again after the victory.[37] COMMENTARY ON DANIEL 12.1-3.[38]

TEACHERS. JEROME: In accordance with the merits of each, some shall rise up to eternal life and others to eternal shame. But the teachers shall resemble the very heavens, and those who have instructed others shall be compared with the brightness of the stars. For it is not enough to know wisdom unless one also instructs others; and the tongue of instruction that remains silent and edifies no one else can receive no reward for labor accomplished. COMMENTARY ON DANIEL 12.1-3.[39]

APOSTLES AND PRIESTS ALSO SHINE. AMBROSE: Is he not good, who exalted the earth to heaven, so that, just as the bright companies of stars reflect his glory in the sky, as in a mirror, so the choirs of apostles, martyrs and priests, shining like glorious stars, might give light throughout the world. ON THE CHRISTIAN FAITH 2.2.24.[40]

THE WISE ARE ASCETICS. PACHOMIUS: Quick,

---

[33]FC 64:130-31*. [34]Mt 13:43. [35]1 Cor 15:41. [36]PG 81:1536-37; cf. WGRW 7:319. [37]1 Macc 2. [38]JCD 145-46*. [39]JCD 146*. See also Letter 53.3, to Paulinus, NPNF 2 6:97-98. [40]NPNF 2 10:226*.

flee from sin, think at once of death, for it is written, "The prudent person treats sin harshly, and the face of ascetics will shine like the sun." INSTRUCTIONS 1.32.[41]

BECOMING GLORIFIED IN HEAVEN. IRENAEUS: The person who loves God shall arrive at such excellence as even to see God, and hear his word and from the hearing of his discourse be glorified to such an extent that others cannot behold the glory of his countenance. AGAINST HERESIES 4.26.1.[42]

AFTERLIFE IS BETTER. AMBROSE: Death . . . is entered on for a time and then . . . is put aside. He has shown, too, that the course of the life that is to be after death will be better than that which before death is passed in pain and sorrow. For the life after death is compared with the stars, while our life here is condemned to misery. ON HIS BROTHER SATYRUS 2.66.[43]

12:4 Seal the Testimony

BEFORE FULFILLMENT, PROPHECY SEEMS ENIGMATIC. IRENAEUS: And Jeremiah also says, "In the last days they shall understand these things."[44] For every prophecy, before its fulfillment, appears to people to be full of enigmas and ambiguities. But when the time has arrived and the prediction has come to pass, the prophecies have a clear and certain meaning. AGAINST HERESIES 4.26.1.[45]

MATTERS OF SECRECY. JEROME: He who had revealed manifold truth to Daniel now signifies that the things he has said are matters of secrecy, and he orders him to roll up the scroll containing his words and set a seal on the book, with the result that many shall read it and inquire as to its fulfillment in history, differing in their opinions because of its great obscurity. . . .

Also in the Revelation of John, there is a book seen that is sealed with seven seals inside and outside. And when no one proves able to break its

seals, John says, "I wept terribly; and a voice came to me, saying, 'Weep not: behold the Lion of the tribe of Judah, the Root of David, has prevailed to open the book and break its seals.'"[46] But that book can be opened by one who has learned the mysteries of Scripture and understands its hidden truths and its words that seem dark because of the greatness of the secrets they contain. He it is who can interpret the parables and transmute the letter that kills into the spirit that gives life. COMMENTARY ON DANIEL 12.4.[47]

THE BOOK IS SEALED UNTIL A PROPER TIME. THEODORET OF CYR: He says, "Add to the book the seals of obscurity, and do not make matters clear to all until knowledge is increased and the whole earth is filled with the knowledge of the Lord," like deep water covering the seas, in accordance with the prophecy. The grace of the divine Spirit along with the appearance of our Savior has removed the seals and has made clear to believers what had been unclear. COMMENTARY ON DANIEL 12.4.[48]

PERSUADING THE WEAK. ISHO'DAD OF MERV: He orders him to "seal the book," that is, with the seal of obscurity, and to avoid revealing it to anybody, so that its memory may not be lost and the nations may not be overwhelmed with fear and renounce to ascend to the promised land; and, at the same time, in order that the weak ones of the people, by learning about the affliction that will befall them, may not be held back from going up from Babylon to Jerusalem. "Many will look for"[49] God, "and the knowledge will increase"[50] and will abound all over the world. COMMENTARY ON DANIEL 12.4.[51]

KNOWLEDGE SHALL BE MANIFOLD. BEDE: The same knowledge from which Scripture itself was

---

[41]CS 47:27*. [42]ANF 1:497*. [43]FC 22:226; cf. NPNF 2 10:184. [44]Jer 23:20. [45]ANF 1:496*. [46]Rev 5:4-5. [47]JCD 147-48**. [48]PG 81:1537; cf. WGRW 7:319. [49]This is the reading of the Peshitta (CSCO 328:132). [50]This is the reading of the Peshitta (CSCO 328:132). [51]CSCO 328:132.

originally composed is always increased and never ceases to be multiplied. . . . Moses acquired more knowledge than the patriarchs. . . . Likewise the Lord himself declares the apostles to have known greater things than the prophets. . . . "Many prophets . . . desired to see the things you see and did not see them. . . ."[52] But he also promises them still greater grace of knowledge after his resurrection and ascension. ON THE TABERNACLE 1.5.19.[53]

---

[52]Mt 13:17. [53]TTH 18:18-19.

12:5-13 DANIEL'S VISION ON THE BANK OF THE RIVER

[5]*Then I Daniel looked, and behold, two others stood, one on this bank of the stream and one on that bank of the stream.* [6]*And I*[h] *said to the man clothed in linen, who was above the waters of the stream, "How long shall it be till the end of these wonders?"* [7]*The man clothed in linen, who was above the waters of the stream, raised his right hand and his left hand toward heaven; and I heard him swear by him who lives for ever that it would be for a time, two times, and half a time; and that when the shattering of the power of the holy people comes to an end all these things would be accomplished.* [8]*I heard, but I did not understand. Then I said, "O my lord, what shall be the issue of these things?"* [9]*He said, "Go your way, Daniel, for the words are shut up and sealed until the time of the end.* [10]*Many shall purify themselves, and make themselves white, and be refined; but the wicked shall do wickedly; and none of the wicked shall understand; but those who are wise shall understand.* [11]*And from the time that the continual burnt offering is taken away, and the abomination that makes desolate is set up, there shall be a thousand two hundred and ninety days.* [12]*Blessed is he who waits and comes to the thousand three hundred and thirty-five days.* [13]*but go your way till the end; and you shall rest, and shall stand in your allotted place at the end of the days."*

h Gk Vg: Heb *he*

OVERVIEW: The vision most likely takes place along the banks of the Tigris River. The angel treading on the water is the same angel who presented Daniel's prayers to God, while the angel of Persia was opposing him (JEROME). Others suggest that the one standing on the water was the Son of God (HIPPOLYTUS). "A time" is a year; therefore, "a time, times and half a time" is three and a half years (THEODORET, HIPPOLYTUS, JE-ROME, AUGUSTINE). This period pertains not to Antiochus but the reign of the antichrist (JEROME, THEODORET). Daniel did not understand the reality of things to come because he had not heard the name of those involved (JEROME). As attested by the Jewish historian Josephus, this did not diminish his reputation as a great prophet and righteous man (THEODORET). God tells Daniel that the words are sealed (IRENAEUS). The customary practice of offering sacrifices each evening and dawn were described as the "continuity" because they were frequent and unceasing (CHRYSOSTOM). The removal of daily sacrifice either refers to Antiochus' desolation of the temple (EPHREM, Porphyry via JEROME) or the period in which the antichrist forbids the worship of God (THEODORET, JEROME). Clement of Alexandria argues that this refers to the Nerodian persecution of the early church. The one who endures will be blessed (CYRIL OF JERUSALEM). The chapter concludes with the promise given to Daniel that he will participate in the resurrection at the end of the world after the fulfillment of all the visions he recorded (THEODORET, ISHO'DAD).

12:5-6 *Angels Standing by the River*

ANGELS BY THE TIGRIS. JEROME: Daniel saw two angels standing on either side on the bank of the river of Babylon. Although it is mentioned here without specifying its name, I suppose that in line with the preceding vision it would be the Tigris River, which is called *Eddeqel* in Hebrew. Yet Daniel does not address his question to those who were standing on either bank but rather to the one whom he had seen at the beginning, who was clothed in vesture of linen or *byssus,* which is called *baddim* in Hebrew.

And this same angel was standing on the waters of the river of Babylon, treading on them with his feet. From this fact we understand that the former pair of angels whom he saw standing on the bank and did not question or deem worthy of interrogation were the angels of the Greeks and Persians. But this first angel was the gracious one who had presented Daniel's prayers before God during the twenty-one days while the angel of the Persians was opposing him. And Daniel was asking him about these wonders spoken of in the present vision, as to the time when they should be accomplished. COMMENTARY ON DANIEL 12.5-6.[1]

ANGELS SYMBOLIZE KNOWLEDGE AND QUES-

TIONS. EPHREM THE SYRIAN: That is, when that angel, who talked to me, left, and appeared to have entered the riverbed, to look for a place to ford. Suddenly two others appeared, standing on the opposite banks. Therefore the angel, while he proceeded in the riverbed and trod the stream in safety, played the role of he who knows the depth of the mysteries of God. So "the one standing on this bank of the stream and the one on the other" represent the symbol of the faculty to ask questions omitted by the prophet, which has been granted to them both. For this reason, as if they had received the faculty to do so, they question the other angel. COMMENTARY ON DANIEL 12.5.[2]

THE SON OF MAN WILL HAVE AUTHORITY. HIPPOLYTUS: And who is the one standing "above the water" other than this very one, concerning whom these very prophets had proclaimed long ago, who at the end of time was about to be attested to by the Father at the Jordan river and to be shown boldly to the people by John, who wore the band of a scribe around his loins and the linen and was clad in an intricate long robe? The two men saw him and asked him because "all rule and authority was given" to him. Hence they asked from him more precisely when he would bring the world to judgment and when the things he had spoken would be fulfilled. But he wished to persuade these men in every manner and lifted up "his right hand and his left hand to heaven and swore by the living One forever." Who swore, and by whom did he swear? The Son swore by the Father, when he said that the Father lives "forever." Most surely, "they will know all these things when the scattering will be accomplished in a time, times and half a time." COMMENTARY ON DANIEL 4.57.3-6.[3]

12:7 *Swore by Him*

---

[1]JCD 148*. [2]ESOO 2:232. [3]TLG 2115.30.4.57.3.1-6.4.

THE ONE SWEARS BY THE LORD. THEODORET OF CYR: Here we learn accurately that the one speaking at the time was not the Lord. For as the holy apostle says, "Since the Lord could not swear by anything greater than himself, he swore by himself, saying, 'as I live, says the Lord.'"[4] And blessed Moses shows him to say, "I will lift my hand to heaven, and I will swear by my right hand and say, 'As I live forever.'"[5] The man in our text is one of those subjected and well disposed to the Lord.

"When the scattering of the holy people. . . ." The scattering of the sanctified people will prevail for three and a half years, and all these things will be accomplished. Then they will know the holy One. He alludes here to the great Elijah; around the end of the antichrist's reign, great Elijah will appear and proclaim the second coming of our Savior. COMMENTARY ON DANIEL 12.7.[6]

12:7 Time and Times and Half a Time

THE NUMBER OF "TIMES" CLARIFIED. AUGUSTINE: The word *times* may seem an indefinite plural in our language [Latin], but the Greek texts (and, so I am told, the Hebrew texts as well) show that "times" is written in the dual number and so means "two times." CITY OF GOD 20.23.[7]

THE ANTICHRIST WILL PREVAIL FOR A PERIOD. JEROME: Porphyry interprets a time and times and half a time to mean three and a half years; and we for our part do not deny that this accords with the idiom of sacred Scripture. COMMENTARY ON DANIEL 12.7.[8]

THE SAINTS REIGN FOR MORE THAN A THOUSAND YEARS. AUGUSTINE: The last of all persecutions, the antichrist's, is to go on for three and a half years. . . . Now the question, quite reasonably, presents itself: Should these three and a half years, brief as they are, be included in the thousand years of the devil's binding and the saints' reign with Christ, or are they outside the thousand and superadded to them? . . . We conclude that the reign of Christ with his saints will be longer than the devil's bonds and imprisonment, for, even when he is released, they will continue to reign with their King, the Son of God, for these three and a half years. CITY OF GOD 20.13.[9]

12:8 I Did Not Understand

DO NOT PRESUMPTUOUSLY EXPOUND. JEROME: The prophet wished to comprehend what he had seen, or rather, what he had heard, and he desired to understand the reality of the things to come. For he had heard of the various wars of kings, and of battles between them and a detailed narrative of events; but he had not heard the names of the individual persons involved. And if the prophet himself heard and did not understand, what will be the case with those people who presumptuously expound a book that has been sealed, and sealed until the time of the end, a book that is shrouded with many obscurities? But he comments that when the end comes, the ungodly will lack comprehension, whereas those who are learned in the teaching of God will be able to understand. "For wisdom will not enter the perverted soul."[10] COMMENTARY ON DANIEL 12.8-10.[11]

12:9 The Words Are Sealed

UNDERSTANDING RECEIVED FROM ABOVE. THEODORET OF CYR: Not in vain have I said these rather obscure matters and put obscurity on these words as if they were seals, for divine matters must not be imparted to all indiscriminately, but the wise will understand it through the knowledge imparted to them from above. Those who pass their life in folly and impiety will not be able to understand any of the things contained here. And whenever the matters come to pass, then they will clearly learn the prophe-

---

[4]Heb 6:13-14. [5]Deut 32:40 LXX. [6]PG 81:1537-40; cf. WGRW 7:321-23. [7]JCD 148. [8]JCD 148. [9]FC 24:284-85*. [10]Source unknown. [11]JCD 150*.

cies concerning these things. The workers of iniquity will be separated from the just, for fire will test all things. COMMENTARY ON DANIEL 12.9-10.[12]

12:10 Many Will Purify Themselves

GNOSTIC INTERPRETATION. IRENAEUS: "The words are sealed up until those who are intelligent understand and those who are white are made white."[13] [The Gnostic Marcosians] boast that they themselves are the ones who are white and quite intelligent. AGAINST HERESIES 1.19.[14]

BELIEVE IN THE WORD OF TRUTH. HIPPOLYTUS: And who are they who are chosen but those who believe the word of truth, so as to be made white thereby, and to cast off the filth of sin and put on the heavenly, pure and glorious Holy Spirit, in order that, when the Bridegroom comes, they may go in immediately with him? SCHOLIA ON DANIEL 12.9.[15]

12:11 The Abomination of Desolation

THE DAILY SACRIFICE. CHRYSOSTOM: Next, in predicting the length of time these evils would last, Daniel's angel said, "From the time of the changing of the continuity." The daily sacrifice was called the continuity, for what is continuous is frequent and unceasing. And among the Jews it was customary to offer sacrifice to God in the evening and about dawn each day; this is why they called that daily sacrifice a continuity. But when Antiochus came, he completely did away with this practice. DISCOURSES AGAINST JUDAIZING CHRISTIANS 5.8.3-4.[16]

THE PROPHECY CONCERNS ROMAN EMPERORS. CLEMENT OF ALEXANDRIA: Daniel said there were 2,300 days from the time that the abomination of Nero stood in the holy city, till its destruction. . . . [This] makes six years and four months, during the half of which Nero held sway, and it was half a week; and for a half, Ves-

pasian with Otho, Galba and Vitellius reigned. . . . After the 1,335 days . . . war ceased. STROMATEIS 1.21.[17]

TWO DIFFERENT ABOMINATIONS. HIPPOLYTUS: Daniel speaks, therefore, of two abominations: the one of destruction, which Antiochus set up in its appointed time and that bears a relation to that of desolation, and the other universal, when antichrist shall come. For, as Daniel says, he too shall be set up for the destruction of many. SCHOLIA ON DANIEL 12.11.[18]

THE CHURCH'S WORSHIP DISRUPTED. THEODORET OF CYR: He calls the antichrist "the abomination of desolation." He calls the order of the church's worship, which would be disrupted and made to cease by the madness and raving of the antichrist. COMMENTARY ON DANIEL 12.11.[19]

ANTIOCHUS BLASPHEMES THE LORD. EPHREM THE SYRIAN: He signifies the times of Antiochus, when the impious king will take away the regular burnt offering, and will set up the abomination that desolates and will try to overturn the people of God and to corrupt his religion. Therefore 1,290 days will fill that entire space of time, when the Jews are afflicted by the harshest calamities, and the temple is violated and inside the secret recesses blasphemous and impious people dare raise an altar to their gods. COMMENTARY ON DANIEL 12.11.[20]

ANTIOCHUS'S DESOLATION LASTED THREE YEARS. JEROME: Porphyry asserts that these 1,290 days were fulfilled in the desolation of the temple in the time of Antiochus, and yet both Josephus and the book of Maccabees, as we have said before, record that it lasted for only three

---

[12]PG 81:1540; cf. WGRW 7:323. [13]Irenaeus is following Theodotion's version of Daniel 12:9-10 here, according to ACW 55:221 n. 7. [14]ACW 55:76. [15]ANF 5:191*. [16]FC 68:125. [17]ANF 2:334*. [18]ANF 5:191*. [19]PG 81:1541; cf. WGRW 7:323. [20]ESOO 2:233.

years. From this circumstance it is apparent that the three and a half years are spoken of in connection with the time of the antichrist, for he is going to persecute the saints for three and a half years, or 1,290 days, and then he shall meet his fall on the famous, holy mountain. And so from the time of the removal of the *endelekhismos*, which we have translated as "continual sacrifice," namely, the time when the antichrist shall obtain possession of the world and forbid the worship of God, unto the day of his death, the three and a half years, or 1,290 days, shall be fulfilled. COMMENTARY ON DANIEL 12.11.[21]

12:12 Blessed Is One Who Waits

WE MUST HIDE AT THAT TIME. CYRIL OF JERUSALEM: "Blessed is he that waits." . . . That is why we are to go into hiding and take to flight. For quite likely "we shall not have gone over the cities of Israel till the Son of man comes."[22] Who are the "blessed" that bear witness devoutly for Christ? I tell you that those who are martyrs at that time take precedence over all other martyrs. For . . . the martyrs under antichrist do battle with Satan in his own person. . . . [The antichrist will] show illusory signs and wonders. . . . May it not enter into anyone's heart to ask, "What did Christ do greater than this? For what power enables this man to do such deeds? Unless God willed it, he would not have allowed it." CATECHETICAL LECTURES 15.16-17.[23]

THE ONE WHO ENDURES WILL BE SAVED. THEODORET OF CYR: He suggests and indicates that when this person sustains a divine blow, the great Elijah will continue preaching the remaining forty-five days when the Lord will appear, borne on the clouds of heaven, and will crown those who kept inviolate their treasure acquired by patience. Also the Lord says this in the holy Gospels: "Whoever endures to the end will be saved."[24] COMMENTARY ON DANIEL 12.12.[25]

THE MEANING OF THE ADDITIONAL DAYS.

JEROME: He means that one is blessed who waits for 45 days beyond the predetermined number, for it is within that period that our Lord and Savior is to come in his glory. But the reason for the 45 days of inaction after the slaying of the antichrist is a matter that rests in the knowledge of God; unless, of course, we say that the rule of the saints is delayed in order that their patience may be tested. Porphyry explains this passage in the following way: that the 45 days beyond the 1,290 signify the interval of victory over the generals of Antiochus or the period when Judas Maccabeus fought with bravery and cleansed the temple and broke the idol to pieces, offering blood sacrifices in the temple of God. He might have been correct in this statement if the book of Maccabees had recorded that the temple was polluted over a period of three and a half years instead of just three years.[26] COMMENTARY ON DANIEL 12.12.[27]

THE WISE FIGHT BACK. CHRYSOSTOM: The conflict lasted a month and a half, and in that time the victory became complete, as did also the deliverance of the Jews from the evils that weighed heavy on them. And when he said, "Blessed is the one who stands firm 1,335 days," he revealed their deliverance. He did not simply say, "the one who attains," but "the one who stands firm and attains." The reason for this is that many of the unholy ones saw the change, but he does not call them happy; he calls blessed only those who gave witness during the time of troubles, who did not desert their religion and who then found abatement of their ills. DISCOURSES AGAINST JUDAIZING CHRISTIANS 5.8.4.[28]

WHEN JESUS WILL APPEAR. ISHO'DAD OF MERV: Blessed are those who will go through the days mentioned before[29] and will exceed them by 45 days; that is, When the evils are completed, there will be rest for the people and the end of

---

[21]JCD 150*. [22]Mt 10:23. [23]LCC 4:161**. [24]Mt 10:22. [25]PG 81:1541; cf. WGRW 7:323-25. [26]1 Macc 4. [27]JCD 151*. [28]FC 68:126*. [29]Antiochus's persecution of the Jewish people.

their afflictions. According to others: 1,335 days, that is, "Jesus Christ, Great Savior"—if you count the letters of these four words, they give the name cited above; that is, [Daniel] has received the revelation that he will encounter and see Jesus, etc. Severus[30] says, "Happy are those who persevere" in order to see the days in which his economy is fulfilled, after his baptism to his ascension, and in which he has been pleased with his aspect and miracles, [days] that will make 1,335. Theodoret[31] asserts that these three years and a half constitute the time when the antichrist will reign at the end, and the 45 days the time beginning from the moment in which "the son of perdition"[32] will be condemned, and Elijah will triumph and will drive all people away from the [antichrist], will admonish the Jews and will pray our Lord until he appears from heaven. COMMENTARY ON DANIEL 12.12.[33]

12:13 Your Allotted Place

HE WILL RULE IN THE FUTURE. IRENAEUS: "All dominions shall serve him."[34] Lest this promise should be understood as referring to this time, the prophet declared, "Stand in your place at the consummation of days." AGAINST HERESIES 5.34.2.[35]

RESURRECTION AT THE END OF LIFE. THEODORET OF CYR: "And as for you, rest and rise at your time"—a more correct reading would be "for your inheritance," as will become clear from the things that follow—"at the end of the days." He says in effect, "Now you must receive the end of your days; but you will rise—and not merely rise but rise for your inheritance, that is, with the company of like-minded people." And once he has shown this, he adds, "at the end of the days." So the divine archangel clearly taught the resurrection through the blessed, no, thrice-blessed Daniel. COMMENTARY ON DANIEL 12.13.[36]

JOSEPHUS TESTIFIES TO DANIEL. THEODORET OF CYR: We have learned these things from the divine oracle of Daniel. The Jews mourned him as a righteous man, although they dare to place this divine prophet outside of the list of prophetic books. And yet from experience they have learned the truthfulness of this prophecy. . . . The Hebrew Josephus is a noteworthy witness that Jews of previous generations called blessed Daniel the greatest prophet. Josephus, to be sure, does not accept Christian teaching, but he cannot allow the truth to be hidden. In the tenth book of his *Jewish Antiquities*, Josephus said many other things about blessed Daniel but then adds the following: "Everything was freely given to him unexpectedly, as to one of the greatest prophets. During his lifetime he enjoyed honor and glory, both with kings and the common people. Although he died, his immortal memory lives on. The books that he composed and left behind are still read among us even now, and we have come to believe from them that Daniel consorted with God. Not only did he spend his time foretelling future events, as did the other prophets, but also he marked off the time when these things would take place." COMMENTARY ON DANIEL 12.14.[37]

THE GENERAL RESURRECTION. ISHO'DAD OF MERV: The words, "You shall rise at the end of the days," through the previous sentence shows him that he will not be forever tested by the afflictions of the people. Through this sentence he says to him that, at the fixed and appointed time, at the end of the world, he will receive the expected resurrection, which Christ will perform at his second coming. COMMENTARY ON DANIEL 12.12.[38]

---

[30]Probably Severus of Antioch, according to CSCO 328:132. [31]PG 81:1541, A13-B7; cf. WGRW 7:323-25. [32]2 Thess 2:3. [33]CSCO 328:133. [34]Dan 7:27. [35]ANF 1:564**. [36]PG 81:1541. [37]PG 81:1544. [38]CSCO 328:133.

Early Christian Writers and the Documents Cited

The following table lists all the early Christian documents cited in this volume by author, if known, or by the title of the work. The English title used in this commentary is followed in parentheses with the Latin designation and, where available, the Thesaurus Linguae Graecae (=TLG) digital referenences or Cetedoc Clavis numbers. Printed sources of original language versions may be found in the bibliography of works in original languages.

Ambrose

Death as a Good (De bono mortis)	Cetodoc 0129
Duties of the Clergy (De officiis ministrorum)	Cetodoc 0144
Jacob and the Happy Life (De Jacob et vita beata)	Cetodoc 0130
Letters (Epistulae; Epistulae extra collectionem traditae)	Cetodoc 0160
On His Brother Satyrus (De excessu fratris Satyri)	Cetodoc 0157
On Paradise (De paradiso)	Cetodoc 0124
On the Christian Faith (De fide libri v)	Cetodoc 0150
On the Faith (De fide)	Cetodoc 0150
On the Holy Spirit (De spiritu sancto)	Cetodoc 0151
On Virginity (De virginitate)	Cetodoc 0147
The Prayer of Job and David (De interpellatione Job et David)	Cetodoc 0134

Ammonas

Letters (Epistulae)

Ammonius of Alexandria

Commentary on Daniel (In Danielem)	TLG 2724.002
Fragments on Daniel (Ammonii Eremitae epistolae)	

Andrew of Caesarea

Commentary on the Apocalypse (Commentarii in Apocalypsin)

Aphrahat

Demonstrations (Demonstrationes)

Athanasius

Festal Letters *(Epistulae festalis)*	TLG 2035.014
Letter to the Bishops of Egypt *(Epistula ad episcopos Aegypti et Libyae)*	TLG 2035.041
On Synods *(De synodis Arimini in Italia et Seleuciae in Isauria)*	TLG 2035.010

Augustine

Against Faustus, a Manichean *(Contra Faustum)*	Cetodoc 0321
Against Julian *(Contra Julianum)*	Cetodoc 0351
City of God *(De civitate Dei)*	Cetodoc 0313
Confessions *(Confessionum libri tredecim)*	Cetodoc 0251
Enchiridion *(Enchiridion de fide, spe et caritate)*	Cetodoc 0295
Explanations of the Psalms *(Enarrationes in Psalmos)*	Cetodoc 0283
Harmony of the Gospels *(De consensu evangelistarum)*	Cetodoc 0273
Homilies on 1 John *(In Johannis epistulam ad Parthos tractatus)*	Cetodoc 0279
Letters *(Epistulae)*	Cetodoc 0262
On Genesis Against the Manichaeans *(De Genesi contra Manichaeos)*	Cetodoc 0265
On Grace and Free Will *(De gratia et libero arbitrio)*	Cetodoc 0352
On Lying *(De mendacio)*	Cetodoc 0303
On the Christian Life *(De vita christiana)*	Cetedoc 0730
On the Literal Interpretation of Genesis *(De Genesi ad litteram libri duodecim)*	Cetodoc 0266
On the Merits and Forgiveness of Sins and Baptism *(De peccatorum meritis et remissione et de baptismo parvulorum)*	Cetodoc 0342
On the Predestination of the Saints *(De praedestinatione sanctorum)*	Cetodoc 0354
On the Trinity *(De trinitate)*	Cetodoc 0329
On Various Questions to Simplician *(De diversis quaestionibus ad Simplicianum)*	Cetodoc 0290
Proceedings of Pelagians *(De gestis Pelagii)*	Cetodoc 0348
Sermon on the Mount *(De sermone Domini in monte)*	Cetodoc 0274
Sermon 397 *(De urbis excidio)*	Cetodoc 0312
Sermons *(Sermones)*	Cetodoc 0284
Tractates on the Gospel of John *(In Johannis evangelium tractatus)*	Cetodoc 0278

Basil of Seleucia

Homily *(Sermones)*	TLG 2080.002

Basil the Great

Homilies on the Psalms *(Homiliae super Psalmos)*	TLG 2040.018
Homily on the Words "Give Heed to Yourself" *(Homiliae in ilud: Attende tibi ipsi)*	TLG 2040.006
Letters *(Epistulae)*	TLG 2040.004
The Long Rules *(Asceticon magnum sive Quaestiones [regulae fusius tractatae])*	TLG 2040.048
On the Holy Spirit *(De spiritu sancto)*	TLG 2040.003

Bede

On the Tabernacle *(De tabernaculo et vasis eius ac vestibus sacerdotum libri iii)*	Cetodoc 1345
The Reckoning of Time *(De temporum ratione liber)*	Cetodoc 2320

Benedict
Rule of St. Benedict (*Regula*)   Cetodoc 1852

Caesarius of Arles
Sermons (*Sermones Caesarii Arelatensis*)   Cetodoc 1008

Cassian, John
Conferences (*Collationes xxiv*)   Cetodoc 0512
Institutes (*De institutis coenobiorum et de octo principalium vitiorum remediis*)   Cetodoc 0513

Cassiodorus
Exposition of the Psalms (*Expositio psalmorum*)   Cetodoc 0900

Chromatius of Aquileia
Tractate on Matthew (*Tractatus in Matthaeum*)   Cetodoc 0218

Clement of Alexandria
Christ the Educator (*Paedagogus*)   TLG 0555.002
Stromateis (*Stromata*)   TLG 0555.004

Clement of Rome
1 Clement (*Epistula i ad Corinthios*)   TLG 1271.001

Constitutions of the Holy Apostles (*Constitutiones apostolorum*)   TLG 2894.001

Cyprian
Exhortation to Martyrdom (*Ad Fortunatum*)   Cetodoc 0045
The Lapsed (*De lapsis*)   Cetodoc 0042
Letters (*Epistulae*)   Cetodoc 0050
To Demetrian (*Ad Demetrianum*)   Cetodoc 0046
Works and Almsgiving (*De opera et eleemosynis*)   Cetodoc 0047

Cyril of Alexandria
Commentary on Luke (*Commentarii in Lucam*)   TLG 4090.030
Letter 50 (*Ad Valerianum episcopum Iconii*, in *Concilium universale Ephesenum*)   TLG 5000.001

Cyril of Jerusalem
Catechetical Lectures (*Catecheses ad illuminandos*)   TLG 2110.003

Didache
Teaching of the Twelve Apostles (*Didache xii apostolorum*)   TLG 1311.001

Ephrem the Syrian
Commentary on Daniel (*In Danielem*)
Commentary on Tatian's Diatessaron (*In Tatiani Diatessaron*)

Hymns on Paradise (*Hymni de Paradiso*)
Hymns on the Nativity (*Epiphania*)

Epiphanius of Salamis
On Weights and Measures (*De mensuribus et ponderibus*)

Epistle of Barnabas (*Barnabae epistula*)   TLG 1216.001

Eusebius
Ecclesiastical History (*Historia ecclesiastica*)   TLG 2018.002
Proof of the Gospel (*Demonstratio evangelica*)   TLG 2018.005

Eznik of Kolb
On God (*De Deo*)

Fastidius
On the Christian Life (*Liber de Vita Christiana*)

Fulgentius of Ruspe
To Monimus (*Ad Monimum libri III*)   Cetodoc 0814
To Peter on the Faith (*De fide ad Petrum seu de regula fidei*)   Cetodoc 0826

Gregory of Nazianzus
In Defense of His Flight to Pontus, Oration 2 (*Apologetica [orat. 2]*)   TLG 2022.016
On His Father's Silence, Oration 16 (*In patrem tacentem [orat. 16]*)   TLG 2022.029
On Theology, Theological Oration 2(28) (*De theologia [orat. 28]*)   TLG 2022.008

Gregory of Nyssa
On the Baptism of Christ (*In diem luminum [vulgo In baptismum Christi oratio]*)   TLG 2017.014
On the Soul and the Resurrection (*Dialogus de anima et resurrectione*)   TLG 2017.056
On Virginity (*De virginitate*)   TLG 2017.043

Gregory the Great
Dialogue (*Dialogorum libri iv*)   Cetodoc 1713
Forty Gospel Homilies (*Homiliarum xl in evangelica*)   Cetodoc 1711
Homilies on Ezekiel (*Homiliae in Hiezechihelem prophetam*)   Cetodoc 1710
Pastoral Care (*Regula pastoralis*)   Cetodoc 1712

Hilary of Poitiers
On the Trinity (*De trinitate*)   Cetodoc 0433

Hippolytus
Against Noetus (*Contra haeresin Noeti*)   TLG 2115.002
Commentary on Daniel (*Commentarium in Danielem*)   TLG 2115.030
Fragments

On the Antichrist (*De antichristo*)   TLG 2115.003
Scholia on Daniel (*Scholia in Danielem*)

Ignatius of Antioch
Epistles (*Epistulae vii genuinae*)   TLG 1443.001

Irenaeus
Against Heresies (*Adversus haereses, livres 1-5*)   Cetodoc 1154 f-g

Isaac of Nineveh
Ascetical Homilies (*De perfectione religiosa*)

Isho'dad of Merv
Commentary on Daniel (*Commentarii in Danielem*)

Isidore of Seville
Etymologies (*Etymologiarum sive Originum libri xx: Recognovit brevique adnotatione
    critica instruxit*)   Cetodoc 1186

Jacob of Sarug
On the Establishment of Creation (*Homiliae Selectae Mar Jacobi Sarugensis*)

Jerome
Against Jovinianus (*Adversus Jovinianum*)   Cetodoc 0610
Against the Pelagians (*Dialogus adversus Pelagianos*)   Cetodoc 0615
Commentary on Daniel (*Commentarii in Danielem*)   Cetodoc 0588
Commentary on Ezechiel (*Commentarii in Ezechielem*)   Cetodoc 0587
Homilies on Mark (*Tractatus in Marci evangelium*)   Cetodoc 0594
Homilies on the Psalms (*Tractatus lix in psalmos*)   Cetodoc 0592
Homilies on the Psalms, Alternate Series (*Tractatuum in psalmos series altera*)   Cetodoc 0593
Homily 87 (On John) (*Homilia in Johannem evangelistam [1:1-14]*)   Cetodoc 0597
Letters (*Epistulae*)   Cetodoc 0620
Homily 94 (On Easter Sunday) (*In die dominica Paschae, II*)   Cetodoc 0604

John Chrysostom
Against the Anomoeans 2 (*De incomprehensibili dei natura*)   TLG 2062.012
Baptismal Instructions (*Ad illuminandos catecheses 1-2 [series prima et secunda]*)   TLG 2062.025
Commentary on Daniel (*Interpretatio in Danielem prophetam [Sp.]*)   TLG 2062.209
Concerning the Power of Demons (*De diabolo tentatore [homiliae 1-3]*)   TLG 2062.026
Discourse on Blessed Babylas (*De sancto hieromartyre Babyla*)   TLG 2062.041
Discourses Against Judaizing Christians (*Adversus Judaeos [orationes 1-8]*)   TLG 2062.021
Homilies Concerning the Statues (*Ad populum Antiochenum homiliae [de statuis]*)   TLG 2062.024
Homilies on 1 Corinthians (*In epistulam i ad Corinthios [homiliae 1-44]*)   TLG 2062.156
Homilies on Ephesians (*In epistulam ad Ephesios [homiliae 1-24]*)   TLG 2062.159
Homilies on Genesis (*In Genesim [homiliae 1-67]*)   TLG 2062.112

Homilies on Repentance and Almsgiving (*De paenitentia [homiliae 1-9]*)	TLG 2062.027
Homilies on the Acts of the Apostles (*In Acta apostolorum [homiliae 1-55]*)	TLG 2062.154
Homilies on the Gospel of John (*In Joannem [homiliae 1-88]*)	TLG 2062.153
Homilies on the Gospel of Matthew (*In Matthaeum [homiliae 1-90]*)	TLG 2062.152
Homilies on 2 Timothy (*In epistulam ii ad Timotheum [homiliae 1-10]*)	TLG 2062.165
Homilies on Titus (*In epistulam ad Titum [homiliae 1-6]*)	TLG 2062.166
Letter to the Fallen Theodore (*Ad Theodorum lapsum [lib. 2]*)	TLG 2062.001
None Can Harm Him Who Does Not Injure Himself (*Quod nemo laeditur nisi a se ipso*)	TLG 2062.086
To Stagirius (*Ad Stagirium a daemone vexatum, lib. iii*)	TLG 2062.006
On the Epistle to the Hebrews (*In epistulam ad Hebraeos [homiliae 1-34]*)	TLG 2062.168

John of Damascus

Barlaam and Joseph (*Vita Barlaam et Joasaph*)	TLG 2934.066
On Divine Images (*Oratio apologetica adversus eos, qui sacras imagines abiciunt*)	TLG 2934.004
Orthodox Faith (*Expositio fidei*)	TLG 2934.004

Julian of Toledo

On the Confirmation of the Sixth Age (*De comprobatione sextae aetatis libri tres*)	Cetodoc 1260

Justin Martyr

First Apology (*Apologia*)	TLG 0645.001
Dialogue with Trypho (*Dialogus cum Tryphone*)	TLG 0645.003

Lactantius

Divine Institutes (*Divinae Institutiones*)	Cetodoc 0085

Leander of Seville

The Training of Nuns (*De institutione virginum et contemptu mundi*)

Leo the Great

Letters (*Epistulae*)	Cetedoc 1657
Sermons (*Tractatus septem et nonaginta*)	Cetedoc 1657

Martyrdom of Polycarp (*Martyrium Polycarpi*)	TLG 1484.001

Maximus of Turin

Sermon (*Collectio sermonum antique*)	Cetodoc 0219a

Methodius

On the Resurrection (*De Resurrectione*)	TLG 2959.003
Symposium, Or Banquet of the Ten Virgins (*Symposium sive Convivium decem virginum*)	TLG 2959.001

Nemesius of Emesa

On the Nature of Man (*De natura hominis*)	TLG 0743.001

Novatian
On the Spectacles (*De spectaculis*)
On the Trinity (*De trinitate*)   Cetodoc 0071

Origen
Against Celsus (*Contra Celsum*)   TLG 2042.001
Commentary on the Epistle to the Romans, Books 1-5 (*Commentarii in epistolam ad Romanos*)
Commentary on the Gospel According to John, Books 1-10
    (*Commentarii in evangelium Joannis*)   TLG 2042.005
Exhortation to Martyrdom (*Exhortatio ad martyrium*)   TLG 2042.007
Fragments on Ezekiel (*Selecta in Ezechielem*)   TLG 2042.062
Fragments on Psalms (*Selecta in Psalmos [Dub.] [fragmenta e catenis]*)   TLG 2042.058
Homilies on Exodus (*Homiliae in Exodum*)   Cetodoc 0198 5 (A)
Homilies on Ezekiel (*Homiliae in Ezechielem*)   TLG 2042.027
Homilies on Genesis (*Homiliae in Genesim*)   TLG 2042.022
Homilies on Leviticus (*Homiliae in Leviticum*)   Cetodoc 0198 3 (A)
                                                                                              TLG 2042.024
Homilies on Numbers (*In Numeros homiliae*)   Cetodoc 0198 O (A)
On First Principles (*De principiis*)   Cetodoc 0198 E (A)
                                                                                              TLG 2042.002
On Prayer (*De oratione*)   TLG 2042.008

Pachomius
Instructions (*Catechesis*)
Letters (In *Catecheses*)
Life of Pachomius (Bohairic) (*Vita Pachomii*)

Pacian of Barcelona
On Penitents (*De paenitentibus*)

Paulinus of Nola
Poem (*Carmina*)   Cetodoc 0203

Peter Chrysologus
Sermon (*Collectio sermonum a Felice episcopo parata sermonibus extravagantibus adjectis*)   Cetodoc 0227

Possidius
Life of Augustine (*Vita Augustini*)   Cetodoc 0358

Primasius
Commentary on the Apocalypse (*Commentarius in Apocalypsin*)   Cetodoc 0873

Pseudo-Clement of Rome
2 Clement (*Epistula ii ad Corinthios*)   TLG 1271.002
Pseudo-Clementine Homilies (*Homiliae*)   TLG 1271.006

Pseudo-Dionysius
Celestial Hierarchy (*De caelesti hierarchia*)   TLG 2798.001

Pseudo-Hegesippus
On the Jewish War by Josephus Flavius (*Flauius Iosephus sec. transl. et retract.*
  Hegesippi - Historiae libri V)   Cetodoc 0190a

Pseudo-Macarius
Fifty Spiritual Homilies (*Homiliae spiritualis 50*)   TLG 2109.002

Quodvultdeus
The Book of Promises and Predictions of God (*Liber promissionum et praedictorum Dei*)   Cetodoc 0413

Romanus Melodus
Kontakion on the Three Children (*Cantica*)   TLG 2881.001

Rufinus of Aquileia
Commentary on the Apostles' Creed (*Expositio symboli*)   Cetodoc 0196

Salvian the Presbyter
Four Books of Timothy to the Church (*Adversus avaritiam libri quatuor*)
The Governance of God (*De gubernatione Dei*)   Cetodoc 0485

Symeon the New Theologian
Discourses (*Catecheses*)
The Practical and Theological Chapters (*Capita practica et theologica*)

Tertullian
Against Marcion (*Adversus Marcionem*)   Cetodoc 0014
An Answer to the Jews (*Adversus Judaeos*)   Cetodoc 0033
The Chaplet (*De corona*)   Cetodoc 0021
On Fasting (*De ieiunio adversus psychicos*)   Cetodoc 0029
On Idolatry (*De idololatria*)   Cetodoc 0023
On Penitence (*De paenitentia*)   Cetodoc 0009
On Prayer (*De oratione*)   Cetodoc 0007
On Purity (*De pudicitia*)   Cetodoc 0030
On the Resurrection of the Flesh (*De resurrectione carnis*)
On the Soul (*De anima*)   Cetodoc 0017
To the Martyrs (*Ad martyras*)   Cetodoc 0001

Theodoret of Cyr
Commentary on Daniel (*Interpretatio in Danielem*)   TLG 4089.028
Commentary on Ezekiel (*Interpretatio in Ezechielem*)   TLG 4089.027
Commentary on the Psalms (*Interpretatio in Psalmos*)   TLG 4089.024
Lives of Simeon Stylites (*Historia religiosa*)   TLG 4089.004

Valerian of Cimiez
Homilies *(Homiliae)*

Victorinus of Petovium
Commentary on the Apocalypse *(Commentarii in Apocalypsim Joannis)*

Biographical Sketches & Short Descriptions of Select Anonymous Works

This listing is cumulative, including all the authors and works cited in this series to date.

Abraham of Nathpar (fl. sixth-seventh century). Monk of the Eastern Church who flourished during the monastic revival of the sixth to seventh century. Among his works is a treatise on prayer and silence that speaks of the importance of prayer becoming embodied through action in the one who prays. His work has also been associated with John of Apamea or Philoxenus of Mabbug.

Acacius of Beroea (c. 340-c. 436). Syrian monk known for his ascetic life. He became bishop of Beroea in 378, participated in the council of Constantinople in 381, and played an important role in mediating between Cyril of Alexandria and John of Antioch; however, he did not take part in the clash between Cyril and Nestorius.

Acacius of Caesarea (d. c. 365). Pro-Arian bishop of Caesarea in Palestine, disciple and biographer of Eusebius of Caesarea, the historian. He was a man of great learning and authored a treatise on Ecclesiastes.

Adamantius (early fourth century). Surname of Origen of Alexandria and the main character in the dialogue contained in *Concerning Right Faith in God*. Rufinus attributes this work to Origen. However, Trinitarian terminology, coupled with references to Methodius and allusions to the fourth-century Constantinian era bring this attri-bution into question.

Adamnan (c. 624-704). Abbot of Iona, Ireland, and author of the life of St. Columba. He was influential in the process of assimilating the Celtic church into Roman liturgy and church order. He also wrote *On the Holy Sites*, which influenced Bede.

Alexander of Alexandria (fl. 312-328). Bishop of Alexandria and predecessor of Athanasius, on whom he exerted considerable theological influence during the rise of Arianism. Alexander excommunicated Arius, whom he had appointed to the parish of Baucalis, in 319. His teaching regarding the eternal generation and divine substantial union of the Son with the Father was eventually confirmed at the Council of Nicaea (325).

Ambrose of Milan (c. 333-397; fl. 374-397). Bishop of Milan and teacher of Augustine who defended the divinity of the Holy Spirit and the perpetual virginity of Mary.

Ambrosiaster (fl. c. 366-384). Name given by Erasmus to the author of a work once thought to have been composed by Ambrose.

Ammonas (fourth century). Student of Antony the Great and member of a colony of anchorite monks at Pispir in Egypt. He took over leadership of the colony upon Antony's death in 356.

He was consecrated by Athanasius as bishop of a small unknown see. He died by 396. Fourteen letters and eleven sayings in the *Apophthegmata Patrum* are attributed to him, although it is unlikely that all of the identified sayings are his.

Ammonius (c. fifth century). An Aristotelian commentator and teacher in Alexandria, where he was born and of whose school he became head. Also an exegete of Plato, he enjoyed fame among his contemporaries and successors, although modern critics accuse him of pedantry and banality.

Amphilochius of Iconium (b. c. 340-345, d.c. 398-404). An orator at Constantinople before becoming bishop of Iconium in 373. He was a cousin of Gregory of Nazianzus and active in debates against the Macedonians and Messalians.

Andreas (c. seventh century). Monk who collected commentary from earlier writers to form a catena on various biblical books.

Andrew of Caesarea (early sixth century). Bishop of Caesarea in Cappadocia. He produced one of the earliest Greek commentaries on Revelation and defended the divine inspiration of its author.

Andrew of Crete (c. 660-740). Bishop of Crete, known for his hymns, especially for his "canons," a genre which supplanted the *kontakia* and is believed to have originated with him. A significant number of his canons and sermons have survived and some are still in use in the Eastern Church. In the early Iconoclastic controversy he is also known for his defense of the veneration of icons.

Antony (or Anthony) the Great (c. 251-c. 356). An anchorite of the Egyptian desert and founder of Egyptian monasticism. Athanasius regarded him as the ideal of monastic life, and he has become a model for Christian hagiography.

Aphrahat (c. 270-350; fl. 337-345). "The Persian Sage" and first major Syriac writer whose work survives. He is also known by his Greek name Aphraates.

Apollinaris of Laodicea (310-c. 392). Bishop of Laodicea who was attacked by Gregory of Nazianzus, Gregory of Nyssa and Theodore for denying that Christ had a human mind.

Aponius/Apponius (fourth–fifth century). Author of a remarkable commentary on Song of Solomon (c. 405-415), an important work in the history of exegesis. The work, which was influenced by the commentaries of Origen and Pseudo-Hippolytus, is of theological significance, especially in the area of Christology.

Apostolic Constitutions (c. 381-394). Also known as *Constitutions of the Holy Apostles* and thought to be redacted by Julian of Neapolis. The work is divided into eight books, and is primarily a collection of and expansion on previous works such as the *Didache* (c. 140) and the *Apostolic Traditions*. Book 8 ends with eighty-five canons from various sources and is elsewhere known as the *Apostolic Canons*.

Apringius of Beja (middle sixth century). Iberian bishop and exegete. Heavily influenced by Tyconius, he wrote a commentary on Revelation in Latin, of which two large fragments survive.

Arethas of Caesarea (c. 860-940) Byzantine scholar and disciple of Photius. He was a deacon in Constantinople, then archbishop of Caesarea from 901.

Arius (fl. c. 320). Heretic condemned at the Council of Nicaea (325) for refusing to accept that the Son was not a creature but was God by nature like the Father.

Arnobius the Younger (fifth century). A participant in christological controversies of the fifth century. He composed *Conflictus cum Serapione*, an account of a debate with a monophysite monk in which he attempts to demonstrate harmony between Roman and Alexandrian theology. Some scholars attribute to him a few more works, such as *Commentaries on Psalms*.

Athanasius of Alexandria (c. 295-373; fl. 325-373). Bishop of Alexandria from 328, though often in exile. He wrote his classic polemics against the Arians while most of the eastern bishops were against him.

Athenagoras (fl. 176-180). Early Christian philosopher and apologist from Athens, whose only authenticated writing, *A Plea Regarding Christians*, is addressed to the emperors Marcus Aurelius and Commodius, and defends Christians from the common accusations of atheism, incest and cannibalism.

Augustine of Hippo (354-430). Bishop of Hippo and a voluminous writer on philosophical, exegetical, theological and ecclesiological topics. He formulated the Western doctrines of predestination and original sin in his writings against the Pelagians.

Babai (c. early sixth century). Author of the Letter to Cyriacus. He should not be confused with either Babai of Nisibis (d. 484), or Babai the Great (d. 628).

Babai the Great (d. 628). Syriac monk who founded a monastery and school in his region of Beth Zabday and later served as third superior at the Great Convent of Mount Izla during a period of crisis in the Nestorian church.

Basil of Seleucia (fl. 444-468). Bishop of Seleucia in Isauria and ecclesiastical writer. He took part in the Synod of Constantinople in 448 for the condemnation of the Eutychian errors and the deposition of their great champion, Dioscurus of Alexandria.

Basil the Great (b. c. 330; fl. 357-379). One of the Cappadocian fathers, bishop of Caesarea and champion of the teaching on the Trinity propounded at Nicaea in 325. He was a great administrator and founded a monastic rule.

Basilides (fl. second century). Alexandrian heretic of the early second century who is said to have believed that souls migrate from body to body and that we do not sin if we lie to protect the body from martyrdom.

Bede the Venerable (c. 672/673-735). Born in Northumbria, at the age of seven, he was put under the care of the Benedictine monks of Saints Peter and Paul at Jarrow and given a broad classical education in the monastic tradition. Considered one of the most learned men of his age, he is the author of *An Ecclesiastical History of the English People*.

Benedict of Nursia (c. 480-547). Considered the most important figure in the history of Western monasticism. Benedict founded many monasteries, the most notable found at Montecassino, but his lasting influence lay in his famous Rule. The Rule outlines the theological and inspirational foundation of the monastic ideal while also legislating the shape and organization of the cenobitic life.

Besa the Copt (5th century). Coptic monk, disciple of Shenoute, whom he succeeded as head of the monastery. He wrote numerous letters, monastic catecheses and a biography of Shenoute.

Book of Steps (c. 400). Written by an anonymous Syriac author, this work consists of thirty homilies or discourses which specifically deal with the more advanced stages of growth in the spiritual life.

Braulio of Saragossa (c. 585-651). Bishop of Saragossa (631-651) and noted writer of the Visigothic renaissance. His *Life* of St. Aemilianus is his crowning literary achievement.

Caesarius of Arles (c. 470-543). Bishop of Arles renowned for his attention to his pastoral duties. Among his surviving works the most important is a collection of some 238 sermons that display an ability to preach Christian doctrine to a variety of audiences.

Callistus of Rome (d. 222). Pope (217-222) who excommunicated Sabellius for heresy. It is very probable that he suffered martyrdom.

Cassia (b. c. 805, d. between 848 and 867). Nun, poet and hymnographer who founded a convent in Constantinople.

Cassian, John (360-432). Author of the *Institutes* and the *Conferences*, works purporting to relay the teachings of the Egyptian monastic fathers on the nature of the spiritual life which were highly influential in the development of Western monasticism.

Cassiodorus (c. 485-c. 580). Founder of the monastery of Vivarium, Calabria, where monks transcribed classic sacred and profane texts, Greek and Latin, preserving them for the Western tradition.

Chromatius (fl. 400). Bishop of Aquileia, friend of Rufinus and Jerome and author of tracts and sermons.

Clement of Alexandria (c. 150-215). A highly educated Christian convert from paganism, head of the catechetical school in Alexandria and pioneer of Christian scholarship. His major works, *Protrepticus, Paedagogus* and the *Stromata*, bring Christian doctrine face to face with the ideas and achievements of his time.

Clement of Rome (fl. c. 92-101). Pope whose *Epistle to the Corinthians* is one of the most important documents of subapostolic times.

Commodian (probably third or possibly fifth century). Latin poet of unknown origin (possibly Syrian?) whose two surviving works suggest chiliast and patripassionist tendencies.

Constitutions of the Holy Apostles. *See Apostolic Constitutions.*

Cosmas of Maiuma (c. 675-c.751). Adopted son of John of Damascus and educated by the monk Cosmas in the early eighth century. He entered the monastery of St. Sabas near Jerusalem and in 735 became bishop of Maiuma near Gaza. Cosmas in his capacity as Melodus ("Songwriter") is known for his canons composed in honor of Christian feasts. An alternate rendering of his name is Kosmas Melodos.

Cyprian of Carthage (fl. 248-258). Martyred bishop of Carthage who maintained that those baptized by schismatics and heretics had no share in the blessings of the church.

Cyril of Alexandria (375-444; fl. 412-444). Patriarch of Alexandria whose extensive exegesis, characterized especially by a strong espousal of the unity of Christ, led to the condemnation of Nestorius in 431.

Cyril of Jerusalem (c. 315-386; fl. c. 348). Bishop of Jerusalem after 350 and author of *Catechetical Homilies.*

Cyril of Scythopolis (b. c. 525; d. after 557). Palestinian monk and author of biographies of famous Palestinian monks. Because of him we have precise knowledge of monastic life in the fifth and sixth centuries and a description of the Origenist crisis and its suppression in the mid-sixth century.

Diadochus of Photice (c. 400-474). Antimonophysite bishop of Epirus Vetus whose work *Discourse on the Ascension of Our Lord Jesus Christ* exerted influence in both the East and West

through its Chalcedonian Christology. He is also the subject of the mystical *Vision of St. Diadochus Bishop of Photice in Epirus.*

Didache (c. 140). Of unknown authorship, this text intertwines Jewish ethics with Christian liturgical practice to form a whole discourse on the "way of life." It exerted an enormous amount of influence in the patristic period and was especially used in the training of catechumen.

Didascalia Apostolorum (Teaching of the Twelve Apostles and Holy Disciples of Our Savior) (early third century). A Church Order composed for a community of Christian converts from paganism in the northern part of Syria. This work forms the main source of the first six books of the *Apostolic Constitutions* and provides an important window to view what early liturgical practice may have looked like.

Didymus the Blind (c. 313-398). Alexandrian exegete who was much influenced by Origen and admired by Jerome.

Diodore of Tarsus (d. c. 394). Bishop of Tarsus and Antiochene theologian. He authored a great scope of exegetical, doctrinal and apologetic works, which come to us mostly in fragments because of his condemnation as the predecessor of Nestorianism. Diodore was a teacher of John Chrysostom and Theodore of Mopsuestia.

Dionysius of Alexandria (d. c. 264). Bishop of Alexandria and student of Origen. Dionysius actively engaged in the theological disputes of his day, opposed Sabellianism, defended himself against accusations of tritheism and wrote the earliest extant Christian refutation of Epicureanism. His writings have survived mainly in extracts preserved by other early Christian authors.

Dorotheus of Gaza (fl. c. 525-540). Member of Abbot Seridos's monastery and later leader of a monastery where he wrote *Spiritual Instructions.* He also wrote a work on traditions of Palestinian monasticism.

Ennodius (474-521). Bishop of Pavia, a prolific writer of various genre, including letters, poems and biographies. He sought reconciliation in the schism between Rome and Acacius of Constantinople, and also upheld papal autonomy in the face of challenges from secular authorities.

Ephrem the Syrian (b. c. 306; fl. 363-373). Syrian writer of commentaries and devotional hymns which are sometimes regarded as the greatest specimens of Christian poetry prior to Dante.

Epiphanius of Salamis (c. 315-403). Bishop of Salamis in Cyprus, author of a refutation of eighty heresies (the *Panarion*) and instrumental in the condemnation of Origen.

Epiphanius the Latin. Author of the late fifth-century or early sixth-century Latin text *Interpretation of the Gospels,* with constant references to early patristic commentators. He was possibly a bishop of Benevento or Seville.

Epistle of Barnabas. See Letter of Barnabas.

Eucherius of Lyons (fl. 420-449). Bishop of Lyons c. 435-449. Born into an aristocratic family, he, along with his wife and sons, joined the monastery at Lérins soon after its founding. He explained difficult Scripture passages by means of a threefold reading of the text: literal, moral and spiritual.

Eugippius (b. 460). Disciple of Severinus and third abbot of the monastic community at Castrum Lucullanum, which was made up of those fleeing from Noricum during the barbarian invasions.

Eunomius (d. 393). Bishop of Cyzicyus who was attacked by Basil and Gregory of Nyssa for maintaining that the Father and the Son were of different natures, one ingenerate, one generate.

Eusebius of Caesarea (c. 260/263-340). Bishop of Caesarea, partisan of the Emperor Constantine and first historian of the Christian church. He argued that the truth of the gospel had been foreshadowed in pagan writings but had to defend his own doctrine against suspicion of Arian sympathies.

Eusebius of Emesa (c. 300-c. 359). Bishop of Emesa from c. 339. A biblical exegete and writer on doctrinal subjects; he displays some semi-Arian tendencies of his mentor Eusebius of Caesarea.

Eusebius of Gaul, or Eusebius Gallicanus (c. fifth century). A conventional name for a collection of seventy-six sermons produced in Gaul and revised in the seventh century. It contains material from different patristic authors and focuses on ethical teaching in the context of the liturgical cycle (days of saints and other feasts).

Eusebius of Vercelli (fl. c. 360). Bishop of Vercelli who supported the trinitarian teaching of Nicaea (325) when it was being undermined by compromise in the West.

Eustathius of Antioch (fl. 325). First bishop of Beroea, then of Antioch, one of the leaders of the anti-Arians at the council of Nicaea. Later, he was banished from his seat and exiled to Thrace for his support of Nicene theology.

Euthymius (377-473). A native of Melitene and influential monk. He was educated by Bishop Otreius of Melitene, who ordained him priest and placed him in charge of all the monasteries in his diocese. When the Council of Chalcedon (451) condemned the errors of Eutyches, it was greatly due to the authority of Euthymius that most of the Eastern recluses accepted its decrees. The empress Eudoxia returned to Chalcedonian orthodoxy through his efforts.

Evagrius of Pontus (c. 345-399). Disciple and teacher of ascetic life who astutely absorbed and creatively transmitted the spirituality of Egyptian and Palestinian monasticism of the late fourth century. Although Origenist elements of his writings were formally condemned by the Fifth Ecumenical Council (Constantinople II, A.D. 553), his literary corpus continued to influence the tradition of the church.

Eznik of Kolb (early fifth century). A disciple of Mesrob who translated Greek Scriptures into Armenian, so as to become the model of the classical Armenian language. As bishop, he participated in the synod of Astisat (449).

Facundus of Hermiane (fl. 546-568). African bishop who opposed Emperor Justinian's *post mortem* condemnation of Theodore of Mopsuestia, Theodoret of Cyr and Ibas of Edessa at the fifth ecumenical council. His written defense, known as "To Justinian" or "In Defense of the Three Chapters," avers that ancient theologians should not be blamed for errors that became obvious only upon later theological reflection. He continued in the tradition of Chalcedon, although his Christology was supplemented, according to Justinian's decisions, by the theopaschite formula *Unus ex Trinitate passus est* ("Only one of the three suffered").

Fastidius (c. fourth-fifth centuries). British author of *On the Christian Life*. He is believed to have written some works attributed to Pelagius.

Faustinus (fl. 380). A priest in Rome and supporter of Lucifer and author of a treatise on the Trinity.

Faustus of Riez (c. 400-490). A prestigious British monk at Lérins; abbot, then bishop of Riez from 457 to his death. His works include *On the Holy Spirit*, in which he argued against the Macedonians for the divinity of the Holy Spirit, and *On Grace*, in which he argued for a position on salvation that lay between more categorical views of free-will and predestination. Various letters and (pseudonymous) sermons are extant.

The Festal Menaion. Orthodox liturgical text containing the variable parts of the service, including hymns, for fixed days of celebration of the life of Jesus and Mary.

Filastrius (fl. 380). Bishop of Brescia and author of a compilation against all heresies.

Firmicus Maternus (fourth century). An anti-Pagan apologist. Before his conversion to Christianity he wrote a work on astrology (334-337). After his conversion, however, he criticized paganism in *On the Errors of the Profane Religion*.

Flavian of Chalon-sur-Saône (d. end of sixth century). Bishop of Chalon-sur-Saône in Burgundy, France. His hymn *Verses on the Mandate in the Lord's Supper* was recited in a number of the French monasteries after the washing of the feet on Maundy Thursday.

Fructuosus of Braga (d. c. 665). Son of a Gothic general and member of a noble military family. He became a monk at an early age, then abbot-bishop of Dumium before 650 and metropolitan of Braga in 656. He was influential in setting up monastic communities in Lusitania, Asturia, Galicia and the island of Gades.

Fulgentius of Ruspe (c. 467-532). Bishop of Ruspe and author of many orthodox sermons and tracts under the influence of Augustine.

Gaudentius of Brescia (fl. 395). Successor of Filastrius as bishop of Brescia and author of twenty-one Eucharistic sermons.

Gennadius of Constantinople (d. 471). Patriarch of Constantinople, author of numerous commentaries and an opponent of the Christology of Cyril of Alexandria.

Gerontius (c. 395-c.480). Palestinian monk, later archimandrite of the cenobites of Palestine. He led the resistance to the council of Chalcedon.

Gnostics. Name now given generally to followers of Basilides, Marcion, Valentinus, Mani and others. The characteristic belief is that matter is a prison made for the spirit by an evil or ignorant creator, and that redemption depends on fate, not on free will.

Gregory of Elvira (fl. 359-385). Bishop of Elvira who wrote allegorical treatises in the style of Origen and defended the Nicene faith against the Arians.

Gregory of Nazianzus (b. 329/330; fl. 372-389). Cappadocian father, bishop of Constantinople, friend of Basil the Great and Gregory of Nyssa, and author of theological orations, sermons and poetry.

Gregory of Nyssa (c. 335-394). Bishop of Nyssa and brother of Basil the Great. A Cappadocian father and author of catechetical orations, he was a philosophical theologian of great originality.

Gregory Thaumaturgus (fl. c. 248-264). Bishop of Neocaesarea and a disciple of Origen. There are at least five legendary *Lives* that recount the events and miracles which led to his being called "the wonder worker." His most important work was the *Address of Thanks to Origen*, which is a rhetorically structured panegyric to Origen and an outline of his teaching.

Gregory the Great (c. 540-604). Pope from 590, the fourth and last of the Latin "Doctors of the Church." He was a prolific author and a powerful unifying force within the Latin Church, initiating the liturgical reform that brought about the Gregorian Sacramentary and Gregorian chant.

Heracleon (fl. c.145-180). Gnostic teacher and disciple of Valentinus. His commentary on John, which was perhaps the first commentary to exist on this or any Gospel, was so popular that Ambrose commissioned Origen to write his own commentary in response, providing a more orthodox approach to the Fourth Gospel.

Hesychius of Jerusalem (fl. 412-450). Presbyter and exegete, thought to have commented on the whole of Scripture.

Hilary of Arles (c. 401-449). Archbishop of Arles and leader of the Semi-Pelagian party. Hilary incurred the wrath of Pope Leo I when he removed a bishop from his see and appointed a new bishop. Leo demoted Arles from a metropolitan see to a bishopric to assert papal power over the church in Gaul.

Hilary of Poitiers (c. 315-367). Bishop of Poitiers and called the "Athanasius of the West" because of his defense (against the Arians) of the common nature of Father and Son.

Hippolytus (fl. 222-245). Recent scholarship places Hippolytus in a Palestinian context, personally familiar with Origen. Though he is known chiefly for *The Refutation of All Heresies*, he was primarily a commentator on Scripture (especially the Old Testament) employing typological exegesis.

Horsiesi (c. 305-c. 390). Pachomius's second successor, after Petronius, as a leader of cenobitic monasticism in Southern Egypt.

Ignatius of Antioch (c. 35-107/112). Bishop of Antioch who wrote several letters to local churches while being taken from Antioch to Rome to be martyred. In the letters, which warn against heresy, he stresses orthodox Christology, the centrality of the Eucharist and unique role of the bishop in preserving the unity of the church.

Irenaeus of Lyons (c. 135-c. 202). Bishop of Lyons who published the most famous and influential refutation of Gnostic thought.

Isaac of Nineveh (d. c. 700). Also known as Isaac the Syrian or Isaac Syrus, this monastic writer served for a short while as bishop of Nineveh before retiring to live a secluded monastic life. His writings on ascetic subjects survive in the form of numerous homilies.

Isaiah of Scete (late fourth century). Author of ascetical texts, collected after his death under the title of the *Ascetic Discourses*. This work was influential in the development of Eastern Christian asceticism and spirituality.

Isho'dad of Merv (fl. c. 850). Nestorian bishop of Hedatta. He wrote commentaries on parts of the Old Testament and all of the New Testament, frequently quoting Syriac fathers.

Isidore of Seville (c. 560-636). Youngest of a family of monks and clerics, including sister Florentina and brothers Leander and Fulgentius. He was an erudite author of comprehensive scale in matters both religious and sacred, including his encyclopedic *Etymologies*.

Jacob of Nisibis (d. 338). Bishop of Nisibis. He was present at the council of Nicaea in 325 and took an active part in the opposition to Arius.

Jacob of Sarug (c. 450-c. 520). Syriac ecclesiastical writer. Jacob received his education at Edessa. At the end of his life he was ordained bishop of Sarug. His principal writing was a long series of metrical homilies, earning him the title "The Flute of the Holy Spirit."

Jerome (c. 347-420). Gifted exegete and exponent of a classical Latin style, now best known as the translator of the Latin Vulgate. He defended the perpetual virginity of Mary, attacked Origen and Pelagius and supported extreme ascetic practices.

John Chrysostom (344/354-407; fl. 386-407). Bishop of Constantinople who was noted for his orthodoxy, his eloquence and his attacks on Christian laxity in high places.

John of Antioch (d. 441/42). Bishop of Antioch, commencing in 428. He received his education together with Nestorius and Theodore of Mopsuestia in a monastery near Antioch. A supporter of Nestorius, he condemned Cyril of Alexandria, but later reached a compromise with him.

John of Apamea (fifth century). Syriac author of the early church who wrote on various aspects of the spiritual life, also known as John the Solitary.

Some of his writings are in the form of dialogues. Other writings include letters, a treatise on baptism, and shorter works on prayer and silence.

John of Carpathus (c. seventh/eighth century). Perhaps John the bishop from the island of Carpathus, situated between Crete and Rhodes, who attended the Synod of 680/81. He wrote two "centuries" (a literary genre in Eastern spirituality consisting of 100 short sections, or chapters). These were entitled *Chapters of Encouragement to the Monks of India* and *Chapters on Theology and Knowledge* which are included in the *Philokalia*.

John of Damascus (c. 650-750). Arab monastic and theologian whose writings enjoyed great influence in both the Eastern and Western Churches. His most influential writing was the *Orthodox Faith*.

John the Elder (c. eighth century). A Syriac author also known as John of Dalyatha or John Saba ("the elder") who belonged to monastic circles of the Church of the East and lived in the region of Mount Qardu (northern Iraq). His most important writings are twenty-two homilies and a collection of fifty-one short letters in which he describes the mystical life as an anticipatory experience of the resurrection life, the fruit of the sacraments of baptism and the Eucharist.

John the Monk. Traditional name found in *The Festal Menaion*, believed to refer to John of Damascus. *See* John of Damascus.

Josephus, Flavius (c. 37-c. 101). Jewish historian from a distinguished priestly family. Acquainted with the Essenes and Sadducees, he himself became a Pharisee. He joined the great Jewish revolt that broke out in 66 and was chosen by the Sanhedrin at Jerusalem to be commander-in-chief in Galilee. Showing great shrewdness to ingratiate himself with Vespasian by foretelling his elevation and that of his son Titus to the imperial dignity, Josephus was restored his liberty after 69 when Vespasian became emperor.

Julian of Eclanum (c. 385-450). Bishop of Eclanum in 416/417 who was removed from office and exiled in 419 for not officially opposing Pelagianism. In exile, he was accepted by Theodore of Mopsuestia, whose Antiochene exegetical style he followed. Although he was never able to regain his ecclesiastical position, Julian taught in Sicily until his death. His works include commentaries on Job and parts of the Minor Prophets, a translation of Theodore of Mopsuestia's commentary on the Psalms, and various letters. Sympathetic to Pelagius, Julian applied his intellectual acumen and rhetorical training to argue against Augustine on matters such as free will, desire and the locus of evil.

Julian the Arian (c. fourth century) Antiochene, Arian author of *Commentary on Job*, and probably a follower of Aetius and Eunomius. The *85 Apostolic Canons*, once part of the *Apostolic Constitutions*, and the Pseudo-Ignatian writings are also attributed to him.

Justin Martyr (c. 100/110-165; fl. c. 148-161). Palestinian philosopher who was converted to Christianity, "the only sure and worthy philosophy." He traveled to Rome where he wrote several apologies against both pagans and Jews, combining Greek philosophy and Christian theology; he was eventually martyred.

Lactantius (c. 260-c. 330). Christian apologist removed from his post as teacher of rhetoric at Nicomedia upon his conversion to Christianity. He was tutor to the son of Constantine and author of *The Divine Institutes*.

Leander (c. 545-c. 600). Latin ecclesiastical writer, of whose works only two survive. He was instrumental in spreading Christianity among the Visigoths, gaining significant historical influence in Spain in his time.

Leo the Great (regn. 440-461). Bishop of Rome whose *Tome to Flavian* helped to strike a balance between Nestorian and Cyrilline positions at the Council of Chalcedon in 451.

Letter of Barnabas (c. 130). An allegorical and typological interpretation of the Old Testament with a decidedly anti-Jewish tone. It was included with other New Testament works as a "Catholic epistle" at least until Eusebius of Caesarea (c. 260/263-340) questioned its authenticity.

Letter to Diognetus (c. third century). A refutation of paganism and an exposition of the Christian life and faith. The author of this letter is unknown, and the exact identity of its recipient, Diognetus, continues to elude patristic scholars.

Lucifer (d. 370/371). Bishop of Cagliari and vigorous supporter of Athanasius and the Nicene Creed. In conflict with the emperor Constantius, he was banished to Palestine and later to Thebaid (Egypt).

Luculentius (fifth century). Unknown author of a group of short commentaries on the New Testament, especially Pauline passages. His exegesis is mainly literal and relies mostly on earlier authors such as Jerome and Augustine. The content of his writing may place it in the fifth century.

Macarius of Egypt (c. 300-c. 390). One of the Desert Fathers. Accused of supporting Athanasius, Macarius was exiled c. 374 to an island in the Nile by Lucius, the Arian successor of Athanasius. Macarius continued his teaching of monastic theology at Wadi Natrun.

Macrina the Younger (c. 327-379). The elder sister of Basil the Great and Gregory of Nyssa, she is known as "the Younger" to distinguish her from her paternal grandmother. She had a powerful influence on her younger brothers, especially on Gregory, who called her his teacher and relates her teaching in *On the Soul and the Resurrection*.

Manichaeans. A religious movement that originated circa 241 in Persia under the leadership of Mani but was apparently of complex Christian origin. It is said to have denied free will and the universal sovereignty of God, teaching that kingdoms of light and darkness are coeternal and that the redeemed are particles of a spiritual man of light held captive in the darkness of matter (*see* Gnostics).

Marcellus of Ancyra (d. c. 375). Wrote a refutation of Arianism. Later, he was accused of Sabellianism, especially by Eusebius of Caesarea. While the Western church declared him orthodox, the Eastern church excommunicated him. Some scholars have attributed to him certain works of Athanasius.

Marcion (fl. 144). Heretic of the mid-second century who rejected the Old Testament and much of the New Testament, claiming that the Father of Jesus Christ was other than the Old Testament God (*see* Gnostics).

Marius Victorinus (b. c. 280/285; fl. c. 355-363). Grammarian of African origin who taught rhetoric at Rome and translated works of Platonists. After his conversion (c. 355), he wrote against the Arians and commentaries on Paul's letters.

Mark the Hermit (c. sixth century). Monk who lived near Tarsus and produced works on ascetic practices as well as christological issues.

Martin of Braga (fl. c. 568-579). Anti-Arian metropolitan of Braga on the Iberian peninsula. He was highly educated and presided over the provincial council of Braga in 572.

Martyrius. *See* Sahdona.

Maximinus (the Arian) (b. c. 360-65). Bishop of an Arian community, perhaps in Illyricum. Of Roman descent, he debated publicly with Augustine at Hippo (427 or 428), ardently defending Arian doctrine. Besides the polemical works he wrote against the orthodox, such as his *Against the Heretics, Jews and Pagans,* he also wrote fifteen sermons that are considered much less polemical, having been previously attributed to Maximus of Turin. He is also known for his twenty-four *Explanations of Chapters of the Gospels*.

Maximus of Turin (d. 408/423). Bishop of Turin. Over one hundred of his sermons survive on Christian festivals, saints and martyrs.

Maximus the Confessor (c. 580-662). Palestinian-born theologian and ascetic writer. Fleeing the Arab invasion of Jerusalem in 614, he took refuge in Constantinople and later Africa. He died near the Black Sea after imprisonment and severe suffering, having his tongue cut off and his right hand mutilated. He taught total preference for God and detachment from all things.

Melito of Sardis (d. c. 190). Bishop of Sardis. According to Polycrates, he may have been Jewish by birth. Among his numerous works is a liturgical document known as *On Pascha* (ca. 160-177). As a Quartodeciman, and one involved intimately involved in that controversy, Melito celebrated Pascha on the fourteenth of Nisan in line with the custom handed down from Judaism.

Methodius of Olympus (d. 311). Bishop of Olympus who celebrated virginity in a *Symposium* partly modeled on Plato's dialogue of that name.

Minucius Felix (second or third century). Christian apologist who was an advocate in Rome. His *Octavius* agrees at numerous points with the *Apologeticum* of Tertullian. His birthplace is believed to be in Africa.

Montanist Oracles. Montanism was an apocalyptic and strictly ascetic movement begun in the latter half of the second century by a certain Montanus in Phrygia, who, along with certain of his followers, uttered oracles they claimed were inspired by the Holy Spirit. Little of the authentic oracles remains and most of what is known of Montanism comes from the authors who wrote against the movement. Montanism was formally condemned as a heresy before by Asiatic synods.

Nemesius of Emesa (fl. late fourth century). Bishop of Emesa in Syria whose most important work, *Of the Nature of Man,* draws on several theological and philosophical sources and is the first exposition of a Christian anthropology.

Nestorius (c. 381-c. 451). Patriarch of Constantinople (428-431) who founded the heresy which says that there are two persons, divine and human, rather than one person truly united in the incarnate Christ. He resisted the teaching of *theotokos,* causing Nestorian churches to separate from Constantinople.

Nicetas of Remesiana (fl. second half of fourth century). Bishop of Remesiana in Serbia, whose works affirm the consubstantiality of the Son and the deity of the Holy Spirit.

Nilus of Ancyra (d. c. 430). Prolific ascetic writer and disciple of John Chrysostom. Sometimes erroneously known as Nilus of Sinai, he was a native of Ancyra and studied at Constantinople.

Novatian of Rome (fl. 235-258). Roman theologian, otherwise orthodox, who formed a schismatic church after failing to become pope. His treatise on the Trinity states the classic western doctrine.

Oecumenius (sixth century). Called the Rhetor or the Philosopher, Oecumenius wrote the earliest extant Greek commentary on Revelation. Scholia by Oecumenius on some of John Chrysostom's commentaries on the Pauline Epistles are still extant.

Olympiodorus (early sixth century). Exegete and deacon of Alexandria, known for his commentaries that come to us mostly in catenae.

Origen of Alexandria (b. 185; fl. c. 200-254). Influential exegete and systematic theologian. He was condemned (perhaps unfairly) for maintaining the preexistence of souls while purportedly denying the resurrection of the body. His extensive works of exegesis focus on the spiritual meaning of the text.

Pachomius (c. 292-347). Founder of cenobitic monasticism. A gifted group leader and author of a set of rules, he was defended after his death by Athanasius of Alexandria.

Pacian of Barcelona (c. fourth century). Bishop of Barcelona whose writings polemicize against popular pagan festivals as well as Novatian schismatics.

Palladius of Helenopolis (c. 363/364-c. 431). Bishop of Helenopolis in Bithynia (400-417) and then Aspuna in Galatia. A disciple of Evagrius of Pontus and admirer of Origen, Palladius became a zealous adherent of John Chrysostom and shared his troubles in 403. His *Lausaic History* is the leading source for the history of early monasticism, stressing the spiritual value of the life of the desert.

Paschasius of Dumium (c. 515-c. 580). Translator of sentences of the Desert Fathers from Greek into Latin while a monk in Dumium.

Paterius (c. sixth-seventh century). Disciple of Gregory the Great who is primarily responsible for the transmission of Gregory's works to many later medieval authors.

Paulinus of Milan (late 4th-early 5th century). Personal secretary and biographer of Ambrose of Milan. He took part in the Pelagian controversy.

Paulinus of Nola (355-431). Roman senator and distinguished Latin poet whose frequent encounters with Ambrose of Milan (c. 333-397) led to his eventual conversion and baptism in 389. He eventually renounced his wealth and influential position and took up his pen to write poetry in service of Christ. He also wrote many letters to, among others, Augustine, Jerome and Rufinus.

Paulus Orosius (b. c. 380). An outspoken critic of Pelagius, mentored by Augustine. His *Seven Books of History Against the Pagans* was perhaps the first history of Christianity.

Pelagius (c. 354-c. 420). Contemporary of Augustine whose followers were condemned in 418 and 431 for maintaining that even before Christ there were people who lived wholly without sin and that salvation depended on free will.

Peter Chrysologus (c. 380-450). Latin archbishop of Ravenna whose teachings included arguments for adherence in matters of faith to the Roman see, and the relationship between grace and Christian living.

Peter of Alexandria (d. c. 311). Bishop of Alexandria. He marked (and very probably initiated) the reaction at Alexandria against extreme doctrines of Origen. During the persecution of Christians in Alexandria, Peter was arrested and beheaded by Roman officials. Eusebius of Caesarea described him as "a model bishop, remarkable for his virtuous life and his ardent study of the Scriptures."

Philip the Priest (d. 455/56) Acknowledged by Gennadius as a disciple of Jerome. In his *Commentary on the Book of Job*, Philip utilizes Jerome's Vulgate, providing an important witness to the transmission of that translation. A few of his letters are extant.

Philo of Alexandria (c. 20 B.C.-c. A.D. 50). Jewish-born exegete who greatly influenced Christian patristic interpretation of the Old Testament. Born to a rich family in Alexandria, Philo was a contemporary of Jesus and lived an ascetic and contemplative life that makes some believe he was a rabbi. His interpretation of Scripture based the spiritual sense on the literal. Although influenced by Hellenism, Philo's theology remains thoroughly Jewish.

Philoxenus of Mabbug (c. 440-523). Bishop of Mabbug (Hierapolis) and a leading thinker in the early Syrian Orthodox Church. His extensive writings in Syriac include a set of thirteen *Discourses on the Christian Life*, several works on the incarnation and a number of exegetical works.

Photius (c. 820-891). An important Byzantine churchman and university professor of philosophy, mathematics and theology. He was twice the patriarch of Constantinople. First he succeeded Ignatius in 858, but was deposed in 863 when Ignatius was reinstated. Again he followed Ignatius in 878 and remained the patriarch until 886, at which time he was removed by Leo VI. His most important theological work is *Address on the Mystagogy of the Holy Spirit*, in which he articulates his opposition to the Western filioque, i.e., the procession of the Holy Spirit from the Father and the Son. He is also known for his Amphilochia and Library (Bibliotheca).

Poemen (c. fifth century). One-seventh of the sayings in the *Sayings of the Desert Fathers* are attributed to Poemen, which is Greek for shepherd. Poemen was a common title among early Egyptian desert ascetics, and it is unknown whether all of the sayings come from one person.

Polycarp of Smyrna (c. 69-155). Bishop of Smyrna who vigorously fought heretics such as the Marcionites and Valentinians. He was the leading Christian figure in Roman Asia in the middle of the second century.

Possidius (late fourth-fifth century). A member of Augustine's monastic community at Hippo from 391, then bishop of Calama in Numidia sometime soon after 397. He fled back to Hippo when Vandals invaded Calama in 428 and cared for Augustine during his final illness. Returning to Calama after the death of Augustine (430), he was expelled by Genseric, Arian king of the Vandals, in 437. Nothing more is known of him after this date. Sometime between 432 and 437 he wrote *Vita Augustini*, to which he added *Indiculus*, a list of Augustine's books, sermons and letters.

Potamius of Lisbon (fl. c. 350-360). Bishop of Lisbon who joined the Arian party in 357, but later returned to the Catholic faith (c. 359?). His works from both periods are concerned with the larger Trinitarian debates of his time.

Primasius (fl. 550-560). Bishop of Hadrumetum in North Africa (modern Tunisia) and one of the few Africans to support the condemnation of the Three Chapters. Drawing on Augustine and Tyconius, he wrote a commentary on the Apocalypse, which in allegorizing fashion views the work as referring to the history of the church.

Proclus of Constantinople (c. 390-446). Patriarch of Constantinople (434-446). His patriarchate dealt with the Nestorian controversy, rebutting, in his *Tome to the Armenian Bishops,* Theodore of Mopsuestia's Christology where Theodore was thought to have overly separated the two natures of Christ. Proclus stressed the unity of Christ in his formula "One of the Trinity suffered," which was later taken up and spread by the Scythian monks of the sixth century, resulting in the theopaschite controversy. Proclus was known as a gifted preacher and church politician, extending and expanding Constantinople's influence while avoiding conflict with Antioch, Rome and Alexandria.

Procopius of Gaza (c. 465-c. 530). A Christian exegete educated in Alexandria. He wrote numerous theological works and commentaries on Scripture (particularly the Hebrew Bible), the latter marked by the allegorical exegesis for which the Alexandrian school was known.

Prosper of Aquitaine (c. 390-c. 463). Probably a lay monk and supporter of the theology of Augustine on grace and predestination. He collaborated closely with Pope Leo I in his doctrinal statements.

Prudentius (c. 348-c. 410). Latin poet and hymn-writer who devoted his later life to Christian writing. He wrote didactic poems on the theology of the incarnation, against the heretic Marcion and against the resurgence of paganism.

Pseudo-Clementines (third-fourth century). A series of apocryphal writings pertaining to a conjured life of Clement of Rome. Written in a form of popular legend, the stories from Clement's life, including his opposition to Simon Magus, illustrate and promote articles of Christian teaching. It is likely that the corpus is a derivative of a num-

ber of Gnostic and Judeo-Christian writings. Dating the corpus is a complicated issue.

Pseudo-Dionysius the Areopagite (fl. c. 500). Author who assumed the name of Dionysius the Areopagite mentioned in Acts 17:34, and who composed the works known as the *Corpus Areopagiticum* (or *Dionysiacum*). These writings were the foundation of the apophatic school of mysticism in their denial that anything can be truly predicated of God.

Pseudo-Macarius (fl. c. 390). An anonymous writer and ascetic (from Mesopotamia?) active in Antioch whose badly edited works were attributed to Macarius of Egypt. He had keen insight into human nature, prayer and the inner life. His work includes some one hundred discourses and homilies.

Quodvultdeus (fl. 430). Carthaginian bishop and friend of Augustine who endeavored to show at length how the New Testament fulfilled the Old Testament.

Romanus Melodus (fl. c. 536-556). Born as a Jew in Emesa not far from Beirut where after his baptism later he later became deacon of the Church of the Resurrection. He later moved to Constantinople and may have seen the destruction of the Hagia Sophia and its rebuilding during the time he flourished there. As many as eighty metrical sermons *(kontakia, sg. kontakion)* that utilize dialogical poetry have come down to us under his name. These sermons were sung rather than preached during the liturgy, and frequently provide theological insights and Scriptural connections often unique to Romanus. His Christology, closely associated with Justinian, reflects the struggles against the Monophysites of his day.

Rufinus of Aquileia (c. 345-411). Orthodox Christian thinker and historian who nonetheless translated and preserved the works of Origen, and defended him against the strictures of Jerome and Epiphanius. He lived the ascetic life in Rome, Egypt and Jerusalem (the Mount of Olives).

Sabellius (fl. 200). Allegedly the author of the heresy which maintains that the Father and Son are a single person. The patripassian variant of this heresy states that the Father suffered on the cross.

Sahdona (fl. 635-640). Known in Greek as Martyrius, this Syriac author was bishop of Beth Garmai. He studied in Nisibis and was exiled for his christological ideas. His most important work is the deeply scriptural *Book of Perfection* which ranks as one of the masterpieces of Syriac monastic literature.

Salvian the Presbyter of Marseilles (c. 400-c. 480). An important author for the history of his own time. He saw the fall of Roman civilization to the barbarians as a consequence of the reprehensible conduct of Roman Christians. In *The Governance of God* he developed the theme of divine providence.

Second Letter of Clement (c. 150). The so-called *Second Letter of Clement* is an early Christian sermon probably written by a Corinthian author, though some scholars have assigned it to a Roman or Alexandrian author.

Severian of Gabala (fl. c. 400). A contemporary of John Chrysostom, he was a highly regarded preacher in Constantinople, particularly at the imperial court, and ultimately sided with Chrysostom's accusers. He wrote homilies on Genesis.

Severus of Antioch (fl. 488-538). A monophysite theologian, consecrated bishop of Antioch in 522. Born in Pisidia, he studied in Alexandria and Beirut, taught in Constantinople and was exiled to Egypt.

Shenoute (c. 350-466). Abbot of Athribis in Egypt. His large monastic community was known for very strict rules. He accompanied Cyril of Alexandria to the Council of Ephesus in 431, where he played an important role in deposing Nestorius. He knew Greek but wrote in Coptic, and his literary activity includes homilies, catecheses on monastic subjects, letters, and a couple of theological treatises.

Shepherd **of Hermas** (second century). Divided into five *Visions*, twelve *Mandates* and ten *Similitudes*, this Christian apocalypse was written by a former slave and named for the form of the second angel said to have granted him his visions.

This work was highly esteemed for its moral value and was used as a textbook for catechumens in the early church.

Sulpicius Severus (c. 360-c. 420). An ecclesiastical writer from Bordeaux born of noble parents. Devoting himself to monastic retirement, he became a personal friend and enthusiastic disciple of St. Martin of Tours.

Symeon the New Theologian (c. 949-1022). Compassionate spiritual leader known for his strict rule. He believed that the divine light could be perceived and received through the practice of mental prayer.

Tertullian of Carthage (c. 155/160-225/250; fl. c. 197-222). Brilliant Carthaginian apologist and polemicist who laid the foundations of Christology and trinitarian orthodoxy in the West, though he himself was later estranged from the catholic tradition due to its laxity.

Theodore of Heraclea (d. c. 355). An anti-Nicene bishop of Thrace. He was part of a team seeking reconciliation between Eastern and Western Christianity. In 343 he was excommunicated at the council of Sardica. His writings focus on a literal interpretation of Scripture.

Theodore of Mopsuestia (c. 350-428). Bishop of Mopsuestia, founder of the Antiochene, or literalistic, school of exegesis. A great man in his day, he was later condemned as a precursor of Nestorius.

Theodore of Tabennesi (d. 368) Vice general of the Pachomian monasteries (c. 350-368) under Horsiesi. Several of his letters are known.

Theodoret of Cyr (c. 393-466). Bishop of Cyr (Cyrrhus), he was an opponent of Cyril who commented extensively on Old Testament texts as a lucid exponent of Antiochene exegesis.

Theodotus the Valentinian (second century). Likely a Montanist who may have been related to the Alexandrian school. Extracts of his work are known through writings of Clement of Alexandria.

Theophanes (775-845). Hymnographer and bishop of Nicaea (842-845). He was persecuted during the second iconoclastic period for his support of the Seventh Council (Second Council of Nicaea, 787). He wrote many hymns in the tradition of the monastery of Mar Sabbas that were used in the *Paraklitiki*.

Theophilus of Alexandria (d. 412). Patriarch of Alexandria (385-412) and the uncle of his successor, Cyril. His patriarchate was known for his opposition to paganism, having destroyed the Serapeion and its library in 391, but he also built many churches. He also was known for his political machinations against his theological enemies, especially John Chrysostom, whom he himself had previously consecrated as patriarch, ultimately getting John removed from his see and earning the intense dislike of Antioch Christians. He is, however, venerated among the Copts and Syrians, among whom many of his sermons have survived, although only a few are deemed authentically his. His *Homily on the Mystical Supper*, commenting on the Last Supper, is perhaps one of his most well known.

Theophilus of Antioch (late second century). Bishop of Antioch. His only surviving work is *Ad Autholycum*, where we find the first Christian commentary on Genesis and the first use of the term *Trinity*. Theophilus's apologetic literary heritage had influence on Irenaeus and possibly Tertullian.

Theophylact of Ohrid (c. 1050-c. 1108). Byzantine archbishop of Ohrid (or Achrida) in what is now Bulgaria. Drawing on earlier works, he wrote commentaries on several Old Testament books and all of the New Testament except for Revelation.

Tyconius (c. 330-390). A lay theologian and exegete of the Donatist church in North Africa who influenced Augustine. His *Book of Rules* is the first

manual of scriptural interpretation in the Latin West. In 380 he was excommunicated by the Donatist council at Carthage.

Valentinus (fl. c. 140). Alexandrian heretic of the mid-second century who taught that the material world was created by the transgression of God's Wisdom, or Sophia (*see* Gnostics).

Valerian of Cimiez (fl. c. 422-439). Bishop of Cimiez. He participated in the councils of Riez (439) and Vaison (422) with a view to strengthening church discipline. He supported Hilary of Arles in quarrels with Pope Leo I.

Verecundus (d. 552). An African Christian writer, who took an active part in the christological controversies of the sixth century, especially in the debate on Three Chapters. He also wrote allegorical commentaries on the nine liturgical church canticles.

Victorinus of Petovium (d. c. 304). Latin biblical exegete. With multiple works attributed to him, his sole surviving work is the *Commentary on the Apocalypse* and perhaps some fragments from *Commentary on Matthew*. Victorinus expressed strong millenarianism in his writing, though his was less materialistic than the millenarianism of Papias or Irenaeus. In his allegorical approach he could be called a spiritual disciple of Origen. Victorinus died during the first year of Diocletian's persecution, probably in 304.

Vincent of Lérins (d. before 450). Monk who has exerted considerable influence through his writings on orthodox dogmatic theological method, as contrasted with the theological methodologies of the heresies.

Timeline of Writers of the Patristic Period

Location	British Isles	Gaul	Spain, Portugal	Rome* and Italy	Carthage and Northern Africa
Period					
2nd century				Clement of Rome, fl. c. 92-101 (Greek)	
				Shepherd of Hermas, c. 140 (Greek)	
				Justin Martyr (Ephesus, Rome), c. 100/110-165 (Greek)	
		Irenaeus of Lyons, c. 135-c. 202 (Greek)		Valentinus the Gnostic (Rome), fl. c. 140 (Greek)	
				Marcion (Rome), fl. 144 (Greek) Heracleon, 145-180 (Greek)	
3rd century				Callistus of Rome, regn. 217-222 (Latin)	Tertullian of Carthage, c. 155/160-c. 225 (Latin)
				Minucius Felix of Rome, fl. 218-235 (Latin)	
				Hippolytus (Rome, Palestine?), fl. 222-235/245 (Greek)	Cyprian of Carthage, fl. 248-258 (Latin)
				Novatian of Rome, fl. 235-258 (Latin)	
				Victorinus of Petovium, 230-304 (Latin)	

*One of the five ancient patriarchates

Alexandria* and Egypt	Constantinople* and Asia Minor, Greece	Antioch* and Syria	Mesopotamia, Persia	Jerusalem* and Palestine	Location Unknown
Philo of Alexandria, c. 20 B.C. – c. A.D. 50 (Greek)				Flavius Josephus (Rome), c. 37-c. 101 (Greek)	
Basilides (Alexandria), 2nd cent. (Greek)	Polycarp of Smyrna, c. 69-155 (Greek)	*Didache* (Egypt?), c. 100 (Greek)			
Letter of Barnabas (Syria?), c. 130 (Greek)		Ignatius of Antioch, c. 35–107/112 (Greek)			
Theodotus the Valentinian, 2nd cent. (Greek)	Athenagoras (Greece), fl. 176-180 (Greek)	Theophilus of Antioch, c. late 2nd cent. (Greek)			*Second Letter of Clement* (spurious; Corinth, Rome, Alexandria?) (Greek), c. 150
	Melito of Sardis, d.c. 190 (Greek)	*Didascalia Apostolorum*, early 3rd cent. (Syriac)			
Clement of Alexandria, c. 150-215 (Greek)	*Montanist Oracles*, late 2nd cent. (Greek)				
Sabellius (Egypt), 2nd–3rd cent. (Greek)					Pseudo-Clementines 3rd cent. (Greek)
			Mani (Manichaeans), c. 216-276		
Letter to Diognetus, 3rd cent. (Greek)	Gregory Thaumaturgus (Neocaesarea), fl. c. 248-264 (Greek)				
Origen (Alexandria, Caesarea of Palestine), 185-254 (Greek)					
Dionysius of Alexandria, d. 264/5 (Greek)					
	Methodius of Olympus (Lycia), d. c. 311 (Greek)				

Timeline of Writers of the Patristic Period

Location	British Isles	Gaul	Spain, Portugal	Rome* and Italy	Carthage and Northern Africa
Period					
4th century				Firmicus Maternus (Sicily), fl. c. 335 (Latin)	Isaiah of Scete, late 4th cent. (Greek)
		Lactantius, c. 260-330 (Latin)		Marius Victorinus (Rome), fl. 355-363 (Latin)	
				Eusebius of Vercelli, fl. c. 360 (Latin)	
			Hosius of Cordova, d. 357 (Latin)	Lucifer of Cagliari (Sardinia), d. 370/371 (Latin)	
		Hilary of Poitiers, c. 315-367 (Latin)	Potamius of Lisbon, fl. c. 350-360 (Latin)	Faustinus (Rome), fl. 380 (Latin)	
				Filastrius of Brescia, fl. 380 (Latin)	
			Gregory of Elvira, fl. 359-385 (Latin)	Ambrosiaster (Italy?), fl. c. 366-384 (Latin)	
			Prudentius, c. 348-c. 410 (Latin)	Faustus of Riez, fl. c. 380 (Latin)	
			Pacian of Barcelona, 4th cent. (Latin)	Gaudentius of Brescia, fl. 395 (Latin)	Paulus Orosius, b. c. 380 (Latin)
				Ambrose of Milan, c. 333-397; fl. 374-397 (Latin)	
				Paulinus of Milan, late 4th-early 5th cent. (Latin)	
5th century				Rufinus (Aquileia, Rome), c. 345-411 (Latin)	
	Fastidius (Britain), c. 4th-5th cent. (Latin)	Sulpicius Severus (Bordeaux), c. 360-c. 420/425 (Latin)		Aponius, fl. 405-415 (Latin)	
				Chromatius (Aquileia), fl. 400 (Latin)	
		John Cassian (Palestine, Egypt, Constantinople, Rome, Marseilles), 360-432 (Latin)		Pelagius (Britain, Rome), c. 354-c. 420 (Greek)	Augustine of Hippo, 354-430 (Latin)
				Maximus of Turin, d. 408/423 (Latin)	Possidius, late 4th-5th cent. (Latin)
					Luculentius, 5th cent. (Latin)
		Vincent of Lérins, d. 435 (Latin)		Paulinus of Nola, 355-431 (Latin)	
		Valerian of Cimiez, fl. c. 422-449 (Latin)		Peter Chrysologus (Ravenna), c. 380-450 (Latin)	Quodvultdeus (Carthage), fl. 430 (Latin)
		Eucherius of Lyons, fl. 420-449 (Latin)		Julian of Eclanum, 386-454 (Latin)	

*One of the five ancient patriarchates

Alexandria* and Egypt	Constantinople* and Asia Minor, Greece	Antioch* and Syria	Mesopotamia, Persia	Jerusalem* and Palestine	Location Unknown
Antony, c. 251-355 (Coptic /Greek)	Theodore of Heraclea (Thrace), fl. c. 330-355 (Greek)	Eustathius of Antioch, fl. 325 (Greek)	Aphrahat (Persia) c. 270-350; fl. 337-345 (Syriac)	Eusebius of Caesarea (Palestine), c. 260/ 263-340 (Greek)	Commodius, c. 3rd or 5th cent. (Latin)
Peter of Alexandria, d. c. 311 (Greek)	Marcellus of Ancyra, d.c. 375 (Greek)	Eusebius of Emesa, c. 300-c. 359 (Greek)			
Arius (Alexandria), fl. c. 320 (Greek)	Epiphanius of Salamis (Cyprus), c. 315-403 (Greek)	Ephrem the Syrian, c. 306-373 (Syriac)	Jacob of Nisibis, fl. 308-325 (Syriac)		
Alexander of Alexandria, fl. 312-328 (Greek)	Basil (the Great) of Caesarea, b. c. 330; fl. 357-379 (Greek)	Julian the Arian (c. fourth century)			
Pachomius, c. 292-347 (Coptic/Greek?)	Macrina the Younger, c. 327-379 (Greek)				
Theodore of Tabennesi, d. 368 (Coptic/Greek)	Apollinaris of Laodicea, 310-c. 392 (Greek)				
Horsiesi, c. 305-390 (Coptic/Greek)	Gregory of Nazianzus, b. 329/330; fl. 372-389 (Greek)	Nemesius of Emesa (Syria), fl. late 4th cent. (Greek)			Maximinus, b.c. 360-365 (Latin)
Athanasius of Alexandria, c. 295-373; fl. 325-373 (Greek)	Gregory of Nyssa, c. 335-394 (Greek)	Diodore of Tarsus, d. c. 394 (Greek)		Acacius of Caesarea (Palestine), d. c. 365 (Greek)	
Macarius of Egypt, c. 300-c. 390 (Greek)	Amphilochius of Iconium, c. 340/ 345- c. 398/404 (Greek)	John Chrysostom (Constantinople), 344/354-407 (Greek)		Cyril of Jerusalem, c. 315-386 (Greek)	
Didymus (the Blind) of Alexandria, 313-398 (Greek)	Evagrius of Pontus, 345-399 (Greek)	Apostolic Constitutions, c. 375-400 (Greek)			
Tyconius, c. 330-390 (Latin)	Eunomius of Cyzicus, fl. 360-394 (Greek)	Didascalia, 4th cent. (Syriac)			
		Theodore of Mopsuestia, c. 350-428 (Greek)		Diodore of Tarsus, d. c. 394 (Greek)	
Ammonas, 4th cent. (Syriac)	Pseudo-Macarius (Mesopotamia?), late 4th cent. (Greek)	Acacius of Beroea, c. 340-c. 436 (Greek)		Jerome (Rome, Antioch, Bethlehem), c. 347-420 (Latin)	
Theophilus of Alexandria, d. 412 (Greek)	Nicetas of Remesiana, d. c. 414 (Latin)				
Palladius of Helenopolis (Egypt), c. 365-425 (Greek)	Proclus of Constantinople, c. 390-446 (Greek)	Book of Steps, c. 400 (Syriac)	Eznik of Kolb, fl. 430-450 (Armenian)		
	Nestorius (Constantinople), c. 381-c. 451 (Greek)	Severian of Gabala, fl. c. 400 (Greek)			
Cyril of Alexandria, 375-444 (Greek)				Philip the Priest (d. 455/56)	
	Basil of Seleucia, fl. 440-468 (Greek)	Nilus of Ancyra, d.c. 430 (Greek)			
				Hesychius of Jerusalem, fl. 412-450 (Greek)	
	Diadochus of Photice (Macedonia), 400-474 (Greek)				
				Euthymius (Palestine), 377-473 (Greek)	

Timeline of Writers of the Patristic Period

Location / Period	British Isles	Gaul	Spain, Portugal	Rome* and Italy	Carthage and Northern Africa
5th century (cont.)		Hilary of Arles, c. 401-449 (Latin)		Leo the Great (Rome), regn. 440-461 (Latin)	
		Eusebius of Gaul, 5th cent. (Latin)			
		Prosper of Aquitaine, c. 390-c. 463 (Latin)		Arnobius the Younger (Rome), fl. c. 450 (Latin)	
		Salvian the Presbyter of Marseilles, c. 400-c. 480 (Latin)		Ennodius (Arles, Milan, Pavia) c. 473-521 (Latin)	
		Gennadius of Marseilles, d. after 496 (Latin)		Epiphanius the Latin, late 5th–early 6th cent. (Latin)	
6th century		Caesarius of Arles, c. 470-543 (Latin)	Paschasius of Dumium (Portugal), c. 515-c. 580 (Latin)	Eugippius, c. 460- c. 533 (Latin)	Fulgentius of Ruspe, c. 467-532 (Latin)
			Apringius of Beja, mid-6th cent. (Latin)	Benedict of Nursia, c. 480-547 (Latin)	
			Leander of Seville, c. 545-c. 600 (Latin)	Cassiodorus (Calabria), c. 485-c. 540 (Latin)	Verecundus, d. 552 (Latin)
					Primasius, fl. 550-560 (Latin)
				Gregory the Great (Rome), c. 540-604 (Latin)	
		Flavian of Chalon-sur-Saône, fl. 580-600 (Latin)	Martin of Braga, fl. 568-579 (Latin)		Facundus of Hermiane, fl. 546-568 (Latin)
				Gregory of Agrigentium, d. 592 (Greek)	
7th century			Isidore of Seville, c. 560-636 (Latin)	Paterius, 6th/7th cent. (Latin)	
			Braulio of Saragossa, c. 585-651 (Latin)		
	Adamnan, c. 624-704 (Latin)		Fructuosus of Braga, d.c. 665 (Latin)		
8th-12th century	Bede the Venerable, c. 672/673-735 (Latin)				

*One of the five ancient patriarchates

Alexandria* and Egypt	Constantinople* and Asia Minor, Greece	Antioch* and Syria	Mesopotamia, Persia	Jerusalem* and Palestine	Location Unknown
Ammonius of Alexandria, c. 460 (Greek)	Gennadius of Constantinople, d. 471 (Greek)	John of Antioch, d. 441/2 (Greek)		Gerontius of Petra c. 395-c. 480 (Syriac)	
Poemen, 5th cent. (Greek)		Theodoret of Cyr, c. 393-466 (Greek)			
		Pseudo-Victor of Antioch, 5th cent. (Greek)			
Besa the Copt, 5th cent.		John of Apamea, 5th cent. (Syriac)			
Shenoute, c. 350-466 (Coptic)					
	Andrew of Caesarea (Cappadocia), early 6th cent. (Greek)				
Olympiodorus, early 6th cent.	Oecumenius (Isauria), 6th cent. (Greek)	Philoxenus of Mabbug (Syria), c. 440-523 (Syriac)	Jacob of Sarug, c. 450-520 (Syriac)	Procopius of Gaza (Palestine), c. 465-530 (Greek)	Pseudo-Dionysius the Areopagite, fl. c. 500 (Greek)
	Romanus Melodus, fl. c. 536-556 (Greek)	Severus of Antioch, c. 465-538 (Greek)	Abraham of Nathpar, fl. 6th-7th cent. (Syriac)	Dorotheus of Gaza, fl. 525-540 (Greek)	
		Mark the Hermit (Tarsus), c. 6th cent. (4th cent.?) (Greek)	Babai the Great, c. 550-628 (Syriac)	Cyril of Scythopolis, b. c. 525; d. after 557 (Greek)	
			Babai, early 6th cent. (Syriac)		
	Maximus the Confessor (Constantinople), c. 580-662 (Greek)	Sahdona/Martyrius, fl. 635-640 (Syriac)	Isaac of Nineveh, d. c. 700 (Syriac)		(Pseudo-) Constantius, before 7th cent.? (Greek)
	Andrew of Crete, c. 660-740 (Greek)			Cosmas Melodus, c. 675-751 (Greek)	Andreas, c. 7th cent. (Greek)
	John of Carpathus, 7th-8th cent. (Greek)	John of Damascus (John the Monk), c. 650-750 (Greek)	John the Elder of Qardu (north Iraq), 8th cent. (Syriac)		
	Theophanes (Nicaea), 775-845 (Greek)		Isho'dad of Merv, d. after 852 (Syriac)		
	Cassia (Constantinople), c. 805-c. 848/867 (Greek)				
	Arethas of Caesarea (Constantinople/Caesarea), c. 860-940 (Greek)				
	Photius (Constantinople), c. 820-891 (Greek)				
	Symeon the New Theologian (Constantinople), 949-1022 (Greek)				
	Theophylact of Ohrid (Bulgaria), 1050-1126 (Greek)				

Bibliography of Works in Original Languages

This bibliography refers readers to original language sources and supplies Thesaurus Linguae Graecae (=TLG) or Cetedoc Clavis (=Cl.) numbers where available. The edition listed in this bibliography may in some cases differ from the edition found in TLG or Cetedoc databases.

Ambrose. "De bono mortis." In *Sancti Ambrosii opera*. Edited by Karl Schenkl. CSEL 32, pt. 1, pp. 701-53. Vienna, Austria: F. Tempsky; Leipzig, Germany: G. Freytag, 1897. Cl. 0129.

———. "De excessu fratris Satyri." In *Sancti Ambrosii opera*. Edited by Otto Faller. CSEL 73, pp. 207-325. Vienna, Austria: Hoelder-Pichler-Tempsky, 1895. Cl. 0157.

———. "De fide libri v." In *Sancti Ambrosii opera*. Edited by Otto Faller. CSEL 78. Vienna, Austria: Hoelder-Pichler-Tempsky, 1962. Cl. 0150.

———. "De interpellatione Job et David." In *Sancti Ambrosii opera*. Edited by Karl Schenkl. CSEL 32, pt. 2, pp. 211-96. Vienna, Austria: F. Tempsky; Leipzig, Germany: G. Freytag, 1897. Cl. 0134.

———. "De Jacob et vita beata." In *Sancti Ambrosii opera*. Edited by Karl Schenkl. CSEL 32, pt. 2, pp. 1-70. Vienna, Austria: F. Tempsky; Leipzig, Germany: G. Freytag, 1897. Cl. 0130.

———. "De officiis ministrorum." In *De officiis*. Edited by Maurice Testard. CCL 15. Turnhout, Belgium: Brepols, 2000. Cl. 0144.

———. "De paradiso." In *Sancti Ambrosii opera*. Edited by Karl Schenkl. CSEL 32, pt. 1, pp. 263-336. Vienna, Austria: F. Tempsky; Leipzig, Germany: G. Freytag, 1897. Cl. 0124.

———. "De spiritu sancto." In *Sancti Ambrosii opera*. Edited by Otto Faller. CSEL 79, pp. 5-222. Vienna, Austria: Hoelder-Pichler-Tempsky, 1964. Cl. 0151.

———. "De virginitate." In *Opere II/2: Verginità e vedovanza*. Edited by F. Gori. Opera omnia di Sant'Ambrogio 14.2, pp. 16-106. Milan: Biblioteca Ambrosiana; Rome: Citta nuovà, 1989. Cl. 0147.

———. "Epistulae; Epistulae extra collectionem traditae." In *Sancti Ambrosii opera*. Edited by Otto Faller and Michaela Zelzer. CSEL 82. 4 vols. Vienna, Austria: F. Tempsky; Leipzig, Germany: G. Freytag, 1968-1990. Cl. 0160.

Ammonius of Alexandria. *Ammonii Eremitae epistolae*. Edited by Michael Kmoskó. Patrologia Orientalis 10, pp. 555-675. Paris: Firmin-Didot, 1915.

———. "In Danielem." In *Opera quae Exstant omnia*. Edited by J.-P. Migne. PG 85, cols. 1364-81, 1823-26. Paris: Migne, 1864. TLG 2724.002.

Andrew of Caesarea. "Commentarii in Apocalypsin." In *Studien zur Geschichte des griechischen Apokalypse-Textes, part 1*. Edited by Josef Schmid. MTS 1 Sup 1. Munich, Germany: K. Zink, 1955-56.

Aphrahat. "Demonstrationes (IV)." In *Opera omnia*. Edited by R. Graffin. Patrologia Syriaca 1, cols. 137-82. Paris: Firmin-Didor, 1910.

Athanasius. "De synodis Arimini in Italia et Seleuciae in Isauria." In *Athanasius Werke*, vol. 2.1, pp. 231-78. Berlin: De Gruyter, 1940. TLG 2035.010.

———. "Epistula ad episcopos Aegypti et Libyae." In *Opera omnia*. Edited by J.-P. Migne. PG 25, cols. 537-93. Paris: Migne, 1857. TLG 2035.041.

————."Epistulae festalis." In *Opera omnia.* Edited by J.-P. Migne. PG 26, cols. 1351-1444. Paris: Migne, 1887. TLG 2035.014.

Augustine."Confessionum libri tredecim." In *Sancti Augustini Opera.* Edited by Lucas Verheijen. CCL 27. Turnhout, Belgium: Brepols, 1981. Cl. 0251.

————."Contra Faustum.î In *Sancti Aureli Augustini.* Edited by Joseph Zycha. CSEL 25, pp. 249-797. Vienna, Austria: F. Tempsky, 1891. Cl. 0321.

————."Contra Julianum." In *Augustini opera omnia.* Edited by J.-P. Migne. PL 44. Paris: Migne, 1845. Cl. 0351.

————. *De civitate Dei.* In *Aurelii Augustini opera.* Edited by Bernhard Dombart and Alphons Kalb. CCL 47 and 48. Turnhout, Belgium: Brepols, 1955. Cl. 0313.

————."De consensu evangelistarum." In *Sancti Aurelii Augustini.* Edited by F. Weihrich. CSEL 43. Vienna, Austria: F. Tempsky, 1904. Cl. 0273.

————. "De diversis quaestionibus ad Simplicianum." In *Sancti Aurelii Augustini.* Edited by Almut Mutzenbecher. CCL 44. Turnhout, Belgium: Brepols, 1975. Cl. 0290.

————. *De Genesi ad litteram libri duodecim.* Edited by Joseph Zycha. CSEL 28, pt. 1, pp. 3-435. Vienna, Austria: F. Tempsky, 1894. Cl. 0266.

————."De Genesi contra Manichaeos." In *Augustini opera omnia.* Edited by J.-P. Migne. PL 34, cols. 173-220. Paris: Migne, 1861. Cl. 0265.

————."De gestis Pelagii." In *Sancti Aurelii Augustini.* Edited by Karl Franze Urba and Joseph Zycha. CSEL 42, pp. 51-122. Vienna, Austria: F. Tempsky, 1902. Cl. 0348.

————."De gratia et libero arbitrio." In *Augustini opera omnia.* Edited by J.-P. Migne. PL 44, cols. 881-912. Paris: Migne, 1845. Cl. 0352.

————."De mendacio." In *Sancti Aurelii Augustini.* Edited by Joseph Zycha. CSEL 41, pp. 413-66. Vienna, Austria: F. Tempsky, 1900. Cl. 0303.

————."De peccatorum meritis et remissione et de baptismo parvulorum." In *Sancti Aurelii Augustini.* Edited by Karl Franze Urba and Joseph Zycha. CSEL 60, pp. 3-151. Vienna, Austria: F. Tempsky, 1913. Cl. 0342.

————. "De praedestinatione sanctorum." In *Augustini opera omnia.* Editd by J.-P. Migne. PL 44, cols. 959-92. Paris: Migne, 1845. Cl. 0354.

————."De sermone Domini in monte." In *Aurelii Augustini opera.* Edited by Almut Mutzenbecher. CCL 35. Turnhout, Belgium: Brepols, 1967. Cl. 0274.

————."De Trinitate." In *Aurelii Augustini opera.* Edited by William John Mountain. CCL 50 and 50A. Turnhout, Belgium: Brepols, 1968. Cl. 0329.

————."De urbis excidio." Edited by M.-V. O'Reilly. In *Aurelii Augustini opera.* CCL 46, pp. 249-62. Turnhout, Belgium: Brepols, 1969. Cl. 0312.

————."De vita christiana." In *Augustini opera omnia.* Edited by J.-P. Migne. PL 40, cols. 1031-46. Paris: Migne, 1861.

————."Enarrationes in Psalmos." In *Aurelii Augustini opera.* Edited by Eligius Dekkers and John Fraipont. CCL 38, 39 and 40. Turnhout, Belgium: Brepols, 1956. Cl. 0283.

————."Enchiridion de fide, spe et caritate." Edited by E. Evans. In *Aurelii Augustini opera.* CCL 46, pp. 49-114. Turnhout, Belgium: Brepols, 1969. Cl. 0295.

————. *Epistulae 31-123.* In *Sancti Aurelii Augustini.* Edited by A. Goldbacher. CSEL 34. Vienna, Austria: F. Tempsky; Leipzig, Germany: G. Freytag, 1898. Cl. 0262.

————. *Epistulae 185-270.* In *Sancti Aurelii Augustini.* Edited by A. Goldbacher. CSEL 57. Vienna, Austria: F. Tempsky; Leipzig, Germany: G. Freytag, 1911. Cl. 0262.

————."Epistulae nuper in lucem prolatae." In *Sancti Aurelii Augustini.* Edited by J. Divjak. CSEL 88. Vienna, Austria: F. Tempsky, 1981. Cl. 0262.

———."In Johannis epistulam ad Parthos tractatus." In *Augustini opera omnia*. Edited by J.-P. Migne. PL 35, cols. 1977-2062. Paris: Migne, 1861. Cl. 0279.

———."In Johannis evangelium tractatus." In *Aurelii Augustini opera*. Edited by R. Willems. CCL 36. Turnhout, Belgium: Brepols, 1954. Cl. 0278.

———."Sermones." In *Augustini opera omnia*. Edited by J.-P. Migne. PL 38 and 39. Paris: Migne, 1845. Cl. 0284.

Barnabae epistula. In *Épitre de Barnabé*. Edited by Pierre Prigent and Robert A. Kraft. SC 172, pp. 72-218. Paris: Éditions du Cerf, 1971. TLG 1216.001.

Basil of Seleucia."Sermones." In *Opera omnia*. Edited by J.-P. Migne. PG 85, cols. 399-426. Paris: Migne, 1864. TLG 2080.002.

Basil the Great."Asceticon magnum sive Quaestiones (regulae fusius tractatae)." In *Opera omnia*. Edited by J.-P. Migne. PG 31, cols. 901-1052. Paris: Migne, 1885. TLG 2040.048.

———."De spiritu sancto." In *Basile de Césarée: Sur le Saint-Esprit*. Edited by Benoit Pruche. SC 17. Paris: Éditions du Cerf, 2002. TLG 2040.003.

———."Epistulae." *Saint Basil: Lettres*. Edited by Yves Courtonne. Vol. 2, pp. 101-218; vol. 3, pp. 1-229. Paris: Les Belles Lettres, 1961-1966. TLG 2040.004.

———."Homiliae in illud: Attende tibi ipsi." In *L'homélie de Basile de Césarée sur le mot 'observe-toi toi-même,'* pp. 23-37. Edited by S. Y. Rudberg. Stockholm: Almqvist & Wiksell, 1962. TLG 2040.006.

———."Homiliae super Psalmos." In *Opera omnia*. Edited by J.-P. Migne. PG 29, cols. 209-494. Paris: Migne, 1857. TLG 2040.018.

Bede."De tabernaculo et vasis eius ac vestibus sacerdotum libri iii." In *Bedae opera*. Edited by D. Hurst. CCL 119A, pp. 5-139. Cl. 1345.

———."De temporum ratione liber." In *Bedae opera*. Edited by C. W. Jones. CCL 123B, pp. 263-544. Turnhout, Belgium: Brepols, 1977. Cl. 2320.

Benedict."Regula." In *La règle de Saint Benoît*. Edited by A. de Vogüé. SC 181, pp. 412-90; SC 182, pp. 508-674. Paris: Éditions du Cerf, 1971-72. Cl. 1852.

Caesarius of Arles. *Sermones Caesarii Arelatensis*. Edited by Germain Morin. CCL 103 and 104. Turnhout, Belgium: Brepols, 1953. Cl. 1008.

Cassian, John. *Collationes xxiv*. Edited by Michael Petschenig. CSEL 13. Vienna, Austria: F. Tempsky; Leipzig, Germany: G. Freytag, 1886. Cl. 0512.

———."De institutis coenobiorum et de octo principalium vitiorum remediis." In *Johannis Cassiani*. Edited by Michael Petschenig. CSEL 17, pp. 1-231. Vienna, Austria: F. Tempsky; Leipzig, Germany: G. Freytag, 1888. Cl. 0513.

Cassiodorus. *Expositio psalmorum*. Edited by Mark Adriaen. CCL 97 and 98. Turnhout, Belgium: Brepols, 1958. Cl. 0900.

Chromatius of Aquileia. "Tractatus in Matthaeum." In *Chromatii Aquileiensis opera*. Edited by R. Étaix and Joseph Lemarié. CCL 9A, pp. 391-442; CCL 9A Supplement, pp. 624-36. Turnhout, Belgium: Brepols, 1974-1977. Cl. 0218.

Clement of Alexandria. "Paedagogus." In *Le pédagogue [par] Clement d'Alexandrie*. 3 vols. Translated by Mauguerite Harl, Chantel Matray and Claude Mondésert. Introduction and notes by Henri-Irénée Marrou. SC 70, 108 and 158. Paris: Éditions du Cerf, 1960-1970. TLG 0555.002.

———."Stromata." In *Clemens Alexandrinus*, vol. 2, 3rd ed., and vol. 3, 2nd ed. Edited by Otto Stählin, Ludwig Früchtel and Ursula Treu. GCS 15, pp. 3-518 and GCS 17, pp. 1-102. Berlin: Akademie-Verlag, 1960-1970. TLG 0555.004.

Clement of Rome."Epistula i ad Corinthios." In *Clément de Rome: Épitre aux Corinthiens*. Edited by Annie

Jaubert. SC 167. Paris: Éditions du Cerf, 1971. TLG 1271.001.

Constitutiones apostolorum (fort. compilatore Juliano Ariano). In *Les constitutions apostoliques*. 3 vols. Edited by M. Metzger. SC 320, 329 and 336. Paris: Éditions du Cerf, 1985, 1986, 1987. TLG 2894.001.

Cyprian. "Ad Demetrianum." In *Sancti Cypriani episcopi opera*. Edited by Manlio Simonetti. CCL 3A, pp. 35-51. Turnhout, Belgium: Brepols, 1976. Cl. 0046.

———. "Ad Fortunatum." Edited by R. Weber. In *Sancti Cypriani episcopi opera*. CCL 3, pp. 183-216. Turnhout, Belgium: Brepols, 1972. Cl. 0045.

———. "De lapsis." Edited by M. Bévenot. In *Sancti Cypriani episcopi opera*. CCL 3, pp. 221-42. Turnhout, Belgium: Brepols, 1972. Cl. 0042.

———. "De opera et eleemosynis." In *Sancti Cypriani episcopi opera*. Edited by Manlio Simonetti. CCL 3A, pp. 53-72. Turnhout, Belgium: Brepols, 1976. Cl. 0047.

———. "Epistulae." In *Sancti Cypriani episcopi opera*. CCL 3B-C. Edited by G. F. Diercks. Turnhout, Belgium: Brepols, 1994-1996. Cl. 0050.

Cyril of Alexandria. "Commentarii in Lucam." In *Opera omnia*. PG 72, cols. 476-949. Edited by J.-P. Migne. Paris: Migne, 1864. TLG. 4090.030.

———. "Ad Valerianum episcopum Iconii, epistula 50." Found in "Concilium universale Ephesenum anno 431." In *Acta conciliorum oecumenicorum*, vol. 1.1.1-1.1.7. Berlin: De Gruyter, 1927. TLG 5000.001.

Cyril of Jerusalem. "Catecheses ad illuminandos 1-18." In *Cyrilli Hierosolymorum archiepiscopi opera quae supersunt omnia*, vol. 1, pp. 28-320; vol. 2, pp. 2-342. Edited by W. C. Reischl and J. Rupp. Munich: Lentner, 1848 and 1860; reprinted, Hildesheim: Olms, 1967. TLG 2110.003.

Didache xii apostolorum. In *La Didachè. Instructions des Apôtres*, pp. 226-42. Edited by J. P. Audet. Paris: Lecoffre, 1958. TLG 1311.001.

Ephrem the Syrian. "Epiphania." *Des Heiligen Ephraem des Syrers Hymnen de Nativitate (Epiphania)*. Edited by Edmund Beck. CSCO 186 (Scriptores Syri 82). Louvain: Secrétariat du Corpus SCO, 1959.

———. "Hymni de Paradiso." In *Des Heiligen Ephraem des Syrers Hymnen de Paradiso und Contra Julianum*. Edited by Edmund Beck. CSCO 174 (Scriptores Syri 78), pp. 1-66. Louvain: Imprimerie Orientaliste L. Durbecq, 1957.

———. "In Danielem." In *Sancti patris nostri Ephraem Syri Opera omnia*, vol. 2. Edited by J. A. Assemani. Rome, 1737.

———. "In Tatiani Diatessaron." In *Saint Éphrem: Commentaire de l'Évangile Concordant – Text Syriaque (Ms Chester-Beatty 709)*, vol. 2. Edited by Louis Leloir. Leuven and Paris: Peeters Press, 1990.

Epiphanius of Salamis. "De mensuribus et ponderibus." In *Symmicta*, pp. 211-25. Edited by Paul de Lagarde. Göttingen: Dieterich, 1877. TLG 2021.035 to 041.

Eusebius. "Demonstratio evangelica." In *Eusebius Werke, Band 6: Die Demonstratio evangelica*. Edited by I. A. Heikel. GCS 23, 1-492. Leipzig: Hinrichs, 1913. TLG 2018.005.

———. "Historia ecclesiastica." In *Eusèbe de Césarée. Histoire ecclésiastique*. Edited by G. Bardy. SC 31, pp. 3-215; SC 41, pp. 4-231; SC 55, pp. 3-120. Paris: Éditions du Cerf, 1952-1958. TLG 2018.002.

Eznik of Kolb. *De Deo*. Armenian and French. 2 vols. Edited by Louis Mariès and Charles Mercier. PO 28/3 and 28/4. Paris: Firmin-Didot, 1959.

Fastidius. "Liber de Vita Christiana." *Opera omnia*. Edited by J.-P. Migne. PL 50, cols. 383-406. Paris: Migne, 1865.

Fulgentius of Ruspe. "Ad Monimum libri III." In *Opera*. Edited by John Fraipont. CCL 91, pp. 1-64. Turnhout, Belgium: Brepols, 1968. Cl. 0814.

———. "De fide ad Petrum seu de regula fidei." In *Opera*. Edited by John Fraipont. CCL 91A, pp. 711-60. Turnhout, Belgium: Brepols, 1968. Cl. 0826.

Gregory of Nazianzus. "Apologetica (orat. 2)." In *Opera omnia*. Edited by J.-P. Migne. PG 35, cols. 408-513. Paris: Migne, 1857. TLG 2022.016.

————. "De theologia (orat. 28)." In *Gregor von Nazianz: Die fünf theologischen Reden*, pp. 62-126. Edited by Joseph Barbel. Düsseldorf: Patmos-Verlag, 1963. TLG 2022.008.

————. "In patrem tacentem (orat. 16)." In *Opera omnia*. Edited by J.-P. Migne. PG 35, cols. 933-64. Paris: Migne, 1857. TLG 2022.029.

Gregory of Nyssa. "De virginitate." In *Grégoire de Nysse. Traité de la virginité*. SC 119, pp. 246-560. Edited by Michel Aubineau. Paris: Éditions du Cerf, 1966. TLG 2017.043.

————. "Dialogus de anima et resurrectione." In *S. P. N. Gregorii*. PG 46, cols. 12-160. Edited by J.-P. Migne. Paris: Migne, 1863. TLG 2017.056.

————. "In diem luminum (vulgo In baptismum Christi oratio)." In *Gregorii Nysseni opera*, vol. 9.1, pp. 221-42. Edited by E. Gebhardt. Leiden: Brill, 1967. TLG 2017.014.

Gregory the Great. "Dialogorum libri iv." In *Dialogues*. Edited by Paul Antin and Adalbert de Vogüé. SC 251, 260 and 265. Paris: Éditions du Cerf, 1978-1980. Cl. 1713.

————. "Homiliae in Hiezechihelem prophetam." In *Opera*. Edited by Mark Adriaen. CCL 142, pp. 3-398. Turnhout, Belgium: Brepols, 1971. Cl. 1710.

————. "Homiliarum xl in evangelica." In *Opera omnia*. Edited by J.-P. Migne. PL 76, cols. 1075-1312. Paris: Migne, 1857. Cl. 1711.

————. *Regula pastoralis*. Edited by Floribert Rommel and R. W. Clement. CCL 141. Turnhout, Belgium: Brepols, 1953. Cl. 1712.

Hilary of Poitiers. *De trinitate*. Edited by P. Smulders. CCL 62 and 62A. Turnhout, Belgium: Brepols, 1979-1980. Cl. 0433.

Hippolytus. "Commentarium in Danielem." In *Hippolyte. Commentaire sur Daniel*. Edited by Maurice Lefèvre. SC 14, pp. 70-386. Paris: Éditions du Cerf, 1947. TLG 2115.030.

————. "Contra haeresin Noeti." In *Hippolytus of Rome. Contra Noetum*, pp. 43-93. Edited by R. Butterworth. London: Heythrop College (University of London), 1977. TLG 2115.002.

————. "De antichristo." In *Hippolyt's kleinere exegetische und homiletische Schriften*. Edited by Hans Achelis. GCS 1.2, pp. 1-47. Leipzig: Hinrichs, 1897. TLG 2115.003.

————. [Fragments.] In *Hippolyt's kleinere exegetische und homiletische Schriften*. Edited by Hans Achelis. GCS 1.2. Leipzig: Hinrichs, 1897.

————. "Scholia in Danielem." In *Opera omnia*. Edited by J.-P. Migne. PG 10, cols. 669-88. Paris: Migne, 1857.

Ignatius of Antioch. "Epistulae vii genuinae." In *Ignace d'Antioche: Polycarpe de Smyrne: Lettres: Martyre de Polycarpe*. 4th ed. Edited by P. T. Camelot. SC 10, pp. 56-154. Paris: Éditions du Cerf, 1969. TLG 1443.001.

Irenaeus. "Adversus haereses, livres 1-5." In *Contre les hérésies*. Edited by Adelin Rousseau, Louis Doutreleau and Charles A. Mercier. SC 34, 100, 152-53, 210-11, 263-64 and 293-94. Paris: Éditions du Cerf, 1952-82. Cl. 1154 f-g.

Isaac of Nineveh. "De perfectione religiosa." In *Mar Isaacus Ninivita. De perfectione Religiosa*, pp. 1-99. Edited by Paul Bedjan. Paris, 1966.

Isho'dad of Merv. "Commentarii in Danielem." In *Commentaire d'Iso'dad de Merv sur l'Ancien Testament, V. Jérémie, Ezécchiel, Daniel*. Edited by C. Van den Eynde. CSCO 328 (Scriptores Syri 146), pp. 101-35. Turnhout, Belgium: Brepols, 1972.

Isidore of Seville. *Etymologiarum sive Originum libri xx: Recognovit brevique adnotatione critica instruxit*. Edited by W. M. Lindsay. 1911. Reprint, Oxford: Oxford University Press, 1989. Cl. 1186.

Jacob of Sarug. *Homiliae Selectae Mar Jacobi Sarugensis*, vol. 3, pp. 4-27. Edited by Paul Bedjan. Paris and

Leipzig: Harrassowitz, 1907.

Jerome. "Adversus Jovinianum." In *Opera omnia*. PL 23, cols. 211-338. Edited by J.-P. Migne. Paris: Migne, 1865. Cl. 0610.

———."Commentarii in Danielem." In *S. Hieronymi Presbyteri opera*. Edited by F. Glorie. CCL 75A. Turnhout, Belgium: Brepols, 1964. Cl. 0588.

———."Commentarii in Ezechielem." In *S. Hieronymi Presbyteri opera*. Edited by F. Glorie. CCL 75, pp. 3-743. Turnhout, Belgium: Brepols, 1964. Cl. 0587.

———. *Dialogus adversus Pelagianos*. Edited by Claudio Moreschini. CCL 80. Turnhout, Belgium: Brepols, 1990. Cl. 0615.

———.*Epistulae*. Edited by I. Hilberg. CSEL 54, 55 and 56. Vienna, Austria: F. Tempsky; Leipzig, Germany: G. F. Freytag, 1910-1918. Cl. 0620.

———."Homilia in Johannem evangelistam (1:1-14)." In *Opera, Part 2*. Edited by Germain Morin. CCL 78, pp. 517-23. Turnhout, Belgium: Brepols, 1958. Cl. 0597.

———."In die dominica Paschae, II." In *Opera, Part 2*. Edited by Germain Morin. CCL 78, pp. 548-51. Turnhout, Belgium: Brepols, 1958. Cl. 0604.

———."Tractatus in Marci evangelium." In *S. Hieronymi Presbyteri opera*. Edited by Germain Morin. CCL 78, pp. 451-500. Turnhout, Belgium: Brepols, 1958. Cl. 0594.

———."Tractatus lix in psalmos." In *S. Hieronymi Presbyteri opera*. Edited by Germain Morin. CCL 78, pp. 3-352. Turnhout, Belgium: Brepols, 1958. Cl. 0592.

———."Tractatuum in psalmos series altera." In *S. Hieronymi Presbyteri opera*. Edited by Germain Morin. CCL 78, pp. 355-446. Turnhout, Belgium: Brepols, 1958. Cl. 0593.

John Chrysostom."Ad illuminandos catecheses 1-2 (series prima et secunda)." In *Opera omnia*. Edited by J.-P. Migne. PG 49, cols. 223-40. Paris: Migne, 1862. TLG 2062.025.

———."Ad populam Antiochenum homiliae (de statuis)." In *Opera omnia*. Edited by J.-P. Migne. PG 49, cols. 15-222. Paris: Migne, 1862. TLG 2062.024.

———."Ad Stagirium a daemone vexatum, lib. iii." In *Opera omnia*. Edited by J.-P. Migne. PG 47, cols. 423-94. Paris: Migne, 1863. TLG 2062.006.

———."Ad Theodorum lapsum (lib. 2) († Epistula ad Theodorum monachum)." In *Jean Chrysostome. A Théodore*. Edited by J. Dumortier. SC 117, pp. 46-78. Paris: Éditions du Cerf, 1966. TLG 2062.001.

———."Adversus Judaeos (orationes 1-8)." In *Opera omnia*. Edited by J.-P. Migne. PG 48, cols. 843-942. Paris: Migne, 1862. TLG 2062.021.

———."De diabolo tentatore (homiliae 1-3)." In *Opera omnia*. Edited by J.-P. Migne. PG 49, cols. 241-76. Paris: Migne, 1862. TLG 2062.026.

———."De incomprehensibili dei natura (& Contra Anomoeos, homiliae 1-5)." In *Jean Chrysostome. Sur l'incompréhensibilité de Dieu*. Edited by A.-M. Malingrey. SC 28 bis., pp. 92-322. Paris: Éditions du Cerf, 1970. TLG 2062.012.

———."De paenitentia (homiliae 1-9)." In *Opera omnia*. Edited by J.-P. Migne. PG 49, cols. 277-348. Paris: Migne, 1862. TLG 2062.027.

———."De sancto hieromartyre Babyla." In *Opera omnia*. Edited by J.-P. Migne. PG 50, cols. 527-34. Paris: Migne, 1862. TLG 2062.041.

———."In Acta apostolorum (homiliae 1-55)." In *Opera omnia*. Edited by J.-P. Migne. PG 60, cols. 13-384. Paris: Migne, 1862. TLG 2062.154.

———."In epistulam ad Ephesios (homiliae 1-24)." In *Opera omnia*. Edited by J.-P. Migne. PG 62, cols. 9-176. Paris: Migne, 1862. TLG 2062.159.

———."In epistulam ad Titum (homiliae 1-6)." In *Opera omnia*. Edited by J.-P. Migne. PG 62, cols. 663-700. Paris: Migne, 1862. TLG 2062.166.

———. "In epistulam ad Hebraeos (homiliae 1-34)." In *Opera omnia*. Edited by J.-P. Migne. PG 63, cols. 9-236. Paris: Migne, 1862. TLG 2062.168.

———. "In epistulam i ad Corinthios (homiliae 1-44)." In *Opera omnia*. Edited by J.-P. Migne. PG 61, cols. 9-382. Paris: Migne, 1859. TLG 2062.156.

———. "In epistulam ii ad Timotheum (homiliae 1-10)." In *Opera omnia*. Edited by J.-P. Migne. PG 62, cols. 599-662. Paris: Migne, 1862. TLG 2062.165.

———. "In Genesim (homiliae 1-67)." In *Opera omnia*. Edited by J.-P. Migne. PG 53 and 54, cols. 385-580. Paris: Migne, 1859-1862. TLG 2062.112.

———. "In Joannem (homiliae 1-88)." In *Opera omnia*. Edited by J.-P. Migne. PG 59, cols. 23-482. Paris: Migne, 1862. TLG 2062.153.

———. "In Matthaeum (homiliae 1-90)." In *Opera omnia*. Edited by J.-P. Migne. PG 57, cols. 13-472 and 58, cols. 471-794. Paris: Migne, 1862. TLG 2062.152.

———. "Interpretatio in Danielem prophetam [Sp.]." *Opera omnia*. Edited by J.-P. Migne. PG 56, cols. 193-246. Paris: Migne, 1859. TLG 2062.209.

———. "Quod nemo laeditur nisi a se ipso." In *Lettre d'exil à Olympias et à tous les fidèles*. Edited by A.-M. Malingrey. SC 103, pp. 56-144. Paris: Éditions du Cerf, 1964. TLG 2062.086.

John of Damascus. "Expositio fidei." In *Die Schriften des Johannes von Damaskos*, vol. 2. Edited by B. Kotter. Patristische Texte und Studien 12, pp. 3-239. Berlin: De Gruyter, 1973. TLG 2934.004.

———. "Oratio apologetica adversus eos, qui sacras imagines abiciunt." In *Opera omnia*. Edited by J.-P. Migne. PG 94, cols. 1227-1420. Paris: Migne, 1862. TLG 2934.004.

———. "Vita Barlaam et Joasaph." In *Barlaam and Joasaph*. Edited by G. R. Woodward and H. Mattingly. LCL 34. Cambridge, Mass.: Harvard University Press, 1914. Reprint, 1983. TLG 2934.066.

Julian of Toledo. "De comprobatione sextae aetatis libri tres." In *Sancti Juliani Toletanae sedis episcopi Opera*. Edited by J. N. Hillgarth et al. CCL 115, pp. 143-212. Turnhout, Belgium: Brepols, 1976. Cl. 1260.

Justin Martyr. "Apologia." In *Die ältesten Apologeten*, pp. 26-77. Edited by E. J. Goodspeed. Göttingen: Vandenhoeck & Ruprecht, 1915. TLG 0645.001.

———. "Dialogus cum Tryphone." In *Die ältesten Apologeten*, pp. 90-265. Edited by E. J. Goodspeed. Göttingen: Vandenhoeck & Ruprecht, 1915. TLG 0645.003.

Lactantius. "Divinae Institutiones." In *L. Caeli Firmiani Lactanti Opera omnia*. Edited by Samuel Brandt. CSEL 19, pp. 1-672. Vienna, Austria: F. Tempsky; Leipzig, Germany: G. Freytag, 1890. Cl. 0085.

Leander of Seville. "De institutione virginum et contemptu mundi." In *El "De institutione virginum" de San Leandro de Sevilla, con diez capítulos y medio inéditos*. Edited by A. C. Vega. El Escorial, 1948.

Leo the Great. "Epistulae." In *Opera omnia Leonis Magni*. Edited by J.-P. Migne. PL 54, cols. 581-1218. Paris: Migne, 1846. Cl. 1657.

———. *Tractatus septem et nonaginta*. Edited by Antonio Chavasse. CCL 138 and 138A. Turnhout, Belgium: Brepols, 1973. Cl. 1657.

"Martyrium Polycarpi." In *The Acts of the Christian Martyrs*, pp. 2-20. Edited by H. Musurillo. Oxford: Clarendon, 1972. TLG 1484.001.

Maximus of Turin. *Collectio sermonum antiqua*. Edited by Almut Mutzenbecher. CCL 23. Turnhout, Belgium: Brepols, 1962. Cl. 0219a.

Methodius. "De Resurrectione." In *Methodius*. Edited by G. Nathanael Bonwetsch. GCS 27, pp. 226-420 *passim*. Leipzig: Hinrichs, 1917. TLG 2959.003.

———. "Symposium *sive* Convivium decem virginum." In *Opera omnia*. Edited by J.-P. Migne. PG 18, cols. 27-220. Paris: Migne, 1857. TLG 2959.001.

Nemesius of Emesa. "De natura hominis." In *Nemesius of Emesa* (typescript), pp. 35-368. Edited by B. Einarson. Corpus medicorum Graecorum (in press). Berlin. TLG 0743.001.

Novatian. "De spectaculis." In *Opera*. Edited by Gerardus Frederik Diercks. CCL 4, pp. 167-79. Turnhout, Belgium: Brepols, 1972.

———."De Trinitate." In *Opera*. Edited by Gerardus Frederik Diercks. CCL 4, pp. 11-78. Turnhout, Belgium: Brepols, 1972. Cl. 0071.

Origen."Commentarii in epistolam ad Romanos." In *Commentarii in epistolam ad Romanos/Römerbriefkommentar*, 5 vols. Edited by Theresia Heither. Fontes Christiani 2. Freiburg im Breisgau: Herder, 1990–96.

———."Commentarii in evangelium Joannis (lib. 1, 2, 4, 5, 6, 10, 13)." In *Origene. Commentaire sur saint Jean*, 3 vols. Edited by Cécil Blanc. SC 120, 157 and 222. Paris: Éditions du Cerf, 1966-1975. TLG 2042.005.

———."Contra Celsum." In *Origène Contre Celse*, 4 vols. Edited by M. Borret. SC 132, 136, 147 and 150, pp. 64-476, 14-434, 14-382 and 14-352. Paris: Éditions du Cerf, 1967-1969. TLG 2042.001.

———."De oratione." In *Origenes Werke*, vol. 2. Edited by Paul Koetschau. GCS 3, pp. 297-403. Leipzig: Hinrichs, 1899. TLG 2042.008.

———."De principiis." In *Origenes Werke*, v ol. 5. Edited by Paul Koetschau. GCS 22. Leipzig: Hinrichs, 1913. Cl. 0198 E (A). TLG 2042.002.

———."Exhortatio ad martyrium." In *Origenes Werke*, vol. 1. Edited by Paul Koetschau. GCS 2, pp. 3-47. Leipzig: Hinrichs, 1899. TLG 2042.007.

———."Homiliae in Exodum." In *Origenes Werke*, vol. 6. Edited by W. A. Baehrens. GCS (CB) 29, pp. 217-30. Leipzig: Teubner, 1920. Cl. 0198 5 (A).

———."Homiliae in Ezechielem." In *Homélies sur Ézéchiel*. Edited by Marcel Borret. SC 352. Paris: Éditions du Cerf, 1989. TLG 2042.027.

———."Homiliae in Genesim." In *Origenes Werke*, vol. 6. Edited by W. A. Baehrens. GCS (CB) 29, pp. 23-30. Leipzig: Teubner, 1920. Cl. 0198 6 (A). TLG 2042.022.

———."Homiliae in Leviticum." In *Origenes Werke*, vol. 6. Edited by W. A. Baehrens. GCS (CB) 29, pp. 332-34, 395, 402-7and 409-16. Leipzig: Teubner, 1920. Cl. 0198 3 (A). TLG 2042.024.

———."In Numeros homiliae." In *Origenes Werke*, vol. 7. Edited by W. A. Baehrens. GCS 30, pp. 3-285. Leipzig: Teubner, 1921. Cl. 0198 O (A).

———."Selecta in Ezechielem." In *Opera omnia*. Edited by J.-P. Migne. PG 13, cols. 767-826. Paris: Migne, 1862. TLG 2042.062.

———."Selecta in Psalmos [Dub.] (fragmenta e catenis)." PG 12, cols. 1053-1320, 1368-69, 1388-89 and 1409-1685. Edited by J.-P. Migne. Paris: Migne, 1862. TLG 2042.058.

Pachomius. "Catechesis." In *Oeuvres de s. Pachôme et de ses disciples*. Edited by L.-Th. Lefort. CSCO 159 (Scriptores Coptica 23), pp. 1-26. Louvain: Imprimerie Orientaliste, 1956.

———."Vita Pachomii." *Le corpus athénien de saint Pachome*, pp. 11-72. Edited by F. Halkin. Cahiers d'Orientalisme 2. Genève: Cramer, 1982.

Pacian of Barcelona."De paenitentibus." In *Las obras de Paciano publicadas por V. Noguera y edición crítica del Liber de paenitentibus*. Translated by Angel Anglada Anfruns. Valencia: Universidad de Valencia, 1982.

Paulinus of Nola. "Carmina." In *Sancti Pontii Meropii Paulini Nolani Carmina*. Edited by W. Hartel. CSEL 30, pp. 1-3, 7-329. Vienna, Austria: F. Tempsky, 1894. Cl. 0203.

Peter Chrysologus. *Collectio sermonum a Felice episcopo parata sermonibus extravagantibus adjectis*, 3 vols. In *Sancti Petri Chrysologi*. Edited by Alexander Olivar. CCL 24, 24A and 24B. Turnhout, Belgium: Brepols, 1975-1982. Cl. 0227.

Possidius. "Vita Augustini." In *Vita di Cipriano / [Ponzio]. Vita di Ambrogio / [Paolino]. Vita di Agostino / [Possidio]. Vita dei santi* 3, pp. 130-240. Edited by A. A. R. Bastiaensen. Milan: Fondazione Lorenzo Valla, 1974. Cl. 0358.

Primasius. *Commentarius in Apocalypsin.* Edited by A. W. Adams. CCL 92. Turnholt: Brepols, 1985. Cl. 0873.

Pseudo-Clement of Rome. "Epistula ii ad Corinthios [Sp.]." In *Die Apostolischen Väter,* pp.71-81. 3rd ed. Edited by K. Bihlmeyer, W. Schneemelcher and F. X. Funk. Tübingen: Mohr, 1970. TLG 1271.002.

Pseudo-Clementine Homily. "Homiliae (Sp.)." In *Die Pseudoklementinen I. Homilien.* 2nd ed. Edited by B. Rehm, J. Irmscher and F. Paschke. GCS 42, pp. 23-281. Berlin: Akademie-Verlag, 1969. TLG 1271.006.

Pseudo-Dionysius. "De caelesti hierarchia." In *Corpus Dionysiacum ii: Pseudo-Dionysius Areopagita. De coelesti hierarchia, de ecclesiastica hierarchia, de mystica theologia, epistulae.* PTS 36, pp. 7-59. Edited by G. Heil and A. M. Ritter. Berlin: De Gruyter, 1991. TLG 2798.001.

Pseudo-Hegesippus. "Flavius Josephus sec. transl. et retract. Hegesippi—Historiae libri V" (Additamentum). Edited by V. Ussani. CSEL 66. Vienna: F. Tempsky, 1932. Cl. 0190a.

Pseudo-Macarius. "Homiliae spiritualis 50." In *Die 50 geistlichen Homilien des Makarios.* PTS 4. Berlin: De Gruyter, 1964. TLG 2109.002.

Quodvultdeus. "Liber promissionum et praedictorum Dei." In *Opera Quodvultdeo Carthaginiensi episcopo tributa.* Edited by R. Braun. CCL 60, pp. 1-223. Turnhout, Belgium: Brepols, 1976. Cl. 0413.

Romanus Melodus. "Cantica." In *Romanos le Mélode: Hymnes.* Edited by J. Grosdidier de Matons. SC 99, 110, 114, 128 and 283. Paris: Éditions du Cerf, 1964-1981. TLG 2881.001.

Rufinus of Aquileia. "Expositio symboli." In *Opera.* Edited by Manlio Simonetti. CCL 20, pp. 125-82. Turnhout, Belgium: Brepols, 1961. Cl. 0196.

Salvian the Presbyter. "Adversus avaritiam libri quatuor." In *Opera omnia.* Edited by J.-P. Migne. PL 53, cols. 173-238. Paris: Migne, 1859.

———. "De gubernatione Dei." In *Ouvres.* Vol. 2. Edited by G. Lagarrigue. SC 220, pp. 95-527. Paris: Éditions du Cerf, 1975. Cl. 0485.

Symeon the New Theologian. "Capita practica et theologica." In *Chapitres théologiques, gnostiques et pratiques.* Edited by J. Darrouzès. SC 51. Paris: Éditions du Cerf, 1957.

———. "Catecheses." In *Catecheses 1-5.* Edited by Basil Krivochéine and Joseph Paramelle. SC 96. Paris: Éditions du Cerf, 1963.

Tertullian. "Ad martyras." Edited by E. Dekkers. In *Tertulliani opera.* CCL 1, pp. 3-8. Turnhout, Belgium: Brepols, 1954. Cl. 0001.

———. "Adversus Judaeos." Edited by E. Kroymann. In *Tertulliani opera.* CCL 2, pp. 1339-96. Turnhout, Belgium: Brepols, 1954. Cl. 0033.

———. "Adversus Marcionem." Edited by E. Kroymann. In *Tertulliani opera.* CCL 1, pp. 437-726. Turnhout, Belgium: Brepols, 1954. Cl. 0014.

———. "De anima." Edited by J. H. Waszink. In *Tertulliani opera.* CCL 2, pp. 781-869. Turnhout, Belgium: Brepols, 1954. Cl. 0017.

———. "De corona." Edited by E. Kroymann. In *Tertulliani opera.* CCL 2, pp. 1039-65. Turnhout, Belgium: Brepols, 1954. Cl. 0021.

———. "De idololatria." Edited by August Reifferscheid and George Wissowa. In *Tertulliani opera.* CCL 2, pp. 1101-24. Turnhout, Belgium: Brepols, 1954. Cl. 0023.

———. "De ieiunio adversus psychicos." Edited by A. Reifferscheid and G. Wissowa. In *Tertulliani opera.* CCL 2, pp. 1257-77. Turnhout, Belgium: Brepols, 1954. Cl. 0029.

———. "De oratione." Edited by Gerardus Frederik Diercks In *Tertulliani Opera* CCL 1, pp. 255-74. Turnhout, Belgium: Brepols, 1954. Cl. 0007.

———. "De paenitentia." Edited by J. G. PH. Borleffs. In *Tertulliani Opera.* CCL 1, pp. 299-317. Turnhout, Belgium: Brepols, 1954. Cl. 0009.

————."De pudicitia." Edited by E. Dekkers. In *Tertulliani opera*. CCL 2, pp. 1281-1330. Turnhout, Belgium: Brepols, 1954. Cl. 0030.

————."De resurrectione carnis." In *Tertullian's Treatise on the Resurrection (1960) Q. Septimii Florentis Tertulliani de resurrectione carnis liber*, pp. 4-186. Edited by Ernest Evans. London: SPCK, 1960.

Theodoret of Cyr."Historia religiosa." In *Théodoret de Cyr, Histoire des Moines de Syrie*, 2 vols. Edited by P. Canivet and A. Leroy-Molinghen. SC 234 and 257. Paris: Éditions du Cerf, 1977-1979. TLG 4089.004.

————."Interpretatio in Danielem." In *Opera omnia*. Edited by J.-P. Migne. PG 81, cols. 1256-1546. Paris: Migne, 1864. TLG 4089.028.

————."Interpretatio in Ezechielem." In *Opera omnia*. Edited by J.-P. Migne. PG 81, cols. 808-1256. Paris: Migne, 1864. TLG 4089.027.

————."Interpretatio in Psalmos." In *Opera omnia*. Edited by J.-P. Migne. PG 80, cols. 857-1997. Paris: Migne, 1860. TLG 4089.024.

Valerian."Homilia." *Opera omnia*. Edited by J.-P. Migne. PL 52, cols. 691-758. Paris: Migne, 1845.

Victorinus of Petovium. *Commentarii in Apocalypsim Joannis*. Edited by Johannes Haussleiter. CSEL 49, pp. 14-154. Vienna: F. Tempsky; Leipzig: G. Freytag, 1916.

Bibliography of Works
in English Translation

Ambrose. "Death as a Good." In *Seven Exegetical Works*, pp. 69-113. Translated by Michael P. McHugh. FC 65. Washington, D.C.: The Catholic University of America Press, 1972.

————. "Duties of the Clergy." In *Select Works and Letters*, pp. 1-89. Translated by H. De Romestin. NPNF 10. Series 2. Edited by Philip Schaff and Henry Wace. 14 vols. 1886-1900. Reprint, Peabody, Mass.: Hendrickson, 1994.

————. "Jacob and the Happy Life." In *Seven Exegetical Works*, pp. 117-84. Translated by Michael P. McHugh. FC 65. Washington, D.C.: The Catholic University of America Press, 1972.

————. *Letters*. Translated by Mary Melchior Beyenka. FC 26. 1954. Reprint, Washington, D.C.: The Catholic University of America Press, 1987.

————. "Letters." In *Early Latin Theology*, pp. 184-278. Translated by S. L. Greenslade. LCC 5. Philadelphia, Westminster Press: 1956.

————. "Letters." In *Select Works and Letters*, pp. 411-473. Translated by H. De Romestin. NPNF 10. Series 2. Edited by Philip Schaff and Henry Wace. 14 vols. 1886-1900. Reprint, Peabody, Mass.: Hendrickson, 1994.

————. "On His Brother Satyrus." In *Funeral Orations by Saint Gregory Nazianzen and Saint Ambrose*, pp. 159-259. Translated by John J. Sullivan and Martin R. P. McGuire. FC 22. Washington, D.C.: The Catholic University of America Press, 1953.

————. "On His Brother Satyrus." In *Select Works and Letters*, pp. 159-73. Translated by H. De Romestin. NPNF 10. Series 2. Edited by Philip Schaff and Henry Wace. 14 vols. 1886-1900. Reprint, Peabody, Mass.: Hendrickson, 1994.

————. "On Paradise." In *Hexameron, Paradise and Cain and Abel*, pp. 287-356. Translated by John J. Savage. FC 42. 1961. Reprint, Washington, D.C.: The Catholic University of America Press, 2003.

————. "On the Christian Faith." In *Select Works and Letters*, pp. 199-314. Translated by H. De Romestin. NPNF 10. Series 2. Edited by Philip Schaff and Henry Wace. 14 vols. 1886-1900. Reprint, Peabody, Mass.: Hendrickson, 1994.

————. "On the Holy Spirit." In *Select Works and Letters*, pp. 91-158. Translated by H. De Romestin. NPNF 10. Series 2. Edited by Philip Schaff and Henry Wace. 14 vols. 1886-1900. Reprint, Peabody, Mass.: Hendrickson, 1994.

————. *On Virginity*. Translated by Daniel Callam. Toronto: Peregrina Publishing, 1996.

————. "The Prayer of Job and David." In *Seven Exegetical Works*, pp. 329-420. Translated by Michael P. McHugh. FC 65. Washington, D.C.: The Catholic University of America Press, 1972.

Aphrahat. "Demonstrations." In *Gregory the Great, Ephraim Syrus, Aphrahat*, pp. 345-412. Translated by James Barmby. NPNF 13. Series 2. Edited by Philip Schaff and Henry Wace. 14 vols. 1886-1900. Reprint, Peabody, Mass.: Hendrickson, 1994.

Athanasius. "Festal Letters." In *Selected Works and Letters*, pp. 506-553. Translated by Payne Smith. Edited by Archibald Robertson. NPNF 4. Series 2. Edited by Philip Schaff and Henry Wace. 14 vols. 1886-1900. Reprint, Peabody, Mass.: Hendrickson, 1994.

————. "Letter to the Bishops of Egypt." In *Selected Works and Letters*, pp. 223-35. Translated by M. Atkinson. Edited by Archibald Robertson. NPNF 4. Series 2. Edited by Philip Schaff and Henry Wace.

14 vols. 1886-1900. Reprint, Peabody, Mass.: Hendrickson, 1994.

————. "On Synods." In *Selected Works and Letters*, pp. 451-80. Translated by John Henry Newman. Edited by Archibald Robertson. NPNF 4. Series 2. Edited by Philip Schaff and Henry Wace. 14 vols. 1886-1900. Reprint, Peabody, Mass.: Hendrickson, 1994.

Augustine. "Against Faustus, A Manichaean." In *The Writings Against the Manichaens and Against the Donatists*, pp. 156-345. Translated by Richard Stothert. NPNF 4. Series 1. Edited by Philip Schaff. 14 vols. 1886-1889. Reprint, Peabody, Mass.: Hendrickson, 1994.

————. *Against Julian*. Translated by Matthew A. Schumacher. FC 35. Washington, D.C.: The Catholic University of America Press, 1957.

————. *Confessions*. Translated by Vernon Bourke. FC 21. Washington, D.C.: The Catholic University of America Press, 1953.

————. "Confessions." In *Divine Providence and Human Suffering*, pp. 25-30. Translated by James Walsh and P. G. Walsh. MFC 17. Wilmington, Del.: Michael Glazier, 1985.

————. *City of God: Books 1-7, Books 8-16* and *Books 17-22*. Translated by Gerald G. Walsh, Daniel J. Honan and Grace Monahan. FC 8, 14 and 24. Washington, D.C.: The Catholic University of America Press, 1950-1954.

————. "Enchiridion." In *The Enchiridion on Faith, Hope and Love*, pp. 1-141. Translated by J. F. Shaw. Edited by Henry Paolucci. Chicago: Henry Regnery Company, 1961.

————. "Explanations of the Psalms." See *Expositions on the Book of Psalms*. Edited from the Oxford translation by A. Cleveland Coxe. NPNF 8. Series 1. Edited by Philip Schaff. 14 vols. 1886-1889. Reprint, Peabody, Mass.: Hendrickson, 1994.

————. "Harmony of the Gospels." In *Sermon on the Mount, Harmony of the Gospels, Homilies on the Gospels*, pp. 77-236. Translated by S. D. F. Salmond. NPNF 6. Series 1. Edited by Philip Schaff. 14 vols. 1886-1889. Reprint, Peabody, Mass.: Hendrickson, 1994.

————. "Homilies on 1 John." In *Homilies on the Gospel of John, Homilies on the First Epistle of John, Soliloquies*, pp. 451-529. Translated by H. Browne. NPNF 7. Series 1. Edited by Philip Schaff. 14 vols. 1886-1889. Reprint, Peabody, Mass.: Hendrickson, 1994.

————. "Homilies on 1 John." In *Later Works*, pp. 259-348. Translated by John Burnaby. LCC 8. London: SCM Press, 1955.

————. "Letters." Vols. 1, 2, 4, 5 and 6. Translated by Wilfred Parsons and Robert B. Eno. FC 12, 18, 30, 32 and 81. Washington, D.C.: The Catholic University of America Press, 1951-1989.

————. "Lying." In *Treatises on Various Subjects*, pp. 53-110. Translated by Mary Sarah Muldowney. FC 16. Washington D.C.: The Catholic University of America Press, 1952.

————. "On Genesis, Against the Manichaeans." In *On Genesis Against the Manichees and On the Literal Interpretation of Genesis: An Unfinished Book*, pp. 47-141. Translated by Roland J. Teske. FC 84. Washington, D.C.: The Catholic University of America Press, 1991.

————. "On Grace and Free Will." In *Anti-Pelagian Writings*, pp. 443-65. Translated by Peter Holmes and Robert Ernest Wallis. NPNF 5. Series 1. Edited by Philip Schaff. 14 vols. 1886-1889. Reprint, Peabody, Mass.: Hendrickson, 1994.

————. "On Grace and Free Will." In *The Teacher, The Free Choice of the Will, Grace and Free Will*, pp. 250-308. Translated by Robert P. Russell. FC 59. Washington, D.C.: The Catholic University of America Press, 1968.

————. "On the Christian Life." In *Treatises on Various Subjects*, pp. 9-43. Translated by Mary Sarah Muldowney. FC 16. Washington D.C.: The Catholic University of America Press, 1952.

————. "On the Literal Interpretation of Genesis." See *The Literal Meaning of Genesis, Vol. 2*. Translated and annotated by John Hammond Taylor. ACW 42. New York: Newman Press, 1982.

————. "On the Merits and Forgiveness of Sins and On Infant Baptism." In *Anti-Pelagian Writings*, pp. 15-78. Translated by Peter Holmes and Robert Ernest Wallis. NPNF 5. Series 1. Edited by Philip Schaff. 14 vols. 1886-1889. Reprint, Peabody, Mass.: Hendrickson, 1994.

————. "On the Trinity." In *On the Holy Trinity, Doctrinal Treatises, Moral Treatises*, pp. 1-228. Translated by Arthur West Haddan. NPNF 3. Series 1. Edited by Philip Schaff. 14 vols. 1886-1889. Reprint, Peabody, Mass.: Hendrickson, 1994.

————. "Predestination of the Saints." In *Four Anti-Pelagian Writings*, pp. 218-70. Translated by John A. Mourant and William J. Collinge. FC 86. Washington, D.C.: The Catholic University of America Press, 1992.

————. "Proceedings of Pelagians." In *Anti-Pelagian Writings*, pp. 178-212. Translated by Peter Holmes and Robert Ernest Wallis. NPNF 5. Series 1. Edited by Philip Schaff. 14 vols. 1886-1889. Reprint, Peabody, Mass.: Hendrickson, 1994.

————. "Sermon on the Mount." In *Commentary on the Lord's Sermon on the Mount with Seventeen Related Sermons*, pp. 19-199. Translated by Denis J. Kavanagh. FC 11. Washington, D.C.: The Catholic University of America Press, 1951.

————. *Sermons.* Translated by Edmund Hill. WSA 1-11. Part 3. Edited by John E. Rotelle. New York: New City Press, 1990-1997.

————. *Tractates on the Gospel of John 28-54.* Translated by John W. Rettig. FC 88. Washington, D.C.: The Catholic University of America Press, 1993.

Basil the Great. "Homilies on the Psalms." In *Exegetic Homilies*, pp. 151-359. Translated by Agnes Clare Way. FC 46. Washington, D.C.: The Catholic University of America Press, 1963.

————. "Homily on the Words 'Give Heed to Thyself.'" In *Ascetical Works*, pp. 431-446. Translated by M. Monica Wagner. FC 9. New York: Fathers of the Church, 1950.

————. *Letters.* Vol. 1. Translated by Agnes Clare Way. FC 13. Washington, D.C.: The Catholic University of America Press, 1951.

————. "Letters." In *Letters and Select Works*, pp. 109-327. Translated by Blomfield Jackson. NPNF 8. Series 2. Edited by Philip Schaff and Henry Wace. 14 vols. 1886-1900. Reprint, Peabody, Mass.: Hendrickson, 1994.

————. "The Long Rules." In *Ascetical Works*, pp. 223-337. Translated by M. Monica Wagner. FC 9. New York: Fathers of the Church, 1950.

————. *On the Holy Spirit.* Translated by David Anderson. Crestwood, N.Y.: St. Vladimir's Seminary Press, 1980.

————. "On the Holy Spirit." In *Letters and Select Works*, pp. 1-50. Translated by Blomfield Jackson. NPNF 8. Series 2. Edited by Philip Schaff and Henry Wace. 14 vols. 1886-1900. Reprint, Peabody, Mass.: Hendrickson, 1994.

Bede. *On the Tabernacle.* Translated by Arthur G. Holder. TTH 18. Liverpool: Liverpool University Press, 1994.

Benedict. *The Rule of St. Benedict.* Edited by Timothy Fry et al. Collegeville, Minn.: The Liturgical Press, 1981.

Caesarius of Arles. *Sermons.* Vol. 1, 2 and 3. Translated by Mary Magdeleine Mueller. FC 31, 47 and 66. Washington, D.C.: The Catholic University of America Press, 1956-1973.

Cassian, John. *Conferences.* Translated and annotated by Boniface Ramsey. ACW 57. Mahwah, N.J.: Paulist Press, 1997.

————. *Conferences.* Translated by Colm Luibheid. The Classics of Western Spirituality. Mahwah, N.J.: Paulist Press, 1985.

————. "Institutes." In *Sulpitius Severus, Vincent of Lerins, John Cassian*, pp. 201-290. Translated by Edgar

C. S. Gibson. NPNF 11. Series 2. Edited by Philip Schaff and Henry Wace. 14 vols. 1886-1900. Reprint, Peabody, Mass.: Hendrickson, 1994.

Cassiodorus. *Expositions of the Psalms*. Vol. 1, 2 and 3. Translated and annotated by P. G. Walsh. ACW 51, 52 and 53. Mahwah, N.J.: Paulist Press, 1990-1991.

Clement of Alexandria. *Christ the Educator*. Translated by Simon P. Wood. FC 23. Washington, D.C.: The Catholic University of America Press, 1954.

———. "Stromateis." In *Fathers of the Second Century: Hermas, Tatian, Athenagoras, Theophilus and Clement of Alexandria (Entire)*, pp. 299-556. Translated by Frederick Crombie et al. ANF 2. Edited by Alexander Roberts and James Donaldson. 10 vols. 1885-1887. Reprint, Peabody, Mass.: Hendrickson, 1994.

Clement of Rome. "1 Clement." See "The Epistle to the Corinthians." In *The Apostolic Fathers, Justin Martyr, Irenaeus*, pp. 1-21. Translated by Alexander Roberts and James Donaldson. ANF 1. Edited by Alexander Roberts and James Donaldson. 10 vols. 1885-1887. Reprint, Peabody, Mass.: Hendrickson, 1994.

———. "1 Clement." See "The Letter of the Church of Rome to the Church of Corinth, Commonly Called Clement's First Letter." In *Early Christian Fathers*, pp. 43-73. Translated by Cyril C. Richardson. Philadelphia: Westminster Press, 1953.

"Constitutions of the Holy Apostles." In *Lactantius, Venantius, Asterius, Victorinus, Dionysius, Apostolic Teaching and Constitutions, 2 Clement, Early Liturgies*, pp. 385-508. Translated by W. Whiston. Revised by Irah Chase. ANF 7. Edited by Alexander Roberts and James Donaldson. 10 vols. 1885-1887. Reprint, Peabody, Mass.: Hendrickson, 1994.

Cyprian. "Exhortation to Martyrdom." In *Treatises*, pp. 313-44. Translated by Roy J. Deferrari. FC 36. Washington, D.C.: The Catholic University of America Press, 1958.

———. "The Lapsed." In *Treatises*, pp. 57-88. Translated by Roy J. Deferrari. FC 36. Washington, D.C.: The Catholic University of America Press, 1958.

———. *Letters 1-81*. Translated by Rose Bernard Donna. FC 51. Washington, D.C.: The Catholic University of America Press, 1964.

———. "To Demetrian." In *Treatises*, pp. 167-91. Translated by Roy J. Deferrari. FC 36. Washington, D.C.: The Catholic University of America Press, 1958.

———. "To Quirinus: Testimonies Against the Jews." In *Hippolytus, Cyprian, Caius, Novatian*, pp. 507-57. Translated by Ernest Wallis. ANF 5. Edited by Alexander Roberts and James Donaldson. 10 vols. 1885-1887. Reprint, Peabody, Mass.: Hendrickson, 1994.

———. "Works and Almsgiving." In *Treatises*, pp. 225-53. Translated by Roy J. Deferrari. FC 36. Washington, D.C.: The Catholic University of America Press, 1958.

Cyril of Alexandria. "Commentary on Luke." See *Commentary on the Gospel of Saint Luke*. Translated by R. Payne Smith. N.p.: Studion Publishers, 1983.

———. *Letters 1-50*. Translated by John I. McEnerney. FC 76. Washington, D.C.: The Catholic University of America Press, 1987.

Cyril of Jerusalem. "Catechetical Lectures." In *Cyril of Jerusalem and Nemesius of Emesa*, pp. 64-192. Translated by William Telfer. LCC 4. Philadelphia: Westminster Press, 1955.

———. "Catechetical Lectures." In *Cyril of Jerusalem, Gregory Nazianzen*, pp. 1-157. Translated by Edwin Hamilton Gifford. NPNF 7. Series 2. Edited by Philip Schaff and Henry Wace. 14 vols. 1886-1900. Reprint, Peabody, Mass.: Hendrickson, 1994.

———. "Catechetical Lectures." In *The Works of Saint Cyril of Jerusalem*. Translated by Leo P. McCauley. FC 61 and 64. Washington, D.C.: The Catholic University of America Press, 1969.

Ephrem the Syrian. *Hymns on Paradise*. Translated by Sebastian Brock. Crestwood, N.Y.: St. Vladimir's Seminary Press, 1990.

———. "Hymns on the Nativity." In *Gregory the Great, Ephraim Syrus, Aphrahat*, pp. 223-62. Translated by

J. B. Morris and A. Edward Johnston. NPNF 13. Series 2. Edited by Philip Schaff and Henry Wace. 14 vols. 1886-1900. Reprint, Peabody, Mass.: Hendrickson, 1994.

———. *Saint Ephrem's Commentary on Tatian's Diatessaron: An English Translation of Chester Beatty Syriac MS 709.* Translated by Carmel McCarthy. *Journal of Semitic Studies* Supplement 2. Oxford: Oxford University Press, 1993.

"Epistle of Barnabas." In *The Apostolic Fathers*, pp. 191-222. Translated by Francis X. Glimm. FC 1. New York: Christian Heritage, 1947.

Eusebius of Caesarea. "Ecclesiastical History." In *Eusebius: Church History, Life of Constantine the Great and Oration in Praise of Constantine.* Translated by Arthur Cushman McGiffert. NPNF 1. Series 2. Edited by Philip Schaff and Henry Wace. 14 vols. 1886-1900. Reprint, Peabody, Mass.: Hendrickson, 1994.

———. *Proof of the Gospel.* 2 vols. Translated by W. J. Ferrar. London: SPCK, 1920. Reprint, Grand Rapids, Mich.: Baker, 1981.

Eznik of Kolb. *On God.* Translated by Monica J. Blanchard and Robin Darling Young. Leuven: Peeters, 1998.

Fastidius. "On the Christian Life." In *Divine Providence and Human Suffering*, pp. 98-100. Translated by James Walsh and P. G. Walsh. MFC 17. Wilmington, Del.: Michael Glazier, 1985.

Fulgentius of Ruspe. "Letters." In *Selected Works*, pp. 280-565. Translated by Robert B. Eno. FC 95. Washington, D.C.: The Catholic University of America Press, 1997.

———. "To Monimus." In *Selected Works*, pp. 187-275. Translated by Robert B. Eno. FC 95. Washington, D.C.: The Catholic University of America Press, 1997.

———. "To Peter on the Faith." In *Selected Works*, pp. 59-107. Translated by Robert B. Eno. FC 95. Washington, D.C.: The Catholic University of America Press, 1997.

Gregory of Nazianzus. "In Defense of His Flight to Pontus, Oration 2." In *Cyril of Jerusalem, Gregory Nazianzen*, pp. 204-227. Translated by Charles Gordon Browne and James Edward Swallow. NPNF 7. Series 2. Edited by Philip Schaff and Henry Wace. 14 vols. 1886-1900. Reprint, Peabody, Mass.: Hendrickson, 1994.

———. "On His Father's Silence, Oration 16." In *Cyril of Jerusalem, Gregory Nazianzen*, pp. 247-54. Translated by Charles Gordon Browne and James Edward Swallow. NPNF 7. Series 2. Edited by Philip Schaff and Henry Wace. 14 vols. 1886-1900. Reprint, Peabody, Mass.: Hendrickson, 1994.

———. "On Theology, Theological Oration 2(28)." In *Christology of the Later Fathers*, pp. 136-59. Translated by Charles Gordon Browne and James Edward Swallow. LCC 3. Philadelphia: Westminster Press, 1954.

Gregory of Nyssa. "On the Baptism of Christ." In *Dogmatic Treatises, Etc.*, pp. 518-24. Translated by William Moore and Henry Austin Wilson. NPNF 5. Series 2. Edited by Philip Schaff and Henry Wace. 14 vols. 1886-1900. Reprint, Peabody, Mass.: Hendrickson, 1994.

———. "On the Soul and the Resurrection." In *Ascetical Works*, pp. 198-272. Translated by Virginia Woods Callahan. 1967. FC 58. Reprint, Washington, D.C.: The Catholic University of America Press, 1999.

———. "On Virginity." In *Dogmatic Treatises, Etc.*, pp. 343-71. Translated by William Moore and Henry Austin Wilson. NPNF 5. Series 2. Edited by Philip Schaff and Henry Wace. 14 vols. 1886-1900. Reprint, Peabody, Mass.: Hendrickson, 1994.

Gregory the Great. *Forty Gospel Homilies.* Translated by David Hurst. CS 123. Kalamazoo, Mich.: Cistercian, 1990.

———. "Forty Gospel Homilies." In *Be Friends of God: Spiritual Reading from Gregory the Great.* Translated by David Hurst. Revised by John Leinenweber. Cambridge, Mass.: Cowley Publications, 1990.

———. "Homilies on Ezekiel." See *The Homilies of St. Gregory the Great on the Book of the Prophet Ezekiel.*

Translated by Theodosia Gray. Etna, Calif.: Center for Traditionalist Orthodox Studies, 1990.

———. *Pastoral Care.* Translated and annotated by Henry Davis. ACW 11. New York: Newman Press, 1978.

Hilary of Poitiers. "On the Trinity." In *Hilary of Poitiers, John of Damascus,* pp. 40-233. Translated by E. W. Watson and L. Pullan. NPNF 9. Series 2. Edited by Philip Schaff and Henry Wace. 14 vols. 1886-1900. Reprint, Peabody, Mass.: Hendrickson, 1994.

Hippolytus. "Against Noetus." In *Hippolytus, Cyprian, Caius, Novatian,* pp. 223-31. Translated by S. D. F. Salmond. ANF 5. Edited by Alexander Roberts and James Donaldson. 10 vols. 1885-1887. Reprint, Peabody, Mass.: Hendrickson, 1994.

———. "Commentary on Daniel." In *Hippolytus, Cyprian, Caius, Novatian,* pp. 177-194. Translated by S. D. F. Salmond. ANF 5. Edited by Alexander Roberts and James Donaldson. 10 vols. 1885-1887. Reprint, Peabody, Mass.: Hendrickson, 1994.

———. "On the Antichrist." In *Hippolytus, Cyprian, Caius, Novatian,* pp. 204-19. Translated by S. D. F. Salmond. ANF 5. Edited by Alexander Roberts and James Donaldson. 10 vols. 1885-1887. Reprint, Peabody, Mass.: Hendrickson, 1994.

———. "Scholia on Daniel." In *Hippolytus, Cyprian, Caius, Novatian,* pp. 185-191. Translated by S. D. F. Salmond. ANF 5. Edited by Alexander Roberts and James Donaldson. 10 vols. 1885-1887. Reprint, Peabody, Mass.: Hendrickson, 1994.

Horsiesi. "Regulations." In *Pachomian Koinonia.* Vol. 2, pp. 197-223. Translated by Armand Veilleux. CS 46. Kalamazoo, Mich.: Cistercian Publications, 1981.

Ignatius of Antioch. "Epistles." In *The Apostolic Fathers, Justin Martyr, Irenaeus,* pp. 49-96. Translated by Alexander Roberts and James Donaldson. ANF 1. Edited by Alexander Roberts and James Donaldson. 10 vols. 1885-1887. Reprint, Peabody, Mass.: Hendrickson, 1994.

Irenaeus. "Against Heresies." In *The Apostolic Fathers, Justin Martyr, Irenaeus,* pp. 315-567. Translated by Alexander Roberts and W. H. Rambaut. ANF 1. Edited by Alexander Roberts and James Donaldson. 10 vols. 1885-1887. Reprint, Peabody, Mass.: Hendrickson, 1994.

———. "Against Heresies." In *Early Christian Fathers,* pp. 358-97. Translated by Cyril C. Richardson. LCC 1. Philadelphia: Westminster Press, 1953.

———. *Against the Heresies.* Vol. 1. Translated and annotated by Dominic J. Unger and John J. Dillon. ACW 55. Mahwah, N.J.: Paulist Press, 1992.

———. "Epistle to Abba Symeon of Caesarea." In *The Ascetical Homilies of Saint Isaac the Syrian,* pp. 427-448. Brookline, Mass.: Holy Transfiguration Monastery, 1984.

Isaac of Nineveh. "Ascetical Homilies." In *The Ascetical Homilies of Saint Isaac the Syrian,* pp. 3-385. Brookline, Mass.: Holy Transfiguration Monastery, 1984.

———. "Mystical Treatises." See "Discourse 12." In *The Syriac Fathers on Prayer and Spiritual Life,* pp. 252-263. Translated by Sebastian Brock. CS 101. Kalamazoo, Mich.: Cistercian Publications, 1987.

———. *On Ascetical Life.* Translated by Mary Hansbury. Crestwood, N.Y.: St. Vladimir's Seminary Press, 1989.

Jacob of Sarug. "On the Establishment of Creation." In *Biblical Interpretation,* pp. 184-202. Translated by Joseph W. Trigg. MFC 9. Wilmington, Del.: Michael Glazier, 1988.

Jerome. "Against Jovinianus." In *Letters and Selected Works,* pp. 346-416. Translated by W. H. Fremantle et al. NPNF 6. Series 2. Edited by Philip Schaff and Henry Wace. 14 vols. 1886-1900. Reprint, Peabody, Mass.: Hendrickson, 1994.

———. "Against the Pelagians." In *Dogmatic and Polemical Works,* pp. 230-378. Translated by John N. Hritzu. FC 53. Washington, D.C.: The Catholic University of America Press, 1965.

———. *Commentary on Daniel.* Translated by Gleason L. Archer Jr. Grand Rapids, Mich.: Baker, 1958.

———."Homilies on Mark." In *The Homilies of Saint Jerome*. Vol. 2, pp. 121-92. Translated by Marie Liguori Ewald. FC 57. Washington, D.C.: The Catholic University of American Press, 1966.

———."Homilies on the Psalms." In *The Homilies of Saint Jerome*. Vol. 1. Translated by Marie Liguori Ewald. FC 48. Washington, D.C.: The Catholic University of America Press, 1964.

———."Homily 87 (On John)." In *The Homilies of Saint Jerome*. Vol. 2, pp. 212-220. Translated by Marie Liguori Ewald. FC 57. Washington, D.C.: The Catholic University of American Press, 1966.

———."Homily 94 (On Easter Sunday)." In *The Homilies of Saint Jerome*. Vol. 2, pp. 251-54. Translated by Marie Liguori Ewald. FC 57. Washington, D.C.: The Catholic University of American Press, 1966.

———."Letter 68." In *Divine Providence and Human Suffering*, pp. 95-97. Translated by James Walsh and P. G. Walsh. MFC 17. Wilmington, Del.: Michael Glazier, 1985.

———."Letters." In *Letters and Selected Works*, pp. 1-295. Translated by W. H. Fremantle et al. NPNF 6. Series 2. Edited by Philip Schaff and Henry Wace. 14 vols. 1886-1900. Reprint, Peabody, Mass.: Hendrickson, 1994.

John Chrysostom. "Against the Anomoeans." In *On the Incomprehensible Nature of God*. Translated by Paul W. Harkins. FC 72. Washington, D.C.: The Catholic University of America Press, 1984.

———. *Baptismal Instructions*. Translated by Paul W. Harkins. ACW 31. New York: Newman Press, 1963.

———."Concerning the Power of Demons." In *On the Priesthood, Ascetic Treatises, Select Homilies and Letters, Homilies on the Statues*, pp. 178-86. Translated by T. P. Brandram. NPNF 9. Series 1. Edited by Philip Schaff. 14 vols. 1886-1889. Reprint, Peabody, Mass.: Hendrickson, 1994.

———. *Discourses Against Judaizing Christians*. Translated by Paul W. Harkins. FC 68. Washington, D.C.: The Catholic University of America Press, 1979.

———."Discourse on Blessed Babylas." See "Homily on the Holy Martyr, Saint Babylas." In *On the Priesthood, Ascetic Treatises, Select Homilies and Letters, Homilies on the Statues*, pp. 141-43. Translated by T. P. Brandram. NPNF 9. Series 1. Edited by Philip Schaff. 14 vols. 1886-1889. Reprint, Peabody, Mass.: Hendrickson, 1994.

———."Homilies Concerning the Statues." In *On the Priesthood, Ascetic Treatises, Select Homilies and Letters, Homilies on the Statues*, pp. 331-489. Oxford translation revised by W. R. W. Stephens. NPNF 9. Series 1. Edited by Philip Schaff. 14 vols. 1886-1889. Reprint, Peabody, Mass.: Hendrickson, 1994.

———."Homilies on Ephesians." In *Homilies on Galatians, Ephesians, Philippians, Colossians, Thessalonians, Timothy, Titus and Philemon*, pp. 49-172. Oxford translation revised by Gross Alexander. NPNF 13. Series 1. Edited by Philip Schaff. 14 vols. 1886-1889. Reprint, Peabody, Mass.: Hendrickson, 1994.

———."Homilies on 1 Corinthians." In *Homilies on the Epistles of Paul to the Corinthians*. Oxford translation revised by Talbot W. Chambers. NPNF 12. Series 1. Edited by Philip Schaff. 14 vols. 1886-1889. Reprint, Peabody, Mass.: Hendrickson, 1994.

———. *Homilies on Genesis, 18-45 and 46-67*. Translated by Robert C. Hill. FC 82 and 87. Washington, D.C.: The Catholic University of America Press, 1990-1992.

———. *Homilies on Repentance and Almsgiving*. Translated by Gus George Christo. FC 96. Washington, D.C.: The Catholic University of America Press, 1998.

———."Homilies on 2 Timothy." In *Homilies on Galatians, Ephesians, Philippians, Colossians, Thessalonians, Timothy, Titus and Philemon*, pp. 475-518. Oxford translation edited by Philip Schaff. NPNF 13. Series 1. Edited by Philip Schaff. 14 vols. 1886-1889. Reprint, Peabody, Mass.: Hendrickson, 1994.

———."Homilies on the Acts of the Apostles." In *Homilies on the Acts of the Apostles and the Epistle to the Romans*, pp. 1-328. Translated by J. Walker et al. NPNF 11. Series 1. Edited by Philip Schaff. 14 vols. 1886-1889. Reprint, Peabody, Mass.: Hendrickson, 1994.

————. "Homilies on the Gospel of John." In *Saint John Chrysostom: Commentary on Saint John the Apostle and Evangelist, Homilies 1-47 and 48-88.* Translated by Thomas Aquinas Goggin. FC 33 and 41. Washington, D.C.: The Catholic University of America Press, 1957-1959.

————. *Homilies on the Gospel of Matthew.* Translated by George Prevost. Revised by M. B. Riddle. NPNF 10. Series 1. Edited by Philip Schaff. 14 vols. 1886-1889. Reprint, Peabody, Mass.: Hendrickson, 1994.

————. "Homilies on Titus." In *Homilies on Galatians, Ephesians, Philippians, Colossians, Thessalonians, Timothy, Titus and Philemon,* pp. 519-543. Oxford translation revised by Philip Schaff. NPNF 13. Series 1. Edited by Philip Schaff. 14 vols. 1886-1889. Reprint, Peabody, Mass.: Hendrickson, 1994.

————. "Letters to the Fallen Theodore." In *On the Priesthood, Ascetic Treatises, Select Homilies and Letters, Homilies on the Statues,* pp. 91-116. Translated by W. R. W. Stephens. NPNF 9. Series 1. Edited by Philip Schaff. 14 vols. 1886-1889. Reprint, Peabody, Mass.: Hendrickson, 1994.

————. "None Can Harm Him Who Does Not Injure Himself." In *On the Priesthood, Ascetic Treatises, Select Homilies and Letters, Homilies on the Statues,* pp. 271-84. Translated by W. R. W. Stephens. NPNF 9. Series 1. Edited by Philip Schaff. 14 vols. 1886-1889. Reprint, Peabody, Mass.: Hendrickson, 1994.

————. "On the Epistle to the Hebrews." In *Homilies on the Gospel of Saint John and the Epistle to the Hebrews,* pp. 363-522. Oxford translation revised by Philip Schaff. NPNF 14. Series 1. Edited by Philip Schaff. 14 vols. 1886-1889. Reprint, Peabody, Mass.: Hendrickson, 1994.

John of Damascus. *Barlaam and Joseph.* Translated by G. R. Woodward and H. Mattingly. LCL 34. Reprint, Cambridge, Mass.: Harvard University Press, 1937.

————. "Orthodox Faith." In *Hilary of Poitiers, John of Damascus,* pp. 1-101 (part 2). Translated by S. D. F. Salmond. NPNF 9. Series 2. Edited by Philip Schaff and Henry Wace. 14 vols. 1886-1900. Reprint, Peabody, Mass.: Hendrickson, 1994.

————. "Orthodox Faith." In *Writings,* pp. 165-406. Translated by Frederic H. Chase Jr. FC 37. Washington, D.C.: The Catholic University of America Press, 1958.

————. *On the Divine Images: Three Apologies Against Those Who Attack the Divine Images.* Translated by David Anderson. Crestwood, N.Y.: St. Vladimir's Press, 1980.

Justin Martyr. "Dialogue with Trypho." In *Writings of Saint Justin Martyr,* pp. 147-366. Translated by Thomas B. Falls. FC 6. New York: Christian Heritage, 1948.

————. "First Apology." In *Writings of Saint Justin Martyr,* pp. 33-111. Translated by Thomas B. Falls. FC 6. New York: Christian Heritage, 1948.

Lactantius. "Divine Institutes." In *Lactantius, Venantius, Asterius, Victorinus, Dionysius, Apostolic Teaching and Constitutions, 2 Clement, Early Liturgies,* pp. 9-223. Translated by William Fletcher. ANF 7. Edited by Alexander Roberts and James Donaldson. 10 vols. 1885-1887. Reprint, Peabody, Mass.: Hendrickson, 1994.

Leander of Seville. "The Training of Nuns." In *Iberian Fathers.* Vol. 1, *Martin of Braga, Paschasius of Dumium, Leander of Seville,* pp. 183-228. Translated by Claude W. Barlow. FC 62. Washington, D.C.: The Catholic University of America Press, 1969.

Leo the Great. *Letters.* Translated by Edmund Hunt. FC 34. Washington, D.C.: The Catholic University of America Press, 1956.

————. *Sermons.* Translated by Jane Patricia Freeland and Agnes Josephine Conway. FC 93. Washington, D.C.: The Catholic University of America Press, 1996.

Martin of Braga. "Reforming the Rustics." In *Iberian Fathers.* Vol. 1, *Martin of Braga, Paschasius of Dumium, Leander of Seville,* pp. 71-85. Translated by Claude W. Barlow. FC 62. Washington, D.C.: The Catholic University of America Press, 1969.

————. "Sayings of the Egyptian Fathers." In *Iberian Fathers*. Vol. 1, *Martin of Braga, Paschasius of Dumium, Leander of Seville*, pp. 17-34. Translated by Claude W. Barlow. FC 62. Washington, D.C.: The Catholic University of America Press, 1969.

"Martyrdom of Polycarp." In *The Apostolic Fathers*, pp. 109-117. Translated by J. B. Lightfoot. Edited by J. R. Harmer. 1891. Reprint, Grand Rapids, Mich.: Baker, 1983.

Maximus of Turin. *The Sermons of St. Maximus of Turin*. Translated by Boniface Ramsey. ACW 50. Mahwah, N.J.: Paulist Press, 1989.

Methodius. "On the Resurrection." In *Gregory Thaumaturgus, Dionysius the Great, Julius Africanus, Anatolius and Minor Writers, Methodius Arnobius*, pp. 364-77. Translated by William R. Clark. ANF 6. Edited by Alexander Roberts and James Donaldson. 10 vols. 1885-1887. Reprint, Peabody, Mass.: Hendrickson, 1994.

————. "Symposium, Or Banquet of the Ten Virgins." In *The Symposium: A Treatise on Chastity*, pp. 38-162. Translated by Herbert Musurillo. ACW 27. New York: Newman Press, 1958.

Novatian. "On the Spectacles." In *The Trinity, The Spectacles, Jewish Foods, In Praise of Purity, Letters*, pp. 123-33. Translated by Russell J. DeSimone. FC 67. Washington, D.C.: The Catholic University of America Press, 1974.

————. "On the Trinity." In *The Trinity, The Spectacles, Jewish Foods, In Praise of Purity, Letters*, pp. 23-111. Translated by Russell J. DeSimone. FC 67. Washington, D.C.: The Catholic University of America Press, 1974.

Origen. "Against Celsus." In *Tertullian, Part Fourth; Minucius Felix; Commodian; Origen, Parts First and Second*, pp. 395-669. Translated by Frederick Crombie. ANF 4. Edited by Alexander Roberts and James Donaldson. 10 vols. 1885-1887. Reprint, Peabody, Mass.: Hendrickson, 1994.

————. "Against Celsus." In *The Writings of Origen: Volume 2, Origen Contra Celsum Books 2-8*. Translated by Frederick Crombie. ANCL 23. Edinburgh: T & T Clark, 1894.

————. *Commentary on the Epistle to the Romans, Books 1-5*. Translated by Thomas P. Scheck. FC 103. Washington, D.C.: The Catholic University of America Press, 2001.

————. *Commentary on the Gospel According to John, Books 1-10*. Translated by Ronald E. Heine. FC 80. Washington, D.C.: The Catholic University of America Press, 1989.

————. "Exhortation to Martyrdom." In *An Exhortation to Martyrdom, Prayer and Selected Works*, pp. 41-79. Translated by Rowan A. Greer. The Classics of Western Spirituality. New York: Paulist Press, 1979.

————. "Homilies on Exodus." In *Homilies on Genesis and Exodus*, pp. 227-387. Translated by Ronald E. Heine. FC 71. Washington, D.C.: The Catholic University of America Press, 1982.

————. "Homilies on Genesis." In *Homilies on Genesis and Exodus*, pp. 47-224. Translated by Ronald E. Heine. FC 71. Washington, D.C.: The Catholic University of America Press, 1982.

————. *Homilies on Leviticus*. Translated by Gary Wayne Barkley. FC 83. Washington, D.C.: The Catholic University of America Press, 1990.

————. "Homilies on Numbers." In *An Exhortation to Martyrdom, Prayer and Selected Works*, pp. 245-69. Translated by Rowan A. Greer. The Classics of Western Spirituality. New York: Paulist Press, 1979.

————. *On First Principles*. Translated by G. W. Butterworth. London: SPCK, 1936. Reprint, Gloucester, Mass.: Peter Smith, 1973.

————. "On Prayer." In *An Exhortation to Martyrdom, Prayer and Selected Works*, pp. 81-170. Translated by Rowan A. Greer. The Classics of Western Spirituality. New York: Paulist Press, 1979.

Pacian of Barcelona. "Letters." In *Iberian Fathers*. Vol. 3, *Pacian of Barcelona, Orosius of Braga*, pp. 17-70. Translated by Craig L. Hanson. FC 99. Washington, D.C.: The Catholic University of America Press, 1999.

————. "On Penitents." In *Iberian Fathers*. Vol. 3, *Pacian of Barcelona, Orosius of Braga*, pp. 71-86. Translated by Craig L. Hanson. FC 99. Washington, D.C.: The Catholic University of America Press, 1999.

Pachomius. "Instructions." In *Pachomian Koinonia*. Vol. 3, pp. 13-49. Translated by Armand Veilleux. CS 47. Kalamazoo, Mich.: Cistercian Publications, 1982.

————. "Letters." In *Pachomian Koinonia*. Vol. 3, pp. 51-83. Translated by Armand Veilleux. CS 47. Kalamazoo, Mich.: Cistercian Publications, 1982.

————. "Life of Pachomius (Bohairic)." In *Pachomian Koinonia*. Vol. 1, pp. 23-266. Translated by Armand Veilleux. CS 45. Kalamazoo, Mich.: Cistercian Publications, 1980.

Palladius of Helenopolis. "Lausiac History." See "The Paradise of Palladius," pp. 77-281. In *The Paradise of the Holy Fathers*. Vol. 1, *Containing the Life of St. Anthony, by Athanasius Archbishop of Alexandria; Histories of the Fathers by Palladius Bishop of Helenopolis; The Rule of Pachomius; St. Jerome's History of the Fathers*. Translated by Ernest A. Wallis Budge. 1907. Reprint, Seattle: St. Nectarios Press, 1984.

Paulinus of Nola. *The Poems of St. Paulinus of Nola*. Translated by P. G. Walsh. ACW 40. New York: Newman Press, 1975.

Peter Chrysologus. *Selected Sermons*. Vol. 2. Translated by William B. Palardy. FC 109. Washington, D.C.: The Catholic University of America Press, 2004.

————. "Sermons." In *Saint Peter Chrysologus: Selected Sermons and Saint Valerian: Homilies*, pp. 25-282. Translated by George E. Ganss. FC 17. New York: Fathers of the Church, 1953.

Philoxenus of Mabbug. "On the Indwelling of the Holy Spirit." In *The Syriac Fathers on Prayer and Spiritual Life*, pp. 106-127. Translated by Sebastian Brock. CS 101. Kalamazoo, Mich.: Cistercian Publications, 1987.

Possidius. *The Life of Saint Augustine*. Translated by Matthew O'Connell. Edited by John E. Rotelle. Augustinian Series 1. Villanova, Penn.: Augustinian Press, 1988.

Pseudo-Clement of Rome. "2 Clement." In *Early Christian Fathers*, pp. 193-202. Translated by Cyril C. Richardson. LCC 1. Philadelphia: Westminster Press, 1953.

"Pseudo-Clementine Homilies." In *The Twelve Patriarchs, Excerpts and Epistles, The Clementina, Apocrypha, Decretals, Memoirs of Edessa and Syriac Documents, Remains of the First Ages*, pp. 223-346. Translated by Thomas Smith et al. ANF 8. Edited by Alexander Roberts and James Donaldson. 10 vols. 1885-1887. Reprint, Peabody, Mass.: Hendrickson, 1994.

Pseudo-Dionysius. "Celestial Hierarchy." In *Pseudo-Dionysius: The Complete Works*, pp. 143-91. Translated by Colm Luibheid. The Classics of Western Spirituality. Mahwah, N.J.: Paulist Press, 1987.

Pseudo-Macarius. "Fifty Spiritual Homilies." In *Pseudo-Macarius: The Fifty Spiritual Homilies and the Great Letter*, pp. 37-246. Translated by George A. Maloney. The Classics of Western Spirituality. Mahwah, N.J.: Paulist Press, 1992.

Romanus Melodus. "Kontakia." In *Kontakia of Romanos, Byzantine Melodist*. Vol. 2, *On Christian Life*, pp. 136-49. Translated by Marjorie Carpenter. Columbia, Mo.: University of Missouri Press, 1973.

Rufinus of Aquileia. "Commentary on the Apostles' Creed." In *Theodoret, Jerome, Gennadius, Rufinus: Historical Writings, Etc.*, pp. 541-63. Translated by W. H. Fremantle. NPNF 3. Series 2. Edited by Philip Schaff and Henry Wace. 14 vols. 1886-1900. Reprint, Peabody, Mass.: Hendrickson, 1994.

Sahdona. "Book of Perfection." In *The Syriac Fathers on Prayer and the Spiritual Life*, pp. 202-237. Translated by Sebastian Brock. CS 101. Kalamazoo, Mich.: Cistercian Publications, 1987.

Salvian the Presbyter. "Four Books of Timothy to the Church." In *The Writings of Salvian, the Presbyter*, pp. 269-371. Translated by Jeremiah F. O'Sullivan. FC 3. Reprint, Washington, D.C.: The Catholic University of America Press, 1962.

————. "The Governance of God." In *The Writings of Salvian, the Presbyter*, pp. 27-232. Translated by Jeremiah F. O'Sullivan. FC 3. Reprint, Washington, D.C.: The Catholic University of America Press, 1962.

"Sayings of the Holy Fathers." In *The Paradise of the Holy Fathers*. Vol. 2, *The Counsels of the Holy Men and the Questions and Answers of the Ascetic Brethren Generally Known as the Sayings of the Fathers of Egypt*. Translated by Ernest A. Wallis Budge. 1907. Reprint, Seattle: St. Nectarios Press, 1984.

Symeon the New Theologian. "Discourses." See *Symeon the New Theologian: The Discourses*. Translated by C. J. deCatanzaro. The Classics of Western Spirituality. New York: Paulist Press, 1980.

———. "The Practical and Theological Chapters." In *Symeon the New Theologian: The Practical and Theological Chapters and the Three Theological Discourses*, pp. 33-103. Translated by Paul McGuckin. CS 41. Kalamazoo, Mich.: Cistercian Publications, 1982.

"Teaching of the Twelve Apostles." In *Lactantius, Venantius, Asterius, Victorinus, Dionysius, Apostolic Teaching and Constitutions, 2 Clement, Early Liturgies*, pp. 377-82. Translated by Isaac H. Hall and John T. Napier. ANF 7. Edited by Alexander Roberts and James Donaldson. 10 vols. 1885-1887. Reprint, Peabody, Mass.: Hendrickson, 1994.

Tertullian. "Against Marcion." In *Latin Christianity: Its Founder, Tertullian*, pp. 269-474. Translated by Peter Holmes. ANF 3. Edited by Alexander Roberts and James Donaldson. 10 vols. 1885-1887. Reprint, Peabody, Mass.: Hendrickson, 1994.

———. "An Answer to the Jews." In *Latin Christianity: Its Founder, Tertullian*, pp. 151-73. Translated by S. Thelwall. ANF 3. Edited by Alexander Roberts and James Donaldson. 10 vols. 1885-1887. Reprint, Peabody, Mass.: Hendrickson, 1994.

———. "The Chaplet." In *Disciplinary, Moral and Ascetical Works*, pp. 231-67. Translated by Edwin A. Quain. FC 40. Washington, D.C.: The Catholic University of America Press, 1959.

———. "On Fasting." In *Tertullian, Part Fourth; Minucius Felix; Commodian; Origen, Parts First and Second*, pp. 102-114. Translated by S. Thelwall. ANF 4. Edited by Alexander Roberts and James Donaldson. 10 vols. 1885-1887. Reprint, Peabody, Mass.: Hendrickson, 1994.

———. "On Idolatry." In *Early Latin Theology*, pp. 83-110. Translated by S. L. Greenslade. LCC 5. Philadelphia: Westminster Press, 1956.

———. "On Idolatry." In *Latin Christianity: Its Founder, Tertullian*, pp. 61-76. Translated by S. Thelwall. ANF 3. Edited by Alexander Roberts and James Donaldson. 10 vols. 1885-1887. Reprint, Peabody, Mass.: Hendrickson, 1994.

———. "On Penitence." In *Treatises on Penance: On Penitence and On Purity*, pp. 14-37. Translated and annotated by William P. Le Saint. ACW 28. New York: Newman Press, 1959.

———. "On Prayer." In *Disciplinary, Moral and Ascetical Works*, pp. 157-188. Translated by Emily Joseph Daly. FC 40. 1959. Reprint, Washington, D.C.: The Catholic University of America Press, 1985.

———. "On Prayer." In *Latin Christianity: Its Founder, Tertullian*, pp. 681-691. Translated by S. Thelwall. ANF 3. Edited by Alexander Roberts and James Donaldson. 10 vols. 1885-1887. Reprint, Peabody, Mass.: Hendrickson, 1994.

———. "On Purity." In *Treatises on Penance: On Penitence and On Purity*, pp. 53-125. Translated and annotated by William P. Le Saint. ACW 28. New York: Newman Press, 1959.

———. "On the Resurrection of the Flesh." In *Latin Christianity: Its Founder, Tertullian*, pp. 545-594. Translated by Peter Holmes. ANF 3. Edited by Alexander Roberts and James Donaldson. 10 vols. 1885-1887. Reprint, Peabody, Mass.: Hendrickson, 1994.

———. "On the Soul." In *Latin Christianity: Its Founder, Tertullian*, pp. 181-235. Translated by Peter Holmes. ANF 3. Edited by Alexander Roberts and James Donaldson. 10 vols. 1885-1887. Reprint, Peabody, Mass.: Hendrickson, 1994.

Theodoret of Cyr. "Commentary on Daniel." Translated by Robert C. Hill. WGRW 7. Boston: Brill, 2006.

————. "To the Martyrs." In *Disciplinary, Moral and Ascetical Works*, pp. 17-29. Translated by Rudolf Arbesmann. FC 40. Washington, D.C.: The Catholic University of America Press, 1959.

————. *Commentary on the Psalms*. Translated by Robert C. Hill. FC 101. Washington, D.C.: The Catholic University of American Press, 2000.

————. *The Lives of Simeon Stylites*. Translated by Robert Doran. CS 112. Kalamazoo, Mich.: Cistercian Publications, 1992.

Valerian. "Homilies." In *Saint Peter Chrysologus: Selected Sermons and Saint Valerian: Homilies*, pp. 299-435. Translated by George E. Ganss. FC 17. New York: Fathers of the Church, 1953.

Authors/Writings Index

Subject Index

Scripture Index